Contemporary Authors

Autobiography Series

ISSN 0748-0636

Contemporary Authors

Autobiography Series

Joyce Nakamura
Editor

volume **13**

 Gale Research Inc. · *DETROIT* · *LONDON*

The paper used in this publication meets the minimum requirements of American National Standard for Information Sciences—Permanence Paper for Printed Library Materials, ANSI Z39.48-1984. ∞™

Copyright © 1991
Gale Research Inc.
835 Penobscot Bldg.
Detroit, MI 48226-4094

Library of Congress Catalog Card Number 84-647879
ISBN 0-8103-4512-9
ISSN-0748-0636

Printed in the United States of America

Published simultaneously in the United Kingdom
by Gale Research International Limited
(An affiliated company of Gale Research Inc.)

Contents

Preface

Each volume in the *Contemporary Authors Autobiography Series (CAAS)* presents an original collection of autobiographical essays written especially for the series by noted writers. *CAAS* has grown out of the aggregate of Gale's long-standing interest in author biography, bibliography, and criticism, as well as its successful publications in those areas, like the *Dictionary of Literary Biography, Contemporary Literary Criticism, Something about the Author, Author Biographies Master Index,* and particularly the bio-bibliographical series *Contemporary Authors (CA),* to which this *Autobiography Series* is a companion.

As a result of their ongoing communication with authors in compiling *CA* and other books, Gale editors recognized that these wordsmiths frequently had more to say—willingly, even eagerly—than the format of existing Gale publications could accommodate. Personal comments from authors in the "Sidelights" section of *CA* entries, for example, often indicated the intriguing tip of an iceberg. Inviting authors to write about themselves at essay-length was the almost-inexorable next step. Added to that was the fact that the collected autobiographies of current writers were virtually nonexistent. Like metal to magnet, Gale customarily responds to an information gap—and met this one with *CAAS.*

Purpose

This series is designed to be a congenial meeting place for writers and readers—a place where writers can present themselves, on their own terms, to their audience; and a place where general readers, students of contemporary literature, teachers and librarians, even aspiring writers can become better acquainted with familiar authors and make the first acquaintance of others. Here is an opportunity for writers who may never write a full-length autobiography (and some shudder at the thought) to let their readers know how they see themselves and their work, what carefully laid plans or turns of luck brought them to this time and place, what objects of their passion and pity arouse them enough to tell us. Even for those authors who have already published full-length autobiographies there is the opportunity in *CAAS* to bring their readers "up to date" or perhaps to take a different approach in the essay format. At the very least, these essays can help quench a reader's inevitable curiosity about the people who speak to their imagination and seem themselves to inhabit a plane somewhere between reality and fiction. But the essays in this series have a further potential: singly, they can illuminate the reader's understanding of a writer's work; collectively, they are lessons in the creative process and in the discovery of its roots.

CAAS makes no attempt to give an observer's-eye view of authors and their works. That outlook is already well represented in biographies, reviews, and critiques published in a wide variety of sources, including *Contemporary Authors, Contemporary Literary Criticism,* and the *Dictionary of Literary Biography.* Instead, *CAAS* complements that perspective and presents what no other source does: the view of contemporary writers that is reflected in their own mirrors, shaped by their own choice of materials and their own manner of storytelling. Thanks to the exceptional talents of its contributors, each volume in this series is a unique anthology of some of the best and most varied contemporary writing.

Scope

Like its parent series, *Contemporary Authors,* the *CA Autobiography Series* aims to be broad-based. It sets out to meet the needs and interests of the full spectrum of readers by providing in each volume about twenty essays by writers in all genres whose work is being read today. We deem it a minor publishing event that twenty busy authors from throughout the world are able to interrupt their existing writing, teaching, speaking, traveling, and other schedules to converge on a given deadline for any one volume. So it is not always possible that all genres can be equally and uniformly represented from volume to volume, although we strive to include writers working in a wide spectrum of genres, including fiction, nonfiction, and poetry. Like most categories, these oversimplify. Only a few writers specialize in a single area. The range of writings by authors in this volume also includes drama, translation, and criticism as well as work for movies, television, radio, newspapers, and journals.

Format

Authors who contribute to *CAAS* are invited to write a "mini-autobiography" of approximately 10,000 words. In order to give the writer's imagination free rein, we suggest no guidelines or pattern for the essay. The only injunction is that each writer tell his or her own story in the manner and to the extent that each finds most natural and appropriate. In addition, writers are asked to supply a selection of personal photographs, showing themselves at various ages, as well as important people and special moments in their lives. Barring unfortunate circumstances like the loss or destruction of early photographs, our contributors have responded graciously and generously, sharing with us some of their most treasured mementoes, as this volume readily attests. This special wedding of text and photographs makes *CAAS* the kind of reference book that even browsers will find seductive.

A bibliography appears at the end of each essay, listing the author's book-length works in chronological order of publication. If more than one book has been published in a given year, the titles are listed in alphabetic order. Each entry in the bibliography includes the publication information for the book's first and most recent printings in the United States. Generally, the bibliography does not include later reprintings, new editions, or foreign translations. Also omitted from this bibliography are articles, reviews, and other contributions to magazines and journals. The bibliographies in this volume were compiled by members of the *CAAS* editorial staff from their research and the lists of writings provided by many of the authors. Each of the bibliographies has been submitted to the author for review. When the list of primary works is extensive, the author may prefer to present a "Selected Bibliography." Readers may consult the author's entry in *CA* for a more complete list of writings in these cases.

Each volume of *CAAS* includes a cumulative index that cites all the essayists in the series as well as the subjects presented in the essays: personal names, titles of works, geographical names, schools of writing, etc. The index format is designed to make these cumulating references as helpful and easy to use as possible. For every reference that appears *in more than one essay*, the name of the essayist is given before the volume and page number(s). For example, W.H. Auden is mentioned by a number of essayists in the series. The index format allows the user to identify the essay writers by name:

Auden, W.H.
  Allen **6**:18, 24
  Ashby **6**:36, 39
  Bowles **1**:86
  Burroway **6**:90
  Fuller **10**:120, 123
  Hall **7**:58, 61
  Hazo **11**:148, 150
  Howes **3**:143
  Jennings **5**:110
  Jones **5**:121
  Kizer **5**:146
  Major **6**:185-86
  Rosenthal **6**:282
  Shapiro **6**:307-08
  Simpson **4**:291
  Sinclair **5**:272
  Symons **3**:383, 385
  Wain **4**:327

For references that appear *in only one essay,* the volume and page number(s) are given but the name of the essayist is omitted. For example:

Stieglitz, Alfred **1**:104, 109, 110

CAAS is something more than the sum of its individual essays. At many points the essays touch common ground, and from these intersections emerge new mosaics of information and impressions. *CAAS* therefore becomes an expanding chronicle of the last half-century—an already useful research tool that can only increase in usefulness as the series grows. And the index, despite its pedestrian appearance, is an increasingly important guide to the interconnections of this chronicle.

Looking Ahead

All of the writers in this volume begin with a common goal—telling the tale of their lives. Yet each of these essays has a special character and point of view that set it apart from its companions. Perhaps a small sampler of anecdotes and musings from the essays ahead can hint at the unique flavor of these life stories.

Kofi Nyidevu Awoonor, recounting his father's frugality: "When I was set to go to Zion College, I received a prospectus of things to acquire. My father checked the list meticulously, cancelling items he considered superfluous, for example, toothbrush. He insisted our traditional chewing stick would do. It still is the better way of cleaning one's teeth. When he came to an item dubbed 'Achimota sandals,' I saw my father frown. He asked me to describe it. It was a type of open sandal with cover for the heel, rubber-soled and made with leather. It was specially designed by Bata Shoe Company for African secondary-school boys. After my description, my father smiled. He had a friend, a shoemaker, one Mr. Agbleta, who could make it. So I was the only one in the school with 'Achimota sandals' made of cured northern sheep leather. It was not uncomfortable. But it made such an infernal noise, literally bleated, when you walked. For the first term, other boys would follow me wherever I went, annoyingly imitating my bleating sandals!"

Hal Bennett, remembering religion in the South, as it was embraced by some: " 'If religion ain't loud and scary,' an aunt of mine asserted, 'then it ain't good religion. Just like medicine that don't taste bad ain't good medicine.' What she and others like her wanted was the *real* thing, as they called it: a barely literate preacher as handsome as sin and as polished as a peeled onion, standing halfway between being a pimp on the one hand and a bootlegger on the other; the majority of the congregation drunk, or partly drunk and rid of its inhibitions, to make the circus more amusing; the agonized shouting and shameful convulsions calculated to terrify and excite the sinner simultaneously; the women usually wearing the most makeup and the shortest dresses—and with absolutely nothing on underneath, it was said—fainting always with their opened legs aimed like cocked shotguns at the rooster in the pulpit; other men and women frothing like mad dogs at the mouth, babbling in supposedly unknown tongues, wide-eyed and rolling scandalous hips; and, most important, the tender emotions of all of us to be spattered against the stern church walls like carelessly thrown eggs, then scraped up and lard-fried for God's greedy gusto."

Elizabeth Jolley, describing an experience that provided creative inspiration: "Once when I was almost the last person to leave the beach at Bunbury, in the southwest of Western Australia, I saw the sun go down leaving only a long red line of sky far out over the water, which was rolling up as if boiling over, dark, along the deserted sands. In this turmoil of waves, where the sea was meeting the shore, some thin white fingers reached up out of the water as it ran pouring up and out over the sand before swirling back into itself. The thin white fingers grasping the froth of the wave offered me a character that evening. I did not see the person they belonged to—only the animation expressed in the hands reaching up out of the sea at dusk. The thin white fingers, gleaming as they did in the dark waters as the evening rapidly moved towards night, gave me more than a character; they presented a family and, in addition, this family's place in society and their efforts towards survival."

W. A. Swanberg, sharing a scene from downtown London during World War II: "Soon I was working in OWI publications in Grosvenor Square, across from the U.S. embassy, a unit headed by Harold Guinzburg, owner of Viking Press and the most benign of men. Visible from our office were blitz-ruined mansions of this loveliest of Mayfair squares. The top two stories of one four-story building were totally gone, and the only evidence of its original height was a fourth-story porcelain water closet supported only by its vertical piping. The hard-pressed Britons had had manpower only for meager emergency repairs. The WC, swaying slightly, was proof of this and of the excellence of British plumbing. The Toilet, as our group of editor-writers capitalized it, was a rousing symbol of durability and courage etched against the sky, heedless of danger and giving promise of victory. Yet rusting pipes would inevitably topple it. Imagine the ignominy of the unlucky passerby flattened by the falling Toilet instead of being gallantly erased by a buzzbomb."

Donald E. Westlake, recalling one of his grandmother's eccentricities: "My paternal grandmother's maiden name was one of the most beautiful I've ever heard: Annie Tyrrell. There's a lilt to it, like a quick little mountain stream; you can't say it aloud without a ripple. Annie Tyrrell came from Dublin, and when I knew her she was tiny and wise and humorous; a fairy-tale grandmother. She fumbled about for a number of years without making any fuss about the fumbling, and then one day, out walking, she spied a pair of eyeglasses discarded in somebody's trash, tried them on, and was delighted. She could see! The glasses were lopsided, and one wing was repaired with tape, but she could see so much better with them on that she wore them ever after....I decided after a while, when I'd grown used to my grandmother's smiling, wrinkled face behind the lopsided glasses, that a leprechaun had left them for her; professional courtesy. I still believe it."

These brief examples can only suggest what lies ahead in this volume. The essays will speak differently to different readers; but they are certain to speak best, and most eloquently, for themselves.

Authors Forthcoming in *CAAS*

Bella Akhmadulina
Russian poet, translator, and
short-story writer

Mulk Raj Anand
Indian novelist, nonfiction writer,
and critic

Russell Banks
American novelist

Marvin Bell
American poet and editor

Elizabeth Brewster
Canadian novelist, poet, and
short-story writer

Dennis Brutus
African poet and political activist

Algis Budrys
American science-fiction writer and
editor

Ed Bullins
American playwright

Louis Dudek
Canadian poet

Cyprian Ekwensi
Nigerian novelist and short-story
writer

Paul Engle
American poet and educator

Philip Jose Farmer
American science-fiction writer

Leslie Fiedler
American critic, novelist, and editor

Charles Gordone
American playwright, actor, and
director

Daniel Halpern
American poet and editor

Michael S. Harper
American poet

John Hollander
American poet

Steve Katz
American novelist, playwright, and
poet

Etheridge Knight
American poet

Walter Laqueur
German-born historian, journalist, and
novelist

Jessica Mitford
English essayist and journalist

Bharati Mukherjee
Canadian novelist and short-story
writer

Harry Mark Petrakis
American novelist and screenwriter

James Reaney
Canadian poet and playwright

Alastair Reid
Scottish poet, essayist, and translator

Edouard Roditi
French-born poet

Ernesto Sábato
Argentinean novelist and essayist

Antonis Samarakis
Greek novelist and short-story writer

Sonia Sanchez
American poet

Eve Shelnutt
American poet and short-story writer

Anne Waldman
American poet

Acknowledgments

We wish to acknowledge our special gratitude to each of the authors in this volume. They all have been most kind and cooperative in contributing not only their talents but their enthusiasm and encouragement to this project.

Grateful acknowledgment is also made to those publishers, photographers, and artists whose works appear with these authors' essays.

Photographs

Ai: p. 1, Ed Putzar.

Michael Andre: pp. 18, 20, 22, Anne Turyn/*Unmuzzled Ox.*

Kofi Nyidevu Awoonor: p. 29, Fernando Lezcano.

Franco Beltrametti: p. 58, E. Secco D'Aragona; p. 62, Gary Snyder; p. 65, Christophe Beriger; p. 67, Lloyd Kahn; p. 68, Giovanni Giovanetti, copyright © 1985; p. 69, Luca Barberis; p. 70, Fabrizio Garghetti; p. 71, Giona Beltrametti, copyright © 1987.

Hal Bennett: p. 73, copyright © 1972 by *Playboy.* Photo by Vernon L. Smith.

Brendan Galvin: p. 89, Ellen Galvin; p. 91, F. N. Joslin Company.

Matthew Mead: p. 126, reprinted by permission of Deutsche Verlags–Anstalt, Stuttgart.

John N. Morris: p. 166, Walter Scott Shinn.

Fernand Ouellette: p. 180, painting by Gaston Boisvert.

Robert Phillips: p. 193, Geoffrey Kerrigan; p. 197, Olan Mills.

Carolyn M. Rodgers: p. 247, *Negro Digest.*

W. A. Swanberg: p. 259, Christopher Lukas; p. 262, Golling.

Karen Swenson: p. 307, David Gottlieb; p. 310, O. E. Flaten; p. 313, Fred Pleasure; p. 314, © 1986 Layle Silbert.

Frank Waters: pp. 319, 323, copyright © 1989 by Joe Backes; p. 326, copyright © Marcia Keegan.

Donald E. Westlake: p. 329, copyright © 1989 by Matthew Seaman/Lightworker Photography; p. 343, Photo by Bob Serating.

Text

Contemporary Authors

Autobiography Series

Ai

1947-

ARRIVAL

*Ai, photographed by Edward Putzar, who taught her Japanese
at the University of Arizona*

When I was a kid, growing up in Tucson, Arizona, I believed in the cowboy code of behavior. It involved acting honorably and being kind to women and children. I was not particularly kind to other children, but I loved my mother and my grandmother. I don't remember how honorably I conducted myself either. After all, I was only four years old. My prairie consisted of four acres of mostly rocks and dirt and assorted nasty critters, who occasionally got into the house. Once we found a Gila monster climbing the dining-room drapes.

My mother, grandmother, and step-grandfather had moved to Arizona from San Antonio, Texas, in 1945. In Tucson, my mother met and decided to marry a man the family considered beneath her. When she threatened to run away with him, my grandparents gave their consent. She was sixteen and had graduated from high school when she was fifteen (she kept her diploma on the wall beside the bed). However shallow my grandparents' objections about the man—he was not of our class, nor (of all things) was he multiracial, which we were, and (worst of all) his family had picked cotton—they were right in that he was the wrong man. My mother ended up having an affair with a Japanese man. She got pregnant with me and when my natural father, the Japanese, found

1

out, he told her to go home to her family. Finally, after the man she was married to beat her and she tried to abort me by throwing herself down a stairway, she called an uncle and he took her back to Arizona.

I was born barely seven months later, on October 21, 1947, in my great-grandmother's house in Albany, Texas. My mother had gone there to keep from losing me. My great-grandmother Maggie was Irish and African-American. My great-grandfather was Dutch and Choctaw Indian. My mother's father was African-American. My great-grandfather's mother, who was Choctaw, and his father, who was Dutch, had moved to Texas from Oklahoma, where many Choctaws had been relocated by Andrew Jackson. The Cherokees, Choctaws, Creeks, and Chikasaws all made the trek along the Trail of Tears. In the 1860s or 1870s, my great-grandparents moved to Texas. We now think because his family was there, but we have no proof. All I know is my great-grandfather's family name was Waggoner, but when he was born, the birth certificate was changed and his last name became Smith, because they said Waggoner was a white man's name. My own birth certificate lists me as the child of my mother's husband, with a *C* I assume for "Colored" under race.

When the doctor came to see me, he told my great-grandmother, "Maggie, she's not going to live," but my great-grandmother said, "Yes, she will." She put me in a shoebox by the heater and fed me hot toddies. Someone told me that happened to Willie Shoemaker, the jockey, too—the toddie part, that is. They always said my great-grandmother was a nurse. I don't know if that was true, but she knew how to keep me alive. When I was well enough to travel, my mother moved back to Arizona and returned to her husband, but by the time I was eight months old, he'd tried to strangle me because I wasn't his, and when my mother became pregnant with his child, he said he wasn't the father and kicked her in the stomach. She lost the baby. My mother left him for good and we went to live with my grandparents in Tucson, where my memories begin.

I remember being strongly encouraged to read and aside from coloring, which was my favorite activity, reading gave me the most pleasure. I had two books of Japanese fairy tales that contained haiku. I loved those books. One had a red cover and one had a blue cover. I used to sit for hours looking at the drawings and being read to, until I could read on my own. I also learned to spell. A detergent commercial on the radio soaps spelled out the word *Tide*. I'll never forget. I nearly drove my mother crazy spelling

that word. I think that's really why I learned to spell and read so early. In the interest of preserving her sanity, my mother made sure I learned to spell some more interesting words, and to keep me occupied, she taught me to read. We got our first Siamese then, too. His name was Lately, because he was born last. He was a good companion and even kept a scorpion at bay while I stood on a chair, until my grandmother came and killed it. We had chickens, pigeons, pigs, dogs. It was a great life for a kid. Alas, that came to an end when my mother met a new man. When I was five, they got married. He was in the army and stationed at Fort Reilly, Kansas, so we left my grandparents. My mother had a baby girl and I saw snow for the first time. I also started school. My stepfather had been stationed in Japan and had had a Japanese girlfriend, who'd had a son by him. My mother showed me a photograph of her once. She was wearing high heels and white socks. Later, I saw a photo of a little boy. He was fat and cute and my mother said he looked like my stepfather. I was far too young to know. In fact, I think I only know about the little boy because I heard my mother and grandmother discussing it.

I was always listening in. They said you had to watch what you said around me, and since I could spell, they couldn't get away with that much anymore; although even if I could spell, I didn't know what half the stuff meant. Finally, they started spelling backwards. I learned how to do that too, so things were just not said with me around after that. But if anyone was discussing me, I never heard even a whisper. I did not know I was half-Japanese. I thought that fellow she'd divorced and whom I did not remember was my father. It's hard to believe now that I would be twenty-six before I knew the truth. Although I realized as I got older that that man couldn't be my father, I was never able to confront my mother, and she never volunteered anything until I was seventeen, and she did it in such a way that I still couldn't question her. If only she had told me all when I was a child, it would have saved me a lot of confusion and pain.

I didn't know I was half-Japanese, but the fifth-grade African-American girls at Sacred Heart in San Francisco knew. We went there after my stepfather came back from the Korean Conflict, and after we'd spent about a year living in Las Vegas with my grandmother and her new husband, who was in construction. Day after day, the girls would say, "Get away from us, Nigger Jap, you can't play with us, Nigger Jap." Finally, I told my mother and she went to school and told the nuns I had Indian blood and that the kids were mistaking that for Japanese. I suppose it was acceptable, because the taunting stopped. I used to beg my mother to let me go to the Catholic school where all the Catholic Asians went.

By now, I was reading about the lives of the saints and the knights of the Round Table. I liked Saint Teresa best, then the Blessed Virgin, but even so, they came well after the Mickey Mouse Club. I guess I didn't read poetry that I remember, although when I was about six, my mother read me Gray's "Elegy Written in a Country Churchyard" and "The Road Not Taken" by Frost. She also liked Langston Hughes and held him in very high esteem. She wanted me to be an English teacher, because that's what she would have been if she hadn't gotten married. She told me again and again how important it was to get an education, so that by the time I entered high school, I was set on the path to college, at least in my mind. I think if she had not held literature in such high regard, I might not have become a writer, but I can't say that with any real certainty. What I do know is that, by the age of ten, reading was a major activity of mine. I preferred to read rather than play, and when I was twelve she signed me up in a book club, but it took a couple more changes of residence from California to Arizona and back to Los Angeles before I actually wrote something I made up.

In 1959, we moved to LA from Tucson. My stepfather was in the California National Guard by then and we were enrolled in Holy Name School. One day, Sister told us to go home and pretend that we were martyrs and that the next day we'd be fed to the lions, and to write our last letter. She had me read mine to the class. I was mortified. Now I realize she thought it was good. After that, she had us memorize "Captain, My Captain" and some of the Gettysburg Address. Another assignment was to write our own version of "Jabberwocky." She also had us write poems. I don't have them and I don't know what I thought about them. I do remember feeling pleasure when I was writing. I felt a kind of satisfaction I hadn't before. Unfortunately, my mother removed me from that school because of problems my stepsister was having with a lay teacher, so I never got my poems back and I didn't write a poem again until I was thirteen. The shock of going to public school and all was too much for me.

But one day, I saw a flyer announcing a poetry contest. The poem had to be about something historical and I remember failed efforts, especially one about Abraham Lincoln. My mother and stepfa-

ther had split up and we were having a difficult time financially, so we moved back to Tucson and I enrolled in Tucson High School. I was miserable, lonely, and given all these absurdly easy courses because my mother had not brought my files from school in California. What a wasted, boring semester. Luckily, my sophomore year, I took World History, my straight-*A* course, the only one I had in high school. I got a good English class and teacher, and the next time I saw an ad for a poetry contest, I entered it. The poem was very Edgar Allan Poeish. I called it "Le Mort." The teacher asked me why French and I told her I thought it sounded better (I was studying French). I didn't win, but I kept on writing. I would request extra assignments so I could do some creative writing. I discovered the Romantics then and began to imitate Shelley and Keats. Around that time, a Mormon spiritualist my mother and grandmother were friends with gave me a tiny leather-bound set of the Shakespeare plays, and I spent one whole summer reading them. I especially loved the tragedies. I also read the Catholic Bible every night before I went to bed. I watched TV a lot, there being no restrictions

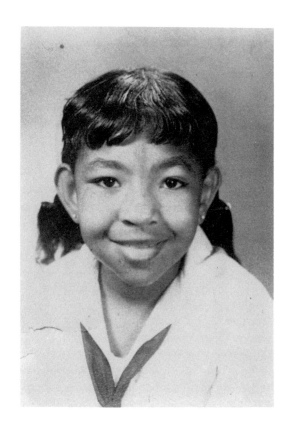

Ai, age nine, in California

on that activity. My mother had given up trying to control me that way, partly because I was the family brain and I would someday become an _English Teacher,_ make a decent living, support my mother, and be a credit to the family and the race(s). So I was accorded certain privileges like watching TV till all hours, not cooking, and doing a minimum of housework, whereas my stepsister learned to cook, clean, and sew, and had to pick up the slack whenever I had extra studying, etc., etc. Although my stepsister is a working woman, she is rather traditional. I guess those roots are hard to kill off, or maybe she really was more domestic than I.

I wrote some fiction, but it didn't interest me as much as poetry. I must say that I developed my interest in moral ambiguity from fiction, though, and also from _film noir,_ which my mother loved and which I also came to enjoy and love now that I am older. I was fascinated by _The Scarlet Letter._ As I didn't know about my own illegitimacy, I can't say that that had anything to do with it. No, I was just fascinated by the story and the characters and the judgement meted out to them by society, acting as God's henchmen. I have never lost that desire to understand how certain people can set themselves up as guardians of morality. Illegitimacy _was_ an issue then, though. There's such a high birthrate among young unmarried African-American women now that nobody seems to remember a time when it was unacceptable, but believe me, it was. In Tucson, there was a caste system among African-Americans too. The Mexican-African-American mixtures, Filipino-African-American, and Indian-African-American, as well as a few very well-off full-blooded African-Americans, comprised the African-American upper class in Tucson. That's the class I come from. We were better off financially, at least in how we saw ourselves, though really we would be called lower-lower-middle class today. The closest thing, I think, to my family and the society they inhabited was probably the Creole society of New Orleans. Needless to say, welfare was a no-no. Only the most pathetic people were thought to need welfare and people on it were disapproved of, if not downright shunned.

My mother was quite strict and I could only go out on double dates (once in a while) with my cousin John. I never had a single date until I was a freshman in college, so one can't totally judge the scene by me, and indeed by my freshman year in college in 1965, the social stigma against out-of-wedlock pregnancy had eased enough that several young women got pregnant and dropped out. They got married,

though, because things hadn't changed quite that much yet.

College was a terrible shock for me. I didn't write at all my first year. I missed my friends from high school. I hated science. I got a _D_ in typing. I failed biology, which I hated. I dropped botany and finally found my niche in geology. I did not like my freshman English class, but I loved my major, which, surprisingly to some people, was Japanese. One night before registration, I'd been reading the college catalog, assuming I'd be majoring in English, when I happened on Oriental Studies. I can't explain the feeling that came over me when I read the description of courses in Japanese. I can only describe it as a kind of peace. That night, I made my decision, not knowing whether in the end it would make a difference because I had not been able to save enough money for registration and my latest stepfather, a barber, would not lend it to me. The fee was $125! In those days, I barely had five dollars a month to spend. My mother did housework and I worked as a janitorial assistant for the Neighborhood Youth Corp. Right after graduation, someone stole my purse at Woolworth's and my last paycheck for $90 was in it. That was all I had for the summer and I couldn't find anything else. There weren't all these fast-food places then and such. It was tough, especially if you were a minority, and of course it still is, probably more so. If I couldn't afford college, what was I going to do? Finally, I applied for a job as a Playboy Bunny. They were interviewing in Phoenix and I figured I could work and pay for school. Ha! After looking at myself with the blinders off, I had to admit that I did not have the boobs for it. There I was looking just like the stereotypical flat-chested Japanese woman. They'd never hire me, I thought. Anyway, I was only seventeen. Looking back, even if I had had boobs, I would never have lasted among those chauvinists, but remember, it was still only 1965. My consciousness hadn't been completely raised yet. It's funny too that my mother, who was so strict, only smiled when I showed her the card from Playboy, inviting me to a get-acquainted party. She knew I'd come to my senses, as moms often do, but if she'd railed against it, I'm sure I would have gone. I'd never thought of doing anything but teaching. What would I do? On the last day of registration, I was lying in bed depressed when my grandmother came over. "Get up," she said, "I got the money for you." I couldn't believe it. I jumped up, dressed, and rushed to campus. I still needed books and such and I don't remember now how I got them, but I did. The second semester, I tried to get on work-study, but they said my stepfather made too much money, and although he gave me nothing (my mother bought our food), they would not accept me, so I started to do housework. My grandmother would drop me off on her way to work and pick me up on her way home. I was quite timid and I remember my grandmother asking me what the woman had me do. When I told her, she was really angry, because I was doing more than I was supposed to for the money. One day she said, "You don't have to do this." She dressed up in her uniform and took me to the work-study office. She practically begged the director to let me on the program. He was from Georgia and kept calling my grandmother girl, though they were about the same age. She was at her most humble, most subservient, and she got me on work-study. Later, we went home so she could, as she put it, take off that goddamn uniform. It was her day off.

Oriental Studies hired me as a filing and research assistant. I mostly worked for a professor who was compiling a bibliography of Indian literature. I spent hours and hours at the library. I also got coffee for all the professors, made mimeos, and filed cards. I worked twenty hours a week and carried eighteen credits. It was hard at first. I had also decided to be a double major; my other field was English. My sophomore year, I told the Oriental Studies secretary, Cindy, that I wrote poetry and she told me she had a great teacher, Dr. Byrd Granger, and that I should show her some of my poems. I did, and eventually, Dr. Granger became my first mentor. She was so supportive and she was honest. I like to think that that's the kind of teacher I am today. She wasn't a woman who expected her students to love her, but she demanded their respect and she got it. It takes a lot of courage to not care whether your students like you and a lot more to let them develop as thinking individuals and not mere regurgitators. I had two other teachers like that in my freshman and sophomore years. One of them, Edward Putzar, taught me Japanese. He would take us out for coffee. He didn't believe in tests because he didn't think they necessarily showed that you had *learned* anything. He required long papers instead. He got in trouble with the chairman because students complained. They preferred tests! The other great teacher was Mr. Moynihan, who taught expository writing. He was a real wild man in a time when almost everyone conformed. His classes were always a surprise. You never knew what he'd do. Some days, he would leave his desk and come sit in the back of the room with me, Vince Peluso from New Jersey, and Nancy Giguerre, a

straight-ahead intellectual who was into Beckett when hardly anybody on campus had ever heard of him, teachers included. When he brought a spokesperson from the NAACP to a class to talk about civil rights and prejudice on campus, the president's wife demanded to speak to the class. She claimed that Mr. Moynihan was rude and disrespectful to her, and he was fired.

The summer before my junior year began, I won a National Defense Foreign Language Fellowship to Columbia University to study Japanese in an intensive ten-week program. I had never been East and never traveled alone, so I was very excited and scared. My mother's marriage was breaking up and things were in complete chaos at home, but I didn't care, I just wanted out. I started hanging out with my friends more and more. They were experimenting with grass and the hippie life-style, but I was merely an onlooker. I kind of regarded it all as a thing white people did. I felt like they could afford to slack off. They were not from poor families and I thought they'd never know what it was like to do without. I was wrong to stereotype them and that's unfair, I know; but at the time, I couldn't understand giving up on your education, which to me was my one chance to make it. Actually, I worked with a white guy who was poor, and we both used to work our asses off day after day. We'd sit outside at break and watch the fraternity and sorority types driving their Corvettes and GTOs. "God, I hate 'em," he'd say. I couldn't even afford a suitcase for the trip. One of the professors gave me fifteen dollars and I went to a discount store and bought one and a footlocker, which I just threw away about a month ago. June 1967 and I was on a train to New York City and then I was there! A girlfriend from Arizona was a student at the Brooklyn Jewish Hospital School of Nursing in Bedford Stuyvesant. She had an Italian father and an African-American mother. She did not look African-American and that was always painful to her, because she wanted to. She was a Bobby Kennedy freak and had an extremely dirty mouth, huge boobs, and a wicked sense of humor. I found her totally intimidating. I was so shy then, you see.

It was that summer, holed up in Johnson Hall of Columbia, ignoring my class work, that I began seriously to read Beat poetry. I listened to the radio, wrote Beat poems, read the *East Village Other*. I went to see the Doors at Steve Paul's club, The Scene. I even got their autographs, plus Robby Kreiger asked if I wanted to have a drink, but I didn't drink and I was too shy. I got Jim Morrison and John Dinsmore mixed up and they signed each other's names and they never let on. I was mortified later when I realized it. They could have made fun of me, but they didn't. I saw the Four Tops, the Fugs, and Frank Zappa. I bought a tape recorder, Haitian beads, a dirty novel about homosexual brothers. In other words, I was getting an education, one that was 90 percent fun, 10 percent work, and of course, ultimately, got me a *B-* average. I got called into the office and told to shape up or ship out. I could have buckled down, but I didn't want to. I found the constant testing agonizing. I was not used to the high-pressure kind of college most of the other kids came from, like Dartmouth and Harvard. I had the weekend to change my mind and might have, but my cousin John was killed in Vietnam. The trip back was so upsetting. On the way out to New York, there'd been the Arab-Israeli War. Now, going back, there were riots in Cleveland. The African-American train attendant seemed less friendly, seemed angry, though not at me, of course, but definitely at the white people. In fact, he told me he was. I was mostly numb. John and I were ten months apart; he was older, but I was ahead of him in school. He was the one who chaperoned me, even the night I graduated from high school. My mother walked me to his car and made me go to the big party with him. Now he was gone forever. I kept remembering the last time I'd seen him. The family let me go to the station alone to see him off. He was wearing his uniform. We really didn't have a lot to say to each other. The family disapproved of his girlfriend, so we talked about her mostly and mutual friends. I watched him climb up the steps of the Greyhound and I never saw him alive again.

My mother was divorced now and things should have been more peaceful at home, but they weren't. My stepfather had gone into the house and put all the furniture in storage, and we couldn't afford to get it out, so relatives gave us odds and ends. In the end, we had everything but a refrigerator and a car. I bought a car with the last of the fellowship money. An Olds for $150. We kept milk in a Styrofoam chest and the other perishables at my grandmother's. We managed. My mother was going through a crisis about turning forty and was crying all the time, and when she wasn't, she was partying with a twenty-year-old man. We were scandalized. My grandmother, my great aunts, her girlfriends were all upset. Now that I'm her age, I don't see anything wrong with it, but then . . . She was neglecting us, though. She stopped working too, and my stepsister and I paid all the bills. I took care of the house payment and bought most of the food.

My junior year had begun and I had decided to take a poetry class for the first time. I signed up with Richard Shelton. I got to be friends with the narrative-writing teacher and Steve Orlen, a poet from the Iowa Workshop. Those two saw something in my work and took me under their wings. Now I got to go to parties with them. I had literary fellowship at last. That's so important for a young writer and I think really necessary to one's growth and the growth of one's work. People were very supportive and there was this feeling of excitement in the air. The antiwar movement was going full throttle. Even in apathetic Tucson, people were dropping out, doing drugs, discovering themselves. Whether you chose one path or another, they were all connected, all part of the sixties thing, which was really a time like no other in the history of this country. No matter how you feel about that period, you can't deny that there was a vitality, a willingness to risk everything, that is gone now.

I hadn't paid a lot of attention to the whole Vietnam thing. I don't know, maybe I can be condemned for that, but after John was killed, I went on my first peace march. I started reading I. F. Stone, the *Real Paper,* the *Catholic Worker* even. I decided to drop the English major and minor in creative writing. I was devoting less and less time to Japanese studies, but I didn't care. I really had found, or rather rediscovered, my calling.

In the spring of 1968, I met Galway Kinnell. He came to give a reading at the Poetry Center. It was customary for the poet to give a reading, visit a class, and have conferences with students. When he came to class, we were in awe. I had moved away from home, and my roommate and I decided to have a party for Galway. I don't remember talking to him at all that night, but the next day, we had a conference scheduled. First, I went to a sorority house to pick up something the dean of women said they had for me. When I got there, it turned out that four of us were the recipients of awards given to the underprivileged! I think we were all embarrassed. The housemother spoke at a microphone. She said how well we'd done, considering our backgrounds, etc., etc. The African-American maid was smiling as she served the girls and their guests, pausing to give me a special pat on the shoulder. The housemother frowned at her as she disappeared into the kitchen with her tray. I mumbled a thank you and sat back down, only to find myself completely ignored, so I left. I opened the envelope outside. It contained a check for seventy-five dollars. I called my mother and told her, then I went to have my talk with Galway. He was very generous, very interested in what I was doing, and at the end of the conference asked me to send him a poem I was working on when I finished it. I never did, but I began to send him poems. When he had time, he'd send them back with comments. It was really great. I had such a crush on him. All the women did, men too. I used to walk around with a copy of *Body Rags*, and a couple of guys I knew did too. For months after Galway left, we'd talk about the reading, the party, the poems. It was the best time I had as an undergraduate. Galway really seemed like some kind of heroic figure from all our imaginations, especially after he read "The Bear" to us. I read W. S. Merwin for the first time and James Wright. Along with Galway, they were my favorite poets. I had a list of one hundred poets Dick Shelton had given the class, and I read at least one book by each of them. It really was one of the richest times in my life. I was learning so much and it was a pleasure. It was the way education ought to be for students, a joyous, almost sexual experience that leaves one wanting more.

I was also taking short-story courses, but only because one had to in order to minor in creative writing. I just wasn't interested in writing fiction. It's funny though, looking back, how I kind of played at poetry right up to the time Galway came to town. I went from my Beat poems to writing horror poems to writing folk songs, but one day I had a conference with Dick, and he said if I wanted to write songs, I had to be as good as Bob Dylan or better than he was. After I thought about it, I decided to get serious about poetry. I didn't really want to write songs or horror poems. I wanted to write poetry with a capital *P*, and that's what I tried to do. I have to give Galway credit for seeing something in all that nonsense, because I would probably have said, "Geez, what a loser," if I'd been honest with myself. And I was finally when I really began to work at my craft. On the other hand, I was writing much better stories. I wrote a takeoff on *The Scarlet Letter* that my teacher thought was good. He was from Mississippi and everyone in class was afraid of him, not only because he was unfriendly and a tough teacher, but also because he looked like a cadaver. I had my own fears about Southern whites and felt he could not possibly want me in his class, although I never once felt anything like that from him. Anyway, it was in that class that I started to use the male and female voices that would crop up in *Cruelty*. I didn't feel comfortable with more than two characters and was not great

at dialogue, so I mainly stuck with narrative, when I could get away with it.

I applied for and got a scholarship to a writer's conference near Potsdam, New York. I got a ride there with a faculty member in the English department. I slept in the car and he slept out under the stars. Bobby Kennedy was assassinated while we were going across country. Martin Luther King had already been killed earlier that year. I wasn't very political, but I remember this heavy depression settled over me, which really had begun the summer before with the death of my cousin. I think I owe the workshop for lifting me out of it. There at the lake, up near the Canadian border where one couldn't even pick up radio, I let go of the outside for awhile. Krishna Vaid, a novelist from India, was director of the conference. Alan Dugan was there the whole two weeks, and Peter Davison and Laurence Lieberman came, as well as Vance Bourjaily. Needless to say, there was some hanky-panky, and I was shocked, because I had never seen adults outside my own family behaving badly, or rather in a way of which I disapproved. It seems pretty tame now, but I sure had stories to tell when I got back to Arizona.

My senior year began and I started to think about graduate school. It was clear that I would not get a master's degree in Oriental Studies, so I started thinking about getting a master of fine arts in writing. Steve Orlen recommended Iowa and I sent for an application, but I chickened out. Then I decided I wanted to go to Columbia University. I had no money, so I would have to get some kind of financial aid. I put off making a decision, though, as long as I could. That fall, W. S. Merwin came to read. He was beautiful, like you'd imagine Byron looked. I got a huge crush on him, but it was different from Galway. You see, Galway was a kindred spirit. Not in his work or his philosophy exactly, but from the first I think we knew it, though it remained largely undefined. It just was. I'm still trying to figure it out. For me, it was a kind of spiritual-father thing, though now it's more brother-sister. It is a kinship of some sort. Hell, I guess it's just the fellowship of poetry, but it's stronger between some people than others. I'm not saying it was the same for Galway, though. After all, he was the master and I was the apprentice. It became over the course of the past twenty-one years the major literary relationship of my life. That's why I call Galway my mentor. I never even saw him that often, but it made an enormous difference that this poet was out there reading my work and encouraging me. I always felt that he would give me an honest opinion.

Finally, I applied to Columbia and the University of Oregon at Eugene. Eugene had a good program then and one of the poets at the University of Arizona, William Roecker, had gotten his degree there. A woman my grandmother worked for, Mrs. Brophy, helped me get a Ford Foundation Scholarship to Columbia. It wasn't enough money, so I was agonizing over that when Galway invited me to come visit him in California for Easter. When I met his graduate students, they said I should come there to the University of California at Irvine. Galway had read them some of my poems and he had also shown them to Jim McMichael, a fellow faculty member. Galway was a Visiting Writer and was leaving in June, but Jim said he'd help me if I wanted to come there. When I got home, I had a letter saying I'd received a teaching assistantship at Eugene, but I was completely sold on Irvine. I told Galway to go ahead and get things started, and I applied for a graduate research assistantship.

That last semester, I'd enrolled in an independent-study course in African history. I did a paper on West African religion, but I wasn't happy with it. I asked the professor if I could give him a poem instead, and he said I could. The first really successful poem I wrote was "Warrior." The professor gave me an *A.* "Warrior" was also the first poem I got published in a real magazine. When I visited Irvine, the students told me to send something to a magazine called *Lillabulero.* They said the editor, William Matthews, was a great guy and open to work by unknowns. I also wrote "Hangman," "The Root Eater," and "Cannibal" that spring. Those poems were all accepted by magazines. It was a very exciting and unbelievable thing to have happen. I really didn't make much of it, though. I was happy, but more concerned with graduating and getting into Irvine. Even though I wanted an M.F.A. and all, I was not career oriented. I just wanted to write and get my degree, so I could teach and support myself. I didn't even call myself a poet yet. I didn't think I had the right.

I also experimented with what I called lyrical poems. I liked them, but nobody else seemed to. The last poet who came to read that spring was Allen Ginsberg. I gave him some poems, but I didn't have a conference with him. Later, he sent them back with comments. I still have the poems and the letter with his suggestions. I appreciated them, but I'd already decided to abandon that form and was back writing my narratives. I hadn't really begun to think of my poems as persona poems, or dramatic monologues, yet. I kind of fell into the form, because Dick Shelton

once said the "I" point of view was sometimes the stronger, more immediate voice in the poem. "Warrior" was not a monologue at first, but when I *became* the warrior, I thought it was a better poem. That happened time after time, and I guess I figured that I should always write monologues. It didn't happen all at once. At some point, I realized that not only was the "I" poem better, but that I personally found it more satisfying to write. I loved being someone else. I loved disappearing into character, but I never considered those characters masks. They were characters and not a way of avoiding my own life in my work. For me, working in the confessional form, for example, would have been impossible. I had no skill at it, no interest in writing it, although I loved reading Sylvia Plath and Robert Lowell. No, I wanted to be someone else, live some other life, and then return to my own when I was done with the poem. Maybe if I were a playwright, I wouldn't have to explain why creating characters is so important to me.

When summer began, my best friend, who was no longer (as he put it) into material things, rang my doorbell one day, and when I opened the door, he was gone, but there was an envelope containing a round-trip air ticket to Rhode Island in it. I'd met a guy the summer before at the writer's conference and he'd invited me out for a few weeks. One day he called to say he'd gotten tickets to some concert called Woodstock.

I was so excited about my first trip on an airplane, I didn't do much writing. I certainly didn't write once I was in Rhode Island. It was a strange situation. He was a WASP and his girlfriend was Vietnamese. She lived in New York City and wasn't going to Woodstock with us. When we got to Woodstock, we ended up being stuck on the highway for about twelve hours. People were getting more and more hostile and we just said fuck it and asked a farmer how to get out. He showed us a back road through the woods and eventually we escaped. Boy did we ever feel like fools when we heard how great it was. We should have gotten out and walked to the field, but we were too chicken. When we went to New York to see Josie, his girlfriend, we tried to make up for missing Woodstock by seeing Van Morrison and Led Zeppelin, but it wasn't enough. We were so embarrassed that we'd say Woodstock was great, if anybody asked.

When I got back to Arizona, I still hadn't heard from Irvine. It was down to the wire on Columbia and Eugene. I turned down Eugene first, then Columbia. Finally, I got word that I was in at Irvine. I'd gotten

$2700 a year for two years, plus I wouldn't have to pay out-of-state tuition either. Galway was gone, but Charles Wright was back at Irvine. Jim McMichael put me and my Siamese, Baby, up until I could find an apartment. I guess not many people can say that Charles Wright took them apartment hunting. Those guys were great. They really went the extra mile for me. I finally found an apartment in Laguna Beach. What a shock California was. I was terribly homesick. I can't imagine how I would have fared in New York, because I found Laguna too fast. Nobody in the workshop seemed to like my poems. I wasn't satisfied with what I was writing. I even thought of going back to Arizona, but Dick Shelton said an M.F.A. was better (the University of Arizona only had a master's then) and that I needed new teachers. He was right and I'm glad I took his advice and stayed.

All the poems I sent out were rejected and I was very depressed. I'd done so well until then. I didn't know what had happened. Some students liked Charles Bukowski a lot and said they were sure he'd love my work, so I sent him some poems. He edited a magazine then. When the poems were finally sent back, the envelope was all crushed as if he were going to throw it away but changed his mind, and the poems just had the word "reject" written on them in red crayon! I was devastated. I didn't even want to write. I started hanging out at the Hare Krishna Temple in Laguna and going to LA to see the Swami when he was in town and chanting, etc. One Sunday, Timothy Leary drove by the temple, just gazing out the window at us as we sat on the steps outside. After about two months, I decided enough was enough and I stopped going. Around that time, I got word that Robert Mezey and Denis Saleh had taken some poems of mine for *Just What the Country Needs: Another Poetry Anthology.* I was the youngest poet in the anthology and the only woman. In those days, poetry was still basically an all-male field in that it was harder to get published, hell, even read, if you were a woman. I got my confidence back and started writing again, without caring too much anymore about what other people thought, at least at the time.

It was around this time, too, that I finally decided to publish under a pen name. I had used my sister's father's surname all my life. My first name was Florence and my stepfather's surname was Haynes, but when I started Irvine, I decided to use the name on my birth certificate. That name was Anthony. I thought it sounded more poetic. My mother was very upset, but I didn't know why. Of course, now that I know about my natural father and all, I understand her objections. But I really wanted a pen name for

some reason. I finally decided on Ai, which means "love" in Japanese.

Donald Justice was the Visiting Writer the second year and I took a workshop with him. We got a few new students from the East, who seemed supercritical to me, but I was tougher and was able to stand up to them most of the time. I knew by then that I'd never survive the workshop without unleashing my ego. I wrote a poem a week then. I'd sit up until 4 A.M. or so every night. I settled into the monologue form for good that year. I reached the point, too, where I knew I was on track and that no matter what anybody said, I'd never stop writing. I still had no career plans exactly. I was getting my thesis ready and thinking about finals. In April 1971, Galway came to do a reading. One day, he asked me if he could have a copy of my thesis. It was called "Slice." I gave him one and didn't think about it anymore. I applied for some jobs. I also sent my thesis out to a press, but they weren't publishing any more poetry. Charles was giving me a ride to school the day of my finals (I didn't drive and still don't), but he was late. I was so upset that they let me reschedule and I did fine, and then it was time to start my adult life. I thought. I could not find a teaching job and I was quite worried. For awhile, I thought I'd stay in California, but I was too scared. I'd finally succeeded in losing my virginity to a creep (naturally), and I was depressed because he'd dumped me. I thought I might feel better if I went back to Tucson, so my stepsister and her husband came and got me. It was more of the same in Tucson, though. No work. I later heard that there were rumors that I was too unstable to teach at the U of A! What a joke. I've outlasted most of the people I started out with in poetry class. You can't last in this field if you don't have some core of stability in yourself that keeps you together. Maybe I would have shorted out without poetry, but it meant and means so much to me that I consider it my salvation. I know it isn't like that for everybody, but in my case poetry was my guardian angel and helped me walk the mighty fine line between self-destruction and survival. I'd say that when your art does that for you, you're truly blessed and you owe it to that art to look after yourself, to treat yourself and it with respect, and that includes whatever emanates from that art too, that gift. In September 1971, I got a job working for Model Cities as the Recreation and Culture specialist. I led the task force in Tucson. I set up recreational and cultural activities through organizations like the Boy Scouts. The residents of neighborhoods would tell you what they wanted and then you would try to help them. I started at $10,000. My family was so proud. I was bored. I hated city government. I was totally unprepared for how political even my position was. If you didn't scratch the right back, eat lunch with the African-Americans instead of the Mexicans, it could be a problem. To complicate matters, one man who could have been an ally was said to be a lech, so I tried to avoid him. I also hated my boss, a woman who would accuse me of not paying attention during our assertiveness-training sessions. One day, she said the wrong thing to me and I knocked a file off her desk. Needless to say, my contract was terminated. I got a job at a junior college teaching one freshman comp class, and I worked as a file clerk the rest of the time. Although I made a lot less money, it was much better for me.

That September, I'd gotten a letter from Arabel Porter at Houghton Mifflin, saying Galway had given her my thesis. She said she wanted to see a new manuscript, or new poems that could be added to "Slice." I was so preoccupied with earning a living that I didn't even answer. It wasn't until I started teaching that I started to write again. After being uninspired for a long time, I was suddenly starting a poem as soon as I finished one. I wrote about three-quarters of the poems that ended up in *Cruelty* in the spring of 1972. In May, I wrote Houghton Mifflin and told Arabel that I had a new manuscript. I asked if she still wanted to see it and she said she did, but just because Galway had put us in touch, I shouldn't expect it to mean they'd want to publish me. In June, I mailed the manuscript. In October 1972, I got a telegram from Houghton Mifflin saying they wanted to publish my manuscript, which was called "Wheel in a Ditch." The wheel represented Ezekiel's wheels, and that in turn represented the spirit trapped by circumstances. It was also the title of a Neil Young song. Once the process of putting the book together began, Arabel told me she thought that the title was too prosey. I tried to come up with something, but nothing satisfied me. What title from what poem would work? I couldn't decide. One night, she called and said she'd read the table of contents to Galway and that he'd suggested "Cruelty," which was the title of a poem in the manuscript. I said it was fine with me.

We did disagree about my pen name. That was the only name I wanted on the book, but Arabel insisted on putting my so-called real name on it. By then, I was sure my mother had something to tell me about my natural father and I realized there was more to her not wanting me to use the surname Anthony. I even wrote Arabel and told her, but I was

so young and powerless that she got her way. It caused me a lot of problems later, because people thought I was abandoning my background or something, when (quite the opposite) I was trying to claim it. It's taken me years to try and erase that surname from people's minds, and even the *New York Times* review of *Sin* had the name Florence Anthony in parentheses. I must say, though, that when I wrote and complained, the *Times* published my letter. Imagine being Florence Haynes until you were twenty-two, then on a whim using the name Anthony, which had no meaning for you anyway, and having people insist on using it. What a drag. If I was anybody, I was Florence Haynes, but that wasn't legal. Anthony was, but it was a lie.

Houghton Mifflin sent a copy of the manuscript to the *American Poetry Review* and they wrote and asked me to pick some poems for them to publish. They also said they'd put my photo on the cover. They had a photographer from the local newspaper come to my house. They even paid me! I already had an advance on *Cruelty*. Whoa, I thought, what a fairy tale.

The State University of New York at Binghamton had hired me as a creative-writing instructor, so I moved that fall. I was teaching there when *Cruelty* came out in October 1973. I didn't feel that great or anything, because I was so far from home and my friends. When the first copies of the book came, I held one in my hands as if it were glass or something. I kept looking at the back and the front. I really couldn't believe it. That was really the most exciting thing, just holding it in my hands.

When the review in the *New York Times Book Review* came out, I started getting calls about readings for the first time. I'd only done two professionally. Philip Levine, whom I'd met at Irvine, gave me my first reading for money in the spring of 1972. He also offered to give my manuscript to Harry Ford at Atheneum, but it was already at Houghton Mifflin. I'd also read at the U of A. Now calls were coming in from places like Missouri and Austin.

The book was getting reviewed all over the country. If it got slammed at all, it was usually because the reviewer thought there was too much sex and violence in my poems. I didn't think of them that way. Actually, I always saw them as sexual more than anything, and the violence came out of the situations, or so I hoped. In graduate school, I felt that violence was the one thing I did not handle well in my work, but I felt that our society was indeed quite violent. I needed to be able to understand it, and I tried by dealing with it in my poems, if it had some place in the characters' lives. I hoped I'd learn something from my exploration of the outward violence, which was really a manifestation of inner violence.

The other thing the reviewers did that bothered me was that they were always calling me a black poet. I didn't object if someone else wanted to be labeled that way, but I preferred not to be. My family had always been so careful to speak of themselves as being multiracial, or at least in recognizing and honoring their multiethnicity, that I wanted to do the same thing. Why couldn't I claim what was rightfully mine? I must say that reviewers in the South never referred to my race and never questioned the violence in my poems. Interesting, isn't it? The people one most expected to point out race never did.

On Christmas Eve night, 1973, my mother phoned me to tell me finally about my natural father. "I have to tell you," she said, "your father was Japanese." Even though I knew there was a secret about my conception, it was still a shock to hear it like that. I was so far away. This was the first Christmas away from my family. I don't know how I got through that holiday. After all those years, I knew the story. Although she said he was dead, I didn't believe her. I tried to find him, but I only got as far as the name of a Japanese minister who supposedly knew all the Japanese families who'd lived in Denver around the time I'd been conceived. I finally got in touch with him, but he said all the Japanese with that name had moved away. He did not say he didn't know any Ogawas and I felt he knew more than he was willing to tell me. I think I almost felt more alone than before. I did try to claim him as my father by legally changing my surname to his. I also made Ai my legal middle name. It was something I needed to do at the time and I have not called myself Florence either since 1981. I don't even feel the need for my father's surname anymore, but I certainly had to use it in order to know. I'm content just being Ai. Maybe it's spiritual or something. I'm sure that in the Book of Life that's my name, and the other was just a vehicle to get me here.

Virtually from the moment *Cruelty* was published, I had a name. I don't think I understood what that meant exactly. On some level, I felt threatened by all the attention. I'd always been so shy. When I read at Cornell, they told me the last poet had taken off all his clothes during his reading. I wrote a reviewer and told him to go to shit. I wouldn't do that now. I was very naive, too. I thought all that attention meant something, but in truth you're only as good as your last book. People want to get on board the latest big bus and ride for awhile, but they get off at their stop; they are not along for the whole trip, and if you think they are, you end up very disappointed and alone. I had acquired such a big ego that when I turned down another year at Binghamton, I expected to find work right away. What a shock when June came and I had nothing for fall. I was devastated. It would take me years to realize that my career as a poet and my career as a poet who teaches are not the same thing. The value you are accorded as a writer more often than not is meaningless to English departments, unless you've won something like a Pulitzer, or you're a novelist. However, I think poetry was of much more value in the marketplace then. I think we were on a fairly equal level with fiction writers then, but not now.

July came, then August. For awhile, I lived off the money I'd saved. I had terrible anxiety and migraines. I also couldn't write because I was so upset. Finally, that fall, I got work in the Poetry in the Schools Program. The master poet, who trained new people, was a graduate student in the M.F.A. program at the U of A. I also got an application from the Guggenheim Foundation. Galway had asked them to send it to me. They warned me not to expect to win one if I applied, but they needn't have. I really couldn't imagine winning, especially so soon, but I trusted Galway. If he thought I had a chance, I was willing to try.

The master poet, Lawrence Kearney, and I had talked a few times before our first job. He was separated from his wife and had two-year-old twin boys. When we got to the Hopi/Navajo school for our first residency together, the people thought I was his wife and they put us in the same tiny room. By now, we were attracted to each other, but he wanted his marriage to be really over before we got involved. In the end, though, we couldn't wait. When I got back to Tucson, I was in love and I moved in with Lawrence and the boys. I had three Siamese and he had a dog. Suddenly, I had a family. I certainly didn't write much then. Also, I was in some kind of slump. If a poem sounded to me too much like a poem in *Cruelty,* I'd put a mental X across it. I just didn't know where I was going with my work or how I'd even get there. I was very depressed. I was also getting criticism from a friend that I think I was taking too much to heart because I'd lost my confidence. I don't think I was even sending Galway anything. I had applied for a National Endowment for the Arts Fellowship, which I didn't get (it took three tries). I also applied to Yaddo and MacDowell. MacDowell wrote and said that just because I could get recommendations from Galway, Merwin, and Michael Harper, that wasn't going to get me in and they rejected me, but Yaddo didn't. I decided against going there because I couldn't take the cats, and I have not applied to a writer's colony since. In April, I won a Guggenheim. That was so fantastic. For once, I could live in Tucson without being poor. Lawrence and I started buying antiques at the flea market. We also sold stuff. It was like a serious hobby with us. His wife came and took the kids and started divorce proceedings. Then Lawrence won a fellowship to the Fine Arts Work Center in Provincetown and I was invited to apply for a Bunting Fellowship. Though I didn't win any money, I became an affiliate, which meant that I could use the Harvard libraries and have a private office at Radcliffe.

After we moved, I was writing again but I wasn't satisfied. In 1976, I taught at the University of Massachusetts at Amherst as a visiting assistant professor for one year. After that, we moved to Detroit, where I taught at Wayne State University. In November 1977, I came out of my slump. I wrote the poems "Killing Floor" and "Nothing But Color." By April, my second book was finished.

In June, I read at an international poetry conference at SUNY at Stony Brook. It was the first time I'd ever appeared on a roster that included Galway. When we got back to Detroit, I got a phone call from Marie Bullock at the Academy of American Poets. She said, "Are you sitting down?" I said I wasn't, and she said, "Well, sit down," so I did. Then she told me that I'd won the Lamont Prize for the best second book published that year. I still get chills when I think about it. My new editor, Jonathan Galassi, called and

congratulated me. I was so happy, because it had been such a struggle getting those poems in *Killing Floor* out of myself.

I hated Detroit, and although I had a tenure track position, once I won the Lamont, I decided to resign and move to New York. You might call that the end of innocence for me. It was time for me actually to enter the world of poetry, the showbiz end, if you will. That's the part that kills your work if you're not careful, when you can let it all go to your head and writing can become secondary to the role one is playing of being a poet. I survived my success, but the marriage didn't. I have absolutely no regrets about that. When I gave my reading at the Donnell Library to celebrate having won the Lamont, I stood there looking out at the packed auditorium and all I thought was what a long way I'd come.

BIBLIOGRAPHY

Poetry:

Cruelty, Houghton, 1973.

Killing Floor, Houghton, 1979.

Sin, Houghton, 1986.

Cruelty/Killing Floor (reprint of titles, bound together), Thunders Mouth Press, 1987.

Fate, Houghton, 1991.

Contributor of articles and poems to magazines, including *Ms.*

Michael Andre

1946-

OF FABULOUS JANE AND JEZEBEL

"Me today, by Jane"

I

Poetry is unfortunately or not the most important thing in my life. What do we remember in fiction? The poetry. But family, religion, and the state dwarf poetry. Sex got me interested in verse. Here I am merely in my mid-forties and I already have an ex-girlfriend, an ex-wife, and an ex-lover. I don't know if any of the poetry I wrote as a boy for Marie's approval is around in print, but as an adult I published *Unmuzzled OX* with my wife Erika Rothenberg.

Before Erika and between the Cambodian incursion and the Christmas bombing I edited the first six numbers. The very first *OX* was keyed to an interview with Robert Creeley; my dissertation at Columbia, which I was writing at the time, was "Interviews and Essays with 7 American Poets." The first *OX* looked like hell but the buyer at the Gotham Book Mart was very impressed by the quality of the contributors and I decided that my public life had begun. Ah! To live in public and get paid for it!—every poet's dream. Unfortunately actors, politicians, and mass murderers have a similar dream.

OX is my very own poetry TV station on which the program of my own poetry regularly runs. Erika Rothenberg in 1972 was an art director—"print" and TV—at McCann-Erickson. I was writing regularly for *ARTnews,* something poet graduate students at Columbia did regularly, on the David Shapiro through John Ashbery connection. *ARTnews* and McCann were in the same building, which Erika and I discovered several years into our relationship when I went to drop off my copy with her when she went to work; New York is bigger than Kingston, Ontario.

I moved to Chicago in August 1968. Al Capone had been replaced by Richard Daley. Erika was there already, at the University of Chicago from whence she was expelled; I was amused reading her antics in the *Chicago Daily Maroon* for which I wrote film criticism; these antics foretold her career as a "Guerrilla Girl, conscience of the art world." The New Chicago School of Poets was an invention of the *Maroon* and of Radio Free Europe, which, through the university, broadcast "culture" as propaganda. I also hosted my own radio show, to be followed by a second show at Columbia a few years later; radio if you're the host is no harder than telephone. A hand

signal to the engineer in the glass booth and you get a promo during which you can calm your guest and ready him for the next hard question. We must murder to dissect other poets in public. None of my best friends are novelists; poetry is a harder row to hoe and I would never sadistically embarrass a poet; nevertheless I was surprised twenty years ago when Robert Creeley refused to discuss in public Charles Bukowski whom he loathed.

On the train from Montreal to Chicago I read Ezra Pound but hummed Bob Dylan. The French in Montreal wanted their fleur-de-lis to bloom and the police in Chicago were polite and the National Guard well armed. I learned my French at the Berlitz School in Paris in the summer of 1967. Is Quebec too far north for the lily to bloom?

> Mon pays ce n'est pas un pays
> c'est l'hiver
> Mon jardin ce n'est pas un jardin
> c'est la blanche

If Gilles Vigneault's jukebox "pays" was Canada, it was an "Anthem for a Doomed Nation." De Gaulle

"Jane"

just got carried away, according to *Le Monde,* and really didn't mean to shout from the balcony of Montreal's city hall, Vive le Quebec libre.

Canadian patriotism like feminism is an obvious lost cause. Erika and I were having dinner with Dan Berrigan and she asked him if there was any group on the left he disliked. Feminists, he said.

Erika equated religion and insanity. Erika was not stupid, just the daughter of Jewish atheists. I could not father her child if I was crazy, therefore I must undergo psychoanalysis. In 1979 we published *The Poets' Encyclopedia* and Erika's mother's press agent definitely helped and I listed Erika for the first time as coeditor; and we believed our reviews. She became more certain I was nuts and I saw she did not want a child, at least not with me—is that marriage? I took a lover who already had a child, and who had a husband she despised. My lover said she wanted another child. Erika said she wanted a divorce.

Why me? Why was my lover stupid? It seemed to take her a long time to get divorced. She seemed to have escalating needs. She didn't read very much—was she dyslexic? Her son was lovely and I didn't mind paying more and more of his expenses—much. But I found it harder and harder to get the magazine together and her friends weren't stupid enough to help. Six years into our relationship I came back early from visiting my parents in Kingston and discovered the obvious. Reading *Seven Types of Ambiguity* little prepared me for living with a deceiver like Ms. Reagan-Helms. Jezebel is of course not her real name, but liars deserve false or allegorical names. I tore up every picture of Jezebel and, the same night, every picture of Erika, and every painting, drawing, and sculpture I owned by Erika. Love is foolish but so is hate. "A Comparison of Her and the Madonna" on the surface claimed to be a comparison of Erika and Jezebel, but was in fact a prayer that the same end would not befall both relationships; it did. "Reasons for the Emergency," one of my few short stories, describes moment by moment the evening Erika found out about Jezebel: I told her. We are victims of our feelings. Marie's mother committed suicide.

I was a freshman at McGill. The funeral mass was at Saint Joseph's back in Kingston; the casket was closed. The sound of gunfire on the porch one time when Marie and I were making out at the cottage meant Dad knew we were there and decidedly disapproved. The sound of gunfire on Lispenard Street where Erika and I lived for eight years multiplied till quietus and one cop said to the other, "Did you get him Joe?"

"I got him," said Joe.

Ostensibly my father was just doing winter target practise. Marie and I made out there during Kennedy's November funeral. Such was high school. Marie was a year older and liked Steven McNamee, who liked poetry and, God knows, may have introduced her to poetry. Steven showed me a copy of Joyce's *Ulysses* which he was trying to read; I eventually read *Portrait of the Artist* and *Dubliners* in high school, and that confirmed me in my alternate vocation. Steven and I, like Stephen, attended a Jesuit high school.

Do love and education interact? Marie attended Notre Dame Convent when I was at Regiopolis College; the Jesuits are prohibited from teaching women; Marie induced me to write poetry. At McGill my very first lover taught me a little German, her first language. I never met Erika at Chicago; at Chicago I dated Diane Radycki, now an art historian at Harvard. Love acts, education directs.

Graduating from McGill, my first job was film critic for the *Montreal Gazette.* The Film Society at Queen's University, where I saw film in high school, and the Film Society at Lincoln Center share their total donkeydom. Linda Gillin, the actress who played Sister Anne Montgomery in my play *How I Blew Up the World,* like any honorable working actress, disliked my feelings about film; but she also disliked Jezebel, and one night in a Chinese restaurant she did Jezebel to my delighted laughter. Art can pinpoint problems before you feel them. Linda saw Jezebel's leisure-class values years before they messed up my life.

These various women got in each other's hair in various ways. Writing art criticism for *ARTnews* and the *Village Voice* myself after sliding out of Columbia, I attended with Erika a lecture on Paula Mödersohn-Becker given by Diane Radycki. Erika was not yet at that point a prominent artist. Thus Diane thought she was doing Erika a favor when she placed Diane's views in Erika's mouth in a subsequent article about Mödersohn-Becker. Erika probably would have been happy had it not represented the precise opposite of her own belief.

Intercession between feuding heterosexuals is a good way to get your fingers broken. Robert Creeley wrote *Presences* supposedly about the sculpture of Marisol. She didn't think so. Marisol hangs out in Puffy's, the same bar where I met Jezebel. Creeley introduced Marisol and me, and after about ten years I got so tired of hearing her complain about his book I decided to write a column in the *Small Press Review* about it. Creeley read it, and apparently didn't like it; and furthermore it emboldened Marisol to deny Creeley reprint rights. And thus it is that the man who keyed the first issues of *Unmuzzled OX* will no longer contribute.

My middle finger is broken and therefore I must state my resentment at the mealy-mouthed French diplomacy of Ashbery, Creeley, et al. I suppose I liked W. H. Auden because I was too young to have any kind of normal man-to-man expectations. When I phoned Ezra Pound, Olga Rudge answered. "You wish to speak to Mr. Pound?" she asked.

I wished to *be* Mr. Pound.

Eliot was already dead. I was in Florence. Pound was moving from Venice to Rapallo, an annual move, the next day, she said. I learned he was dead watching television with Erika back in New York six months later. That, indeed, was the night Erika and I met; her boyfriend at the time, Carl Desens, said Pound was the last.

Who was the weird redhead with pluckt eyebrows and dyed hair? Some non-Pre-Raphaelite Beauty who'd stared too long at Burne-Jones?

I'll never know since for the last six years she's refused to communicate with me in any way. The competition between poets is as bitter as that between ex-spouses; yet artists and poets get along well. My best friend, Robert Buecker, is a gay artist and harpsichord maker. He's the executive-director of the SoHo Baroque Opera Company and I'm the treasurer; the opera company publishes *Unmuzzled OX*. I plan to pirate some Auden librettos. The best thing Auden said to me was, "No tape recorders!"

He was self-conscious about his wrinkles. Laurie Anderson, who was my semi-roommate at the time, drew for the cover of *OX* "two linear portraits of W. H. Auden, who wasn't, as Russell suggests, born five minutes ago." I always suspected Russell was Bertrand Russell but have never inquired, even though, twenty years later, I still see Laurie every now and then trudging these TriBeCa streets. Laurie, like David Shapiro, that other friend of 1972, hacked away regularly at the violin. In 1976 I took up the flute. After I published an article in the *Village Voice* about his gallery, Robert Buecker invited me to join the board of the SoHo Baroque Opera Company. I became treasurer, and Andrew Bolotowsky the flutist is president. For many years Andrew toured playing duets with Jane Adler. As I write this way late in 1990 Jane is pregnant and I'm the Dad.

II

I was born in Halifax. My mother's father was a writer. In Jane's tummy via ultrasound I've seen my child swimming, like a trout in an aquarium.

"Me and Granddad. This must have been shortly after my schizoid pal and I burnt down the shed."

Grandfather Warburton missed that thrill, but he did hear the big guns of World War I from a trench in France; and was shot in the head. He recovered, enough anyway to edit various newspapers in Canada; the wound looked like a third eye. But then in 1919, with my mother still a toddler, his wife was carried away by Bright's disease. He was writing for the Kingston *Whig-Standard* at the time, and my mother's maternal grandparents were also in Kingston; my great-grandfather Tierney, after a career as a mess sergeant in the Royal Dublin Fusiliers, had opened a restaurant in Kingston. Religion was the first important thing in my life.

My mother was born in Blackpool, England, across the Irish Sea. Her father was English, educated, and Anglican, but her mother was Irish Catholic. When her mother died, her Irish grandparents raised her, taking her to Saint Mary's Cathedral on Sundays and sending her to Notre Dame for school, the same school Marie and my sister attended thirty years later. My father was also the child of a mixed marriage. His mother was Anglo-Irish and quite Protestant. She had that native Irish gift for the quarrel, and while my father was at Queen's University, his parents were, like me, divorced.

My paternal grandfather's biography says a great deal about the Canadian body politic. Andre is a

French name; in all written communications from the Canadian government, they add an accent to the final *e*. My grandfather was born in New York City, but his father was born in Paris, France. This man, Alexandre Andre, my great-grandfather, was a carpenter and contractor in New York City. He had a son, Thomas, and two daughters; and he was bilingual. In the 1890s, when Sergeant Tierney was fighting in the Boer War, Alex took a job in Ottawa, the federal capital, where bilingualism counted.

Kingston, Ontario, was the first capital of the united British provinces of Upper and Lower Canada. Many federal institutions, as well as Queen's University, remain. Alex and his son, Tom, soon moved south from Ottawa to Kingston; given the jig north of the Saint Lawrence River, Kingston, besides, was about as close psychologically to New York City as you can get in Canada. My great-aunts stayed in New York, married, so they say, two Jews, and moved ultimately to Beverly Hills, California. I've never met them, but Erika Rothenberg, my own Jewish ex-wife, now lives in Los Angeles.

The construction business is political. My grandfather developed my great-grandfather's business. My father is a civil engineer and my uncle Jack a carpenter. After the Second World War, my parents returned from Halifax to Kingston. My father, uncle, and grandfather incorporated as "T. A. Andre & Sons, General Contractors & Engineers." They prospered through the fifties. My grandfather ran for public office as a Liberal.

Politics and the media are not easy. Uncle Jack was also a Liberal. In the late fifties and early sixties, Diefenbaker, a Tory, was prime minister. My father contributed equally to both mainstream parties; the New Democrats, allied with organized labor, were alone anathema. Many Fridays my mother would take me from school, and we'd drive to Ottawa, where tenders were due at 3:00 P.M. Then, for the weekend, while my parents stayed at the Château Laurier, Parliament Hill became a favorite solitary playground. My grandfather was public utilities commissioner, and rival industrialists had submitted bids for a Frontenac County power development. Alone together in my grandfather's office one of them offered him a $10,000 bribe. Enraged, he ordered the man from his office.

Enraged, Granddad told a reporter from the *Whig-Standard*. The headline that day was "Andre Offered $10,000 Bribe." The headline the next day was the industrialist's defense, "Andre Demanded Bribe." The bottom line was zero, in that the other

industrialist got the contract and my grandfather was not reelected.

Soon after my father bought out his brother and father. Uncle Jack moved to Orillia, started various construction companies, and was eventually elected mayor. My father never felt he could afford political opinions. At McGill I brought him a petition against the war and asked him and a business buddy in Montreal to sign. Neither would.

"Generation gap" was the appropriate phrase used by *Life* magazine back then in the spring of 1967. I spent May to September in Europe with a French Canadian writer, Bernard Robitaille. "Two solitudes" is Hugh MacLennan's annoyingly appropriate phrase for the gap between me and Bernard, between the English and the French Canadian. I learned to introduce myself in French, Je m'appelle Michel, but the charm of this rhyme would wear thin quickly if I then attempted to excuse my English accent by saying my family was *assimilé*. But how else could I explain that last name without the accent?

By 1968 people were fighting in the street over such things.

III

From February to August 1968 I was in three riots. The first was at McGill. It was, as the Beach Boys put it, "student demonstration time." Through my years at McGill I had marched rather pointlessly, gathered petitions uselessly against the war in Vietnam. My favorite book was Mao's little red book in French!—it seemed a camp poetry of the current mess. They were commonplace in Paris in the summer of 1967. I had spent my mornings there at the Berlitz School, my afternoons at un-subtitled French movies; but in the evenings I distributed antiwar pamphlets to American tourists with a group of young Parisian Maoists. Frustration with Lyndon Johnson's war was worldwide.

Then in February 1968, John Fekete, who like myself was in Honors English at McGill, reprinted an obscene article from Paul Krassner's *Realist*—in the *McGill Daily*. The call-in talk-show hosts were outraged. The principal of McGill announced that Fekete would have to be disciplined. The usual circular march in front of Dawson Hall developed into a sit-in at the administration building. That went on for a month or so; Suzanne Grugel and I broke up over my excess—Suzanne was twenty-seven, I was only twenty-one. Then, as I was studying in my rue Hutchison bachelor apartment one freezing dreadful *echt* Canadian night, David McPherson—also in Honors English and still one of my closest friends—phoned to say the demonstrators had broken into the principal's office, were reading outrageous private correspondence to a talk show, the police had been called, and we had to get to the campus and stop the police from arresting the students. We rushed over, then froze for hours, razzing the police. Abruptly the police lines turned into flying wedges of club-swinging maniacs, and the sit-in demonstrators were carried away in paddy wagons.

This did not end the war in Vietnam. But when I graduated in April, I moved in with Pat Woodsworth and his fiancee, Judy. Pat's great uncle had led the Winnipeg General Strike in 1923 and helped found CCF, the party which preceded the socialist New Democrats. Pat had lots of French Canadian friends, including the novelist Russell Marois. French was finally useful that summer, for I dated French Canadian women. On June 24 Saint Jean-Baptiste Day, the national holiday of Quebec, my girlfriend took me to LaFontaine Park where Pierre Trudeau would review the parade. Pop bottles started flying,

"Andy Warhol reads and endorses by his hipness your author's magazine; he took the photo."

many filled with gasoline and burning wicks. The mounted police charged, but our surprising counter-charge overwhelmed them. Police cars were flipped and burned. I was terrified and exhilarated. The whole thing was on national TV. Alone among Canada's elite politicians and police Pierre Trudeau sat courageous. On the way home I got to hear a lecture from my gal on the abhorrent *mentalité anglaise.*

The next day was the federal election. I voted New Democrat of course, and watched the CBC returns in the Woodsworth family home in Montreal West. Everyone in the room seemed secretly glad Trudeau was elected; it was the summer of Trudeau-mania.

Judy Woodsworth helped me type up *Sequences,* a collection of my first poems, everything I had written that seemed worthwhile; I guess I'm glad they were never printed, except for one long poem by the English department; the poems were not particularly good. I was filled with youthful pride writing film, culture, and book articles for the *Gazette,* but things were slow that summer after Expo '67; and as the summer wore on, assignments got fewer. And so I went to the University of Chicago, and the great epoch-making riots at the Democratic Convention.

In Chicago, however, I kept missing the real violence. I spent an afternoon in Lincoln Park, listening to a poetry reading by Robert Lowell and a speech by Eugene McCarthy, then took the Illinois Central back to Hyde Park and saw on the International House television absolute mayhem where a half-hour before I'd lolled and listened. Such was my naivete as a Canadian that I then thought I'd just walk to the actual convention. An armored column passed me heading in the same direction. I had no idea that in big American cities there were areas called "ghettoes": they didn't have them in London, Paris, or Montreal; what would be the problem walking to the convention?

If the French and English sometimes squared off in Montreal, that summer Blacks and whites were twice as hostile in Chicago. I got about halfway to the convention and was not exactly mugged but cajoled out of money. A Chicago police car pulled up. One officer was white, the other Black. They wanted to know what exactly I thought I was doing. I said I didn't rightly know. They were quite nice. They drove me back to the university.

IV

I'm no revolutionary but there is experience, I hope, behind my political writing and editing. America was given the dismal choice between Gerald Ford and Jimmy Carter in 1976. I was at my cockiest in 1976. I interviewed Andy Warhol and ran pieces on him in *ARTnews, Small Press Review,* and *Unmuzzled OX.* Warhol administered dollops of pathetic snobbery and useful confidence. I decided what this country needed was a poet as president; I took the Metroliner to Washington and interviewed Eugene McCarthy, who was running as an independent.

I suppose Warhol and McCarthy had met, but Lou Reed had never met McCarthy; McCarthy had never heard of Lou Reed.

Andrew Wylie, who's turning into the Swifty Lazar of the postmodernist generation, gave me a book of Lou Reed's poems to consider for *OX.* I published two. One won a Coordinating Council of Literary Magazines (CCLM) Award. CCLM had read my interview with McCarthy, and asked him to give Reed the award. I got my picture in *Rolling Stone* standing between Lou and Clean Gene.

But Erika Rothenberg voted for Jimmy Carter.

Her career as an art director at McCann-Erickson was peaking; I wanted her to quit and be a painter; so did Malcolm Morley, another crazed friend from 1976. Erika and her copywriter were working on McCann's *pro bono* American Cancer Society account when her father was diagnosed with lung cancer. Erika herself at the time smoked about a pack and a half of Merits everyday. Advertising is the grease of capitalism.

Erika's true best friend and partner was her copywriter. Her copywriter's husband owned a string of radio stations. He paid Erika for doing the visuals of his wife's ad copy by taking us to Nantucket for the Bicentennial July 4. It was foggy. In November Clean Gene lost, Jimmy won, and McCann dropped the American Cancer Society for Parliament cigarettes. Deep profiles of Parliament cigarette smokers made fascinating reading on the plane to Tampa where her father lay dying.

Every now and then Erika would shoot a commercial in Los Angeles. We'd play tennis when we travelled to Kingston or Sudbury, where my sister lived, or Tampa or Delray Beach, where my parents had a condo. The summer of 1977 was humid in Tampa but we played tennis anyway; we decided, since we were down there, to fly over to Mérida and see the Mayan ruins Erika's Dad and stepmother used

to visit when she was a kid; but one day her Dad's eyes rolled up, and as the male nurse said, he's going.

V

Andrew W the artist inadvertently wrecked my friendship with Andrew W the agent. I won't rehash that here; but Warhol proved troublesome. The "Andy" entry in *The Poets' Encyclopedia* featured a Lita Hornick text and a Jimmy deSana photo of Warhol photographing Victor Hugo nude and, worse, tumescent. Printers dislike erections; that page cost an extra two thousand dollars and six months.

In 1978 for the New York Small Press Book Fair I asked Warhol to do a billboard on space a bank had donated. He agreed, providing, of course, *Interview* could participate. The committee that ran the book fair, including Erika, had asked me to ask Warhol; but, proud of my fait accompli, I neglected to attend the next meeting, and various left-wingers on the board hated Warhol and voted to refuse *Interview*'s applications. Why would people hate Andy Warhol?

Andy invited me to interview anybody I wanted for his magazine. But I had grown tired of interviewing people, it's just a way to meet interesting people, and movie stars and the usual *Interview* staples are not my bread and butter. During dinner with Dan Berrigan one night in 1979, however, Dan told me about sneaking into a General Electric plant and destroying two nuclear warheads. Terrorists are conceivably as smart as Jesuits, so I found this not merely alarming; it took over my life.

So I interviewed Dan for *Interview.* I like Dan, he is in fact my favorite celebrity, perhaps because he is friends with Jesuits who taught me in high school; but nobody hates Dan Berrigan. Dan, though he'd like to be, is not a saint. Everytime he poured himself another Scotch during that interview, he'd turn off the tape recorder, and get a little looser, and at one point he explained to me what he thought Andy Warhol stood for, which was not good. These words were tactless and interesting. Unfortunately, even to save the world from nuclear holocaust, *Interview* will not publish attacks on Andy Warhol.

Nobody is too big for me to attack. Nobody is too small for the big guys to disdain crushing. Erika and I did a flyer announcing a national boycott of GE. Since GE had been Mr. Ronald Reagan's bigbuck employer after he washed up as a pretty-boy actor, it seemed unimportant when someone leaked to the *Village Voice,* after his election, that the National Endowment for the Arts would no longer give grants

"Allen Ginsberg covets the Lone Ranger's mask—Y. U. Puck?"

to *Cover,* a magazine I contributed to, or *OX,* because "they were too political."

Money is always important.

John Cage is, with Dan, a favorite celebrity; I find I argue with Allen Ginsberg real easy. In any case, I started enlisting everyone to support the Plowshares 8, which is what Dan and Phil Berrigan, Anne Montgomery, and the other defiant missile busters called themselves. I started trekking around the country with these people, who tended to be Catholic radicals; Erika started to feel abandoned. No Jew wants to be the only Jew at a party. I'd sleep in church basements, then in the morning think about the mystery of the nativity. We took to arguing about condoms.

David Rosenberg and I took Erika to *Oh, God!* starring John Denver and George Burns in the title role. Rosenberg had dodged the Yankee draft in 1968 by moving to Toronto while I moved to Chicago. We got to chatting at a collating party at Saint Mark's Poetry Project. Learned squash together. Published some of his translations in *OX.* When Harper and Row decided to remainder his *Job Speaks,* we bought up the copies, reissued them with an attack

on Harper and Row as an issue of *Unmuzzled OX.* But Erika thought the Old Testament was an excuse for Israeli militarism, which, with David, it sometimes so seems.

Joe Papp invited me to read at the Public Theater, so David, Senator McCarthy, Dan, and I orchestrated religio-political visions. At a Village Halloween Parade, Ginsberg and I excoriated the nuke-entranced masses (Allen is always helpful and in a bad mood). I started getting written up in *Ms.* or the *Times* or the *Voice* at a rate of one notice a week, and since Jezebel lived in the building where *OX* has its office, I'd show her as my head swelled.

VI

Jezebel was pregnant, I was in Ireland to read my verse at the University of Cork, and Andy Warhol died. I write the "New York Letter" column for *Small Press Review,* and wrote an obituary notice; and produced for German TV a piece involving Victor Bockris, Gerard Malanga, Lou Reed, Carter Ratcliff, and other "superstars."

Jezebel's son said, "Mommy was sick this afternoon," and I knew she'd just had an abortion.

VII

Just because he was dead didn't mean he was not still a problem. John Cage refused to even meet Dan Berrigan because he disapproves of politics. But the Plowshares 8 project had grown into an *Anti-Warhol's Interview OX*. Who wants to attack the dead? Besides, it was the managing editor of *Interview*, not Andy, who decided not to run the Berrigan piece; and I am not Ezra Pound; knottily enough, for four issues I pretended I was and renamed that issue *Ezra Pound's Interview*. Ezra Pound spent most of his life being a problem.

My own verse is self-explanatory. I hate a problematic rhyme. Everything I write is as clear as a Mapplethorpe photo. Speaking of the late Bob the porn-man and his onetime squeeze, Patti Smith, the heroin addict and former recording artist, why do such lovely people entropize? But Gregory Corso, who's been a drug addict longer than I've known him, still seems as young as I was when I met him. "Crack, crack," he said to me the other day, "everybody talks about crack; where can I get some?" I didn't know. Are beatniks still hip? Until they're dead.

At least Gregory has gotten less euphemistic. He used to say, "Gee, I feel sick, and need some money to buy some medicine." Why lie? Now he says he needs money to go down to Atlantic City for the weekend, and waste it. Gregory could title his autobiography Portrait of the Poet as a Conspicuous Consumer.

I wish Mapplethorpe hadn't died of AIDS. Brian Buczak, with whom I wrote *It as It*, died of AIDS July 4, 1987; it's a painful death. But if Mapplethorpe had died of something else, his retrospective would not have to include the photos Holly Solomon refused to exhibit in 1977. And then the NEA might change its mind and give me some money. Gregory, who may have gotten through grade ten, has married a Du Pont, a Rothschild, and a pastry cook. Veblen, Veblen, everybody quotes him, we all embody him; the beat parodies him.

Putting aside such themes and picking up, again, the chain of events, my sister was born in Kingston in June 1939. Between us, World War II occurred. Then I was born in Halifax; my father was the engineer on a new hospital. My first memories are of a bungalow on Cooper Street in Kingston: delicious

warm lamp in the room my sister and I shared; burning down a shed in the backyard with an older boy who went on to schizophrenia.

We moved in 1949 to the last house my father built, on Churchill Crescent. My mother loved "Winnie"—indeed, they had the same birthday. Dad kept a rifle in the trunk but only carried a pistol during union negotiations. My first memory of war and TV is the same: John Cameron Swayze discussing Korea on our "first TV in the neighborhood." On Labour Day all the cannons in town were fired in the general direction of the United States, the obvious enemy. Mass Sunday mornings started out as a good excuse to nuzzle my mother's fur coat, but by 1959 it was time engineering: which mass—low (short) high (long)—at which church? If it was the cathedral, my mother and I were obliged to visit my grandmother where I could play in the attic with my uncle's toys from the twenties and thirties.

January 1, 1959, Batista fled Havana and my father and I played hockey on the bay of Lake Ontario behind my grandfather's house. We had our own rules, and tried to cheat. The rules for ice

"Nuclear family on Cooper Street"

hockey were first written down in the nineteenth century for a game in Kingston between Queen's and Royal Military College. One rainy day or snowy eve my mother taught me to type; and another night she let me use carbon paper to start a sports newspaper. Copies were a nickel but you could only borrow them. In 1969 when the Miracle Mets won the world championship I didn't have a TV and watched the games, like many New Yorkers, on the TVs in store windows.

In 1979 I was birding on Hawk Mountain with the poet Warren Woessner and birdwatchers would constantly disparage a particular bird as a TV: the turkey vulture. I had a poem called "Letter Home" published in the *Canadian Forum* a few years earlier, and so that fall Jim Mele of Cross Country Press, New York and Montreal, published a collection of my poetry called *Letters Home;* Sylvia Plath's collected letters with the same title came out the same week. Ray Johnson the founder of the New York Correspondance [*sic*] School did the cover, leaving a space between the And and re to pun: Letters Home by Michael and Ray.

I spent New Year's Eve 1989 at a macrobiotic party on Staten Island listening to Chaliapin and Gigli recordings. I suppose by 1999 I'll think macrobiotics are pretty silly, but not as silly as *2001: A Space Odyssey,* by Arthur C. Clarke. As Socrates said, You never know. I don't know what happened let alone what will. I'm a member of the Reality Club. Former presidents Abbie Hoffman and Heinz Pagels probably do know since they're dead; the club is biased towards science, meeting at the New York Academy of Sciences and Rockefeller University; John Brockman, the literary agent, bankrolls the club. In reality, we never really know how the imagination narrates.

II

I have by heart the openings in the original of *The Iliad, The Aeneid, Paradiso,* and *Faust.* My Italian is atrocious; Rosanna Chiesi, a unilingual Italian art dealer who put Erika and me up for a week, was delighted after my recitation. Dante, she guessed. Right, sweetheart, I shoulda' said in Italian, you get a wooden lira. My German's not so good either, but it helps to hear Gounod and Boito put it to music. But I've had German lovers. The Jesuits made me memorize the first few hundred lines of Virgil back in high school; Charlie Doria taught me classical Greek using Clyde Pharr's *Homeric Greek.* I tried to use the first few pages of Cervantes as a Spanish grammar but it's too damn quixotic.

"Rodney Dangerfield has great taste in dogs if not magazines"

III

Poetry is not much like anything else. It's more like painting than music, in that an "original" manuscript is worth more at the bank than the publishing "rights." Auden's fee for first serial rights, for instance, is less than what Bob Wilson of the Phoenix Bookshop paid him for the drafts and notes in his half-legible script. Brockman told me I could pick my publisher, Random House or Doubleday or Morrow, provided I could guarantee sales. Vanity! Some poets carry their economic clout beyond agreeing to buy their unreadable tomes retail. What publisher would not print James Merrill and nice books about James Merrill when Jimmy Merrill's family business is Merrill Lynch, and a sell recommendation from that corporation could instantly bankrupt them? *Unmuzzled OX,* that's who! The Lowell family fortune and vanity pales at Merrill, yet such now is the might of Mitsubishi I fear the NEA may shortly fund only haiku.

IV

There was a young poet in Limerick who got off the plane sick. He hates to travel. His brain unravels. Nor's Northworst the airline to pick.

There is, however, more to Lima than its beans. Sendero Luminoso resembles the IRA, which no doubt resembles the RIN; fortunately I was already living in New York when Trudeau passed the War Measures Act and arrested everybody back in my RIN cell in Montreal: from political club to jail cell in forty-eight hours. Inventory your itineraries and it adds up to here. I feel freest in New York, although I have been taken in chains to Saint Vincent's during a hurricane.

COP: What'll it be, Saint Vincent's or Bellevue?

ME: My psychiatrist is affiliated with Saint Vincent's.

COP: Vinnie's it is!

Psychiatrists are all crazy. The cop got him on the phone, and the psychiatrist asked, "Has he been drinking?"

COP: Definitely.

"Tell him not to drink," said the psychiatrist.

Not drink as I travel this hard road of life? Sure, and pay them one hundred dollars an hour once a week for less happy results.

"First Communion in front of Dad's Coupe de Ville, that artifact of the fifties," Churchill Crescent

Why was I arrested in a hurricane and why have a psychiatrist affiliated with Saint Vincent's anyhow? Ah, the tale of me and madness is not a happy one. Marie's mother was paranoid and shot herself. Insanity is interesting to students at McGill, Chicago, and Columbia. My friend from McGill, David McPherson, became chief psychiatric resident at Bellevue, and I worked on Admissions with him out of curiosity. Most people who show up voluntarily are homeless and are diagnosed with "undifferentiated schizophrenia" and given no help—not even a subway token to the men's shelter.

In my quest to be a Daddy, I agreed to Erika's demand that I see an analyst—specifically, as it turned out, Alan Bass, Derrida's translator. I was not a committed patient. The best way to get Alan's attention was to attack Derrida; Alan, however, had little experience with hospitals or true mental illness, if anything's true in this eschew world.

Erika and I had filed for divorce and I was living with Jezebel and her little boy; he was four. Every other weekend he'd sleep with his father, literally in his father's bed; then during the week Jezebel and I would try to convince him to sleep in his bed. Jezebel referred to Alan as Dr. Bass. A presummer bad weekend in Raghampton with Jezebel, her son, and Jezebel's mom drifted to its unhappy conclusion. I had been kept up the previous night and was supposed to read a poem at Rose Drachler's memorial service in a church on Gramercy Park. We parked in front of the church and I watched various friends of Rose go in and out; Rose had been a friend of Erika's equally, although I knew she would not be at the service. Erika's mother's house in Raghampton, however, was less than a mile from Jezebel's mother's. Finally I told Jezebel, forget it, let's go home, but then friends showed up from Washington to be "entertained" and put up for that night. Monday morning they left, Jezebel took her son to preschool, and, as yet unemployed herself, said, maybe I should see Dr. Bass.

Jezebel is committed to romance, expensive treatments, and little else, but how was I to know this then? Jezebel wants to meet Him Most Fishy in the Disarray of Deconstruction? Why not?

There are only two intelligent people in Jezebel's family, a Harvard-educated uncle who manages the family fortune and her oldest sister, a writer and hence troublesome. Whenever the dumber members of Jezebel's family would get mad at this writer, they'd commit her, and have her pumped full of drugs for a few months so that she would *behave*. Jezebel has a charming way of keeping secrets and demanding private audiences. A private audience with Alan was followed by a trip back crosstown to Vinnie's. The psychiatrist affiliated with Saint Vincent's would not admit me, but then, at his suggestion, she dragged me back across town to Bellevue Admissions. It was Monday at 5:00 P.M. and my last good night's rest had been Friday.

Bellevue Admissions had been reconstructed since I'd last been there as Dr. Andre. By 8:30 I was finally so tired I was practically hallucinating and an intern from India thrust a paper at me, and I signed. Jezebel disappeared. I was handcuffed to a gurney, and shot full of Thorazine—there were of course no beds available. One side-effect of Thorazine, in about 25 percent of its users, is dyskinesia, a form of Parkinson's disease. Hospitals are good places to go if you want to die. In my case, however, it was just an interesting break.

V

Stay out of hurricanes, the psychiatrist at Saint Vincent's might equally have told the arresting officer. A hurricane in Manhattan is far superior to camping in the Adirondacks. In case of floods, the city lays plywood sheets across the subway vents and sandbags them down; giant clouds moor like zeppelins to the southwest corners of the World Trade Center twin towers. For fear of floods this particular night, I induced a friend at Puffy's, the corner bar, to help me move the entire inventory of *Unmuzzled OX* Books and Magazine onto pallets.

Whiskey peps me up. My friend had mice, he told me as we lugged boxes of books, and Jezebel's son was allergic to cats—so I gave him my dear old cat Pest.

Unfortunately whiskey dulls my hearing. Alone at last I turned on the stereo—a bit loud perhaps. The window was open so that I might better hear the hurricane's howling wind. A neighbor phoned to complain. This triggered lickety-split bizarre interventions and unwarranted blows rivalling, in my surprised and battered head, a Chaucerian fabliau. But it'd take pages to set up this story, and since this is an autobiography, and so many actual people, especially me, behaved so foolishly, I have to draw a veil over it all—except to note two things.

The neighbor was actually feuding with Jezebel. 105 Hudson Street is a thirteen-storey nineteenth-century "beaux arts pile" designed by Carrère and Hastings, who also designed the Frick and the New York Public Library. It became a mixed-use co-op in the late seventies, with the lower floors used as spaces

"Dan Berrigan, your author, miscellaneous lawyers at one of Dan's billion trials. He was fined ten dollars."

by small arts organizations like *OX* and the upper floors used as large residential lofts. Artists Space on the second floor held many benefits for the Plowshares 8. Mahogany trim and transoms, red maple floors, slate sills and baseboards, all of which Erika and I restored as well as the arched windows and marbled public spaces please me still after twelve years; I don't mind either the cheap maintenance and unexpected quiet, for Manhattan, of TriBeCa. The building is the *OX. ZerOX 105,* a limited edition series of reprints, takes its name from this address.

The other thing that's odd, and rather nice, is that when you get arrested in New York for disorderly conduct, they apparently don't take you to jail—you go to the hospital.

VI

If only hospitals were good places to go if you wanted to die!

Tom Wirth worked with me as managing editor of *OX* (he had briefly been managing editor of Grove

Press). He was gay, he had AIDS, he signed a living will saying he wanted no drugs, no intravenous feeding, no respirators—essentially no treatment. His friends were enlisted to be with him until he died; I phoned, on the morning of July 1, 1987, prior to going over to Tom's—and there was no answer!

The people with him the night before had panicked. Tom could no longer speak. An ambulance took Tom to Bellevue. New York State did not recognize the living will. The doctors had an arsenal of machines and drugs to fire on Tom. "Don't do it or we'll sue," we said. "Go right ahead," said the doctors.

What ensued was grist for tabloids and television. The mob of reporters and TV cameramen as I approached the State Supreme Court astonished me. "Living will" that summer entered the national vocabulary. The doctors claimed Tom had a terminal not a fatal disease, a distinction I'm still trying to figure.

We lost the case, but a photographer slipt into Tom's room and took a picture of Tom on the machines which, with the headline "Forced to Live," became the front page of the next day's *New York Post.* After that there were guards and security checks to keep people out of the AIDS ward. Governor Cuomo at last signed some paper which, among other things, granted preliminary status to living wills; they let Tom die; and I wrote "Elegy for Two Who Died of AIDS," which so far has only appeared in a memorial book on Brian Buczak, who also died that struggling summer.

VII

I don't know what moral this is supposed to illustrate; I'm no hero, as should be plain by now. Basking in reflected glory will hang over in a pall of low self-esteem. Tom's death was no victory, I was the last person to see him alive. I could see the eyes rolling up into his forehead, like Erika's father. Tom was raised a Catholic, but abjured it, as he abjured the Midwest, because neither the Church nor his small hometown would accept his homosexuality.

Seeing Tom dying frightened me, particularly alone on a dumb hot dirty New York City morning; and therefore I went to the nurse's station, and told them Tom was a Catholic and Get Him a Priest! They did, they said.

My first book published by a stranger was *My Regrets.* That was in 1974, and since then I've acquired cabinets of new regrets. Extreme Unction counts if the corpse is still warm.

I have, as should be plain by now, a morbid sense of humor.

Here's a favorite stunt.

I enjoy watching birdwatchers. Everybody wishes they knew birds, and so I have taken unsuspecting nature lovers like Jane up to the Central Park Ramble armed with two guides, Peterson and the superior Golden Guide, and two sets of binoculars, my good pair and a better looking German set that has never worked. I'll show her a redstart, then maybe a ground-dwelling ovenbird. Then I'll spot a Norwegian Brown and bring her closer to this ground-dwelling mammal which, since they're furtive, she never sees. I don't see it, Jane says.

When Michael Tarachow came to New York, Erika and I took him to a restaurant near Bloomingdale's; Michael published *My Regrets.* Dustin Hoffman, who is short, walked by with two tall blondes on either hand. Robert De Niro lives in TriBeCa across the street at 110 Hudson. Celebrities are as much a part of New York as the Statue of Liberty. You want visitors to see at least one celeb, as Robert Wilson offhandedly calls them.

Nobody, even Jane, wants to see Norwegian Brown rats in their habitat, which is all five boroughs.

I published Robert Mapplethorpe and I don't like Jesse Helms but I regret, in a way, the number of columns I sent Len Fulton, editor of the *Small Press Review,* about my loathing for that fat brown rat; I regret it because Len won't publish them.

It's my green card which made a coward of me. I don't get arrested—except once—because I'm afraid of being sent to the Northwest Territories, i.e., back to Canada. I like the imagined spectacle of Dan Berrigan getting arrested again and again. Dan says he hates it. *Studying the Ground for Holes,* published by Larry Zirlin's Release Press in 1976, had, said Erika, a perfect title—I liked to hide in books, she meant. As Faust says—

> Habe nun, ach! Philosophie,
> Juristerei und Medizin,
> Und leider! auch Theologie
> Darchaus studiert, mit heissem Bemuhn.
> Da steh ich nun, ich armer Thor!
> Und bin so klug, als wie zuvor. . . .

Calling someone a Nazi is more insulting than calling an African a nigger. My next book after *Letters Home, Jabbing the Asshole Is High Comedy,* was censored.

This publisher, whose name shall be ever veiled, who had published numerous poems of mine in her magazine, was leaving the Commonwealth Edison grant committee, happy at her annual allotment when, suddenly, one of New York's guardians of power spotted a poem of mine. Debate ensued. She agreed to no longer publish such filth. I published *Jabbing the* —————, as it appears in bibliographies, myself using simply the Print Center as its address.

My next book, *Social Work*, does not appear in my bibliography because, though a contract was signed, the League of Canadian Poets reneged. Now, of course, if a publisher tried such a shenanigan, I'd have one of my free lawyers/agents nip them on the —————.

I wanted the *Village Voice* to endorse the *OX*/Plowshares 8 boycott of General Electric. Guy Trebay, my editor, agreed; then the publisher told him the *Village Voice* does not boycott its advertisers. I was angry, and didn't understand this, and stopped reading the *Voice*, which had been an important outlet. When RR succeeded JC, there was an article in the *Voice*, leaked by —————, saying *OX* would no longer get grants because it had endorsed a presidential candidate.

Politics is always for profit. It would have profit-ed me greatly to read that article, but I never have; I haven't talked to Guy in ten years.

Writers crave readers. Lawyers are liars and doctors make me sick. Poetry is the best, most difficult science of the mind.

Psychiatry is a wisp, the hope for a science of mind: Prozac, Thorazine, and Valium are every bit as hip as cocaine, marijuana, and LSD. I'm no hero, I avoid all six. Lithium, that silly salt, makes a man less lively. People say they dislike depression but they dread mania. Yet it's easier when racing to slow than, when depressed, to start. Doctors, as Freud said, enjoy the observation of suffering; all doctors, he wrote, are latently sadists. I'm my own Doctor.

That's what I told the medical crew at Bellevue who insisted on keeping Tom Wirth alive. Jean-Noel Herlin, a book dealer and another friend of Tom's, told Dr. Cohen he was acting just like Adolf Eichmann. Erika and I essentially were divorced in landlord/tenant court, in that our only valuable possession was the lease to my loft. Whose loft? I can almost hear Erika say now, ten years later. The judge decided it was hers.

"Father, Mother, Joan, Andre"

Jezebel is guilty but not really so bad. She doesn't read the Bible, though when we talked about getting married, I talked about Catholic weddings; and she got a dumpster's load of books On Being a Jew. Jane's Jewish too. Jezebel's favorite JAP joke went, how did the JAP commit suicide? She put all her clothes on her bed and jumped off.

I could write a comic short story about Jane and me called Doctor Zauberflote and his cook Shakuhachi.

One bibliographical anomaly is my two plays *How I Blew Up the World* and *King of Prussia*. After I quit writing for the *Voice,* but before I published a final cartoon there, I wrote a poetry column for the *SoHo News;* even the name of that periodical is probably unfamiliar to you but for a while the publisher positioned the *SoHo News* as a rival of the *Voice.* My editor at the *News* was the late Ron Whyte, a playwright. Lee Strasberg gave Ron directorship of the playwrights and directors workshop at the Actors Studio; there I converted an extremely long short story from my unpublished collection into a play. Erika's stepfather was a TV screenwriter and he lent me various copyrighted TV teleplays. I found I could collage *How I Blew Up the World* into any of these TV shows and people would respond. Then the Plowshares 8 business came and I took the transcript from the trial which Dan Berrigan lent me and crafted it into a play called *King of Prussia*. King of Prussia, Pennsylvania, is the town where GE makes nosecones for the MX missile. Sometimes, in bibliographies, it is listed as a collaboration between me and Dan.

There are seventeen skeletons in my closet but like Jezebel I let the bed clothe the dead.

Another anomaly, this one in the fabliau, is numerical. Canadians do not normally study nineteenth-century American classics, and thus I have never read *Moby Dick;* don't call me Ahab. Don't allude either. Ahab was married to Jezebel, of course. I wish Jezebel lived in L.A. with the ex-wife but, alas, I see her bedroom light on now as I write and I know she's in Massachusetts. These memories are confused by the present. I've published under fifty? pseudonyms. You can add. Befuddled by intellect, Y. U. Puck, whose author's photo resembles McGill grad

S. I. Hayakawa, lied in his "All New Illustrated History of Ideas, Part I." Laura LeNail is such a feminist I've gotten masher notes from lesbians. Jezebel must have sublet. Is real estate destiny?

Memory is such a mystery I can't remember why anyone bothers. One last thing. The reason I let the police into my office back in that hurricane is because a poet's son beat me up, and I was bleeding, and confused. Shortly thereafter Jezebel commenced a secret affair with his business partner. The illusion was perfect. What man would imagine the woman he loved was sleeping with the only man who ever tried to murder him?

BIBLIOGRAPHY

Poetry:

My Regrets, Pentagram Press, 1977.

Studying the Ground for Holes, Release Press, 1978.

Letters Home, Cross Country Press, 1979.

Jabbing the Asshole Is High Comedy, Print Center, 1981.

It as It, Money for Food Press, 1983.

Editor:

(With Erika Rothenberg) *The Poets' Encyclopedia,* Unmuzzled Ox, 1979.

Gregory Corso, *Writings from Ox,* Unmuzzled Ox, 1981.

The Cantos (121-150) Ezra Pound, Unmuzzled Ox, 1986.

Author of plays "How I Blew Up the World" and "King of Prussia."

Work has been included in many anthologies, including *Scenarios* and *The Literature of SoHo,* edited by Richard Kostelanetz, *Contemporary American Fiction,* edited by Douglas Messerli, and *Up Late* and *Stiffest of the Corpse,* edited by Andrei Codrescu. Contributor to magazines, including *Quarry, Canadian Forum, Queen's Quarterly, Periodics, Montreal Gazette, File, Abraxas, Zymergy, O. ARS, Lightworks, Spectacular Diseases, Mudfish, Exquisite Corpse, Little Magazine, New Lazarus Review, Telephone,* and *Konglomerati.* Associate editor of *ARTnews,* 1971–1977. Editor of *Unmuzzled Ox.*

Kofi Nyidevu Awoonor

1935-

I must have been born sometime before the first sowing season of 1934 or 1935. Instinct tells me it was 1934, because my elder half-brother who must have been only a year older was born in 1933. For the purpose of going to school, my parents inexplicably settled on 1935 for me, the month of March, and the thirteenth day of that month. Anyone versed in the now-prolific trade of horoscope reading using dates and stars will certainly have a difficult time reading mine. But something, my excessive love of the sea and all bodies of water, tells me I am a sea-creature—Pisces? Well.

I come from a typical mid-twentieth-century African family with an illiterate mother. This social condition is ominous and deadly, but it is as African as our cyclical droughts, the crop failures, the locusts, the petty wars, venal presidents, the IMF, and the debt that afflicts our continent. My mother records her birth from the time she was a little girl when the cassava war (Great War of 1914–1918) came. For my people, time or a date is a magical union between place and event. I had a granduncle whose "drinking" name was Gambia who confirmed the period of my mother's birth because he was a young man when it happened. He remembered the First World War very vividly, because on a dusty market day at Adzanu, in the then-German territory of Togoland, where he had gone to sell his handwoven cloths, he and the other young men from our village, Wheta, were press-ganged by the Germans into head-carriers for the German troops. Under constant abuse with the whip, they were kept in that forced service for over two years, fed on hard biscuits and the lash. That too was a regular feature of blessed colonialism that came in the wake of Christ's message to "redeem" my pagan folks from their "dark, satanic" ways! My mother was born before this significantly dismal event. By my calculations, she was born around 1910 or 1911.

The year of my birth could have been recorded by my father, because he could read and write, having had a little elementary education. But he did not. I was baptised in the little Presbyterian church at Dzodze, where my father was a tailor. I once checked the record in our big town, Keta, my father's town,

Kofi Awoonor

settled sometime early last century or even earlier by his great-grandfather. The record was an interesting exhibition of fine calligraphy; it was however an obvious repository of false information. It gave my baptismal date, somewhere in May 1935, as my year of birth. My mother did say that I received the first holy sacrament when I was one year old.

I was born in the *ablada*, the anteroom, of my maternal grandfather's bedroom, he who was called by his fighting and drinking name, *Nyidevu medaa kevu o; agavenyiwo dae wofe ko koe yi to:* "The canoe-upsetting hippo does not upset the canoe with the sandload; the hippos of Agave attempted it; they broke their necks as a result."

"My uncle the diviner-chief Dzebubu and my brother Besa in front of the hut where I was born"

He was a sub-chief of Asiyo, a division of Wheta, of the line of Ashiagbor, reputed to have been a descendant of one of the founders of Wheta. When the Anlo sojourners moved on the last stage of their historic migration from Ketu near the Niger River in modern-day Nigeria in the early fifteenth century, there were many stopping points. Wheta was one last point from which, at Adudu near Atiteti, they built canoes and crossed the great lagoon to the coastal areas, leaving settlements dotted along their route until they reached Anloga, and later Anyanui on the estuary of the Volta River, or the Amu as my people call it. The story of the last lap in that historic migration is retold during our great festival Hogbet-sotso, celebrated sometime in November every year in the royal town of Anloga. It is a colourful folk saga of that journey remarkable for its display of heroism, determination, and survival in which the women played the major role as pathfinders, and sustainers of the various clans on the march. Its reenactment in a solemn drama of their escape from the clutches of the wicked host King Agokoli of Notsie, in present-day Togo, is a riveting pageant of original theatre and the dramatization of a people's history. My maternal ancestors were among the leading clans on that journey. When they reached the vast valley just before the marshes that turned into the Keta Lagoon, from where they could cross further southwards, they camped, building there a town called Wheta, at the head of the valley. Others believe that its name is derived from its historical claim as a major camping site for all the clans; it was the last place where all of them were together before dispersing and fanning out into the coastal strips that separated the vast lagoon from the sea.

Wheta is still a very traditional African town, with numerous shrines for the thunder gods Yeve and So, the one the Yorubas call Shango. We must have descended from a tributary of the great Yoruba-Benin civilization. Yoruba remains the language of the secret cult Afa (Ifa), the divination cult of the Benin-Yoruba peoples. There are two elementary schools, a Presbyterian church, a clinic, and one water pump drawing water from an underground well.

Childhood, as it must have been for many Africans of my generation and peasant background, was for me a time of general poverty and deprivation, even though it was relieved by the warmth of a doting extended family. The persons who linger most lovingly in my memory are my maternal grandmother and grandfather. My grandmother called Afedomeshi was a vibrant, tall (to my child's eye), and graceful woman who hailed from Anloga. Theirs was obviously, as is still common among our people, an arranged marriage. This kind of marriage normally occurs among members of the extended family who are sometimes separated by distance. It is designed to affirm existing ties across distances marked by the large lagoon and the never-ending grassland that edges this little inland sea, running along the intervening space that separates it from the mighty Atlantic Ocean. It is still a land of breathtaking beauty, especially when the lagoon is in full flood—the canoemen do a bustling business ferrying the women to and from the many market towns around it, and fishermen are seen in clusters retrieving their crab and shrimp traps, and the white sails of the canoes vanish in the evening light as they float gently and silently into the towns across the eight-or-so-mile stretch of water.

My grandmother Afedomeshi (the name means "the steadfast female base of the homestead") at the beginning of every vacation waited for my homecoming from Dzodze, where I had begun school in 1939 at the Roman Catholic Mission School. The journey to Wheta, a distance of eleven miles, was always by foot, as there were no lorries on that path in those days. And for a six-year-old boy, it could be a difficult trip. My late uncle Kowu used to come and fetch me. I would tie my few clothes into a neat bundle, using one of my mother's headkerchiefs, and happily trudge off behind him on the journey home to the person who seemed to love me most in the whole big and sometimes unsure world. The trip was always an expedition, a hunting one at that, since my uncle Kowu was the best catapult shot I have ever known. Bird life was abundant. There were also wild fruits whose trees studded the edge of the path; in season, these supplied enough sweet or sour fruits to the travellers till we entered the division of our village, Asiyo. I remember one very distinct landmark on the very outskirts of the village.

I sometimes walk past it in my adult dreams even today. It was the burial ground. In those days, the graves were not covered with cement; they were six-foot-long earthen mounds on top of which would be perched a cooking pot, a wooden ladle, and a few articles of daily domestic life. Even in my adult dreams, I still experience the slight chilly fear that always gripped me when I walked past this graveyard as a child. Our people believe that the world of the dead, *awlime*, is linked with the world of the living,

kodzogbe, in a complementary relationship. The dead transact their affairs at night; they farm, cook meals, go to the market, and care for their children at night time when we are asleep. So the night is peopled by them, the night-walkers. That is why the living are enjoined not to walk in the night, for fear of bumping into the real owners of the night. The night also belongs to the spirit forces and the gods, who are the lords of the invisible world.

My grandmother appears in several of my poems, the main focus of my sentimental recall of childhood. She went away to join the ancestors in 1946:

> Where did grandmother, a tall gazelle
> the only ancient tree when the hippo left
> pass with those interminable dirges
> waiting for us to come home
> with briars for her corn-wine
> picked beneath harvest moons
> that come home with us
> from grandfather's farm far away?

I asked this in a 1969 poem, "To Those Gone Ahead." She used to brew the famous corn-beer we call *aliha*. She also made a wine called *tadiha*, pepper wine, good for curing coughs.

My grandfather Besa Nyidevu occurs in my poems as a warrior, a great paterfamilias, a man reputed to be endowed with magical powers which he used for good. His memory remains strong and

"Graveyard of the ruined chapel of Keta. Among them lie buried some of my ancestors on the paternal side."

revered in Asiyo even today, more than forty-five years after his death. He was a sub-chief. He died during a raging smallpox epidemic that is said to have swept through the land around 1940 or so. He was a man of solid reputation, an intrepid farmer and a custodian of the old ways. It is a pity I did not know him well; he lingers large, powerful, stern, and loving in my infant memory. He fathered many sons and daughters. Of his children, only my mother, another sister, Masa, and my uncle the diviner and present regent of the chiefly title Kwaku Dzebubu are alive. My uncle remains the main anchor of my maternal family now, he whom I described in one poem as:

> the godlike ram of sacrifices
> the only tree of the homestead now.

He is uneducated in the ways of the Europeans, but a sharp intellectual whose grasp of the contemporary world is no less deep than his abiding and devoted dedication to the ancestral ways. He is the custodian of the family shrine. He is a farmer and a diviner of the shrine of Afa, the divination god.

I must not forget to mention my cousin Dede, who died when we were children. She was the daughter of my mother's second sister, Abla. She died in 1953. Dede remains a special personality in my poetry. In "Hymn to My Dumb Earth," we are seen together playing, making

> wattles and palm leaves
> into mats rested upon the matted earth
> of mud dried by the receding lagoon
> one harmattan noon many seasons ago
> we cannot remember
>
> She said an animal, any animal
> delivered a child that day noon in the forest;
> waterstones fell, hail stones fell upon our land
> we raced to pick them up.
> They melted.
> We cried in the rain of the harmattan sun.

She must have been my first love. She returns into my poems in the form of a persistent, recurrent persona of innocence, beauty, yet of a tragic fate. In my novel *This Earth, My Brother,* she merges into the mythic woman of the sea, the ultimate mother, the tragic heroine, Africa, who is raped in her infancy and dies of a curable ailment—intestinal disorder—as her land supplies the wealth of the conquering nations of the world. Even though tragic, she remains the lyrical centre of my poetry, supremely feminine, loving, caring, and in the truest spiritual sense, undying,

immense, nubile, yet mature and childbearing, virginal, yet a mother. She is also a gatherer and custodian of all the heirlooms of our people—the beads, the precious stones, the rare spices that are mixed with the pomades to be rubbed on the bodies of the young girls at the puberty rites, and the special herbs gathered by her ancestral hands. In the last encounter, the reunion between her and the main protagonist, the carrier and the atoning persona in *This Earth, My Brother:*

> She rose now up upon the waves, her breasts bare, her nipples blacker than ever. On her face a little smile; the sun gave out a radiance that recalled the bright sunshine of the butterfly field and the hunt of childhood and her first epiphany. There an eerie silence clung to the earth and the sea, over the memorial booms of the ceaseless waves echoes of the muskets of her funeral procession. In the company of one lovely gorgeous star she rose. She walked on the sand, her arms outstretched; she strode towards him, a smile on her face; her breasts bobbing softly. From his island of solitude and joy, utter indescribable joy, he moved towards her. . . . He sank upon his knees. She enveloped him in her warm embrace. Her smell was of cinnamon and wild flowers, ancient smells of treasure well kept for the children of the future.

There were other members of that large extended yet closely knit family who remain mere childhood memories, like my uncle Dogbe Kundo:

> chanting a dirge
> till dawn in his armchair
> into death's cold arms
> at dawn.

My mother still swears he was poisoned by his drinking companions, as my uncle loved his home-made gin. All these memories coalesce into a persistently pleasurable yet significantly sad childhood:

> What happened to that laughter
> of childhood, the banana trees
> watered by roots of bath
> and birth waters flowing from
> our ancient rivers
> in dead groves?

Of the other side of my family, my father's, my consciousness was hazy, except when, once in a while, he would herd us children to his maternal hometown, Anyako. It is still a famous Christianized village, even as it clings to its original African ways, typified by a few thunder-god shrines, and the famous Kleve sacred grove on its outskirts. Anyako is picturesquely perched on a strip of land which is almost an island on the edge of the Keta Lagoon. There is a vast marshland that separates it on the northern side from its blood-related villages of Nolopi and Abolove. The German missionaries from Bremen, after they had built the church in Keta in 1847, crossed the lagoon to Anyako. In spite of some early hostile acts meted out to them because of the nineteenth-century European missionaries' characteristic insensitivity to the African's religious ways, and what many will call their zeal to gain the crown of martyrdom in "darkest" Africa, the Presbyterian church at Anyako took root and flourished, producing great African evangelists and translators of hymns and a writer such as L. P. Tosu.

This was our immediate second home, even though our visits were far in between. We relished the thought of going, particularly the canoe ride across what to our childhood eyes was an enormous sea of never-ending water.

Anyako used to be a pig-rearing town, and in the extensive and complex ecological logic of our people, the pigs fed partly on human waste. As little visiting boys, the thrill was, when on the job, with your back

to the cooling salt-lagoon, to keep the hungry pigs at bay with a stick as they snortingly waited for you to finish. It was an exciting yet rather frightening experience. There were stories of men or boys whose members were snapped off by ravenous feeding pigs! Over the years, Anyako abolished pig-rearing as an agricultural enterprise. I grew up believing that shit was pig fodder. And for that reason I still don't eat pork; this was reinforced later by a religious taboo enjoined on me against it.

Keta, my paternal hometown, was a bustling commercial town when I was growing up. My great-great-grandfather was said to have drifted there, perhaps at the tail-end of the eighteenth century, and his sons became the pillars of the then-rapidly modernising town after the coming of the Bremen missionaries of the Lutheran persuasion. The town used to boast a Danish fort, Prindsensteen, built around 1784 or so as a slave fort, where the various European factors put together their dismal new world-bound human cargo. It was one of the most important forts in the centre of the sadly named Slave Coast, which stretched from east of the estuary of the Niger River to the western reaches of present-day Ivory Coast, with its most active epicentre in present-day Benin, once called Dahomey, "the home of the snake," because of the proliferation of snake cults.

The fort served as the seat of the British administration in the district when I was a boy. The British had taken it from the Danes around 1874 in the shifting ownership programme that was an aspect of the European enterprise in Africa. It also housed a prison, where local criminals spent months of incarceration for petty thievery, or disturbing the peace.

Those days, as in other important "port" towns, the steamers came with European goods, and took away copra, palm kernel, and oil. It was the era of the surf-boats. It was cheaper than building a harbour. The British empire was constructed on acute parsimony and stinginess. Otherwise the profits would not have been good enough to sustain the empire on which the sun was hoped never to set. The ships anchored in deep water about a mile or two at sea, depending on the tides. The surf-boats, rowed by men with some of the most enormous chests you could imagine, went to collect the goods and brought them ashore. The goods consisted mainly of cement, bales of Manchester cloth, casks of South African sweet wine, salted beef, cabin biscuits, hair cream, and all the trifles the colonial economy came to dump in Africa in return for the continent's gold, diamond, palm oil, cocoa, bauxite, cotton, and other products for which it was "opened up" and "discovered."

*"Fort Prindsensteen in ruins, built in 1784
by the Danes"*

The coming of the ships was always a time of infinite excitement. The town would take on a near-festive atmosphere, because the boatmen, normally fishermen on the large canoes that dared the ocean for fish, would be making more money than they had ever known. Then the sailors—mostly Greeks, Spaniards, and other Mediterraneans—would descend on our little town. The drinking bars would do a roaringly brisk and lucrative trade. Once in a while fistfights would break out between the sailors and the local toughs. And we would cheer our local boys on until the police arrived, blowing their whistles and swinging their truncheons. Then hell would break loose as everyone ran for dear life.

Keta, alas, today is a dying town. It has transpired that the founding ancestors built the town on a sandbar between the raging Atlantic and the lagoon formed by the many rivers struggling to enter the sea. The meaning of the very name Keta is "the head of the sand." My father said that when he was a boy, the location where the old fort now stands, destroyed recently by the sea, was about eight miles or more from the sea. The sea has carried on a relentless assault upon the town; because of the lagoon, Keta has not been able to expand except laterally, as a long town of now over five miles, with narrow stretches of barely three yards of land between the two waters. My now rather famous poem which has been inflicted upon many West African secondary-school children, "The Sea Eats the Land," is perhaps as vivid and lyrical a record of the tragic story of Keta as any. Keta, even today, waits sadly for a solution. The market which used to be the biggest fish-distribution centre in the eastern board of Ghana, supplying smoked and dried fish to countries as far as Niger, is now a shadow of itself. All the young people are gone. Only the very young and the very old are left. The fort has been destroyed. So has been the old Presbyterian church built by German and African artisans one-and-a-half centuries ago. Only the churchyard remains. A building constructed fifty years later to commemorate the coming of the church called Jubilee Hall remains. It now serves as the chapel. My old school, the famous Keta Presbyterian School, is an assortment of half-destroyed buildings now face to face with the sea waiting its turn. My poem is more in anger and anguish than in nostalgia for a proud, defiant, and noble town which has suffered the ravages of nature thanks to many years of well-orchestrated conspiracies on the part of officialdom and the loss of social consciousness on the part of its remaining inhabitants. Recently, during the rains in mid-1989, half the town was underwater, and there were tilapia swimming in the floodwater that had inundated many homes, including ours. My mother, like many members of her generation, refused to be moved elsewhere. The sea continues to pound the remnant narrow strip of land; the lagoon, though tranquil, is capable of its own mischief, particularly when the rivers from the north are in full flood. With the construction of the Akosombo dam, the entry of the great river Volta into the sea has become blocked; the rivers that normally would have emptied into the sea during the rainy seasons seek refuge on the flat, low-lying land, destroying more than a century-old culture of shallot farming, the mainstay of the villages to the west of the town all the way to the marshes of the estuary, apart from dwelling houses and other farming activities.

Of my paternal grandparents, only my grandmother lingers as a real but a dim character. She came from Anyako from the royal clan of Lashibi. I only remember her when she was very old and lived with us at Dzodze.

She carried on interminable quarrels with my mother, whom she accused consistently of starving her, even right after she had had a meal which I myself had carried to her. She could no longer walk in her old age, and I believe she must have been a little off, because she made a regular racket particularly in the night made up of a long ululation, chants, and prayers to a household god called Mamagbo, whose devotee she was. When she died, my father found a lorry to take her home to Anyako. I remember my father and I walked the distance, over twenty-five or so miles, for some reason which I cannot now recall. We buried her at the cemetery on Moduikpota, a hillock on the northern outskirts of the town, according to the old African religious rites.

My grandfather Robert Brigas was a surveyor who was reputed to have planned many towns in the Gold Coast (now Ghana) in the early part of this century. He, together with three brothers, studied in England at the turn of the century. One of them, Moses, was a Cambridge blue in boxing and a very successful lawyer who died rather early at the age of thirty-nine.

Another brother, Francis, the youngest (my grandfather Robert Brigas being the eldest), died about twenty years ago of old age after a fruitful life as a lawyer, a notorious anglophile, and a reputedly reactionary politician. It was he who is said to have written the letter on behalf of the United Gold Coast Convention, the first nationalist movement to emerge in the country after the apparent demise of the

Aborigines Rights Protection Society of last century, to invite Kwame Nkrumah, who became the first president, to return to the country in 1947. He also served as the first treasurer of the movement when it was founded in that year.

Their father, George, was one of the merchant princes of the Gold Coast, with vast commercial enterprises and trading ventures that covered almost the entire West Coast of Africa, with active centers in Gambia, Sierra Leone, Togo, and the Gold Coast. He also had a familial base in Sierra Leone where it is established that his Dahomean ancestor, after having been rescued during a war from imminent slavery, was repatriated to Sierra Leone. This ancestor must have been the first Robert, with his wife Videawu; both became Christianized and sought to return home to Wuiddah in present-day Benin. Their son George was the one who made good and became, as the family stories had it, very wealthy by the middle of last century. The family became prosperous enough to dabble in slavery of the domestic type. When I was growing up, there were two old women, one with the "tribal" marks of the northern peoples; they were obviously the last people left of the old household. They were whispered to be the last of the domestic slaves of the wealthy George. But they were family, very close family. One of them, Nyekowowo, was the last wife of Robert Brigas my grandfather. It is he who is accused by everyone of laying waste the family fortune through excessive litigation. He was obviously a rapacious cad who sowed confusion and quarrels in the family, appropriating things which were not his. Even the family land on which my father later built his house he bought from his father! His mother, that is, my great-grandmother, was called Nugbolo from a leading family in Glidzi and Agbedrafo in Togo. She was a wealthy woman in her own right, being a famous maker and trader in beads. Quite a few coconut plantations and land holdings were left to the family in present-day Togo. The fate of these today is not very well known. Grandfather Robert Brigas sold the major property holdings in Keta, Koforidua, and elsewhere. And by the time he died in 1955, there was hardly any sign of that famous wealth. The last time I saw him, in 1953, I had gone to pay my respects. He was having lunch. The table was loaded with a wide assortment of dishes. His manservant Abotsi, as old as grandfather himself, was serving. I stood at reverent attention as he told me of a family scholarship tenable at the London School of Tropical Medicine and Hygiene which I must work hard at my books to take up. I was fascinated yet awed by this tall, gaunt old man who

spoke the King's English impeccably, and once in a while seemed to stray into the Anexo dialect of the Ewe language. You could see he was a well-travelled and polished gentleman of the old school, Victorian to the core, a product indeed of the European entry into Africa, a cultural mulatto, part of the generation that took to the white man's ways, and then developed strategies of eliminating him from its economic and political life out of sheer self-interest. Its members were the ones whom the British resented most, for they not only aped them, but also dared to challenge them, because they had travelled to England, where they had seen them stripped of all those superior airs with which the entire dismal colonial enterprise was masked, with its mindless cruelty, studied hypocrisy, and rapacious greed. Of my father's family the only decent man remaining is my uncle Kwasi, a gentle, kind, and wonderful soul who has assumed the entire burden of family head both in Keta and across the border in Togo. May he live, as our people say, to "grow gray hairs on his teeth."

My family background has given me, and my immediate generation within it, a fairly broad African character. I have relations who are Fanti, Nzema, and Ada; I have other relatives scattered across the whole of West Africa and in three or four countries. Mine is one of the few truly Pan-African families!

Keta was a very busy commercial and "cosmopolitan" town. To it had flocked many other ethnic groups, from as far as Ashanti and near as Ada, who are our neighbours to the west on the Volta River estuary. Today, I speak two other Ghanaian languages, apart from my own native Ewe, with great fluency, which surprises native speakers who know that I was not born into these languages. I learnt all of them in the bustling and ethnically integrated town of Keta in the decade of the forties.

But it is Wheta, my natal village, which remains my spiritual hometown. Most of my childhood memories are records of returns to this village, with its narrow lanes, numerous shrines, and ancestral ways. I recall most vividly my grandfather's farm village, Lave, where I used to accompany the old man in the company of my uncles. We would cross a little river, Aka, it was called, pass through copses of bush and elephant grass, startling a bird, an antelope, or a grasscutter here and there. There were always tracks of warthogs who came to drink water from the low-lying distant hills. My grandfather's farm hut built with mud still stands. There is still standing the silk-cotton tree under which we used to share our meals, and rest in-between hoeing or harvesting. It is now

Houses destroyed by the sea at Keta

old and enormous, a veritable guardian and custodian of my family. I still go to Lave; it is for me a place of pilgrimage. I go to sit under the tree, communicate with the past, when my grandfather tilled the ancestral land. A great portion of the family land was acquired by the central government for an irrigation project built with Chinese expertise. The animals are all gone. Only a few water birds come along when the dam is full, and the voices of rice-planters or harvesters are heard till last light.

Wheta has not changed much since I was a boy. The village remains as ancestral as its shrines and holy groves. There are a few modern-type houses built with cement and roofed with iron or aluminum sheets. There are still the little markets that sell food, matches, kerosene, and other odds and ends. These transform into almost magical places at evening, with each stall lit by naked homemade lamps whose glow reveal animated faces caught in chatter or haggling. These markets, common all over West Africa, are ancient community centres, places of gossip, news, and elaborate village romances. I almost forgot the police station that was not there when I was a boy. It is housed in a building which, when I last looked in, was in a desperate state of disrepair, as the owner had refused to spend money, complaining that the rent he

charged was not enough even to buy a piece of roofing sheet or a pair of hinges. One morning, about five years ago, the policemen, led by the inspector, simply moved away from the town to a location five miles away. The villagers were outraged, as, so they claimed, theft of fowls, goats, and sheer malcontentedness and rascality increased. Petitions were sent to the police boss in the faraway capital. And one day the inspector and his boys marched sheepishly back into the town into their still-unrepaired building. Before that event there was an inspector, an old gentleman who had a running battle with homemade gin, in charge of the station ten years or so ago. He was totally incoherent with booze, night or day. It could have been bureaucratic cynicism or disrespect for small villages such as Wheta that sent a police chief who was literally in the last stages of alcoholic dementia to head a squad of law-enforcement officers. The fact of course was that crime is still a minor problem, limited to an occasional theft of livestock, or spontaneous fistfights as the result of too much homemade gin being consumed, particularly at funerals.

I have been helping the village of late. I was involved in reviving the clinic and repairing the water pump; both had not functioned for over fifteen years.

I started school in 1939 at the Roman Catholic Mission School in Dzodze. My father, after three or four years of elementary school, went to his mother's town with his mother when the marriage broke down in around 1919 or so. The collapse of the marriage I suspect was largely because my grandfather, a successful surveyor and an overseas-educated African of the old school from a solid upper-class background, had gone in for an educated lady from Cape Coast, whom he wedded in church. I believe he consequently neglected his elder and illiterate wife. At Anyako, my father fished, and was later apprenticed as a tailor. His maternal uncle Adebi Ackuaku took him with him to Dzodze, over twenty-five miles further inland. Dzodze was then a bustling market and farming town on the road to Ho, the regional capital. Dzodze is the fictional Deme in my novel *This Earth, My Brother*. My father practised his trade as a tailor; it was during this tailoring period that I was born. He met my mother, Kosiwo, who had gone to the Dzodze market from Wheta with her mother. There was some period of courtship, which ended with my father's uncles taking to my mother's people the appropriate "door knocking" drinks. With this, they declared my father's intention to marry my mother. The marriage was sanctioned by my mother's people, who accepted the gifts of drinks, cloth, beads, silk kerchiefs, a trunk box, gold trinkets, and an amount of money. It is these things that would have to be returned by my mother's people should any divorce proceeding instituted by my father against her succeed. The marriage lasted for forty-four years, till my father's death in 1977. There were quite a few dramatic periods in that marriage; for example, it must have been 1938 or so when, after a particularly violent quarrel—my father possessed a raging temper—my mother put me on her back and went home to her people. Months after, my father, contrite and obviously missing his wife, came to Wheta with a delegation made up of his people to plead that my mother return to the marriage home. There was a family court on which sat representatives of both sides. My father was found guilty. He was made to pay a fine of one ram and six bottles of homemade gin. The ram was slaughtered and there was a great reconciliation feast. My father was sternly rebuked, and told that should he ever lift up his hand against my mother again, she would be permanently taken away from him by her people. This shows that in our culture, a woman does not lose her personality, identity, or rights when she marries. No married woman bears the name of her husband. The rights and claims of her own family on her remain very strong. They are the essential features of the protection she enjoys even as she lives in her husband's house. Our people understand the fickleness of love relationships, and not being afflicted with any widely proclaimed romantic ideas, they make provisions for the day a marriage may break down. They also understand that there are great periods of stress, pain, and sometimes deep sorrow in the relationship between a man and a woman. During those periods the woman, who leaves her parents and family house to marry sometimes a perfect stranger, is assured that she does have a place where she and her children always belong. It is the same principle that underlies the maternal factor as the main determinant in our lives. Mother's house is the last and unambiguous place of refuge, the place we go to when sorrows mount.

Dzodze Roman Catholic School in 1939 was a little school mainly for the children of those who had become converted to Christianity. I was baptised into the Presbyterian church since my father's people were Presbyterians. In the Presbyterian churchyard in Keta, in the shadows of the now-crumbling chapel built by the missionaries from Bremen, lie two of my paternal great-granduncles, whose family was said to have ceded part of their land to the German missionaries in 1847.

The Catholics were kind enough to accept a few Presbyterian children into their schools, even though the historic rivalry between the churches manifested itself now and then in unseemly quarrels over proselytising rights. The Presbyterian church school at Dzodze was only at the kindergarten stage.

The Catholic mission run by Dutch priests was an expanding evangelising enterprise which preached vigorously against "idol worship," to which the African was supposed to be eternally addicted. There had been a general assault upon holy places and shrines in the area a few years earlier led by an English district officer called John Miller. He went around destroying them. The effort to wean the African away from his religion was a fundamental aspect of the colonial enterprise; this too was an instrument of the "civilizing mission," a veritable alibi for exploitation and profit.

The Reverend Father James, head of the church in 1939, was a tall, bearded Dutchman with an enormous nose and what looked like two pinkish flapping bowls sticking out at both sides of his head in place of ears. I was eternally petrified of the man. But he was ever so gentle and kind when he spoke to us now and then whilst we weeded his compound or cleaned the chapel. During his time, Bishop Herman, now blessed by the Vatican, used to come to the school. A little, bearded man of boundless energy, he always carried sweets in his pocket. These he threw around to us as we followed him everywhere on the mission compound.

I remember most vividly the huge portrait of God in the chapel. He was a large, bearded white man, not very old, obviously in his sixties, with two sharp and penetrating eyes that stared at you everywhere you went. He used to frighten me enormously. I still cannot understand how a God who was said to be full of love could be made to look so fierce.

Then one day Father James was transferred to Togoland, at that time mandated by the French. In his place came Father Zystra. He had a deformity in both arms. He was very cruel. I remember one day a group of us were marched to the headmaster's office by Father Zystra. We were given twelve lashes each because we had made noises under the reverend father's window whilst he was having his afternoon siesta.

Missionary education in Africa was accompanied by a sadistic use of the lash. Many boys and girls did not complete school in those days because of the excessive caning that was resorted to by the teachers at the slightest provocation. In chapter three of *This Earth, My Brother,* I recreated the atmosphere of extreme brutality that regularly accompanied colonial education. It was, alas, an aspect of the whole dismal and brutish enterprise which was anything but benign, with cruel laws and a harsh, pitiless police apparatus.

Our teacher, Mr. Dowu, was a tall, gentle Yoruba man whose father had settled in Dzodze and was a successful corn-miller. Kindergarten, or *abordzokpo,* meaning "the grasshopper class," was really playtime, time for learning songs. It was also storytelling time.

"Baa Baa Black Sheep" was part of the repertoire. Later on in primary school we graduated to more complicated songs, as I learnt later, with bizarre racist connotations, like:

ten little nigger boys fighting over wine
one got so jolly tight leaving only nine
nine little nigger boys then have lost their mate

I cannot recall the last line. This song was obviously designed to teach counting. At the end of the song, all the ten little nigger boys were absolutely tight!

One of the great sports of kindergarten was when we marched off to catch and bring to school by

Mother, Kosiwo

force boys who played truant. Quite a few boys, out of sheer fear of the cane, would cut school and go into hiding for days. The school had instituted an arrest-and-deliver programme to which, because of the thrill of the hunt, we all became enthusiastic policemen. The culprit, once apprehended, was carried aloft by all of us and, sniffing and weepy, would receive a few lashes and a stern admonition as to the consequences of a repeat incidence of truancy.

I fell in love with school from the first day I set foot there. It was a wonderful place of childhood camaraderie, mischief-making, laughter, and occasional tears.

In school we broke the taboo of telling stories during the daytime at the instigation of our teachers. On rainy days we huddled together in our mud-built classrooms and listened with attention to the exploits of the spiderman and his family. Ayiyi or Ananse, the spider, is the archetypal Ghanaian folk hero and antihero rolled in one. A small creature, his life underscores the survival principle that is the bedrock of the African world. He survives by his ingenuity, guile, wit, and sometimes sheer mendacity. Even publicly acknowledged negative tendencies upon which the culture frowns become a common store from which he borrows articles for his survival. The African world was, and alas still is, a difficult one. Many of the stories speak of periods of great famine, slave raids, and migrations. The search for food and a place of solace are recurrent motifs. On a larger plane, the stories are grave morality plays that reinforce the community's solidarity, dramas of the conflict between good and evil, perpetual sagas of man's efforts to cope with his individual and collective destiny in a harsh and difficult world.

One of the stories that used to send shivers down our infant spines was the story about the boy who was born after seven days of conception. Predictably he was called Kofi, as the Friday-born boy is believed to be strong-willed and rather stubborn. After tormenting his father, mother, and the entire family for days, and in response to a rebuke to mend his ways, Kofi sets out on a journey. He is going to do the final outrage: go to the land of Death and conquer him. Armed with magical powers given him by the gods, he arrives in Death's village, fights him for days, and defeats him. Then he ties him up, carries him squealing in a wicker basket, and brings him into the village. The village gathers around to see the "warrior" Death himself finally in thrall, his eyes as red as the earth. In the night Death breaks the ropes and escapes. From that day, he stalks all of us, hiding on the very outskirts of our villages and behind every door or gate. And no one sees him until he strikes. His war upon humanity has become pitilessly relentless.

School was quite a learning period. We learnt not always silly poems, arithmetic (which I dreaded), reading, and writing, but also how to weave baskets and mats, how to prepare the elephant grass for thatching, how to lay bricks. We were an unpaid labour gang that built new classroom blocks and sold our services to any local entrepreneur for a fee. The monies that accrued were naturally kept by the teachers and the headmaster. At the end of every year, we were given a doughnut each for our toils. In Keta, where I moved in 1944, we spent days mining salt, an arduous job if you ask me. We had neither shoes nor gloves. Mining flatland salt in temperatures averaging ninety degrees Fahrenheit can be cruel on little boys. We would be at it for days. We sold this salt on the market, sometimes storing it for months for export to Nigeria and elsewhere. We knew the price of salt since our various households also organized salt-winning expeditions during the season. But we never received anything beyond the eternal single doughnut at the end of the year.

In 1944 my father decided to send me to his paternal hometown, Keta, to continue my education. The Second World War had been raging in Europe and elsewhere. It did affect us, the colonial subjects. As schoolboys in Dzodze, we spent days in the wild palm groves collecting palm-nuts. These we then shelled and bagged for shipment to England as part of our war effort. We also donated pennies which we earned from little labours. African subsidy of Europe was not limited to peacetime exploitation of our resources nor to forcible supply of soldiers. We also directly financially subsidised the wars fought there to "make the world safe for democracy."

I recall the never-ending convoys of military trucks full of African soldiers passing through Dzodze raising an eternal cloud of dust, as the road was never tarred until after independence. After heavy tropical downpours, this road would be closed for days, as it was totally impassable.

The army recruiters used to come. Village boys, many of them refugees from the lash-dominated schools, the arduous fishing chores, and the family farms, would line up to "have their names written down" to be soldiers. In a week or two, trucks would come with a platoon or two to collect the new recruits, who had received five shillings as inducement fees to join the army. Half of them would vanish into the bush. And the hunt for them would be on for days. There were military boots trampling and whistles blowing in the nights; then you would know an unwilling recruit who had taken the king's money and did not want to go fight the king's war had been cornered. Some sought refuge in distant villages, or crossed the border into Togo and simply kept on going.

Many Gold Coast families lost sons in East Africa, North Africa, and Burma. I had three uncles who went to Burma. Only one returned. They were part of the African troops whose heroic role as infantrymen in the British Eighty-first and Eighty-second Divisions in the Southeast Asia theatre and contribution to the defeat of Japan are still yet to be accorded a significant recognition. At the end of the war, fifty thousand Gold Coast soldiers were demobilized without receiving even a one-hundredth fraction of what was paid to the European troops.

Because the Germans were said to have a design to recapture their former colony, Togoland, which they lost in 1919, Keta was put on war footing. A siren from the post office blew alerts and calls for attack drills. A British warship plied the adjacent sea. There were stories of some of our fishermen being fired upon by German torpedoes. The Royal Air Force planes would come dropping leaflets on which were written slogans such as "We Will Win," "V for Victory," "Help Buy British Bombers to Bomb Berlin." Many of the leaflets also carried the picture of a smiling white man, with a big cigar stuck in his fat face, and his right hand held up, the index and the forefinger forming a V sign! It was the great imperialist Winston Churchill himself urging us, the subjects of the empire, on to victory.

I entered standard one of the Junior School in the Bremen Mission School of Keta in 1944. Even though my blood relatives were around, as this was my father's paternal town, my father put me in the care of an Ashanti trading family headed by Opanin (Elder) Sarpong Akosah. I was the domestic servant to one of the many younger brothers, called Kofi Firi. He was a kind master who never raised his voice. He died rather young. Come to think of it, this arrangement was more a commercial transaction than anything else. It was common in those days for a father to put his boy or girl in the care of a family of sometimes perfect strangers for the purpose of being brought up well. For my father, my going into "service," as it were, at the age of nine was more of an economic arrangement which took care of one more mouth to feed, and more important sealed a deal he had made with the trading family, by name Kotoko Company, by becoming a storekeeper in its expanding enterprise. The war had made trade goods very scarce. As a result there were enormous profits to be made. My father was ambitious both for himself and his children. He was determined to make good in spite of or perhaps because of the poor start and the neglect he had suffered in early life. In the end, he made it, becoming a successful trader, a leader in his community, a great paterfamilias who took seriously his responsibility as family head, acquired some amount of immovable property, educated all his twelve children, and left behind a solid reputation as a hard-working gentleman who breached the gap between the old and the new societies with admirable but well-worked effort.

I was an avid reader at Keta Bremen Mission School. I read everything I came across; I devoured all those tales "retold for easy reading": *The Great Stone Fall, The Jungle Books, Mill on the Floss, Treasure Island, Ivanhoe, Great Expectations.* So Kipling, George Eliot, R. L. Stevenson, Charles Dickens, Walter Scott, and many other classics of the English

language found in me, a slightly underfed African boy in a little coastal town in the corner of the British colony called the Gold Coast, an enthusiastic companion. With them and many others I held a long and exciting dialogue of the imagination; I travelled to faraway lands: I was with Robinson Crusoe on his amazing island of Rousseauian simplicity, shared with him his preternatural fear of the cannibals, and admired the heroic loyalty of Friday, that redeemed sinner who was an echo of my people and my culture in the European imagination. *Robinson Crusoe* remains the most classic novel of colonial conquest and enterprise, with its well-designed assumptions of racial superiority and elaborate Christian hypocrisy. It is the novel of discovery and exploitation of the entire "primitive" world of which I and my people had been assumed to be part. It remains the most superb commentary on the European mercantile philosophy that has taken over the world.

I also read the *Arabian Nights,* translated into my language, Ewe, by the Reverend C. G. Baeta, *Nomalizo* by a South African evangelical writer, also made available in my language. The main literary fare of course was the Bible; *Biblia,* as it was called in Ewe, had been translated last century by a team of German and African linguists under the impetus of the Bremen Missionary Society. The hymns had also been translated. An assortment of devotional prayers, they were as German as the original Lutherans who wrote them. They also, apart from being mainly praises and prayers to God, contained the most gratuitous insults ever launched upon our people. The most famous hymn in this genre is "Thy Kingdom Come, Oh God." The sixth stanza goes:

> O'er heathen lands afar
> Thick darkness broodeth yet
> Arise O morning star
> Arise and never set!

Obviously someone forgot to inform us where these heathen lands were over which the morning star was being so passionately implored to rise and never set. Another of these hymns is "On Greenland's Icy Mountain." African Christians are still lustily singing these insults directed at their people. These hymns provided me with a wonderful recipe for repartee, irony, echoes, double-meaning, and cultural assertion in a 1969 poem, "Hymn to My Dumb Earth," a long poem of 372 lines. So the Bible and the hymns were for me consistent sources of poetic derivation, not because they supplied any devotional edge to my verse, but mainly because they served as a wonderful resource for poetic cadence and riposte, fashioning a verbal magic at their most cantatory best, and in thematic terms, a marvellous source of self-descriptive cultural irony.

Keta was also a period of my coming to know, love, and fear the sea in its most elemental form, and in its reverberative and destructive relationship with my little town. I remember the night I arrived. It was magical, riding in the mammy truck into town at a snail's pace with the night market alive at Awusawoto, the Moslem sector. I did not hear the boom until I had curled on my little mat. It was like the firing of muskets, with rumblings tailing off into enormous booms that again rumbled on till another boom. Forever and forever. I realized the next day that we were right at the seashore. The sand-strip was wide white stretching into coves at whose edge the ceaseless waves carried out their musketry. I would come to know this beach, with a single copse of Indian almond trees, as both playground and workplace, a mythical meeting point with my eternal earth and sea mother who is the central persona of *This Earth, My Brother.*

The long seine nets which our people still use landed there. I learnt to be a fairly good fishing hand. This type of net always needed many hands to help pull it ashore. Sometimes, we fished with the longer variety designed to catch the large mackerel when in season, September to October. This chore might take hours. When the ropes were in, and the net portion began to arrive, men were needed to carry these on

"Remnants of the Presbyterian church built in 1847 by the missionaries from Bremen"

their backs and move up and down as the waves and the fishermen determined. It was after this that the large bag, what our people call *voku* ("testicle"), came ashore with the catch. It was a very arduous and sometimes profitless way to catch fish, for the *voku* would sometimes hit the shore and contain only seaweed and a dismal assortment of inedible stingfish. When the catch was good, our reward was given us in fish. This you took home to supplement the day's protein supply.

Then there was the wide and exciting lagoon, which has a large variety of talapia, blue-claw crab, and shrimp. As little boys, you began with the bottle trap. Then you graduated to the palm-frond trap, mainly for more tricky catches, such as shrimp. The hook and line were more sporting and long-drawn propositions. You had to run away from home for an entire day to carry out this thrilling occupation. You escaped punishment if the catch you brought home was good. If it was not, your behind bore witness to your profitless truancy.

I dwell on these geographical and cultural realities of my life because they constitute the original source for my work as a writer. Landscape intertwines with the most fundamental framework of our existence; language in its entire operation is a focus of daily existence and deep ritual and religious anchorage. The Zulu poet Masizi Kunene and I, perhaps, are the "elder" modern African poets who turned to our oral poetic traditions for direction. In my critical study of African culture and literature, *The Breast of the Earth,* I indicated how the generality of our literary efforts in the mid–twentieth century sought an umbilical link with the aboriginal literatures of our people. That is how it should be, for as we say, "you weave the new rope where the old one left off." But we cannot make any claim that we are the first to have done this. Homer's epics were derived from original Greek orature, just as the best of Shakespeare, Tagore, T. S. Eliot, Walt Whitman, and many other "good" writers was derived from and part of a chain of original literary and cultural materials. This is so in order that literature will not become a desiccated set of exercises created by isolated men and women. The full resource of original culture must be riffled, raided, and used by all our writers. We are lucky that we come from an oral literary tradition. For our peoples the "word" remains magical, ominous, and immense. It is defined by a ritual dimension; every word is both sacred and profane. The line between these two had long been obliterated, since the gods themselves spoke the tongues of men, and men assumed divine roles in their spiritual state, when mortals were no longer flesh and blood. So life and death are commanded, directed, nay even controlled by the word.

I began my writing career at the age of fifteen when a school friend and I filled an exercise book with poems. They were immature, infantile, but responding to the voracious and indiscriminate reading we did in British colonial literature. Echoes and even memories of those childhood poems have vanished forever. Just as well.

In 1950, in my last year at elementary school, I sat for the Common Entrance Examination, a nationwide examination for all elementary-school leavers who wish to enter any of the few secondary schools. It was highly competitive. I was called to Ho for an interview. For this great occasion, my father, who believed that shoes actually spoiled children, bought me a pair of brown canvas shoes for the journey. I acquired from my own earnings as a loader in the market a yellow shirt of some silvery net material and set out on the journey from Dzodze to Ho.

I do not know what happened, but I never entered Achimota the following year. My father later told me he could not afford the thirty pounds sterling I was supposed to pay to cover part of the half-scholarship I had won to go to Achimota.

So, in January 1951, having successfully passed standard seven, I was taken to Anloga. There, my father talked the Reverend Dr. Fiawoo into admitting me to his Zion College of West Africa at a fee of eight pounds a year. I was to stay with a friend of my father's—one Mr. Beckley, who was a storekeeper for the United Africa Company, a giant British trading conglomerate which is now a major subsidiary of the multinational company Unilever. I did not last there, since I could not combine my studies with domestic chores as a houseboy. I persuaded my father to move me to the boardinghouse at an additional cost of four pounds a year.

Zion College was a private educational enterprise founded by the Reverend Dr. Fiawoo, who held a Ph.D. in theology from the University of Chicago and was a minister of the African Methodist Episcopal Zion Church, the black American church that has carried out missionary work in many parts of Africa since last century. It was, compared to the secondary schools run by the colonial government or the other missions, a very poor school. The teachers were barely qualified to teach. Some of our teachers regularly sat the Cambridge School Leaving Certificate examinations with us, and sometimes failed. Most of them were dedicated; but because they were badly

paid, or had other ambitions, they were perpetually moving on. So we studied on our own. There was no science laboratory in the school. But we studied chemistry, physics, and general science, all from books. We learnt everything by rote. It was a pathetic but a brave attempt to get education by many of us who could not afford the better schools because we were too poor.

But it was perhaps the period that toughened me up, gave me a self-assuredness and resourcefulness that developed my instincts for independent thought and action. I showed early signs of rebellion against what was at times a capricious and insensitive school authority which, in the best tradition of colonial education, often sought to humiliate and dehumanize us. There was a particular headmaster, a Presbyterian minister, who took a perverse pleasure in the use of the cane and in mental cruelty. I left the school as his bitterest enemy, even though he claimed I was one of the best pupils that passed through its gates.

Anloga, the Anlo-Ewe royal town, is an old town founded by the sojourners from Notsie about whom we have already heard. Though a modern town, it is very steeped in tradition, and very conservative. As the seat of the Anlo paramountcy and the centre of Anlo culture, the town has always resisted change. Even today, no one can ride a horse into Anloga because it is believed that Nyigbla the ancestral god rides into the town regularly on horseback, and no one must compete with him.

In 1953, the townspeople staged a riot against government taxes. Our school was the first target, as the Reverend Dr. Fiawoo, under the internal independence parliament of 1951, became the Deputy Speaker of the National Assembly. He was personally held responsible for the taxes by the people. They set fire to his house and made a bonfire of his books, including the manuscripts of his play *Tuinese,* already a success on the stage after the great triumph of his first play, *Tokoatolia,* translated into English from Ewe as the *The Fifth Landing State.* The next targets were the students' hostels. We had to flee the town at dusk, because it was obvious that, as poor as we were, our boxes and few clothes were targets of envy. I rode the first truck, together with three other students, to scout our route of escape westwards across the estuary of the Volta River in a dugout canoe. The night we fled, the town went up in flames and the special riot police force arrived. A few people, obviously rivals in old clan disputes, were set upon and murdered. Many of the ringleaders were later tried and hung in Accra.

The school relocated later that same year in Keta, twelve miles east of Anloga. A few of us, hungry for education, went back under very difficult conditions, including walking five miles every day at noon to use the classrooms which a primary school was persuaded to vacate for us in the afternoon. On Sundays we marched eight miles, without shoes, to the AME Zion Church at the eastern end of town for worship.

I forgot to mention my first leather sandals. When I was set to go to Zion College, I received a prospectus of things to acquire. My father checked the list meticulously, cancelling items he considered superfluous, for example, toothbrush. He insisted our traditional chewing stick would do. It still is the better way of cleaning one's teeth. When he came to an item dubbed "Achimota sandals," I saw my father frown. He asked me to describe it. It was a type of open sandal with cover for the heel, rubber-soled and made with leather. It was specially designed by Bata Shoe Company for African secondary-school boys. After my description, my father smiled. He had a friend, a shoemaker, one Mr. Agbleta, who could make it. So I was the only one in the school with "Achimota sandals" made of cured northern sheep leather. It was not uncomfortable. But it made such an infernal noise, literally bleated, when you walked. For the first term, other boys would follow me wherever I went, annoyingly imitating my bleating sandals!

In 1954, I sat for the Cambridge School Leaving Certificate and the Sixth Form Entrance Examinations. I passed both rather well. I was among the first fifty in the whole country.

I was called for an interview to enter Achimota—a school my father had always dreamt I must go to by all means, because his half-brother, the son of the wedded wife, had gone there!

I entered Achimota in January 1955 for a two-year sixth-form course which would prepare me for university.

The difference between my old school, Zion College, and Achimota was like the difference between a poor man's hovel and a palatial mansion. Achimota was conceived as a British public school, with girls thrown in almost as an afterthought. The halls were solid edifices; there were spires over every building, wide avenues planted with acacia, open fields where the sport of kings, cricket, was played by boys and masters in immaculate white, a swimming pool (the only one in the whole country at the time), a zoo, a hospital, a music school with a resounding piano and instruments for the school orchestra, a dining hall where some of the best meals I'd ever eat as a boy were served, a well-stocked library, and a respectable Anglican (high) chapel. Who said colonialism had no conscience? It salved it—after the annexations, the bloody wars it fomented among the "tribes," and the shameless support it gave to naked plunder—with occasional grand gestures such as Achimota. But these gestures were also largely disguised insults, notable proclamations of cultural superiority and arrogance of power. The colonial subjects were expected to be very grateful for them.

But Achimota had its graces and virtues, including a misguided attempt to make the African children stick to their culture—drumming and dancing. Sadly, this is the conception of culture that many educated Africans are stuck with—folkloric, picturesque, quaint, and as one recent government-sponsored tourist poster termed it, "exotic." They compounded this with dividing us into our "tribal groups." I ended up being the tribal head of the Ewes in my last year, a semi-prefect position mainly designed to organise "tribal drumming."

It was a happy if at times frustrating period, during which I came face to face with the colonial educational apparatus, with young English boys and girls fresh from Oxford or Cambridge not only hectoring us, the students, around, but also exhibiting the most revolting acts of racial snobbery and cultural arrogance towards Africans as a whole. In the main, they had the full run of the place. The headmaster was an ex–army type, straight-laced and positively certain that Britain had a gift to give to us hapless African boys and girls. When the two years came up for me to leave, I was glad to do so, even as I was aware that I needed a lifetime's studied effort to live down the "Achimota syndrome," typified by an actively obscene old-boy network and a fairly pompous superiority complex. I stay away from all old-boy associations by deliberate choice. A good deal of them are incestuous, self-aggrandizing, and blatant self-exhibitions designed to proclaim that our school days were golden and our old schools veritable abodes of unadulterated happiness and joy. These associations simply indicate a pathetic refusal to grow up, elaborate efforts to construct nostalgia into an eternal barrier against maturity and ultimate physical extinction. The most famous hymn we sang in Achimota was in Latin: *Gaudeamus igitur juvenes dum summus*. That is the crux of the matter—an epicurean philosophy that injects into childhood, even ours, which was deprived, poor, malnourished, the nonsensical musings of upper-class English boys!

I entered the University College of Ghana in 1957, one of the eight Independence Scholars from the entire country. I had wanted, in fulfilling my father's wish, to go to England to study law. But that year, there were no scholarships for law. I attended an interview for a scholarship to study "cost and works accountancy" in Manchester. One of the members of the panel whom I met the afternoon of the interview told me I had topped the list but they didn't think I should be made an offer. The alternative, of course, had always been to go to the University College of Ghana at Legon. Legon was founded in 1948 from an intermediate academic programme which was part of Achimota College, which in turn was founded as Prince of Wales College in 1927. Remember the smiling prince who as King Edward VIII gave up a throne for "the woman he loved"? Such were the ties that bound the various and sometimes disparate strands of the imperial enterprise. Legon is a cross between Oxford, Cambridge, and London Universities. Built on a beautiful hill ten miles from the capital, Accra, its architecture is redbrick oriental; the mud huts which were bulldozed to make way for it are not reflected in any of the buildings nor in the phallic arrogance of the Great Hall atop the highest point on the hill. In 1957 it was manned by academics and administrators from Britain, dutiful intellectual mentors of the future middle-class of Ghana, with a handful of subservient Africans who actually believed that they were Englishmen.

The syllabus for the honours degree in English was a precious trip through the "best" that those islands, Great Britain, had produced. From *Beowulf*, through Chaucer, Shakespeare, Defoe, Richardson, Keats, Dickens, Tennyson, Hardy, T. S. Eliot, James Joyce, E. M. Forster, Conrad, to Harold Pinter. The amazing thing was how our literary formation was expected to be fashioned entirely by the literature of the British Isles. That is part of proprietarian patronage of colonialism. We were, after all, British subjects. So from Tolstoy, Balzac, Maupassant, Dreisser, Chekhov, Whitman, Poe, Goethe, Stendhal we were supposed to be entirely shielded. The same thing went for students of economics, political science, philosophy, and theology. The syllabus for the last subject was a barely disguised programme for the study of the Bible.

There was a strange Scotsman on the departmental staff called Tom Dunne, a lively, irreverent iconoclast and Scottish nationalist whose anti-English moods and diatribes perfectly suited my anticolonial sentiments. He gave me books to read, mainly forbidden literature. He encouraged me to send in poems for the University Gurrey Prize, which I won the following year.

My entry was made up of translations of the funeral dirges and war songs I had heard since a boy, following the manner of J. H. Nketia's *Funeral Dirges of the Akan People,* which had just been published. The Anlo-Ewe dirge is an old, traditional form called *Agoha,* performed at funerals. Song is equivalent to the poem, as it is a composition arranged in stanzas. It employs such literary devices as alliteration, repetition of words and lines for emphasis, assonance, and double-meaning. Such other elements as elaborate imagery and symbolism are also its major attributes. This poem is then married to music, to a simple melody which is given form by voice and accompaniment of an ensemble of drums, rattles, and gongs. In its finest expression, it achieves a union with the dance, body movement which not only accentuates the rhythm, but also gives meaning to each word in elaborate and intricate interpretive movements.

The poet-cantor or *heno* ("the mother of songs") among the Anlo-Ewe is an important social person, a creative artist whose resources are the general store of both linguistic and cultural communal holdings. He is also, contrary to what many outsiders believe, a man apart, tormented sometimes by ennui, loneliness, and imbued with a deep sense of his individuality. But he is essentially a communally driven creative person whose work follows laid-down traditional forms, even when he puts his individual stamp upon it. One of the most important of the *henowo* ("poets") of the Ewe tradition was Vinoko Akpalu, who died in 1974 at the age of ninety. He took the traditional *agoha* ("sorrow song") and expanded it, stamping on it for all time his individual talent. Today his name, Akpalu, is synonymous with this particular genre of funeral poetry, or the dirge. Here is a short sample of Akpalu's work:

> Xexeame fe dzogui dzie nyea mele
> nye mele amewoamewo kasa o
> Mesio nye klamatowo
> Wo kpo do me no
> He no anyi de me nu
>
> I am on the world's extreme corner
> I am not in the row with the eminent
> Those who are lucky
> Sit in the middle
> And prop their backs against a wall.

The theme of loneliness in the midst of life, the solitariness of the act of dying itself, and the need for communal warmth and human companionship are all expressed in this Akpalu dirge poem with such force. What is missing on the flat page is the cadence of the

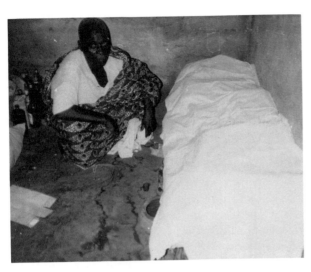

"My uncle Dzebubu consulting the 'elders.'
The white cloth covers divine representations
of our ancestral gods."

chanting voice, the solemn atmosphere of the funeral as the body is laid out in a room, the compound bustling with mourners coming and going, and the artists given pride of place in a prominent corner to perform, not only to honour the dead but to reassure the living, particularly the bereaved. All the artists are normally part of the extended family, related to the dead by complex lineage and marriage patterns.

This piece and others formed the source and resource for my early writing. I was not merely translating. I was reworking original oral poems into literary pieces that sought to expand one language into another, very severely unrelated—the ideas, the speech forms, and the rhetoric of an old mythopoetic tradition that has served as a sustaining aesthetic and philosophical force for our people through centuries of travail and suffering. It is poetry of survival, which is, as I wrote some time ago, "more than a matter of hope—anchored in faith, belief and the certainty that life is a cyclical process; we fulfil our turn with drums, laughter and tears, and pass on inevitably to our ancestorhood, to sustain those we leave behind on this wayside farm we call life."

My first book, *Rediscovery* (Mbari, 1964), was a slim volume, experimental, tentative if you like, but very much an effort to move the oral poetry from which I learnt so much into perhaps a higher literary plane, even if it lost much in the process. The opening poem, "My God of Songs was Ill," records the tradition of the *hadzivodu* ("god of songs") among the

Anlo-Ewe. The poet-cantor, having spent a period of apprenticeship, is helped to install this god as a personal deity to help him in his performances. He "seats" him in a brass pan, and supports him with daily offerings and observances of certain taboos. The famous poet-cantor Akpalu and the old poets such as the late Komi Ekpe of Tsiame, with whom I worked in 1970, had gods of songs. The god supports the poet in his public appearances, guarantees him a clear voice, and gifts him compositions when he is asleep if the poet is at peace with him. If he neglects to observe the prescribed taboos or offends the god in any way, he loses his voice, suffers ill health, or dries up as a creative artist. In this poem, celebrating the relationship between the muse and the creative artist, I employ the age-old motif of this god:

> Go and tell them that I crossed the river
> While the canoes were still empty
> and the boatman had gone away
> My God of songs was ill
> And I was taking him to be cured.

In the poem, the song god, suffering some offence, had refused to let the poet sing. He took him groaning and crying to the house of the cure god:

> "Come in with your backside,"
> The cure God said in my tongue.
> So I walked in with my backside.
> The poet placed the ailing song-god on the
>   stool.
> The bells rang and my name was called thrice
> My God groaned amidst many voices.
> The cure God said I had violated my God
> "Take him to your father's gods"
> But before they opened the hut
> My God burst into songs, new strong songs
> That I am still singing with him.

I sought in this poem to define the communal and spiritual dimensions of original poetry, the relationship between the poet and that fine divine essence that encompasses our lives, the interdependence of the waking and the spiritual world, the bridging role of the true poet between those worlds, and the harmony that is mandated between the living, the ancestors, and the divinities. There is a covenant between the poet and the community. He breaks it at his peril. His voice is borrowed from the people; its resonance and eloquence derive from them. His individual gift is granted him by the gods to be used in the service of the people. In the long poem, a dirge, *I Heard a Bird Cry,* the poet laments that: "The singing voice which the Gods gave me / Has become the desert wind." But to restore that voice, he needs to become reintegrated. There occurs a vision of the people returning, limping, weeping, towards the fetish hut. The poet joins the mourners:

When you started the song
I sang it with you
My steps fell in
With the movement of your feet to the drums
I put my hand in the blood pot with you.

My poetry has sought not only to achieve this reintegration, an "atonement" (at-oneness) with my culture, but also to make that the elemental basis of my literary statement, to "Sew the Old Days," torn and tattered, so "that we can wear them under our new garment / for the new season that is coming."

Some critics have sought to highlight the so-called "clash of cultures" theme in my work. Certainly it exists, in the projection of the historical contact and confrontation between Europe and Africa. But sheer pursuit of this theme can lead into a *cul de sac,* can become an endless, meaningless chase of an irrelevant if even an obvious aspect of a fairly complex corpus of poetry. Indeed, persistent images of the anvil and the hammer, the crucifix and the ancestral herbal pot, the Christian minister and the traditional priest, and such binary elements that characterize the African reality today are at work in my poetry. But they do not always clash, for the poet seeks to work out a harmony, an amalgamation of the various sensibilities that accompany them, fiercely rejecting the superior and sometimes destructive death-dealing tendencies of the other for an assertion of the life-affirming communal and survival intentions of the original.

In 1967 I left Ghana to live abroad for the first time. My road, as for all ex-British colonials of the dying empire, led of course to London. There was an attempted coup led by some young officers from the Ho military barracks in April 1967. As my rotten luck would have it, I had spent a weekend in that camp two weeks prior to the abortive attempt to topple the generals. I was a well-known Nkrumahist; I was a part-time teacher at the Kwame Nkrumah Ideological Institute at Winneba. I had been appointed by Nkrumah at the tender age of twenty-nine to head the Ghana Film Industry Corporation in 1964 on secondment from the University of Ghana, where I held a research fellowship in African literature. I was

in short a CPP activist, and to the right-wing generals a flaming Communist!

I was briefly arrested after the failed coup. My house and office were thoroughly searched for subversive materials. I was let go. I then decided that I needed to return to the academic world, where I felt I had always belonged. Longmans, the publishers, gave me a generous grant for a fellowship at University College, London, where I was to work with the noted linguist Professor Randolph Quirk. So I took the offer and left with my wife and infant daughter of three years in the fall of 1967.

I had taken up the fellowship to work towards a deeper understanding of the English language as it affected me, an African. But it was also, alas, a period of exile, not in the Joycean sense, but in the definition, accentuation, and recollection of absent places and people. This definition was sharpened, thrown into bold relief, by the "alien" climate of England. Even as a "privileged" and sufficiently well-provided-for Longmans Scholar, I came to dread the racially defined stares and the manifest rejection on the trains, the sidewalks, the shops, and even in the lofty and hallowed halls of University College off Malet Square. One old man, about eighty, visibly shaking with the palsy, on a bleak winter day came up to me at a bus stop in Upper Norwood to ascertain from me whether I was part of "a conspiracy by coloured people to violate English women"! Suddenly, in England I realised I was "black," a racial category which makes me not only invisible but also an object of indifference and vicarious insults. I do not know any white person who is "white." Pink, maybe. I am brown, dark brown; but all these labels, with the exception of "white," define historical and cultural systems with pejorative connotations. They have been imposed upon the world by Europe—"black hordes," "red devils," "yellow peril," "white man's burden,"—in her atavistic claims of superiority. Even today, perhaps more fiercely than ever, to be "black" means to be underdeveloped, carrier of AIDS, hungry, ignorant, unintelligent. I have had white people say to me after a brief conversation, "Oh, you are so intelligent." I resent the assumptions, the historical arrogance, and the insult that this supposed compliment implies. I insist I am African, West Coast variety; my forebears and their kinsmen faced Europe squarely; some died on slave ships; but those who survived did so by dint of their own energy, their own intelligent appraisal of the Universe; they did so in spite of the European. The global apartheid that deepens the racial divide today was not installed by the African at home or abroad. It was constructed around theologies of white supremacy, racial superiority, and an elaborately wrought, exploitative machine based on sheer unadulterated and unashamed greed.

As soon as I could, I fled London. One year was enough if I was not to spend my days writing indifferent short stories to be sold to the transcription center, Radio Deutchvelle, and the BBC. When your fellowship dries up, you need to make a living. With a wife and two kids, it can be tricky when you have no obvious and saleable skills, and when the capricious racial factor is sprung into action if you "merely" want to teach kindergarten in Britain.

So I fled to America in 1968. In America I could become anonymous, because my people had been there for four hundred years. It began with an invitation from the Poetry Center to join "world" poets for a reading. I was expected to bring my "British African robes" along.

In London I had kept up my poetry, done a reading at the Round House, and skirted gingerly on the edge of a beginning "black" arts movement in Britain. But it was a doomed cause, as Britain remains one of the countries most intolerant of the global racial mix in its midst. The African people there know. If you are black and run for Britain at the Olympics, you are called a Briton, but if you shoplift, you are a Jamaican immigrant! Its attitudes towards Africans and Asiatics are part of its barbaric past, when it plundered these "lesser breeds" to sustain a pathetic empire over which the sun did actually set.

> So I fled to America where
> they fired guns for cameras
> and buried food in Whitman's field
> in (the) year of locusts
> dust in eyes
> and death in the desert.

> ("On Killing of Cattle, Hogs,
> and Sheep in Minnesota,"
> from *House by the Sea*, Fall 1974)

I spent seven years in what for me was a "farther" exile in time and space, during which I sought to understand the mightiest power on earth, grasp my own place as an African, nay a "black man," in the global scheme of things, and expand perhaps the frontiers of human understanding and our common destiny.

The height of my brief visit in the summer of 1968 was the well-attended Poetry Festival at Stony Brook on Long Island. I gave a reading and a statement. The company was made up of some of the best names in American poetry. Louis Simpson, the

prime mover of the festival, received enthusiastic support for its organization from Dean Herbert Weisinger, one of the finest literary minds I was later to know and love as a great humanist and scholar. On hand was Jack Thompson, poet and scholar and a dear friend if I ever had one in America, who had an extensive experience of Africa, where he worked for the Farfield Foundation in the sixties. Among the poets were the inimitable Allen Ginsberg, who chanted Hopi poems to my Ewe songs; Gary Snyder, a superb poet of landscape and the Native American sensibility; Galway Kinnell; Robert Duncan; Jerry Rothemberg, with whom I later collaborated in the production of a most important magazine, *Alcheringa*, a literary landmark in the search for an exposition of the truest poetry of our planet. *Alcheringa*, an aboriginal Australian word meaning "dream time," carried articles on original poetries with samples from all our survived cultures which had, thanks to nineteenth-century European anthropology, been dubbed "primitive" or worse. Rothemberg's own work in this field, culminating in his large work *Shaking the Pumpkin*, is a wonderful tribute to the underlying strength of these aboriginal cultures, and a recognition of the lessons they have to teach a world gone giddy with its material achievement, with civilizations that, in the process of accomplishing the destruction of man, are destroying the very earth on which they thrived. In this day of screaming ecological causes, perhaps a pause will be made to ponder the fate of nations and peoples whose life-styles sought to preserve the world, and yet who were rolled over in the mad rush towards the material paradise because they were "primitive" and "savage."

The excitement of Stony Brook was its luring call for new teachers who were creatively engaged by the magic of "letters" and by the process of creativity itself as a vital and integral part of human existence. In short, real teachers.

After the festival, I was made an offer to join the staff at Stony Brook in the fall of 1968. This offer, generous and warmly made by Dean Weisinger, I accepted with great expectation. The seven years I spent in America, from 1968 to 1975, have come to signify the most creative period of my literary career so far, the period when my political and social consciousness became dramatically deepened.

Richard Nixon was winning the general elections when I arrived in the USA in November 1968. I remember the man vaguely as the gentleman who represented his country at our independence celebrations in 1957. I had a friend who was aide to him during the celebrations and thought the man was God's brother, if not God himself.

The Vietnam War was in its most escalatory phase, and the American nation was poised for a massive act of striptease and soul-searching. Even more significant from my point of view was the simmering revolt of African-American youth. Martin Luther King, Jr., the apostle of nonviolence, had just been murdered on the balcony of a Memphis hotel; some of the inner cities had gone up in flames. The radical Black Panther party, under the militant leadership of Huey P. Newton, was getting geared for a showdown with the forces of law and order under the famous FBI director J. Edgar Hoover. The legacy of Malcolm X, whom I met in Ghana in 1964, it seemed had been inherited by this new, openly armed group, using a California state law to parade the streets in defence of their right to full American citizenship.

I took a small apartment on 149th and Broadway on the edge of Harlem, and within Spanish Harlem. I commuted by train to Stony Brook, seventy miles away on Long Island. Harlem was closeby, volatile, exciting, and reminiscent of my distant homeland, at least its urban portions, with its proverbial African flamboyance and love of colours and its original addiction to loud music.

In "Harlem in Summer," I tried to record all this:

> A splash of colours
> and battered speech tilted
> like stormed cotton fields;
> the pavements, the primal
> corridors of heaven
> heaves blows puffs
> anxious waiting for the flash of knife
> borne by an avenging angel

I met the Yoruba god Ogun in Harlem

> drink(ing) blood openly defiantly
> in large calabash-fuls, as he grins,
> the chief celebrant over this festival

Harlem, alas, was also

> huddled pavements, dark
> grey alleys of anonymity
> the dark dirge America
> mean alleyways of poverty
> dispossession, early death
> in jammed doorways and creaking
>   elevators,

> glaring defeat in the morning
> of this beautiful beautiful America

America is an entire experience which one needs to write about. I still have a manuscript somewhere entitled *Where Is the Mississippi Panorama*, completed in 1974. The title was borrowed from my good friend Louis Simpson, who was an ex-colonial, like me, but from Jamaica, of an impeccable European Jewish pedigree, a soldier in the last war, and a Pulitzer poet.

I don't know whether his question is a takeoff from some line in Whitman, perhaps the best poet America has produced. I too came to discover Whitman, the poet of the American psyche, steeped in the lore of journeys and encounters, victory, conquest, and also enormous blood. I used to play a trick on students in my poetry classes. We would close the windows on winter mornings, put out the lights. Then I would ask them to listen to what the ghosts of massacred Native Americans (foolishly called Indians) were whispering. This used to bother many of them. I used to see above the crowds of Madison or Fifth Avenue a small group of weeping Native Americans in full war regalia floating above the skyscrapers and wailing plaintively that: "All things shall die / except the earth and the hills." But even they, the aborigines of America, in their penetrating wisdom could not foresee how their earth would be scarred and the hills blasted by the newcomers with pale faces whose symbol is the cross, whose metal is gold, whose guardian deity is greed.

In my poem "Departure and Prospect" I summarised my American sojourn. Exciting, creative, it was the period of some everlasting contacts with peoples, sensibilities, and places, memories of which remain deeply lodged in my soul. There, I "sold my fear forever / for a mess of potage in the American wolf's lair."

By the eve of my departure for home in September 1975, it seemed I had prophetically made a tryst with my proper destiny, which was waiting for me at home in Ghana. The snake that died on the tree was finally falling upon the earth. On my way to fulfil that destiny, I affirmed that

> I shall not pass through Barcelona
> or Paris; I will avoid London
> and Malmo . . .
> I will leap in the exuberant nights
> of my flight like a crocodile
> I once knew as I leap
> for victory and death

This poem is crammed with bits of personal history, the people I met, the places I came to know and love, and the images that are stuck in my memory as they seek to mesh with the originals I had brought with me from home in Africa.

I spent a wonderful visiting year in Austin, Texas, in the company of such superb poets as David Wavill and Christopher Middleton, two Englishmen who seem to be paying for their colonial sins in one of the few civilized spots in Texas. I also read with Voznesensky there. Austin is a wonderful intellectual oasis in the vast American anti-intellectual desert, where ignorance is sometimes made into a virtue, a survival line, an insulation belt against outside contamination. Someone once left a note in my mailbox in Stony Brook accusing me of being a Communist and an outside agitator. He was really complimenting me, raising me to a level of political consciousness which my "radical" friends at home sometimes deny me. I am, and will remain, an ardent African nationalist, riveted by the struggle and prospect for African economic and cultural emancipation. We cannot fully share in the world's fare if we are kept underdeveloped, economically exploited, and culturally bombarded by a monologue of Western Christian and racial superiority. This is the crux of my political commitment, both at home and abroad. I only hope my poetry and all my writings lend a hand in that struggle.

I had carried with me, in exile, memories of where I came from, recollections of the salt flats and the wide valley of my birthplace and early childhood, parabolic, and immense remembrances of that Africa:

> once a memory and a song
> now a place felt
> in the marrow
> of the absent bone,

Recollections of my father who

> spoke, as always, of how I am
> the one who must resurrect
> ancient days, raise again those
> misty glories of men and women
> who linger vaguely in the memorials of the tribe

All these were anticipating my homecoming, my return to the native land I had left eight years earlier, when the political dreams we built in the shadow of

"Ocean-going canoes, used as ferries for European goods in the 1940s"

Kwame Nkrumah were shattered by the right-wing military coup d'état of 1966. Perhaps the creative process itself must always mirror the reality of the poet's entire existence; truth and adherence to truth must map out the journey along the road of individual and collective consciousness; creativity itself must become a testimony to the truth, the swearing of an oath, as I said, to shout for struggle, victory, and survival, that "we cannot die of thirst / when our palm trees are prospering." The true poet perhaps is the one who bears witness at the court of human conscience, across the bars of a divided and tortured history and the strife of claims and counterclaims. My work is made easier because of who I am and where I come from, and for this, "praise be to my ancestors."

I left America in late August 1975. I chose to go home by a slow Ghanaian freighter of the Black Star Line, founded by Nkrumah in redemption of Marcus Garvey's dream. The *Oti River* was carrying lager beer to Nigeria. Nigeria was experiencing an oil boom. And it was spending money to buy canned beer from the United States! That too is part of the underdevelopment syndrome. An African-American family in New Jersey was worried when I told them the ship was manned by Africans. They were sure I would not reach my home.

I had a small but a comfortable cabin. I took with me for the seventeen days' journey an assortment of books, mainly on philosophy, a subject that I had always wanted to read more systematically. From Plato to Santayana. I would seek to enter the Western intellectual mind in a more leisurely manner. I also took along Marx and a few volumes of the best of Lenin. After a trip to China in 1963 as a member of the Afro-Asian Writers' Bureau, I had become fascinated with Mao Tse Tung and his peasant Marxist revolution. So he too came along with me. But I was being overly optimistic. Seventeen days is too short to cover so many tracts of exciting, disparate, and sometimes impenetrable treatises. There were other attractions, mainly the deep blue Atlantic Ocean and the eternally fascinating flying fish. I could not help but think of the famous Middle Passage as we floated in our reversal journey. In my long prison poem, *The Wayfarer Comes Home,* a poem in five movements, I wrote of

the single way journey upon the sea
my companions the flying fish
heading towards the coast of Senegal.
    we rode, we rode
    taking the waves

as we traced the Middle Passage backwards
in the smell of vomit
our light bent for home
grey in the August moon.

I had pleaded for and been offered a lectureship at our third university, the University of Cape Coast in the Central Region. I was drawn to this university partly because it had the most picturesque compound facing the Atlantic Ocean. Antelopes still roamed the campus where virginal bush had not been cleared. It was a new university, founded in 1962 by Nkrumah. Besides, I had hoped it had not contracted some of the diseases that afflicted the University of Ghana at Legon, where meaningless intellectual snobbery had become erected into a way of life. Cape Coast was set up to train science teachers for the secondary schools and teacher training colleges. After Nkrumah's overthrow, at the behest of the "intellectual giants" of the older University at Legon, Cape Coast was reduced to a small liberal-arts college graduating hundreds of students with degrees in classical civilization and religious studies (they added Islam to the syllabus under duress). Science education, for which the university was set up, still receives a halfhearted support as it stagnates between the intellectual backwardness of its leaders and the developmental myopia of the successive governments.

I was coming from America with a variety of experiences, apart from a Ph.D. and five books under my belt. I was going to be a missionary returning home to work among my people, to preach the good word of national cultural and intellectual redemption. We would work to mould new African minds as to the tasks that faced us. I was a member of what I call the transition generation. I was twenty-two when independence came. I had witnessed the colonial era, with its warped and oppressive agenda designed purposely to keep us in thrall. I had witnessed, as a young lad, our national struggle for freedom. My father was an ardent nationalist, a staunch supporter of the United Gold Coast Convention when Nkrumah returned from America and Britain to lead it. And when he broke with the UGCC to found the radical and revolutionary Convention People's Party, my father was an immediate supporter. I saw the rallies and heard some of the most stirring speeches of the epoch. I was in Accra in January 1950 when Nkrumah launched his Positive Action against the British in his last effort to dislodge them. This was the action that led him to jail. I was part of the independence experiment as a young undergraduate, participating in breaking the barriers erected by the British and their African collaborators to keep the CPP and its radical nationalism out of the university campus. Legon was and is the seat of Ghanaian political reaction of the most persistent and virulent type. There were African professors who had no respect for the university they were teaching in, considering it as only a vague echo or at least inferior copy of the Oxford or Cambridge from where they had received their indifferent degrees. As for degrees from America, forget it. The British traditional snobbery and anti-Americanism was part of the colonial intellectual programme. So Nkrumah, a US-trained intellectual, was looked down upon by the products of Britain's universities. The same contempt he suffered from his anglophile peers in the UGCC, who all, to a man, were sponsored to Britain by rich relatives. In England they rubbed shoulders with the British upper class in the universities and the Inns of Court at the same period when Nkrumah was washing dishes, waiting table on a Mexico-bound pleasure boat, carrying offal in a soap factory, or working night shift at a shipyard in Chester, Pennsylvania. The personality of the anglophile intellectual African expresses itself not only in a dismal self-abasement, but in a cringing attachment to British institutions, manners, and ideas. The contest in Africa between the radical nationalist perspective exemplified by people like Nkrumah and Nyerere, and the reactionary, subservient, pro-European outlook which was embraced by people like Tafawa Belewa of Nigeria and Houphouet Boigny of the Ivory Coast, underscores a historical and continuing struggle that finds echoes in Africa's universities, which have all been largely anti-progressive, and in many instances rejected an African agenda for a so-called universal system which is essentially European. That contest equally underscores the issues of true African independence, or subservience that in turn defines the dependence syndrome in its most classical form. The liberation of the African can only begin with the liberation of his mind from centuries of intellectual consumerism.

It was to contribute my modest quota to this work of fundamental and mental liberation that I made the decision to leave for home. I had interacted with some of the best minds in America, I had "touched base" with my brothers from whom centuries had separated me, beginning with Langston Hughes and James Baldwin, whom I had met on African soil; to the young poets such as Michael Harper, Calvin Canton; the fine dramatist George Macbeth; the enterprising dance choreographer Carmen Moore, who put my long poem *I Heard a Bird Cry* to music and dance and braved a performance

one summer in Central Park; the young black militants at Stony Brook who, after Vietnam, were facing Babylon head on and belching fire. To these I became a guru, teacher, and moderator as we crafted together the Black Studies Program, one of the finest to be spawned across America's university campuses, in a search to assuage black hunger for self-pride and identity.

I was gearing myself for the ultimate African discourse and the debate as to which way we would go, as a people, as a civilization. The political climate in Ghana had undergone some changes since the rightist military takeover of 1966, the development that originally had prompted my leaving the country. By the time I was returning home in September 1975, another military coup had taken place, but this time against the rightist Busia administration, which was not only inept but manifestly corrupt and anti-African. General Acheampong's early days revealed a strong streak of nationalism, exuded a wonderful spirit of pride and self-reliance. There were rumours of corrupt practices, but they were merely rumours, which seem to be the main source of information in the underdeveloped world. But there was a purposeful edge to the regime, as it sought to tackle fundamental questions of food production and general development.

My suspicion of military regimes remains intact even today. The armies of Africa created out of the colonial enterprise do actually believe that they have a mandate to take over and run countries. In spite of my personal dislike of government by any form of physical coercion, I am however reconciled to the thought that military governments are also part of the historical struggle for a political system that will answer the yearnings of the people. They too, if one can believe the difficult, can be instruments of creating that equitable system a people desire, particularly a people such as ours, who have suffered so much for so many centuries.

I arrived at home in September 1975 and assumed work as a lecturer at the University of Cape Coast. On December 31, 1975, at about 5 A.M., I was arrested by the intelligence police called the Special Branch. I was to spend ten months in the maximum prison of Ussher Fort in Accra, seven of those months in solitary confinement. The story of the arrest and incarceration I have already told in my book *The Ghana Revolution*, a book that has become notoriously controversial. There is nothing in that book I would change if I were writing it today. It is a truthful account of the various events, historical and personal,

Houses flooded by the Keta Lagoon

and an honest if perhaps a little embittered record of the darker period of recent Ghanaian history.

The House by the Sea (1978) is the poetic record of that imprisonment. It explores not merely the psychological pain of incarceration, but also the larger issues of freedom within the framework of political action. It is the book that brought my tentative political position in my earlier poetry boldly into the open, with it an undisguised option for radical action and the call for the creation of a humane society. It is poetry marked by defiance and denunciation, proclaiming that:

> though our bones cruch
> our spirit will not break
> until we make a
> reckoning in the red bright book
>   of history
>
> . . . .
>
> for as all die, so shall we
> but it is not dying that should pain us
> it is the waiting, the
> intermission when we cannot act,
> when our will is shackled by tyranny.

The house by the sea is the prison fort of Ussher, built by the Dutch in the seventeenth century to hold slaves before the transatlantic journey; the imagery of this house is explored through a series of linking motifs of "long rows of ancient walls," "a line of assorted flowers," "prison cats in heat," "executioners, heroes, condemned men," the gulls that sail over its sky, a flying jet plane—all accentuating the will to survive, affirming for the poet

> That so much freedom means
> that we swear we'll postpone dying
> until the morning after.

The last line became the title of a book of selected poems published in 1986 by the Greenfield Review Press in upstate New York.

Some critic wrote that I was a poet of death. I deny this most vehemently. How can any serious poet write merely of death? Though I wrote of death as an overhanging presentiment of our common human condition, my poetry speaks of life and hope for a better life, an immense love "that will defy dying / and Death," rejects death as "terminal and deadly," opts for the blossoming tree, the transformation of death into birth,

> any place of birth where
> my tree will blossom
> . . . .
> (and) crumble this wailing wall.

In prison I took a great interest in a subject around which I had skirted all my life, the subject of mystery, the Universe and God. In solitary I had a visitation from my grandfather Nyidevu, who had then been dead over thirty years. He was sitting in a reclining chair at the foot of my bed. He said to me I would soon be leaving the prison. I upon release should consult my mother, who would take me to a certain shrine near my birthplace. Then he was gone. I was not asleep: it was like one of those waking dreams in which all your senses are alert, and you believe what you are seeing is actually occurring. It was so brief.

When I came out of solitary confinement and prison a few months after that revelation, I did go to the shrine with my mother. I have since been back within the ambit of my ancestral religion.

I was born with the blessing of my ancestral deities. As a boy I had been taken before them many occasions. But school and Christianity had claimed me in a concerted conspiracy to wean me, like most African children, from our ancestral ways. I became a serious Christian, even though at the age of fifteen I refused to take the first Lord's Supper. I did not show up at the church service devoted to giving this important sacrament, specially prepared for boys and girls of my age. I must have been severely punished for this serious infraction. But I never took the sacrament. I suppose this does not make me a Christian at all.

I have since embraced, from the base religion of my African ancestors, a universal God. Many non-Africans believe Africans are polytheistic. This is simply not true. The African religious outlook centres around a Supreme Being who is the creator of the Universe. This outlook further assigns to the divine hand of the creator the creation of intermediate divinities who dwell on earth with man. These are sometimes represented by natural phenomena such as rivers, mountains, groves, thunder, the rainbow. Their role is to intercede between man and God. They are visible; it is through them that the Supreme Being speaks and acts. So the African never erects temples to the Supreme God. It would be presumptuous. He communicates with him through His numerous agents. The ancestors also have a place in this hierarchy of divine beings, and act on behalf of their offspring still in the living world, who too are spiritual entities.

I have also ventured into the study, however haphazardly, of world religions. Hinduism and its theology of predestination, Buddhism and its reflective philosophy constructed around a moral order, Islam and its combination of worldliness and mystical revelation; all have come to attract in me a yearning for an answer to the mystery of life itself on the bedrock of the brotherhood of man. I am equally renewed in my fascination for the militant Christ, who abhors injustice, loves the poor, and seeks to alleviate their suffering. I remain suspicious of the opulence, the attendant arrogance and tendentious hypocrisy and immorality of organized Christianity, whose hand I see glaringly in my historical despair. What I claim ultimately is a common humanity, and decency of treatment, a theology of liberation for all, an end to oppression, especially the type that derives its logic from racism and the imperative economic exploitation structured around unmitigated greed.

In sum, I have sought to write poetry that will supplement my quest for individual and collective redemption, a return to a humane society, free and unfettered. It is this some writers have seen as the politics in my poetry. I have been political, even taken part in founding a political party. But I have also insisted that writing poetry cannot be a substitute for political action. My poetry remains ego-centred, that is, derives its ultimate energy from my personal being. Even when it clenches its fists and clamours for a march or a war for liberty, it does so from that intimate recess of my soul which too had known fetters and sorrow. In a 1986 poem, "Grains and Tears," I wrote in the style of the message to the ancestors, using the same inspiration of the oral poem I have come to love so much:

> Go and tell them I paid the price
> I stood by the truth
> I fought anger and hatred
> on behalf of the people
> I ate their meager meals in the barracks
> Shared their footsteps and tears
> in freedom's name.
> I promised once in a slave house at Ussher
> to postpone dying until
> the morning after freedom.
>   I promise.

My recent poetry, inspired by my diplomatic sojourn in Latin America, propels me further towards social themes, centering around the struggle between power and deprivation, oppression and poverty. The grim reality of this other America of José Martí, Bolívar, Sandino, San Martín, Fidel Castro, Che Guevara, Daniel Ortega, and all the historical forces of political revolution have come to signify for me deeply felt symbols of that eternal human resistance. I am persuaded more to speak of struggles and victory, of faith, of the starred, defiant flags of freedom, and of the love supreme that underlies this. It is not new poetry; it is a new direction in my old poetry which, even in defeats, sees banners waving again, as the people, all our people, march to a better day. I affirm that:

> What consoling of the people we need do
> let us do it now
> as our road will surely end
> in the man's inordinate field.

Havana, April 1990

BIBLIOGRAPHY

Poetry:

Rediscovery and Other Poems, Mbari (Nigeria), 1964, Northwestern University Press, 1964.

(Editor with G. Adali-Mortty) *Messages: Poems from Ghana,* Heinemann, 1970, Humanities, 1971.

Night of My Blood, Doubleday, 1971.

(Translator) *Guardians of the Sacred Word: Ewe Poetry,* NOK, 1974.

Ride Me, Memory, Greenfield Review Press, 1974.

The House by the Sea, Greenfield Review Press, 1978.

(Translator) Vinoko Akpalu, *When Sorrow-Song Descends upon You,* Cross Cultural Review, 1981.

Until the Morning After: Selected Poems, Greenfield Review Press, 1987.

Fiction:

Ancestral Power [and] *Lament* (plays), Heinemann, 1970.

This Earth, My Brother: An Allegorical Tale of Africa, Heinemann, 1970, Doubleday, 1971.

Nonfiction:

The Breast of the Earth: A Survey of the History, Culture, and Literature of Africa South of the Sahara, Doubleday, 1974.

In Person: Achebe, Awoonor, and Soyinka at the University of Washington, University of Washington African Studies Program, 1975.

The Ghana Revolution: Personal Perspective (essays), Oases, 1984.

Ghana: A Political History, Woeli Accra, 1990.

Contributor to *African Commentary, Africa Report,* and *Books Abroad.* Associate editor, *Transition, World View,* and *Okike.*

Franco Beltrametti

1937-

Franco Beltrametti's grandfather Giuseppe Beltrametti, Mendocino County, California, about 1905

The winter of 1989–1990 has been dry, with many forest fires and a drought from Sicily to the Alps. Since December the golden calycanthus flowers light up when the sun rises above the roof lines of the courtyard from the cliffs of Monte Generoso. I've been living here on and off for nineteen years. My neighbours Laurie and Giovanni have this old electric typewriter, which I'm using now. I like its typefaces, its hum and metallic noises. A ten-thousand-word autobiography sounds like ten thousand rivers and mountains. I'll try.

I was born on Lago Maggiore, October 7, 1937. My father worked for the Swiss railways. I guess I was born in Locarno because my mother's mother, Anita Sala, moved there from Sestri Levante, Liguria, after her husband, Hervé Fragnière, died in 1930. Earlier he too was in the railways. My father's father, Giuseppe, was a farmer. He migrated in 1899 from

Cadenazzo, Ticino, to California, had a dairy farm in Point Arena, Mendocino County, on the Pacific. His wife, Lucia, had four daughters and two sons: Americo and my father, Giovanni, the elder. My grandfather came back from California in 1909 to see his savings vanish in the bankruptcy of a local Swiss bank. His second son, Americo, went to California too. He'd a reputation as a troublemaker. Everybody in the family would say that I looked just like him. He died at twenty-two from gangrene in Santa Maria, California, in 1931. As a kid I would often visit my grandfather's farm in Cadenazzo. A stone house, a garden, some cows and a horse, an orchard and vineyard on the slope of Monte Ceneri's chestnut woods, and some fields out in the Magadino plain. He told me of the San Francisco fire, of trains into the city, of riots in Chinatown and other things, letting me dream that the world was wide and available. He had a black hat and a red bandana, kept tight by an empty matchbox. He was an Anarchist at heart and gave me, probably without counting on it, a desire to travel, to go away, to move on. I'm fifty-three and I'm still like that. My mother's name is Linda. She attended the Scuola d'Arte del Costume in Milano near the *Duomo*. Nowadays it's called stylism. While visiting relatives in Cadenazzo during September 1933 she got a love letter. The messenger was my father. In 1936 they married, moved from one railway town to the next, and finally separated when I was sixteen.

The language of southern Switzerland, Ticino, was Italian and of local dialects. You could tell where everybody came from by their accent. Tiny differences did matter. I have forgotten many dialects and only speak some with my father, now eighty-three. My mother always spoke Italian with me. (They were unlikely persons to be together. I'm their only child. I too have one son, Giona. He was born in Kyoto, Japan, in 1966. His mother's name is Judith Danciger.)

I should say something about my grandma Anita. She always took me mushroom hunting and also to the pastry shops and beer halls she was fond of.

In April 1945 the war was over. The Antifascists hunted down the local Fascists. I assisted at the mobbing of a tobacco shop under Locarno's *portici*. The owner got an ear cut in the fight. Some Fascist bosses' villas burnt. I didn't disapprove. Switzerland had been officially neutral but thousands of runaway Italian, French, and German Jews were driven back at the border and handed to the slaughter. Call it neutrality! In the middle of the night you could hear swarms of airplanes. You could tell from the red sky that Milano was being bombed. My man was Stalin. I thought of myself as a Communist and an Anarchist.

Life was boring in Chiasso, a small railway border town where we moved in 1946. Thank God we had gangs, street fights, soccer games, and the "2 movies 2" in Ponte Chiasso across the border. Como was near for Westerns, and more movies with the Neapolitan actor Totò. When my parents split up I was the first to go. I rented a room in Lugano, where I was stranded studying at the *Liceo*. I wasn't a good student. Mnemonic systems were horrors. I loved languages, art history, and whatever art and literary news I could get. The professor of French, Pericle Patocchi, was sharp on Provençal poetry and on Ronsard, Louise Labè, Rabelais, Verlaine, Baudelaire, and Apollinaire. It took two years more than had been foreseen to finish the damn school. Life was so much more enticing, and books. Sartre, Camus,

Villon, Ungaretti, Dino Campana, Vittorini, Pavese, Melville, and Hemingway were my heroes, along with Lucio Fontana, Yves Klein, and Pollock, whose shows in Milano I didn't miss. My mother had moved there with her new man, Edo. The city was good for bars, galleries, bookstores, music, and action. Lugano was a sort of weekly exile. When I moved to Zürich in 1958 to study architecture I was very much on my own. My father and my mother always helped; they weren't wealthy. I think they were and still are exceptional in their quiet ways.

A few hours ago I told my mother about this autobiography. "Oh, you forget so many things. I've a better memory than you," she laughed on the phone. My standard excuse for my poor memory is that I met so many people and got involved with so many different places, situations, jobs, and events that the nowness of it all took over.

In spring 1939 my parents went on a trip to Interlaken and Lausanne. I was left with my grandma Anita, and remember huge blue hydrangea flowers (in Kyoto, 1967, I'd see them again on LSD) and alleys lined with strawberries. For the first time my parents weren't there. That was in Cadenazzo in the large country house of my mother's wealthy relatives. At my grandad's farm a few hundred yards uphill the scene was radically different, a small fireplace with a coffeepot always on. But there were hydrangeas there too.

I remember my grandma Anita's pâté and anchovies. She was a gourmet, even spent days preparing my aunt Carla's wedding banquet. There was a mountain girl helping in the house. I forget her name. Sometimes she would play with my little thing and I would touch her. I must've been four or five since my uncle Fredi was often away in the army. Those days Fredi was quite outgoing. We would visit another young lady on the opposite shore of the lake. She had several fox skins. Once the tin ocean-liner toy which we'd borrowed from zia Carla sunk. That almost caused a breakup. My uncle used me as his hunting dog, I would rescue the warm, tiny birds from under the brush. I remember him shooting a large green woodpecker. I remember not liking that, but I liked my uncle. My career as hunting dog came to a sudden end after I caught pneumonia from sleeping out in wet clothes. Fredi also caught trout with his hands in the Isorno river gorges of Loco, Onsernone Valley. His father, Venanzio, a retired railway engine driver, had the most monumental white mustaches ever and collected old weapons. They never impressed me though I liked to play duels with Fredi with real swords. We were careless but it all worked out.

Flashback: Winter 1940, I am walking on a frozen fountain. The ice breaks. A farmer rescues me and brings me to his kitchen, lit up by a roaring fire. His wife takes off my icy wet clothing, lays me naked on the large wooden table for a massage with grappa till I am red. I don't even catch a cold. At age five, near the railway yards of Castione, Bellinzona, behind the kindergarten fence, a man is castrating cocks. Feathers fly all over. Another time a stoneworker saves me from drowning in a fast-running creek. (I've a terrific collection of straw pets: Miki the dog, a giraffe, a horse, Mumo the huge teddy bear, a tiger, and an elephant. I also am fond of a doll and knit several clothes for her: I remember a blue skirt with pink flowers.) The Swiss army marching up and down the dirt road into town. To school, the smell of ink, the beauty of metal nibs. The uncomfortable wooden benches. I hate to sit there, eternally. Soldiers shaving along rows of wooden sinks on freezing mornings. One good day, no school: the building is crowded with British Sikh soldiers and other war refugees. It's 1943 or 1944. We spend a summer, my mother and me, with relatives in Indemini, a lonely mountain village. I help make wooden charcoal. A long white worm scares and puzzles me: it vanishes in an invisible hole. Mystery. Age seven: my father has to move again, I change school three times in second grade. In Locarno the teacher shuts me in a closet. A daily routine. I eat all his hidden stash of dry figs; my grandmother moves me to another school. 1945: war is over. I'm on my father's shoulders watching a crowd with red flags feasting in Piazza della Colleggiata, Bellinzona. Finally my parents find a house in downtown Chiasso, where a year before my father's freight train was machine-gunned by two U.S.A. war planes.

Flashback: 1945, still in Ravecchia, Bellinzona. I remember the last time my dad played soccer with me in the corridor. I remember his geographical maps, was excited by those faraway names, faraway places. I remember a Christmas. My father was away working, my mother couldn't hide her sadness. She was very young and beautiful. She has an oblong beauty mark on her right calf. She dressed well, with Italian taste. Everybody else seemed clumsy, except for the women farmers in long, flowery skirts.

The border opened, the family could trade visits. I remember the fantastic smell of fresh color ink from *Il Corrierino dei Piccoli*, Bibì and Bibò, the cartoon adventures of il Signor Bonaventura, who always won a million lire. In those early postwar days, a mythical apparition: my Sicilian uncle, Achille Viola, a lawyer at Milano's market. He had fine mustaches, brought oranges at each visit, even rented a box at the La

"My father, Giovanni 'John' Beltrametti (left) with two railway colleagues," Basel, Switzerland, 1934

Scala opera house. He was the third husband of my grandmother Anita's sister, Carolina. But zio Achille died before he could take me down to Palermo. Zia Carolina went broke, would become blind, and moved back to Ticino. She stayed very elegant till the end. My mother was living with her while studying in the city.

In 1946 my parents rented a place for the summer in Bordighera, near the French-Italian sea border. The long trip by train was a treat. Bombed bridges were reinforced with wooden structures. In Genova, for the first time, the sea: silver light on pale turquoise waves. The beds of the rented cottage turned out to be full of fleas. We move to Pensione Aurora, where we'd go back for a few summers. A table was reserved for two men who detected and unprimed mines. One had a face ruined by metal splinters. He introduced me to Ping-Pong. (Ping-Pong: one of the things I like best in life. This very afternoon I played several games with my son, Giona.) I learned to swim; what a change the Mediterranean was from the granite pools of freezing mountain water where we used to go. I still visit those remote waterfalls and emerald green pools.

Well, Chiasso was a funny, swampy place, large meadows with grey Alpine cows were hidden by the "downtown" buildings near the station. Lots of charcoal smoke in the air from the railway engines. I could watch the wide railway yards from my fifth-floor windows. The landlord had a cigar factory. There were many cigar factories. They're all gone.

Women working tobacco had tanned fingers. There were lots of full- and part-time smugglers. They would carry backpacks loaded with cigarettes, chocolate, and watches over the ridges into Italy. At thirteen I learned to play decent poker in a bar which is being taken down right now. The village where I'm writing all this is about ten miles north of Chiasso, at the southern tip of Lugano Lake. But that Chiasso town, in spite of its adventurous activities on the border, was dull, and from the beginning I felt a stranger. I still am a stranger. I didn't learn its dialect, and immediately took a strong liking to Italians. The locals thought, and to a degree still think, they are more Swiss than the Swiss. Everybody else must be uncivilized and inferior. My friends were Italians, sons of border guards, smugglers, forwarding agents, and railway workers. Our gang was the downtowners. A Calabrian kid lost an eye, hit by an umbrella rib used as an arrow. We were pretty wild and ritualistic. At some point I met Floretta; she could outplay the boys at soccer. Flora and I are still friends. She owns the courtyard, fixed the buildings one by one in the early seventies, and now teaches architecture in Zürich and Rome. Her husband, André Ruchat, was my best friend in Chiasso. He went down in 1961 with a Swiss army airplane. Their daughter Anna will be a mother soon. Flora has some of my best paintings in her house. (Yes, I'm a visual artist too.)

For summer vacations we later moved to Nervi, east of Genova. I remember blinding afternoon light, large processions of red and black ants, cicadas in the pine trees. I bought my first poetry book there, *Il Dolore* by Ungaretti, and couldn't get over the impact: I built a special place for poetry in my mind and wrote hermetic attempts. It took years to find out some basics: the only way to write is to write. Later on in Japan, when at twenty-eight I still was very shy regarding poetry, Philip Whalen confirmed it: in order to write you've got to sit down and do it.

When I was thirteen or fourteen, I often cycled to swim and read by the Breggia River, now covered by the main highway. All I wrote, all I painted, and I did paint a lot as a kid, is gone. First by selective destruction of unsatisfying work, and finally at twenty-three in Fredi's garden above Locarno, I burned everything thoroughly and happily. By then my mother had moved back from Milano and worked for her sister and Fredi's clothing shop. She somehow managed to save two paintings from the fifties. Strangely enough they remind me of Tancredi, whom I didn't know at all. In Ascona there was a gallery, la Cittadella, run by Gisèle Réal, showing Ecole de Paris abstract work. Gisèle had the best art

mags of the time. Through her I met Raffaello Benazzi and through Raffaello, Julius Bissier, the German painter. In April 1965, just before leaving for Japan, I visited him. "It's a long way," was his last greeting at the gate of the garden. When I arrived in Tokyo his wife wrote that he'd died. His art is light and transparent, spirit and hand are one.

I was overeducated, had to go a long way away from all of it to begin to see through. Life is interesting because it is complicated, as Ted Berrigan was fond of saying, using the same wording which I also used in Italian. Complications? Complexities? Whatever it is it's been a long way, endlessly surprising, never predictable.

It's a miracle how lightly I went through the architecture studies, hardly attending twelve hours of *Vorlesungen* (lectures) over five years. I even got scholarships and a degree in spite of my loose ways. Paris, 1960 and 1961: it was easy for somebody as determined as I was to find work. I knew Paris from previous visits. When I moved there it felt like home. Evelyne followed soon. She was a Zürich photographer. We moved from one hotel to the next. The best

Mother, Linda Fragnière, Milano, Italy, 1934

was Hotel Henry IV, place Dauphine, with windows on the Seine and Le Pont Neuf. The first was near la Contrescarpe. I was working for Candilis and Woods's atelier, 18 rue Dauphine, and nighttimes I was trying to paint, in a general Michaux plus Tobey direction. My readings were the preSocratics, Lao-tzu, D. T. Suzuki, Lévi-Strauss, Genet, and Rimbaud. In the atelier I met Li Yen, a Chinese just in from London. Li introduced me to more Taoism and Zen, and also to Ezra Pound, Saint John Perse, Max Picard, Mao Tse-tung, and to new American writers. I'd already read the Italian version of Kerouac's *Subterraneans* with my sculptor friend Raffaello Benazzi, with whom I often stayed in the pine forest near Massa Carrara, where I designed a children's sea camp for the Anarchists, coming and going from my Zürich rooms in Niederdorf, the old section of town. I got more leads from Giovanni Blumer, an autodidact heavily into Marcel Duchamp, Lautréamont, Ludwig Hohl, and everything marginal and intelligent. For a while we'd a girlfriend in common, Irene Aebi, now singing with Steve Lacy. In Naples, Irene met an American navy kid, went to San Francisco, and came back with news from the West Coast, of Jack Spicer and his circle of poets.

You see: I can't be linear even if I try. Back to Paris. The main things were making love to Evelyne, wandering with Li Yen, and discovering that architecture as it was practiced wasn't my way. Too square, too hectic, too abstract, too many phone calls, too much sitting around drawing tables, too many straight lines with too many rapidographs, far from the streets and reality. The atelier was a friendly and fairly well-paid setup, but Li and I quit and found jobs on our own. The main one was remodeling a studio in rue d'Amsterdam for Henry Meerson, a worldly fashion photographer doing covers for *Harper's Bazaar* and such. Evelyne worked for him in the darkroom, and he was fond of saying that his young architects combined Chinese and Italian subtlety with British rigour and Swiss precision. What an optimist! Our Algerian carpenters were passionate but rough, yet Meerson never blinked. We hung out with his models, saw lots of movies, were wandering scholars. The Algerian liberation was near, bombs would explode often in the deserted Quartier Latin. Li gave me the first rudiments of English while I tried to improve his French. At the beginning of spring I left Evelyne, moved back to Zürich for exams, passed through Paris in summer, read Gregory Corso's *Happy Birthday of Death* and Kerouac's *Dharma Bums*. Meerson gently paid cash for our project of a summerhouse on the Côte d'Azur which was never

built, and I moved to London into Li Yen's flat while Li used mine in Zürich on Rindermarkt. I found work with the Smithsons, designing details for their Saint James Towers. It was a part-time job so I'd time to wander. The British Museum became familiar, including the nearby teahouses. Coomaraswamy, several Kenneth Rexroth, and D. T. Suzuki on Japanese art were among the books which I stole in Charing Cross. On Hampstead Heath, Chinese flew kites from the large grass terrace overlooking London. (One can cut another's kite loose by hitting its string with a tenser string, using the wind.) By the end of 1961 I was back in Zürich. I got my degree in architecture at Eidgenössische Technische Hochschule (Swiss Federal Institute of Technology) in 1963. I traveled a lot, mainly to Italy, France, Spain, and Tangier. It is a mystery how I could work, study, lead a dense bar life day and night, go through girlfriends, sometimes heartlessly, read steadily, and be on the move all the time. *Flashback: Life in Zürich around 1963, springtime. I'm living at Professor Alfred Roth Dolder's house overlooking a creek in the forest. You can hear it all the time, running from waterfall to waterfall.*

Christophe Beriger, the architect, had moved back to Zürich from Paris and offered a job and also helped my degree project for a conservatoire, drawing technical details. Leo Zanier, now living with Flora, helped with statics. I got a letter from Irene, who was in Rome, her new fiancé was an engineer, Bubi Fiorenzi. I moved there and we became friends instantly. After two months of traveling in Greece I rented and repaired with them a tufa tower in Isola Farnese, above the Etruscan ruins of Vejo, seventeen kilometers north of Rome. There was no running water in the village. In order to get it, along with a bus line, Isola joined Rome. For the feast Rome sent a Bersaglieri band. More musicians than inhabitants to feed. A firework hit a barn in the night, lots of firemen arrived, also hungry; the barn was ashes. In winter I worked again in Zürich with Christophe, Li Yen, and a young Tokyo architect, Minoru Shimoda. We always had green tea and Remy Martin cognac on the draft tables. Some of the projects got built eventually by Christophe's father's firm. *Flashback: Lots of Jean-Luc Godard's movies. The frozen lake of Zürich. A girl in München, Berta. We'd met in Greece, Mikonos. Her father was a Second World War Prussian general who liked Minoru better than me. Several trips to Paris and Provence. Spring 1964 comes: back to Rome and Isola. We've credit at the grocer's, at the bar, and at a restaurant in Trastevere, da Lucia. I work with Bubi remodeling attics in Campo dei Fiori and Trastevere. With a zoning plan for Sperlonga, half the way down to*

Naples, we save the Grotta di Tiberio beach from speculation and cement. Irene and Bubi tell of an American girl named Judy. One morning she arrives in her mother's sports car. She's studying to be an interpreter in Geneva, Switzerland, and comes and goes from there to her mother's place in Rome.

Flashback: Judy suddenly crying out of happiness after moving in. We go for long hikes and drives, visit Bagnaia, Bomarzo, and Viterbo, Siena, and the Etruscan graves of Tarquinia, and the frescoes which I'd seen at seventeen. We visit Sperlonga, swim in the sea, swim in Vejo's river and waterfall. She has a younger sister, Lizzi; her stepfather, Doctor Hirshman, had died a few weeks before we could meet. Leila, her mother, is a Hungarian-Latvian Jew born in Paterson, New Jersey, and has grey eyes like a gentle wolf. My studies of the English language become steadier. Judy writes poetry, she types the texts carefully, which I never did. We listen to records: Vivaldi, Bach, Bob Dylan, and Roberto Murolo's Vecchia Napoli *(an LP which actually I'm playing right now.)*

Flashback: My father, throughout these years, keeps visiting me. In Zürich we used to meet at the Hauptbahnhof, where he would arrive with his train on the job. He comes to Isola too, goes to Sperlonga, meets my new friends. I've a "London smoke" suit. Sometimes I wear the coat with white jeans. Fredi and my mother tailored that suit. My mother never visits. I always visit her. She keeps private, rarely goes out of her way, some kind of strange dignity and shyness.

Flashback: Judy opens her light blue eyes, I call her Judy girl, the best in the ring. At the beginning our common language is French, which we both speak fluently, then Italian and American. After the fast turnover of girlfriends, Judith Mary Danciger is a radical change. Summer is over, Li Yen and Christophe arrive and want me back for work, so Judy and I move to Zürich for six months, go through several borrowed houses, including a sandstone cottage in a quarry near Regensberg, and end up with our luggage and growing collection of books under a roof on Oberdorfstrasse. In the streets I would meet Koebi, a welder, walking a variety pack of expensive dogs, all pets of Niederdorf's hookers.

There were only a few boutiques and galleries; it was a section of Zürich full of old bars and artisans' workshops. Sometimes we would drink with Friedrich Kuhn, the fabulous painter. I was working hard, paid as usual by the hour. Judy was learning German and was wearing a long camel-hair overcoat. Leila, Bubi, and Irene visited from Rome. I started feeling restless, the drive to see Japan took over. Spring came, 1965. We spent two weeks in Ticino visiting my parents, Flora and Anna, Solange and Lio Galfetti, the architect, Benazzi and Bissier.

With Irene Aebi and Bubi Fiorenzi (kneeling), near Rome, 1963

In my early days in Zürich I met Alfred Giedion, the historian, and his wife, Carola Welcker, and Alberto Giacometti, the sculptor, at Caffee Odeon, a classy, Viennese-style hangout. I also met the architects Alvar Aalto and Richard Neutra and listened to their monologues. Giacometti was very silent, our meetings fast but intense. Well, all that was over, I was an architect, was living with a woman I loved, and was leaving Europe. Judy came along till Venice. For a week we roamed all over and rode boats to the islands. She waved me good-bye at the station. I was off to Vienna, Moscow, and the Japan of my mind. In Moscow, Majakovskji's grave was covered with flowers. May 9 I saw the military Day of Victory Parade in the Red Square, twenty years after the fall of Berlin. While the Trans-Siberian train was leaving Moscow I shared a bottle of vodka offered by a grey-eyed Red Army veteran. On the train everybody was visiting from one compartment to another, in pyjamas and dressing gowns. A drunk general distributed his decorations to several kids. Days later, an hour before he'd to get off, everybody looked for his scattered medals. I was second class, had food stamps, which would provide two daily bottles of cognac to share with Volodja, a Vladivostok cannery worker, and Simeon, a Siberian Yupik whaler from the Bering Strait on his way home after a recovery period in Crimea. With his new Turkish rifle he shot rocks from the train windows. Volodja and Simeon spoke some German from their army days in Eastern Germany. I showed them a recent photo of Judy, they approved. Simeon had a picture of his father in white furs and seal skins. We parted our ways in Khabarovsk on the Amur River. The main buildings were neoclassic, Europe had extended so far. But from the train occasional Mongolian yurts and camps filed by with endless, rolling, bare hills. Every morning a different landscape and different springtimes. Khabarovsk had a large, modern, new hotel, the waitresses in miniskirts had a Marilyn Monroe–*Niagara Falls* look.

A new model train took me to the harbor of Nakodka and a Russian ferry to Yokohama, through the Tsugaru Kaikyo, crowded with small wooden fishing boats. Along the eastern coast of Honshu you can see many villages under steep green mountains, just like in classic Far Eastern painted scrolls. That's why landscape is called *sansui:* mountains and waters. In Yokohama, Minoru and Günter Nitschke, a friend from London, were waiting. They took me to eat sushi and to a public bath, and finally to a cottage in Tokyo's Nishi-Ogikubo. Günter's girlfriend Fujiko spoke German and English. After two weeks of hanging out in Shinjuku's bars and Tokyo's various districts, I moved in with Minoru in a one-floor guesthouse where I started studying spoken Japanese and Chinese ideograms and Eastern literature, including *Genji Monogatari,* Osamu Dazai and Fenollosa's art books. I daily went to museums and Noh theatre, the Kanze Kaikan. Noh is a healing performance, knots vanish through living tragic deeds again. Enlightenment through voice, music, and dance.

On the crowded sidewalk outside Shinjuku's Fugetsudo coffeehouse I met Nanao Sakaki, the Japanese wandering poet, and soon his informal Bun Academy. Nanao had and still has a remarkable social mobility. Homeless people under bridges would offer tea and next we were sitting in some hidden luxury mansion. He'd translated Milarepa in Tokyo dialect; many thought that he himself was Milarepa. Then I met a young weaver named Akiko Sato and when she moved to Kyoto it was time to move too. Unexpectedly Minoru quit his job and came along. Akiko later rented part of a farmhouse in the country, in Ohara Mura north of Kyoto.

I'd to make up my mind; in the fall Judy arrived. We rented a four-and-a-half mat tatami room (which is nine square yards) in an apartment house on a backpath near Ginkaku-ji, the Silver Pavilion Temple. Minoru got a room next door. Judy too liked Japan immediately, started giving English lessons to students provided by Minoru and his Zengakuren friends. She also started studying weaving with Akiko. Winter was wonderful but the Zürich money was gone. Through old Isaburo Ueno, the rationalist architect married to a Viennese designer named Lizzi-san, I worked as an architect in buzzing Osaka, a striking contrast with quiet Kyoto. In Osaka I also taught French to a fashionable Ikebana teacher, who wanted to learn how to spell Chardin, Dior, Champs-Elysées, and such. One day, in the sushi restaurant where the lesson would usually finish, he told me that I was a beatnik. We parted friendly and never met again. Meanwhile for the Osaka firm my approach to design was too Japanese. They'd enrolled a European to get the new dope, but even the Honda skyscraper for Kobe was too Japanese. At that point I got wind of an exchange scholarship between my Zürich school and Kyoto University, and thanks to Gaudenz Domenig, the architecture anthropologist, I met the outgoing Masuda-sensei, who was lecturing every Saturday afternoon on traditional art and culture to a few foreign students. I got the scholarship and was able again to do what I wanted.

One spring afternoon Nanao came visiting, along with Gary Snyder, who introduced me to Philip Whalen, the poet living nearby across the Shirakawa (White River) of our poems. Phil soon introduced me to Cid Corman, a long-time resident. There I was in the middle of three poets who talked shop talk. I began to type things. Phil would elaborate thoroughly every question I'd on any disparate subject. Gary was very active, had sound views on the alternative movement, tribal communes and stuff. Cid was quieter and witty, had European links which I appreciated. In a way these new friends broke the enchanted isolation where Judy and I were living with Akiko and Minoru. At Gary's place I met Rexroth and others. Spring 1966 came. Judy was pregnant. We moved to a larger place near Nanzen-ji, overlooking a park daily trimmed by many gardeners. Dry pine needles were picked one by one. The year in our tiny paradise room was over. There were no sleazy tourist traps then along the Philosopher's path on the canal under Higashiyama, steep forest of cedars, pines, and rhododendrons.

*Philip Whalen (center) and Beltrametti (right),
Kyoto, 1966. Photo by Gary Snyder.*

Giona was born October 9, 1966, in the Baptist Hospital built in the thirties by Ueno-sensei, who invited me to his International Design Institute. Every Monday I made the students design their dream house and build large models. Ueno approved, we were far from those pseudo-modern speculators of Osaka. Japanese homes are modulated on 3' x 6' tatami-mat patterns, articulating light wooden frames. A complex case in point to focus on. *Flashback: Playing with little Giona on our terrace. Throwing him in the air and watching him fall back laughing from the sky into my stretched arms.*

Phil would visit us, announcing his arrival by blowing a conch shell. He gave me Gertrude Stein, Olson, and Blake to read and I went several times through his own books, like *Every Day*. Oral transmission. Now he's a Roshi, a Zen teacher in San Francisco, Soto lineage. My practice has always been rather informal, walking meditation is my way; I've a strong refusal for anything formally set up. Yet the *Diamond Sutra* is a daily study along with Lao-tzu. I try to practice their essence in art and life, which have

become very much the same, a daily thing, renewed by necessity and chance. I love chance, in its John Cage and Duchamp connotations. *Flashback: Nanao, Gary, Phil, Giona baby, and Judy on a wooden deck above the Kamo River western bank. Min Min, a popular Chinese restaurant. Kyoto is the* ville toute proustienne, *the ancient capital of our mind. Cid keeps more to himself, is busy writing and editing* Origin *magazine. We've long* tête-à-tête *talks, since then we've been corresponding almost weekly throughout the years. Suddenly I get an invitation to teach design in Iowa. Flashback: My grandparents' marriage certificate framed in their entrance hall. Mendocino Co.—only later I discovered that Co. meant County. Everybody in the family would say, oh we got a letter from Mendocino Co., and that was it. Grandpa never explained. He was proud of his cows' beauty, they got prizes for the best-looking horns, the certificates hung in his neat stone stable. Anyway Iowa was given up since another teaching gig opened at San Louis Obispo's Cal Poly.*

The same week our money disappeared from a book where it was hidden, Cid offered the sum which was repaid with the first Californian paychecks. With Gary I went to Kagoshima, Kyushu, and to Suwanose Jima, a volcano island part of the Ten Islands Archipelago extending towards Okinawa. I helped Nanao and his friends to build a straw shed. We cleared a bamboo forest for a sweet-potato field. Meanwhile Judy waited with Giona at Gary's house north of Daitoku-ji temple. Buying strong paper, tape, and rope to mail our packages to Europe and California I realized that I was speaking fluent Japanese and that just then I was leaving. Our plan was to be back in Kyoto within two years. It didn't happen. (I returned after nineteen years for an intense month of hikes, visits, readings, and shows. Kyoto always feels like home. Other places which kind of feel like home: Ticino at large, Milano, Venezia, Rome, western Sicily, Paris, San Francisco, and California at large.)

The Washington Bear cargo ship at Kobe harbour: everything was huge. Fridges with pounds of roast beef, gallons of milk and juices: America. Used to tight spaces and small dishes and cups, the boat largely anticipated America's big spaces. Asked by Phil and Gary, James Koller, the poet, was waiting for us at Pier 40, San Francisco harbour. He was editing *Coyote's Journal* and *Books,* had a face which seemed cut with an ax, and we've been the closest friends since. Jim drove us in his green 1965 Chevy pickup to Mill Valley across the Golden Gate Bridge. The Mahalila Great Delight Society, Hisayo and Albert Saijo, Jim Hatch, Jay Blaise. Smoking grass was the main activity with designing posters for rock bands. There I met the poets Lew Welch and Joanne Kyger.

After a week of feeling out the new continent, we got a ride to San Louis Obispo. The artificial lawns and uptight buildings of the campus froze me. We bought an old VW bug, rented half of a duplex cottage in the Mexican section close to the Southern Pacific Railway's tracks. The hooter announcing endless freight trains made me feel better. I was an extreme teacher, gave out my energy trying to always learn something. A few students became part of the family. Giona started walking and talking. He used to climb any wall or tree he could get near. Jim Koller came down visiting, the second time with Phil back from Japan to edit his collected poems, which Bill Brown named *On Bear's Head*. In SF Phil introduced us to Richard Brautigan, Lawrence Ferlinghetti, and Michael McClure, and Allen Ginsberg looked us up at the Swiss American Hotel on Broadway. "That's America," he smiled, taking me to a drugstore lined with porno mags. My American was shaping up, though I still speak with an Italian accent. Jaime de Angulo became another hero of mine. His adventurous and tragic life, his writing, drawings and notations of native music are unique. Teaching wasn't leaving enough time to write, so in spite of Dean George Hasslein's dismay I gave up after a year. "You're going to starve," he said, smiling a sad Armenian smile; "Anytime you want back I'll've a job for you." In the early seventies I went back twice for weekly terms and five hundred bucks.

My friend in San Louis Obispo was a sculptor of kinetic flags and metal fishes sounding rib to rib in the wind. Jack Augsburger died in 1979. At the opening of my show at Loeb's in Bern, I cried. Lewis MacAdams and Kathy Acker were there. Jack died, I explained, but they didn't know him. In San Francisco I heard Janis Joplin at the Fillmore; she was dynamite. Jerry Garcia, the Fugs, and Jimi Hendrix I heard in Santa Barbara. My students printed fake tickets to get in; they were very political about prices. In Bolinas, Bill Brown was a writer and a gardener, Jim and Jack Boyce, the painter, were working for him. When in the city, Bill used to drink at the San Gottardo on Columbus Avenue, whose owner went to school with my father back in Ticino. My father wrote its address as a good hotel but the San Gottardo had just a zinc bar, and had become a winos' hangout. Jim had a large Malamute dog named Thomas Thomas and soon a new girl, Cassandra. She later became a famous bartender in Santa Fe's La Fonda Hotel.

It was time to see Europe again. We mailed everything and somehow the painting which Yves Klein gave me in January 1957 in Milano disappeared forever. The small blue thing is now worth a fortune. It was a magic reminder of our meeting at Galleria Apollinaire, a token of vision and generosity. Klein died in June 1962. So in San Francisco we said good-bye to Phil and flew to Denver and Colorado Springs, where we wrecked Judy's uncle's Cadillac. Then to Memphis, Tennessee, to see her grandfather Zeide Nash, who disapproved of Judy's marriage to a non-Jewish person. But when Zeide saw little Giona from his redbrick tenement window he waved us up. He lived surrounded by music scores and books in Hebrew, Yiddish, Latvian, and Russian, several musical instruments, and a collection of cactus. His neighbours were black people, the tiny old Latvian was the only white man on the block. As a young man he'd to flee the Czar's military repression following the failed 1905 revolution, first to England then to New York and onwards doing all kind of jobs. From Memphis we flew to New York, which was torrid, so we visited Vermont. The second time in the city was better but we had to leave for Southampton. The liner was a feeble remake of Céline's boat ride in *Voyage au Bout de la Nuit*. Everybody stood up for national anthems and the captain was playing them all. We never stood up and were removed to the bar for meals. Leila meanwhile had moved to Brighton with her new English husband, who was running a language school; that marriage didn't last long. Later that uptight Englishman was killed in his trailer in southern France. London again. *Flashback: Riding buses on Oxford Street, Charing Cross Road, etc. Giona is twenty-two months old and enjoys himself immensely. In Zürich, Christophe is at the airport, drives us to Saanen, Bernese Oberland, where he rents rooms in a châlet with Li Yen and Kim Lawrence. We attend Krishnamurti talks; he has things to say even on the recent Paris May 1968 events and transmits breakthrough insights. I hear him again in 1972 in Ojai, California. A blue jay flies in front of him just when he is pronouncing the word "bird." Silence.*

In Zürich, Giovanni Blumer, who had been living in Shanghai, told me, "This is no time for poetry but for revolution." I did what I could but went on writing. After a long visit to Ticino we moved to Zürich at Christophe's on 38 Forchstrasse. Giona was very lively; he and Luca Zanier would throw wooden toys on the roofs of trams and on the sidewalk below. Blond Friulano Luca and dark Italian-Swiss-American Giona had wild fights; we separated them only when needed. Nice kids. At Christophe's, besides doing our projects, we were busy with the immigrant Italian workers and within the extraparliamentary Left, already divided into several factions. I met Urban Gwerder, the poet, prepared several pages for his underground paper, *Hotcha!*

When spring came once again we visited Ticino. My first architect teacher, Rino Tami, offered to collaborate in designing the Chiasso—San Gottardo highway. I was adamant. I needed all my time. We moved to Rome, rented a walk-up flat near Judy's old family friend Zev in Trastevere, where I wrote my first prose book, *Nadamas.* I was attending Steve Lacy's rehearsals, in the ground-floor place which he inherited from the Musica Elettronica Viva people. There I met many musicians, including Cornelius Cardew and Mal Waldron, the pianist. Steve's soprano sax inspired the rhythm of my book. We'd met earlier in Milano at Ettore Sottsass and Fernanda Pivano's house. Nanda encouraged me to write down what I was saying; she was friends with Whalen and got me to translate Burroughs, Brautigan, and others for her anthology *L'Altra America.* I suggested that she include Joanne Kyger and James Koller and she did.

Giona was spending his time playing in Piazza Santa Maria di Trastevere, also begging and reselling balloons with his babysitter Marino Zanier. Edoardo Cacciatore, the poet, came visiting with Leila. I was typing. "A poet," he said, "what a destiny!" From Edoardo I first heard of Adriano Spatola. I met Giulia Niccolai, also translating for Nanda's anthology. Giovanni Blumer visited from the north. He had to see Nanni Balestrini, the poet who was running the monthly *Quindici.* I went along and we ended up at Adriano Spatola's, which turned out to be around the corner from our place and, surprise, Giulia was living with him. At the second meeting Adriano asked what was I doing. After reading some he said, "I'm going to publish it. Title: *One of Those Condor People.*" After a few weeks we left for Naples and by boat to Palermo and western Sicily. We lived for a year in Partanna in shack number 492 among the people who lost houses and everything in the 1968 earthquake.

I learned to drive at the Leonardo da Vinci Driving School and worked with a leftist group, the Centro Studi e Iniziative della Valle del Belice, trying to set up people's co-ops for the reconstruction, and freewheeling for organizations, ideas, posters, etc.

In Partanna, 1969–1970, we met Franco Giuliani from Trieste, Sonia Trincanato and Gianantonio Pozzi from Venice, Neno Negrini, now a farmer in Bolivia, and Pietro Gigli, the free-lance photoreporter. The group was a splinter from Danilo Dolci's nonviolent enterprises. We started antidraft movements, promoted "no taxes to this state," blocked the main roads when needed, organized manifestations for the reconstruction for the people by the people, and for new jobs. Almost 100,000 people were living in the shacks, often in desperate conditions. The local mafia, the authorities, the carabinieri, and the landlords didn't like our activities. Springtime 1970 my father came and bought a large fridge for our community kitchen. Christophe repaired the doors and windows of our shacks. Bubi Fiorenzi visited from Siracusa, where he'd refixed a ruin on the cliffs of the bay.

Late spring my book, published by Adriano's Edizioni Geiger, arrived. Positive reactions came in with letters by Mary de Rachelwiltz and Nelo Risi. Adriano moved the tiny book all over Italy and kept publishing my work. Adriano was a large, pink-faced, and jovial man, central to poetry experiments and experiences, in love with Giulia, chess, poker, and alcohol. He had just published *Towards Total Poetry,* later developed into performance poetry. By 1971 we

Judith Mary Danciger and Giona, Kyoto, 1967

(Adriano, Giulia, Corrado Costa, and myself) were involved with Adriano's *Tam Tam* magazine, designed by Giovanni Anceschi, the son of Professor Luciano. Somehow I'd become part of the Italian avant-garde poetry scene.

In late summer I'd a dream on mescaline: splashes of frozen blood in a glacier. I announced to the Sicilian comrades that in a month I would quit. They were involved in endless arguments and meetings, fighting on the political line. It wasn't fun. I loved Sicilians and our cheap, prefab shack, the thin, green walls, its rattling metal roof, the ancient Arab walls and dirt roads lined with prickly-pear rows, the almond orchards, the ruins of Partanna, the blue sky, the Greek temples of Selinunte and Segesta. But we had to leave. I edited a report, *Belice lo stato fuorilegge,* promptly published by Feltrinelli in Milano. Adriano printed my second poetry collection, *Another Earthquake,* and helped in editing and published the Roman prose book *Nadamas.*

We moved to Venice, staying at Sonia's and Gian's in San Tomà with Maurizio Allegretto. I was completely and maniacally absorbed by writing. Judy worked as an interpreter for Buckminster Fuller's talks. We were introduced to Ezra Pound, by then totally silent. I felt respect for the fragile old man; we never got beyond eye contact. I was also playing chess with the gondoliers of the bar Trento. Giona was very popular with his Sicilian accent. We couldn't find a place to rent in Venice and in winter 1970–1971 a vacation cottage above Lugano proved to be the right place to get very depressed, entangled in knots of my own making. Judy bravely protected me and took Giona sledding. My father's wordless concern was solid. I moved back to Zürich and worked while Giona and Judy were mostly in London at Leila's. It was really a bad winter. From California, issue number nine of Koller's *Coyote's Journal* arrived with some early poems of mine and gave me a lift. I wrote a key poem:

> My demons
> I see coming out
> even from where
> I thought them exorcised
> they say they're feeling well
> we're getting to be friends.

Adriano published it, and so did Jim, and Tim Lonville in his *Grosseteste Review* in England. Spring 1971 came, an offer from Flora Ruchat became real. There was a place for us in the complex of old houses surrounding a courtyard in Riva San Vitale. (I'm still

With Adriano Spatola and Giulia Niccolai,
Mulino di Bazzano, Parma, 1973.
Photo by Christophe Beriger.

there. There is also a large garden and a creek with trout often poisoned by chemicals from the many factories upstream.) We moved in rapidly and spent the rest of the summer back in Sicily. We edited our multilingual poetry magazine, *Montagna Rossa,* named after the cliffs of Monte Generoso. By Christmas we were back to California house-sitting Gary Snyder's new house, Kitkitdizze. It was a winter of snowstorms, writing, and brush-clearing the property. Nanao and Allen Ginsberg visited us. Spring came in the Sierra Nevada foothills with manzanita flowers and tiger lilies. On a trip to the Southwest and Los Angeles with Marian and Chuck Dockham, a friend from Japan, we saw a UFO in Arizona's Prescott National Forest while camping out. We visited Phil and Joanne in Bolinas, met Robert Creeley, stayed with Jack Boyce in his cabin built with used lumber from the Oakland Bridge railway.

Back to Europe in early summer 1972: I edited most of issue 3/4 of Adriano's *Tam Tam* magazine. Judy's name doesn't always show in those publications yet she was central to everything I was doing. We also translated into Italian Jaime de Angulo's *Indian Tales*, and spent time again in Rome, Sicily, and Sperlonga. Suddenly Chuck wrote of some available land next to Gary's; we bought it with Leila's help. I'd gone through that land in my winter hikes, knew China Flats meadow, black oaks and digger pines, and the Yuba river's boulders far below. That's where Lew Welch went and probably shot himself. He was never found. Believe it or not, that winter he visited Kitkitdizze, asked Judy for coffee, left thanking her, passing right through the closed door. Giona and I were at the mailbox, five miles of dirt road away.

In 1973 I asked for an immigration visa. Endless hassles with red tape. When the paper arrived in spring 1974 Judy and I had separated. We painfully felt that we couldn't grow further together. The breakup was hard on Giona, who was seven, attending second grade in Riva. I left with a broken heart for Sicily, stayed at Bubi's in Siracusa and then at Vreni and Claudio Volontè's in Capena near Rome when Judy phoned that my green card had arrived. From San Francisco airport Richard Baker Roshi, the Zen master, drove me to Green Gulch in Marin County to wait for my lost leather backpack. By Greyhound I arrived in Nevada City and hitchhiked Gold Rush Highway 49 to the Ridge and through the diggins' moonscape to our land, Elakawee. Nobody knew I was coming, everybody was stunned but warm. I helped Snyder build his garage shed and a ramada, learning some basic carpentry. Gary is a very concrete and capable man. Then I worked with a local carpenters' crew till I felt ready to build independently, overcoming my hangups about practical matters. With Chuck I built a light nine-poles frame, with a long skylight over the ridgepole and large eaves. It looks like a bird ready to fly away. It's still there with the many additions constructed by Judy. The sandcasted lagbolts were rescued from a ghost gold-mine flume in the higher Sierras.

Many people helped, some I can't recall since my journal of summer 1974 got stolen. I remember Neal Pinholster, Bob Erikson, Nebraska Bill, Peter Orlovsky, Lloyd Kahn, Piero Resta, Peter Warshall, Steve Sanfield, Joel Goodkind, Dale Pendell, Jack Augsburger, Peter Blue Cloud, Robby Thompson, Tania the belly dancer, Fred Brunke, Cathérine and Hélène Attié, and others whose names I forget. For the *San Francisco Chronicle* we were Rattlesnake Hippies. By the early fall Hélène, age eighteen from Paris, was hanging her silk skirt in the doorless doorway. I was gone to the Bay Area, Bolinas, San Louis Obispo, Big

Sur, and Los Angeles; some of it is told in my second novel, *Quarantuno*. By the end of winter I flew from San Francisco to Geneva, rode a train south till Montélimar, a bus and a taxi to the village of Ardèche, where Judy had moved.

It was raining hard in La Bastide de Virac when Giona came out running from an old stone house. We circled and embraced many times holding tight together and laughing under the pouring rain. I stayed two weeks, cut wood for the fireplace and stove, then headed back to Riva. Our two rooms were empty, things had been stolen, I felt a total stranger. Gianantonio arrived from Venice with a Fiat 500. We drove all over northern and central Italy; he was shooting a 16-mm movie, *Al Paese dei Balocchi*. More magazines and books were coming out here and there, others were being worked on, word by word like stone on stone or wave after wave. Next winter I decided to return to California. I visited Paris and attended Le Havre 1975 Book Fair, reading with Giulia and Adriano. So I met Julien Blaine, another life friend.

The night before leaving by air from Luxemburg I got in a car crash with Giovanni Blumer; Marcello Angioni was driving. He's a Sardinian poet and a translator for the Common Market. I was the only one hurt and spent three months at Sainte Elisabette Hospital. Marcello brought books, drinks, and food every day. We planned an international poetry magazine, *Abracadabra*, which went on till issue number five. Harry Hoogstraten, another friend from Japan days, and Suse Hahn hitchhiked down from Amsterdam and became very much part of the project. Steve Lacy, Adriana Casellini, Udo Breger, and my father visited. When I got out of the hospital my right foot was crooked forever and I couldn't walk. After two weeks at Marcello's, supervised by his five children and his Swedish wife, Louise Gigia, I rode a train home. It took months of therapy to finally walk without crutches. Robby Thompson visiting from California was of great help.

Several persons started buying my paintings. I went back into painting while building the cabin. Once I was sick from a lymph-glands poisoning caused by lizards. A country-medicine book perused by Marian had the remedy; doctors couldn't figure the cause of those swollen glands.

Anyway, it was late 1976. I could walk again and I visited Suse and Harry in Amsterdam. *Abracadabra* number one came out in April 1977. Renée and Maurice Ziegler in Zürich offered to do my first show at their gallery, which worked with artists like Meret Oppenheim, Jean Tinguely, and Kimber Smith.

While the show was on I visited Giona and Judy in Ardèche and Julien in Marseille. Jim arrived in Europe; we drove with Harry in a red rented car with a coyote's paw sign on the windshield from one reading to the next: Amsterdam, Rotterdam, Haarlem, Zürich, Biasca, Venice, Ferrara, München . . . The response was strong. *Flashback: In München I dream of a poetry festival to be called P77, outline a programme and team, call Gian and Armando Pajalich in Venice, Giovanni d'Agostino in Santa Maria, Codifiume near Ferrara. They all go for it. Giovanni d'Agostino is an artist of the lighter kind, inserts in wax blades of grass, burns, pine needles, and poppy petals. His woman Giovanna Manduca is a fine and solid person. In their beaten-up Ford we drive to Marseille, see Julien, pick up Giona in La Bastide, visit caves and canyons, drive back to Riva for the summer. Ping-Pong and visitors, like Jos Knipscheer, the Dutch publisher, and his large family. In September Judy moves out of France, I suggest California and the empty cabin.*

P77 was on, poets came from all over: Spatola, Niccolai, Costa, Angioni, Blaine, Lacy, Hoogstraten, MacAdams, Breger, Gerald Bisinger, Giovanni Anceschi, Milli Graffi, and many others, including Michael Köhler doing *S-Press* tapes in Germany; Uwe Möntmann and Pietro Gigli were the photographers. We gathered a fine attendance for eight days, a small-press bookstore, movie projections, and free places to stay in private houses. *P77* was a turning point. A Dutch friend of Nanao came too; Soyo Benn Posset would organize *P78* in Amsterdam at the Cosmos, then *One World Poetry* at the Meelkweg. Jean-Jacques Lebel, whom I knew from Paris in 1958, started *Polyphonix* in Paris; Gianni Sassi started *Milano. poesia;* Julien Blaine, the Cogolin, then Tarascon, *Rencontres Internationales.* The new festival chain born in Venice at the Saloni del Sale is still spreading, though not everybody knows the lineage: it was a necessity in the air anyway. Through the readings and festivals I'd meet many artists, like Anne Waldman, Bernard Heidsieck, Valeria Magli, the *ZAJ* people Juan Hidalgo, Walter Marchetti, and Esther Ferrer (I'm very fond of Esther), Baruchello, Amelia Rosselli, Elio Pagliarani, Joëlle Léandre, Ma Desheng, Haroldo de Campos, Pierre Joris, Joël Hubaut, Claude Pélieu, Arnaud Labelle-Rojoux, Jean Daive, Claude Royet-Journoud, Philippe Castellin, Philip Corner, and Tom Johnson.

"The handmade cabin in Nevada County," 1974. *Photo by Lloyd Kahn.*

With Giovanni d'Agostino, Milano, 1985. Photo by Giovanni Giovannetti.

I came back exhausted to Riva, saw off Judy and Giona heading to California. *Quarantuno,* the second novel, came out in Milano thanks to Nanni Balestrini's enterprise with Gianni Sassi, *Ar&a,* and won me a new friend, Virgilio Gilardoni, the Marxist historian, whose writing I'd followed since I was a teenager. After a quiet winter in Riva, Rome, and Naples at Bubi's place in Posillipo, Harry and I caught up with Jim in Maine. A week of merry snowstorms in Jim's A-frame on Georgetown Island near Bath and off we went on several reading tours coast to coast. In NYC I met, through Joanne, Ted Berrigan and Alice Notley. At our Saint Mark's performance Ted said he'd written many poems in his head while listening to mine. We kept seeing each other in the Lower East Side, Amsterdam, Zürich, and Boulder, Colorado, where I met Ed Dorn and Jenny Dunbar doing *Rolling Stock.* Ted died in 1983; he was pure verbal energy and I miss his sharp wit and warmth. I dedicated a show of my *Tibetan Papers* to his last postcard: "Absolutely yes anytime! 21/IV/83."

Poetry in its various aspects: from aloud composition to writing to editing to publishing to readings to performances to actions to painting to collages to traveling. I became a wanderer; by 1978 poetry and art had taken over my life. At Sassi's in Milano I met Demetrio Stratos, researching progress in regress of the voice as daring experimental singer for Cage's *Mesostics* and as leader of the progressive rock band Area. Stratos died in NYC in 1979. (Now I'm living with Daniela Ronconi, the woman he was married to. Life's interwoven threads are surprising.)

Spring 1978: in NYC I met Annabel Levitt Lee. We translated some Blaise Cendrars together; she was to publish my *Airmail Postcards* for her fine *Vehicle Editions.* Somehow New York became familiar too. Summer was busy in Riva, Ping-Pong games, Giona visiting, and a flow of visitors. In the fall I drove, with Corrado Costa, to Amsterdam for *P78,* organized by Benn, Harry, and Jos. They flew in Jim, Joanne, Bill Berkson, Lewis, Tom Pickard, Harris Schiff, Nanao, Anne Waldman, Reidar Ekner, Brion Gysin, William Burroughs, and others. At a breakfast Ted introduced me to a shy, very sharp-looking British poet: Tom Raworth. Tom has become so much part of my concerns; we continue meeting, reading, and doing things together. One fine summer day in Riva his wife, Val, was the laughing witness as we improvised

The Thoughts of Captain Alexis, a collab which developed into an English-Italian-French two-voices performance. We are still at it: *Mail, Horses, Camels,* etc. In a few weeks we'll be in Marseille's new Centre International de Poésie at Le Refuge and visit Callelongue again. Also with Jim I do written and visual collabs like *Graffiti Lyriques* and *The Possible Movie.*

Ten thousand words can't tell it all, and go by fast.

P79 in Amsterdam: Jim, Harry, Giulia, Adriano, Julien, Anne, Kathy, Steve, Ed Dorn, John Giorno, Diane di Prima, Udo, Gysin, Burroughs . . . with Giovanni d'Agostino and Gianantonio, who has changed his name to John Gian, I did *Tales by Three,* a performance of signs and words. The *P79* festival was such a success that later it sort of went commercial, excluding research as the crucial meeting ground. In 1980 Jim and I zigzagged once more across the States. Besides Jim's wry "We're opening new trails," and my "Another day, another dollar LESS," and besides having a tough go, I saw new places: the Juan de Fuca Strait, Seattle, Idaho, and Oregon. We visited Creeley in Placitas, camped in the stormy Rio Grande Canyon, saw Taos again, met Nanao, and

were in Albuquerque and Santa Fe (didn't make it this time to Drummond Hadley's ranch nor to Keith Wilson's place in Las Cruces, New Mexico.) I was rather worn down when we arrived at Don Guravich and Joanne's friendly house in Bolinas. Then I visited Giona and Judy; the Ridge gave us a fine welcome. We read on a deck under the stars and visited Phil in the city.

Giona is back here since October after years of coming and going to and from California. Tonight he fixed a Chinese meal; he's twenty-three and works as an electronics technician and copywriter nearby. He studied electronics in San Francisco with his grandfather's help. My father never failed us and though his family is scattered he acts the old ways.

In 1979–1980 I rented a house in Sperlonga, came and went from our seaside winter headquarters with Gian, Rita degli Esposti, and Giovanni d'Agostino, edited the anthology *Sperlonga Manhattan Express* and *Scorribanda Productions.*

Life through the eighties wasn't an easy ride. I kept learning the hard way how to survive without going out of my concerns. It takes obstinacy,

"The old pier," Riva San Vitale, Switzerland, 1981. Photo by Luca Barberis.

"My father with Tom Raworth and Mimi," Riva San Vitale, 1987. Photo by Fabrizio Garghetti.

integrity, and discipline: money made with poetry and art is rare and you can't buy poetry grocery, no, you've got to buy grocery grocery. But since the almost-deadly car crash in Luxemburg 1975, I feel that I'm just going on the ways indicated by my dead friends and teachers. Make it new, give what you know and learn what you don't. (In 1982 I met a local longhair named Gian Pio Fontana, who looked like a Sioux; he asked about Jaime de Angulo. He's a farmer, an artist, and a freewheeling scholar, and since then we've been very close.)

Julius Bissier's greeting, "It's a long way." Yves Klein's visionary extremism. Andrè Ruchat's tenderness. Jack Boyce's straightforwardness. Ted's laugh. Brion Gysin's almost cynical elegance hiding his vulnerable openness. Bubi's generosity. All my dead friends have taught me to fight it on the ground. Wordslingers, signslingers. Ueno-sensei's understanding; Lizzi called him the Chief Monkey. I carry them with me as I carry the tattoo eye which Claudio Volontè did on my left biceps. Claudio died too. Tragedy, passion, confusion, and despair are also part of it, part of my being still here. As Jim wrote on a spray painting hanging in the kitchen, "We are old

enough to know that . . ." That what? To know that. Years ago I met Patrizia Vicinelli, a sidewalk epic poet, and through her man Gianni Castagnoli, the xerox artist, I met Dario Villa, a young Milano poet-translator of Basil Bunting. Dario has a sharp eye on visual art too. Adriano also died; almost two years ago his generous heart exploded. Dario wrote a fine piece on my show with Tom at Adriano's gallery in the country near Reggio Emilia, on the same Enza river where he and Giulia had moved, further upstream in Mulino di Bazzano, in the early *Tam Tam* days. As Heraclites pointed out, you can't step in the same water twice.

Nineteen eighty-six: finally back in Kyoto. After an evening with Minoru, Shizumi, and Cid Corman, I thought to meet Lady Murasaki:

> same face
> same soul
> 1000 years later.

I dedicated the poem to Duncan McNaughton, the American poet I have cared for since we met in 1974.

Years ago Giona, then studying graphics, looked at me and jokingly said, "Why are you sitting doing nothing? Do another magazine." "There's no money for it." "Do it small!" he laughed, going out in the courtyard to play. Within fifteen minutes I designed the graphic grid and the logos for *mini*, "the smallest magazine of the world." I've done twelve issues so far and mailed them all over. It's light and fast, full of real people and their traces of poetry, visuals, scores, and objects, for anybody concerned or even only curious. This morning I was training for the Milano presentation of my latest book, *Niente da*, which is *Nothing to*. I'll paint words on a large scroll and go over them at the end with a huge X done with a wet sponge.

Flashback: I'm twelve, my young and beautiful mother is running after me with a carpet-beater, trying to reinforce the law, upset because the wet pen which I'd thrown at il Signor Chiesa, the schoolteacher, splashed black ink on his grey suit.

I was a very temperamental kid, always in trouble with school and restrictions. That was in Chiasso, maybe 1949. Many times she pointed out the advantages of education. I couldn't have cared less, but she managed to see me through to where further education starts. My mother was really elegant and at seventy-three still cares for style. When I translate this passage for her she'll smile. *Flashback: Grandfather Giuseppe after my parents' separation, "Stay close to your father, he needs you."*

A few minutes ago I called Jim Koller in Maine. "What's up?" he asked. "I'm finishing that autobiography thing," I said. "That's good," he said. Now I'll walk out in the cold, clear, February night and see Orion. Back to the humming electric typer, I can't quit. Writing is writing about writing the writing one is writing. It is also recording a voice. I finish this ten-thousand-word movie with a 1969 poem:

there is not much to understand
just pay attention.

Riva San Vitale, 20-23/II/1990

In Chicago with James Koller, 1987. Photo by Giona Beltrametti.

BIBLIOGRAPHY

Poetry:

Uno di quella gente condor, Geiger, 1970.

Un altro terremoto, Geiger, 1971.

Face to Face, Grosseteste, 1973.

One of Those Condor People, Blackberry-Salted in the Shell, 1974.

(Translated by Paul Vangelisti) *Another Earthquake,* Red Hill Press, 1976.

In transito, Geiger, 1976.

Ein anderes Erdbeben, Nachtmaschine, 1978.

Oog in Oog, in de Knipscheer (Haarlem), 1978.

Airmail Postcards, Vehicle Editions, 1979.

No Difference Here: It's a Fact, edited by Donald Guravich, Evergreen, 1980.

Ibernazione, Cervo Volante, 1981.

Target: 13 Poems and Inks for Annabel Levitt, Grosseteste, 1981.

E allora, Tam Tam, 1982.

Il libro delle x, Scorribanda, 1983.

A, Manicle, 1984.

Per adesso, Campanotto, 1984.

1984, Tam Tam, 1985.

19 permutazioni, Edizioni Inedite, 1986.

Surprise, Coyote, 1987.

Nado Nado, Nèpe Zéroscopiz, 1988.

Tutto questo (poems 1977–1988), Supernova, 1990.

Translator:

Tam Tam (Cid Corman, Gary Snyder, Philip Whalen, and James Koller), 1, 2, 3/4, Mulino di Bazzano, 1971–1974.

L'Altra America (Ted Berrigan, Richard Brautigan, W. S. Burroughs, and James Koller), edited by Nanda Pivano, Officina Rome, 1972, Formichiere, Milano, 1979.

Cid Corman, *Gratis,* North, 1977.

Gary Snyder, *24 poesie di Han Shan,* North, 1977.

Joanne Kyger, *Sulla mia Costa,* Caos, 1978.

Jaime de Angulo, *Don Bartolomeo,* La Frontiera, 1985.

James Koller, *Fortune,* Supernova, 1987.

Tom Raworth, *Il Grande Giorno Verde,* Supernova, 1988.

Other:

(Editor) *Belice lo stato fuorilegge,* Feltrinelli, 1971.

Nadamas (novel), Geiger, 1971.

Fur Book (object book), 1973.

(With Joanne Kyger and Piero Resta) *Trucks: Tracks,* Mesa Press, 1974.

(Editor) *An Alleghany Star Route Anthology,* Grosseteste, 1975.

Quarantuno (novel), Cooperativa Scrittori and Ar&a, 1977.

(With Harry Hoogstraten and James Koller) *Andiamo* (poems), Great Raven Press, 1978.

(Editor with Giovanni d'Agostino) *Sperlonga Manhattan Express,* Scorribanda, 1980.

El Tibetano (three novels), in de Knipscheer, 1981.

(With Donald Guravich and Ken Botto) *Snapshots,* Evergreen, 1983.

(Editor with Patrizia Vicinelli) *c/o,* Scorribanda, 1984.

(With Tom Raworth) *Mail,* Scorribanda, 1984.

Più e meno di quanto incontra l'occhio, Zum Strauhof, 1984.

Banana Story Eccetera (three novels), La Frontiera, 1985.

(With Raworth) *The Thoughts of Captain Alexis,* Scorribanda & Infolio, 1987.

(With Koller) *Graffiti Lyriques,* Avida Dollars, 1988.

(With Julien Blaine, Koller, and Raworth) *A Gang of 4,* Coyote's Journal, 1989.

Niente da (three novels), Corpo 10, 1990.

Contributor to many publications, including *Grosseteste Review, Coyote's Journal, Tam Tam, Abracadabra, Montagna Rossa, Invisible City, Doc(k)s, Mgur, Infolio,* and *il Verri.*

Beltrametti has exhibited his work in many one-man shows, including *Journal of Signs,* Zürich, 1977; (with d'Agostino) *Tales by Two,* Zürich, 1980; *Sperlonga Work,* Zürich, 1980; *Flowers & Tibetan Papers,* Genova, 1983; (with Nanni Balestrini and Corrado Costa) *Tibetan Papers, Pastels & Décollages,* Milano, 1983; *More (& Less) Than Meets the Eye,* Zürich, 1984; *Choses,* Paris, 1986; (with Koller) *Graffiti Lyriques,* Milano, 1987; (with Blaine, Costa, Koller, and Raworth) *La Bande des Cinq,* Marseille, 1991.

Hal Bennett

1930-

THE VISIBLE MAN

"There, there, dear boy . . . she restored a more affectionate note to her voice . . . the things you do and say in America are sometimes a little puzzling to a funny, old lady brought up in Central Europe, but you have made me very happy here, you Americans, and I will not complain. Do and say what you like. Be as odd as you please and I will try to understand. After all the way of two races are different. . . ."

—The Gräfin Adele von Pulmernl und Stilzernl,
in Carl van Vechten's *Parties* (1930)

I

In the green, semitropical summers of the late 1930s, when I was nine years old, I prayed for Second Sunday and the beginning of church revival as passionately as drought-stricken farmers pray for rain. Revival began each year on the second Sunday in August and lasted the whole week, during which a new crop of backsliders and sinners was expected to be entered, by foul means or fair, into the ranks of the Christian converted. To assist in this procedure, there would be plenty of free food, along with preaching, praying, singing, lovemaking out in the woods behind the church, and abundant drinking, although all alcoholic beverages were supposedly forbidden by the Baptist church.

But there were certain sensational drunkards among the members of Saint Joy Baptist Church—this was in Buckingham, Virginia, where I was born April 21, 1930—and during revival the little store across the road from the church did a thriving business selling corn whiskey underneath the counter and cold beer on top of it. Also, my cousin Fred Bryant assured me that the head usher at Saint Joy—she who was always so perfectly starched and pressed in her snowy white uniform, her breath reeking bountifully of chewed sassafras root as she whispered Christian platitudes, conducting us to our seats—that this personage was, in fact, one of Buckingham's biggest drunks and manufactured her own homebrew, as many professionally pious people apparently

Hal Bennett, 1972. Copyright © 1972 by Playboy. *Photo by Vernon L. Smith.*

did in Virginia during those days of the Great Depression.

It was even rumored with a certain amount of pride up and down the red dirt roads, the sun-drenched countryside, that the present minister was an accomplished drunk, as well as a very successful womanizer. But the Reverend Mr. Fleming of my memories was tall, sober, handsome, stately, friendly—indeed, almost saintlike in that hell of liars, whoremongers, and hypocrites which was black Buckingham in those days. For one thing, Mr. Fleming didn't try to frighten sinners into the arms of God by hurling medieval imprecations at us like knuckleballs from the pulpit. Also, he was a teetotaler and did not appear to be diseased with that fever for any kind of woman which affects a great number of preachers in Baptist churches. Indeed, Mr. Fleming seemed moderate, educated, and nicely restrained, which of course were prominent reasons for certain factions in the congregation to hotly dislike him.

"If religion ain't loud and scary," an aunt of mine asserted, "then it ain't good religion. Just like medicine that don't taste bad ain't good medicine." What she and others like her wanted was the *real* thing, as they called it: a barely literate preacher as handsome as sin and as polished as a peeled onion, standing halfway between being a pimp on the one hand and a bootlegger on the other; the majority of the congregation drunk, or partly drunk and rid of its inhibitions, to make the circus more amusing; the agonized shouting and shameful convulsions calculated to terrify and excite the sinner simultaneously; the women usually wearing the most makeup and the shortest dresses—and with absolutely nothing on underneath, it was said—fainting always with their opened legs aimed like cocked shotguns at the rooster in the pulpit; other men and women frothing like mad dogs at the mouth, babbling in supposedly unknown tongues, wide-eyed and rolling scandalous hips; and, most important, the tender emotions of all of us to be spattered against the stern church walls like carelessly thrown eggs, then scraped up and lard-fried for God's greedy gusto.

I did not know then that, for blacks, the hysterical taking on of Christianity, with all its sexual innuendos, was probably the first important step in our long and painful pilgrimage towards immense self-hatred. And this accompanied, of course, by the standard minstrel-show clowning and the most rhythmic fingersnapping and body-moving music imaginable, certainly to keep our minds off the fact that we were slouching towards Bethlehem and a deliberate kind of cultural slaughter. In Saint Joy, this journey began on a mourner's bench set like a broad, polished electric chair to the front of the church, where my brother Jesse and I were plumped down to mourn for our sins and to pray desperately for the Holy Ghost to enter our unworthy souls. I am pleased to report that it never entered mine, despite all the whooping and hollering done over our bowed heads.

The music, the stomping, and the shouting were so commanding that whites parked their vehicles on the road and came in to be a part of it, but kept to the back seats to show that not even they were above the ceremonies of the very segregation which they themselves had long ago imposed. Their presence seemed to animate the congregation and to elevate the choir, accompanied by a stomping little band made up of piano, trumpet, saxophone, guitar, drums, and tambourines that kept the old church reeling and rocking as though drunk on its own juices. Sitting next to me on the mourner's bench, my brother—who was three years older—held his eyes squeezed shut, sweat erupting on his cheeks and forehead like the chicken pox as his thick lips moved, fabricating begging prayers, he told me later. But I watched the proceedings through parted fingers, convinced somehow that this ignominious business of "getting religion" and giving my puny, hungry, black self to an infinite God was not exactly my cup of tea.

Furthermore, except for the question of color—fifty years ago, I was convinced that if God exists at all, he was undeniably white; I am not sure that my opinion is very much different today—but, except for the question of color, God sounded suspiciously like my evil grandfather and my evil grandmother rolled into one. Obviously, God despised my brother and me, for whatever reason it is that God despises defenseless and impoverished people; but it took me some years to realize that my grandparents despised us, too, because they had been taught by religion and by the system of American apartheid to harbor an intense dislike for themselves and for all things even vaguely resembling their hated color.

Inasmuch as we were helpless and of their black blood—and it seemed a foregone conclusion on their part that we black pickaninnies were going squarely to hell on the next Greyhound bus—our grandparents felt obliged to starve, whip, torture, abuse, and otherwise demean us as much as they could in order to collect the compensations awaiting them in heaven for putting up with us in the first place. In effect, my brother and I were deliberate millstones around our grandparents' necks, symbolic crowns of thorns mashed into their heads to toughen them up for the deluxe golden crowns when they got to heaven to sing and shout. Even the Reverend Mr. Fleming, as sensible as he seemed to be, talked about this system of celestial bribery in well-crafted sermons that caused some of his partisans, and even some of his enemies, to weep for sheer joy.

Gilmore Bennett, our grandfather, was clearly bucking for a golden crown and a cushy throne at the right hand of God. Big, brutal, and extremely black, he was said to be a former slave, and seemed imbued with a bitterness and self-loathing that seeped in to his very bones. And he treated all of his tribe with the cheerful cruelty of a patriarch who has one mad eye on his heavenly reward and the other one fastened to his workers. While he feasted right under our noses on ham, bacon, eggs, hot biscuits dripping with wild honey and home-churned butter, my brother and I were kept almost exclusively to a diet of rough cornbread and buttermilk, the same that was fed to the hogs, the dogs, and the cats. I have described elsewhere[1] how my brothers and sisters and I, half-crazed with hunger and on the razor's edge of starvation before we were taken off to New Jersey, waged war with our grandfather's hogs down in their muddy pen for the cabbages he gave them by the ton. But perhaps it was precisely my grandfather's niggardliness which enabled him to put together one of the largest and richest of all black-owned estates in Virginia; how he managed to do it, I have never known, nor have I ever heard it talked about.

Since my brother and I had left Buckingham four years earlier to go to school in New Jersey, our summers in Virginia were a terrible throwback to an almost unbearable primitiveness: from asphalt streets and electric lights to kerosene oil lamps and red dirt roads; from trolley cars and buses to mules and buggies and tale-telling on mosquito-plagued porches in nights that were so hot, black, and thick that you could stir them with a spoon. We had retrogressed from big-league baseball games to playing with inflated pig bladders left over from the previous winter's killing; from Joe Louis and Marian Anderson, and Orson Welles and Mickey Mouse and Baby Snooks and Shirley Temple, back to the barefooted wilderness of Buckingham, Virginia, where two or three dozen eggs could be traded at the general store for a pair of shoes, or any other merchandise inside that bartering range; and ghosts (*h'ants*, people called them—cousin Fred Bryant called the Holy Ghost the Holy H'ant) could be seen walking in graveyards or climbing trees buck naked, carrying coffins on their heads; and people still used smelly outhouses where men were warned to hold their genitals up to protect them from tenant rats, and the Sears Roebuck catalogue hung from a handy nail to be used for toilet paper in the better places, with corn shucks or dried grass available in the lesser ones.

Since God and "thy neighbor" were the only things most church people ever talked about loving in my presence, our grandfather made certain that if we could not love him—and he was probably the most hateful human being I have ever known in my life—then we certainly would never be permitted to love

ourselves. So he taught us fear instead, and a terrible sense of our own unworthiness; he certainly made us regret our foolish idea that we had somehow escaped him and his evil ways by crossing state boundaries. As soon as he got his hands on us again, he put us side by side with grown men and women in the fields, especially in tobacco, which is filthy and grueling work. For one thing, the tobacco plant oozes a juice which gums up the hair, so my brother and I had our heads shaved against that eventuality. Other people wore hats or headrags in the tobacco field, but no one bothered to consult us about our choice. Also, large, ugly, greenish white worms inhabited the tobacco plants and had to be taken off and killed in a sordid daily ritual, each carcass yielding quantities of disgusting juices and yellow guts. Excepting myself, everyone else did this murdering with their bare hands; I knocked the worms off the leaves with a stick and beat them to death with a rock, weapons carried especially for that purpose. When the rock was too gut-stained to be handled decently, I quickly found another.

My grandmother was especially amused by what she considered my lack of manliness in the matter of the worms, obviously overlooking the fact that I was just nine years old. On those occasions when she worked with us in tobacco, she squashed the vile creatures between her fingers as though God had made her just for that particular pleasure; I was certain it was something that she and my grandfather had enjoyed doing together on dates, centuries ago before they got married. She also sniggered when sheer frustration pushed me into imitating parts of radio programs that we used to listen to in New Jersey—"The Shadow," "The Green Hornet," "I Love a Mystery"; Kate Smith singing "God Bless America," and Stella Dallas wrapped in endless conflicts with her mannish voice. My grandmother was a small, sinewy black woman eternally complaining about her "nerves" and aching joints. Bullied unmercifully by my grandfather, she called him Mr. Bennett until the day he died, in 1941. She might have been a radio victim herself, and neighbors steeped her with remedies to improve her lack of appetite, which was another of her complaints. But I do know that on at least one occasion I surprised her wolfing down good, solid food in the kitchen during a time when she was complaining far and wide that her "nerves" permitted her only a few sips of sweet milk from time to time. Whether on orders from my grandfather, or because of her own innate meanness, she fully participated in starving my brother and me,

---

[1] *The Black Wine*, New York: Doubleday, 1968.

and set the same food before us that she had prepared for the animals.

She also turned all the mirrors in the big old house to the wall when a rainstorm blew up; Fred Bryant suggested that she did so to keep from seeing how ugly and frightened she looked, but I believe it was because mirrors were thought to attract lightning. And there was tremendous lightning during those bombastic Virginia storms, slicing past the drawn curtains and shades and exploding spitefully in our faces like spastic dynamite. Our poor grandmother jumped ten feet, and put her false teeth in her apron pocket to keep from swallowing them. Then came the thunder's basso roll, which we had been assured were the footsteps of an angry God about to mash nigger children into the dirt. Ready to jump out of her skin by then, my grandmother would scurry off in her felt slippers to hide in the safest clothes closet, leaving us heathen pickaninnies pitifully unprotected while she cowered among the hanging clothes. I do not remember my grandfather ever being around during a storm, and Fred Bryant hinted that the old man was also cowardly hiding somewhere. But it occurred to me that perhaps my grandfather was offstage causing the turbulence himself, hurling thunderbolts at us, wildly splashing water, beating enormous kettledrums with his big black fists to frighten all of us out of our wits, and especially our grandmother hiding in the closet. I will say that she at least had the sensitivity to look foolish when she came out, after all the danger was over. So much for her Christian faith.

The coming of revival was important, then, because we did our chores early that Sunday morning, then washed up, dressed in our Sunday best, and filed off to church on the first day in a caravan of our grandfather's very best buggies. During the week, we would quit work in the fields around noon and go to church. So, revival was respite from punishing work and from our grandparents' tortures and aggressions against our personal dignity, showing very clearly that they themselves had none that amounted to anything. Also, revival gave us a wonderful chance to get away from them for a while, since they would be busy hobnobbing with the few people who liked them, or pretended to, because most people did not.

And there would be large tables lined up every day underneath the shade trees to the side of the church grounds and groaning under the weight of succulent home-cured hams, fried chicken, biscuits, cornbread, cakes, puddings, pies; and all of it free. The Great Depression might have been flaying the nation, but there was small evidence of it in Bucking-

ham that I remember. My brother and I stuffed ourselves like pigs from the tables of people really pleased to see us back again from New Jersey, although some laughingly accused us of talking "funny." By this, they meant that, under Northern provocation, we were gradually learning how not to talk through our noses and what sounded like great barrier reefs of Virginia snot. Revival also meant that our mother and father and the rest of the family would be coming home for the church affair, along with dozens of other dispersed blacks who chose this time of the year to come back to Buckingham, proving perhaps the popular saying that you can take people out of Virginia but you can't take Virginia out of the people.

So, Second Sunday came at last, dawning cool and bright, with the early morning sky painted pale blue around us, though it was obvious that the day would be a scorcher later on. Cousin Fred Bryant, who was a few months older than my brother Jesse, had managed to spend the night at our house among all the people sleeping on pallets on the parquet floors. There were even people sleeping on blankets in the front flower garden, and on the porch, and in their cars out near the woodpile. It was always like this every year at Second Sunday, with people drawn back home like refugees for the revival meeting, staying at the old homestead, as they called my grandfather's house. It was the only time that I ever saw him and my grandmother act really happy; sometimes they tried to smile—which was a pitiful thing to see—and they even put on a show of liking my brother and me for the benefit of the crowd. "They getting paid for grinning," Fred Bryant asserted. But I wasn't so sure that he was right. Even monsters like my grandfather and my grandmother had exaggerated ideas about Virginia hospitality—except, of course, when it came to children—and they probably fell into the part of being good hosts, even against their will.

Even Fred Bryant was somewhat welcome with so many other people about, and my grandmother shrewdly enlisted him to bring meat from the smokehouse and butter and cream from the spring, as though to keep Jesse and me from knowing the full extent of their wealth. Fred was son to Nancy Bryant, who was the daughter of my grandfather's sister, which made Fred first cousin once removed to my father, and second cousin to me. It was important to know things like that, lest we forgot who we were. But the most important thing I knew about Fred was that he was my very best friend from the first time we laid eyes on each other. He taught me how to fish, and to swim, and to dance, and instructed me in the proper way to approach the first girl I ever had a date with. It seemed to me that he knew everything, and I was willing to follow him to hell and back, if need be. More than anything else, he always hung around my brother and me when we were in Virginia, and no amount of name-calling or rock-throwing on the part of my grandfather or my grandmother ever made him go away.

That morning of Second Sunday, it was Fred who took me out to the great cluster of cars parked around the woodpile and showed me the familiar big black Oakland with the Jersey license plates. Suddenly, he and I were hugging each other, and hitting each other on the back in thanksgiving. As regular as clockwork, my mother and father, along with five of the other children, had got in from New Jersey during the night. My parents would stay until the beginning of September, when they would carry my brother and me back to New Jersey to school.

"Where are they?" I said, feeling suddenly wonderful. "Where is my family?"

Fred grinned. "They upstairs sleeping in the hallway, some of them. Miz Bennett, she in Aunt Delilah's room with the girls and some other women. Your Daddy, he out somewhere with your granddaddy, looking at that combine they bring over this morning."

I thought it was a miracle that Fred Bryant knew so much. "A combine?" I asked. "What's a combine?"

His grin disappeared, as though cut off by a switch. "You going to find that out tomorrow, you and your brother Jesse. Right now, you got to eat breakfast and get ready for church. But tomorrow, you going to be working with that combine. You just wait and see."

He looked very somber then, almost funereal. "You my favorite friend," he said, "even if you is my cousin, and young, and scrawny. You just make sure you don't get yourself kilt tomorrow, you hear me, pal?"

"I hear you," I said, anxious to see my mother, and to get dressed up and go to church for Second Sunday and its festival of delicious foods. So, skipping away, I really didn't hear Fred Bryant at all.

And, next day, I came face to face with what I believe to be every man's terrible dilemma, no matter what his color: that we are viciously forced into the most readily available manhood, like being required to wear shoes that fit too loosely or too tightly, even before we have fully been children.

II

Second Sunday always seemed to be a kind of summer Christmas, generating a special feeling of love, family, and warmth, which I suppose all people demonstrate, to a greater or lesser degree, on days laid aside for such institutionalized displays. So, at my grandfather's that Sunday morning, our brothers and sisters greeted Jesse and me with the usual self-conscious joviality called for by the occasion. Our father told us how much uglier and blacker we'd gotten—I privately thought the same about him—while our mother thumped us very positively on the head and spun us around like tops, exclaiming at how much we'd grown. Then, after breakfast and the morning's chores, we all got dressed up and went to church for the first day of revival.

The feeling of false holiday was especially strong there, and expressed itself in hugs, kisses, and loud, brassy chatter in the churchyard and out under the shade trees, where the tables of food were being set up. Fred Bryant was all dressed up and captive to his half-blind aunt, whom he led good-naturedly by the arm from one bunch of people to another. There was more kissing and screeching when folks met who hadn't seen each other since last revival. Our father, who paraded around looking like a younger version of his father, was pressed and polished, pulling dangerously at the ends of his big mustache, winking roguishly at every young woman he saw. Accustomed to this, my mother carefully ignored him, and did her own share of hugging, and kissing, and backslapping; and the standard Virginia exclamation—"Why, I certainly do declare!"—was heard everywhere, said always in ritual tones of utmost pleasure and shocked disbelief. My mother was part white and part American Indian, and had married my father when she was fourteen, to get away from a white family in Lynchburg to whom she had been sold by her father. She had lovely dark eyes, the color of haunted chestnuts, I sometimes used to think, and she was beautiful that day in a navy blue dress with a large white lace collar, black patent-leather pumps, and a small blue hat balanced like a pancake on top of her head.

But there was more than the usual excitement that Second Sunday in 1939, for a wealthy white farmer in Buckingham—I shall call him Mr. Harriman—had agreed to rent my grandfather his combine for three whole days, and the machine had already been delivered to our farm, as Fred Bryant had said. Heretofore, Mr. Harriman had not trusted any Negro farmers enough to rent them his precious machine, which could do work in three days, it was

The author, in a sketch by Sue d'Avignon

said, that eight or ten Negroes would require three to four weeks to complete. That a man of Mr. Harriman's "white" category had finally condescended to rent such a valuable piece of property to my grandfather was delicious news that buzzed all over the church ground like excited bees. My grandfather strutted around like the cock of the walk, my grandmother noticeably put on more than her usual airs, and all the rest of us relatives, far and near—and this included myself, and my mother as well, I must say—all of us seemed glorified in my grandfather's reflected light.

As for my mother, it made me feel good to stand somewhere away from her and watch the expressions on her lovely face, and the way her delicate hands moved in contained little flights as she talked animatedly to some neighbor or relative. Still, from time to time, her eyes swept the crowd like a searchlight, seeking out each of her children in turn. A thrill always shot through my body when her eyes lighted on me, a small smile playing with her lips as if to say, *You and I have a special understanding, my youngest son.* It was true that we shared secrets that the rest of the

family probably knew nothing about. For one thing, when we were in New Jersey, my mother sometimes turned off the lights and combed her long black hair so that I could see the sparks shoot from it in the dark. More seriously, I had already read my first book, *Anna and the King of Siam,* which my mother had smuggled from the house where she worked for a wealthy Irishwoman in East Orange. And I had become completely addicted to *National Geographic* magazines, which my mother brought to me rather than throwing out in the Irishwoman's garbage. She also saved newspaper clippings for me about unusual events—one told the story of a young white girl who had been secretly feeding a huge snake underneath the house; when the horrified family found out and killed the snake, the girl had died, too.

My mother had her day off on Thursdays, and when she came home to see us, Brother and Alberta stopped their usual bickering and fighting and seemed to curl around her like cats around a favorite leg. Alma, who went to vocational school and was considered dumb by some stupid people, pulled out lacy doilies that she crocheted with incredible skill, and beamed as my mother praised them. Jean, who was the baby, and spoiled rotten, got her fair share of the attention, although she almost stood on her head to try and hog it all. Even Jesse came home from out carousing with his friends, and usually stood with me at the outer edge of those Thursdays when my mother gave of herself, her money—she earned five dollars a week in those Depression days—the little food we had in the house, the house itself, when people poorer than ourselves were thrown out of theirs.

We lived in Orange, New Jersey, on the lower part of Parrow Street, around the corner from Oakwood Avenue School. The tall old house was decrepit looking but not especially ugly, with peeling gray clapboards, a stoop on the second floor, and a large oak tree in the backyard. The furniture was also old, but substantial and comfortable, bought piece by piece by my mother from Good Will or the Salvation Army. My brother Jesse and I shared a bedroom off from the kitchen, and there were enough rooms on the two floors for everybody else. We even had a separate dining room, which meant that we did not have to always eat in the kitchen, as most other people did in those days.

It was our mother who had brought us out of the Egypt of Virginia into the Promised Land of New Jersey. She had gone to the North herself to work and pay for a mule, which we desperately needed in Virginia. "A family without a mule," as the saying went, "might just as well lay down and die." Well, we did not quite die in those days, although we were sometimes very close to it. As for lying down—that is, giving up, throwing in the towel—this was strictly forbidden by my mother, once she had us all around her. And if my father continued to chase women— which he did up until a few weeks before he died, at the age of eighty-six—it was my mother who kept us together as some kind of family, and encouraged each and every one of us to be a little better than we thought we could be.

She was an intelligent, self-educated woman, while my poor father was actively illiterate and never made any attempt that I know of to correct the situation. When World War II came along, and my three brothers and one of my sisters went into the military services, my mother dictated letters to me for them and asked me to read their answers, smiling sometimes in her slow, gentle way, which, I came to understand, showed her pleasure that I was indeed the different one among her brood, and that she had done her best to cause the distinction. And it does not seem too farfetched to suppose that she read to me while I was in her womb, and patted me through the layers of her belly with hands intended to inspire more than the usual mediocrity which branded most Negroes in those days.

We indeed had a special understanding between us, my mother and me, probably the more intense because we never talked about it. I am sure that because of our relationship I was able to go through the ordeal with the combine which began the day following that Second Sunday. Nor would my mother have tried to stop it, not even for my benefit, for, insofar as I know, she never openly interfered with my ideas or anybody else's. But she did sometimes try to subvert some of my more ridiculous notions in her unobtrusive way. A couple of months earlier, for example, I had strutted about in New Jersey bragging that I was a Bennett and that black people were the really superior beings on this earth. I do not remember what it was that had inspired such hogwash; but, as I spouted it one day, my mother put her hand on my head, almost like a benediction, and said quietly, "One day, my dear son, you're going to find out that Negroes ain't worth a damn, and the Bennetts ain't either." Her awkward double employment of *ain't,* her use of profanity—which was certainly not her way—shocked me deeply, and was obviously designed to do so.

Was it true, then, that Negroes were not worthwhile people? And that we Bennetts, so honored and even envied by many in both our Buckingham and New Jersey communities, that we were hardly worth the talking about? And if Negroes in general weren't worth a damn, what about twenty-five-year-old Joe Louis Barrow, who had been heavyweight boxing champion of the world for two years then, after knocking out Jim Braddock, a white man, in a Chicago fight? And what about Marian Anderson, possessed by a contralto voice which Toscanini himself said happened only once in a hundred years? Marian Anderson would sing with extraordinary success at the Lincoln Memorial, following the personal intervention of Mrs. Eleanor Roosevelt after the Daughters of the American Revolution had denied their facilities in Washington to the Negro artist.

And wasn't Paul Robeson mesmerizing predominantly white audiences with his exceptional singing and acting abilities? And Louis Armstrong blowing his trumpet, showing all his teeth? And what about Bill Robinson, tap dancing in motion pictures with little Miss Shirley Temple, the outstanding white ingenue of the moment? Not to mention Lena Horne and Eddie "Rochester" Anderson, and Hattie McDaniel, and dozens of other outstanding Negroes of the day. So, what on earth had my mother meant by her shocking comment?

It would take me nearly fifty years to find out about blacks in general; I would need far less time than that to find out that she was absolutely right about the Bennetts. But none of this had come to pass that day of the combine. Although a person more gifted than myself might have foreseen even then that immense tragedies for our family waited in the background, just as even greater calamities awaited the nation, and the world.

Following that Second Sunday's eating orgy, my brother and I crawled from our pallets early Monday morning as fat as bloated chipmunks. When we stumbled downstairs to help our grandmother with the business of putting together breakfast for over two dozen guests, I was surprised to find that my father, my grandfather, and several more of his sons had already been fed. My mother and some other women were helping my grandmother in the spacious kitchen; and our mother served Jesse and me each a big plateful of ham, eggs, hominy grits, and hot biscuits with honey and butter.

It was certainly the best breakfast we'd ever eaten at our grandfather's, and our mother kept a careful eye on us, as if to make sure that no one would try to take it away. Then, my grandfather bellowed for us from the porch, where he and the other men had been chatting and smoking or chewing tobacco. Before we left the house, our mother put her hand on my head, then on Jesse's. "You children be careful today," she said. "You all hear me?"

"Yes, Mama."

She looked at us both for a few seconds, then went back to the kitchen, where breakfast was already being prepared for the next shift of eaters.

It was still early as my brother and I followed the men out of the house and down to the low ground, where strange tracks, almost like those of a tractor, but not quite, had been gouged into the soil. The sun was already up, slicing like a hot knife at an angle over the tops of the tall pines; roosters crowed, and birds twittered up in leafy trees and down in the underbrush, about their morning chores. The air was perfumed with the hot, sweet smell of honeysuckle, ripening muskmelons, dew-damp grass, and the rich male odors of sweat and tobacco, which came from the men's overalls as they clumped in their heavy clodhoppers down to the wheat field.

Bouncing barefooted behind them, trying to match their long strides, my brother and I were both numb with excitement, for it was the very first time that we had been so solidly included in the company of the Bennett men. Our father looked back over his shoulder from time to time, as though he might be sizing us up. The rest of the expedition—three of our uncles, and our grandfather—marched along with intense and dramatic purpose. Neighbor men almost certainly would have been with us as well, but I am sure that my grandfather had forbidden their presence to keep the ensuing affair as something which belonged to our family alone. A stout brown-and-white partridge fluttered up from a little clump of bushes to the side of the road, surely trying to divert our attention from her precious young left somewhere in a nest nearby. I'd slowed down to watch the bird when Jesse tugged me by the elbow and said in a low, choked voice, "Look yonder, pal." I looked, and saw the famous combine for the first time.

Nearly as tall as a barn, it had an array of pipes on its top that appeared to be either chimneys or smoke stacks, or were designed for other purposes. They stuck straight up from the combine's huge, hulking body, which seemed to be a cross between a tractor, a truck, and one-half of a metal mule's ass, as Fred Bryant would describe it later. Resting on hard rubber wheels that had made the dinosaur imprints on the road, it faced the wheat field with what resembled a large paddle wheel that was wider across than the whole machine itself, the paddle wheel at first reminding of the delicately structured wings of an enormous dragonfly. There were also lesser pipes, and pulleys, chains, rachets, steps, chutes, and platforms everywhere. And, very high up, extended outward like a metal baseball glove, there was a slotted seat where presumably the operator of all this splendor would sit.

Even the wheat field, nodding and waving for glorious acres and acres ahead, seemed impatient to have the combine begin its ministrations. For, obviously, this marvelous contraption was intended for the wheat. But, for the moment, it sat there at the field's edge as though sizing things up, some of its metal gleaming, some of it subdued, all of it imposing. And even at that early age, I could sense something about the machine that smacked of pure menace, inspiring great unease, as the English governess had felt when she first met the King of Siam.

As for Jesse, he stayed with our grandfather and the other men around the combine as they patted its sides, wheels, blades—these were very cleverly hidden away among the paddle wheels—and other obtrusions, in the same way I'd seen prospective buyers inspect a mule or a horse to test its qualities. Again, I caught my father casting surreptitious glances at me, and wondered what they signified. The sun had heated considerably by then, and the morning was bright and clear as my grandfather took a step or two into the tall wheat, tested the golden heads with expert fingers, and said, "It's dry enough to begin, boys." Coming back to the combine, he slapped its monstrous side. "Start her up!" he cried, rearing back reverentially to gaze up at the beast.

One of my stringy uncles clambered to the mitt-shaped seat as agilely as a monkey, fumbled with one thing and another for a few tense moments, and then the great machine shuddered into life with tremendous vibrations that seemed to make the entire earth shake. My uncles cheered in a chorus, my grandfather grinned—it was something he did very rarely—and our father came over to talk to Jesse and me. He put a big hand on each of our shoulders and pulled us closer to him, an ominous sign in itself, since he almost never touched us in affection. Looking thoroughly untrustworthy—he was a big, good-looking man with a small gap between his teeth, called a lie gap by some people in Buckingham—he raised his voice so that we could hear him above the noise of the machine.

"Your granddaddy's got a real important job for you boys to do," he said, and his thick lips split in his famous, insincere grin. "Mr. Harriman's combine here, we've got to send it back in the same condition we got it, or even better. First thing is not to break the blades. That'd be real bad for Daddy, and he'd make it bad for everybody else, you all know how he is.'' He rolled his eyes comically at the menace of our grandfather's wrath falling on all of our heads. "So you boys got to walk in front of the combine and pick up any rocks that might break the blades.'' Then he closed one handsome eye in a sly wink, as though we were a cabal of conspirators. "Now, you boys can surely do that, can't you?''

"Yassir!" Jesse and I both sang it out together, so impassioned by our father's taking us into his confidence and giving us this most important of all missions—to maintain the integrity of Mr. Harriman's combine, and to send it back to him spanking brand-new, as it were, as if we had not used it at all. After giving my brother and me another healthy squeeze on our shoulders, and another confidential wink, our father swaggered back to the other men. Jesse and I grinned unbelievingly at each other—a stranger watching us might have thought that we had just been commissioned to go out and fetch the Holy Grail back from the heathens all by ourselves—not knowing then that we had just been sold for thirty pieces of silver, our father's unaccustomed hands on our shoulders being nothing more than the ignoble touch of Judas.

I am paying so much attention to this incident because the kind of calculated treachery which sent my brother and me out in front of the white man's combine, for example, was the same kind of deceit that blacks had used, centuries earlier, to sell other blacks into one kind of slavery or another. The practice was still alive and well that hot August morning when our father conned us into picking up rocks in front of a white man's machine to keep the blades from being broken; and this selling out of one another in the black community continues up to the present day. From this same treachery, our own distaste for ourselves and for each other, comes our disunity, our need for pain, and all the other many evils that black flesh is heir to in America. And even as we point our fingers at white society for what we are doing to ourselves, we are still so consumed by self-loathing that we continue to have no strong, proud racial personality of our own upon which to hang our hats, especially among young blacks.

Is there a solution? A liberal white woman from Tennessee recently told me: "Blacks have to do what they ought to do, or we're just going to have to make them.'' Looked at carefully, this is of course a monumental statement for a white woman to make and for a black man to digest. What is it that the Tennessee lady is saying that black Americans "ought

to do''? What will white Americans "make" us do, if we don't do what we ought to do? I do not know the answers to these questions—although the white lady was kind enough to give me a few clues—but I can of course speculate. First, however, the scene with the combine might open the door to other possibilities.

III

With a loud, muscular roar, the combine lurched into the field, almost like a staggering man, and my brother and I raced around in front of it to begin our search for dangerous rocks. The paddle wheel began turning, slowly at first, then with a speed that was astonishing and terrifying. And, in the space of a few seconds, my brother and I were running back and forth through the golden wheat, removing dangerous rocks from the path of the combine.

They lay among the wheat stalks like land mines, some of them partly hidden by dirt; turned up by plows during sowing, they had obviously not been removed then because no one had anticipated that the harvesting would be done by Mr. Harriman's wonderful combine. Now it moved with a kind of slow, contemptuous dignity, like some enormous royalty accompanied by the grinding of gears, the insistent creak of the paddle wheel as its blades reached out, captured the stalks of wheat, and nicely sliced their heads off. The grain was gulped into the guts of the machine, where the chaff was separated and blown to the wind, while the wheat poured into bags that were automatically tied, and then kicked to the ground by my uncles to be retrieved later by crews on wagons. As for the wheat straw, it was mechanically bound into sheaves and also kicked off for later pick up.

I was to learn all of this later on from Fred Bryant, because there was only time in the field to dart back and forth in front of the combine, picking up rocks from the machine's path and throwing them out of the way. But all we did was to throw them into other lanes, where they would have to be picked up later on and thrown back to where we'd picked them up in the first place. All this time, the combine moved forward like a juggernaut, smoke pouring from one pipe, chaff from another, skinned wheat running like golden water into bags from still another, the blades grinding inexorably as our father, or grandfather, or one of the uncles, yelled down at us from their vantage point atop the combine, and alerted us to the presence of yet another rock among the wheat stalks.

I got dizzy. My stomach felt tight and sick. My legs and arms ached. My vision blurred, and my eyes stung from the sweat that dripped into them. But there was no stopping, not even for a second, as the combine ground on. The men yelled and laughed sometimes at the spectacle of my brother and me racing back and forth in front of the combine, throwing rocks to other areas where we'd have to pick them up again and again out of the path of Mr. Harriman's precious combine. When my grandfather finally bellowed for the machine to stop, it was for himself and the other men to take a drink of water, to check the combine itself, to insure that its powers had not been overly exerted, or that no nicks had appeared in its blades.

No one paid any attention to either my brother or me while we gulped down some water, breathing like pack mules and looking at each other with the sure understanding that we really didn't count at all with these men, that they didn't even *like* us, not to mention love. If it hadn't been for the fact that doing so might have harmed Mr. Harriman's blades, we could just as easily have had our heads cut off, along with the wheat, and been shot out with the other chaff. The Baptist church had sowed the seeds of my self-loathing, my sense of my own lack of worth; the day of the combine fortified it, gave it roots, leaves, disgusting white worms. Nobody really loved me, except perhaps my mother. And, did she *really* love me? If so, why was she home only on Thursdays when we were in New Jersey, bringing me magazines from some white woman's garbage can? And why was she letting this terrible thing happen to us today, without lifting one finger to try and stop it?

The machine rattled to life again, and the operation began again. Sweating and scrambling, my brother and I knew now that we might be accidentally murdered out there. We could feel a breeze from the paddle wheel breathing down our necks, as though to remind us that we were so imminently mortal. "Jump!" somebody would shout. So my brother and I jumped like jackrabbits to keep ourselves from getting cut up and killed, while the men of our family, of our race and same blood, sat upon a white man's machine—certainly worth far more than two sweating, terrified pickaninnies were—and laughed at us uproariously as though we were an amusement. Then, mercifully, we would rest for a few more minutes. Water and gasoline were given to the combine; our grandfather patted it complacently while my father and his brothers inspected it again for possible damage. Then our father yelled to Jesse and me to get ourselves ready.

Again we trotted around in front of the hated thing. The engine roared, the paddle wheels jumped

sprightly into action as the combine moved forward again and the men on top laughed again in loud, lusty voices at the marvel of it all. This went on for the three days during which Mr. Harriman had rented his combine to our grandfather. When Jesse and I stumbled up to the house, our mother received us with eyes full of pain and comprehension. But she never consoled us, or showed by any act or comment that she knew the horror which was taking place in the wheat field. Then we dragged off to do other chores, and to wash up, and then off to church where it seemed that everybody was getting religion that summer except for my brother and me.

As with all things, that summer of 1939 in Buckingham finally came to a close. Neither Jesse nor I had to work in front of the combine after that, but its coming to our grandfather's, and my own realization of how completely worthless and unloved I was, except perhaps by my mother—but why did she never *tell* me, not once in her entire life, that she did love me?—these remain in my memory as that summer's outstanding revelations. The agony may have left me eternally wounded by my own people— my uneasy encounters with the white world would come later on—but the ecstasy of it all, especially my mother's gently guiding hand, undoubtedly turned me into a writer. And I shall always thank God as I know God—hollow-voiced and masked, mysterious forces, wearing buskins and draped in white Grecian robes—I shall always thank God for that.

On September 1, 1939, Hitler's armies marched into Poland; two days later, our family arrived back in New Jersey, just as Britain and France declared war on Germany. Up and down Parrow Street, people huddled around their radios, looking at each other with frightened eyes, for it was certain that America would have to become involved in the conflict. When that happened, near the end of 1941, two of my brothers were drafted immediately, while my sister Alberta went into the Women's Army Auxiliary Corps (WAAC) as a nurse. Other women from our neighborhood worked in defense plants making either munitions or plastics, the latter being the case with my sister Alma, who made Lucite at the nearby Du Pont plant, where she probably contracted the cancer which would kill her some twenty-five years later. My mother left the Irishwoman's employment and went to work in the diet kitchen at Orange Memorial Hospital.

Jesse and I kept on with school, where we made wooden silhouettes in carpenter shop for aircraft spotting, collected tinfoil for the war effort, and knitted Afghan squares for blankets for our Russian allies. After school I worked up the street in the grocery store of an old Jew named Hyman Mayer. Mr. Mayer and his family became a treasured second family to me; every single day at least one of them would pat me on the head and tell me to "get an education." I loved them with a desperation that probably would have surprised them, had they known, and I was absolutely convinced that they loved me. But if race, creed, and color were not a problem in most places in America in those days, it was because circumstances had squeezed all of us like sardines into a reasonable semblance of brotherhood, especially in that first year or so of the war, when it sometimes seemed probable that the Allies might actually lose to Hitler and Tojo.

Still, we blacks on Parrow Street were intensely aware that we were important parts of the war effort, primarily because whites began looking at us as though we might be good for something after all. Caught up in the unaccustomed headiness of patriotism, we cheerfully hated the Japanese, the Germans, the Italians, and all other villains that the government named for us to hiss and boo. When the national anthem was played in school, we did our best to sing louder and more patriotically than the whites, to show that it was our national anthem, too—although the "Negro National Anthem," by James Weldon Johnson, could frequently be heard in all-black gatherings:

> *Lift every voice and sing,*
> *Till earth and heaven ring,*
> *Ring with the harmonies*
> *Of Liberty. . . .*

But it was really the radio which was our contact with the larger world, and that period's great equalizer. Everybody thrilled to Ed Murrow broadcasting from Britain in the middle of a blitz. And to Myra Hess, the concert pianist, playing "Jesu, Joy of Man's Desiring," with such majestic serenity. And Winston Churchill's defiant, erudite drawl as he urged the English-speaking world on to fiercer efforts. And President Roosevelt's carefully aristocratic tones in his fireside chats to the nation. And Gabriel Heatter's optimistic pessimism. And Kate Smith, singing "God Bless America" in her roly-poly voice that seemed fat with gold. And Adolph Hitler, of course, curling the airwaves with speeches that seemed to slice the radio like a demon's vile lash. We even enjoyed it when Bob Hope was cut off the air for telling a dirty joke, and giggled at his audacity until the next time. All too infrequently, Marian Anderson sang, our true voice of hope, turning our darkness into light.

Then, President Roosevelt died in April of 1945. My mother looked stunned, then burst into tears when I dashed into the house with the news. Germany surrendered in May. The dropping of the atomic bomb on Japan that following August brought the war to an end; in Orange High School, Doc Ensminger instructed us to open our chemistry books and cross out the statement that atoms were the smallest particle of matter. The splitting of the atom to make the bomb had rendered that theory obsolete. Truly, we had entered the Atomic Age.

I had been writing all that time, and sold my first short stories, when I was thirteen, to the *AFRO-American Newspapers* for two dollars more per story than Jack London got when he sold his first stories. Fred Bryant told me that interesting piece of trivia; his blind aunt in Buckingham had died, and he had migrated to New Jersey to live with another aunt in Orange. He became one of the high school's star athletes before dropping out in his junior year to go into the navy. Columned, corniced, and pedimented like a Greek temple of learning, Orange High School in those days seemed crammed with talented and dedicated teachers. One of those was Miss Mary Fiend, who was my greatest inspiration. With her encouragement, I became the school's first black editor of the yearbook, and also won several awards in the *Scholastic* magazine writing contests. I was also working part time on the Newark *Herald News*, writing feature articles on old local sports figures for Oliver "Butts" Brown, a former sports figure himself who was then the paper's editor.

Despite scholarships to several colleges, I joined the air force after graduation in 1948. For four years, I worked as chief writer in public information offices, was a string correspondent for *Stars and Stripes* in Japan, editor of a base newspaper there, and a sometimes combat correspondent in Korea after the war broke out in 1950. In 1952, I was discharged from the air force with ulcers and a small pension. My mother died of a cerebral hemorrhage the next year; she was barely forty-six years old, and had gone back to Buckingham for her health. Her funeral, which was large and vulgar, was the only one I have ever attended in the United States. My single consolation, among all the gaudy tears—I myself was dry-eyed—was that my mother had lived long enough to see me become a writer.

Shortly after my mother's death, two other former air force writers and I founded a weekly newspaper in Westbury, New York, which promptly flopped. I became an assistant editor at the *AFRO-American Newspapers* in Baltimore, then escaped to

"With Martha Domínguez Cuevas, executive secretary of the Centro Mexicano de Escritores, in Mexico City, 1957, just prior to that year's devastating earthquake"

Mexico three years later, where I have more or less lived ever since. I studied briefly at Mexico City College on the GI Bill, then received two fellowships from the Centro Mexicano de Escritores. Founded in 1951 by an American writer named Margaret Shedd, and financed in part at that time by the Rockefeller Foundation, the CME gave me the most thorough background in writing I had had up to that point.

Now, safe inside my exile, it would be easy to go into the stories of my clashes with white Americans, and of their clashes with me. The actual truth is that I have had far more problems with black Americans, especially my own family, than with whites. This is not to say that I "hate" blacks, as some of them have absurdly accused. But, my mother's cryptic comment that long-ago day about blacks not being worth a damn seems to make perfectly good sense today. Entertainers in the main—and this includes athletes, popular singers and musicians, dancers, comedians— we still form a kind of unending American minstrel show which will never earn us either a solid economic base or solid respect, this continuous singing, dancing, ball-playing, grinning, jiggabooing, hip-shaking,

and finger-popping. While a great part of this has to do with buying our way out of the ghetto, I believe that another part has to do with our idea that we are invisible—thanks in part to Ralph Ellison's *Invisible Man*—suggesting, of course, that we can do anything we want to and get away with it, since nobody sees us anyway. Everybody at one time or another, especially chicken thieves, has played this child's game of If-I-don't-want-to-be-seen-then-nobody-can-see-me.

While Ellison implies that we are invisible because whites refuse to see us as human beings, I suggest that Ellison's blacks are invisible because they cannot bear the idea of being seen, hating themselves as they do. But, contrary to Ralph Ellison, I personally am not and never have been invisible; indeed, I have always been the most visible of all men; and if it is true that some people seem to stare through me, it is merely an illusion on my part, and theirs, for the human eye cannot see through flesh. They see me, all right, sometimes so clearly that I sometimes wish I could become invisible.

The main error in believing in our invisibility is that black youth, especially, will do practically anything to achieve a visibility which they already have. It is the same thing that happens with black entertainers trying to keep our so-called betters pleased and amused, lest they do us violent damage. But I further suggest that we play our children's games because the games of the majority adults—job, family, home, responsibility—are generally denied us. It follows, then, that we are a race which has never matured, because that also has been denied us, as much as by ourselves as by anybody else. If we are to survive in America, we must grow away from these childish things, and see ourselves as we really are, rather than as others think they see us.

As for white Americans, it would please me to believe that the liberal lady from Tennessee, who gave the dire warning about blacks, was thinking along lines similar to the ones I have mentioned. But I doubt that she was, for I have seen that even as white women demand their "rights," burn their bras, and storm about, calling themselves "the new niggers"—are we old-style niggers that out of sync?—they seem to be incapable of understanding the true nature of their bondage, or of ours, either. But I do know that the lady's male companion indicated that the country would be better off if whites began lynching blacks in shopping malls. A lot of people might find such a new fad far more amusing than women's liberation marches, or playing electronic games, including some blacks themselves. Since slavery is not so easily expunged from the racial memory, I am convinced that a fair number of blacks still yearn to be physically owned and taken care of by whites. Failing this, we find other slow and painful ways to kill ourselves—with drugs, crime, liquor, poverty, ignorance, laziness, madness—while certain whites look on with guilt and dismay, in many cases harboring a keen sense of gratitude that we have had the good taste, if not the good sense, to lynch ourselves.

IV

Is there a solution?"
I asked Fred Bryant this the last time I saw him in Buckingham. I was discussing the race question and other things, while Fred lay flat on his belly nearby, like a faithful black dog, chewing on a piece of broomstraw. We had both become middle-aged men, but we had already discussed the fact that both of us looked far younger than we really were. Talking about the race issue, we had the self-satisfied air of veterans who had somehow managed to come out somewhat intact from a war with few real survivors.

For my oldest sister had dropped dead of a heart attack while cleaning fish in her backyard in Buckingham. My oldest brother had also died of a heart attack, alone in a small rented room in Newark, his heart pills and a quart of liquor on the bedside table. My sister Alma had died of breast cancer, all but abandoned by her husband and her children. My father, age eighty-six, had died in a kind of regal splendor at the University of Virginia hospital, attended by Jewish doctors from New York City and white Southern nurses who had the added quality of being pretty. One of my father's legs had been cut off years before because of gangrene, but his death was the result of a heart that "was like a can of worms," according to one of his doctors.

Would any of my family have died more comfortably if we had been owned by other than white men? If they had been less visible? More invisible? So far, Fred and I had survived, while others were falling around us like flies. If my scars were less visible than Fred's, I knew that his were nonetheless still there. By that time, I was already living in Mexico, and had dropped in to Buckingham just to see how things were. "When that mess was going on in Little Rock," I told Fred, "where they didn't want that little colored girl to go to a white school, and Eisenhower called out the troops? Well, the President of Mexico invited all black Americans to come and live there."

Fred snuffled out a laugh. "And you took him up on his offer?"

"I suppose I did. Why don't you come on down, too, Fred? You could live with me, and you'd be living in a country where they like black people." There was no need to tell him about the Mexicans who really didn't like black people.

But I could see that Fred would never leave America, as I had. The land really meant far more to him than it did to me. He had married, had four children who lived and worked in the North, and a divorced wife who was somebody's maid in Richmond. Fred had come back to Virginia after the divorce, and was living on his navy pension there in the shell of my grandfather's house, paying rent of exactly five dollars a month. The tenants before him had almost torn the place down for firewood, taking out even the parquet floors to burn in the massive fireplace.

This was the most shocking thing I'd found when I went back—that my grandfather's house and what was left of his land had fallen into wrack and ruin, and absolutely nobody seemed to care. When my grandfather died in 1941, I hugged myself in pure joy that he had finally ceased to exist. My grandmother came to the North then and worked for a couple in West Orange that she claimed were the parents of the actor Henry Fonda, because they had the same surname. She became rather stylish in New Jersey, and kicked up her old heels, as they say, with a very handsome and very smooth numbers writer named Mr. Oliver. When I went back to Buckingham on a brief visit, after being discharged from the air force, my grandmother was back home again, looking even worse than she had when my grandfather was living. She had cancer, and was nearly blind, and I suppose I knew enough by that time not to laugh at the spectacle of anyone's death.

The land was left to a bunch of heirs, including my father, his brothers, and one of Fred's aunts. They sold some of it off in little bits and dabs to "housing developers," who put up little clapboard boxes side by side, with a few five feet in between, and sold them at high prices on the installment plan to workers at the new factories that were springing up near Buckingham, and out in Dillwyn, Lynchburg, and Appomattox. So, a number of people sold off their farms and went to work in the factories, while other little ticky-tacky houses were put up for them to buy as substitutes. What land there was left, like my grandfather's, had turned to weeds.

"It would take years of nothing but fertilizer to get this land right again," Fred said. "And who's got the time and the money for that?" He dug his hands into the red dirt, and they looked like black crabs holding something that was bloodied and abused far more than he and I were or ever could have been. "You going to revival today?" he asked me, changing the painful subject.

"I suppose so," I said.

He had already confessed to me that he had become a Christian in the navy; I had gotten baptized—slapped indifferently in the forehead with ill-aimed water—as a political move in 1948, since a scholarship to Lincoln University in Pennsylvania apparently depended on my being Presbyterian. As it happened, I didn't use the scholarship anyway, but I suppose I had been "saved," as Fred said, with his marvelous grin. "You going?" I asked him.

He nodded in that slow, easy way he had, and chewed on his broomstraw.

"Is there a solution?"

Fred and I were lying in what had been the old wheat field where my brother Jesse and I had gone through that awful ritual nearly forty years ago. Jesse was married now, living in New Jersey, as was Jean, the baby girl, who had become quite Christian and quite matronly. Looking out over the injured, un-loved fields, it seemed impossible that so many years had slid by, so many people dead, so many more being born, to die. The day of the combine was still vivid in my memory, and I felt a sense of hot hatred flash through me when Fred brought the subject up.

"You know why you never had to work in front of that combine again?" he said.

I shook my head. I'd hoped it was because I had done such a sorry job those three days back in 1939; but I'd come to believe that the whole miserable business had been some kind of rite of passage, to move little black boys into black manhood, assuring at the same time that we would always live with the sense of menacing men and machines behind us.

"Why wasn't I invited back?" I said sarcastically.

Fred grinned. "Because your Mama, man, she had a *fit,* let me tell you. Man, she stomped her foot, she put her finger in your granddaddy's face, and she told him she'd *murder* him if he *ever* put you and Jesse in front of that combine again. Your Daddy, he just stood there like a bump on a log."

"You're kidding!" I shot up straight on the ground. Not because my father had done nothing. But, my gentle *mother?* Shaking her finger in my *grandfather's* face? And the evil old man backing down? The whole picture seemed so unbelievable that I felt like laughing. I cried, instead.

Fred immediately scooted over and wrapped a long arm around my shoulders. "What you crying about, pal? You still remembering all them hateful, hurtful things? Well, you know what you got to do? You got to forget them, pal, that's what. You hear me? You got to forget everything that don't suit you, and that don't serve you."

Those are not his exact words, but they are close enough. I remember that I pulled away from him, and walked around in a kind of growing amazement. And, later on, when Fred and I stripped and splashed about in the snake-filled creek, the water so cold and delicious that it made my teeth ache, I was still puzzling over his words.

Their true meaning came to me that afternoon at church, where the ritual of handshaking, backslapping, and I-do-declares picked up again as though no time at all had come in between, as though all of us had gone from being unloved children to being unloved old folk all in the same summer's afternoon.

Fred was talking about forgetting everything that had happened that hadn't suited me, that hadn't served me. He was talking about amnesty, which means forgetting. It is a kind of trade-off done by nations and people, when to keep on remembering does far more harm than the act of forgetting does.

The jacket cover from Bennett's fifth novel, 1976

Amnesty. It was a wonderful word, a wonderful understanding. Across the church ground, Fred Bryant looked at me and winked, nodding his head. The August day was mild, peaceful, the revival a lot poorer than before, since everything had to be bought at stores. But the tables were still there underneath the same shade trees, although the food had come mostly from cans, packages, plastic containers. Snazzy new cars and trucks were parked where horses, wagons, and buggies used to be. There were fewer people than before, since most of the young left Buckingham as soon as they were able, and didn't bother to come back, not even for revival.

Inside the church, the choir started singing, and people began going in. The service was about to begin; the old woman that Fred said got drunk off her own homebrew was still there, still starched and pressed, probably still drunk. Watching her as she came and went from the door, conducting people to their seats, I thought about my father, my grandfather, my mother, my grandmother. And about the men and women everywhere—black, white, yellow, whatever color—who had trespassed against me, as I

most probably had trespassed against them, or others like them.

And I promised to forget about the hurt; I suppose that I even forgave them for it, I suppose that is what I am saying. I forgave them their pain and their trespasses, and found myself hoping—I suspect that I was really praying, but I am too much of an atheist to ever publicly admit such a thing—I found myself hoping that all the people I have sinned against, would somehow forgive me, as I forgave them.

Getting involved in forgiving and forgetting the so-called bad times, it is amazing how we find that good has been hiding underneath them all the while, like a sumptuous feast covered by a shabby cloth. Hadn't my father, for example, held me once in his brawny arms, a worried look on his handsome face, when I'd accidentally been hit in the head by a broomstick that we used for a baseball bat? And hadn't we gone on Sunday rides, as happy as lords, in our old Oakland, up to Eagle Rock with Brother driving and Daddy admonishing him not to speed; then back down to Orange again like a roller coaster, my mother flushed and laughing nervously, joyously, and all of us with her? And hadn't my mother hugged me hysterically in a tremendous grip, when I came back home from Korea, and cried in my arms and screamed thanks to the Lord that *her baby son* had come home safe from the war?

I ambled over to Fred, and we just stood there, grinning at each other. Both of us were a little high on jackleg peach brandy, which really is the only decent way to go to revival. The choir was singing "Come to Jesus," in voices so angelic and sweet that they hurt the heart. Inasmuch as Fred and I had already been saved, we went inside. Some white people were already there, comfortably sitting on the segregated back benches. We smiled at them, and they smiled and nodded at us. After all, the ways of different people are different.

BIBLIOGRAPHY

Fiction, unless otherwise noted:

The Mexico City Poems [and] *House on Hays* (latter a play in verse), Obsidian Press, 1961.

A Wilderness of Vines, Doubleday, 1966, Cape, 1967.

The Black Wine, Doubleday, 1969, Sphere, 1974.

Lord of Dark Places, Norton, 1970, Calder & Boyers, 1971.

Wait until the Evening, Doubleday, 1974.

Seventh Heaven, Doubleday, 1976.

Insanity Runs in Our Family (contains "Black Wings," "Insanity Runs in Our Family," "Where Are the White People?" "The Ghost of Martin Luther King," "Dotson Gerber Resurrected," "Whatever Happened to Henry Oates?" "Million Dollar Baby," "The Abominable Snow Man," "The Woman Who Loved Cockroaches," "The Mountain to Mohammed," "The Judgment of Father Anselmo," "The Day My Sister Hid the Ham," "Second Sunday," "Also Known as Cassius," and "Sightless"), Doubleday, 1977.

Brendan Galvin

1938-

Sometime around my fiftieth birthday, I walked into the room I write in and found the sun shining on my desk, illuminating a well-scribbled page of the 14-by-11-inch sketch pad I use to nudge vague ideas and images toward possibilities for poems. What entered my head quite involuntarily was, "My God, that's the most beautiful sight in the world!" If I ever wondered whether drifting into poetry as a lifetime obsession was the wrong route for me, I haven't since that morning, with its revelation in that almost corny mellow autumn light. Since then I've asked myself how many others react the same way to seeing the tools of their trades after nearly thirty years.

For me poems often begin with the psychic center of my work, the water, the sand, and the pine-covered square miles comprising the towns of Wellfleet, Truro, and Provincetown, out on the end of Cape Cod. I grew up out there, or my senses did, in ways that they didn't around Everett, the boring, blue-collar suburb north of Boston where I spent most of the non-summertime of my first twenty-two years. My work still involves the sensory pleasures of those few miles of the Cape I know well, and I am with Faulkner and William Carlos Williams in this: the universal is only real and significant when it springs out of the local, and never when it's the product of the mind alone, uncorroborated by external experience. Only recently have I realized that there's something Celtic about this connection with landscape, something operating at the genetic level, perhaps. In the chance pairing of a writer with a home place, I have been lucky beyond luck.

It must have been sometime near the beginning of this century that my grandfather went sailing out of Boston on a friend's boat and fetched up on those outer reaches of the Cape. Whether they rounded Jeremy Point and saw the white churches and houses of Wellfleet huddled down the bay, or threaded the channel into Pamet Harbor in Truro, or swung around Long Point into Provincetown, I do not know. What I have been told is that the unbroken line of dunes and beaches reminded Ned McLaughlin of those on the coast of Donegal, Ireland, where he was born, and which he appears to have missed after his

Brendan Galvin, 1990

immigration to America sometime in the last quarter of the nineteenth century. It's as if his silence on the subject of the place of his birth were a way of countering the pain of having left; no one in the family can tell me the name of his native townland.

Eighty years later, my children have done part of their growing up within walking distance of where my mother did hers, for my grandfather soon began packing his wife and young daughters onto the Boston-Provincetown steamboat each summer for the trip to Pond Village, in North Truro. One of those girls would later marry into a local family, and her husband, my Portuguese uncle, Gib Sylva, would coax me to eat Wellfleet oysters off the half shell by feeding me a chocolate between each one. A hard measure indeed, though I'm happy to say I soon kicked the chocolate part of the habit.

By the 1920s Ned McLaughlin had bought property in South Wellfleet. His great-great-grandchildren live there year round now, and his vegetable garden, ditched to draw the waters of a marsh pond, plowed and planted until a few years ago, is still in the family. Because he rarely saw eye-to-eye with Mary Ann McElenney Barr McLaughlin, the young Donegal widow he'd married in Boston in 1895, he went native on the Cape at some point, and had to be driven back to Boston for holidays and family occasions by the connivance of his daughters, or so I am told. Cape Codders are notorious for their treatment of "washashores," and can turn a mean back on outsiders, but in my youth I knew men who spoke well of him. Apparently he could hold his own with local Yankees.

Home is always partly a matter of names and their resonances. So is poetry. Horse Leech Pond, Shirttail Point, Paine Hollow (we used to call a lethal home brew we concocted Paine Hollow Beer). Then there's Dogtown, where my brother Bill used to live, and The Gut, Wilder Dyke, Thumpertown, High Toss Bridge, even Hitler Road, though God knows why. And always out there was a sense of community I never ran across in Greater Boston. Once you could ring up the local operator and ask her to connect you with Captain Teabag or Joe Boofer, and she'd put the call through for you.

This is changing rapidly, of course. Tourism used to evaporate out there on the day after Labor Day, as though the Cape were some sort of motorized island that parted from the mainland and anchored, unreachable, in the Atlantic until the following July. Now I don't recognize most people on the streets of Wellfleet, where I spent my summers, or in Truro, where I manage to spend a good part of each year in a house my wife Ellen and I had built in a pine grove above a salt marsh more than twenty years ago. One April night when I was nineteen I walked the white centerline of Route 6, on a bet, from Wellfleet Center to South Wellfleet (the Paine Hollow made me do it) and never met a car. If I did that tonight I'd be holding up some commuter traffic.

I write this from Durham, Connecticut, where I've lived for thirteen years. It's a mixed town of commuters and dairy farmers, and its official emblem is a Holstein cow. A half hour away is Central Connecticut State University, where I've been on the English faculty since 1969, teaching mostly Freshman Composition, Creative Writing, and Modern British and American Poetry. It appears I will have spent my working life in the trenches of Academe, with students not unlike I was at Boston College in the late fifties: a diamond in the rough, and first member of my side of the family to graduate from college. There I earned a B.S. in Natural Sciences, and was on my way out to St. Louis University's Dental School when, after a summer of intense concentration on the idea of spending my life looking into other people's mouths, I decided I wanted to get an M.A. in English, and so gave up the idea of drilling by day to support writing by night. At Boston College I had taken mostly courses in biology, chemistry, and physics, hardly the raw materials for poetry, one might think, and only after a long apprenticeship in writing did I realize how helpful those science courses actually were. For one thing, they forced me to write accurately, since we were graded down for inexactness, and then again, they generously gave me a vocabulary most poets don't have. It has always seemed natural to me to use a word like "meniscus" in a poem, therefore, and in writing about the natural environment I've never left the sciences behind. I want what I say to be scientifically correct, if possible, and to that end I've learned to research things, to check them out and to get useful information I don't have in my head. When I'm working on a poem I'm often educating myself, and perhaps the reader as well. I can sympathize with the occasional reviewer who laments that my work sends him to the dictionary or encyclopedia.

Sometimes, in the back of a physiology lab for instance, while others were cutting through the plastron of a turtle to get at its heart and increase its heart rate with chemicals fed through an eyedropper, I'd find myself noodling away at a poem in the back of a notebook. Sporadically, from high school on, I'd been writing poems and other "things." At Malden Catholic High I was on the football team that won the state championship in my junior year, and my first rejection came when I submitted a poem to the school newspaper's poetry column. It was about sending away for a ray gun from the back of a cereal box and vaporizing my mother and father with it—the teenager in revolt. The final couplet went: "This gun you may have over-rated / But there they are disintegrated." Both the faculty advisor, Brother Michael, and the editor loved it, but somehow couldn't believe a football lineman had written it. I think they thought I took it away from someone on the bus to school.

Boston College had developed almost a proprietary interest in Robert Frost sometime in the fifties, and while I was there he was driven over from

Galvin, about 1939

Cambridge to give an annual reading. I knew a lot of his work by heart then, and could impress or annoy a coed by mumbling it just under my breath as he read it from the podium. Since I worked my way through college on a tar truck in those summers, oiling roads all over Frost's New Hampshire, I had seen many of the places he wrote about, and could imagine his poems happening in the White Mountain towns I worked in and passed through. Inevitably, he was the first poet I imitated, to be replaced later by Robert Lowell, whose Boston I also roamed and connected with.

It was Thomas Merton whose poems and meditations grabbed me in my brief bohemian period after college. I had decided to be a writer (it was actually that vague), and had moved with a Cape friend, Jack Gregory, an art student at the Boston Museum School, into a fourth-floor apartment on Symphony Road in the Back Bay, behind Symphony Hall. Thirty-seven Symphony Road was an experience. My younger brother looked around and called me Junior Beatnik. There were cockroaches wall-to-

wall, rats in the kitchen at night, and you never knew what you'd run into on the stairs. Maybe a half-wild city dog going through garbage bags left out by the various denizens of the building, most of whom we never actually saw during the year we lived there. We heard them though, and used to tape the drunken arguments of one couple and play them back at their window across the air shaft at top volume the next morning. The bathtub would clog recurrently, the trashmen collecting in the public alley behind the building would deliberately clash cans to wake everyone at 5:00 A.M., and one morning I was awakened by a pigeon walking around my bedroom. The street itself was lined with nearly identical buildings from the nineteenth century, firetraps all, and it was a rare week when the thrumming red trucks of the Boston Fire Department didn't pay it a visit. This gave my father and mother some sleepless hours, I do not doubt.

It is one of those quandaries of the human personality that even as I read Merton I was also going to parties with girls from Fairfield County and Newton, art students who wore the then-*outré* uniform of scratchy black stockings and eyes made up to look like a cat's. I drank a lot of beer and wine, too, while living on the savings of my job on the asphalt truck the previous summer. I wrote a few poems, and worked on my magnum opus, a play called "The Bluebird Man," full of songs and characters based on some of the odder inhabitants of Symphony Road. The only characters I remember now are a crone named Miss Mehitable Scrod, and of course The Bluebird Man himself, whose theory was that all the world's problems could be solved if everyone was given a bluebird to take care of. Such are the philosophical capacities of some twenty-two-year-olds. Needless to say, the play was never finished, and if I remember correctly, never even made it to the first-act curtain.

Tuition and frivolity dissipated my funds by midwinter. I was taking four English courses at Boston College and a creative-writing course at the Harvard Extension, where I got some good advice on a one-acter, some poems redolent of Merton, and a short-short story or two. I found a part-time job mornings from six to ten at Jordan Marsh, vacuuming floors before the store opened. You haven't lived until you've waited for the train underground at the old Symphony Station at 5:00 A.M. of a February morning, while water dripped from cracks in the ceiling and a wind blew through the tunnel all the way from the Pole. Or operated a vacuum cleaner, hungover, in a showroom full of mannequins and mirrors where, from a corner of your eye, a reflected arm or head seemed to move, or a Doberman appeared from nowhere leading a security guard on a leash, a jump start for your still-sleeping heart.

It surprises me yet that I relish the taste of Kraft macaroni-and-cheese dinners, which became a staple of our diet. They cost fifteen cents then, and I judge the inflation rate to this day by them. Last time I looked they'd gone up to fifty-two cents a package. In the late sixties I even wrote an ode to them. Jack Gregory and I had befriended a group of nursing students that year. They lived one street over and owned a TV and cooked elaborate meals, financed as they were from home, and were angels of mercy to us. On weekends when they went home they'd leave us a key so we could catch the Red Sox on their TV set, and never complained when we borrowed from their cupboards. I think of them kindly to this day.

The most useful thing I brought away from that year was that living in a garret wasn't a smart way to become a writer. When you have to scrounge for basic necessities and dodge the rent collector there isn't a lot of time to cogitate. In early June I went back to Wellfleet and moved into a shack on Long Pond, and went to work at the local First National Store, grinding hamburg and learning to become a meatcutter, a summer job that stood me in good stead for several years after. On some of those Saturdays, I'd spend eight full hours in the cold chest, grinding hamburg the tourists snatched from the meat case so quickly I couldn't keep up with them. There were days when I created literally a ton of the stuff. There were other days when I quartered chickens on the band saw for hours, or cut whole swordfish into steaks. My friend Joe O'Brien worked there as well, and we paid four dollars a week apiece on the shack, which he named the *Dreckhaus.* We slept in the living room, which was screened but had no windows. There was an outhouse off in the woods a little way, and the water was hand-pumped through a rusting pipe, which provided more iron than we needed and resulted in a new taste in our Kraft dinners. At night we lit kerosene lanterns and a candle or two. One of the perks of working in a supermarket was that we could buy ageing meat cheaply, and sometimes when a lobster began showing signs of its demise in the tank we'd rush it home and boil it on the ancient gas stove before rigor mortis set in. When we had girls coming over for dinner, we'd even pull the plug on the lobster tank for a little while: symbolic redistribution of the wealth.

Our transportation that summer was a prewar Plymouth owned by our third roommate, Foster

"Family summer house, South Wellfleet, Massachusetts, soon after purchase in 1935"

Wolfe. It had no gas tank, so the fuel line ran under the front seat into a five-gallon can hidden under a rug in the back. On hills the passenger had to reach over the seat and shove the copper line all the way into the gas can. Our favorite gag was to pull up to a gas station and tell the attendant to fill 'er up; another was to pick up a hitchhiker and explain why he shouldn't smoke in that car, which gave "flaming youth" a whole new meaning.

Although I had spent most summers of my twenty-two years in South Wellfleet, it was during 1961 on Long Pond that I think I first took notice of the Cape's natural beauty in a serious way. I could hear the sound of Atlantic surf, less than a mile away, breaking through the trees. I had always heard it as a kid, but never felt it with the intensity I did now. Sometimes, skinny-dipping in the pond below the house, an astonishingly full moon rose at the far end of the water. Those woods were full of birdsong, and we waked to squirrels skittering across the tar-paper roof we had put on before we moved in. In the morning, someone's wayward hound might be watching over our sleep a few inches away on the other side of the screen. Since we paid so little rent, our landlord thought it only fitting that we become surrogate parents for his pregnant cat. On quiet afternoons off, I began my first serious attempts at poems, before the social life of the evening began. We seemed never to be without someone dropping in, a bass player from a local night spot, some waitresses, a biker nobody seemed to know, and occasionally the drunken mate on a charter boat, who'd stay over in the spare bedroom and inevitably wake screaming, nightmaring his Korean War combat.

After completing two English courses nights at Boston University, I was accepted into the M.A. program across town at Northeastern, and there under three outstanding teachers, Raymond Blois, Jane Benardete, and Samuel French Morse, I began to see new possibilities for myself. It was a small program with small classes, and was probably begun as a way of providing the cheap labor of teaching fellows for the Freshman Composition program, the kind of place where everyone knew everyone else, which incubated both close friendships and fierce competitions. The years 1962–1964 were my happiest as a student. I believe that Ray Blois, had he chosen to write criticism, might have rivaled Northrop Frye. Instead he passed everything on to us in courses on Chaucer, Milton, and the American Romantics. He had a lot to say about the right and wrong ways of term papers, too. He really wanted to teach bowling, though, and was nearly unbeatable at it. Jane Benardete's discussions of Emerson, Thoreau and Whitman, Twain and James, and her probing questions, always seemed to leave me on the edge of my chair and the edge of my mind, reaching out for something beyond myself that I couldn't quite formulate yet. Since she was my advisor, she gave me helpful tips about teaching and writing, too. The late Sam Morse was the only true Yankee patrician I've had the privilege of knowing, wonderful on Wallace Stevens, a terror in Writing Poetry, where we'd leave the class groaning over how much crow we'd eaten, and the person who first said, "You ought to send some of these out."

As a teaching fellow in 1963–64, I had two sections of Freshman Comp, thirty-five business students to a section, a grammarian's nightmare finally capped by a five-week Intro to Lit course for P.E. majors, where I salvaged the year by discovering that I could probably teach literature to anyone. Along with the M.A. in English, in the spring of '64 I was given a one-year appointment as instructor, and got to teach not merely two, but four sections of Freshman Comp, young engineers this time, and fairly logical writers compared to the business administration groups. That year I red-penciled fifteen hundred student essays, letting them pile up on the kitchen table of my apartment until the mound collapsed onto the floor and I dove in and eventually got to the bottom. I was writing poems daily then, making time for myself. For the first time in my life I was coming home from work as clean as I'd left, not reeking of asphalt or meat or fish. I owned a dark blue suit and several sports jackets, a fifty-dollar FM radio and a hi-fi.

In November of 1964 one of my stamped, self-addressed envelopes came back. The *Atlantic* had accepted two of the four poems I'd submitted and suddenly I was two feet taller. "I can't recall anything like this happening here," an elderly colleague told me, and at the department Christmas party the chairman said, "You'll find it gets harder the more you write." A poet himself, he'd been trying to crack the *Atlantic* for fifteen years, but never rose higher than the *Christian Science Monitor*. This must have been my first encounter with literary envy, and the second came soon after. Another department member, also a poet, simpered and said, "Two swallows don't make a summer, you know." I was totally unprepared for these remarks, assuming as I did that professors would be delighted to have a poet as a colleague. Over time I've discovered that the opposite is generally true, that academics can become positively enraged when a colleague has the temerity to publish poetry or fiction. Later I'd discover that other poets and writers resent it as well. There is no such thing as a brotherhood of the craft in this business. Recently a Guggenheim recipient told me that less than a year after his award two out of his four recommenders were no longer speaking to him.

Of my experience as a graduate student at the University of Massachusetts in Amherst I have less to say. I was filling in the blanks in my knowledge of the history of English and American literature, in preparation for comprehensive exams, and so ended up in a number of courses I wouldn't have taken otherwise. I don't care if I ever read the *Faerie Queene* again, and I feel the same about a lot of minor Middle English literature. I had intended to become a Chaucerian, but the man I was to do my dissertation with proved to be both stultifying and bitter, and anyway by that time I'd decided to write on Theodore Roethke, whom I had discovered one Saturday in the employees' lounge of the First National Store in Wellfleet, back around 1962 or 1963. I had bought a copy of the *New Yorker* off the store rack that morning, and there found one of his North American Sequence, "The Rose," perhaps, or "Meditation at Oyster River." I had never seen anything like it before, and I immediately realized that I might be able to write about my experience of my own home place as he had done with his adopted Pacific Northwest. Since that time I had been soaking myself in his poems, and I

At about age ten

can recall Saturday nights when my greatest pleasure was to read him at the kitchen table.

While I worked on the Ph.D. requirements I was also doing an M.F.A. in Creative Writing. UMass was the only Ph.D. program I had applied at, and when they offered me a University Graduate Fellowship in English, all expenses paid, I had jumped at the offer. Since I had no duties except to attend class and show up once a month to collect my stipend, I had lots of time to write poems as well as do my coursework. I completed the M.F.A. in February 1968, and the Ph.D. in May 1970. I also became friends with the poet Thomas Reiter, with whom I still exchange work, and whose incisive critical comments have helped over the past twenty years to show me what my weaknesses and strengths as a writer are.

In Amherst I met, fell in love with, and married on August 1, 1968, my wife, the former Ellen Baer. Ellen is behind every poem I've written since then, in ways only a writer can understand. I am not a practical person when it comes to dealing with everyday life. Although I am glad to know that I get a check from my employer every two weeks, I am not much interested in what happens to it after that. Ellen deposits it, and pays the bills, and balances the checkbook, and has managed to keep us on a firm financial basis over the years. I am sure that without her I'd be lost on a sidewalk somewhere in my bare feet. This must be disconcerting to anyone of a younger generation who has grown up in a climate of marriage contracts and shared household responsibilities, but as a division of labor it has worked well. She cooks with verve, sees to the house and its cash requirements, and is at least as handy as I am with small repairs. She is also fine to have around the woodpile. I teach the courses and write the poems. She listens to the poems and makes suggestions. There's only one dinner I'm capable of, a personal version of veal milanese. She's a great sounding board and has more often than not dissuaded me from a wrong course. We have spent more time together than any other couple I know, and it works. I have been as lucky in my wife, and it can only be called luck if I won't call it grace, as in my work and my home place.

Our children are Peter, twenty-nine, a son I adopted from my wife's previous marriage, and Anne, our daughter born in 1971. At this writing Peter is on the computer-science staff at Brown University, and does to giant systems apparently marvelous things, which I can neither understand nor explain. His wife, Carla Rissmeyer, is employed at Wesleyan in a similar capacity. Anne is a sophomore at Wheaton College. Given the family of my childhood, I am constantly surprised to find myself in the midst of this warm group.

I wish I could say that my mother and father were happy together, but I can only conclude from my experience of them that they weren't. For one thing, my father was frustrated in his work. As a letter carrier for the Post Office, he never developed his native intelligence to anywhere near its capacity, I believe. A substitute carrier who had done his route once told me that someone who'd never delivered on it could finish it in a half hour. That left a lot of free time to kill in an eight-hour day, and too often some of it was spent in bars.

James Russell Galvin hadn't started out with the idea of a civil service job. It was the Depression and its psychological aftermath that led him into thirty years in the Post Office, along with his marriage to Rose Marie McLaughlin and a growing family. In high school and forever after he had been known as "Porky," not because of any corpulence on his part, but because another, unrelated Galvin in Malden, Massachusetts, had the same nickname. At Malden

High he had starred in football, baseball, and track, and although he weighed only 145 pounds and was below average height, he went on to play halfback on the freshman football teams at Boston College, Niagara University, and Providence College. I do not know if I have the order of institutions right, or even whether he lasted out the year at any of them, but somewhere in there the Depression struck. In my youth there were stories of Civilian Conservation Corps camps he had worked in. In the thirties he was in local Democratic politics in Malden, a member of the city council, still "Porky," still trading on his reputation as a high-school athlete, as he would in various ways throughout his life. Apparently he was considered a possible nominee for the Massachusetts House of Representatives, too. There's a story that he was somehow finagled out of running, but I can't credit that, and another story that he wanted to start an insurance business but that my mother talked him out of it. Therefore, the Post Office. His brother Bill had been a lawyer, his sister Kathleen rose to principal of a grammar school in Rhode Island and has another named for her there. Another sister, still

living, was for many years a buyer for one of the more elegant Boston retail stores. Not bad for first-generation Americans, the children of parents from County Cork, Ireland. My paternal grandmother was a Sexton, dead before I was born. Her husband, William Galvin, was a member of the Knights of Saint Finbar in Cork, and that's how I almost came to be named for that saint. The priest who performed my baptism talked my parents out of it. It's the name I've given the younger of my Border collies. As with my mother's side, I know nothing about the townland the Galvins came from, though I conclude it was Cork City itself, since Saint Finbar is the patron of the place and his handsome cathedral occupies one of its hillsides. I wish we had talked more about the Galvins and McLaughlins, especially now that I'm middle-aged. But there was a regrettable reticence on both sides, perhaps Catholic in origin, as though such talk might be tantamount to a dangerous self-regard.

Rose McLaughlin never finished Everett High School. She became a hairdresser and owned a beauty parlor in Malden Square, where she apparently met my father. They were married in 1937, and I was

The Galvin family, 1951: James, Rose, Brendan, Kevin, Terry (standing in front of James),
uncle Arthur O'Leary (kneeling), and Bill

born on October 20, 1938. My brother Kevin was born in 1940, James, called Terrance (his middle name), six years later, William Francis two years later, and Eileen Bernadette shortly after. Eileen died, I believe of some form of leukemia, though it was never discussed with the other children, at the age of three. She had spent much of her brief life in Boston Children's Hospital. If one of the themes in my poems is the victimization of innocence, it begins with the death of that poor little girl. And though I was too young to see the depth of it and probably entangled in the snares of my own puberty, my sister's death must have caused enormous suffering for my mother and father. My mother frequently consulted a parish priest, I know, since he asked after her welfare later on. My father had always been devout in his own quiet way, but I suspect that at this time my parents began to drift apart, the seemingly little they had in common beginning to break down. Perhaps in a different generation they might have divorced, though I can't say that with any certitude. The level of frustration in their household can be assessed by the amount of bickering that went on, unless I am wrong and it was just another Irish-American sport.

For one thing, my father would never again have the adulation he got as a high-school athlete. As each of his boys grew he hoped that we would somehow equal or better his own abilities, but it wasn't to happen. His two middle sons didn't play organized sports at all, and my youngest brother, who had strengths as both a pitcher (he threw no-hitters in Little League) and quarterback, decided he wanted to play ice hockey instead. My mother, on the other hand, wanted what she thought was intellectual achievement, meaning children in the professions, which resulted in my remaining in the natural sciences rather than majoring in English as an undergraduate. Because of this pull in two directions, my brothers pretty much gave up trying to please them and went their own ways. In the case of my own children, I have never pressured them in any direction, and it has worked out for the best.

As I see it now, the fact that my mother's family were dour country people from the stony pastures of Donegal in the northwest of Ireland and my father's folks were from the milder southwest of County Cork had a lot to do with the polar differences operating in our family. The McLaughlins, or those I knew, seem to have been teetotallers and relatively chilly personalities, while some of the Galvins were given more to the pleasures of the bottle and on occasion to a bit of extramarital sex. Two out of three of my McLaughlin aunts never married. The name itself means some-

As a member of the Malden Catholic High School football team, 1956 (front row, far right)

thing like "from the great fiord land," and crossed the water to Ulster from Scotland sometime around the twelfth century. Its origin is supposedly Norse, which may help explain a dollop of ice I detect in the McLaughlin blood. Oversimplification? Perhaps, but I find those two poles tugging in myself, and the fact that I quit drinking about ten years ago indicates to me that my mother's side won out on that score. Nothing sinister here, by the way. I had simply begun to drink less and less, and around the time I gave it up several acquaintances ran afoul of alcohol in ways that deeply affected their lives, one quite finally. I could also see that liquor might poison a writer's life from observing firsthand a couple of poets who wasted their energies trying to recover from hangovers. Another I knew failed to live up to his early notices and took to booze as an escape. Anyone considering quitting should be aware that when he does he becomes a threat to his drinking friends, however. He may also discover just how boring cocktail parties truly are.

It is interesting to me how many writers have had murderous or absconding fathers, or ineffectual and frustrated ones, and I suppose I belong to this latter group, given that once in conversation when I was about twenty my dad told me that his work didn't require any particular talents and that he hoped I wouldn't fall into similar circumstances, the Post Office in particular. Even before that I had decided I'd do something different, try to make my mark on the world in a way that would justify my existence and say that it mattered that I was here, though I'm sure I didn't put it so clearly at the time. "You'll probably work in an office," I was told by the woman from the State of Massachusetts who administered aptitude tests to us in high school. This angered me, and I gave her whatever the 1955 version of "No Way!" was. The idea of working at a desk eight hours a day loomed as a defeat. One of the things I was qualified for, according to my test results, was Creative Writing. Interestingly, none of my brothers went for the nine-to-five, forty-hour week either. Kevin is a professional photographer, Terry a self-employed builder and restorer of houses, and Bill a reporter and newspaper editor.

Another salient event of my youth was that at age twelve or so I was sent upstairs to the third floor of the triple-decker we lived in, to the flat of my aunt Margaret McLaughlin, where I slept in the bedroom of my late aunt Mary, who had died years before. My parents' first-floor apartment consisted of five rooms, and with four growing sons we were elbow-to-elbow and wall-to-wall. I lived upstairs until I graduated from Boston College and left home. Aunt Margaret and I weren't exactly at each other's throats, but it was always touch and go, since I was a growing boy and she, in her fifties and unmarried, was set in her own ways. She left little notes for herself in shorthand all over the house (she was a secretary), and messages in English for me, mostly warnings not to touch certain foods in her refrigerator. It was tough on a growing boy, and I often succumbed to temptation.

Brendan and Ellen Galvin, 1986

Aunt Margaret was also my first encounter with censorship, since she edited anything with a suggestive cover out of my growing paperback library. If you recall the paperbacks of the fifties, you'll know this included *Lord Jim, Cat on a Hot Tin Roof,* practically anything. They simply disappeared. No explanations were given, nor did I require any. I had been an inveterate reader for as long as I can remember, and I simply replaced the missing books with others. Although I took my meals downstairs with my family, there must have been a feeling of separation and even rejection in this setup, though under the circumstances what else could have been done? We lived rent-free in Aunt Margaret's house, willed to her for her security as the unmarried daughter, and so we were in many ways under her cold thumb. But when I left home and my room was empty, I talked my parents out of letting my brother Terry, Aunt Margaret's favorite, move into it.

At the summer place in South Wellfleet this crowd-management situation was even more intense. As many as thirteen people spent weekends in that house, which had six bedrooms. There were my mother and father and their four kids, my aunt Margaret, my aunt Helen and uncle Gib, their daughter Lou and her husband Arthur, and eventually their two kids, Arthur and Noel. Where did we all sleep? This feat of proximity inevitably led to colossally petty feuds, not uncommon in Irish-American families anyway, and I believe that my defense of my privacy to this day stems in large part from the overdose of propinquity I got in those years. I am a regular avoider of crowds, not to say agoraphobic, and have learned to appreciate solitude and the pleasures of isolated work. I have recently completed a book-length monologue spoken by an early Irish monk.

In my poems, too, that loner streak runs deep. They are often about an individual consciousness encountering the natural environment as opposed to other humans. This obsession with the natural puts me beyond the pale of main currents in contemporary poetry, I realize. Many poets today tend to write, largely in the negative, about their relations with other people, and often shamelessly trash their families in their work. I might have gone confessional and abused familial relationships for the frisson of some audience, and to authenticate myself as a Modern, but from the beginning I've avoided that route. I do not see myself as a victim, and I have to regard some of the choices and errors made by my family as emblems of their human frailty, not as deliberate moves against me. If the overused word "compas-

With daughter, Anne, age fourteen

sion" means anything anymore, it means that they are forgiven for being mortals, and that we are all operating with defective, mortal equipment, and are therefore not to be abused in print. My father got up early every morning and went to work to support us, and my mother was strong on the value of an education. That's the other side of the way things were. There is no overriding reason why I had to be born, and I am happy to be here and lucky to be who I am, so I am not going to rend the nightfalls lamenting my rash concerns.

A few weeks ago, after a reading at a local library, an elderly man told me he liked my poems because the things in them were real. He could see them and feel them, he said. He turned out to be an organic farmer, and that compliment is the finest I've ever received. It is worth any number of rave reviews, because it came from someone with nothing to gain in pronouncing it, and because he is close enough to elemental things in his own life to be capable of verifying his responses. He is not concerned with the Meaning of Meaning, or Ironic Juxtaposition, or the Agon between the Me and the Not-Me. I am delight-

ed that my poems are about man's place in the natural environment, and that quite without realizing it or establishing it as a program I have been led in this direction by the poems themselves. In the late seventies, when I began to put my third collection together, I noticed that I had been writing directly about birds, or that bird imagery was prominent in many of the poems, so I called that book *Atlantic Flyway*. As with any poet who sees he has stumbled onto a good thing, I *then* began to research the habits of birds, to read up on them, beginning with the great horned owls that nested in our woods in Truro for several years. As a kid in South Wellfleet I could identify nothing more exotic than a catbird. If anyone had told me when I began writing seriously in the sixties that I'd be writing about birds a few years later, I'd have laughed them out of the room. But without realizing it I had produced a book full of poems about them. Never mind that my publisher, Paul Zimmer of the University of Georgia Press, began a running joke with me about *Atlanta Flyweights*, the best book yet written on boxing in the South.

My training as a biologist had crept in the back door of consciousness and intended to stay. In the last few years I've read numerous books by and about eighteenth-century natural historians in order to write *Wampanoag Traveler,* a book-length poem composed of letters from a mythical "pilgrim forager" named Loranzo Newcomb, a kind of Johnny Appleseed in reverse who gathers specimens of New World flora and fauna for shipment to members of the Royal Society in England. Lately I've completed *Saints in Their Ox-Hide Boat,* a book-length monologue spoken by the Irish Saint Brendan, a seagoing monk and abbot of the sixth century who may have sailed as far as America. For this I researched early Irish monastic lore, the history of sailing, especially on the North Atlantic, and Celtic mythology. Both works have allowed me to write in voices other than my own, a pleasure after twenty-five years of hearing a modern speaker in my work who purports to be me.

Research has taught me that I don't have to rely solely on what's in my own head, but that I can both expand my own knowledge—as I've said, a poem ought to teach its author as well as its reader something—and provide an authentic dimension. It's also a way of continuing to follow out in my work the things I'm interested in, rather than psyching out what a particular audience wants and writing to that group. Fully 85 percent of Americans now live in urban areas, and know very little about the environ-

With novelist George Garrett, Durham, Connecticut,
1985

ment. Recently I've noticed that even a few poets, usually those associated with the Big Apple, have been making statements to the effect that all birds are flamingoes (wrong!), or saying that if they want to know about birds they'll go not to poems but to the Bronx Zoo. I could multiply such examples, but their drift indicates that there are writers who seem not merely to be worried that there's stuff living, flying, and growing out there whose names they don't know: they seem absolutely incensed, outraged, that such beings actually exist! How can we hope to preserve the environment if even our poets, the lightning rods of the race, don't know anything about it?

I believe part of the problem is that these writers have bought into the bourgeois notion that anyone who writes about the biosphere also presses lilies in books and is of questionable masculinity. Otherwise, what can explain this attitude? Certainly it's not intelligent to think that all that green stuff out there and those flying and creeping things have nothing to do with us, and that we can forget about them in favor of concentrating on the Self and its "desires," its "gestures," and so on. As if the environment in which these cerebrations take place is mere handy backdrop (if it's acknowledged at all), similar to the landscapes in which advertising models pose, showing themselves to Nature for its edification. Several years ago I began to notice that the models in those ads were invariably using the wrong equipment. Here was this Ralph Lauren-accoutred Hunk in the surf, fishing with a spinning reel attached to a boat rod, a freshwater fly tied to the end of the line without a leader, and about a foot of monofilament dangling from the knot. To carry home whatever he would catch with this rig, he had a freshwater creel about the size of a loaf of Pepperidge Farm bread over his shoulder.

The wrong equipment for the job. I had to wonder what would happen had he really needed to survive by catching fish with such an outfit, and it struck me that metaphorically many, perhaps most, American poets now are in the same position. They know nothing about the reality of the natural world, what it takes to live in it, the rhythmic possibilities in "the life of muscles rocking smooth." So we get the imagery of Museum Chic: the sheen of dolphins is like that of "Etruscan mirrors," and from his apartment the poet telephones a friend who hikes in the mountains a lot and says, "Phil, I need a two-syllable name of a bird who lives up there. Quick!"

Robert Lowell's skunks were real. You can smell them in the poem. As with Frost, Roethke, James Wright, and James Dickey, most of the poets I read

"On Yeat's Tower, Thoor Ballylee, County Galway, Ireland," 1988

and admire even today are rooted in a locale they convey sensually. I'm thinking of Elizabeth Bishop, Richard Wilbur, Ted Hughes, Seamus Heaney, Phillip Booth, Derek Walcott, and a few others. I wish more of them were Americans, but twenty years after the first Earth Day most American poets consider the idea that there's a world out there less important than sneaking up on their own consciousnesses, as if the human mind could exist all by itself in space.

I have already said that my poems generally begin in a sketch pad, and perhaps more about my work habits is in order here after the diatribe above. I am a morning person. My friends generally know that if they call me up after 9:00 P.M. I will answer them out of one of the byways of sleep. I get up early and try to work most days of the year. The exceptions are Sundays, when I catch up on the week's news in the *New York Times* and the *Boston Globe,* and those Tuesdays and Thursdays when I teach morning classes. Some mornings I may never write a word, but simply stare at the page. If nothing else, I always try to add a few words to what's already there, and may move from page to page in the pad if nothing

happens to attract me to any particular thing-in-progress. After more than twenty-five years I know that I have to be sitting there in order to have the twenty or so good mornings each year when things really connect for me. An event I can only describe metaphorically as setting a foot on the surface of a pond, then another foot, and discovering that I'm not sinking but walking across the top of something very deep all the way to the other shore. That's what it feels like when I'm working well, and it, too, is local. It's Duck Pond in South Wellfleet, where I swam every summer day as a kid. Nobody else is around, only pines and water and the sound of surf through the trees from the ocean a mile away, and when I set foot on the opposite shore a draft of the poem is finished. Usually when things are happening on the page I find I'm doing a lot of recombining of experience, too. I take something from 1955 and set it with something invented and something I read about last week, and I'm off and running.

There's an annual cycle involved, too. I know not to worry if poems don't stir at certain times of the year. I work every day all summer long, and can accurately predict that the poem I do around Labor

Day will involve signs of the coming fall. The flowering of sickle asters on the edge of the marsh by Corn Hill Road, for instance, or the first sighting of black-and-white warblers on their way south. I have dated the arrival of exotic species in one of my birdbooks for some years now, and can nearly predict to the day when each one will arrive. Fall is a time for revising the summer's poems, so not much that's new happens until around Thanksgiving. Probably it's the shock of returning to the classroom and more human interaction than I've had all summer that slows the imaginative faculties down in autumn. Or maybe they just need time for a little rest and recreation of their own.

From mid-May until September I stay pretty close to our Cape place. I have never used it to socialize with summering writers, and a former colleague once remarked, "But you never go to the beach!" I do, of course, but not while tourists are splashing coconut oil on their flesh. I've been to a place where I know I can see a flock of black-crowned night herons coming in off the bay like a graveyard shift going home in the early morning. In fall I've been out on those flats at low tide, spotting the south-going plovers and turnstones, my car the only one in the parking lot. A few weeks ago, in April, as Ellen and I walked toward the mouth of the Pamet River with our dogs Patches and Finnbarr, the rubbery head of a harbor seal poked up. It followed us, maybe fifty feet away, swimming leisurely and disappearing from time to time, for a good half mile, interested, something in its countenance disturbingly nonanimal, maybe even superhuman.

My reclusiveness has created rather funny situations for my family. When my daughter, Anne, was younger, she and Ellen spent a lot of time on the beach for Anne's swimming lessons. After awhile, whenever Ellen mentioned her husband she found she was getting strange looks from the other mothers, since none had ever seen me and were beginning to wonder if I wasn't a figment of her imagination. Then again there are the times in July and August when I get in the car and have to think how to start it: I discover to my pleasure that I haven't been in it for more than a week.

Sometime in November I begin kicking a poem around the page, trying to nudge it in some coherent direction, all the while knowing that in six months or maybe eighteen I'll return to it and get it right in a single morning. Even though I know that, I may still continue to kick it around, since I've found that it's better to have that fragment and be teasing it out than to have nothing. When I've finished a poem there's always that moment of panic when I wonder what comes next, especially if there isn't a half-baked lump of language somewhere in the sketch pad. Generally though, there's nothing painful to me about writing. To be able to disappear outside of time into words on a sheet of paper for six hours or so is deeply pleasurable for me. I distrust the popular image of the artist as someone in the throes of agony over a work—Charlton Heston as Michelangelo—and am surprised that some poets also retail that kind of experience as their own. Maybe it impresses women, or helps poets justify to a dubious public how they spend their time? By February or so the sap is beginning to rise again, and new ideas and a few complete poems are beginning to appear as I get ready to head for Truro and a summer of writing, and so the cycle has accomplished itself more or less over the last quarter of a century.

In June of 1986 my wife, daughter, and I went to Ireland for the month, my first trip abroad. Ellen and I returned there again in 1988. I have always been leery of Irish-American chauvinism, and of Irish-Americans in general, since I am one, grew up among them, and wasn't really looking forward to spending a month among a people who might only display more intensely their worst characteristics. In my own family, for instance, talking about doing something was often confused with actually doing it. I was delighted to be proved wrong: the Irish are a warm, helpful people much more often than not, so that when you encounter the rare exception, you are quite surprised. We visited Cork and Donegal, and so had a firsthand look at ancestral terrains, climbed to hill forts like Dun Aengus on the Aran Islands and into 3500-year-old passage graves in Sligo. We lived for a week on a small island off the west coast, spent another week in the Burren in County Clare, and a day in Dublin. There I stood on the steps of Eason's Bookstore on O'Connell Street, across from Trinity College, where we'd just seen a page of the Book of Kells. Smoking a genuine Havana cigar, I watched the faces of the passing crowd for an hour or so while Ellen and Anne were in Eason's. I think I will remember that hour all my life because of the sense of a wordless eternal energy I caught from that crowd, and because those faces brought back those of my childhood and youth in Boston. My friend Jack Flavin passed about seven times, and Paddy Harrington, a grade-school classmate I had forgotten, among others. In the next few weeks this was to happen to me all over Ireland, and once, rounding a corner in Sligo town, I pulled up short and stunned even as the man approaching from the other side did the same: we had met our bearded doppelgangers.

There are seven Brendan Galvins in the Irish telephone directory, and probably more around the country, since the Irish don't go in for phones that much. The country is more complex than I had realized, I've discovered in reading about its history. I can understand better the connection between Irish writers and their landscapes, and perhaps a little more about my own affinity with mine, and why. When I went I had no intention of writing poems about the place or my ancestry, but I had the first few already in my head nearly word-for-word before I returned, and could see that I'd been given a new fascination. Reading Irish history and folkways gave me some insights into my own family, too. In the old days Irish parents didn't praise their children because they were afraid they'd be overheard by the Little People, who'd steal the best kids and leave Changelings in their places. Then there were the potato famines, especially in the last century. It wasn't wise for a mother to grow too attached to children she might have to lay in their graves. My grandmother

McLaughlin believed in the Little People, and lost her sons to childhood diseases early in this century.

Quite by accident, our first time in Ireland we spent a week in Clare, by the ruins of the medieval Cistercian abbey of Corcomroe. Objectively that ruin isn't as spectacular as Jerpoint or some of the earlier Celtic monastic sites in Kerry, but something about it kept drawing me back to hang around the place. Third try lucky, as they say, I even managed to find the well, frigid and flowing up out of a cleft in the Burren limestone among the hoofprints of a herd of cows. It was scummy with chloroplasm and I didn't drink from it. I should have chanced it though, since in my subsequent reading I discovered that the Galvins had fought for the last time as a clan there at Corcomroe, before they broke into factions and began fighting among themselves.

Although I do not regularly have face-to-face contact with other writers and poets, when I look at the mail that piles up on my desk waiting to be answered I have to admit that most of my friends are in fact writers and poets. I have been as lucky in this

Addressing graduates, upon receipt of a Guggenheim Fellowship,
Central Connecticut State University, 1988

regard as in most others, beginning with my meeting Jack Flavin in the fall of 1965, in a creative-writing class at UMass. Our heavy literary discussions usually were carried from there to Barselotti's or one of the other Amherst bars. We still get together several times a year, even though Jack has retired from throwing Rod McKuen's books into the trash at the Springfield Public Library, and has taken over the editorship of the wonderful and entirely necessary parody tabloid *Poultry, a Magazine of Voice*.

I have already mentioned Tom Reiter, with whom I've exchanged poems for twenty years, and whose generosity of attention I can never repay no matter what advice I give him about his own work. In addition, I've been lucky to have as an editor Paul Zimmer, who brought out my first four books, two at Pittsburgh and two at Georgia, and without whom it's safe to say my writing life would have been considerably different. Then there's Larry Lieberman, poetry editor at the University of Illinois Press, and one of the most original poets writing now, who quite by surprise drew *Great Blue: New and Selected Poems* out of me, gave me his best opinions on the shape of it, and saw it through to a handsome reality. Nor can I omit Martha Christina, Peter Makuck, Phil Paradis, Rick Simpson, Dorie LaRue, Richard Dillard, and Neal Bowers, whose lives and various arts I much admire, or the late Howard Moss for his many kindnesses. Murray Westinghouse must be given a nod, too—though his friendship may make a martyr of me yet—because of his unerring ability to detect nonsense.

And since angels still tread the earth, isn't it clever of one to don the disguise of George Palmer Garrett and travel among the literary spheres arranging things, introducing people who ought to know one another, sending great scrawled yellow letters and tape recordings, buying the books of friends and distributing them where they might do some good, and making everyone's ribs ache because he understands that, for the gall and heartburn of lit-biz, laughter is the quickest antidote? Without him we wouldn't know who the Bill Blass and Old Possum of American Poetry are, and we might be as career-ridden and jumpy as they are.

In Wellfleet when I was a kid I got my first look at a real writer in the person of the novelist Edwin O'Connor, Pulitzer Prize winner and author of *The Last Hurrah*, a masterpiece that has to be reckoned with in any discussion of the American political novel. Smooth, devout, clean-cut, his is the singular image of self-control I can summon from my youth. And I suspect that if I could get back there I'd find that

somewhere in my convoluted kid-thoughts was the idea that if I could become a writer I might have that self-possession, too. An impossible ideal, I know. And yet each morning when I sit down to write, on one level what I'm doing is sweeping away a lot of baggage I've lugged across the past thirty years. Old poems, not necessarily mine; all theories; literary slights, hurts, and envies—all in the effort to somehow get in touch with that innocent who picked up a pen and put two words together in a notebook down there in the back of a physiology lab. Lately, I think a lot about all the luck he's had. Here's a new poem about his journey:

Word Cells

To be creased and pressed in all
the right places, able to balance
on the thinnest bicycle I'd
ever seen, to speak in sentences
without involving my hands,
and all winter in the closed
Hotel Billingsgate to knock off
a best seller in a room
I created white and narrow
and furnished with right angles,
pure forms: strict bed and chair,
a table too small for any clutter
of doubts, barely there
myself in cold harbor light
through a wall all window,
a room like a trappist's
where I'd zero in on the page
without leaky engrossments
flapping over my head. I wanted
to be my version of you, Edwin,
to appear chosen in my sense of
self and clear isolation,
devout at Mass, reading steadily
through three meals a day
in the same booth at Winty's,
cured of my need to ride
stolen tricycles into beach party
fires. I would do it right
and with economy, never a wrong
word or dropped fork. No matter
the Mercedes you'd later buy
from a window in Hyannis,
peeling cash from a roll thick as
a register tape, and that first
glimpse of frosted hair
you introduced to Main Street
when you married into the new house
airy as heaven above the ponds.

I was hooked on the rogues gallery
from a paperback cover by then.
They stared, final and minatory
as words over the gates of Hell.
Double-bound in rubber bands
and a back pocket, chewed over,
digested, communal, that anthology
went to parties where one
or another of us could speak the sonnets
in it with eyes closed, his torso
working like a pinball maestro's
for the flash and jing of noun with verb,
a drunk's party trick, but true
down in some girl-forsaken
ventricle. Thirty years on,
after the knowledge that poetry
and pedigree almost rhyme but won't
travel far together, after
the manifestoes of men whose bow-ties
were tourniquets keeping their bodies
from their heads, and the ward-heeling
formalists, the deep imagists
pontificating on the remains of
their earthshoes, the moment I'm after
every morning I sit here among
yawking and flapping distractions
isn't in any white room: it's
a Saturday in the park when that
paperback was the heart of a game
of Who Said It? Patrolling
the lower slopes of Parnassus,
an elderly couple and their dog
point us out to the police, and with
Oscar Williams, a half-gallon
of chablis, in air spondaic

with Punks! Punks!, our word cell
heads for the subway, going
underground for another afternoon.

BIBLIOGRAPHY

Poetry:

The Narrow Land, Northeastern University Press, 1971.

The Salt Farm, Fiddlehead, 1972.

No Time for Good Reasons, University of Pittsburgh Press, 1977.

The Minutes No One Owns, University of Pittsburgh Press, 1977.

Atlantic Flyway, University of Georgia Press, 1980.

Winter Oysters, University of Georgia Press, 1983.

A Birder's Dozen, Ampersand, 1984.

Seals in the Inner Harbor, Carnegie-Mellon University Press, 1985.

Raising Irish Walls, Ampersand, 1989.

Wampanoag Traveler, Louisiana State University Press, 1989.

Great Blue: New and Selected Poems, University of Illinois Press, 1990.

Other:

Massachusetts Story (documentary filmscript), produced by Gordon Massingham, 1978.

Contributor to numerous periodicals, including *American Review, Atlantic, Harper's, Hudson Review, New Yorker, Ploughshares, Poetry, Sewanee Review,* and others.

Elizabeth Jolley

1923-

Elizabeth Jolley, about 1984

All this goes on inside me, in the vast cloisters of my memory. In it are the sky, the earth, and the sea, ready at my summons, together with everything that I have ever perceived in them by my senses. . . . In it I meet myself as well. I remember myself . . .

— St. Augustine

"You must have come to terms with your own sexuality to write about sex the way you do. Can you tell us something about this please?"

"How can someone who looks like you—I mean that lilac shawl, the spectacles, and your hair going grey—how can you, at your age, write about sex?"

"How could *you* have written the filthy scene on page 139?" *(Miss Peabody's Inheritance)*

"Have you had lesbian relationships?" but the question was in the eyes only and came out as "How many grandchildren do you have?"

Sometimes other people in an audience or at a book club answer questions for me.

The washing-up basin in our house, when I was a child, was sacred. One afternoon when my mother was out Françoise, our French governess who had a white mackintosh, took the mackintosh and a nailbrush and the washing-up basin full of hot soapy water into the garden. Until Françoise came to our house I had no idea that there were white mackintoshes. I watched Françoise kneel on the lawn beside the washing-up basin. It seemed then that I had never seen anything quite like this before. The white enamel gleamed on the bed of green. Françoise then spread out the white mackintosh on the grass and began, at once, to dip the little brush in the hot water and, with a slight swaying movement, she set about her scrubbing. She scrubbed in deliciously neat little circles on the mackintosh, a bit at a time, replenishing her tiny brush frequently with quick little dippings into the basin. As I watched I longed to take the delicate brush and have a turn at the scrubbing. It seemed then to be such a nice thing to be doing. I forgot, for a time, about the basin and how it was suddenly in the wrong place, *outside the house and on the lawn.*

My mother would be coming home quite soon. The scrubbing was taking a long time and I became anxious. I ran out to the front gate to look up the street. I did this a few times, darting back and forth, absorbed in the little spreading circles of soap but watching the street.

I did not say anything because what could I say? And then, all at once, I saw my mother coming, walking home from the bus. I ran to and fro several times from the washing-up bowl to the street and back to the washing-up bowl, not knowing whether to tell Françoise to take the bowl back to the sink as quickly as possible or whether to rush up the road to beg my mother not to be cross with Françoise. I was nine then. Ambivalence has pursued me. Indecision, the time waster and the consumer of energy—whether a child should stay in bed or be sent off to school, which dish to use to serve the boiled peas, whether to buy brown onions or white, butternut pumpkin or ironbark—the list is endless.

"Please do not be cross with Françoise . . ." I ran, breathless, up to my mother. I even carried her shopping bag for her. The result was, of course,

terrible. Françoise, weeping and leaning on my father's arm, left for the boat train that evening.

Often something prevents me from writing. There are things I would write, but when I start on one of them clear images come to mind for something else. My pen then becomes half-hearted, as if unsure, not quite certain. It is impossible to write with an uncertain or an unwilling pen. Perhaps it is because of the lace curtains which I put up to hide the walls of the new house next door. Because of this new house it is no longer possible to see my own hands reflected in the green leaves. Sometimes, when I dipped my pen in the ink, it seemed as if my own hand was reaching towards me from the thick foliage immediately outside my window. For many years, until now, I looked through this tall narrow window into the deepest green. Sometimes I caught sight of the corner of a white sheet, pegged and billowing lazily on a clothesline, fresh and damp, against this green background. I have used this image to create the character of Edwin Page in the novel *The Sugar Mother.* He is an elderly academic given to romantic thought and quotation. He is enchanted by the image of this sheet and likes to imagine that green and white were the chosen colours of the Elizabethan court. His area of study being, together with desultory wanderings, the Renaissance.

Vera, in the novel *Cabin Fever,* looking from the upstairs window in the nursing home during the first stage of labour, is amazed that a woman in a nearby garden can, in apparent tranquillity, in spite of the drama in Vera's own body, hang out her washing. Vera notices the gentle rhythm of movement between the clothes basket, the pegs, and the clothesline, a contrast to her own movements and feelings. She notices too that a white sheet folded and pegged to the line is beginning to billow slightly but it is in a leafy green place which is too damp for drying. The same image but used differently and showing different things about the characters. When using an image for a second or a third time I do not, as a rule, remember using it before. It is only after the works are finished that I see this repetition. A repetition with changes.

Perhaps the lace curtains, in spite of their pure clean whiteness and delicate pattern, both of which are attractive in themselves, make me feel shut in.

The new walls of the new building do not offer me the imaginative possibilities of a magic place close to where I am sitting. And I have lost forever the rising sun which, for years, decorated the wallpaper on the opposite wall of my room, a moving, changing pattern of light and shade every morning as the new day came up through the tremulous leaves.

It is New Year's Eve and people are at parties. Once at a party, years ago, all the husbands except mine, at midnight, kissed their wives. I felt really clumsy, not being kissed. Later I thought that these party kisses in public, after lots of wine, were rather superficial. My husband has never done the conventional thing, like putting his hand at my elbow to let me go first through a door or introducing me to people. I think this is a kind of shyness. I made up my mind to go through doors by myself and to tell people what my name was and so on. I have been nursing my husband at home now for many years. He has rheumatoid arthritis and is frail and helpless. I do not mention this in interviews or autobiographical pieces because it would be an invasion of his privacy, but I will just say one or two things here because a long illness in a household affects everyone. It affects the attitudes of other people to the household. The illness has affected my whole life. Recently I was offered respite care in a nursing home for him and I was forced to understand something about myself. Apart from his not wanting to be in a nursing home, even for a short time, I realized that, unless I had some specific travelling to do because of my work, I was absolutely unable to face the idea of having a holiday. A great big empty space seemed to lie before me. I even had dreams in which I was incredibly lonely or lost. I probably need counselling. Awful though it is, I expect it is useful for me to have had this realization. This reflection may be of use to other people. Another thing which might be of help to someone else is that often, it seems to me, it is difficult to divorce the long illness from the person who has it, so that other people, oneself included, blame the person rather than understanding it is the illness which is such a nuisance. And a nuisance most of all to the person who has it. People outside the household, not understanding, might be critical, for example, at a buffet dinner where guests are expected to help themselves. Some women, with feminist leanings, voice their disapproval at the sight of a wife carrying a plate and a glass to a husband.

There are times when I feel I lack grace. Perhaps, because of having a bit extra to do, I have lost the art of the gentle predinner drink, or sitting over a meal in a leisurely way. When people ask me how my husband is I tell them, which is nearly as bad as telling people how you are yourself when they say, "How are you!" I also have a regrettable tendency to tell other women's husbands where and how to park their cars. In addition, as if that is not enough, I read

Mother, Margarethe Knight (née Van Fehr), about 1930

in bed and at mealtimes and often sit with one or both elbows on the table. Most days I have champagne at breakfast, alone—and flat because of it being uncorked days before, and usually in a small glass jar of the kind used for the more precious kinds of jam. I have the idea that this is beneficial.

I have always thought of myself as immortal, and at the same time I am surprised to find that, up to the present, I have lived as long as I have. It seems to me that pleasure in living must come from within. There are certain thoughts and feelings and experiences which are consoling. Over the years I have tried to put these things in particular and known places in my fiction. By giving them to certain characters these consolations are kept as if in a storehouse where they can be found at any time. A sort of scattered catalogue of consolation. This does not mean that the fiction is autobiographical. It simply means that certain truths and moments of awareness are saved for recollection at some time in the future. Memory has an odd way of giving things back to us, not in any chronological sequence and often most unexpectedly.

In my novel *Foxybaby* Miss Porch goes back to her house during a time when she is resident at the school where she works. The way in which "she comes upon" her house is written from an experience I had myself once when, thinking I had forgotten to turn off the water main, I went back to the cottage where our orchard is. I did not drive back but approached from a place where the road curves back near the foot of the property. I walked across an old railway line and down into a gully, across the creek and up the slope of a neighbouring property—as if in a dream, as if in a strange country and then suddenly coming upon my own place from an unaccustomed direction. The cottage looked quite different. It seemed to sink in the grass (which comes up to the walls and the door) as if nestling there. It seemed to be closed up (which it was), but closed up in a secretive way, like an unopened flower. It seemed in its secretiveness to not want anyone to come, and it looked as if no one had been there for years. By giving something of this to

Father, Charles Wilfred Knight, 1930

Miss Porch in creating her character, I hope I was able to show her in such a way that a reader could see all round her, make a picture of her without any judgement offered from me as the writer. (I had, of course, turned off the water.)

It is only now after many years of writing that I begin to understand something of the healing power of certain times and people and places remembered. This power goes in the opposite direction too, and moments of abrasive conflict presenting the destructive side of human life are often the material for the creation of characters, situations, and dramatic incidents. Time spent in experience is never a waste of time.

Some years ago the image of a glass door covered by a lace curtain manifested itself several times, together with the idea of the possibility of peering through the edges of the curtain at the lodger in the room beyond, only his back, as he sat at the table, being visible. When I was a child we played with a little girl who lived across the road. Her father was a stoker in the steam laundry and her mother was a dressmaker. They kept chickens and a lodger. My father was a teacher and we had no lodger and no chickens. The lodger, picking his teeth and reading his newspaper, sitting with something called a cruet at his elbow, was fascinating. At home we did not have a cruet either. For years I wished we had this little collection—the cruet, so neatly held in a special stand, the salt, the pepper, and the sauce bottle. I wished too for a lodger.

An early editor removed the recurring glass door and the lace curtain so that the image would not be repeated after its first appearance. I know now that an image can be repeated often, as a phrase of music can be repeated, perhaps with slight changes of rhythm or key, or it can be written again in its original form. An example being the freshly washed white sheet moving lazily in a damp wind against a dark green background. In this repetition the style of the musician or the writer is formed.

Once when I was almost the last person to leave the beach at Bunbury, in the southwest of Western Australia, I saw the sun go down leaving only a long red line of sky far out over the water, which was rolling up as if boiling over, dark, along the deserted sands. In this turmoil of waves, where the sea was meeting the shore, some thin white fingers reached up out of the water as it ran pouring up and out over the sand before swirling back into itself. The thin white fingers grasping the froth of the wave offered me a character that evening. I did not see the person they belonged to—only the animation expressed in the hands reaching up out of the sea at dusk. The thin white fingers, gleaming as they did in the dark waters as the evening rapidly moved towards night, gave me more than a character; they presented a family and, in addition, this family's place in society and their efforts towards survival.

It has often seemed to me that the fiction writer needs to examine his own place in society before attempting to place his characters. In fiction the writer is able to present reflections from his surroundings. An example of this is Ibsen's character Gina in *The Wild Duck*. She is shown to be a character knowing her own place satisfactorily in a group of emotionally bankrupt people who have lost their way.

To add to the catalogue of consolation is to overcome certain weariness or a sense of futility in a world which contains so much human suffering, in the face of which we seem to be utterly powerless. The Mozart piano concerto which has a certain significance (perhaps mistakenly) for me can always be found now:

> "It's number eight," Daphne said, "number eight in C major, C Dur, the third movement, but it's not as you said. It's not the coming to the mistake and going back and playing over again to correct the mistake. It's not a putting right, not a fresh start— only something going on in the way it has been going. It is the actual music; in the actual music, I should say; it is the way it was written—it's even more inevitable that way."

The picture I have when I listen to this music is of the pianist flipping up his coattails and then leaning forward, with more energy, in order to go back a bit in the music before playing it over again. I gave this idea of correction, being able to correct by replaying, to Edwin Page in the novel *The Sugar Mother*. The music, the phrase from the piano concerto, becomes a metaphor for the mistake Edwin might be making in his life and the possibility of going over a part of his life again to put right the mistake. Daphne, however, corrects him, telling him that the music is not in fact repeating itself in this way. The music and the imagined correction (the metaphor) offer a parallel to events in Edwin's life.

Similarly a game of horses-and-carts parallels the displacement of the boy's aging father in the story "Two Men Running." This game of horses-and-carts was described to me over sixty years ago. I cannot explain why, at the moment when it was useful, the

memory of my father telling me about the game came to me so vividly. It was as if all those years later I could hear his voice telling how he and his sister, when they were children, had a screw-top jar full of screws and nails and nuts and bolts. They put these out on the kitchen table, which was, for their game, the street. They played, moving the screws and things up and down the table, dot dot dotty dot, up and down and to and fro on the table. The horses and carts (as they became) passed each other and turned round in the street. I gave the game to the man in the story, a flashback to *his* childhood. Some things in the story are shown through the progress of the child's game.

When my father told about this I must have been about five or six. He was making cocoa for me and for my sister. My sister, who is fourteen months younger than I am, has no recollection of his telling about the game.

The above is an indication to me that though writing is an act of the will for me, once I have written something, the act of writing unlocks more writing, and the next idea is set free. But *having* an idea is not the same as *developing* it in detail on the page. This is where persistence, the will to write, comes in.

Music can be used to show a great deal about a character. Some phrases of music belong so much to some of my characters that when I hear them it is as if I am still writing about the specific character concerned, and all kinds of details, finished with years ago, come back to me all over again.

When a certain kind of person listens to music a change takes place in their demeanour. Hester in the novel *The Well* is one of my characters shown in part through music:

> On the day of the Borden's party Hester, straight after their early breakfast, listened to Mozart. She knew from listening alone that while she listened her mouth took on a different shape, the lips drawn together and pursed. Once, seeing her music-listening mouth in the rear mirror, while she was driving home with a string quartet in the cassette player she understood the possibility that her whole body was, during the music, different. Without meaning to she knew that it was not only her lips; it was all the seriousness and tenderness which entered and set the bones of her jaw and changed the movement of her eyebrows and the tilt of her head. The first time, the first time while driving home, she had been

Madelaine, Elizabeth, and friend at Flowermead,
Sutton Coldfield, West Midlands, about 1928

taken by surprise and mostly now she did
not think of it.

Hester then remembers going to a quartet from
school and she recalls the players and "the deep
concentration which was evident in the sensitive
movement of the muscles of their faces, particularly
round the mouth." To me equally important as the
forward-going action of the novel is the dwelling in
the novel, the passages which enable a reader to look
about the landscape, to study the situation, and above
all to see all round a character. Hester is not a
particularly pleasant person. By showing her in some
detail of music it is possible that a sympathetic
attitude will be developed towards her. In my fiction I
do not want to offer judgement. When writing,
though I want and hope to avoid plodding prose, I do
not consciously, at the outset, seek to write in a
particular way. On second or third or fourth rewriting I may see what I have done and perhaps will
heighten the effect in some way. Fiction is usually a
reflection from ordinary human life, but a part of the

art of writing is this heightening. On the whole I do
not stop and consider these things except on an
occasion like this when I am actually writing about
writing. Apart from trying to avoid plodding, I do
record in my fiction some things which have special
meaning for me so that they will be in known places
for future reference when I might need the consolation of memories. These include things like the little
roundabout of painted horses which used to be on the
foreshore of the Swan River at Crawley, here in
Western Australia; and a shop in Claremont, quite
near where I live, where it used to be possible to sit on
a broken chair up against the varnished wood of the
counter and keep in touch with countless neighbours:

> The shop was still an emporium, it belonged
> to a time which had gone by. Bolts of cloth
> were on a wide shelf next to cups and dishes
> and a glass case of faded haberdash-
> ery. . . . Sacks of wheat and laying pellets
> stood on the floor next to a modern biscuit
> stand. It was possible to buy an incinerator
> and a birthday card and a pair of stockings
> without moving an inch. You could buy
> kerosene and candles and icing sugar and a
> box of chocolates all in the same breath,
> though chocolates were not a wise choice in
> the hot weather. . . .

These things are in, forever, the short story "A
Hedge of Rosemary" and the little novel *The Newspaper of Claremont Street*, respectively. Both were written
during that strange time of impact shortly after
coming to a new country.

Having only recently written the novel *Cabin
Fever*, I am unable to explain my reason for keeping
the character of Oliver George deliberately, it seems,
vague. I made him from details of his age, expressed
with some horror by Vera's mother, from his white
hair, his russet pullover, his innocent pleasure at
sending flowers to Vera, a certain understood devo-
tion to his elder sister Eleanor, fifteen years his
senior, his narrow single bed which, he explains, he
has always had—and then once more the use of
music. He explains to Vera, before they really know
each other, that he is susceptible to music, which
seems to contain an everlasting youth. He says too
that he responds to music and feels he should not
simply pass on this response to her. He says to her
that she can escape from his room if she wants to. But
Vera does not want to escape. She shamelessly asks
him to make love to her a second time and then a
little later considers her own response:

Somehow it is, just then, as if the remembered reddish colour of his pullover is blending with the glowing floor boards and the cherry wood furniture of the attic bedroom, and I wonder why I should, during the wild sweet moments, consider this woollen garment and the attic chair, the woodwork of the wash stand and the floor boards.

Before this Vera has worked swiftly in sensing Mr. George's susceptibility, and talks about her own feelings over the cello in connection with Staff Nurse Ramsden, an object of her admiration, earlier:

Mr. George is so nice, without meaning to, I go on talking and tell him about Ramsden, Staff Nurse Ramsden, and how I wanted once to tell her about the downward thrust of the cello and about the perfection in the way the other instruments come up to meet the cello. I tell him that I did not feel able to tell her that I thought someone had measured the movements of the notes controlling carefully the going down and the coming up in order to produce this exquisite mixture.

727 Chester Road

I don't, as a rule, write an autobiographical note, but for some reason I remember something which, in reality, came to my mind some time ago, and I gave the two remembered things to two of my characters. I did not try then to write out the actual memory as I am about to do now.

Perhaps my mother was in hospital, or something, but I remember staying with an aunt and uncle who were not really Aunt and Uncle, they were just called that. I was about six. 727 Chester Road was a tall narrow house in a terrace. On the wall by the front door was a brass plate bearing my aunt's name and the qualification which I read as Must Be Singing. I realize now it was an abbreviation for a degree in music with singing attached.

Aunty Mary played something called *Gopak* by Mussorgsky for me on the piano. It seemed to me then, as it does now, to be very special, this having the piano played especially for me. I mean, my being the only person in the room and the piano player turning to me and smiling while she played. Not smiling only with her lips, smiling and smiling with her eyes and

with her shoulders and with her hands. She said the music was a sort of little dance.

Later in the upstairs attic room where the piano was we sat together high up in the window and played a game. Trams did not go along Chester Road but they must have crossed the end of the street, because I remember I liked hearing the grind and screech of the nearby trams and the sound of clocks chiming somewhere through the subdued steady roar of the city. The game we played was invented by Aunty Mary. She took one direction along the road and I took the other, and with pencil and paper (I was very fond of pencils) we counted the cars and lorries and bicycles each from our chosen direction. After a certain time the one with the most traffic on their side won the game. I liked this very much.

I have given the piano playing to Staff Nurse Ramsden in the novel *My Father's Moon,* and the game to Emily Vales and Little Lewis in the radio play and story "Little Lewis Has Had a Lovely Sleep." I hope that by doing this I have been able to show more things about the characters.

Here is the little passage as it is in *My Father's Moon.* The main character is nursing during the war. She has not been at the hospital very long; she is uneasy, it being her first night as Night Runner. She has to prepare the meal for the night staff in the hospital:

This first night it takes me a long time to clear up in the little pantry. When at last I am finished Night Sister Bean sends me to relieve on Bottom Ward. There is a spinal operation in the theatre recovery room just now, she says, and a spare nurse will be needed when the patient comes back to the ward.

On my way to Bottom Ward I wish I could be working with Staff Nurse Ramsden.

"I will play something for you," she said to me once when I was alone and filled with tears in the bleak, unused room which is the nurses' sitting room. She ran her fingers up and down the piano keys. "This is Mussorgsky," she said, "it's called *Gopak,* a kind of little dance," she explained. She played and turned her head towards me nodding and smiling, "do you like this?" she asked, her eyes smiling. It is not everyone who has had Mussorgsky played for them; the thought gives me courage as I hurry along the unlit passage to the ward.

There is a circle of light from the uncurtained windows of the office in the middle of the ward. I can see a devout head bent over the desk in the office. I feel I am looking at an Angel of mercy who is sitting quietly there ready to minister to the helpless patients . . .

The game, Aunty Mary's game comes into the story of Little Lewis, first as a game between Little Lewis and the babysitter and later on as a sinister game of chance between the babysitter and a kidnapper.

My early childhood was contained in my mother's hats. I waited once for my mother to come to fetch me from hospital. I sat high up, pressed close to a tall window looking down to the street below. In all the movement down there I could not see my mother's white hat. My head was wrapped in bandages. She said she would wear the white hat.

"What are these stalks of dry grass here for?" I asked the nurse. She said there wasn't any grass. What I thought was grass, she said, was only the frayed edges of the bandage. I was bandaged because of a mastoid operation. The white hat had a wide soft brim. There was another one, a navy blue velour trimmed with black grosgrain that deepened the shadows round her eyes. It made her face fragile and increased her paleness. I thought she was sad when she wore this hat. There was too a small round hat, light-coloured, a colour as of peaches, and the colour was wrapped in silk softly round the hat. A small veil of dark spotted gauze went with this hat. My mother's eyes shone in the spiderweb of the veil as if they were pleased to be caught there.

When she came that day to fetch me from the hospital she had a new hat. It was a circle of fur all round her head, low, just above her eyes. Her eyes were bright with laughter and tenderness and I tried to melt into her perfume. I was five then.

My mother was an exile because of her marriage. Her homesickness lasted throughout her life. It was a longing for Vienna as it was, not for the Vienna it had become. Her father had been a General in the Imperial Army and he belonged to the great number of people whose reason for existence disappeared with the Emperor.

My father's exile came about because of his beliefs and his ideals. He was a pacifist, and suffered brutal imprisonment in the First World War because he refused to fight. He was disowned by his father because of this (in public, in front of shocked neighbours). He did not help matters by going to Vienna with the Quaker Famine Relief and then bringing back a wife with aristocratic pretensions from the enemy country.

I experienced the migrant's sense of exile in a vicarious way before having the experience myself. I have always been on the edge, in a sense—growing

Elizabeth Jolley (back row, center) with classmates, Sibford School (Quaker boarding school)

up in a German-speaking household in a neighbour-hood, and at a time, where foreigners were regarded with a mixture of curiosity and hostility, being sent to a Quaker boarding school and not being a Quaker by birthright. Then there was the nursing training alongside girls from "good" families, whose mothers kept maids—"county families" in England, where twin-sets and pearls were not just a joke.

Perhaps the adverse, or seemingly adverse, experience can produce an advantage. The person concerned can make for himself the herb of self-heal, as Kenneth Graham (the author of *The Wind in the Willows*) calls it in his autobiography.

It would seem that all writers draw heavily on their early experience but in different ways. It would be interesting to know to what extent migration causes people to look back to events and customs in childhood. Tolstoy, Wordsworth, and Traherne are examples of writers who recall and use childhood experience; Gorky and Dickens too (though one might imagine that both Gorky and Dickens would have obliterated all memory of their childhood). None of these writers migrated to another country.

Nymphomaniacs and murderers, perplexed housewives, greedy spoiled children, unfaithful husbands, and angry maiden aunts inhabited our dolls' houses. Joan, a cleaning lady with loose pink legs too big to fit in any bed, sat all night on a wooden kitchen chair and later rattled her celluloid flesh and bones as she took to the stairs with a dustpan and brush, her energy mounting as she entered the day with gossip. My sister and I played with dolls' houses for many years, an endless story with characters, dialogues, situations, and incidents. When separated from the dolls' houses, that is, when travelling in buses and trains, we drew matchstick people in our drawing books and yelled their conversations across to each other. In crowded buses, being children, we had to stand. We were often at opposite ends of a bus and had then to really raise our voices.

I always thought I came from a family of no consequence and without inheritance. For years I did not understand how things stood with me, but looking back now I remember that when I was about eight years old my father invented heat and light. He wrote two textbooks for schoolchildren; the one on heat had a red cover and the one on light was blue. As for inheritance, what fool would claim, ticking the appropriate boxes on the application form for an exclusive school of nursing, a grandpa who died of blood poisoning following severe scalding from the freshly boiled kettle he was carrying when he fell in his last epileptic fit? Then there was the other

grandpa, who must have owned a disease which, though not acute for himself, destroyed my mother's mother and, subsequently, three stepmothers. (My mother grew up in a convent.) Aunt Maud and a mysterious cousin called Dorothy were talked about in whispers. Both were said to be mad. Who would acknowledge, with irresponsible ticks, the grandfathers, the aunt, the cousin?

Perhaps I was "born like it," as people seem to be, from the cradle—swimmers, actresses, excellent cooks, good at sums, able to draw umbrellas, dogs, and horses . . . I loved pencils and empty pages and had my wrist slapped in Mixed Infants for covering, in five minutes, all the clean pages of a new exercise book with the dots and curves which I took to be writing, before any of us had been shown how and where to make the first pothook.

I have always wanted to write things down, and I never used the box camera Aunty Daisy gave me one Christmas. My mother said I never used it because Aunty Daisy borrowed it back every summer—but I knew differently.

When I was a child I listened to the concerned voices of my mother and my father and their visitors, and especially to the voices of my grandfather, grandmother, and aunt (on my father's side). It was a household of two languages, German and English. Two languages are a disadvantage when it comes to starting school.

During the 1920s many people were out of work and were very poor. The coal miners had their strikes and the Hunger March to London stretched, it seemed, the length of Britain. My father, as a teacher, always had work. In 1929 my parents took in a miner's child. It was meant as an act of kindness. . . . I remember my mother trying to spoon a boiled egg into the little girl's mouth, which was square with crying. My mother tried to push a toffee in with the spoonful of egg but it was no use, the whole lot fell out.

"She's never had an egg before," my grand-mother said. "Give her a piece." The little girl was six, like me, and I could not imagine then how anyone could be six and not know how to eat an egg.

In the late 1930s and later, when Neville Chamberlain's Britain was at war with Hitler, all kinds of people had work—in food offices, in munitions, and in replacing conscripts and those who enlisted.

I was born in 1923 at Gravelly Hill, near Birmingham, England. My parents moved house several times but always we lived within bicycling distance (about four miles) of the Central School for Boys in Bilston, where my father felt he should teach.

In my life with my husband I have had wider moves. He was Librarian at Selly Oak Colleges Library, Birmingham, and then at the Royal College of Physicians in Edinburgh; Deputy Librarian at the University of Glasgow; and finally Librarian at the University of Western Australia.

I have worked at several things besides nursing. I failed in real estate and door-to-door selling (cosmetics and bath salts in plastic urns); I was good at being a Flying Domestic (cleaning houses). And I have been a tutor in the School of Communication and Cultural Studies at Curtin University of Technology (formerly the Western Australian Institute of Technology) for several years. I love my work with the students there. I have been involved too with Arts Access of the Fremantle Arts Centre. This gives me the opportunity to drive into the remote areas of Western Australia, especially the wheat belt, where I conduct drama, literature, and creative-writing workshops.

W e liked our dresses very much. They were blue with little white spots. They were made by our mother's dressmaker. We called them our spotted frocks.

"What pretty dresses," a woman at the shops said, "and matching too. Are you twins?" she asked.

"Our frocks are from Mr. Berrington," I said, "and yes, we are twins," I told her. "I'm ten and she's nine."

It did not seem at all strange then that Mr. Berrington provided new dresses for us . . .

In the long summer of 1938 Mr. Berrington took me and my mother to Europe. I was supposed to be improving my German and my mother was pretending to be finding a suitable place in which I should study music, an ambition she retained even after the war started and even when she knew I could not sing and that after ten years of laborious piano lessons, I had made only the slightest progress.

The following year, on the day war was declared, when we heard Mr. Chamberlain's voice on the wireless say, "Britain is at war with Germany," my father wept. Knowing the suffering brought about by the Great War he could not believe that there would be another one.

"Is Mr. Berrington coming?" I asked my mother while my father was praying in the front room. "Yes," she said, "of course he's coming to lunch as usual." A sense of safety and relief came over me. It was the feeling that, in the familiar shape of Mr.

Nursing at St. Nicholas and St. Martin Orthopaedic Hospital, Surrey, 1940

Berrington, everything was to be "as usual." I have never forgotten this. I was sixteen then.

No one would have guessed Mr. Berrington's occupation from his quiet and ordinary appearance. He came from a long-established professional family. A barrister and a King's Counsel, he was chairman of many legal committees and was on the boards of a number of charities. He played bridge and tennis every week, belonging to exclusive clubs of both. He was my mother's Friend. Both Mr. Berrington and my father loved my mother. And both learned and spoke German.

For as long as I can remember Mr. Berrington came for Sunday lunch. My father and Mr. Berrington exchanged the texts of the sermons at their respective churches during the first course and discussed the weather forecast while the pudding was served.

Mr. Berrington was remarkably generous. I understand now, but did not then, that his generosity enabled my mother to reestablish her own good taste, which she had suppressed in order to fit in with the dreary surroundings in which she found herself. She had her own dressmaker and Mr. Berrington gave the impression, without actually saying anything, that he liked to see her in good quality clothes. I do not know if my father minded. I never heard him make a critical remark. He often paid my mother compliments, perhaps putting into words the things Mr. Berrington did not say. It was some time before I came to the conclusion that Mr. Berrington did admire and praise her but, of course, only when other people were not there.

That summer of 1938, in the luxury of expensive hotels and seeing for myself things only heard about before—like the miracle of the confluence, the apparently inexplicable appearance of the brown water of the river Main meeting and flowing with the blue waters of the Rhine, that unbelievable division actually in the water—seems now to have marked the end of my childhood. I began to understand then that our household, because of having Mr. Berrington, was different from other households.

School

Our headmaster often said he knew which boys and girls would hand in their *Golden Treasury of the Bible* (two volumes) on leaving school and which boys and girls would keep them as a spiritual guide for the rest of their lives.

When I was eleven I was sent to a Quaker boarding school in a small village on the edge of the Cotswolds. Earlier, because my father, in spite of being a teacher, thought that school spoiled children's innocence, he took us away from school. We spent some partly profitable years listening to Sir Walford Davies (the returning phrase of the rondo), Commander Stephen King-Hall (parliamentary affairs), and Professor Winifred Cullis (germs in unwashed vests [singlets] and milk jugs) on the radio. Wireless Lessons, they were called. We had too a succession of governesses from France and Austria. Françoise, Gretel, and Marie. We chased them with spiders and earthworms. And, with my mother, they had *misunderstandings*. They departed in turn, leaning on my father's arm, in tears, to the railway station and the boat train.

The journey to school was always, it seemed, at dusk. My father always came to the station. I remember the afternoons seemed dark before four o'clock. The melancholy railway crawled through waterlogged meadows. Cattle, knee-deep in damp grass, raised their heads as the slow train passed. The level crossings were deserted. No one waited to wave and

curtains of drab colours were pulled across cottage windows.

My father seemed always to be seeing me off at bus stops or railway stations. He paced up and down pavements or platforms to keep warm. My memory is of his white face, his arm raised in farewell, and his body getting smaller and smaller as the distance between us increased.

The quiet autumn-berried hedgerows, the brown ploughed fields sloping in all directions, and the rooks, unconcerned, gathering in the leafless trees made the landscape surrounding the school very different from the narrow street of small houses at home. At the end of our street was a smouldering pit-mound; the coal mine and the brickworks were close by, and we could always smell the bone-and-glue factory. I was unaccustomed to being in a class with other children. But after the bitter homesickness of the first year I liked it very much there. I still have the friends I made at school. Until their deaths recently, I corresponded regularly with my music mistress, known affectionately as the Hag, and with my English mistress, the Bug (also with affection). I think of their teaching with gratitude. I realise too that they can't have been much older than I was.

My sister came to school later. She ran away three times and was brought back from the outskirts of Banbury, eight miles away, by the Bug in her little car. One of the boys, equally unhappy, sent a piece of meat home in a letter to demonstrate the awfulness of the food. The village postmistress brought the envelope, dripping with gravy, back to school, where it was displayed at Morning Meeting. The whole school had to send their sweet allowance to a charitable institution that week. The postmistress also took responsibility for a telegram I tried to send to my father on his fiftieth birthday—but more of this later.

The village was said to be the coldest place, next to Aldershot, in England. It was a point of honour never to wear overcoats except on Sundays to Meeting. (Consequently many of us were obliged to go on wearing school overcoats for many years till they wore out.) There were three springs in the village; water bubbled and flowed cold and clear over pebbles at the side of the street. Villagers fetched their water every day. Later the springs were covered and green-painted hand pumps were placed there. Once during the mobilisation some soldiers camped by the pump immediately outside our school. Though told not to, we could not resist going out after dark into the freezing evening to stand by their fire and to exchange stories and trophies with these handsome men in their new uniforms. We took our supper, slices of dry bread, out to them. They accepted the offering with well-mannered gratefulness, though it was clear they had plenty of nice things, like baked beans, which we did not have. They wrote, in their best writing, in our autograph books: *it's a grand life if you don't weaken* and *fight the good fight but don't fight too hard.* One of them gave me a button off his coat, which I still have. I had no idea then, in spite of the ideals of pacifism, just what pain and mutilation I was to witness in the course of my work not much later on. These men were on their way then to what was to follow as a result of the war.

Because of the strong pacifist attitude, which I shared and still do share, in the school, those of us who had defied authority were subjected to the All Day punishment the next day, supervised by the music mistress, the Hag. The routine began at 7:00 a.m. with an icy strip-wash. Our free time before lunch and before tea, usually given to roller-skating, was occupied by two more of these freezing washings. Pent-up hilarity was in evidence along the row of unprivate washbasins. We were not allowed to speak. Being "on silence" all day was the chief form of punishment at the school. We developed the ability to use the "deaf-and-dumb" alphabet with an efficiency which proved useful in my work later. Other punishments for both boys and girls were cleaning windows with wet newspapers, digging weeds out of the tennis courts, and helping the headmaster's wife to make marmalade.

Because it was a small school there was always the chance to be in the school play, even if you could not learn by heart or act. And to get into the First Eleven hockey team was not impossible. We played matches at country schools and against Village Ladies. Once, in order to avoid showing gaps, we sewed our brown woollen stockings to our knickers. As we ran about the field the result was disastrous.

There is not space to elaborate on my Golden Greetings telegram to my father. The postmistress hovered with her freshly sharpened pencil and crossed out all my best words—*congratulations, venerable, half a century, jubilee, beloved*—reducing the message to *loving birthday wishes,* followed by my name. My first editor? Perhaps.

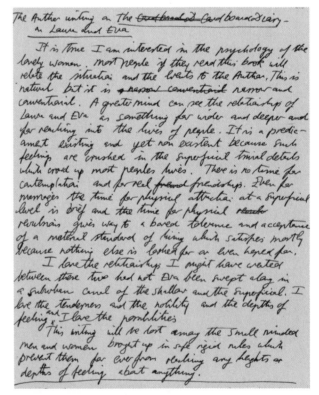

Pages from the original manuscript of Palomino, *1963*

I still have my *Golden Treasury of the Bible,* two grey nondescript books, Part I a fat book of the Old Testament and Part II, slim, the New Testament. There is a pencil drawing of Shirley Temple, or rather her ringlets, in the back of Part I. Part II has pages "The Good Samaritan" and "The Prodigal Son" marked for one of my children in 1950, so I must have looked at it *fairly* recently. . . .

Until now I had forgotten completely Shirley Temple's curls.

When the time came to leave school we all went either to work or to some further study or training. Our headmaster reminded those of us who were leaving that he wanted us to go out into the world with the deepest responsibility for standards and judgements. He wanted us, he said, to believe in the nourishment of the inner life and the loving discipline of personal relationships. He said too that we must always be concerned with the relentless search for truth. After six years of boarding school I left, an idealist, at the end of 1940.

My mother felt that nursing was vulgar in some way and my father said it was God's work. My mother said the striped material for my uniform was pillow ticking. She said she had other things in mind for me, travelling on the continent, "Europe," she said, "studying art and ancient buildings and music."

"But there's a war on," I said.

"Well, after the war."

A letter from the matron of the hospital saying that all probationers were required to bring warm underwear comforted my mother. She said the matron must be a very nice person after all.

My school trunk, in my room at the hospital before me, was a kind of betrayal. When I opened it books and shoes and clothes spilled out. Some of my pressed wildflowers had come unstuck and I put them back between the pages of the exercise book, remembering the sweet wet grass near the school where we searched for flowers. I seemed then to see clearly shining long fingers pulling stalks and holding bunches. Saxifrage, campion, vetch, ragged robin, star-of-Bethlehem, wild strawberry, and sorrel. Quickly I tidied the flowers—violet, buttercup, kingcup, cowslip, coltsfoot, wood anemone, shepherd's purse, lady's slipper, jack-in-the-pulpit, and bryony . . .

I had no idea of what could go wrong with the human body, either from birth or by illness and accident later. At the age of seventeen I had never seen a badly crippled or a really ill person. From the start—an air raid in London, to arriving at the hospital late (the stations not being marked, I missed the one I needed), to going on a ward at half past five in the afternoon, for the first time, when badly burned men from a nearby aircraft factory were being brought in—I thought I would leave the hospital straight away. But I had no idea how to get my school trunk with all my possessions away from there, so I stayed. . . .

I have used as landscape and setting my own experiences during and immediately after World War II in the two novels *My Father's Moon* and *Cabin Fever,* though I am not the character Vera. Without knowing it I suppose I banished those years, and it has taken me a long time to write these two books, about twenty years, while writing other stories and novels. On the whole I prefer to write the imagined rather than the autobiographical. I have to understand that the one cannot be written without the other. Imagination springs from the real experience.

Perhaps there is something invisible which a person is given early in life, a sort of gift, but the giver of it, not expecting any thanks, is never given them.

My father liked what he called a splendid view. He would dismount from his high bicycle and, parting the hedge, he would exclaim on the loveliness of what he could see. We would have to lean our bicycles up against a fence or a gate, scramble across the wet ditch, and peer through the rain-soaked hedge at a sodden field or a dismal hill hardly visible through the rain mist. But first something about his bicycle. This may seem irrelevant but perhaps it is necessary to say that the bicycle was enormous—twenty-eight-inch wheels and a correspondingly large frame. He collected the parts and made it himself, and once, when it was stolen, he went round the barrows and stalls in the Bullring marketplace in Birmingham and bought back all the parts as he recognized them and rebuilt it. I mention this because it shows something of the kind of man he was.

We had to ride bicycles too. When I was six I had a twenty-four-inch wheel with hand brakes, left and right, back and front respectively.

"Never use the right hand brake before you use the left," my father said. Excellent advice, of course, but my problem then was that I was not sure about my left hand and my right. The back mudguard had small holes in it for strings which were meant to keep a lady's skirt from getting caught in the spokes. I was terribly ashamed of these small holes and wished I could fill them in with thick paint or something . . .

The author at her home, Claremont, Western Australia, 1988

The reason that I mention all this is because I believe that my own love of what my father called *scenery* or a *splendid view* comes in part from the bicycle rides he insisted upon. We had to go with him. The bicycle rides through the rural edges of the Black Country in England were his relaxation and pleasure. We stopped frequently while he studied gravestones in small overgrown cemeteries and explained about lych-gates. He told us about turnpike houses and towing paths and locks, those mysterious sluice gates so powerful in altering the water levels in the canals. My own love of the quality of the air comes too, I realise, from my father, who often simply stood at the roadside enjoying what he declared was fresh air, *unbreathed air.* He marvelled at the beech trees in the fenced parklands of the wealthy. He paused before fields and meadows explaining about the rotation of crops and about fallow fields. He was inclined to make a lesson out of everything. To him health and learning were the means to a particular form of freedom, and the bicycle was the way in which to achieve these.

I developed the habit in my letters to my father of describing in detail the places where I lived and through which I journeyed. Wherever I went I was always composing, in my head, my next letter to him . . .

My mother, who loved order, cleared up her house as she moved steadily into old age. Before she died she had, in a sense, tidied up, thrown away, and burned up her household, so that nothing remains of my descriptions posted home every week during all the years.

Migration

In 1959 my husband, who was Deputy Librarian at the University of Glasgow, accepted the post of Librarian at the University of Western Australia. We made this tremendous move by ship with our three children, Sarah 13, Richard 6, and Ruth 4. We brought most of our furniture, the children's bicycles, and almost all our books, which I packed in twenty crates.

I came to Western Australia from Britain in the middle of my life. I never thought of myself as a migrant but that is what we were called. Migrants. I realise that the freshness of my observation can distort as well as illuminate. The impact of the new country does not obliterate the previous one but sharpens memory, thought, and feeling, thus providing a contrasting theme or setting.

During the initial voyage, while the ship was in the Great Bitter Lake waiting to go through the last part of the Suez Canal, I remembered, quite suddenly, my father's hands. Sorrow lay below the wide colourless expanse of water. The picture I had was of his hands cupped, as they so often were, carrying something to show, to describe, to tell about. It seems now, when I think about it all these years later, that he had come part of the way, part of the long journey as he used to come when seeing off a train, "as far as the first stop."

I thought about my father's hands on the ship that day and thought how, in that way, he was, in fact, accompanying me, and it was as if the lake offered from its secretive depths this sudden memory and that pain of homesickness for which there is no remedy.

"A Hedge of Rosemary" is the first story I wrote after arriving in Western Australia. In it there are the two contrasting landscapes, an attempt perhaps to close the enormous space between my two worlds (the journey by ship having taken just over three weeks):

When he [the old man] went out in the evening he walked straight down the middle of the road, down towards the river. The evening was oriental, with dark verandahs and curving ornamental roof tops, palm fronds and the long weeping hair of peppermint trailing, a mysterious profile . . . the moon, thinly crescent and frail, hung in the gum leaf lace . . . the magpies caressed him with their cascade of watery music . . .

On my first evening in Western Australia I went out to post a letter, a short way along the road and round a corner. I walked down the middle of the road; the evening was oriental with dark verandahs and curving ornamental roof tops. Back home again, I wrote the few lines of description and followed these immediately with a few words about the stillness and the eerie quietness. And then I wrote of my own longing for the chiming of city clocks through the comforting roar of the blast furnace and the nightly glow across the sky when the furnace was opened. Recalling the house where I had lived as a child in the

Black Country (the industrial Midlands of England), I wrote that the noise and glow from the blast furnace were like a night-light and a cradle song. I gave these memories to the old man in the story. I doubt that I would ever have written these things down if I had not come to Western Australia. On arrival in a new country, sense of place has to be established by a scrutiny of previous places in comparison with the present one.

I never thought of myself as a migrant. But migration, the travelling, the state of chosen exile, has given me the feeling of inhabiting several worlds. Though the same language is spoken here there are colloquial differences. The climate and the customs and the clothes are different. The bright light and the blue skies in Western Australia made all our clothes seem very shabby. In Scotland (where we lived before changing countries) the doors and windows along the street were kept closed winter and summer. Curtains and blinds covered the windows; these coverings were not intended to keep out the sun in Glasgow! All along Parkway, the little street of houses on campus at the University of Western Australia, there were always women and children moving forever on the grass verges, in and out of each others' gardens and in and out of each others' houses, constant visiting and exchanging of children and dishes and recipes, the doors behind the fly screens always open, winter and summer. There was a greengrocer who came to Parkway with his van; he uttered the famous words, "Whichever house you go to in this street the same woman always comes to the door."

People often ask me if moving from one country to another has affected my writing. What would you have written if you had stayed in England? is their question. My reply is that I have no idea. But what I do know is that, without being disloyal to my previous country, there are certain experiences and observations I would have missed if I had remained in England. Until I came to Western Australia I had no real conception of the importance of water and its effects in and on the earth. In a dry country, water, either the lack of it or sudden floods, can be uppermost in a person's mind. My teaching work in the remote townships and farms in the wheat belt gave me fresh insight. A farmer's wife once described the effects water has on the appearance of a paddock. Later I quickly made a note and gave this passage to my character in "Two Men Running." He is running in his imagination through the remembered landscape of his childhood:

"Grandma and Alice reading Postman Pat," *1989*

"The gravel pits, the hills, the catchment and the foxgloves in the catchment. Did you know," I ask him. "Did you know that where the water collects and runs off the rocks there are different flowers growing there? Did you know that, because of this water, a paddock can be deep purple like a plum? And then, if you think about plums, the different colours range from deep purple through to the pale pearly green of the translucent satsuma before it ripens. Because of water that's how a paddock can look from one end to the other. It's the same with people . . ."

In writing the above I was trying to show something of my character's need to recreate for himself the wholesomeness of this remembered landscape. A consolation for him, as indeed I have come to understand that the earth is consoled with the gift of water—providing it is not too much water.

The ability to make changes and to accept the differences, to be at home in the new country, depends on the development of the person in the country of origin. Exile, if forced, is intolerable for most people. Chosen exile is not easy.

Some of my fiction is based on my experience of exile during the 1930s, when my father and mother were helping refugees to escape from Central Europe. My father would go in the night to meet trains and the people stayed in our house till jobs could be found, usually living-in work—housekeeping and gardening—for people who had never, in their lives, done this sort of work. Many of the people were only part of a family. I remember nights filled with the sound of subdued weeping and the deep voice of my father consoling.

My fiction is not autobiographical but, like all fiction, it springs from moments of truth and awareness, from observation and experience. I try to develop the moment of truth with the magic of imagination. I try too to be loyal to this moment of truth and to the landscape of my own region or the specific region in which the novel or story is set. I have always felt that the best fiction is regional. In Western Australia, in the vastness of this one-third of the whole continent, there are a variety of regions from the seacoast through to the deserts, which separate us from the rest of Australia (port, city, suburbs, river, foreshore, sand plain, escarpment, the partly cleared semi-rural, the rural, the bush, the wheat belt, and the outback). In Western Australia we even have a few mountains. And we have rabbit- and emu-proof fences separating the outreaches of the farming land from the beginnings of the desert.

The landscape of my fiction is not to be found exactly on any map but I am faithful to the landscape and I do not make mistakes. I never have water flowing where it could never flow . . .

I never called myself "writer" till I was called "writer" from outside. For a long time rejection slips and letters poured in. 1963: ". . . I don't think any advice could be offered to the author. This does not appear to be the work of a novelist, or indeed of an imaginative writer of any kind, though it does show a limited talent . . ."

There is an enormous difference between rejection and acceptance. I would have gone on writing in the face of further rejection. The change in status from being an absolutely hopeless case or entirely unacceptable to being accepted is a strange unexpected experience.

For me my character comes before plot and incident. I have always been interested in people. My work, first nursing and now teaching, has been essential. I can never understand why anyone should give up a good job in order to write full-time. As a writer I need people very much. Having enough time for writing is always a problem because writing is time consuming. A senior fellowship from the Literature

Board of the Australia Council a few years ago helped me to buy time in all sorts of ways, for example, to teach for fewer hours a week and to have some domestic help and domestic appliances, which are time-savers.

I have developed the ability to make the quick note while shopping or doing housework. This is very useful, as I would not be able to write if simply confronted with sheets of blank paper and no ideas in my head!

I read a great deal. Reading and discussing literature with students has proved over the years to be the best way for me to study the art of writing. It is one thing to write and another to craft the writing to make it acceptable to readers. I think it is wise not to rush into publication too soon. It pays to write a number of stories or novels in order to discover themes and direction. I always rewrite a great deal. Of course the writer wants to be published. Who would want to build a bridge and have no one walk across it? It has always been my hope that ultimately my work would be published and read with understanding and enjoyment. While I am writing I do not think of a possible readership. To start with I am both writer and reader. When I come to the final draft, or what seems as if it will be a final draft, I do craft the work with a reader in mind. I would like my work to reach all kinds of people. The fiction writer can offer people something entertaining, but at the same time might be able to change a person's outlook on life or their direction, I hope towards the more positive, the more loving and optimistic.

The literary prizes are highlights in a writer's life. The writer does not write in order to win a prize. But if a book wins a prize it is a kind of measurement of success. People like to buy and read a book which has been selected for a prize. Many people do not understand that a book has to be chosen or selected in order to be published at all.

I have always felt grateful for the people who read and select the books, first for publication and then later as prizewinners.

Before being accepted (and I was unacceptable for a very long time) I had no idea of the business of publishing. From the time when a book is accepted for publication till it is on sale in a bookshop a whole lot of people are busy working on the production of that book. The writer, therefore, without actually meaning to be, or realising it, is a sort of primary producer. As a failing orchardist I rather like this idea.

It is thought that I have written a number of books in a short time. This is not the case. Because my work was rejected, and because I went on writing, a bank of material built up. I would have gone on writing in spite of the rejection slips, had they continued.

Characters can sometimes be embarrassing to the author. I do not like to be embarrassed by my characters, either by their actions or by the things they say. If there is something which seems awkward in this way I usually change it. Awkwardness suggests a change is needed.

In the first writings of the novel *Palomino* I tried to place Laura and Andrea during the deepening of their relationship and the realisation of their sensual passion for each other, in direct confrontation. I tried to create dialogue and action for them in these encounters. The result was very wooden indeed—self-conscious conversations and cliched actions, with one character sounding like a missionary from a hundred years ago and the other a rebellious schoolgirl in the 1930s. After many attempts to bring the two characters together satisfactorily (over approximately twenty years of writing) I tried internal monologue, or thought process, as it is sometimes called. The older woman reflects on the speech and actions of the younger woman in relation to her own feelings and this is followed by the thoughts and feelings of the younger woman. Each fragment carries, as heading, the name of the person whose thoughts are offered. Ultimately this seemed the best way to present the material of the novel.

I had no sooner finished writing this novel than it happened that I was to appear on a platform with another writer; we were both to address a group of postgraduate students. The first speaker got up and started off,

"The novel is dead and interior monologue is *out . . .*" I hardly heard the rest of his talk, which was a nuisance because I was supposed to follow him; all I could do was to think of my dead manuscript with its outdated style lying on the table at home ready to be posted off for submission.

It was the fashion for many years for these deaths, either of the novel or the short story, to be announced from time to time.

Miss Thorne in the novel *Miss Peabody's Inheritance* is a character who could be embarrassing because of her large size, her exuberance, her ability to be completely unself-conscious, her desire to initiate, or simply her desires and her behaviour and her use of the idiom of the eternal schoolgirl mixed with the language of an educated well-bred woman. The best way for me to get over the problem of

With grandsons Daniel, Samuel, and Matthew, "making faces!" 1988

awkwardness in the creation of this large and powerful woman and her entourage, and her habit of leaving a trail of broken beds—"It simply is not profitable to spend time wondering why hotels invest in cheap frail furniture "—across the more cultured spots in Europe, was to give her entirely to an imagined novelist, Diana Hopewell, who writes about her in a flamboyant, cliche-ridden style and, above all, in the form of letters. Writing in letters allows a great deal of freedom, repetitions, poor but vivid phrases, purple passages of description—these are all excused in this rapid and personal method of communication. I would like to write another novel in this style but the novelist is expected to come up with something fresh every time. The word novel, after all, does mean "of new kind, strange, hitherto unknown; a fictitious prose tale published as a complete book." A perfect description which must not be betrayed.

My husband once made a profound remark about my father, and it was this: that my father was never able to see the consequences of his good intentions. I suppose in many ways that remark fits me too. It is especially true about children and their

upbringing. The mother is a tower of good intention and is not able to know beforehand the results of her efforts. I think being a mother is one of the hardest tasks with which we are faced. Being a grandmother is an unexpected Blessing. I have four grandchildren: Matthew, Daniel, Samuel, and little Alice. A great many things are in existence by some force beyond us. I have only to look on a newly born lamb or a grandchild to feel humble and amazed and filled with a deep sense of reverence.

BIBLIOGRAPHY

Fiction:

Palomino, Outback Press, 1980, Persea Press, 1986.

The Newspaper of Claremont Street, Fremantle Arts Centre Press, 1981, Viking, 1988.

Mr. Scobie's Riddle, Penguin, 1983, Viking, 1984.

Miss Peabody's Inheritance, University of Queensland Press, 1983, Viking, 1984.

Milk and Honey, Fremantle Arts Centre Press, 1984, Persea Press, 1986.

Foxybaby, University of Queensland Press, 1985, Viking, 1985.

The Well, Viking, 1986.

The Sugar Mother, Fremantle Arts Centre Press, 1988, Harper, 1988.

My Father's Moon, Penguin, 1989, Harper, 1989.

Cabin Fever, Penguin, 1990.

Short story collections:

Five Acre Virgin and Other Stories (also see below), Fremantle Arts Centre Press, 1976.

The Traveling Entertainer (also see below), Fremantle Arts Centre Press, 1979.

Woman in a Lampshade, Penguin, 1983.

Stories (includes *Five Acre Virgin and Other Stories* and *The Traveling Entertainer*), Fremantle Arts Centre Press, 1984, Viking, 1988.

Radio plays, broadcast by ABC:

"Night Report," 1975.

"The Performance," 1976.

"The Shepherd on the Roof," 1977.

"The Well-bred Thief," 1977.

"Woman in a Lampshade," 1979.

"Two Men Running," 1981.

"Paper Children," 1988.

"Little Lewis Has Had a Lovely Sleep," 1988.

Also author of stories and poems broadcast by ABC and BBC, 1966–1982. Work represented in more than twenty anthologies, including *Summer Tales 2, Sandgropers, Australian New Writing, A Taste of Cockroach, The Last Crop,* and *Bill Sprocket's Land.* Contributor to periodicals, including *New Yorker* and *Grand Street.*

Several works have been translated into languages including French, German, Russian, and Spanish.

Work represented in the biographical film *The Nights Belonged to the Novelist.* Film adaptations of *Woman in a Lampshade* and *The Last Crop* are currently in progress.

Matthew Mead

1924-

TRANSLATING BOBROWSKI

Matthew Mead: "a 1970 line-drawing"

swamps and thickets of a grammar, male moon and neuter girls, from which I might never emerge. It was some hours before I again picked up the small book bound in black. Instead of a paper dust wrapper the book had a loose cover of transparent plastic which carried with it the faint suggestion of celluloid. There was no blurb. In red letters on the black ground I read: *Johannes Bobrowski Sarmatische Zeit.* The book had been published by Union Verlag in East Berlin in 1961. We were later to learn that this edition had been preceded by a shorter West German edition. I turned the pages of the book. I could understand words, I could make out some sentences. "I can't understand it," I said to my wife. I continued turning the pages. I had never actually read anything by a socialist poet who lived in a socialist country. This was the chap they were all talking about. "I can't understand it," I said to my wife. "Would it be possible to see what one poem says, in English?" She nodded. I turned back to the front of the book. I read:

Anruf

Wilna, Eiche
du—
meine Birke,
Novgorod—
einst in Wäldern aufflog
meiner Frühlinge Schrei, meiner Tage
Schritt erscholl überm Fluss.

Ach, es ist der helle
Glanz, das Sommergestirn
fortgeschenkt, am Feuer
hockt der Märchenerzähler,
die nachtlang ihm lauschten, die Jungen
zogen davon.

Einsam wird er singen:
über die Steppe
fahren Wölfe, der Jäger
fand ein gelbes Gestein, aufbrannt' es im
Mondlicht.—

In the autumn of 1962 I had married a German wife. We were living in Bad Godesberg, a small town on the river Rhine. At the age of thirty-eight I was attempting to learn German as my first foreign language. I was deep in reflexive verbs and the terrors of gender when my wife arrived home with a small book of verse brought from Leipzig by a friend who had paid a visit to East Germany. Those were the days when the German Democratic Republic was still referred to as "The Zone." The Berlin Wall was about a bitter year old. "This is the chap they are all talking about over there," said my wife. I took the book, looked at the cover, and returned to the

Heiliges schwimmt,
ein Fisch,
durch die alten Täler, die waldigen
Täler noch, der Väter
Rede tönt noch herauf:
Heiss willkommen die Fremden.
Du wirst ein Fremder sein. Bald.

Paraphrasing my wife's line by line translation, several drafts later, I wrote:

Call

Vilna, you
oak—
my birch
Novgorod—
once in the woods the cry
of my springs flew up, my days'
step sounded across the river.

O, it is the bright
glitter, the summer constellation,
given away; by the fire
squats the teller of tales,
those who listened nightlong, the young ones,
went away.

Lonely will he sing:
Across the steppe
wolves travel; the hunter
found a yellow stone,
it flared in the moonlight.—

Holiness swims,
a fish,
through the old valleys, the wooded
valleys yet, the fathers'
words still sound:
Welcome the strangers!
You will be a stranger. Soon.

I had at that time written quite a lot of verse but published little. I thought of myself as a modern poet—the word close to the thing and the written word close to the spoken word; no muck, no padding. I looked at what I had written down at my wife's dictation on this latest page. I wanted to call the poem *Invocation*. I disliked the "O" of line 8. I was uneasy about "Lonely will he sing" but changing it to "Lonely he will sing" was only a minor improvement. I wanted to write "He will sing alone" or "He alone will sing" but that would not translate the original. I wondered why wolves had to "travel" across the steppe. The scene of the poem did not seem modern,

Johannes Bobrowski

it did not seem even contemporary. But then the poem did not seem quite the kind of poem I had encountered before. I let the words "Black Mountain" drift across my mind. *Call*—and the title was Bobrowski's own suggestion—was not published until 1975 but when it appeared in *From the Rivers* changes in the first English version shewn above were few: "over" for "across" in line 7, a semicolon reduced to a comma in line 3 of the third stanza, and "What is holy" for "Holiness" in stanza four. My wife's first impression of the German text was of a "poetic" language which was at the same time most individual. She noticed the two separable verbs, *aufflog* in line 5 and *aufbrannt* in line 18, where in each case the word order made the separation of the prefix unnecessary. Not all the difficulties of translating the poems of Johannes Bobrowski had become apparent during the translation of this first poem. The adjective placed after the noun, or between two nouns to each of which the adjective might apply, the insistent genitive, and the half-secret tense were still to come but would not be long delayed.

If I was not the least suitable person to translate Bobrowski into English my qualifications for doing so were minimal. I lacked even that basic ability insisted on by the late Philip Larkin in one of his asides on the subject of translation—the ability to know a foreign language well enough to make reading poems in it worthwhile. I was myself disinclined to read translations. At that time most of the work of Ezra Pound was on my shelves but I had never found it necessary to purchase his volume *Translations*. I now know that the greatest pleasure of reading a translation is to know both languages well enough to find fault with both the translation and the original. I should not have been able to translate Bobrowski at all without the intimate assistance of my wife. I do not say that translating Bobrowski was a labour of love but it was a labour which took place in the context of love. I stopped words drifting across my mind and went to bed. The next day we turned to the next page.

When I was young and reading for the first time the first poets which I had chosen to read, a poem drenched the mind. I suppose that I read poetry then as I now read a detective story; something that could not have been a plot carried me with it without effort. At the end there are poems or parts of poems or fragments which the living mind does not forget; as if a rhythm had been established for ever. As I grew older and particularly after I had for a short time edited a little magazine, I found it more and more difficult to interest myself in reading new poetry. When my wife and I began to translate Bobrowski I had reached a dead point in my own writing. In translating Bobrowski I had to concern myself neither with poetry nor my own writing but with subject and object, verb and adjective, hidden tenses and floating pronouns. It was only after a poem had been translated that I could read it as a poem. Bobrowski is not a difficult poet but he is a poet of coinings and of unusual grammatical constructions. It was often necessary for us to start with the question: What do the words mean in German? before asking: What is the English equivalent? but sometimes, particularly in the beginning, our difficulty seemed to consist of discovering what was happening in the poem. As we began to trust the poems and to become accustomed to the poet's habits this difficulty largely disappeared and we became at ease in strange clearings and beneath high, inexpressible skies. There are, I suppose, peculiar difficulties in translating from any language into English but we learnt very early on to be wary when translating two particular words from the German. These words were *schon*—"already"

(three syllables for the price of one and the feeling that *schon* was an emphasis-word not really required in English anyway), and *schön*—"lovely" or "beautiful" (two or three syllables and the feeling that *schön* might well be an all-purpose adjective of about the weight of "nice" in English). We did try however to establish a "plot" or primary meaning in our translations. I assumed that there are no fewer types of ambiguity in German than there are in English and that those types are equally difficult to control. My theory was that if a primary meaning could be transferred from one language to another then that meaning, divested of the ambiguities which flashed about it in the original, would regain a cluster of ambiguities, although not necessarily the same cluster, in the language into which it had been translated. When we could not find a primary meaning or establish what was happening in a poem we translated the poem but omitted our version from the small pile of translations which was beginning to accumulate. The next months were months of discovery and detail.

I do not suppose that the process of two people translating a poem can be represented on a one-dimensional page. Tongue, mind, and imagination at the double, jostle each other in a common cause. The following is a simplification and the poem was *Die Jura:*

The Jura, it's a river, I know there's a footnote, waters *hart vor dem Wald*, hart vor, must be "near" make it "by," aber *zurückübersetzt* translated back would it be *vor? unterströmig* is that an adverb, the waters are *unterströmig*, nachgesetzt, placed after the subject like *sommers* two lines on, what's the equivalent for *unterströmig*, look in the dictionary, there isn't an equivalent, undercurrent, try "drifting depths" for now, here comes an archetypal fish climbing to the surface of the water with glancing fins, gleaming?, and climbing at noon, *Nur um Mittag*, only at noon, watch the only, leave it for now, gleaming, pity he doesn't say what sort of fish, must be a pike it's not afraid of the otter, well I suppose *der wilde Otter* can be called "wild," remember Wildfütterung, savage feed, *Er kehrt wieder unterm Mond, Er* is the fish (only at noon/under the moon), it's the otter that dives, plunges *im Wurzelgewirr, tief im Geflecht der Finsternis lärmt*, you go and enforce it, well it's down among the roots and the darkness seems tangled as well and a plunge would make a noise, I am looking for plausibilities:

> He returns
> under the moon. And he does not
>   hasten
> when the wild otter
> in the network of roots
> plunges deep in the tangle of
>   darkness.

In the great stillness I come to you beautiful brother of woods and hills, my god Malcolm won't think much to that, lovely brother any better, not really, the river is the poet's brother or the woods' and hills' brother, probably both, *Beerengesträuch* is going to have to be "berried bushes," where are we going now, going to pieces a bit, there's more over the page, we're on page 15, heartbeat, sudden sound of water, why not "abrupt" for a change, My boat follows your heartbeat, that's the Jura's heartbeat and we go over the page, no before that, "a green as if made of mists," *Und der Tau* And the dew, and there is a "*Graukopf*/greyhead" squatting in the bushes, painting with clammy fingers—it must be the dew—

painting with clammy fingers, sort of misting-in the other colours,

> And the dew. Greyheaded it squats
>   on the overgrown slope
> in front of the village; with clammy
>   fingers
> it paints your red, your green, the
>   strange
> blue, the silver sound.

there ought to have been a colon after "silver sound" not a full stop, *Silberlaut,* silver sound, can't make anything else of it, here we go, my god Gott, Perkun or Pikoll, I'll bet, I spotted them a bit further on, Gott a hardmouthed hyphen I suppose, oldstyle god, sacrifices still greasy, there's the god standing over/above the riverwood, wood by the river, black place of sacrifice gleaming with fat? no, god gleaming with fat, well what is happening here, take it word by word, *sah* saw *in den Wiesen* in the meadows *das rötliche Erz* the reddish ore *und die Quellen* and the springs *schossen hervor* shot out shot forth broke forth and lost his beer money, no it's genitive, the sandy tracks belong to his glance, that would be

> saw in the meadow the reddish ore;
> and the springs broke forth,
> the sandy track
> of his glance.

"A midsixties profile"

one of those miracles I hadn't heard about, you? should it be "meadows"? keep esses to a minimum, does the punctuation after "ore" really need strengthening from a comma to a semi-colon? did that note say anything else, yes, *Nemona* is the Latvian name for the river Memel, from the where to on the Memel, now this is better, this is marvellous—Who lights the late fire of the year where the stream Nemona goes, cries out with straining lungs before the falling ice? Out of open skies *offenen Himmeln stürzt es*, it falls, *aber zurückübersetzt?*, a yellow smoke travels before it, precedes it, drifting, travels, what about stream and goes, wouldn't river and flows be better:

> Who lights the late
> fires of the year, where the stream
> Nemona goes, cries out with
>   straining lungs

before the falling ice? Out of open
skies
it falls, a yellow smoke
travels before it.

Let's leave it as it is for now, we can always
revise it for the Kullekted. What kind of
falling ice anyway?

We had now committed ourselves to the long
trudge through Sarmatia without knowing where or
what Sarmatia was. We were aware that Bobrowski
had dropped more than geographical markers in the
first lines of *Call*—Vilna, Novgorod; but we were
more immediately concerned with the problems of
threading red berries on a grass-blade, plotting the
smells and scents round a log-cabin or defining a
wingbeat moon than with a view of geopolitics. The
poems began to establish a landscape of broad plains
and mighty rivers, a landscape in which the wheel was
a rarity and the Jew going by with his cart an event; or
an event in childhood. I do not propose to offer a
Mead's Tour of the poems in translation; it is no part
of a translator's job to comment on his texts. But I
often wished for a large glossary to the poems—with
maps. The poem *Vilna,* for instance, sets that city in
both time and place; or sets it adrift in both. Vilna
(Wilna) founded in the eleventh century (and one
must add Anno Domini), since 1323 (as Vilnius) the
capital of Lithuania, Russian (as Wilnjus) since 1795
but Polish (as Wilno) between 1920 and 1939, Polish,
except for a short time, just at the only time when a
modern Lithuanian state existed; Bobrowski's name
for the city, Wilna, "City of Kings," has about it a
ring of historical nonexistence or the unlikely echo of
its future as the Soviet city of Vilnius. The poem is a
lament for a past glory reaching back to the *Vorwelt*—
which we felt able to equate with the *Foretime* of
David Jones—and reaching forward an indetermi-
nate moment in time; the poet is there, the Jews are
present in some tense. Pilsudski and Dzerzhinsky
came from around here. No tractor on the plain; no
cavalry on the horizon. The poem contains a word,
Eisgang, for which we could find no English equivalent; the breaking up and drifting of the ice in spring
does not often occur on English rivers. The climate of
Bad Godesberg has been compared to a warm wet
rag, or a cold wet rag, according to the season. That
winter though there were lumps of ice floating on the
river Rhine. Sarmatia. Wherever Sarmatia was it is
also the land and the landscape which Bobrowski
experienced and appropriated in his boyhood and
reexperienced as soldier; a land of myth and history.
Our presence there, or at least mine, was blatantly, in

*Wife, Ruth Mead: "that winter there were lumps of ice
floating on the Rhine," 1962*

the derogatory Marxist sense of the word, "adventu-
ristic."

We worked quickly in those days. Handwritten
drafts were succeeded by typescripts which suffered
heavy correction. We had certainly reached part
three of *Sarmatische Zeit* with its set of poems about
other writers—Jahnn, Villon, Góngora, Günderode,
Kivi, Conrad, Dylan Thomas; some of the names
meant nothing to me—and I believe that I had
recognised the importance of two of the poems, *Lake
Ilmen 1941* and *Kaunas 1941,* as a "way in" to
Bobrowski for an English reader (that English reader
being myself), when we were overtaken in our own
fast lane—we thought at first that we had lapped
ourselves—by the publication of Bobrowski's second
book of poems, *Schattenland Ströme.* This book was
published in West Germany in 1962 and in East
Germany in 1963. Its publication made our task
much easier. It provided us with more poems to leave
out of the small collection we were beginning to think
we might make in English.

Translating verse so much resembles the writing of original verse that it may easily be mistaken by the translator for original work. There are more theories of poetic composition than there are poets but most theories seem to recognise a beginning to composition which occurs outside a poet's control if not beyond his ken, a beginning when either something is "given" or something imposes itself upon the poet who can only rid himself of the imposition by substituting a poem for that imposition. Without the imposition there can be no poem and the imposition cannot be willed. When the imposition occurs then all that follows is the process of composition from the raw state of the imposition to the finished completion of the poem. The imposition, or, alternatively, what is "given," in translation is the poem in the original language. That poem is constantly available however much interpretation it may require. The difference between writing original verse and translating is that if a poet does not write his poems no one else can do it for him whereas many translatable poems, and some untranslatable ones, attract more than one translator. A poem is evidence of the existence of a unique individual. A translation is smaller evidence of a lesser thing. Among the few people who knew my own verse in the early sixties I discerned a lack of enthusiasm about the idea of my translating Bobrowski, and less enthusiasm still at sight of the result. Who, at any time, is not wasting someone else's? Who in his own time is not wasting his own?

Schattenland Ströme (Shadowland Rivers) was similar in physical appearance to its predecessor although bound in a white linenlike substance on which the author's name and the title of the book in blue could be seen quite clearly through the sturdy plastic cover. The contents of the book appeared to increase the amount of work we should have to do if, as it now seemed, we were aiming at translating a representative selection of Bobrowski's poems into English. As I have said, the increased number of poems available for translation made selection easier. Some of the "writer" poems in the second book dealt with subjects better known to us—Else Lasker-Schüler, Nelly Sachs. There was a long *Ode auf Thomas Chatterton*. The poems about Russia in the new book appeared to offer the opportunity of supplementing those poems on the subject which we had already translated. There were again no tractors in sight. There seemed to be no attempt to break out from the guidelines which the poet had laid down for himself on earlier occasions. We continued into a hard winter both on the page and in the river-valley.

In February 1963 we wrote to Bobrowski, telling him that we had translated a large part of his first book of poems, *Sarmatische Zeit,* and some of the poems in his second volume, *Schattenland Ströme.* I introduced myself as a little-known poet. We asked him if he would care to see our translations and whether there were plans for English publication of his work. Bobrowski replied on 27 February. He said that several of his poems had been translated into English by Christopher Middleton and Michael Hamburger and that three translations by Middleton had already appeared in the *Times Literary Supplement.* Bobrowski added that he was not aware that either Middleton or Hamburger intended to translate a whole book of his verse into English. He proposed to write to them on this matter and to tell them what we were about. He added that the English rights to his poems were the property of the Deutsche Verlags-Anstalt in Stuttgart. He said that he would like to see our translations but that his English was only an "average school-English." He concluded by saying that if my wife came from Danzig then she would be better able than he to judge whether we had struck the right note. On 12 March 1963 I replied to Bobrowski's letter, saying that I knew both the original poetry and the translations of Hamburger and Middleton and that I had in the meantime read the translations of his poems which had appeared in the *Times Literary Supplement.* I said that I should be glad if the fact that my wife and I had attempted to translate his poems led to Middleton and Hamburger translating a volume of his poetry since the prospect of publication for a book by these well-known translators would be much greater than for a book translated by us and that I was perfectly agreeable to his writing to them as he proposed. I enclosed with this letter the poems which we had translated from *Sarmatische Zeit.* I added that we had encountered things in his poems, particularly certain poems in *Schattenland Ströme,* which we were not sure we had understood and that if we continued to translate we should be very grateful if we were able to seek his advice. On 10 April we heard from Bobrowski that he had been in touch with Hamburger and Middleton who welcomed the news of our undertaking and had offered to read our translations and assist in finding a publisher. In a further letter dated 17 April Bobrowski acknowledged receipt of the translations we had sent him and was able to suggest a number of amendments. The suggested alteration which we noted immediately concerned the poem *Die Jura* in which we had identified *der Graukopf,* painting with clammy fingers, as the dew. Bobrowski stated that der

Graukopf, the grey-head, was in fact a painter of his acquaintance. He asked our permission to send our manuscript to Hamburger and Middleton. On 22 April we were able to reply that, in accordance with his previous suggestion, a copy of our translations had already been despatched to Michael Hamburger.

In mid-May 1963 we received from Michael Hamburger the comments on our translations which he and Christopher Middleton had made separately and independently. The letter contained the heartening words: "Christopher Middleton agrees with me that your versions are excellent as poems, and we are entirely in favour of publication." The handwritten comments enclosed with the letter were invaluable and the assistance we received from Hamburger and Middleton was an act of extreme generosity.

Our correspondence with Bobrowski, which was conducted in German, was in the main concerned with matters of detail. The first points were raised by him in his letter dated 17 April 1963 after he had begun to examine our translations with the aid of his "average school-English" about which he seems to have been too modest. By mid-July Bobrowski had answered all our questions. I think we had by then translated sufficient poems to make a booklength selection although it was not until the spring of 1964 that such a manuscript was submitted to a well-known English publisher.

I do not think it irrelevant to record here how Bobrowski's poems found English publication. Insofar as the managing director of that publishing house dealt directly with me, I was surprised to find the "negotiations" characterised by indecision and delay. The gentleman appeared to have been told by his literary advisers that Bobrowski poems in our translation were well worth publishing. When considering a book of translations by unknown translators of poems by a little-known German poet, I should have thought that the job of the potential publisher was to estimate how much money he was likely to lose on the book, for surely no profit could be expected, and then to decide whether he was prepared to lose that amount of money. But there was no decision and at one point the very manuscript seemed to have been irretrievably lost. We were able to publish some translations in magazines but to me the delay seemed embarrassing after the optimism about book publication we may well have expressed to Bobrowski. I did not then know that he himself had waited years to publish his first book of poems. One shudders at the thought of the snags and rapids which his manuscript must have encountered in East Germany especially if the poems had to be judged in the dark of what remained of the doctrine of Socialist Realism with its whims requiring a work of art to reflect socialist reality and the socialist way of thinking, to show a positive attitude to the new reality of a collective society, and to be by its very nature and existence optimistic and an affirmation of life. The only effective form of socialism is the communism which has made Russia into a military and imperialist power. Communism is good at silencing poets. In the miserable People's Democracies of Eastern Europe the literati have had to face many difficulties but in the German Democratic Republic these difficulties were increased by the presence of an archaic antifascism which clouded the contours of Marxist-Leninism itself. Something of this same confusion seems to plague socialist theory in general but a particular instance can be found in Alan Bold's *Penguin Book of Socialist Verse* where humanistic aspirations, cries of compassion, and libertarian appeals are presented as socialist verse. Much of what is there is not even political. The poem *Report,* by which Bobrowski is represented in the anthology, is a simple description of an interrogation. The interrogators are German officers and the girl interrogated is Jewish. Poets in the West, people in the West, have only socialist theory and socialist fancy to experience on their home ground. Socialist reality eludes them. To me East Germany is a country of luxury hotels, cold churches, and two dinners a day. But it is reality for those trapped there and the divergence of that reality from socialist theory is one of the elements which has reduced Socialist Realism to half-read rules and awkward bits of barbed wire through which the occasional true poet can slip either naked or disguised as an old clothes' man. I do not think that Bobrowski's poetry reflects socialist reality and Bobrowski does not "dialecticise" in his poems although his months of indoctrination in Rostov and Taliza would have taught him how that was done. Bobrowski's poetry is at its most positive when at its most nostalgic and at its most religious. And as for optimism Bobrowski seems to have been a notable son of Melancholie's house. We must be grateful that in 1960 the escape route of publication in West Germany still existed for East German authors—at whatever risk to the individual author. The difference in attitude to art of state authorities in East and West makes little real difference. In the West one can say what one likes in verse and no one takes any notice. In the East the authorities take notice and no one hears what one wanted to say.

"Donald Carroll: a contender," 1966

I have met very few poets in my time chiefly because I have never thought the literary life worth living; and not only, perhaps, the literary life. Kindly as may be my manner and bright on the page my prose, I am a miserable sod at heart. My contacts have therefore been few. I had however met the man who in 1965 proposed to cut the hybrid knot which had been strangling English publication of Bobrowski's poetry. Donald Carroll may be less familiar as a poet than in some of the other parts he has played. But a poet, an American poet, he was; I have evidence and no doubt in the shape of his poem of some one hundred and fifty lines, *The Biography of a Hymn.* I published it in *Satis,* a little magazine. Its author, when I met him, was a very photogenic young man. There was a a brightness about him. He could have been a contender. In March 1965 he wrote to say that he was setting up in London as a literary agent and asked if there was anything he could do for me. There was and he did it and by August of that year he was proposing to publish a sixty-four-page or eighty-page selection of Bobrowski under the Donald Carroll imprint, an imprint which was to be founded for that purpose. We wrote to Bobrowski asking him to look kindly on any application Carroll might make to purchase the English rights but by the time our letter arrived the poet must have been, unbeknown to us, terminally ill. Johannes Bobrowski died on 2 Septem-

ber 1965 at the age of forty-eight. His death was an occasion for mourning in both German states and most German newspapers. He was buried in Berlin-Friedrichshagen on 7 September. The London *Times* carried an obituary. In a few short years Bobrowski had acquired a European reputation. At the time of his death the only poems which had appeared in English in our translation were those in *Peacock,* an Oxford literary magazine. There was a sense of loss. As a translator one may not necessarily get to know the man but one gets to know his words. Now there was silence. I wrote a poem in memory of Bobrowski in German on a dark evening. It was my last and first poem in German. I reprint it here:

Übersetzer an den Übersetzten

Zum Gedenken an Johannes Bobrowski

Fluss, Ebene,
Baum, im Flug
der Vogel, Benennung
und Wohnstatt, fremd
mir, Dir nie
fremd—des Kindes
Auge, Schritt
des Soldaten,
die bekannte
Schwelle.

Ich ging durch die Ebene,
langsam, sah Dein Feuer
in der Ferne.
Hab ich den Baum
schief an Deinen
Himmel gesetzt,
schwebt Dein Vogel
seltsam?
Liebe
übersetzt sich
als Liebe.
Ihr Lied in einem
fremden Land
gesungen.

Eine Luft, die tötet.

My wife helped with the grammar. Donald Carroll saw to it that the poem was published in the *Times Literary Supplement* in English and in the *Neue Zürcher Zeitung* in English and German.

Shadow Land, a selection of forty-four poems, was published in the spring of 1966 and well received. The selection was mine and designed to provide a way into Bobrowski's landscape by beginning with the poems, *Lake Ilmen 1941* and *Kaunas 1941*, both about the invasion of Russia, and following with *The Road of the Armies* with its Napoleonic parallel. A back-up of names and place-names was intended to provide opportunities for familiarisation by the reader. I do not think there was a bad review of the book. The first review that I saw was by Maurice Wiggin in a Sunday *Times* dated 3 April 1966 bought by chance for a large sum of money from the surly large lady who was then in charge of the newspaper kiosk at the Bad Godesberg railway station. The review was a neat characterisation of the book:

> *Shadow Land* is wound up in strange elemental rhythms, alive with flickering shadows of wolves, boars, badgers; flume of rivers, rustle of birch trees. A strange world indeed, a no-man's-land of longing, insecurity, fear and courage. Latvian, Russian, East German images; fire and snow; alive and kicking.

Shadow Land seems to have been widely reviewed and the review in the *Times Literary Supplement* enabled us to make several textual improvements in the second edition of the book.

In August 1966 the BBC broadcast a bilingual programme called "Poems by Johannes Bobrowski" with an introduction by Michael Hamburger. The poems in German were read by Hans Magnus Enzensberger. An edited edition of this programme with the addition of Bobrowski reading a number of his own poems was repeated at a later date. I have tapes of both programmes. I believe the BBC has erased its tapes. In 1967 there was a second edition of *Shadow Land* complete with a silver cover, a photograph of Bobrowski, an introduction by Michael Hamburger, acknowledgements to two German publishers and to the editors of several English and American magazines in which "some of these poems" were said to have appeared.

In 1964 Bobrowski had published a novel, *Levins Mühle,* which was later turned into a television play and then into an opera. It was suggested that we should translate the novel into English and we had translated the first chapter and been offered £150 to translate the rest before we decided that there were too many words in a novel. The book was eventually translated into English by Janet Cropper.

Bobrowski published two volumes of short stories in 1965, *Mäusefest und andere Erzählungen* and *Boehlendorff und andere.* We translated a number of these stories and published them in magazines but I

was rarely at ease in these translations because I could not be sure that I had found the right note. I was pleased to see, in 1970, the paperback *I Taste Bitterness* translated by Marc Linder whose American English seems at times much closer than our prose to Bobrowski's German. His translation comes close to the "story-teller" manner in which Bobrowski read some of his prose aloud. I did not attempt to publish our versions of other stories after I had seen *I Taste Bitterness.* Looking through our versions again the only story I should have liked to have published in English was "De homine publico tractatus." Bobrowski's recording of the original employed the East Prussian accent which, however wrongly, reminded me of Sir Bernard Miles and the phrase: They reckon that's the finest bit of sharpening stone in Hertfordshire. This in its turn indicated a way of putting Bobrowski's story into English even if that way was valid only for this one story.

In 1966 the volume of poems which Bobrowski had selected for publication but had not prepared for the press, *Wetterzeichen,* was published. Its cover was black. The title, to be read through the clear plastic wrapper, was blue. The poems dated from 1956 to 1965. There were poems of great simplicity in *Wetterzeichen* and poems which seemed almost mystical; poems of great weight and poems with a lightness of touch. As we translated them we were continually reminded that we were translating the poems of a dead man and that everything the dead have to say is true. It is the poet's privilege to speak from the grave. There was an oblique claim to immortality, even resurrection, in the poem *In the Empty Mirror:*

> One day: I shall bring you
> the drink again, I shall fly
> against the skies, one day: but I shall
> descend, you will hear me
> breathing, the fields will hear you
> above the wind, a white light
> will speak to you.

which struck me as eerie. I did not identify "the drink"; it could have been a love potion. There was less of Sarmatia in this posthumously published volume although aspects of that Shadow Land annexed certain poems as if by right:

> Cold. On the tip of a grass-blade
> the emptiness, white,
> reaching to the sky. But the tree
> old, there is
> a shore, mists with thin
> bones move on the river.

Darkness, who lives here
speaks with the bird's voice.
Lanterns have glided above the forests.
No breath has moved them.

I have tried not to allow this essay to deteriorate into a narrative of Bobrowski-publication in English and I cannot recall that we made any attempt to publish the poems we translated from *Wetterzeichen* until 1969 when the question of the publication of a second book of Bobrowski's poems in English arose. I do not know who raised the question; I do not suppose that I did. I have a letter from the successors to Donald Carroll refusing a second volume, I think without seeing the manuscript. I have a letter from Jonathan Cape Ltd. enquiring about the contractual position on "all of Brobowski's (sic) work." It appeared that Penguin Books had acquired the paperback rights to *Shadow Land* at the time of hardback publication. In 1970 I was told by Penguin Books that they would like to publish a selection of Bobrowski's poems together with a selection of poems by Horst Bienek, whose work we had also translated, in one volume in the Penguin Modern European Poets series. I suggested to Penguin that such a joint volume might not be wholly appropriate. Bienek was a much younger man who was later to become a best-selling novelist. I pointed out that sufficient Bobrowski poems were available in translation to fill a whole paperback volume. I gathered that it was at that time Penguin editorial policy to issue joint volumes. I was quite prepared to comply with such a policy so long as my point of view was known; I had, after all, admired Bienek's poetry enough to translate it. I was asked to provide an introduction to the volume and was able to make clear in the opening paragraph of that introduction the difference, which seemed best presented as a difference in age, between the two poets. Since this introduction is now out of print I give it here as it was then printed except that, after the first paragraph, I reprint only what I had to say about Bobrowski.

Johannes Bobrowski and Horst Bienek were both born in that East Germany which is no longer German—the territory of the German Democratic Republic is properly *Mitteldeutschland*—and both were forced by circumstance to spend important years of their lives in Russia. They share certain experiences, not least the experience of exile both east and west of their place of birth. Yet a gap of thirteen years separates them in age.

Nineteen forty-one found Bobrowski a twenty-four-year-old German soldier in Kaunas where he saw the "slavering wolves" of the SS drive the "grey processions" over a hill to death. In 1944 Bienek, on the way to school, "saw the first corpse with a placard round its neck"; it was the corpse of a German deserter. For one there is the nausea of victory, for the other the notation of defeat. Such incidents may be common enough in human history, although perhaps not lately nor so frequently among Anglo-Saxons. Their importance here is that they have become assimilated into poetry; the poet, once again, has become a witness.

There is little that is directly autobiographical in the poems of Johannes Bobrowski. His life followed the pattern of that of most Germans of his age: the short pre-war adulthood, then the war, the years as a prisoner-of-war, the return to a still shattered Germany. It is a process described most succinctly in Sabais's poem *Generation*. But there are several important facts of Bobrowski's life which should be noted here, facts which elucidate the poetry. Johannes Bobrowski was born on 9 April 1917 in Tilsit in East Prussia, and grew up, as he himself said, "on both sides of the Memel." At that time the northern shore of the river was Lithuanian, the southern shore German. The son of a German railwayman, Bobrowski spent part of his boyhood on his grandfather's farm in Lithuania, in an area where Germans, Lithuanians, Poles, Russians, and Jews—the latter forming a large proportion of the population—lived side by side. In one of his novels, set in a similar area at an earlier period of history, Bobrowski notes ironically that the Germans' names were Polish, the Poles' German. He is always a poet of the borderland where frontiers, so clearly drawn on the map, are to be seen only as guesses at some ghostlier demarcation. The accident of geography influences his work in many ways: past and present are defined by no neat division, the dead speak to the living, the living speak with the tongues of the dead, the stranger enters and is no stranger.

Bobrowski was educated in Rastenburg and Königsberg. In 1938 he moved with his parents to Berlin where he began to study the history of art; in 1939 he was conscripted into the army. Bobrowski once said that his choice of theme was something like a war-wound, and that he began to write at Lake Ilmen in 1941 about the Russian landscape, "but as a stranger, as a German." He saw with his own eyes in the Soviet Union the repetition of a process which he already knew historically, "the clash between the Teutonic Knights and the people of the East, Prussian policy in Eastern Europe." And this, he wrote, was a long story of unhappiness and guilt, "for which my people is to blame." Bobrowski was a Christian, a member of the Lutheran church, and his purpose was avowedly didactic: "to tell my countrymen what they still do not know about their eastern neighbours." What he had to say has seemed of first importance both to his countrymen and those neighbours, but for us the interest is in the way the poetry continually transcends the didactic purposes of the poet.

Most of Bobrowski's poems are set in the landscape of a part historical, part mythical, part contemporary, part imagined land—Sarmatia. The name is still to be found in the encyclopedias. It was a land known to Roman historians, a country of nomads stretching from the Vistula and the Danube to the Volga and the Caucasus, an empire founded in 400 B.C. and overthrown eight centuries later by the Goths. *Sarmatian Time* was the title of Bobrowski's first book of poems. In it the time is not that of the history books, yet the poems do not forget how ancient is the land in which they move, nor the

> Image of the hunter, conjuration,
> animal-headed,
> painted in the icy
> cave, in the rock.

It is also the time of childhood:

> When we squatted at the
> edge of the wood,
> threaded red berries
> on a grassblade; the grey Jew
> went by
> with his cart.

But it was a childhood in which "the silver rattle of fear" had already been heard and which a foreknowledge of loss may have rendered more vivid. Although time in this Sarmatia exists on a meridian of its own, it is interrupted by real events: Napoleon drives in retreat down "The Road of the Armies"; German soldiers in 1941 stare out over the waste of Lake Ilmen, aware of an immensity which can hold them for days, nights, years in a confusion of tenses, but where, after they have gone, as though they had not been there, the wolf

> Listens for the bells of winter
> Howls for the enormous
> cloud of snow.

Space too, the vast Sarmatian space, has many dimensions and nomadic journeys. We move from the definite point of Novgorod to an unnamed "Fishingport"; then, suddenly, we are again "In Transit": on the planks of a wooden railway station we meet Tolstoy, a contemporary. And "we" is an "I" and "I" is a footprint drowned by the bog's black water. We were there? Where were we?

> No one will learn where we were,
> dogs with dull eyes
> saw us run down
> past the fences, black the house
> and hilly the land round the source
> of the Volga . . .

Bobrowski's landscape is a peopled, working landscape; we meet the Jewish merchant, the fisherman, the young lovers, the peasant praising the boar which has killed a wolf. The poet is fascinated by Sarmatia and also by his fellow-artists: Conrad (a distant family connection), Chagall, and the two Jewish poetesses, Else Lasker-Schüler who died in Jerusalem, and Gertrud Kolmar who disappeared to an unknown death during the "Final Solution."

Bobrowski's involvement with the German East is well illustrated in the poem *Pruzzian Elegy*, an elegy for that forgotten people which was destroyed as a nation and almost exterminated by the Teutonic Knights. The poem, which itself makes no direct comparison with more recent happenings, must obviously be read in the context of later events and later German guilt with which Bobrowski was so concerned. What was done to the Pruzzians was done in the name of Christianity. The "Son's gallows," the cross, follows the armoured might of the conquerors. The Pruzzians left no monuments and only fragments of their language remain. This brilliant evocation of an extinct people should be set beside the poem *Dead Language* which describes how insidiously a lost tongue affects the unwilling ear. The italicised words in Pruzzian only emphasise how powerfully the dead language once contained and named everything—the door, the river, the crow, the tree. But now it opposes and menaces, in a way which it can itself no longer express, the world of the supplanter. At any moment the woods may take flight, the bird plunge from the air like a stone, and the enormous distance of the endless plain shrink to a narrow clearing in an unknown past. It was part of Bobrowski's genius to explore that past, bringing back from it "news that stays news."

Johannes Bobrowski published his first poems, which he never reprinted, in 1943 in *Das Innere Reich*, the Nazi cultural periodical. His next poems appeared ten years later in the East Berlin Communist magazine, *Sinn und Form*, then edited by Peter Huchel, to whom Bobrowski was to acknowledge an artistic debt. Bobrowski's first collection of poems was published in 1961 in West Germany. East Berlin editions and honours from each of the German-speaking countries followed. In a few short years he achieved, on his own terms, an international reputation as poet, novelist, and story-teller. He died in East Berlin on 2 September 1965, at the age of forty-eight . . .

When Bienek wrote an introduction to an edition of Bobrowski's poems, he noted how the elder poet had sought to avoid becoming "an institution for the two German literatures." He was speaking for them both. Neither of these two poets has written his poems to change the world. Their concern is for what survives the shifts of time, for what endures in the change of names.

I do not think that there is much I would wish to change in the above introduction, although there is much that might be elaborated, except for the statement: "Bobrowski's landscape is a peopled, working landscape. . . ." Bobrowski said that this was so but it seems to me now that the people stand out so vividly in the landscape because there are so few of them; and the work that is being done is preindustrial, sometimes preagricultural.

The Penguin Bobrowski/Bienek selection was published in 1971. In 1970 I had myself become a Penguin Modern Poet when a selection from my first two books of verse, *Identities and Other Poems* and *The Administration of Things*, appeared in *Penguin Modern Poets 16*.

A second instalment of Bobrowski in our translation might have been left to a much later date had it not been for Peter Jay of Anvil Press who suggested that a second book—of poems and stories or of poems only—should be published. In the event *From the Rivers* was not published until 1975. *From the Rivers* was a much quieter book than *Shadow Land* and had a beautifully restrained cover. It was a book of poems made up of some of the remaining translations from *Sarmatische Zeit*—including *Call*—and *Schattenland Ströme* and a first selection of the translations we had made from *Wetterzeichen*. Some of the latter had appeared in Michael Hamburger's bilingual anthology *East German Poetry* in 1972. *From the Rivers* was well enough received although there were fewer reviews than of *Shadow Land*. Michael Vince reviewing the book in *PN Review* made the valid point that without the help of an introduction: "It is easy to assume, for example, that 'Donelaitis' in the poem *Tolmingkehmen Village* is a pagan god, rather than an eighteenth-century Lithuanian poet. Perhaps it was felt that such confusions would not matter, and that Bobrowski's work speaks for itself. . . ." To have included a translation of Bobrowski's note on Donelaitis would have emphasised how many other proper names required explanatory notes of identification and how ill-equipped we were, in the absence of a German critical edition of the poems, to furnish such explanations. The question of allusion is difficult to deal with in the shade of the splintered tree of our knowledge, but the difficulty does not apply only to poetry. "If a man has never seen an elephant the word is obscure to him." In the wet summer of 1988 I said at a dinner table, "Confucius, as you were, Buddha said, 'When Burma is in danger, send for George Orwell,'" and someone laughed. I do not know if the laugher made the connection—France, Foch, Weygand. He had evidently recalled that Orwell had served in Burma in the Imperial Indian Police. Some know where France lies but know

Ruth Mead: ". . . many books . . . ," 1988

nothing of Foch and Weygand. Some do not know where Burma bubbles (Burma was, admittedly, in 1988 emerging from the cloud of its own mosquitoes) and some hold that Burma was once ruled by Mr. Dennis Thatcher. Some people expect a doubtful joke to follow the name, Confucius. Some people have never seen an elephant. George Orwell shot an elephant. Nevertheless Mr. Vince's point was well made and one which we noted for the future, which, as far as Bobrowski was concerned, seemed to stretch unscarred before us. I had myself become so accustomed to obscurities of reference and allusion in all things that I was not always put off by a name I did not know as long as the name could stand just as obscurely in a translation as it had stood, obscure to me, in the original. I am always prepared to assume that a poet knows what he is doing; or thinks he knows. My own verse had attracted adverse comment for its alleged vagaries of reference to people and places that I thought (and think) to be well within the boundaries of common knowledge. A number of people know a great many things, even if they are academics. There are many who do not know what to do with what they know. There are those who

attempt to explain the work by relying upon information about the man. There are those who rely on a blurb. My first book of verse was found by more than one reviewer to owe much to the influence of German verse, and to be the worse for that, when in fact almost all the poems in that first book had been written before I was able to read any German at all. There is no biography of Johannes Bobrowski. I am not myself certain that biographies of poets are necessary; the poems of any poet waste time ridding themselves of their human associations and attachments before they begin to survive, if they do survive, in their own inhuman right. We may with Tennyson thank God day and night that we know so little of Shakespeare. There is no virtue in trying to "explain" the poems by explaining the man who wrote them. And certainly the man cannot be translated. But there is a "snapshot" of Bobrowski at a Group 47 meeting in an obituary notice by Ruth Tilliger in the newspaper *Christ und Welt* for 10 September 1965 (the meeting was the literary bunfight of a now defunct organisation which in its day possessed and could confer great prestige):

It was in the Council Chamber of Aschaffenburg Town Hall in October 1960. The subsequently much-regretted monster-meeting of the Gruppe 47 had reached its lowest point when a small, thickset man took his seat in the "electric chair." He looked more like a workman, or perhaps like a peasant; round face, broad cheekbones, a bit uncouth. Unfashionable clothes, solid footwear. He was introduced as Johannes Bobrowski and hardly anyone in the auditorium, not even the know-it-alls, knew the name. Then, heavily, broadly and quite artlessly, he read aloud a group of poems—and the twenty-second meeting of the Gruppe had found its voice: a poet had been discovered!

With the publication of *From the Rivers* and after our decision not to proceed with the publication of our translations of Bobrowski's short stories it began to become apparent that we were coming to the end of our translation of his work. Bobrowski's second novel, *Litauische Claviere*, was published in 1967. In 1970 I found the eight poems which had been published in *Das Innere Reich* in 1944 reprinted in the magazine *Almanach 4 für Literatur und Theologie*. In 1978 a book of satirical epigrams *Literarisches Klima: ganz neue Xenien, doppelte Ausführung* was published. There seemed to me to be little in these that need be or could be put into English although if the early poems had been more translatable they might have been more than a curiosity in English. I was born in 1924. There have been few men of my age in Germany for over forty years. Many were killed in the war. All the boys in my wife's dancing class were killed. Only two members of Sabais's squadron survived. I did not kill anyone myself. I spent most of my war in the Far East and the loudest bang I heard was at Chinese New Year.

The suggestion for what I came to regard as a "consolidated" Bobrowski in English came from Peter Jay of Anvil Press in, I think, 1983. There were a number of poems from the volume *Wetterzeichen* still to be translated or to be put into final form and we revised the whole text of our translations as we had done for each new collection or edition, making what we believed to be improvements in detail. On this occasion we were urged to give particular attention to hyphenation. We were in this new volume presenting all that we had been able to translate of all the poems which Bobrowski himself had selected for publication. We realised that it was twenty years since we had

begun to translate Bobrowski's poems. He was dead and we were old. After some hesitation, fearing confusion, we called the book *Shadow Lands*. We added a number of notes to those provided in the original by the author. Our notes were based on a need to know, our need to know; what we had had to look up might be useful to others. The production of the volume was all that we could have wished. The Introduction by Michael Hamburger was excellent, the Index of Titles complete. I could not quite make out the photograph on the dust wrapper.

Good reviews of Bobrowski were becoming routine if never unwelcome. Reviewing *Shadow Lands* the *TLS* remarked that thanks to us Bobrowski's reputation in England was secure; that we translated poetry into genuine poetry.

Perhaps translators should be anonymous. They live in the shadow of other men and echo the meaning of other men's speech. They have nothing of their own but words. When we began to translate we did not even own a German dictionary. English/German, German/English, yes; German/German, no. The words seemed fairly sure of their meanings, to have a fussy sense of direction and, as to spelling, steel-sure. I say nothing about the German language. I am only a part-time user and I often break it. There is a German poet called Shakespeare. I imagine the dignity and assurance of the man translating from the classics for his own generation, who can rely on ages of tradition and precedent for support. Up in the moment it is more as if one were a monoglot Hungarian who, having wandered into Lord's cricket ground hoping to learn something of the game, finds himself holding a bat for the first time against the West Indies with ten to make and a match to win; or as if one's own sweaty hands were gripping an Hungarian equivalent of King Willow. Several hundred pages of verse taken from among Bobrowski's papers appeared as volume two of his *Collected Works* in 1987. Translators are not to be trusted; and death is no safeguard against betrayal. Philip Larkin's poems have recently been translated into non-rhyming German. Foreign translators! Translators have nothing but words. The poet sees the moon and writes down his word for moon. The translator does not see the moon, he sees the poet's word for moon. The translator writes down his equivalent for the poet's word for moon. And beyond all this second fiddle an age repeats itself. Too much blood, too many men, a broken generation. Bobrowski was a Lutheran Christian. How much that is worth today in terms of immortality I do not know; for the man, that is. We discern the face of the sky and the signs of the times. I do not like that stigmatum which has turned up on a sunny forehead. The poets are putting it down word by word to survive flesh and blood. The words have nothing but translators; three maidens, a paper moon, a cardboard sea. Bobrowski has been dead for more than twenty years and we too shall be dead pretty soon. There will be poems or parts of poems or fragments which the living mind does not forget; as if a rhythm had been established forever. Schöne Erde Vaterland. And the minds of dead men.

Bad Godesberg, 1988

Biographical Note

An English poet, translator, and editor living in Germany, Matthew Mead was born on September 12, 1924, in Buckinghamshire. Partially due to his desire to divorce autobiography from his poetry as much as possible, details of Mead's early life and career are scarce. He served in the British army from 1942 until 1947, including three years in India, Ceylon, and Singapore, and, although he was not involved in European combat, commentators note that Mead later expressed in his poetry a deep concern with the problems confronting European society in the era following World War II. Mead began writing poetry during the war, but it was not until 1960 that he published his first work, *A Poem in Nine Parts*, and became the editor of *Satis*, a literary journal then based in Newcastle-upon-Tyne. During its three-year existence, *Satis* was marked by a quirky, politically detached editorial policy, and offered a ready outlet for writers of experimental poetry, including a number of contemporary American poets.

In 1962 Mead moved to Bad Godesberg in the Rhine valley of West Germany with his German-born wife, Ruth. With her assistance, Mead commenced his study of the German language and the Meads subsequently began to translate poetry by East German poet and novelist Johannes Bobrowski. Their first collection, *Shadow Land: Selected Poems of Johannes Bobrowski* (1966), initiated a successful and prolific career for the Meads as translators of contemporary German poetry. During the next two decades they collaborated on additional volumes of Bobrowski's poems, as well as works by Heinz Winfried Sabais and poet, novelist, and screenwriter Horst Bienek.

The first major collection of Mead's own poetry, *Identities and Other Poems*, was published in 1967 to mixed critical reception. The concerns of *Identities*

inform much of Mead's subsequent works, often presenting ironic commentary on contemporary society and stressing especially the problem of identity for the modern poet. Other significant volumes of Mead's poetry that appeared during the 1970s include *The Administration of Things* (1970) and *The Midday Muse* (1979), the latter expressing what critics consider a heightened pessimism towards culture and politics. During the 1980s, Mead and his wife pursued further translation projects, and *A Roman in Cologne*, his latest original work, was published in 1985.

Mead has been praised for employing a variety of styles in his poetry, yet his versatility has led to critical uncertainty regarding the diffuse identity presented in his works. Juxtaposing poems of political and social concern with poems addressing more intimate subjects such as love and the conflict between flesh and spirit, Mead's poetry has been particularly lauded for a conciseness of expression and for voicing what A. Kingsley Weatherhead terms a "European consciousness." Currently residing in Bad Godesberg, Mead remains known to a relatively limited audience, yet he is esteemed as a knowledgeable translator and

Matthew Mead: "close of play," 1988

his poetry is considered to well convey the political complexities and the fragmentation of the individual in the contemporary European milieu.

—David Kmenta

BIBLIOGRAPHY

Poetry:

A Poem in Nine Parts, Migrant Press, 1960.

Identities, Migrant Press, 1964.

Kleinigkeiten, Satis Press, 1966.

Identities and Other Poems, Rapp & Carroll, 1967.

The Administration of Things, Anvil Press Poetry, 1970.

(With Harry Guest and Jack Beeching) *Penguin Modern Poets 16,* Penguin, 1970.

In the Eyes of the People, Satis Press, 1973.

Minusland, Satis Press, 1977.

The Midday Muse, Anvil Press Poetry, 1979.

A Roman in Cologne, Satis Press, 1985.

Translator of poetry with wife, Ruth Mead:

Shadow Land: Selected Poems of Johannes Bobrowski, Carroll, 1966, revised edition, Rapp and Whiting, 1967.

Heinz Winfried Sabais, *Generation,* Satis Press, 1967.

(With others) Nelly Sachs, *O the Chimneys,* Farrar, Straus, 1967, published in England as *Selected Poems of Nelly Sachs,* J. Cape, 1968.

Sabais, *Generation and Other Poems,* Anvil Press Poetry, 1968.

Max Hölzer, *Amfortiade and Other Poems,* Satis Press, 1968.

Horst Bienek, Unicorn Press, 1969.

Elisabeth Borchers, Unicorn Press, 1969.

(With Michael Hamburger) Sachs, *The Seeker and Other Poems,* Farrar, Straus, 1970.

Johannes Bobrowski and Bienek, *Selected Poems,* Penguin, 1971.

Sabais, *Mitteilungen/Communications,* Roether, 1971.

Sabais, *Socialist Elegy,* Roether, 1975.

Bobrowski, *From the Rivers,* Anvil Press Poetry, 1975.

Christa Reinig, *The Tightrope Walker,* Satis Press, 1981.

Sabais, *The People and the Stones,* Anvil Press Poetry, 1983.

Gunter Bruno Fuchs, *The Raven,* Satis Press, 1984.

Bobrowski, *Shadow Lands,* Anvil Press Poetry, 1984.

Christian Geissler, *Songs from the Old Folk's Home,* Satis Press, 1988.

Former editor of *Satis* (magazine), Edinburgh, Scotland. Contributor of translations to numerous magazines, including *Peacock, Stand, The Sixties, Quarterly Review of Literature, Transatlantic Review, Art and Literature,* and *Tracks.* Work represented in many anthologies, including *The Penguin Book of Socialist Verse, Penguin Modern European Poets, Poetry of the Committed Individual,* and *Contemporary World Poets.*

Aharon Megged

1920-

(Translated from the Hebrew by Vivian Eden)

Aharon Megged, 1989

In November 1985 I went, for the first time, to Poland, the country where my ancestors had lived for hundreds of years. One cold, grey morning I left Warsaw in a taxi for Wloçlavek, about 220 kilometres northwest of the capital, to see the house where I was born. My father and mother were no longer alive, and the exact address, 2 Piekarska Street, at the corner of Krolowicka Street, was given to me by Professor Uhrbach of Jerusalem, a member of the National Academy of Sciences, who had also lived in that same house and had learned Talmud from my grandfather.

It had snowed all night; the sky was opaque and the fields on either side of the road were white. There was little traffic, and the taxi went slowly because of the snow that had accumulated on the road. I don't know Polish, and the driver, who was accustomed to driving tourists, knew but a few words of English. Whatever I said to him, he'd answer: "No problem," so the time was passed largely in silence. We passed small villages of wooden houses that looked squashed under their straw roofs, high-gabled barns sunk to their waists in snow, solitary churches, crosses, icons of the Holy Mother, carts hitched to mules or oxen, loaded with hay . . . The sights were familiar to me: I had read *The Peasants* by the Polish writer Wladyslaw Reymont, the Nobel laureate (1924), in Hebrew translation when I was fourteen.

We had left Wloçlavek—my father, my mother, my younger brother, and I—to immigrate to Palestine when I was five years old, but pre–World War II Jewish Poland lived on within me. From books by Agnon, Frischmann, Sholem Asch, Peretz, and many others who had accompanied me since childhood, from stories told by my parents and by my grandmothers and by their friends—I knew the scenery of towns and villages very well: the markets, the synagogues, the study houses, and the Jewish quarters of Warsaw, Lodz, Cracow, and the hundred thousands of Jews who lived there, how they acted at home and in the streets. Three million Jews lived in Poland before the war, and they had a rich culture, in Yiddish and in Hebrew: schools, theatres, sports organizations, clubs, trade unions, political parties—a sort of autonomy. In Wloçlavek there were twelve thousand Jews before the war, who constituted about 20 percent of the population, and they had an extensive network of cultural institutions. My father taught in the Hebrew gymnasium.

At two in the afternoon we arrived at the town's central square, where we parked the car. The driver and I waded through snow and slush to find Piekarska Street. No one knew where it was. After about fifteen minutes we found an old woman who explained to us, ironically, that all the street names had been changed to "Socialist names" ever since "the Russian conquest," and Piekarska Street was now Stalingrad Street.

As I stood before the house, a miracle happened to me. Suddenly the memory of childhood returned: yes, yes, this is the house, a brick house surrounding a square courtyard paved in stone, and on the second floor, a wooden balcony all the way around, where I would stand holding onto the railing and look down. On a white winter day like this one—and to this day I feel shame and hurt when I remember this—I fled home from a certain Polish boy who spat at me and called me "Zhid" when I wanted to draw water from the neighborhood well.

On the first floor lived an old man of about eighty, a straight-backed man with a wide handlebar mustache. The door was opened by a woman of about thirty, full-bodied and blonde, who was his granddaughter and understood a bit of English. When I told her who I was, where I had come from, and what our name had been before we had Hebraized it, the old man said: "Ah, Greenberg. I remember. I remember your grandfather and your father. You lived

second floor right, and downstairs lived the Uhrbach family, and next door to them the Bachurskis."

Then he told me—the granddaughter translated—how the Germans had arrived in town, in September 1939, expelled the Jews from their homes, herded them into a few streets near the old market, and surrounded them with barbed wire, and how they set fire to the synagogue, and how in June 1941 they sent most of the Jews to Chelmno, which was a death camp, and how in April 1942 nothing remained of the ghetto but ashes.

I went into the apartment which the old man said had been ours, and where there now lived a young couple, and at once, like an electric shock, my eyes were struck by the sight of the wallpaper strewn with golden peacocks with long tails and beautiful plumage, the same peacocks which, every morning, as I opened my eyes, were the first to greet me, glowing before me like legends of Paradise. Near the back wall of the room stood the tall stove built of white tiles, the same stove that on cold winter days I would stroke with my hands to get warm. For a long moment I was frozen to the spot.

I wanted to meet Jews. We returned to the central square and went into the Polish Tourist Office, Orbis, and I asked whether they knew of any Jews living in the town. They didn't know, but a sympathetic clerk leafed through the telephone book, found the name Abraham Stein, and commented that he was most probably Jewish. She phoned him and said that there was someone here from Israel who would like to see him. About twenty minutes later, a Jew of about sixty arrived at the office. His face was stern and yellow, unsmiling. He spoke Yiddish, and told me that he was one of thirty Jews in the city, those who had fled eastward to Russia when the Germans arrived and thus had survived. After the war they had come back here.

"We have a club. Would you like to visit it?" We walked through a few streets and arrived at an old building. We climbed a rickety staircase to the rear wing. The "club" was a long, narrow room. In its centre stood a long, narrow table with chairs, and next to it a kitchenette with a kettle and some scruffy glasses. Mr. Stein told me that every week a few Jews get together here, drink tea, play cards, talk. Sometimes a performer comes from Warsaw to sing songs in Yiddish.

The week before I had been to Auschwitz, and two days earlier I had been to Maidanek. At the death camp in Maidanek the "blocks" still stand the way they were then, row after row of black huts, like ravens in the snow. In some of them are displays of the hair, the shoes, the hats, the eyeglasses, the suitcases of the tens of thousands of Jews who died there from hunger, from beatings, from shooting, from gas. The gas chambers with the "showers," the canisters of Zyklon B, the crematoria are all in place.

A lame dog prowls through the snow around the huts, sniffing, as if in search of something.

2

On a sunny day in April 1926 we arrived at Jaffa by ship. The sea was rough and the ship anchored at some distance from the dock. A burly Arab sailor lifted me off the deck in his arms and lowered me into the small boat that brought us into port. English officials with yellow mustaches checked our passports and Arab porters carried our trunks. They brought us to the "quarantine"—huge halls with showers—disinfection here, men in that direction, women this way, but my brother and I were sent along with my mother. The sight of the naked women—so many of them!—standing under the showers, with me walking naked between their legs, was the most exciting thing that happened to me that day, my first day in the Holy Land.

In a black coach hitched to a white horse driven by a coachman in a red tarboosh, we were taken from Jaffa to Tel Aviv. Tel Aviv was a small city then of about forty thousand inhabitants, with sand all around it. Its streets, with their white houses two or three storeys high, were open to the sea, and caravans of camels carrying sacks of gravel, bells jingling, passed by.

My aunt, my father's sister, and her husband had come to Palestine two years earlier, and lived in a basement apartment in the center of town. Both of them were working people—she was a seamstress and he was a construction worker—and they took us into their two-room apartment. The fragrance of geraniums pervaded the courtyard from the many flowerpots on the porches all around, and wafted indoors through the windows. When I went outside the following morning, the light blinded my eyes. A strong light, to which I was not accustomed, sparkled from the yellow sand, from the whitewashed walls, from the piles of gravel, from the sidewalks. The people in the streets spoke Hebrew, but it did not sound strange to me, because my father and mother had spoken Hebrew to one another back in Poland.

My father went out to look for work in the only profession he had practiced, teaching, but at the Teachers' Union they told him that his chances were slim. There was an economic crisis and unemploy-

"My parents, Leah and Moshe Megged,"
Poland, 1920

ment was rampant. Morning and evening we ate bread, olives, vegetables, and "leben"—a kind of sour milk—and for lunch my mother cooked semolina pudding and apricot soup, because apricots were very cheap. Three months after we arrived, my sister was born, and we were a family of five. What little money my parents had brought from Poland was running out. My father went to the labor exchange and was given work two days a week paving the road that was the extension of the city's main street. He borrowed khaki clothes and work shoes from my uncle, and for eight hours he would push wheelbarrows full of sand on a track of boards that led from the seashore, in the hot summer sun. When he came home in the evenings, his eyes were extinguished, and his hands, which were unaccustomed to physical labor, were swollen and blistered. He did not complain. The Land of Israel is redeemed through suffering, he said.

One day my father disappeared from the house—we, the children, were not told where he had gone—and came home only ten days later. When he came in, we saw his eyes were alight. He told us that he had wandered the length of the country—on foot, in carts, hitchhiking, because he hadn't any money for fares—and had gone as far as Kfar Gil'adi on the Lebanese border in order to find out whether a teacher was needed anywhere. "And I've found a job!" he kissed us. "I've found a job!"

The post he had found was in a small "moshavah"—agricultural village—called Ra'anana about fifteen kilometres northeast of Tel Aviv. They were about to open a school there, and he would be its first teacher.

We lived in Tel Aviv for six months, and during that time I became a complete "sabra." I spoke Hebrew like all the children I played with, and Polish was completely forgotten, as if an angel had touched me on the nose to make that language fly away from me. I got used to going barefoot, in short pants, without a shirt or undershirt.

3

Old Ra'anana was a single, long street of sand, on either side of which, at a generous distance from one another, were planted about thirty small houses and cabins, and behind them were cow barns and chicken coops. All around were fallow fields, young citrus groves, and eucalyptus copses. On the hills to the south the black tents of the bedouin tribe of Abu-Kishek were pitched, and to the north was a small Arab village of clay houses surrounded by sabras—prickly pear cactus—and fig trees.

The truck which brought stock to the grocery store brought us to the village and unloaded our few possessions onto the sand. My mother carried my baby sister in her arms. When we entered the cabin we had been allotted, and my mother saw the dirt floor, the cracked walls, and the roaches skittering from corner to corner—she came outside, sat down on the bed, and crying bitterly she announced that she was not going to live here.

My mother, Leah, was tempestuous by nature, and impulsive, and very often when she hated something or someone, she would let loose with hard words. My father was a temperate and patient man, and his motto was "This, too, is for the best." With soft words he soothed my mother, until she went inside again and began to scrub the walls with kerosene, against the bugs.

The "school" was just a single room, in the cabin next to ours, with one table and some chairs. My father taught all subjects to a dozen pupils there, six to twelve years old. My mother, who also had

teaching experience, taught them singing and handicrafts, and prepared plays with them for holidays and festivals. On Saturdays, she would take the children out to the eucalyptus copse, spread a tablecloth on the soft grass, set out cookies she had baked, and she and my father would tell stories, or read something that had a moral.

Beyond our yard stood a long cabin with two wings. One wing was the synagogue, and in the other lived ten young men and women, a commune of pioneers who worked in the village citrus groves. In the mornings, when I woke up, and the rays of the sun which came in through the cracks cast stripes of gold on the walls, I would hear the chanting of men at their morning prayers like the whisper of the wind in a forest, and at night, before I fell asleep, I would hear the singing, and the playing of the accordion and the harmonica, and the stamping of the dancing feet of the happy young pioneers. When I grew up—and this memory has always accompanied me—I said to myself: this was the Land of Israel for me—the blending of ancient tradition and youthful, rebellious spirit that aspired to build a new society.

We bought a nanny goat in the Arab village, but after a few days we discovered she was a billy goat, and we exchanged him for a cow. We planted vegetables in the plot of land behind the cabin, and we raised chickens. We lived in poverty, but to me this world to which I had been brought was a wonderland of many enchantments. In the morning the village cowherd made his way down the road and, with his flute, led the cows from all the courtyards to the meadow. At night the jackals' howls could be heard all around as they approached the chicken coops, until the barking of the dogs silenced them. And in the daytime, after school, I could run barefoot through the fields strewn with wildflowers, thistles, and bushes and reach the tents of the bedouin or the eucalyptus copse, which to me looked like a forest. It had in its center a pool of rainwater in which rafts could be floated. Arab peddlers riding donkeys brought juicy figs, bunches of fresh peppermint, eggplants, eggs nestled in straw, colorful textiles from Damascus, Isfahan.

Bit by bit, the village grew and expanded. The main road was paved, and side streets branched out from it. In the centre, a "People's House" was built, which was intended to serve all the civic needs of the inhabitants, and four of its rooms were allotted to the school. The number of pupils increased to several dozen and the number of teachers to four; birds would fly under the roof of our classrooms and leave their droppings on the Bible open before us, between Joseph and Potiphar's wife.

I read books from the moment I learned to read. I would pull a book off the shelves in the living room, sit on the floor, set the book on my knees, and sink into reading. Thus I read nearly all the books in my parents' small library, whether or not I understood them: poems by Bialik and Tchernichovsky, stories by Tolstoy and Turgenev, Herbert Spencer's principles, Nietzsche's *Thus Spake Zarathustra* in Frischmann's excellent translation, a biography of Spinoza . . . In addition, my father took care to broaden my Jewish education. My parents were not religious people, and back in Poland they had rebelled against their parents, who had been very pious. However, they respected tradition, the ceremonies of the Sabbath and the holidays, and my father, who saw religious literature as part of Jewish historical culture, decided that his sons had to learn Talmud. Every Saturday afternoon he would sit me and my brother down at the table, with a volume of Talmud opened before us, and while outside all our friends were playing football, we had to recite verses in Aramaic, with tears in our eyes.

My "literary" writing began with my first love, when I was eleven years old. Esther—who died of tuberculosis five years later—came to us with her family from the big, mysterious city of Jerusalem, which I had not yet seen for myself, and this alone was enough to endow her with a sort of halo around her head. She had grey eyes, the color of a winter sky with white seagulls flying in it, and her lips were thin and pale. Her carriage was upright and proud, and she was the best pupil in the school, beloved of all the teachers.

Two years, day and night, this burning love tormented me. With all my might I tried to attract her attention, to win a few words of affection from her, or the grace of her smile—but to no avail. On Saturday mornings I would sit under the lemon tree in front of our new wooden house and read poetry, because I knew that Esther would pass by on her way to her aunt's house and I thought she would see me like that and think better of me; I would slip her essays I had written which had been marked "Excellent!"; I would utter vows, mutter incantations, stand under her window at night. To no avail. To her, I was just a kid. To assuage my torments and grant them some sort of significance, I wrote poems in secret. Love poems, nature poems, long rhymed ballads. I didn't show them to anyone. I locked them in a drawer, so that my parents and my brother wouldn't find them.

Aharon, age three, in Poland, 1923

During my final year in the school I found a certain solace in a friendship that developed between me and another boy of my age. Yosef was short of stature but broad of shoulder, with calloused hands and a strong will. His parents were poor and he worked in the citrus groves during vacations to help support the family. Late every afternoon we would meet, and on our way to the big eucalyptus wood he would tell me about the books he had read: *The Communist Manifesto* by Marx and Engels, *The Class Roots of the National Problem* by Borochov, *The Sociology of the Jews* by Arthur Ruppin. These were books of whose existence I had been unaware, and they opened before me a world of social thought. I confided my love for Esther to him, and he consoled me with descriptions of the glorious future awaiting humanity after the world revolution. We built ourselves a treehouse in the high branches of a gigantic eucalyptus and decided to write a novel together that would express our desire for the establishment of a just and equal society.

4

There was no high school in Ra'anana yet, and I was sent to study at the most prestigious high school at the time—a sort of Eton of the Land of Israel—the Herzlia Gymnasium in Tel Aviv.

The Gymnasium, which was built like an elaborate castle with three towers in the front, thick walls, arched windows, long corridors, looked like a prison to me, and melancholy descended upon me when I entered it. I was used to the family atmosphere of the village school where I had gone for seven years. There we called the teachers by their first names and we would go on outings and picnics with them. Here there was a Prussian system of strict discipline: you had to stand up for the teacher and address him as "Sir"—while he called you by your surname. You had to report for morning parade, and the fear of examinations, punishments, reprimands, and warnings was always dangling over your head. Most of the students were children of wealthy merchants, bankers, managers of companies, high officials. To them I was a country mouse. I would bring a sandwich spread with white cheese and an orange for the ten o'clock snack, while they would go out to the kiosks in the street and buy whatever they felt like.

During the first year I took the bus every morning from Ra'anana to Tel Aviv, and because the road was bad we sometimes had to get off the bus and push to get it out of the sand. I had to get up at 5:30 in the morning, whatever the weather, and because my parents had taught me good manners, such as to relinquish my seat on the bus to women and to old men, most days I spent the entire journey to school on my feet because there were usually more passengers than seats. The teachers did not take these problems into account, and whenever I was late for the first lesson, I would be sent off to the office of the principal—a prophet of doom and omnipotent ruler at one and the same time—and subjected to reprimands and warnings. In sorrow, I concentrated on my studies.

During the summer vacation—far from the gloomy corridors of the Gymnasium and the piercing eyes of the teachers at their lofty podiums, far from the cynical jokes of my pampered schoolmates—the world was beautiful once more. In the evenings, after several hours of work in our garden, or in the citrus groves to earn a bit of money, I would get together with my friend Yosef again, for long walks on the dirt roads with the stars twinkling above and choirs of crickets sawing away in the grass on either side. The "novel" we had promised ourselves we would write did not get written, but we did, however, clarify the world's problems, and we planned how to solve them.

That summer, when I was about fourteen years old, I enlisted in the Haganah. This clandestine organization—which had started during the twenties as protection against Arab attacks and riots once it became clear that it was impossible to depend on the British, who took a sympathetic stance toward the attackers—had branches in every Jewish settlement, large and small. We met in the evenings in the citrus-packing plant, which stood in the middle of a thick grove, far from inquiring eyes, and by the light of a field lantern the adult instructor taught us how to use a pistol, a tommy gun, a grenade, and how to signal with Morse code and semaphore and so forth. On moonless nights we would go out for field exercises and to guard the fields that bordered on the lands of the Arab village. The underground atmosphere matured us, and I—left-handed though I am—was a distinguished sniper. I regretted that the teachers and

"At age seven (left), with my mother, sister, and younger brother, near our cabin in Ra'anana," 1927

the pupils at the Gymnasium knew nothing about all this.

My second year at the Gymnasium saw an end to my daily bus trip from the village into town. My grandmother, my father's mother, had arrived from Poland and rented a small apartment, one-and-a-half rooms, for herself and her twenty-five-year-old daughter in the commercial quarter of Tel Aviv, and I went to live with them. Below us was a mirror-polishing workshop, and all day long we were deafened by the noise of the whetting and polishing machines. My grandmother was a quiet woman who moved silently through the house, was pious, and knew only Yiddish. Her daughter knew Hebrew and was a member of the Communist party—which was illegal at the time—and I was witness to secret meetings between her and her comrades. When she wasn't home I'd peek into her books: Freud, Hegel, Schopenhauer, Nietzsche, Lenin, Plekhanov . . . What lofty spheres in this noisy and polluted commercial neighborhood!

But "from the dungheaps He lifteth the fallen," and my last two years at the Gymnasium I was fortunate to walk in the shadow of great luminaries. In my search for a place where I could live alone, I ended up in a northern quarter of Tel Aviv, near the sea, adorned with trees and gardens, which was called "Workers' Quarters A," and where the high officials of the Socialist establishment lived. I found a tiny room on the roof of the home of one of the editors of *Davar*, the Labor Federation's daily newspaper, who was also one of the few astronomers in the country. On that same roof stood a large telescope, and Comrade Zakai, a likable man of about fifty with a smiling moon face, would come up every evening to look through the telescope at the stars and the moon in the heavens, passing through my room, which opened at either end. What a great honor had befallen me! In the house to my left lived the secretary general of the Labor Federation, and to his left, Comrade Ben-Gurion; to my right, the director general of the Workers' Bank, and next to him the director general of the Workers' Sick Fund, and so on down the row. These people's children all attended the prestigious Gymnasium, and I frequented their homes. I was lucky enough to see Ben-Gurion himself only four or five times, because as head of the Jewish Agency he spent most of his time abroad, but I frequently encountered his wife, Paula, who spent a lot of time outside. She spoke to everyone she met in the street and she knew what was going on with everyone in the neighborhood. Once she said to me: "You know why you're so skinny? Because you walk

all the way to the Gymnasium and back every day. Here, take seven mil and ride the bus!"

I finished the Gymnasium with honors, but I didn't like it. It was locked into its thick walls and into its system of strict rules and regulations, isolated from the effervescent life outside. However, I was extremely grateful to some of the teachers, who had directed my attention to the great world beyond the confines of the chilly classroom, and especially to the English teacher, who taught Shakespeare with great inspiration and made me love him, and to the mathematics teacher, under whose tutelage this subject ceased to be dry and came closer to philosophy.

A great influence on my life—greater than either my parents' house or the school—was the youth movement. "Mahanot Ha'olim"—"The Ascenders"—was the most authentic movement of Jewish youth in Palestine. It had not been founded by any of the political parties, but had sprung from the young people themselves, pupils in the high schools. Its slogan was "self-fulfillment," and fulfillment, in its terms, was to leave home and parents to go live a life of work and cooperation in a kibbutz. As opposed to the other youth movements, it was completely non-dogmatic, and though it had a Zionist-Socialist outlook, the study of Zionist and socialist thought was not the main thing—but rather education towards manual labor, closeness to nature, love of the land, simplicity, and the renunciation of personal ambition to the needs of the collective. Education took place through hikes all over the country, work camps adjacent to the kibbutzim, free discussions, the encouragement of interest in the arts, literature, music, painting. Formal manners and external appearances were of no importance.

I had joined this movement a year before I went to the Gymnasium. About a quarter of an hour's walk from our little house in Ra'anana, on a hill surrounded by woods, a group of graduates of "Mahanot Ha'olim" had set up its tents and huts and established a kibbutz. The life I saw there when I visited looked to me like the realization of the utopian ideal on earth: the singing that burst forth from the tents and the common showers, the communal meals in the large hut that served as the dining hall, the general meetings where everyone spoke seriously and frankly, the free relationships between the sexes, the enthusiastic dancing on Friday nights, the discussions around the campfire—these people are happy, I said to myself. And when two of them started a branch of the movement in the village, I was among the first to join.

During the four years I was at the Gymnasium, I was active in the movement, in Ra'anana and in Tel

View of Kibbutz Sdot Yam at the sea, in its first year, 1941

Aviv. I went on hikes and to work camps, I was a counselor for younger members, I participated in the many discussions and parties, and while doing so I became familiar with many great works of literature—both Hebrew literature and world literature—which had been skipped over by my formal studies at the Gymnasium: Brenner and Gnessin, Shlonsky and Alterman, Dostoevsky and Chekhov, Gogol and Kafka, Hesse and Schnitzler. We discussed all these at length at meetings, and at parties we would read aloud selections from them. My future was clear to me: I would live in a kibbutz.

5

My parents, cultured people most of whose spare time was taken up by the reading and discussion of books, wanted me to go to university and become a professor. But in those days of high tension, when the "Arab rebellion" against Zionism was raging through the land, and attacks on Jewish settlements occurred every day and every night, and young people had to help defend against the gangs and settle in the valleys and in the hills—only the fainthearted and "careerists" went to warm the benches of the university. I, as a member of a pioneering youth movement, went to a kibbutz.

I first did a year of training—together with a group of fifteen graduates of the movement—at the large and well-established Kibbutz Giv'at Brenner, where there were a thousand people and all branches of agriculture as well as a few factories. Most of its members came from Germany and were people with higher education who whistled Bach's cantatas and Beethoven's overtures while they worked. German was heard outdoors and in the dining hall. In the evenings, the sound of classical music played on gramophones and the aroma of good coffee wafted through the windows of people's rooms. I lived in a shabby little tent, and for most of the year I worked in the citrus groves together with a fellow called Ernst, who would recite to me—in the original and in translation—poems of Rilke and Brecht, and tell me about plays he had seen in Berlin; and with Enzo Sereni, from an aristocratic Italian-Jewish family with ties to the royal family, a brilliant man with original ideas and ambitions for political leadership, who, as we dug around the trees, would lecture us, with great rhetorical ability and enthusiasm, about the nature of Italian fascism and the nature of Jewish socialism as he saw it. (In 1943 he parachuted behind enemy lines on a mission to save Jews. He was caught and executed in Dachau.) This was a joyful year, a year of a feeling of freedom and the outburst of youthful and effervescent powers, and also a year of absorbing cultural treasures, and at its end—in 1938—we, the group of graduates from the movement, joined Kibbutz Sdot Yam.

Sdot Yam was then a young and poor kibbutz of about seventy members which was located, in tents and huts, on the sands of the Haifa bay. The goal it had set for itself was to break into the fields of fishing, shipping, and work on the docks, where there were very few Jewish workers. I, like most of the members of the kibbutz, was slotted into work at the wharf.

In the Haifa port at the time there were hundreds of Arab workers, and the Jews who worked there—a few dozen—were mostly immigrants from the Greek city of Saloniki, husky men, broad-hipped and muscular, who had a great deal of experience as stevedores and porters, because the port of Saloniki had been a "Jewish port" for generations, which rested on the Sabbath. Work in the warehouses, on the decks, and in the holds of the ships was not yet mechanized in those days, and it was all done with human hands and backs. On my first day at the port, faced with the huge ships tied to the dock and the burly Arab and Salonikian stevedores, I saw myself as Gulliver in the land of the giants.

At six o'clock in the morning we would catch the train, which stopped near our temporary encampment, and take it to Haifa. At the dock the work supervisor would direct us to loading or unloading a ship, or unloading sacks and boxes of fruit from railroad cars and taking them to the warehouses. On our backs we would carry sacks of potash and sacks of wheat that weighed a hundred kilos and more, and the work inside the holds of ships would sometimes go on for fourteen or sixteen hours at a stretch. We would return home in the evening utterly exhausted, all our bones aching, and the next day we'd catch the train again.

But there were also times when we had nothing to do, waiting on the dock for a ship that was late in coming. During those hours I'd sit on a pile of sacks of potash or wheat in a warehouse and read Shakespeare's *Julius Caesar* or Goethe's *Faust* in Hebrew translation, and Agnon's *Bygone Days.*

The work was hard, but for me this was a period of powerful experiences which engraved themselves deeply within me. It was my first encounter with a human world full of color and many different types, with social groups so different from the ones I had known in my childhood—with the Arab and Jewish proletariat, with the British clerks and police who ruled the docks, with work supervisors from big companies, with sailors from Denmark, Finland, Japan, Egypt, Russia. At that time, after the war had broken out in Europe, rickety wooden boats began to arrive in port overflowing with destitute Jewish refugees from Nazi persecution. The boats were

"illegal" because the British Mandate's laws limited immigration to Palestine. Now these refugees were taken off the ships—before our eyes—by British police and soldiers and brought to detention camps.

During the hours of waiting on the dock, between one ship and the next, a long story took shape in my head, built of the stuff of the life of the port, and I felt the need to get it down on paper. To write at night after an exhausting day's work as a stevedore was impossible. I asked the secretariat of the kibbutz if I could be put on guard duty for two weeks, and I was. We had a piece of land several kilometres distant from the kibbutz where we grew vegetables and fodder, and I would go out—in a cart hitched to a donkey—to guard it at night. It was winter, and most nights it rained. I sat in the little wooden shed, surrounded by sacks of chemical fertilizer, tools, mice running from corner to corner, and thus, by the light of a field lamp, I wrote on the pages of a notebook, blotted by drops of water that leaked through the roof, the story "A Load of Oxen," the first of my stories to have been printed in a renowned publication.

The story included a realistic-grotesque description of how oxen are unloaded from the hold of a ship and driven to the slaughterhouse, while refugees are taken off a ship and brought to a detention camp. It was written in the Mishnaic Hebrew that I had absorbed in my father's home. It caused a stir when it was published because it was the first Hebrew story "in two thousand years"—as people used to say then—about Jewish dockworkers in the Land of Israel. In addition, a young writer was discovered who had grown up here, in this country, and "his Hebrew is so rooted . . ."

Thus I was endowed with the title "author," though I wasn't particularly proud of this distinction as I saw my writing as a "hobby." Newspapers and journals approached me and asked me to send them material.

6

In the winter of 1941 I moved to the permanent place of settlement of Kibbutz Sdot Yam, at Caesarea. On the ruins of the ancient city of Caesarea, which had been built in the days of Herod and had been a large port city where Jews, Greeks, and Samaritans lived, there was now a small Arab fishing village. Not far from it, in the sands, we put up tents, some stone sheds, and a thatched shelter for boats. The place was exposed to the vagaries of nature: storms that came from the sea, waves that washed over everything on the beach, the salt which consumed whatever we planted, the dune sand scattered over the floors and the furniture, burying tools and crates that were left outside. Everywhere we dug we would find antiquities from the days of Roman and Byzantine rule—temple columns, statues of gods and caesars, stones with Greek and Roman inscriptions, coins and potsherds. Thus we unearthed the Roman amphitheatre, which had been wonderfully preserved, and which is now used for theatrical and operatic performances.

For a while I worked at fishing. We would leave the little bay in two or three boats in the early hours of the evening and set out to sea, cast out our nets and our floating lamps, and in the morning we would pull in the nets and collect our catch, which was mostly pretty poor. The women would sit under the thatch of the boatshed and mend the torn nets, and on stormy days we would help them. When we began to do agriculture, I transferred to work in the vegetable garden, which we cultivated on a piece of land that had once been the Roman hippodrome and where two huge marble columns still lay, as well as the remains of stone benches. When I planted eggplants, I saw in my mind's eye horses galloping over the rows and a Roman crowd cheering them—and me. In the evenings, if the tent in which I lived alone hadn't blown over in a storm, I sat at a rickety table and wrote stories.

After a year of this, I was sent by the kibbutz to Tel Aviv to work in the youth movement's national secretariat. There were seven of us, from various kibbutzim, and we all lived in a rented apartment in the center of town. I edited the movement's monthly journal, I wrote articles and columns for it, I ran discussion groups in the Tel Aviv branch, and I was involved—both as a graduate of the movement and as a member of the Haganah—in the hectic politics of this period of the World War and the struggle against the British Mandate. There were vast disagreements in the labor movement about how to conduct this struggle, about whether to be moderate or to take more extreme action, and I was among the "activists."

Having completed my service in town, I went back to the kibbutz, to manual labor, to writing at night. I separated from the woman to whom I had been married for a year and a half, and a few months later I married eighteen-year-old Eda Zoritte—she is my wife today—who had been in the youth group of which I had been counselor in Tel Aviv. Born in Tel Aviv, she was a graduate of a teachers' seminary and the Ballet Studio. Life in a kibbutz was not to her

liking, so in order to be near me she found a job teaching in Hadera, a large village of private farmers, about ten kilometres from Caesarea. Two or three times a week she would walk from Hadera to Caesarea through the sands and along the seashore in order to get to my tent. Sometimes I would come to meet her in the cart hitched to the donkey, especially during the winter, when the stream that emptied into the sea south of Caesarea would overflow and could not be crossed on foot. This was apparently the pioneering equivalent of the coach and six horses with which the knight would bring his beloved to his castle.

In 1946 I was sent by the kibbutz movement to the United States, together with another five emissaries, in order to establish a youth movement there which would guide its members towards life in a kibbutz in the Land of Israel; the movement was called "The Young Pioneer." My wife joined me three months after I got there.

We lived the life of a commune in a shabby apartment in Boro Park in Brooklyn. In those days, before the establishment of the State, and when the kibbutzim were poor, the emissaries abroad did not receive any salary. They were thrown into the cold water and told to learn to swim by themselves. In looking for ways to earn money to support ourselves, we found out that the Hebrew schools of the United Synagogues of America needed a Hebrew book for beginners. As I was the "author" in the group, I was given the task.

The United Synagogues signed a contract with me to write a story of ten thousand words using a basic vocabulary of five hundred Hebrew words about children in the Land of Israel—and I would get two cents a word.

I wrote that story, an adventure story called *To the Children in Yemen*, and thus it happened that the first book of mine to appear in print came out in the United States, and it was not a book written out of any inner urge, but rather out of the need to earn a living.

(Many years later, in 1965, when I was on a coast-to-coast university lecture tour, I learned that the book had been reprinted many times over the years and distributed in tens of thousands of copies. I went to the United Synagogue offices in New York and asked them whether they didn't think I had some royalties coming to me. They dug through their archives and unearthed the ancient contract, and showed me that in exchange for the two hundred dollars I had relinquished all further rights to the material.)

We were not blessed by great results for all the work we did among the Jewish youth of New York, and my wife and I were sent to Chicago to try our luck there.

We rented a room in a quiet neighborhood on the south side, near the University of Chicago, in the apartment of a sour-faced and bespectacled Jewish widow, a veteran Communist who subscribed to newspapers in Yiddish from Birobidzhan and hated the Zionists. She frowned upon our activities and responded to them with stubborn silence. My wife got a job teaching Hebrew in a Sunday school, with a tiny salary, and after an extensive search I found a part-time job—three days a week—at the dispatchers of the famous Chicago slaughterhouses. The work was not hard, and I, it might be said, had experience: taking down slaughtered cattle and sheep from the hooks in the warehouse and carrying them to the trucks near the platforms. I worked alongside Irish workers, Italians, and Poles, who during every short break in the work would run off to drink beer and bet on horses, and who didn't understand what I was doing there among them. On my free mornings I would sneak into the university to hear lectures on English and American literature, like Rabbi Hillel in his youth, who climbed up onto the roof of the study house and heard Torah through the chimney.

With the help of some local Jews who felt close to the workers' movement in the Land of Israel, we organized a few dozen young people who formed the nucleus of "The Young Pioneer" in Chicago. We would meet them for discussions in parks and in the Poalei-Zion clubhouse. From the Salvation Army we rented a summer camp outside of town, where we held weekend seminars on Zionist-Socialist doctrine for boys and girls of sixteen and seventeen who knew very little about their Judaism, surrounded by crosses, flags, and calls to prepare for the coming of the kingdom of God, and exhortations to march bravely onward as soldiers in the army of Jesus the Savior.

On the twenty-ninth of November we listened to the radio in our room on South Fifty-second Street in Chicago, and heard the good tidings from Lake Success of the United Nations decision on the matter of the establishment of a Jewish state in Palestine. On that night, when thousands danced in the streets of Jerusalem and Tel Aviv, intoxicated with joy, we had a modest celebration, just the two of us. However, in the coming days the American newspapers, and the papers we got from home, were full of terrible news of Arab attacks on Jews in the cities and villages, and about pitched battles all over the country. Long lists of the names of the fallen appeared in the Hebrew

press, and among them we found many of our close acquaintances.

We planned to go home. We left Chicago for New York. My wife was in the last months of her pregnancy. Flying then was transportation for rich people only. We had to wait for the birth. We rented a room on Jane Street in Greenwich Village, in the apartment of a fair young woman, the mother of a little girl. She was separated from her husband, and she used to pour her heart out to us about his threats and extortions. Since Betty's husband was a Jew, we felt guilty about his disgraceful behavior.

On May 15, 1948, the National Council in Tel Aviv declared the establishment of the State of Israel. In New York, in a solemn ceremony in the courtyard of the Israeli legation, Teddy Kollek inducted several dozen young men, including me, who were there on various missions, into the Israeli Army. Five other people and I were set to work packing the arms which had been obtained from contributions by Jews all over the United States to be sent by ship to Israel.

Every morning we reported to a large, secret storehouse in the Bronx, where enormous quantities

As a member of Kibbutz Sdot Yam, 1950

of queer armaments would reach us in trucks, pick-ups, and private cars: pistols of various sorts, antiquated rifles—some of them undoubtedly dating back to the Civil War—obsolete submachine guns and mortars, swords, spears, knives, helmets, compasses, binoculars. All these we cleaned, oiled, wrapped in plastic, packed into metal barrels filled with sand, and brought to the harbor. The Israel Defense Forces, which then faced Egyptian tanks, Iraqi airplanes, and Jordanian artillery, needed weapons, even if they were from the Stone Age.

Three months after the birth of our older son, Eyal, we returned to Israel in an old ship, stopping on the way at five European ports. Those were the final weeks of the War of Independence, which ended in the victory over the seven Arab armies.

<h1 style="text-align:center">7</h1>

My wife, who is very much an individualist and has artistic leanings, was not built for life in a kibbutz. She even used lipstick, an unforgivable sin in the eyes of kibbutz society at the time, which was no less strict than the Jehovah's Witnesses.

In 1950 I left Sdot Yam and went to live in the city—an act that was considered as equivalent to religious conversion. The kibbutz sent bereavement notices to one of the daily papers to mark my "departure." From a surfeit of guilt feelings I broke out in pimples all over, which cleared up only after I stopped spreading my bread with margarine, the preferred spread at kibbutzim.

That same year, my first collection of stories appeared, *Spirit of the Seas,* in which most of the stories centred around the beginnings of an impoverished fishing kibbutz, the sea, and the port.

To Tel Aviv I brought a bed, a table, two chairs, and twenty-five books. The only tool with which I could earn my living was a pen. I was fortunate enough to be taken on as the amanuensis of the most important Hebrew poet of the time, and one of the greatest Hebrew translators ever, Avraham Shlonsky. (He translated Pushkin's *Eugene Onegin* and *Quiet Flows the Don* by Mikhail Sholokhov from Russian, *Colas Breugnon* by Romain Rolland and *Tyl Ulenspiegel* by Charles de Coster from French, Shakespeare's plays from English, and many more great works.) I sat before the maestro with the unruly shock of white hair, a wizard of language and a wise clown, and helped him edit the literary-theoretical quarterly *Orlogin,* in which some of the most important writing of the time was published. As a former kibbutz member, I did not know much about money matters,

"At home in Tel Aviv with my wife, Eda, and our two sons, Eyal (left) and Amos," 1958

and I did not realize that my salary was the same as that of a shoemaker's apprentice.

We rented a rooftop apartment of one-and-a-half rooms in a building on the second floor of which lived four prostitutes. Every Saturday night they held a small party for their clientele. At the end of every party, at midnight, we could hear the enthusiastically rendered strains of the national anthem, "Hatikva," wafting through their windows. Like all of us back then, they were proud patriots.

In the summer of 1951, a group of about twenty young writers got together and decided to put out an independent journal. We had much in common: all of us had been born here, or had come as young children; most of us were graduates of the pioneering youth movements, and some were kibbutz members; most had been in the Haganah or in the Palmach before the establishment of the State and had taken part in the War of Independence; and with respect to literature, our stories and poems were written in living, spoken Hebrew, as opposed to the language of the previous generation of writers who had come from the diaspora, mostly from eastern Europe, and our writing was strongly rooted in the developing Israeli reality. An editorial board of four was elected, and I was given the job of acting editor.

In a short time the bi-weekly *Massa*—which was the journal's name—had become the focus of the new Israeli literature, in which every young writer felt it was a privilege to be published, and once published, he saw himself entitled to stroll down Dizengoff Street with his head held high, and in the evening to go into a cafe frequented by artists and writers in the hope that he would hear some compliments on his story or poem. The offices of *Massa*, two rooms on Rothschild Boulevard, seethed with people coming and going day and night. They came in work clothes from the kibbutzim and the cooperative villages, and in uniforms that had not yet been demobilized from the army, and wearing white shirts and cloche dresses from the cities. A certain poet who had no fixed abode used to sleep on the desk in the office, and in the morning we would find a new poem of his which he was offering for publication. The magazines were snapped up at the kiosks and circulation reached five thousand, an enormous number at the time, when the adult Hebrew-speaking population numbered no more than half a million.

Like most intellectuals in the Western world in the years following the victory over Nazi Germany, we too were dazzled by the "Sun of the Nations" in the East. The establishment of the "popular democracies" in Poland, Romania, Czechoslovakia, and so on looked to us like the dawn of a new and glorious era in which the wolf would dwell with the lamb and the leopard lie down with the kid. Comrade Stalin's fatherly smile under his benevolent mustache promised us a happy future. When, on behalf of the journal, I went to the "Peace Festival" in Bucharest in 1953, in which tens of thousands of youth from five continents participated, I was so drunk from the slivovitz they so liberally dispensed, from the colorful folk dances of seventy nations, from the nostalgic Romanian melodies playing through the loudspeakers in the city's streets, that I did not see the poverty and repression around me at all. (Several years later I expressed the disappointment I experienced at this festival in my novella *Journey to the Land of Gomer*.) Relations between us and the Soviet Embassy, which was located three doors down the street from the *Massa* office, were excellent. We were often invited there for vodka, caviar, and films about the happy land, and the poet Avraham Shlonsky headed the Center for Progressive Culture, which fostered ties with "the world of tomorrow" and ran clubs in Tel Aviv, Jerusalem, and Haifa which sponsored lectures, discussions, and artistic performances in the spirit of "peace, socialism, and the brotherhood of nations."

It was only after the Prague trials of 1952 and 1953 that we woke up from the dream of a Communist paradise, an awakening which caused splits in the Israeli labour movement and in the kibbutz movement. As a result of these divisions the financial backing of *Massa* also broke down, and after three-and-a-half years it ceased to exist as an independent bi-weekly and became the literary supplement of the daily newspaper *Lamerhav*, and I, as its editor, went along too.

During those years my first plays were produced. Two of them—the comedies *Incubator on the Rock* at the Ohel Theatre and *Hedva and I* at the Habimah National Theatre—were hits that ran for over a hundred performances. In 1954 our second son, Amos, was born, and the income from the plays allowed us to buy a flat sufficiently large for me and my desk, my wife and her desk (and her easel), the children and their toys. Everything would have been perfect were it not for the Israeli passion for togetherness. In Israel, the buildings are very close to one another and their windows are open most days of the year. The good people who live there, as they enjoy listening to the radio or watching television, try very hard to share their pleasure with their neighbors, and turn up their sets to maximum volume. It took us six months to convince our neighbors on all sides to spare us their kindness.

8

Despite the recognition I had won, the literary prizes that kept coming in, the income from the plays, the social connections, I felt like an "outsider" in Tel Aviv. Even now I feel like a temporary resident in this city and dream that one day, in ten years' time—or thirty or forty—I will build a house for myself on a hilltop in the upper Galilee or in a desert canyon in the Negev.

During the fifties and the sixties the bohemian life thrived in Tel Aviv no less than in Paris. Every night, in two or three cafes on Dizengoff Street, writers, actors, and artists would gather, joined by military people and politicians who admired artists or had repressed literary tendencies—because among the People of the Book everyone is a potential writer—and pass the time in arguing, drinking, singing, spontaneous oratory, celebrating theatrical premieres or the appearance of a new book until the wee hours. Sometimes, after midnight, everyone would move on to one of the bars near the beach or to a nightclub in Jaffa to dance the tango, the rhumba, and the samba to the strains of the band, mingling with the proletariat.

Late in the evening, when I was tired from writing—I did most of my literary writing in the evening—I too would go down to the cafe to mingle with my own kind. Although exciting things happened there, and words of wisdom were spoken by the great minds of our generation, and wonderful chanteuses crooned nostalgic songs that brought tears to the eyes of all who listened, I felt that I didn't belong to all this; and I would ask myself if I wouldn't be better off back in my study pursuing the intimate and complex relationships I was developing with the characters in my stories, which interested me a great deal despite our frequent disagreements.

The truth is that wherever I was, in any period of my life, I have felt myself an outsider. Among the children at school, among the pupils at the Gymnasium, in the youth movement, at the kibbutz. I did what I had to the best I could, I took on jobs that everyone respected—but I was never "one of the bunch." I stood within and observed from without.

This "existential condition," which is rooted in my character, is what has caused all the heroes of my stories and novels to be antiheroes, characters on the periphery of society, whose prevailing modes are irony or satire. This was the case in my first novel, *Hedva and I* (which became a best-seller right away), a satirical novel about a couple that leaves the kibbutz but can't get accustomed to city life; this was the case in *Fortunes of a Fool* and in *The Living on the Dead,* novels in which the central characters find themselves pushed aside, frustrated and lost as a result of drastic transformations that have taken place in Israeli society, which has changed from a pioneering society with egalitarian ideals to an organized state in which concepts of material success, achievement, and power are supreme. This is also the case in *Heinz, His Son, and the Evil Spirit,* a novella in which the hero is an immigrant from Germany, isolated from society, fighting a quixotic war against the bureaucracy, and in *The Short Life,* a novel about a humble and kind-hearted insurance agent who has a hard time with his wife's ambitions. In the novel *Asahel,* too, the eponymous hero is a minor official, village-born, who feels

"With Eda (left) and fellow writers in the bohemian cafe Kassit," Tel Aviv, 1960

The author (second from left) with colleagues at the Embassy of Israel in London, 1970

out of place in urban society—and antiheroes appear in other works of mine as well.

For thirteen years I edited the literary supplement of *Lamerhav*—where the first stories of several writers who are very well known today appeared, among them A. B. Yehoshua, Amalia Kahana-Carmon, Yoram Kaniuk, Yehoshua Kenaz, and others—and during those years I was involved, unwillingly, by virtue of being an editor, in rivalries between various literary groups, between writers and critics, between megalomaniac poets and arrogant professors. As an editor, you naturally attract grudges, bitterness, the desire for revenge. Suddenly you are astounded to see writer X, who only yesterday sat across the desk at the newspaper office smiling at you, walk past you in the street without even saying hello; suddenly you discover that a critic whose convoluted article you just spent five hours editing and cut by 25 percent has published a murderous attack on you in the journal which he edits, consigning you to Hell. When you free yourself from involvement in these quarrels and jealousies of our literary "shtetl," they look ridiculous. Thus, several years after I stopped being an editor, I wrote the satirical novel *The Flying Camel*

and the Golden Hump, the two protagonists of which are a writer and a literary critic who live in the same apartment building.

9

A year after the Six Day War, in 1968, I was appointed cultural attaché to the Embassy of Israel in London.

I became a diplomat. I wore a suit and a tie. I sat in an office and dictated letters to a secretary. I signed, after extensive negotiations and elaborate refinings of phraseologies, a cultural agreement between Israel and Great Britain, and the signing ceremony was immortalized in a photograph that is filed in the archives of both states. I rented a frock coat from the Moss Brothers shop in the Strand for five pounds fifty pence to wear to a reception for diplomats in Buckingham Palace. I bowed to Queen Elizabeth II, who graciously asked me my name and where I was from, I drank champagne and ate bad meatballs from Lyons, and I waltzed with Lord Mountbatten's granddaughter. Nearly every week we received invitations to dinners from various organizations and associations, with the participation of lords and wealthy donors, and I learned when to wear white tie and when to wear black tie, and my wife learned the art of diplomatic entertaining and in what order to seat guests around a table so that nobody was insulted. I formed connections with famous people, so that during the course of small talk I could let drop—without lying—phrases like: "When I was speaking to Lord Goodman . . . ," or "While dining yesterday with Sir Laurence Olivier . . . ," or "I told Peggy Ashcroft that she was quite wrong about that . . . ," and so on. We went to the theatre, the opera, the ballet, museums, galleries, concerts . . .

But actually, matters of protocol and the cultural delights of London took up only a small part of my time. For seven or eight hours a day I was occupied with tedious office work, with creating ties with cultural institutions and universities, with initiating and organizing Israeli cultural events—poetry readings, concerts, dance performances, exhibitions, and so on—so that most evenings were taken up with engagements related to my work as cultural attaché. I had no time to write.

When I returned to Israel after three years, *Lamerhav* was defunct, and I went to work at *Davar*, the daily newspaper of the Labor Federation, as a columnist. Twice a week, on Tuesdays and Fridays, my column appeared, and I was free to write about whatever I wanted: politics, social topics, the arts. I initiated a series of interviews with ordinary people. I travelled all over the country and interviewed farmers in remote settlements, industrial workers, Arab and Druse villagers, housewives, shopkeepers, cabdrivers, new immigrants. I believed that what they had to say was more interesting than what well-known politicians and intellectuals, who were interviewed day in and day out by all the media, had to say, and the newspaper's readers thought so too, so that after every one of these interviews I would receive dozens of emotional letters.

For twelve years I wrote those columns, a number of which were collected in my book *The Turbulent Zone*, and although this journalistic work was very time-consuming, it was also rewarding: I felt a vibrant connection with people from all segments of the population, and the pulse of the times. And I had always liked to travel around the country. Would I have written the novel *Journey in the Month of Av*, which tells of a father searching for his son "lost" in the Sinai desert, had I not been engulfed by the burning heat of the Arava, and had my face not been struck by the east wind blowing dust from the mountains of Edom on the road to Eilat?

During the sixties and the seventies I went on four lecture tours to the United States, and for a month I was "writer in residence" in the Jewish community of Fort Wayne, Indiana. I remember all this through a dreamlike haze. I was a Luftmensch, up in the air most of the time, hopping from airport to airport. I would land in some city or other on the face of that vast continent, a city whose name was listed on my itinerary, and be taken to a Hyatt hotel, or a Hilton, or a Holiday Inn on the outskirts of a wealthy suburb, where not a pedestrian is to be seen. The room on the twelfth floor is equipped with a television, a radio, a refrigerator with alcoholic beverages, long sterile corridors in which you sink into soft carpets, and downstairs there is a polite and somnolent restaurant, with subliminal background music and smiling waitresses in brown aprons. In the evening I lecture in the hall of a university or a reform synagogue, or at a community center, before an audience of people whom I do not know and who do not know me, on Israeli literature, Israeli culture, Israeli identity, and so forth, and then I have dinner with professors or "professional Jews" and am asked the same questions and give the same answers, and the next morning—or two or three days later—I once again traverse the polished halls of the airport, rushing to catch the plane to somewhere in Arizona or Louisiana, arrive once again at the Hyatt or the Sheraton, and feel like I'm in a satellite in outer space.

I once flew from Savannah, Georgia, to Atlanta in a ten-seater plane which looked like a flying donkey, and I was the sole passenger. Halfway there, a terrible storm broke out: thunder and lightning, and we were tossed like a boat on the ocean waves, and all my seafaring experience as a fisherman was no help at all in assuaging my fear, until I was spewed out onto dry land, like Jonah from the belly of the whale. On another occasion, when I was returning to the hotel in the company of two students, at midnight, from a lecture at Hillel House on the campus of the University of Chicago, at which Saul Bellow had been present, we were stopped by two Black men. One of them brandished a knife at my stomach and ordered: "Gimme a dollar!" I was so surprised that I didn't understand that this was a threat on my life, and I mumbled that I was a stranger in town. He hesitated a moment, and then said to his friend: "Leave 'em alone," and the two of them went on their way down the empty avenue. Two minutes later we heard a horrible scream not far from us, and in the morning,

"With the British writer V. S. Pritchett (left) at the International PEN congress," Jerusalem, 1974

on my way to the airport, I read in the newspaper that a man had been murdered at that very spot.

At the beginning of one of those lecture tours, a small item about me appeared in the *New York Times*. A man named Sonnenfeld, who claimed to be a relative of my mother, the owner of a mirror factory (I appear to be destined for mirrors), tracked down this item, and tracked me down as well, interrogated me as to my itinerary, and out of warm family feeling—which is prevalent among so many American Jews—sent urgent messages to all members of the huge Sonnenfeld tribe across the United States saying that cousin Aharon Megged was now in the country, and would be in such and such a city on such and such a date, and they should welcome me there. Following my lectures in about ten different cities, one of those Sonnenfelds would appear, introduce himself as my relative, and invite me to his home for a reception with the town's leading citizens, which was all prepared . . .

Those lectures, and the receptions afterwards, the luncheons and the dinners with the hosts, the space flights—all these involved a great deal of spiritual tension and an increasing feeling of alienation. To paraphrase the title of Harry Goldin's book *Only in America*, I wanted to write a book called *Lonely*

in America. When I ask myself in retrospect why I took those tours upon myself, which anyway were not very well paid, it seems to me that my motive was a kind of adventurous urge to put myself to the test and do things which are against my nature, together with a constant urge to set sail for unknown territories.

But who can understand the ways of the spirit? In 1957 I went to Spain with the intention of writing a drama about the period of the Inquisition. I never wrote that drama, but the mystical experiences of Spain found their way several years later into my novella about an imaginary journey to Nicaragua. I haven't written a book about America, but experiences from my trips to America have stolen—in various guises—into my novels *Of Trees and Stones* and *Journey in the Month of Av*, as well as into several of my short stories.

Milestones: in December 1973, in the middle of a lecture tour of the United States, the news reached me, by telephone, that I had been awarded the Bialik Prize for my work. In 1977 I was "writer in residence" of the Hebrew department at Oxford University, in England. We lived in a little village, Yarnton, and in that idyllic environment, in the shade of a manor house and a seventeenth-century church, far from the storms ravaging Israel, to the sound of the rustling of the evergreens during the day and the hooting of the owl in the rafters at night, I wrote *Asahel*. In 1979 I was elected to the Hebrew Academy, and in 1980 I was elected president of PEN in Israel, a position in which I served for seven years. In 1983 I was invited to New York to receive the *Present Tense* prize for the novel *Asahel*, which had appeared in English. In 1984 I was invited to Iowa to participate in the International Writing Program headed by Paul Engle. In 1988 we were visiting writers at the Rockefeller Foundation in Bellagio on Lake Como in Italy.

10

We are a "Literary Family"—like the ironic title of a story written by my wife, Eda Zoritte: Eda is a fiction-writer and essayist who has written short stories, three novels, one-act plays, and critical works about contemporary Hebrew poets. Eyal, our first-born son, is a poet who has thus far published ten books of poetry; Amos, our younger son, is a historian whose book about the Spanish conquest of America is about to be published by Cambridge University Press. Each of us has gone his own way, and there are no clashes between us.

Six months after I went to Poland, our son Eyal went there as well, on his own initiative. When he came back, he was very moved. He told us that he had visited the city and the house where I was born, and the small town where my mother—his grandmother—was born and felt as if he had been there before, perhaps in a previous incarnation. I thought about the Jewish "blood-link" passed on from generation to generation. It's been two generations that we have been living here, as free men in our own state, and we did not experience persecutions and pogroms or the horrors of the Holocaust. Nonetheless, the memory of hundreds of years of diaspora seems to flow in our blood. When he was in his twenties, Eyal wrote a poem:

I was in Poland, a holiday in the dream, good
light, an ordinary day, a girl
in a black wooden alley.

If I am a tree; I have a Polish
root in the dream, a handful
of noisy crows
in the window.
Black alleys on a large yellow globe.

As for me, into the pages and between the lines of whatever I write sneak echoes—often unintentional—of the Jewish past, both recent and distant, with its anxieties and its enchantments, from one of my first stories, "The Name," which I wrote in the early fifties, until my most recent novel, *Foiglman*, the hero of which is a Polish-born Yiddish poet, a Holocaust survivor, who tries unsuccessfully to strike roots in the Land of Israel.

I have never felt the need to write an autobiography, because it seemed to me that the experiences of my life, my feelings, and my thoughts are embodied in the books I have written, in various guises. Were it not at the request of the editor of this book, I would not have written these pages. All that remains is for me to quote a few lines from my novella *Of Trees and Stones*, in which a man in his forties, a clerk in the Department of Nature Conservation, during the course of an entire night after a party, confides his sins to a writer who had been his wife's lover. In the second part of the novella, the writer replies to the confidences, and among other things he says:

It is customary to speak of the "autobiographical elements" in a writer's works, as if every character is an incarnation of the writer's self, or a part of that self. You too have mentioned something like that. No, in my work there are only anti-autobiographical elements. Cover-ups, defacing of tracks, disguises, misleadings. Arrows and signposts leading the reader in a direction away from me, just at the moment he thinks he is approaching my hiding-place . . .

Often, all too often, I am the I and I am the Other at one and the same time. That is to say, I see myself from without, as if I were also my own shadow, or a reflection of myself in a mirror. When you see yourself, hear yourself talk, you cannot be honest. You are self-conscious. You perform for the Other, who is you. Feelings are born, as it were, with their doubles. And then two things can happen: either they are alarmed seeing their doubles before them, or they laugh at themselves.

BIBLIOGRAPHY

Fiction:

Ruach Yamim (title means "Spirit of the Seas"; short stories), Hakibbutz Hameuchad (Tel Aviv), 1953.

Hedva Ve-ani (title means "Hedva and I"; novel), Hakibbutz Hameuchad, 1955.

Israel Haverim (title means "Israeli Folk"; short stories), Hakibbutz Hameuchad, 1955.

Mikreh Hakssil (novel), Hakibbutz Hameuchad, 1960, translation by Aubrey Hodes published as *Fortunes of a Fool*, Gollancz (London), 1962, Random House (New York), 1963.

Habrikha (title means "The Escape"; three novellas), Hakibbutz Hameuchad, 1962.

Hachai al Hamet (novel), Am Oved (Tel Aviv), 1965, translation by Misha Louvish published as *Living on the Dead*, Jonathan Cape (London), 1970, McCall (New York), 1971.

Hayom Hasheni (title means "The Second Day"; short stories), Tarmil (Tel Aviv), 1967.

Hachaiyyim Haktzarim (novel), Hakibbutz Hameuchad, 1971, translation by Miriam Arad published as *The Short Life*, Taplinger, 1980.

Hatzot Hayom (title means "Midday"; portable selection), Hakibbutz Hameuchad, 1973.

Makhbarot Evyatar (title means "Evyatar's Notebooks"; novel), Hakibbutz Hameuchad, 1973.

Al 'Etzim Ve-avanim (title means "Of Trees and Stones"; novel), Am Oved, 1973.

Ha'ataleph (title means "The Bat"; novel), Am Oved, 1975.

Heinz U'vno Veharuach Haraah (title means "Heinz, His Son, and the Evil Spirit"; novella), Am Oved, 1976.

Asahel (novel), Am Oved, 1978, translation by Robert Whitehill and Susan C. Lilly, Taplinger, 1982.

Massa Be-av (title means "Journey in the Month of Av"; novel), Am Oved, 1980.

Hagamal Hame'ofef Vedabeshet Hazahav (title means "The Flying Camel and the Golden Hump"; novel), Am Oved, 1982.

Ma'asseh Meguneh (title means "Indecent Act"; three novellas), Am Oved, 1986.

Foiglman (novel), Am Oved, 1987.

Produced plays:

"Incubator 'al Hassela" (title means "Incubator on the Rock"), Tel Aviv, at Ohel Theater, 1950.

"Hedva Ve-ani" (title means "Hedva and I"), Tel Aviv, at Habimah Theater, 1955.

"Baderech Le-Eilat" (title means "On the Road to Eilat"; also see below), Tel Aviv, at Habimah Theater, 1955.

"Hanna Senesh" (also see below), Tel Aviv, at Habimah Theater, 1958.

"I Like Mike" (also see below), Tel Aviv, at Habimah Theater, 1960.

"Hamesh Hamesh" (title means "Tit for Tat"), Tel Aviv, at Ohel Theater, 1960.

"Bereshit" (title means "Genesis"; also see below), Tel Aviv, at Habimah Theater, 1989.

"Ha'onah Haboeret" (title means "The High Season"; also see below), Tel Aviv, at Habimah Theater, 1967.

"El Hatzippor" (title means "To the Bird"), Haifa Theater, 1974.

Published plays:

Baderech Le-Eilat, Sifriat Poalim (Tel Aviv), 1955.

Hanna Senesh, Hakibbutz Hameuchad, 1958.

I Like Mike, Hakibbutz Hameuchad, 1960.

Bereshit, Or Am, 1965.

Ha'onah Haboeret, Amikam, 1967.

"I Like Mike," "Hanna Senesh," and "Bereshit" (translated as "The First Sin") were also produced in New York, Los Angeles, Buenos Aires, Stockholm, and other cities. "The Road to Eilat" was produced in Zürich in German translation by Max Brod.

Nonfiction:

Massa Hayeladim El Ha-aretz Hamuvtahat (title means "The Children's Journey to the Promised Land"), Am Oved, 1984.

Ezor Hara'ash (title means "The Turbulent Zone"; essays), Hakibbutz Hameuchad, 1985.

Shulhan Haktivah (title means "The Writing Table; essays), Am Oved, 1989.

Children's books:

El Hayeladim Beteyman (title means "To the Children in Yemen"), United Synagogues of America (New York), 1948.

Ahavat Ne'urim (title means "Young Love"), Dvir (Tel Aviv), 1979.

Nadav Ve-imo (title means "Nadav and His Mother"), Dvir, 1989.

Contributor to journals and newspapers, often under the pseudonym of A.M.

John N. Morris

1931-

A MESSAGE TO THE FISH: A MEMOIR OF CHILDHOOD

I was born about two in the morning on the eighteenth of June, 1931, in the Acland Nursing Home in Oxford, England, the twelve-pound son of Charles and Charlotte Maurice Morris, married nine months to the day. The birth was difficult, and my enormous pineapple of a head (with red ringlets to the shoulders) a nurse reshaped by hand. For several days my mother ran a fever. "What's that book you're reading?" the doctor asked. For *Anna Karenina* he substituted *Evelina* and *The Vicar of Wakefield* and her temperature subsided. An emblematic nativity.

On the day of my birth my mother's class graduated from Vassar. Now she and Charles (as I was always to call my father) were spending a wedding-present year in Oxford in a small flat above the High near Oriel Lane. A postgraduate student of English, my father had some loose attachment to Merton College, and in Merton College chapel I was christened. This rite was performed by the brother of W. R. Inge, the then famous "Gloomy Dean" of St. Paul's, London—a second-hand connection with second-rate eminence, said ironists on both sides of my family, entirely typical of our dealings with the world.

We were—the two families into which I was born—Old Americans, a fact in which I take pleasure. On my mother's side I must be kin to half the names in the New England hagiology, but after the first Plymouth generation of Brewster and Bradford we produced in my line of descent not a single publicly noticeable figure—no eminent divines, no Signers, no generals or delegates to the Constitutional Convention. Our stock modified by Welsh, Scotch-Irish, Huguenot and New Amsterdam Dutch influence, we were instead intensely and prosperously and almost anonymously respectable. Connecting or disseminating ourselves among similar families from Boston to Savannah and recruiting our strength by marriages to energetic immigrants, in every generation down to about 1900 we did the country's necessary middleclass business as merchants, investors, shipping agents, brokers in cotton or indigo, traders to China. In New York our address would be

John N. Morris in his father's arms, December 1931

Pine or Wall Street, where we lived near or over the office or shop; and we buried us in Trinity churchyard. At last, and just in time, before gentility irremediably set in, one of us—my great-grandfather Charles S. Maurice, an engineer, ironmaster and builder of railroad bridges—in the decades after the Civil War made himself almost seriously rich, a fact with some slight bearing on myself to this day.

The Morrises are another story, at once simpler and more extravagant. "Never have I known a family, whose lineaments either good, or bad, are stamped in more indelible characters." Thus John

Blair Dabney, an Episcopal clergyman of Virginia, who in 1850 interrupts his account of the Dabneys to devote thirty or forty pages to us his cousins. "Hence all that was repulsive and unamiable in their characters stood out prominently on the surface. They were too prone to defy public censure, to take pride in the inflexibility of their own will, to despise the imbecility of those who tamely submit to the dictation of others." The first American of this "race" (as Dabney calls them) was William who in about 1725, accompanied by his son Sylvanus, immigrated to Hanover County, Virginia, from Glamorganshire. This ancestor of mine must have arrived here rich, for he soon owned some 10,000 acres of land. Almost at once the Morrises' "tempestuous and vindictive passions" declared themselves. A widower, William "in the decline of life became enamoured of a servant maid, a member of his household, and regardless of pride and prudence, espoused this menial"—an event to which his son Sylvanus took unforgiving and unforgiven exception. Sylvanus was all but formally disinherited ("I give and bequeath to my son Sylvanus Morris one brindle cow and calf . . . and two steers at Ducking-hole plantation"), and forty slaves and the various "plantations" passed to the grandchildren. (I offer without anachronistic moral comment this piece of William's eighteenth-century testamentary prose: "I give and bequeath to my granddaughters . . . my negro man called big Charles to be equally divided between the three, also each of them a cow and calf . . .")

Plantation—the word has a grand ring to it. But Hanover County is not and never was the South of legend, the South of Tidewater Virginia and the great houses on the James. Taylor's Creek, the house the first William built in 1732, was an altogether simpler affair. When I was two or three my mother and I spent there the winter my mad father was confined in a Richmond hospital. Our daily visits to him I do not recall, but in glimpses I remember the house: the little rooms, dark and cold then, bare yet somehow cluttered with furniture; my cornshuck mattress (can this be right?) loud and hard under me; meals of salty ham and canned tomatoes from the army of jars lining the pantry shelf. Little feeling attaches to these recollections, which nonetheless express a great unhappiness—my mother's certainly, locked up as she must have felt she was in a lonely countryside with only a child and her sick husband's worried aunts for company. Yet as a grown man I have delighted in visiting the place, now much refurbished and the property of our Nelson cousins (the family from whom I take my middle name). On a

rainy afternoon in 1982 eighty or ninety of the Morris connection gathered there to celebrate 250 years of Taylor's Creek. And ourselves. For an hour or two we recognized each other as kin, the children of this handsome simple place, these few rooms the common point of departure to which for perhaps the first or last time we had returned.

Considered simply as a record of fact John Blair Dabney's account displays my ancestors as a succession of worthy but obscure Virginia gentry, well known to their neighbors no doubt but not to any wider world. They preserve the land they hold, most of it, or they add to it by local purchase or Kentucky speculation. Their names are William or Sylvanus (or William Sylvanus) or Richard or Charles or John or James, and they marry among their class or caste (including, perhaps too often, their cousinage). Increasingly the Morrises are not only farmers but doctors (one trains in Edinburgh) or lawyers. Except in the affairs of their county, they are not much given to politics, or not successfully so. One of them—"Great Richard" in the family mythology—is a Federalist at the wrong moment and on this is blamed his failure to be elected to Congress in 1814, though more than once he represents Hanover in the House of Delegates and he is something of a star in the state constitutional convention of 1830. In my great-grandfather's time we begin to set up as academics. In 1859 this Charles, a graduate of the University of Virginia, is professor of law at William and Mary. After Appomattox he returns to Taylor's Creek with a few twenty-dollar gold pieces hidden in the band of his hat, his capital for the new life, and commences schoolmaster. In 1869 he is a professor again—of English and "Belles Lettres" at the University of Georgia. In 1876 he is at home in Virginia once more, the professor now of Greek at Randolph Macon College. In 1882 he returns to Georgia, the professor of English again—*the* professor; as is customary he teaches every undergraduate. His first son, Sylvanus, will become a professor of law at Georgia; his third son, my grandfather John (born on the second day of the battle of Gettysburg), also by training a lawyer, will after a year at the University of Berlin become and remain almost forever professor of German at Georgia, dying at last in 1955. A million miles off, deep in the late twentieth century I bring up the tail of this academic procession.

So much for such appearances on any public record as the Morrises have made. In Dabney's account of us (he leaves off in my great-grandfather's youth) I find recorded traits of character that survive, however tamed and attenuated, in the Morrises I

"My grandfather Maurice and I," 1935

have known, including me. Dabney's is a tale or tally of singularity, of generations of angular personality and exorbitant selfhood expressing itself as acquisitiveness, unchecked frankness, and an arrogant contempt for the views and sensibilities of others. The Morrises, it appears, distinguished themselves from others by "greater inflexibility of purpose, . . . more impetuous passions, less sympathy for human weakness, a more distrustful and censorious spirit, and a keener appetite for acquisition." In them "the sense of justice was more strongly developed than the feeling of benevolence"—justice to themselves in particular, for they were "always tenacious of their interests." Over and over Dabney protests that they are not grasping, not really. They display an "overweening love of money," yes; but as he reports of his Morris grandfather, "while he might be thought rather hard in his dealings," he was never "accused, so far as I know, of seeking his own profit by unfair advantage . . ." That "so far as I know" seems a rather desperate parenthesis. Dabney's pages are full of unconscious comedy as he struggles to set out honestly the Morrises' unamiable qualities while fending off conclusions any reader might reasonably draw. A Colonel Richard Morris was "disposed to be harsh and cynical: and this leaning of his often betrayed him into ridicule and satire for which in common with many of his race he had a peculiar and remarkable talent." He was "tenacious of authority," "a strict disciplinarian," "prone to suspicion," "undu-

ly disputatious and unyielding," and his "habitual distrust . . . repelled the love of his fellow men." Yet to his loyal kinsman Dabney this "unaffected"— for which read stunningly rude—"old fashioned gentleman" seemed somehow "an agreeable companion, a kind relative, an affectionate father, and a hospitable host"; and "when he unbent himself he was extremely social and amusing . . ." Not even his "bitterest enemies" thought him dishonorable.

One such "old fashioned gentleman" after another inhabits Dabney's pages. "Irony had grown so much into a habit with him, that you were at a loss to know when he was expressing his real opinions," he says of one of us, noticing too "a blunt abrupt manner bordering on rudeness." "Notwithstanding his distrust of mankind" he occasionally performed kind and generous actions. Another "hot and hasty" Morris could never "be accused . . . of hiding animosity under a smiling exterior. . . . He had the *fortiter in re* in perfection, but made little pretention to the *suaviter in modo*." The manners of another such upcountry Squire Western were "brusque and unpolished almost to rusticity." Everywhere one reads of "the spirit of opposition," "unbending independence," "a gruff surly manner," "a choleric temper." And so it continues. Even in the 1890s, Dabney having long since fallen silent, my great-uncle Sylvanus records the "one flaw" of my great-grandfather Charles: "He sometimes yielded to gusts of temper, and lost control of himself."

Sylvanus's prose is blander than Dabney's; so nowadays, to my regret, is the character of the Morrises who in the early generations, however insufferable they may have been, were at least men of weight and force. In my father's madness, to be sure, I see suggestions of the inherited temperament that must have made our forebears a torment even to themselves: his sudden glints of mania even in sanity, his overpowering charm that might alter in an instant to intense suspiciousness and a hint of rage barely under control, a large recklessness of feeling that, unbacked by money to protect him from its consequences, made him seem not eccentrically independent like his ancestors but culpably willful, an exasperater, a man for his inferiors (in the family and outside it) to blame or pity or excuse. In dying sane, or almost so, though he left no slightest noticeable mark on the world, my father was, I think, a kind of hero, the not-finally-defeated struggler with an inherited temperament that in others had perhaps been empowering, if only ambiguously so, but which in him was chiefly an obstacle to the use of his gifts and to his granting himself, or even knowing what were, his own deep wishes. Perhaps this view of him is melodramatic or (almost the same thing) sentimental or otherwise false. But in these autobiographical paragraphs I maintain it is the right one.

I did not live long among the Morrises, though I think that in the five or six years of my parents' marriage I became one of them. After the Oxford year my father took up a graduate fellowship at the University of Virginia. I almost remember this Charlottesville time—that is, I remember remembering it, in glimpses and flashes. Our little house on Chancellor Street shook as the trains from the west slowed for the station. Mother walked me on the University grounds. In time I was dictating to her what I called songs, a few of which some university wag made part of a public reading in Richmond as "the work of one of our younger poets." In the closet a cask of bootleg whiskey exploded, ruining my father's new suit. And after a while my father's fellowship was not renewed.

I think it was now that, as cause not consequence, my father first went mad. From a family visit in the Adirondacks a telegram summoned Mother to Washington, where my father had been working at the Library of Congress. She found him in St. Elizabeth's, straitjacketed in a bare cell. What form the affliction took I do not certainly know (though over the years I must have been told a dozen times). I think I remember that after some days or weeks of increasingly agitated excitement he seized on a newspaper

story as accusing him of a murder in Richmond, to which he wished instantly to confess. But this account I am entirely capable of having invented for myself. In any case, my father was soon transferred to the Richmond hospital (as if granted, it now occurs to me, a version of his wish). Perhaps we too, my mother and I, were locked away, shut up in Morris country that winter at Taylor's Creek. Or is this thought too fanciful? "Down the Little Red Lane," Mother would say, tipping the spoonful of codliver oil into my mouth, and the phrase always connects itself with the long driveway of the old place, a narrow track cut deep into the clay, along which one afternoon I tried to escape. Beyond the gate on the far side of the woods stood a scattering of Negro shacks or cabins where for half an hour or so I excited myself with my disobedience among the washpots and half-disassembled cars and unwelcoming, worried civility. In Georgia Professor Morris was reading Freud, hurrying through him in the account I've been given, as if doing so would help his son, believing as professors do that books will save us.

After a few months it seemed that my father's case was not hopeless (and in the longest run it was not). Through some connection of my grandfather's a job was found for him with the Georgia state relief agency. Now we three were once more together, in an apartment in Madison, a small town near Athens and my grandparents. Here my recollections begin to assemble, perhaps not quite at random. I am three, and my father is playing the cello. In the Windsor chair brought home from England, the room lit only by the coal fire, he leans to the instrument, and what I receive is not music but separate impulses, distinct and unresolving vibrations, something in the lowest of registers, reverberations of the walls and floor. Somewhere in the room, though I cannot place them in this memory, hang two pictures that accompany us everywhere: in great slashes of blue and black a print of horses; and a blonde Renaissance serenity, her profiled bust like a brocaded wing chair, the distance behind her deeply wanderable. Much read to, I am a talkative bookish child. Down the stairs from our kitchen to the coalpile in the alley the Young Man in *Alice* threatens to kick Father William. On my tricycle, its front wheel battered out of true, I grind to and fro on the sidewalk, in a rage at some admonishment: "I'm not going to *do* it. I'm not going to *do* it. I'm not going to *do* it—but I *will*." I am especially fond of certain pieces of verse: "I sent a message to the fish. / I told them 'This is what I wish.' / The little fishes' answer was / "We cannot do it, Sir, Because.'" This I have learned from Mother, the comic muse. The others I have by heart from my father: "The Mountain and the Squirrel had a quarrel" and "It was many and many a year ago, / In a kingdom by the sea, / That a maiden there lived whom you may know / By the name of Annabel Lee . . . / *She* was a child and *I* was a child . . ." On my tricycle, as if I already had a history I repeat these lines to myself, penetrated with pleasure. At night, my father absent somewhere, Mother sings me to sleep: "Bye Baby Bunting . . ." I am wholly attended.

In Georgia I almost died, in the first and worst pain I can remember. To my exploring finger, even now unwilling to leave a wound alone, a crevasse opens behind my left ear, a souvenir inscription. That deep infection was then a serious business, one not to be treated as at first mine was with syringes the size, as it seemed to me, of fire extinguishers. The cart to the operating room I recall and the room itself and the ether cone. And then the two or three weeks of hospital recovery. ("Hospital" was a new word and I remember revolving it: hospital, hospitable, hospitality. Was the hospital hospitable? These reflections pleased my elders.) My enormous hurt head ducked away from the doctor's hands and it took him an exasperated hour to change the dressing. From my high bed in the corner room I looked out into the tops of trees—an unexampled view. Mother read to me from *A Child's Garden of Verses:* "I have to go to bed and see / The birds still hopping on the tree, / Or hear the grown-up people's feet / Still going past me in the street." From the sidewalk invisible beneath the trees precisely these sounds reached me.

> I was the giant great and still
> That sits upon the pillow-hill,
> And sees before him, dale and plain,
> The pleasant land of counterpane.

In my sleep a waxy secretion sealed my eyes, and I awoke believing I was blind.

In 1959, in a book of new poems plucked casually from the Columbia University bookstore shelf, these lines:

> Here in the first glass cage
> the little bobcats arch themselves,
> still practicing their snarl
> of constant rage.
>
> The bison, here, immense,
> shoves at his calf, brow to brow,
> and looks it in the eye
> to see what it is thinking now.

These effigies of opposition I recognized at once. Whoever this W. D. Snodgrass might be, in the old state capitol on the campus of the University of Iowa he and his child and my father and I had paid our timekilling visits to the same theatre of taxidermy. "[I]ts guardian, / the patchwork dodo," was unmistakable. In the flesh or feather, at four I had recognized this fabulous bird from an illustration in *Alice,* and here, on a page again, in a new poem, its certain recollection was evoked, vivid almost as life. In first experience and in memory these images of extinction, these shows of life under arrest, charmed me. And the poet on his page seemed, marvellously, to have written, though from the father's point of view, a passage in my autobiography.

Soon after the operation on my head, a sometime teacher of my father's, a professor of American literature named Norman Foerster, arranged for him a fellowship at Iowa, and there that fall my mother and I joined him. The train trip seemed endless. We were undertaking this great journey, I thought, "to see the rabbits"—and in the event, Cedar Rapids was a shocking disappointment. Into the ordinary subur-

"My mother," 1940

Morris, 1941

In Iowa City I saw my parents naked, surprising them by pretended accident. No fuss was made of these occasions. My mother's curious defect bemused me, and as if somehow to simulate it I used now and then to slip on her underpants—electric blue, coldly smooth—and look on myself in their dressing mirror. I remember, too, experiments with her lipstick—cosmetic efforts, like cutting my own hair, not much approved of.

As always I was much read to. And variously: on the one hand, Beatrix Potter, *Little Black Sambo,* pleasant rubbish from the library; on the other, when Mother tired of such things, the *Ancient Mariner* (illustrated by Doré?) or Hilaire Belloc's *Cautionary Tales,* source of the first poem of any length I remember knowing entire.

> John Vavassour de Quentin Jones
> Was very fond of throwing stones
> At Horses, People, Passing Trains,
> But 'specially at Windowpanes.
> Like many of the Upper Class
> He liked the Sound of Broken Glass,
> It bucked him up and made him gay:
> It was his favorite form of Play.
> But the Amusement cost him dear,
> My children, as you now shall hear.

And so on for fifty or sixty lines. This edifying work, I now see, tells the tale of a nurse who inveigles her senile patient into leaving her his fortune—Miss Charming, "Who now resides in Portman Square / And is accepted everywhere"—and it must have amused my parents to hear me recite it. To me it was "About John, Who lost a Fortune by Throwing Stones," and John was the name I liked to find at the center of things, at whatever cost. I might understand hardly a word of it but it sounded fine—and in memory its brisk worldliness sorts healthily with the slightly depressive lonelinesses and nostalgias of *A Child's Garden of Verses,* always congenial to my temperament, or "Annabel Lee," my father's loss-laden favorite.

I set in our house the action of "Rikki-Tikki-Tavi," Kipling's story of the mongoose who saves his human family from the cobra Nag and his yet more sinister consort Nagaina and the twenty-five dangerous eggs about to hatch in the melon-bed at the bottom of the garden. Switching on the light in our kitchen I almost thought I might discover Chuchundra the muskrat, "a brokenhearted little beast" who "whimpers and cheeps all the night, trying to make up his mind to run into the middle of the room." In

ban comfort of our Iowa City house we settled for our last year as a family.

At four I had become, I suspect, a worry to my parents. Until that year I cannot remember having been for so much as an hour in the company of a child. (This cannot be true, but so it seems.) Now this state of affairs was to be set right. In the Psychology Department's kindergarten, as full of rage as the angriest of my ancestors I submitted to be torn from my new playmates to build with awkward blocks under the testing eyes of graduate students or pour sand futilely from one odd-shaped little bucket into another. At rest time I lay rigid on my cot, already in love with the blackhaired girl in the next cubicle, descried dimly through the muslin screen. At the first birthday party I attended, ignorant of the convention I protested that I too should receive presents, loudly drawing the analogy of Christmas. At a party of my own I fell into a fury when someone's older sister—uninvited, foisted upon us—so insisted on the head of the table that I was deposed: my anger can revive to this day.

our bathroom as in the bathroom of the bungalow I listened for "the faintest *scratch-scratch* in the world—a noise as faint as that of a wasp walking on a window-pane—the dry scratch of a snake's scales on brickwork." On the sidewalk in front of our house I greeted a neighbor who, preoccupied, snubbed me. "Good morning," I repeated, persistent. "It is I, John Nelson Morris, who speak." When this oddity was reported to my mother she knew at once that I had been very angry, for I had spoken as the tiger in *The Jungle Book,* Shere Khan, balked of his purpose. It was as if I knew the world only in allusion.

In Iowa City I took to running away—or not away, exactly, for I always circled back to home, where in recollection at the end of one of these adventures a policeman waits with my mother to receive me. Over my mother's relief he is stern. If I do this again, he says, he will arrest me: the word seems enormous and I admire his uniform. And I do it again. In the dark I pause on the road by the frozen river, something I have never seen. Below me dozens of people are skating, cutting figures on the ice. It fascinates me, how they leave these traces behind them. As if the scene requires it, snow is falling through the streetlight as I climb the hill toward home. In case I should meet Goliath, a taller man than my father, I am dragging a gunnysack a quarter full of stones.

My father's fellowship was not renewed; perhaps not reapplied for. I recall nothing of our departure from Iowa City. At some time before the birth of my sister, Anne, in the December of 1936 my parents parted finally. From then until the summer of 1945, when he and I shared a bedroom in a Savannah roominghouse, I saw my father I think only once. From 1936 I grew up, and grew up happily, a member more and more of my mother's family—the son of Charles Morris translated, so to speak, into the son of Charlotte Maurice, with attendant gains and losses. Now I was to be John in another language.

The Civil War ruined the Morrises; the years just after it made the Maurices. In a box of not very interesting letters my great-grandfather Charles Stewart Maurice fails to tell me clearly how he manufactured his fortune. Elsewhere I glean that, Salutatorian of the Williams class of 1861 and a member of Phi Beta Kappa, he trained as an engineer at the Rensselaer Polytechnic Institute and, commissioned in the Union navy, served in the blockade of the Confederacy, duty in which, in the family's irreverent phrase, he "offered up his digestion on the altar of his country." After a peacetime false start or

two, by 1871 he was a prospering partner in a bridgeworks venturous enough to be the second in America to build in steel, a new kind of work requiring, his obituarist wrote, "original designs or improvements on tools already in use." By 1895 when he retired the partnership of Kellogg and Maurice had become the Union Bridge Company; his firm had by then erected bridges across the Hudson at Poughkeepsie, the Niagara river and the Platte and the Tombigbee, the Cairo bridge across the Ohio and the Memphis bridge across the Mississippi, others in Nova Scotia and Brazil, and a section of the Third Avenue El. "The sinking of the caissons for the piers" of the Hawkesbury River Bridge in New South Wales "in the tidal flow of the river was . . . the most hazardous work undertaken by the Company." No doubt the realest risks were run by the Australian construction workers. Still, on such caissons and piers it is respectable to found or erect a fortune, making something besides money. Never mind the dullness of his letters.

I think we never quite recovered from him. Or is this speculation merely a cliché about descendants? He was at any rate unrepeated, his sons declining to contest with him on precisely his terms. My grandfather—George, the second of them—was to be sure himself a civil engineer and a builder of bridges: one across the Susquehanna near Harrisburg I know was still in use in 1958. But about 1912 Grandfather bought 600 cheap acres of land in the Sandhills section of south-central North Carolina and set up as a peach farmer. In the tale we came to tell ourselves about this decision, he borrowed money from his father to disobey his father's advice.

North Carolina was not Grandfather's first choice. Thousands of acres of Louisiana swamp he could have had for the same price; so, too, some great tract in the barren west. My grandmother, a Virginian, thought these places too far from home. The point is, Grandfather was not particularly interested in raising peaches. A generation or so too late he wanted to live as if on a frontier. In this underpeopled, not very fertile part of North Carolina he could in a fashion reinvent the past. In a drama of his own devising he surveyed and cleared the land and constructed his life in the image of an American country gentleman, freestanding and independent. He built his house out of steel and concrete, forthright as any bridge, lovely and serviceable and as lasting (I hope) as stone. Yet in part of his mind, I think, he suspected the whole thing to be a sort of fiction. Grandfather was a latecomer and he knew it.

In manners, conduct and dress a conservative by instinct, Grandfather was nonetheless with almost his whole heart a technological modernizer (witness the materials of his house). A hunter of elk in Wyoming, in his pleasures he was preindustrial, archaic; yet he drove to the wilderness in a Chrysler, approving of every new mile of paved road opening before him. In very old age Grandfather published at his own expense a booklet called *Daniel Boone in North Carolina,* in which he settled to his satisfaction the tiny question of just where that itinerant sojourned in the state. This modest enterprise expresses Grandfather's lifelong interest, not unusual among men of his class and generation, in America in its simpler condition, an interest in the exploration and settlement of the continent. Books on these subjects made up most of his library. This interest was in a first view innocent, even romantic. His booklet displays as epigraph Byron's jaunty stanza about "The General Boone, backwoodsman of Kentucky." Yet the question engaging him was the humblest matter of trivial biographical fact: where *precisely* in Yadkin County did Boone's cabin stand, on what surveyable, what mappable square feet of ground? My grandfather's father had erected bridges, some of them of original and ingenious design, over rivers on the routes of exploration. Perhaps nothing now was left but detail work. In North Carolina Grandfather was filling in the map.

In an old American style Grandfather named his place after one of the family's points of origin: Ballintoy, a village on the Scottified north coast of Ireland. (This was perhaps a doubling gesture of affiliation, for the old settlers of his new section were Scotch-Irish too.) Here after the year in Iowa City I began the process of my own affiliation. In six or seven years under the spell of family and the place I succeeded in becoming imperfectly a Maurice.

Even at first I was not entirely a stranger. Between the Richmond hospital and Georgia my father had been set to sanative hard labor, and in a glimmer of recollection I am proud to watch him plow behind a mule, breaking ground for the new parterre at the bottom of Grandmother's garden. From a yet earlier visit arises what I think is my earliest memory of all: I am climbing into bed in my grandparents' room, my cot set near the fire. This room, thirty or thirty-five feet long by perhaps twenty, I would come to know much better. Against the north wall to the left of the door as one entered stood my grandparents' four-poster. Windows at the gable end looked over the levels of the acre or so of rather formal garden to the pinetrees and blackjack

from which the whole place had been claimed. To the east French doors opened onto a tiny balcony. Beyond the flagstone terrace and the lawn the forest fell away as if it all belonged to us; on the horizon a glint of white picked out a steeple in Carthage, the county seat eleven miles into the distance.

In those days this seemed the center of silence, where even a child might be for an hour or two at a time alone. I remember what seem to be months of the middle of the morning or endless afternoon. Pausing from my moony concentration on this or that I might hear the voice of a dove or a bobwhite or the bird, whatever it was, that by the hour claimed my aunt's attention: "Miss Mau*rice*! Miss Mau*rice*! Miss Mau*rice*!" No human sound anywhere, unless now and then pots clashing in the kitchen or a maid's footsteps on the flagstones on the hall. Listening hard I might just make out, half the house away, the longcase clock in the livingroom, the slow clack of its pendulum, the whir of its machinery gathering strength to strike each quarter of the hour. At noon the dull bell in its cupola on the barn released the hands from work. All morning for years, as it seemed

"My grandfather Maurice," 1943

to me, and uninterruptable, Grandmother sat writing on crinkling paper airmail letters to wisemen in India. In 1989 I sold her chair at auction for some thousands of dollars, the price of perfections invisible to my eye.

In my earliest time in that house such a day might have begun with my tiptoeing in my pajamas toward my grandparents' bedroom (for now of course I had a room of my own) along the gallery above the stairs. There I would join Grandmother in their bed, sharing from her tray her porridge and egg, though not her breakfast drink, warm water and lemonjuice taken for the sake of her bowel. Through the openwork tester or canopy I inspected the grainy plaster of the ceiling and in a sidetable drawer discovered over and over again Grandfather's untouchable .45 pistol. What we spoke of in these comfortable half-hours I wish I could remember, especially since I am alone in not recalling this uniformly kind and gentle woman with a reflex of warm regard. This defect of feeling puzzles and reproaches me.

Or precisely at seven I might join Grandfather at the glimmering long oval table in the diningroom. In memory this meal never varies: an apple, a bowl of oatmeal, a three-minute egg. As in his portrait above the fireplace behind him he is dressed in a Norfolk jacket, riding breeches and boots or puttees. (His costume cannot have been so uniform; perhaps the portrait has frozen the recollection.) Grandfather pares our apples, each peeling a coil single and entire upon the plate. These leavings we preserve as a present to the horses, our first piece of morning business.

My grandfather was a gentleman, certainly, and a farmer, but not a gentleman farmer; there was no rich man's nonsense, no tax loss Kentucky grandeur about the working buildings on the place, a showiness Grandfather would have disdained even if he could have afforded it. The forge or shop, the sheds for the tractor and combine and the trucks and the plows and the harrow, the gashouse and the lubrication ramp or greaserack, the wooden watertower, the dogrun and chickenhouse and pigstye, the corncrib—among these log and pineboard plainnesses I could if I wished pass my day. Over them all the barn, though no great size, seemed to me to loom tremendous. At five I found the horses alarming but, encouraged by Grandfather, on tiptoe I offered from my flinching palm my applepeel to David Gray, Lady or Parfait, their prehending lips and yellow enormous teeth. These tractable animals were trained both to plow and saddle. Great David was my favorite, a vast

dappled beast, but when at six or seven I began to ride, his huge barrel was impossible for my legs to clasp and Parfait, an aged chestnut mare once my mother's, became my horse. Beyond these mild and amiable creatures were stalled a team of white mules, contrary and unrewarding; across from them, beyond the grain bins, stood stanchions for the three cows. The dark loft above all this I never dared to penetrate (rumored home of a blacksnake, a master mouser), though I admired to see our foreman Grady standing in its gable door manhandling with pulleys and grasping tackle a season of hay up from the truck or wagon below.

In a little room to the right of the west door hung the horsecollars, the blackest of flat black, and in festoons the long working reins and traces; to the left in their own compartment (tackroom too grand a term for it) were disposed on long pegs bridles and the cavalry saddles, high at pommel and cantle, that Grandfather preferred to the effete English style. Here hung too, in a place of ironic monitory honor and never used, a single piece of western saddlery, fantastic with horn and skirts and embossing, the Eighty-Thousand-Dollar Mistake as it was known in the family mythology, sole relic of some great-uncle's failure at ranching on the High Plains.

On most days the fire in our forge was out, its rare hours of life therefore drawing me the more strongly. No one man on the place was master there, but almost everyone could turn his hand to tinkering or replace a cast horseshoe between visits from the itinerant smith. Under direction I turned the handle of the mechanical bellows and the coals bloomed and I gazed sleepy and unblinking as the workpiece turned whitehot, till Grady, perhaps, or Robert or Albert or Jesse withdrew it from the fire. Everything I see in this recollection is hard as fact. Yet already I lived in a book, and the hammer I hear rings out in every such memoir as this one. In my overalls I longed to hale from the anvil the authenticating sword in my Howard Pyle version of King Arthur.

The barn, the shop, the sheds, the gashouse— here at every season something was doing, and from a perch in the mulberry tree by the greaserack I looked on, at once fascinated and almost extinguished with boredom. In summer the whole farm gathered purpose. Now a hundred pickers hired by the day swarmed in the orchards, and trucks bound for New York loaded at the packinghouse, a great open shed clattering with machinery. Overhead dangerous-looking leather belts transmitted power from a huge, unmuffled gasoline engine, and for three months a ramshackle factory roared in the middle of miles of country silence. I longed to join the responsible girls deftly culling the bruised or overripe peaches passing rapidly on rollers up an inclined plane before them, and I watched entranced as the fruit rolled across a long, tilted table-like affair, sorting itself by size as it moved through a maze of baffles, to be tumbled at last into fragile-looking springy bushel baskets. And over it all the booming and rattling noise—and a cloud of poisonous, itchy dust, as if from a thousand carpets vigorously beaten. This was a place of work, and it seemed, I think, to the remembered child inexpressibly festive.

Or did so until the summer when, twelve or thirteen, I was set to pasting labels on those baskets, required in hundreds. This task was assigned me—allowed me, really—out of kindness and lasted, I suppose, no more than a couple of weeks; yet it remains, preposterously, my version of the Blacking Factory. In a sort of attic under the peak of the tin roof, in panicky haste I worked in the ridiculous fear that if I fell behind the whole operation below me would halt. Crammed tight in nested stacks, each basket had to be wrenched or wrestled free with a force that might destroy it; so that to succeed was sometimes to fail and I labored under a kind of judgement, hurried and ashamed.

Of this matter imagination made—or makes—enormously too much. I solicit no tears for this fortunate boy. Ballintoy—Home; the House; the Place: always the honoring capitals when any of us spoke or thought of it—seemed a full, perfect and sufficient world to me, a plenitude of fascinations for a noticing child. A noticer, a watcher and listener, is what I think I chiefly was in those years. Uncoaxed by *my* hand, milk drummed against the side of the pail and, carried by others, came to the pantry where, poured into pans, it was set to cool on a shelf in the coldcloset. Cream rose for our tea; or someone churned it into butter for our table. In November, before my eyes a couple of pigs were slaughtered, trussed up and screaming, the blood gathered in a bucket, a black washpot of water boiling for their scalding steaming in the sharp air; and someone taught me to make a whistle of the bladder. Corrupting recollection almost makes a Dutch picture of the scene. Mr. Maddox, Grandmother's gardener, killed us our chickens with an ax. The bodies tumbled and flounced in comic convulsions, and on the separated heads the eyes seemed to stare and widen while the beaks worked silently open and shut. In the kitchen the cook drew their guts, and in her brisk black hand the shining tangle of intestines, all blue and green,

made me think of the water-snakes in the Mariner poem Mother had read me.

In two skills, riding and shooting, I received instruction, if in a rather homemade way. Twenty miles off in Southern Pines and Pinehurst the rich Northern winter people had invented for themselves a horsey society complete with a Master of Fox Hounds and all the rest. This struck me as glamourous, but the family line on it was amused contempt. In this view as in most others we followed my grandfather who in early life had seen more than enough of the rich at this kind of play. Only golf, irredeemably suburban, more deeply stirred his impatience. (To a caller recounting stroke by stroke his assault on this or that hole at Pinehurst I once heard Grandfather respond, "How uninteresting. How very uninteresting," in tones so polite that the narrator refused the evidence of his ears.) For us any pleasure was the better if made to seem useful. In winter Grandfather and I rode to exercise the idle horses, to beat the bounds of the place or to inspect the New Ground, a field freshly taken into cultivation, or the plantation of young pines along the county road. Where the land fell away into deep woods we traced out the firebreaks where tongues of red clay penetrated our sandy geology. Pebbles of white quartz washed out there, and on the lookout for wonders I imagined them to be flecked with gold and was slow to learn from disappointment. Here and there a clearing opened for no apparent present reason, as if the trail were an abandoned road leading us to the site of something. Not only in memory do those hollow lanes seem to have been full of an excitement. Even a child felt that just over the next rise some other life might be detected. Deeper in we might reach the little waterfall, famous in my mother's stories, where as a girl she had walked alone with her excellent dogs Romulus and Remus, creatures of fable.

I never jumped a fence or learned how properly to kick Parfait into a rack or canter. I made a tangle of the reins, the curb and snaffle. Never mind. In recollection, where it never rains, under the high-capped longleaf pines Grandfather and I ride home up half a mile of the white sandy driveway that winds and disappears and then declares itself once more. At the barn, dismounting, I stagger on my own feet, suddenly short again.

From outside our world the sepia Sears-Roebuck catalog offered for sale a Red Ryder BB gun, that dauntless cowboy and his little Indian pal besieged in illustration on the shiny page among the Columbia bicycles and the female models in their countrified, anaphrodisiac underwear. When I was eight Grandfather gave me a real rifle. Once my uncle's, this single-shot Winchester .22 had awaited my coming of sufficient age in a cabinet in the office, Grandfather's business room to the left of the front door, with the rest of our small armory: a pair of English shotguns; a serious hunting rifle (product of Savage Arms: handsome name); a lever-action 38.40, to be mine when I was sixteen; my great-grandfather's Union Navy revolver, a longbarrelled .44; a bolo; one or two other such things. All these we kept ritually clean. The ramrods and pullthroughs, the patches in their tiny boxes held for me the glamour of initiation, the special charm of devoted things, of single and arcane purposes. On the mantelpiece stood a studio photograph of Niblo, a waterdog dead sixty years, and a framed pencil sketch of the U.S.S. *Agawan,* my great-grandfather's Civil War blockader, nosediving into the North Atlantic in a gale off Cape Sable. A little casket made from the planking of the *Constitution* preserved the best of the arrowheads that came to light in clearing the ground for our house, of which there had been so many, and in so many states, as to suggest the site had been an aboriginal arms factory.

Under Grandfather's direction I labored like a recruit at the rifleman's finicking, divisible skill. On my belly in the dust beside the Scuppernong arbor, for hours I shot with pencil and paper. Over and over I Formed the Sight Picture: the black disc balanced on the sightblade; I Tightened the Group, Grandfather marking each Point of Aim. I may have thought my rifle made me a cowboy. In the dull discipline of dry firing Grandfather taught me to be something of a marksman.

Grandfather and I had in mind greater things than targetshooting. But I never became a hunter. The War ended Grandfather's expeditions to Wyoming for his biennial elk. (Now no more ashtrays made from the creature's hooves, exuding the stench of death in damp weather. Even I did not miss them.) And the trip we had once fantastically proposed for ourselves, down the wild Mackenzie River in Canada, was never to be made.

But for some years I had a use for my rifle. With my .22 I was proof against what sometimes seemed the huge boredom of Home. Though I loved every foot of the place, now and then a great dreariness descended. For half an hour or so I might lean against the mailbox kicking the sand in the driveway; or pressing my face hard against the trunk of a pinetree, pick at the layers of bark as if at a scab. In the hot afternoon, useless to myself, I drooped about the place, poking in corners, desultory, selfpitying in Eden, full of a childish Nothing to Do. From the

pasture downhill from the barn might sound once in a long while the single clank of a cowbell. In the house the downstairs rooms were dim, the summer curtains drawn; and every book was unreadable. Upstairs in refuge from the heat Grandmother lay resting, dressed in the lightest, airiest cottons, unapproachable, scarcely breathing. Sometimes I appeased my torpor with Mr. Maddox's ax, raging in the scrubby growth below the dogrun, in twenty minutes laying flat a dozen or fifteen spindly blackjack. More often, savage with this boredom (and yet as if I were suppressing an excitement), for an hour at a time I was absolutely accurate with my rifle. At the end of the lowest level of the garden I set up my targets, a sheet of bullseyes or a tin can wedged between two stones. Flat among the lawn furniture I fired my fifty or a hundred cartridges at the Germans or Japanese arising out of the wilderness beyond the last flowerbed, each round concluding safely in that clutter of trees.

Thus it was I fought the war at Ballintoy—or at the wheel of our Buick baking in the driveway, where I sat at the stick of a Spitfire, the Moore County sky swarming with Messerschmitts. And what, it now occurs to me to wonder, would Grandmother have made of that in her bedroom reading her peaceable Indians and Quakers? We all went to war in our own fashion. Grandfather, that evenhanded man, was president of the county Ration Board, starving his own farm of gasoline to set an example. Once Grandmother crowded the house full of people in evening clothes in support of Bundles for Britain. Grandfather looked splendid in his dinnerjacket—a costume that in time he passed to me. Knotting a black tie was the last male skill he taught me.

This prodigious social exertion I do not remember to have been repeated, or not on anything like that scale, though rumors of earlier formal jollifications echoed to me from the Old Days, that legendary period or heroic age before my birth when every room was full of houspartying young people, friends of my mother's and my aunt Ellen's, visitors from the North, instructors and graduate students from Chapel Hill (among them Charles Morris, my father). Now the tennis court west of the drive between the melonbed (haunt of Nag and Nagaina?) and the dog cemetery was reverting to nature, a rusting, immoveable roller the only sign of former function on the flat expanse of pinestraw. From these more sociable days our swimming pool survived, scene now of my birthday parties and an occasional refuge of snapping turtles. This sizeable construction ("the shape of a baby's stomach," in Grandmother's slightly mysterious phrase) my grandfather had inserted along a contour of the hill below the house. The tar-and-macadam sealer between the slabs of concrete leaked badly, and the pool had constantly to be replenished by pump from a pond deeper in the woods. Every summer or so there would emerge from the supply pipe the head and then, with each pulse of the ram, in increments of inches the whole body of an enraged serpent caught up in the toils of the process. So 1938, say, might be remembered, on something like the Chinese model, as the Year of the Watermoccasin.

In fact the house was often full of visitors still. Cousin Marian was one, a maiden sub-librarian at Vassar, her mouth in constant pursing motion as if she were about to spit out a persimmon. Or Cousin Priscilla, a glamourgirl of sorts, who, refugeeing from the country club rigors of Cedarhurst, Long Island, was to marry first one, then another Yugoslavian. Or Cousin Frazier, a New Yorker, very rich by our modest standard, tall and preternaturally handsome for a Maurice, with an oldfashioned "society" accent in which he recorded books for the blind. His tales of Berlin in the 1920s, even if severely edited, I wish I had retained. And with Frazier his friend Bill C., whose conversation ran too much on his acquaintance among theatre people and the Irish peerage. Any day the guestrooms opening onto the gallery might contain one or another of my aunt Ellen's friends: unpromoteable female associate professors of French or assistant deans of women, full of firm and unusual opinions, oddly and vividly dressed. These persons even a child could almost see were locked into some angular relation with ordinary life yet were (like Ellen) on the whole content. One of them dashingly flew her own airplane. In later life I now and then found my path crossing theirs in strange places—a fact perhaps supporting Ellen's view, often reiterated and half believed, that there are only 415 people in the world.

Such visitors might remain a day or two, a week, rarely a month. From earliest days I faintly recall ancient Aunt Lida, no relation really, who stayed off and on for years, her ashes at last buried in our family plot. A friend of Grandmother's, perhaps an object of her charity, she looked like Mr. Toad in *The Wind in the Willows* and had a Ph.D. in French history from Columbia. Ellen used to recall her strong interest in Marie Antoinette: "The guillotine was Lida's King Charles's head."

Ellen herself, my mother's elder sister, seldom left Ballintoy. Occasional jaunts to Chapel Hill, an expedition to Mexico, another to Bermuda, a yearly month or two at her cottage on the South Carolina coast—these are the only absences I remember. Boarding school had not worked, Ellen returning home almost as soon as deposited, and college was not even attempted. By contrast a winter in Paris in the 1920s loomed in legend as a great success. This venture had been organized to separate my mother from an unsuitable admirer. There one story had my mother confounding herself by undertaking to explain in French to her class of other visiting foreigners the working of the United States Constitution, a document of which she had scarcely heard. Ellen on the other hand was unembarrassable. The Madame Quelque-chose with whom the girls boarded summoned weekly dinnerparties to hear her discourse on any subject whatever in an uninhibited approximate French of the grossest accidental indecency. However infirm her grasp of the language, Ellen formed a lasting friendship with a translator of Faulkner to whom for years she explained by mail locutions like "worm fence" and "split-bottom chair"—terms perhaps opaque enough without a page or two of Ellen's spirited clarification.

Like the rest of the family Ellen assumed that a child was a rational being interested in the sort of things that interested her and wholly conversable. My elders never noticeably adapted their vocabulary to childish capacities. At the same time, if a word or subject puzzled me I had only to ask and a full and courteous explanation was instantly provided. (Most of them had, too, a modest gift for the telling and memorable phrase delivered impromptu and unselfconsciously. "Wrangle windows and divorcement doors," Ellen remarked of her parents' plans for their house.) The brisk good sense of this general family way with the young had a special charm coming from Ellen who retained all her life a childlike freshness of attack in her dealings with the world at large, an enthusiasm and emotional expressiveness. Her arms might fling wildly about and her voice vary widely in loudness and pitch, even roaring or screeching, or break suddenly into alarming loonlike laughter. One of my happiest recollections is Ellen seen from behind as she bustled toward some task, some object. She moved with a sort of vigorous waddle, every limb somehow in independent motion, as if the whole oddly hafted frame were held together inexpertly by wires. Then with a surprising force and deftness, intent, she wrung the neck of her problem. I loved her too in calmer mood—her gestures tamed, her voice resolving into ladylike composure, her face pensive now, lovely with introspection.

Ellen claimed perfect recall of everything read or heard before she was thirty; of nothing at all thereafter. The most remote association evoked from her memory passages of newspaper verse or Shelley, old songs, dialogue out of forgotten novels or Broadway plays, the 1907 summer schedule of trains between Bronxville and Manhattan. Contexts and sources were seldom supplied. In college I was amazed to discover that I had been listening to "Lycidas" all my life. Not surprisingly Ellen was a repository of family lore, a trove of generations of anecdote, a settler of arguments about the provenance of this or that piece of furniture or the precise degree of our relation to some distant cousin. About Family in the snobbish sense she cared only a little, but the family simply *as* family, as an entity, mattered tremendously. Undistinguished we might be; we were nonetheless distinct—our precious collective selves and no one else. Herself stunningly an original, she sometimes sank her own identity in ours, in her ancestors'. In her old age my cousin Tony kindly took her to live with him in Fairfax County, Virginia, where her mother's people came from. There she registered to vote. "And when did you move to the county?" the Registrar inquired. "In 1682," Ellen answered, with no air of saying anything out of the way.

In that old age she once expelled me, otherwise always her bright, particular star, from that company. Across the diningtable at Ballintoy for ten seconds of sudden senility she did not know me: "Who are you? Who *are* you?" A pause full of glittering blankness; then: "*I* know *you.* You're one of those *clever Morrises!*" I am shocked and hurt to remember it.

A Morris I certainly was. Where was the sin? True enough, no one could plausibly accuse the Maurices of whatever unpleasant thing Ellen meant by cleverness. But surely even the Morrises were not so clever as all that? In what did this quality consist? A century or so of provincial professorships? I followed in that train and was pleased to do so. But in the face of one of Grandfather Morris's articles on ringmail in *The Journal of English and Germanic Philology* I was almost as much at a loss as any Maurice. I could as soon bridge the Susquehanna as imitate it. Ellen was wrong: precisely in me one strain of Morris cleverness had run out (though perhaps a whisper of the old high mania remained). And as for the Maurices . . . well, for a generation or so that family had been hard happily to marry into; now it appeared you couldn't even be born one of them. If I, the favored

John N. Morris with his aunt Ellen, 1985

of Heaven, were not one of Us. . . . Let there be no more Maurices! Perhaps at forty-nine it was time to be myself alone. Or so I may have felt for the moment.

On one set of shelves in the livingroom at Ballintoy stood the remnants of a great-great-uncle's learned library—an early Erasmus, a handsome seventeenth-century Tacitus, a few other such things. This Uncle George's career at Trinity College in Connecticut had ended badly, in philology and poetry—a vast, mad work called *Aryan Word-Building* and a volume of *Verses,* both privately printed. No Maurice now concerned himself with such things, but they all were, somehow and unsystematically, decently well read in the oldfashioned English and American classics, particularly of fiction. This knowledge—which is not exactly what it was—they had acquired naturally, as the common mental furniture of their caste or class, and it was an occasion of quiet astonishment to them that in the university these books were the objects of study. Even among the authors they knew best their tastes may seem to the modern enlightened a touch timid or genteel: Trollope they preferred to Henry James; and Dickens was still chiefly a comic writer. Of Jane Austen they had a deeper, though unarticulated understanding. Grandfather read neither Addison nor Johnson but admired Addison more; Swift, though amusing, was unsuitable. But why, he always wondered, had he as a boy been forbidden the tedious Walter Scott? Except with Ellen poetry figured hardly at all, though in college Mother had shared the Vassar passion for Edna Millay and in Oxford she and my father read Housman to each other. Shakespeare was, surprisingly, an almost universal blank, the works of Gilbert and Sullivan having perhaps usurped his place. (Though Mother liked to mangle a quotation to some purpose. A plate of spaghetti once provoked from her "Worms have died, and men have eaten them"; and on parenthood she corrected Lear: "How sharper than a serpent's tooth it is to have a child.") Mother and Ellen ventured more among the modernists than did my grandparents, but not, I think, with any great sense of eager discovery. Books were not meant to be mysterious or excruciating.

What they had cobbled together out of all this was a common fund of allusion and a vocabulary of feeling and social notation subtle and supple enough to seem, falsely, sufficient for most purposes. Certain things they could say perfectly, if only to one another or the few much like them. They did not set out to puzzle, but this was often the result; people found

them quaint who merely failed to understand them. At the same time they shocked by their plainspokenness, their language always vigorous and apt, refusing all euphemism, surprising hearers who mistook direct and accurate speech for wit and outrageousness. In fact, though humorous enough in an old-fashioned sense of the term, they were not particularly witty and were touchingly pleased when others seemed to think them so. To them it was all a matter of simple precision.

On any winter night by the fire they are at liberty in their books. Each sits in a cone of light, alone in concert. On the hooked rug by the hearth a dog groans in his sleep; the pages turn; a quarter hour strikes. Alas for my piety, the work on Grandfather's lap is not Parkman's *Oregon Trail* but *Powder River: Let 'er Buck,* a new volume in the Rivers of America Series, or a Kenneth Roberts novel. Grandmother sets aside some female Theosophist or Schweitzer's little book on the historical Jesus; takes up *Scribner's* or *The Atlantic Monthly.* If Mother is here on one of her visits she is reading *The New Yorker.* On the table beside her sits *I'm a Stranger Here Myself,* by Ogden Nash. Without meaning to, Ellen commits to memory whole paragraphs of a story by "Saki."

If I am old enough this evening I am reading too—Howard Pyle's *Wonder Clock* or *Robin Hood* or *Otto of the Silver Hand.* Or *The X-Bar-X Boys* or one of the Oz books, a recent passion mildly disapproved of. If I am younger, in a minute one of the women will attend to me. If Grandmother tries me again with *The Water-Babies* I may go on strike, preferring Ellen and *Scottish Chiefs.* Otherwise I am almost undistinguishing on anyone's comfortable lap. *Babar* and *The Green Fairy Book* are all one to me. In the mirror in *Tanglewood Tales* I stare again and again at Medusa, and the Dragon's Teeth spring up the same armed men as in Iowa or Georgia. Over and over the King her father returns in *The Princess and the Goblins,* and high in the castle her grandmother sits in a bare room the princess cannot rediscover. John Vavassour de Quentin Jones is very fond of throwing stones. I sent a message to the fish: I told them, This is what I wish.

BIBLIOGRAPHY

Poetry:

Green Business, Atheneum, 1970.

The Life Beside This One, Atheneum, 1975.

The Glass Houses, Atheneum, 1980.

A Schedule of Benefits, Atheneum, 1987.

Other:

(Editor, with M. X. Lesser) *Modern Short Stories: The
Fiction of Experience,* McGraw-Hill, 1962.

*Versions of the Self: Studies in English Autobiography from
John Bunyan to John Stuart Mill,* Basic Books, 1966.

Has written poetry, articles, and reviews for numerous
publications, including *American Scholar, Modern Age,
Nation, South Atlantic Quarterly, Yale Review, Hudson
Review, Georgia Review, Harper's, New England Review,
New Republic, New Yorker, Shenandoah,* and *Sewanee
Review.*

Fernand Ouellette

1930-

(Translated from the French by Antonio D'Alfonso)

Discretion is, as Maurice Blanchot wrote, "literature's locus." Should we then assume that autobiographical writings are just unhealthy transgressions from the genres, wavering between Saint Augustine's confessions and Michel Leiris's heart laid bare? Perhaps . . . But who can claim that such a narrative is not a literary act, that is, more an outburst of fiction than the revelation of true events?

I will skim over this journey of mine and stress the points of interest in my development, making sure, however, that I keep intact my privacy by muffling the violet music of secrets and unreachable silences imbedded in their geodes. In short, I will try to calmly tame certain tendencies as I enter the troubling world of memory, and listen to the commotion made by internal images.

Writing is a subtle play of disclosure and concealment, of moving forwards and backwards. The writer must be able to express what seems impudent and reveal only what can be caught in subdued light or, better yet, what speaks in the stillness of objects and experiences. He should free himself of time and circumstances; he must transmute everything into a space where the *other* can find himself, and where gradually even the impudent aspects of revelation become blurred. The autobiographical text should be a palimpsest for every reader. This then is an attempt at the almost insurmountable challenge of writing about an existence more comfortable with contemplation and suffering than being analyzed under a harsh light which would dull everything.

Furthermore, a writer, with exceptions, does not need to have qualities of a public figure, especially if he is a quiet person and keeps away from the clamor of the literary circles and their institutions. Let him take risks in the forums of confession where every reader may turn out his "bull's horn" (Michel Leiris).

Fernand Ouellette, Turin, 1986

1

I was surely improperly breast-fed by a distracted mother, for I have become fatally impatient. I would not be surprised if I scratched her nipples, for as an older man, I never wanted to let my nails grow. It was only fifty-seven years later, in 1988, after my mother died, that I noticed my nails began to grow, painfully, roughly. It is thanks to impatience and unexpressed aggressivity I am able to walk into my own history, adapting myself to the *other* and to the world.

It all began on September 24, 1930, at 1660 rue Bennett, in a Montreal neighborhood called de Maisonneuve.

If I concentrate on my first memories, three encounters seem to have profoundly affected me, for I am still marked by them.

I must have been three years old when the brother of my mother's father came to visit us from the distant Abitibi region of northern Quebec, telling stories about American Indians. This was a sudden opening up to the *other,* the exotic, a parallel world, the imaginary world, which would bring me closer to my need to write. Still today, I see out of the corner of my eyes the cupboard with a mirror beside which he was sitting. There glittered the small spoons and silver plates we received for our baptism. (I should also speak about the Chinese man who ran a laundry service on Lafontaine Street, a few steps from our house. Every time we walked in front of his shop it sent a shiver down our spines.)

Secondly, how can I forget the hours of enlightenment brought to us by my mother playing the piano, especially when her father came to visit us. The entire household became enveloped by the sounds of celebration. I remember Beethoven's *Appassionata* (for which my mother received her diploma), Chopin's *Scherzo,* Strauss's waltzes, and the *Waltz for Tiny Wooden Soldiers,* not to mention the sentimental songs, such as "Bercés par la houle, ah! qu'il fait bon rêver." Such music deeply marked my sensibility. The manner with which I was to contrast certain images in my poetry was undoubtedly influenced by my constant listening to music and, in particular, to Mozart.

Finally, I should talk about the enormous crucifix on the right side of the entrance to the large church where I was baptized, Très-Saint-Nom-de-Jésus de Maisonneuve. Every time we used to go to mass, I would beg my mother to lift me in her arms so that I could kiss Christ's feet, which had become smooth and shiny under the pious lips of believers.

On another level, I still remember the beating my father gave me because I had shown my penis to my brother. From then on, a dual conscience imposed itself on me—an enormous chasm that lay between myself and my dealings with living, sex, and the body; it would take many years before I could bridge it and free myself from the quicksand in which I slipped every time sexual impulses overcame me. These were possibly the first effects of a more-or-less conscious link, as some claim, with the Transcendent, with God, the one and only.

At first, I went to a boarding school called Saints-Noms-de-Jésus-et-de-Marie, located on Adam Street, in the Viauville district. Was it to be in this school, somewhat refined for the neighborhood, that I received the gift of poetry? When I fell on my head in gymnastics from atop a human pyramid? As if, after an original state of unconsciousness, my brain had found in this intense swirl of neurons a new organization, another and more complex model for the infinite connections of cells. Who knows? Yet I must admit that my mother's mother copied in a notebook poems she read in magazines and newspapers. In all cases, the more important events in my life always struck me like lightning.

Gradually, as a student, I realized that I had great difficulty in finding my place in what was to become, after my family, my first society. I had the gift of setting off my schoolmates with my sharp comments that pierced them like darts. They called me the "irritating" one, the teaser. All in all, I was a boy with a mild case of aggressivity or, should we say, an aggressive but kind boy. Of course, the sort of person that was easy prey for kids. (I was blond, with hair more curly than a girl's.) Later on, I felt more at ease being friends with girls than with boys, even though . . .

2

When I turned nine, my father decided to buy and remodel an old summer cottage on the bank of the Saint Lawrence River, in the far eastern part of Montreal. Being a carpenter and the son of a carpenter and the son-in-law of a carpenter, my father saw the work entailed as a relatively easy task. He knew how to do everything, even how to do the electrical wiring, having been himself an electrician back in 1927, when he got married. He eventually took on more refined jobs as a cabinetmaker for some upper middle-class people in Montreal.

The Second World War prevented us from going to the river. It was only after 1946 that we were permitted to use a motorboat to explore the Saint Lawrence and the neighboring islands up to Sorel. Large freighters from the West Indies, merchant ships, steamships, and transatlantic liners began to moor in our little bay.

How could I forget the way we chased after the wake from the ships, how close we felt to the waves, how carefully we explored the harbor? This was my first real encounter with movement and space, my learning to adapt to nature and, ultimately, to my own freedom. At night, when there was no moon or ships with flashing lanterns to furrow the water, the river seemed to breathe more deeply in the silence. Our consciousness, which had been hovering over the horizon, waited for these moments to connect itself with the infinite. In wintertime the vast field of ice was transformed into a skating rink. A fine powder rose from the snow like a simoon blowing over the Sahara. With the crows, the entire expanse cawed. The icebreakers forced their way through the frozen water to open the channel. This was spring with its immediacy and violence. When the ice melted and flowed out towards the gulf, we would at times have to manoeuvre our motorboats around bruised and bloated corpses that had surfaced.

The river was not only the best initiation to nature we could get, but also to industrial life. Ours was a district of oil refineries and harbors for tankers. Between the river and our house, train boxcars were stagnating on the railway tracks. Wheat-filled trains which had stopped overnight became our playground.

Yes, the river gave us the freedom to tussle with life and death. It was a metaphor of the path to the exotic, our imaginary departure to faraway continents. In my memory, this area, named Terrasse-Vinet, remains an unforgettable little universe. Today it seems to me a privilege that I should have had access to its inexhaustible presence, to have lived far from the city's center, but also to have lived in a place where a multiformity of the earth's representations flourished.

Six years old

3

I do not know in fact what pushed me to go to the Seminary College in Ottawa, in September 1943. It is true that I had attended the Capucins de la Chapelle de la Réparation. At the monastery I enjoyed talking with the Capuchins, walking along the garden paths edged with flowers with enormous birdhouses towering at the end.

At that age I was unaware of the extent to which I was unconsciously attracted by the formal beauty of the monastic life. More than the religious vocation per se, it was the aesthetic vision, the dreamlike dimensions of this life-style that must have made me decide to apply as a seminary student. My whole being turned towards beauty. It was my own secular way of contemplating God. Then again, four years later, as soon as love offered its first glance to me, I immediately quit the seminary—the day before All Saints' Day.

With hindsight I have always considered that the positive aspects of my experiences at the seminary by far outweighed the neurotic ones, which only worsened my natural tendency to live my moral perception and action in a dualistic manner.

Thanks to the Capuchins I learned to look at nature differently. I rediscovered music. It was in 1943, for example, that I heard for the first time on record *Le Sacre du printemps* and the Concerto for Piano in D Minor by Mozart, conducted by Bruno Walter, who was on the piano. We went also as a group to the National Gallery of Canada and the Museum of Natural History. I discovered painting, even though a monk would prevent us from entering the room where large paintings of nudes were exhibited. (Never did I visit with my parents the Montreal Museum of Fine Arts. It was much too intimidating a place, reserved as it was for the anglophone bourgeoisie. I wonder whether my parents could have known what a museum was; it was only much later that they visited the Louvre, the Prado, and the National Gallery in London.)

We were forced to participate in activities dealing with the choral society; this initiated us to the reading of music and, in particular, Gregorian chant. We were asked also to play small roles in the plays of Henri Brochet or Henri Ghéon, who have today become mute fossils. I remember having to read out loud enlightened pages for the members of the college at mealtime. The Father Director had taught us to read without emotion, anticipating the structure of the text with our eyes only. (This experience left me with unpleasant memories; forty years later, when I am invited to dine with monks, I tremble whenever the reading is about to begin. I can no longer endure this suffocating *tone* during the silence of contrition.)

The rule at the college was that we had to participate in the tasks of its daily upkeep by sweeping, dusting, washing the tiles and dishes. This was a concrete way of integrating us into the community.

Of course, our collective life was disciplined. In bed by eight or nine o'clock, depending on your age. Awake at a quarter past five. Mass. Classes. Break. Mealtime. Siesta. Vespers. Etc. Silence when in rank.

A portrait of the author, painted by Gaston Boisvert, 1954

Silence in the refectory or dormitory, except on holidays. And if, in the classroom, we had the thoughtlessness of whispering to our fellow classmate, we were punished. More often than not, we had to kneel in the hall with our face to the wall. This sort of training was something that the monks mastered. It was their way of getting the novitiate used to religious life. We were all destined to be priests. Our classical studies were preparing us for scholastic studies, even though the standard of education was in reality low, considering the level of academic requirements necessary for university. Having come to college on my own accord, at least this is what I believed, wanting to achieve righteousness, never did the idea of revolt ever come to my mind. I would become intolerant of all this much later, when I finally decided to leave the college.

I still remember how we used to celebrate Christmas, with the Christmas Eve dinner followed by night skating. The ceremonies during the Holy Week filled me with lasting joy. Though my relationship with my confessor was simple and innocent, in spite of many things, the overall experiences that were part of my formation at the seminary left me with nervous memories. I used to have nightmares in which I would find myself stuck in a closed room. I came back to Montreal and my family with a paradoxical sense of failure. My parents were silently disappointed by the fact that their son would no longer be a priest, which for a working-class child represented the only way to social mobility.

Only once I had left the college did I get the feeling that I had withdrawn into exile. I suffered from a dulling of the soul, even when surrounded by the people I loved most. Psychologically speaking, this was the most painful period of my life. I was lost, worn out, vulnerable to what would become for me an aggressive world and society.

I was unable to find, for example, the simplicity needed to form a relationship free of tension with a woman. My dualist nature distorted all contact. My shyness suffocated me. I often locked myself in a room to read and listen to music. I lived in a tunnel. Prey to my neuroses, it was as if I was slipping in quicksand. It would take me many years before I found the power to confront the difficulties which grew more out of my own unconscious than the outside world and people. As is often the case, it would be life itself which was going to take me by the collar and push me to my limit, forcing me to react, and mostly to reveal to myself my personal strength, leading me little by little on the road to writing, which, at first, was a life buoy—my way of facing reality—and then a source of underground energy for transformation and humanization. In the end the "monster with many faces" came alive, the one which every writer and artist, not to say every person, conceals within.

It was during this tumultuous period of my life that I read Dostoevsky and Léon Bloy, the terrorist of spirituality. One cannot truly understand me if one neglects the fact that I came alive with Dostoevsky and that it was Bloy who first opened a large hole in me before I was able to free myself. To quote Kundera, I had to learn to live and write without letting the burden of being weigh me down. I had to learn to make myself light as well as hold out against those who believe in a literature of laughter and suspicion.

4

In all honesty, I must admit that it was by fantasizing about a woman that led me to my writing. Every morning, for almost two years, I would see her in the streetcar on my way to the office. Sometimes, I would follow her unawares all the way to her work, never daring to go up to her and even less to speak to her. The first poem I wrote came from the evening light of her eyes. Dante's excitement upon meeting Beatrice comes to mind. Though this woman was only a symbol, in appearing before me she nevertheless helped me to discover my *anima.*

In 1948, I went to a conference where a film was shown by one of the rare Polish survivors of the ten thousand officers killed by the Soviets. That evening I heard for the first time about Nazi concentration camps. I have never been able to eradicate them since. This brutal confrontation against what was senseless is a landmark which permits me to judge and understand the hypocrisy behind what happens in so-called history and for the sake of historical necessity.

At this time I had quit school to work during the day for a stockbroker; evenings, from 1949 on, I took courses in the social sciences. Two years later, I decided to specialize in journalism.

I remember trying to convince one of the few Marxists in Quebec with some irrefutable evidence that God existed. A gesture at once foolish and naive. It was Braque who once said that "evidence makes truth weary."

Charles King, Inc., where I worked, remains for me a privileged place for the important inner things that secretly occurred within me. This was where most of my first poems were written. I was fortunate enough to finish work at two o'clock in the afternoon.

I had met a graduate in medieval studies who encouraged me to read philosophy books, very much at the heart of the changes that took place in contemporary thinking following the event of Auschwitz. I am referring to the works of Garrigou-Lagrange, Jacques Maritain, and Sertillanges. Before these, philosophers based themselves on the concepts and systems of Saint Thomas Aquinas and, more rarely, those of Duns Scotus.

L'idée d'éternité (The concepts of eternity) by Sertillanges, through its relentless meditation on the notions of infinity and eternity, had a major impact on me. I was walking towards light, towards those unknown areas where being suddenly becomes spirit. I felt as if I was able to walk through walls, much like the enlightenment of the *satori* and other forms of illuminations. A number of writers and artists, among others, had similar revelations and, in one way or another, plunged deep into the core of their being. Could we surmise that this was just a momentary letting-go of the protective and fragile devices of the mind? No matter what, this experience was crystallized so strongly in my identification to light that my life, and its hypothetical expression in art, lost its significance if it would orbit away from this vital illumination. More than once I have come back to this unifying source of energy to better seize the meaning of my life and my relationship to the world and God, as though I feared that everything was but an illusion and would vanish during the night.

The three years between 1949 and 1952 were the most significant in my life as a writer. Everything came together: writing, spiritual meaning, love. As a consequence, through my writing I kept at a distance from contemporary life-styles and fashions, though I was still vulnerable to daily life as to the perpetual challenges made by history.

Never have I run away from these three *raisons d'être* which, I admit, converge in me to remodel the person that I am. They kindle my deep-rooted sense of hope in light and its radiance and manifestations: be it in a poem, a musical score, a painting, a landscape, or a pair of eyes. This was why, when it came to music, Mozart represented such a fundamental source of transformation, as if he were the consciousness of light turned into sound. The same would later apply to Vermeer and Corot in painting, and to certain landscapes of Israel, Quebec, Italy, and France. The angel figure which appears in Rilke's *Duino Elegies* spread its presence over the texture of my first collection of poems, published under the title *Ces anges de sang* (These angels of blood). As long as light falls upon the horizons of invention, in my life and literature, I cannot see how fate can lead me astray. I do not want fate to change into an element of drift which I, obsessed, petrified, would scrutinize, unable to act upon it, having myself then turned into "a calm, handsome corpse."

5

I met my wife, Lisette Corbeil, at my friends' house in 1954. I was literally struck by love. That same evening, returning home, I told my mother that I would marry this woman. She was the ideal *anima*. She had large, dark, sad eyes which corresponded in my mind to those of Dostoevsky's Natasia Philippovna. Fifteen days later, I asked her to marry me. We got engaged on April 18 and married on July 9, 1955, in order to respect her parents' social exigencies.

My wife had a heart condition which lingered as a threat over our life-style and her pregnancies. We did nonetheless have three children together. Life could not allow a real relationship free of anguish. This was an essential part of my destiny. Love gave my writing a particular brand of "heaviness," a gravity which, I hope, was tempered by the gracious presence of light.

Needless to say, my wife helped me to liberate myself of the stronghold that a prolonged adolescence and Jansenism had had on me.

After Dostoevsky's "existentialism," it was the reading of Henry Miller's works that had the explosive impact on my inner life. His books made my moral standards simmer with unrest and widened the gap between myself and the world, people, and life. Without my intense rapport with Miller's work, I would never have been the same man. (His influence was human more than literary. I did not possess the artistic temperament to follow him in his Dionysian and baroque experiments. It seems to me that I am still, in many aspects, an Apollonian, if I may say so, evolving under a different kind of light.)

My first book of poems was published a few days before my wedding, and on that day, just as we were about to take the train for our honeymoon, my poet-friend and publisher, Gaston Miron, handed me a copy of *Le Devoir* with the first review of my work. It was an excellent article. The simple link between this first review and the beginning of my married life is very revealing of the sort of life-style we were to have, with our joys and misunderstandings, withdrawn from the world. The writer in me could not be separated from the husband and the father. At times, distant, according to some, at other times, loving and

Fernand and Lisette, the year they were married, Saint-Jean Port-Joli, 1955

gentle, I listen attentively to the *other* according to my own gut feelings.

The first two years of our marriage represent for me what I imagine plenitude to be: an irreverent kind of happiness shared with the loved one; so attuned to one another, we were destined for one another. This was what I considered the ideal fulfilment of *being-with*, which is the essence of being human. One thing I could not have possibly understood in those days was that a couple could not be solely based on love, and that it needed more of the specific dynamic inherent to the family nucleus. Threats and rows come as much from the outside world as from the weaknesses and the individual energies of the lovers themselves.

Tension between us initially manifested itself, I believe, with the birth of our first child. There again this is a story that is commonplace and not very original. It took me many years of training before I grew into my role as father. Writing consumed much of my life. Trouble was inevitable. I resided in my metaphors, my music, my *elsewhere*. A synchronization of an impossible kind connected the strings of my actions as writer and my duties as father. Writing involuntarily removed me from my obligations as parent, so that my wife had to assume practically alone the task of vigilant caring for our children's health as well as their intellectual blossoming. I was not *present*. I also became too impatient, easily intolerant, due to my delicate nerves and no doubt to the manner in which I was breast-fed. I might have had a kind of intolerance related to a need for the absolute which the terrible Léon Bloy had transmitted to me, imbued me with. I would have to fight against this propensity in a person who otherwise could only mumble his faith and who suffered at the sight of people throwing themselves into the abyss. Tolerance is a trait we are not born with. One becomes tolerant only after having steadily worked on clearing things up in oneself, as though inner life, often in a chaotic and rough state, was required to be refined little by little in a crucible before emerging with truly human qualities. The eruption of intolerance is an immutable pitfall, a threat to equilibrium, a sign of our moral atrophy.

6

I left my job at Charles King, Inc., to work as a salesrep, for seven years, at Les éditions Fides in Montreal. This left me with plenty of time to write, besides poetry, a number of portraits of writers for Radio-Canada.

It was at Fides that I met Gaston Miron in 1952. We often talked about poetry and it was he who published my first book of poems. I also knew André Belleau for two years, who remained a close friend until he died. Belleau, along with Gilles Marcotte, was among Quebec's finest professors and essayists.

In those days I had an avid desire to read. In fact, we felt as if we would never come to terms with all of culture, which was slipping through our fingers and becoming a universe of its own. For instance, I discovered surrealism in literature very late by reading the poetry of Pierre Emmanuel. Acquiring this knowledge radically altered my writing. Emmanuel then led to the works of Pierre Jean Jouve, whose works the reading of Baudelaire helped me appreciate. But it was mostly thanks to the poems of Quebec poets, Alain Grandbois and Saint-Denys Garneau, that I got the desire to explore the world through personal vision and poetic language. If Grandbois brought me to the universe of the *other* and his world, then, on the contrary, Garneau seemed to want to smother me. The way he withdrew from life and his quest for spirituality were, even on the formal level, more demanding. Everything within led him to submit himself to the asceticism of one who cares but for the fulgor of solitude. It is obvious today that he

left us with an *oeuvre* that perfectly reflects his intense quest.

Pierre Jean Jouve, however, was to be the real master of poetry; he was the master in *manner*, in "pottery making," master of audacity, of music, of poetry as the landscape for inner life. We enjoyed similar natural affinities, such as an erotic vision, a passion for Mozart, as well as our sense of faith. I met Jouve in Paris in 1967. If I had sent Grandbois my first written poems, it was to Jouve that I handed my first completed manuscript. Both comforted and encouraged me. Jouve said that I possessed a tragic vision, necessary, in his eyes, for the breaking through to true poetry.

My second book of poems, *Séquences de l'aile* (The sequences of wings), was composed during 1955 and 1958. Enthusiasm for the launching of the *Sputnik* in October 1957 was no different from my enthusiam for conquering of the cosmic space underlying certain of the poems. Today, these experiments appear to me somewhat abstract and disembodied. I get a similar impression that the poems about the city—which have become, for certain critics, models for a kind of modernity—are often incomprehensible. If I believe that poetry is to be made from the materials of reality, I am not convinced that it should be organically composed with the technical styles in vogue at any given time. These rapidly become obsolete, entrenching poetry in the important issues of the day, in the stuff that rumor is made out of, in

Daughters, Andrée and Sylvie, and son, Jean, about 1966

With Edgard Varèse, New York, 1960

words imprisoned in their first meanings, in a sort of functional synthesis of conjecture and reality.

In 1958, the year when our first daughter, Sylvie, was born, we founded the magazine *Liberté*. In a society still under the control of reactionary politics but sensitive to the desires of our people, *Liberté* wanted to be an outcry to everyone, the frank expression and circulation of ideas and especially a forum for writing. By asking the questions we did, the magazine was not different from other magazines, such as *La nouvelle relève, Gants du ciel,* and *Cité libre*. *Liberté* followed the tradition, though it dedicated itself to the nationalist question as well as offering a workshop for writers. The first issue appeared in 1959. I am the only surviving founder of the magazine today who is still an active part of the editorial committee. I feel as if I am just the last of the dinosaurs and, after thirty years, sometimes a little distant and weary.

In 1960 our daughter Andrée was born, and in 1962, our son, Jean.

In December 1960 I became director-producer at Radio-Canada. Already in the same department were two other writers: the novelist André Langevin

and the poet Jean-Guy Pilon. Later the novelists Gilles Archambault and André Major would follow. I want to mention this important fact in order to stress the concrete role we had in culture. It would be impossible today for me to dissociate my life from my work at Radio-Canada. I consider myself quite privileged. What can our capitalist society do with poets and novelists? In particular, our fragile North American community of a few million French-speaking people? The British and French models for a state-owned radio station were beneficial to us, in fact. The programs I produced enabled me to come into contact with a culture that became more and more diversified and all-encompassing. I am referring to the forty-two programs that I produced and directed in 1961 dedicated to human knowledge: a wonderful and never-dying utopia of the encyclopedic spirit of the eighteenth century. I am also talking about the fifty-two shows on the different aspects of the "American Man"; or the programs analyzing the use of cybernetics in medicine, law, pedagogy, communications, and art. These programs, directed by André Belleau, in 1968 enabled us to fly to California, where we visited the Rand Corporation and the research staffs at Stanford, UCLA, and Berkeley.

From 1969 onwards, I directed a number of programs which led me to Europe. With the French poet Robert Marteau, whom I met in 1966, I traveled throughout France, visiting the symbolic locations of the Troubadours and produced a series of specialized shows. Later on, throughout a period of several years Richard Salesses and I crisscrossed Europe, and this in spite of the fact that I am not a traveler. I will go on a trip only as an inevitability I accept and reject at the same time. To be and eat alone in an unknown city unavoidably pulls me into a state of depression. It was during one of these trips abroad that I discovered painting and occidental art, namely Roman and Gothic art.

In 1955 I began a five-year correspondence with Henry Miller. He would write to me in French. Thanks to Miller I got to know the composer Edgard Varèse, who then lived in New York. Varèse sent me his first LP. As soon as I heard his music I was convinced that his was more a metaphysical experience through sound than the simple sonorous exploration of our technological civilization. To reduce Varèse to the noises found in his time would be unjust and superficial. A special issue of *Liberté* was dedicated to him.

Once we had published this special issue of *Liberté*, I asked Varèse if I could write his biography. This was totally unconscious and improperly audacious since I was far removed from the human and cultural background of this artist born in Paris in 1883 of an Italian father; an artist who had lived before the First World War eight years or so in Berlin, and who had frequented people such as Busoni, Debussy, Rodin, Hofmannsthal, Mahler, Strauss, Satie, Ravel, Picasso, Apollinaire . . . I never once imagined the kind of labyrinth or Herculean enterprise I had taken on. Varèse never once tried to protect himself from the risk of having me as his biographer. He trusted me totally. I completed the first version of the biography in 1965, a few weeks before he died. He had the time to read it and to send me a telegram describing the work as *magnifique.*

Varèse the man was a marvel of existence. He knew how to talk about facts like no other, abruptly, abrasively. He accepted me as soon as he saw me and, little by little, treated me like a grandson. When I used to meet him in New York, he would show his personal files, allowing me to tape all our conversations dealing with his life. We would eat together, going afterwards for a walk in Greenwich Village.

When we came back, we would listen to music. That was when I heard the famous recording of Roger Désormière's interpretation of Debussy's *Pelléas.*

I learned to live, breathe, and work with Varèse. He would always have the right word that would help solve a problem or get me out of an impasse. He taught me to harden myself and to prepare myself for the different people I would have to meet later on as a producer at Radio-Canada. In 1973, at Saint-Paul-de-Vence, for example, I was able to relate immediately to Chagall, for whose work I had a great admiration. On other occasions, I would be able to very quickly remove the "varnish" on people, to take an image used by Varèse.

7

The biography on Varèse came out in Paris in 1966. The year before I had published my third poetry book, *Le soleil sous la mort* (The sun under death).

These poems were partially filtered with a poetic energy known in Quebec as "poems for the nation." It seems to me that on a certain level this book led me away from my images of the inner world. Over many of the poems linger the threat of nuclear war or the degrading spectacle of dictators and generals, poems which we too quickly label as "militant works." However, the last section of the collection, leaning towards the presence of the sun, foreshadows the next book, *Dans le sombre* (In the dark), published in 1967.

This last collection was supposed to be published by Les éditions du Seuil, in Paris, but for nationalist reasons I rashly decided to take it from Jean Cayrol's hands. I followed my Québecois publisher's advice that literature should first appear in the land for which it was destined. I submitted myself in a somewhat naive manner to the Quebec literary establishment, which claimed itself to be autonomous, as some polemist had decided. We believed no doubt in those days in "the synchronization of the literary, social, and national cause" (Gilles Marcotte).

Strangely enough, most of the poems in that book were written immediately after Varèse's death, in November 1965. I was literally propelled by a fiery charge. The amazing thing was to notice to what extent most of the poems were permeated with eroticism. An unearthing to the core had occurred, a digging into the unknown and the neuroses within me. Progressively I began to move towards a more luminous oneness of the couple. The poems were sufficiently daring for the printer to refuse to print them. Pierre Emmanuel described them as having an "erotic audacity." Pierre Jean Jouve was not unfamiliar with my poetic matter, though my eroticism, its music and light, were necessarily not his. Nevertheless I had appropriated his need for crystallization and his art of contrasts.

From 1963 onwards, I wrote mostly essays on language, bilingualism, tolerance, violence, student power, not to mention my unflinching reading of Kierkegaard's work. Most of these were united and published in my first collection of essays, *Les Actes retrouvés* (Recovered acts).

During those years of unabating work, I felt myself in a whirlwind of a changing Quebec, more and more obsessed by modernity. As many writers, artists, and intellectuals, I was for independence. Political independence appeared to be the only concrete solution to get us out of our weakened position. We were attuned to a collective enthusiasm which a person rarely experiences in his short life. But this did in no way suggest that our thoughts of sovereignty would lead to a closing in on ourselves, even less, becoming xenophobic or sectarian. Most of the leaders were actively and directly communicating with the rest of the world. I am speaking of the folksingers who followed the Parti Québecois, of the many fellow travelers active in the social and intellectual spheres.

We dreamed of being able to transcribe the American experience in French, as others in Latin America had done in Spanish and Portuguese. We were no less American than our neighbors south of the border, but with the haunting nostalgia of an imaginary South. In my opinion, superficially exotic and often diminishing in my bias in literature, the French admire us more for the differences than the similarities between us or for the universal qualities of our works. They become excessively keen on our *joual*, a style that radically corresponds to the stereotypical image they have of North American literature. However this *patois* was mostly the suffering and baroque outbursts of a language profoundly hurt and humiliated in a context of forced bilingualism. The finest writers of Quebec will never be recognized in France—perhaps due to the many writers it already has—unless they publish directly in Paris.

It was not without a realistic hope, nor without an awakened awareness of reality, that many of us became, without being dupes however, friends of the Parti Québecois until we were defeated by the referendum of May 20, 1980. The refusal by a small minority of the population of the very concept of independence broke our innermost momentum, as it

brutally drowned the hope in many people. My father saw his dream vanish a few years before he died. I believe many writers withdrew into their imaginary worlds in order to respect the democratic will of the majority, in spite of the fact the basis for the referendum was not modelled on any democratic spirit, inasmuch as the campaign had been morally tainted by the demagogical violence and immoderate lies on the part of politicians and the business world.

8

The end of the seventies is an open wound in me. No clear-minded person of my generation can ever forget the declaration in 1970 by the Canadian government of the War Measures Act and its consequences. Yes, a British diplomat was kidnapped and a Quebec provincial minister "assassinated"; yet, I remain convinced that the unexpressed reason for all this spectacle—the military deployment and the non-stop hovering of the helicopters in our cities—was a serious misunderstanding which led the Prime Minister to act against the elite, intellectuals, poets fighting for the independence of Quebec. There was a will to want to give us a lesson in history and to discourage the people from blindly following the Québecois elite. This immoderate measure—fundamentally antidemocratic, unthinkable in any other advanced society—did not prevent the Parti Québecois from getting elected in 1976 for the first time in its history. On the contrary, never had the determined militants become so enthusiastic and active. What had always been a democratic vindication finally ended with a democratically voted outcome. That is why all the Democrats sided with independence even after the Yes-to-Separation group lost in the referendum. I firmly believe that we find more of the democratic spirit amongst the Separatists than among the Federalists or the so-called Liberals who had gambled, years earlier, with fear, unwarranted arrests, and democracy itself.

When in 1971 I was given for the first time the Governor General Award for my book of essays *Les Actes retrouvés,* I had no choice but to refuse it. Out of principle, the symbolic gesture was directed against the head of state who had proclaimed the unlawful Measures Act. I could not ignore the fact that my friends had been searched and sent to prison, or that there had been enactments of executions. I had nothing against the award as such, for I would accept it twice in the years to come: in 1985 for my novel *Lucie ou un midi en novembre (Lucie or a November afternoon)* and in 1987 for my book of poems *Les Heures (The hours).*

9

In 1973 I had the pleasure of being invited to Israel as a poet. This trip, which I took with two friends from *Liberté,* André Belleau and Jean-Guy Pilon, has remained of unique significance for me. Never have I found the inner light, the soothing of being, I saw early in the morning, when Jerusalem—a mother to us all—was bathed in a pink nimbus. It was the only time when, serene within, I believed I was going to die. This is enthusiasm or, at least, heedless spontaneity.

That year, thanks to Gilles Marcotte, I published *Depuis Novalis: errance et gloses.* This mysterious book brought me further still into the nationalist question and ideological restlessness. The texts moved towards the spiritual under the poetic eye. Novalis came to me as a master of life, a figure of utmost importance. Perhaps, what I did was take Novalis as an invented character and follow him through his work. The task implied a sensibility specific to the sacred timeless dimension of language.

Depuis Novalis would come out in France only fifteen years later. The idea for the book grew out of a seminar on German Romanticism which I had codirected with my friend André Belleau. The course was so charged with fervor that afterwards the students would come over to our house and listen to German Romantic music. Belleau sang *lieder* by Schubert and Schumann. May every student have the chance of having such a great teacher. Belleau was one of the finest thinkers I have ever met. His death in 1986 was a loss for us. His friendship was one of the many gifts life has offered me.

10

When I look at my past, I notice that I was not very fortunate in friendship (and maybe love). At least I am aware that I do not have the particular sort of genius that changes friendship into a work of art, itself a source of truth and human beauty. I am not, nor ever was, someone with great experience in relationships and so never was able to equal the kind attention others brought to me. I am a solitary man, often lost in my reveries, dissatisfied with life's limits. My eyes are turned towards an Orient that does not

With André Belleau at the grave of Friedrich Hölderlin, Tübingen, 1974

seem to appear. Solitude is a source of strength only if it does not consume us. It is then, and only then, that art might emerge as the "pinnacle of solitude," to quote Beckett.

This intense feeling for my shortcomings is brusquely heightened when I am with a friend of the likes of Robert Marteau, a French poet who lives in Paris behind the Quai Voltaire. He is a thoughtful friend, a prince without the instinct of possession nor the excessive thirst for power. A wonderful alchemist, he has refined my soul. Yes, friendship is creation. Natural too that he is in Paris, and that the Atlantic separates us. The fact that he lived here with us for thirteen years did not make life easier between us. I think I was not present enough in the friendship, in spite of the few bright sparks we shared during our encounters. Yet, I knew that he had great insight and that he had a special passion for language and life. Only once he had left Montreal did I feel a sense of loss, his absence. Before, a phone call sufficed. Unfortunately, the phone has replaced the actual meeting. It is not our custom here to meet people in a café as we would in Paris. The most satisfying, most enlightening times I have spent in Paris were in Robert's company, as when we visited a museum or walked together in the streets of the fifth and sixth *arrondissements,* or when in the evening I was dining with him and his wife. How can I ever forget the riverboats that cast light into their dining room, or forget the silence of the Flore Pavillon near Pont Royal? Every so often Robert sends me admirable texts, fragments of his souvenirs and reveries. It was on a trip with him that I first noticed the Poitou's misty horizon, a distant homeland for us, with the sensation of having seen it before. Thanks to Marteau, ascetic poet *par excellence,* visionary of the world, I have learned what it means to dedicate oneself to the absolute life, to God's light shining through a world wondrously admired.

Ouellette, Robert Marteau, and Yugoslavian poet Miodrag Pavlovitch, about 1975

11

In 1974 I published an autobiography entitled *Journal dénoué* (Unbound diary). The major part of the book had been written eight years before, when I was thirty-five. The ups and downs are limited, as one can well imagine. I do not belong to the tradition of Henry de Monfreid or Jack London, and so my story might sound narcissistic and presumptuous. Many readers undoubtedly dislike this essentially subjective genre; yet we must realize that much of our western literature has for the most part been subjective. To complete the work, I then tried to find a synthesis between myself and people and objects by changing my perspective and focusing on my quests and aspirations. When it comes to judging one's true value, we notice there is all around a "moral fatigue," to quote Lawrence Durrell. Revising the work many years later for a new edition, it occurred to me that when I was younger I did not have the courage to open myself completely and maintain throughout the tension essential to such a venture. In the words of a French critic: How did I dare write such a thing?

I began the book as if it were a story, a work of fiction, which for obvious reasons could never come to an end. By force of circumstances, its form broke up into fragments, undoing itself to widen its horizon. I had reached a nerve center which would lead me to a gap in my fate: a human being short of attaining fulfilment. Understandably so. My goal had been to extend the process of inner evolution to the point of taking the risk with confessional indiscretions and allowing myself to open up more intimately. This is why the book was so warmly received by perspicacious readers such as Henri Guillemin and Robert Mallet. I was coming to grips with my life, my neuroses and my fantasies, and I was wandering beyond our fixed horizons. No matter the process or the nature of my confessions, this book inevitably became a mirror for others trammeled by similar religious atavism, intellectual training, and moral deficiency. With the benefit of hindsight I can say that the form I had chosen was in fact quite modern.

A splintered form, as they say. There was no doubt that this work, due to its style, would bring me directly to the writing of a novel.

I won't say that I followed into the steps of Stendhal, Balzac, or Proust. Rather, I chose to work in the manner of a painter such as Chagall, who had given us *Le double portrait au verre de vin*. The experience of the autobiography had been formally based on the idea of the "double portrait." For instance, I am not sure that my "truth program" on the couple convinced all my readers, especially not the feminists. In all cases, the fundamentally feminist attitude forces us into an ideological position. This was the principle behind my novel *Tu regardais intensément Geneviève (You stared fixedly at Geneviève)*, published in 1978.

Two years later *La mort vive* (Death alive) came out. The theme was all-encompassing, essentially spiritual and poetic. It dealt with a painter in the process of working towards an absolute form. Whatever happened around this main theme was just my compromising to the genre, a dulling of language which slowed down the reader's journey through the novel's spiral. My friend Belleau spoke of this novel as a "fine failure." Was my ambition perhaps too great? It was not in style.

Strengthened by this earlier venture, I came out with a third novel, *Lucie ou un midi en novembre*, a book very similar to Ernesto Sabato's *Angel of Darkness*, although we North Americans have been spared the realities of everyday tortures. My primary connection to such experiences was my religious sensitivity. The story is animated by a fiery passion which forces Lucie to her death. The only question Lucie asks herself is concerning God's presence among us; she is silent in an era of total dehumanization wherein horror, as Edgar Allan Poe wrote, is the product of the soul.

The result—Lucie's sacrifice of her life—is not accidental. She quotes at the very beginning of her entries in her diary a sentence by Euripides which is very helpful in the understanding of the entire novel. The long dream sequence in the middle of the novel, a single sentence three pages long without punctuation, enabled me to push the story forward, quicken the action, as if it were a turntable or, better still, a change of speed or gears, in order to force the reader to participate more actively in the story until its conclusion. Perhaps it would be more correct to call this work a tragedy more than a novel. A critic in fact said that my "literary style consisted of crossing over the borders of the genres."

Between 1971 and 1980, I wrote a number of poems which would appear in different books: *La Terre d'où . . . (The earth from . . .)*, *À découvert (Uncovered)*, *Ici, ailleurs, la lumière (Here, there, the light)*, all of which we collected, along with a few unpublished poems, in a book entitled *En la nuit, la mer (In the night, the sea)*, published in 1981. Two other books of poetry, done in collaboration with painters, Léon Bellefleur and Fernand Toupin, came out as art books. Simultaneously, I published a second book of essays, entitled *Écrire en notre temps (To write in our time)*, a book obsessed by poetry, yes, but more so by the *mal* of our times, by our irrational commotion and by all-prevailing injustice. One must only look at how ideology has the pretention of forcing each one of us to lose our identity, our uniqueness which should shine with all its sacred light. I see how expressing one's yearning for democracy can become monotonous, vain, and ineffective; yet, it is this that shows us how fragile we really are, crammed in as we are, in our times, drifting through history.

12

On July 11, 1984, after a game of golf, my father discovered that he had cancer of the bowel. After a second operation within eight days, my father had to learn to live with a colostomy. It was not before May 1985 that he fully got his strength back. But by then he found out that he had two tumors in the cerebellum and that his lungs were ravaged. He was told that he had six months to live. In reality, he would live only six weeks. He died on June 14, at five o'clock in the morning, after thirteen hours spent in a coma, curled up like a fetus, as if the spirit was entangled in the body. The morning had enveloped him with its light.

My mother would never overcome the death of her husband. Her health dwindled within two years or so; she would never go out of her apartment. After a serious warning of high blood pressure, she was once again hospitalized on January 18, 1988. She died of heart complications on the 22, at six o'clock in the evening.

The morning of May 4, the day of his birthday, my father had broken out in tears when he saw us come in with gifts. I had never seen my father weep. The emotion had been too great for him. And yet he was a courageous man throughout his life, even when ill.

My mother, strangely enough, was serene when she told me that she had only a few days to live, she who had always been afraid of becoming sick and dying. Perhaps the sedatives made her keep calm. She could not accept the fact that she would never see her children again. She had asked many questions on my father's death, on *how* one should die. On the last two days of her life she stayed in bed, lucid, smiling, as she stroked my hand for the last time. I was told that the last words she said were: "I am tired."

Months after my mother died, I tried to find the houses my grandparents, parents, and we ourselves had lived in. I wanted to photograph them and piece together a family album before the images and signs would forever vanish.

For some time now I get the strange sensation of hearing my father walking. I hear him laugh, see his facial expressions. These are maybe the last manifestations of a personal heritage, the last gestures arising from mimetism.

Just before he died, my father gave his golf bag to my younger brother and his paintings to my two sisters. (My second brother had committed suicide in May 1979, after being unable to overcome his alcoholism after unsuccessful treatments.) My father

Parents, Gilberte Chalifour and Cyrille Ouellette, celebrating their fiftieth anniversary, 1977

did not leave me anything, in spite of the fact that it was I who for one year had taken care of him. It was only seven months after he died that he gave a sign of his love for me.

On January 23, 1986, I began to write the poems for my latest book I would entitle *Les Heures*. The writing had the quality of immediacy, as if it had been dictated to me; its inspiration was violent, overwhelming. All the more so because the poems dealt solely with my father's death, from his coma to the after-death, as a kind of mysterious initiation to death itself, as though I had experienced the death of us all. I wrote eighty-two poems up to February 23. Because my father had died at the age of eight-one, I took one of the poems out and prepared the work for publication. The experience is not without resemblance to what happened to Rilke under the spell of his *Elegies*.

In July 1988, I received a letter informing me that the city of Troyes, in France, had awarded me the Premier Grand Prix Francophone. (In November 1987, I had received the Prix David from the Quebec government.) For the occasion, the French publisher asked me to offer him a manuscript. We decided to reprint *Depuis Novalis,* modifying and adding to it a collection of essays, some of which had never been published in Quebec. In a sense, this was a continuation of the autobiography I had published fourteen years earlier. In *Ouvertures,* everything evolves my spiritual development in poetry and art. All converges towards Him, whom I cannot name, to whom I am drawn.

* * *

I recognize the fact that I have little humor and am not ironic, which does not mean that I am not delighted by the fireworks in others. Each one of us kindles a secret light that burns within. Each has his own land, his own paths. I accept myself for being of a spiritual tradition.

I have never tried to seduce many women, though I am attracted to them, by the "littlegod-knowswhat" of their presence, as Borges said. Except for light, nothing in this world is more admirable, I believe, than the body of a woman. (I am aware that saying this may seem for some as a subtle sign of sexism.)

In describing my sense of astonishment, I have no doubt with the blink of an eye toppled over into another galaxy. I have allowed one of the venerated signs to slip away for the never-said. The same applies to most of the important moments of one's life, for

Fernand and Lisette Ouellette with Jean, Sylvie, and Andrée, about 1985

the earthquakes in our consciousness occur in the silence of human beings. People come and go in their intimate suffering, in their miraculous intimacy that no outside look can disrupt. They come and go in the timelessness of their inner spheres. Such are the actions of human beings.

I wrote this text facing the few objects that stand on my bookshelf. There, the imaginary landscape I see on a limestone from Tuscany. This space is a constant reminder that I must cross over the thick fog, like the one over the Styx, before I can catch the distant glimmer. Otherwise, I am condemned to remain beneath the rock, without sign or language, in the immeasurable nothingness of the deceitful dead. Here, erotic brass figurines come from the Ashanti; a gong which Louise Varèse sent me after the death of her husband; finally, a Chinese ivory figurine of a woman with a lily; without mentioning the postcards scattered everywhere on other shelves. A photograph of my parents and another of my friend Belleau are lit by the small Greek funeral lamp from the fourth century B.C., given to me by an antiquarian in Taormina who loved poetry. On my left by the window, I notice the Virginian bean tree we planted

as soon as we moved here in 1966. That tree is my wall for meditation. Most of my books were written when, between sentences, I would stop and look at the tree in search of an image or concept.

If I am not traveling I rarely go out. I am a sedentary, stay-at-home person. I am not the sociable type. It takes all I've got to give a reading. I prefer concentrating on the impenetrable landscape of the limestone, in a kind of "need" atmosphere which comes to me when I am not writing. Like a dry stone. (T. S. Eliot is whispering in my ear that this will not be mentioned in my obituary note.) Have I really come to grips with the eternal dilemma between ethics and esthetics (which was the essence of the work of the likes of Hermann Broch)? One thing is sure: I have never been able to accept that the political realm be dissociated from ethics, as if it had its own absolute sphere of activity.

At times I have lost my footing, imperceptibly. Does my writing move along solid ground? Isn't this the case for our autobiographical writings? Perhaps it is an intrinsic way of establishing a distance with oneself, with the "I" that thinks it is speaking. For who could deny the fact that there is no show in our effort to gather the fragments of our lives, in our attempt to follow the traces within, in order to better become one with ourselves? And who can reassure me that I have not been caught out blatantly babbling about myself, in front of an imaginary mirror, scrutinizing an imaginary person? Is writing but an illusion?

BIBLIOGRAPHY

Poetry:

Ces anges de sang (title means "These angels of blood"), l'Hexagone, 1955.

Séquences de l'aile (title means "The sequences of wings"), l'Hexagone, 1958.

Le soleil sous la mort (title means "The sun under death"), l'Hexagone, 1965.

Dans le sombre (title means "In the dark"), l'Hexagone, 1967.

Poésie: Poèmes 1953–1971, l'Hexagone, 1972, revised edition, 1979.

(With Fernand Toupin) *Errances*, Editions Bourguignon, 1975.

Ici, ailleurs, la lumière (title means "Here, there, the light"), l'Hexagone, 1977.

À découvert (title means "Uncovered"), Éditions Parallèles, 1979.

En la nuit, la mer: Poèmes 1972–1980 (title means "In the night, the sea"), l'Hexagone, 1981.

(With Léon Bellefleur) *Éveils*, l'Obsidienne, 1982.

Les Heures (title means "The hours"), l'Hexagone /Champ Vallon, 1987, l'Hexagone, 1988.

Wells of Light, Exile Editions (Toronto), 1989.

Fiction:

Tu regardais intensément Geneviève (title means "You stared fixedly at Geneviève"), Quinze Editeur, 1978, revised edition, l'Hexagone, 1990.

La mort vive (title means "Death alive"), Quinze Editeur, 1980.

Lucie ou un midi en novembre (title means "Lucie or a November afternoon"), Boréal Express, 1985.

Nonfiction:

(Editor and contributor) *Visages d'Edgard Varèse* (title means "Aspects of Edgard Varèse"), l'Hexagone, 1960.

Edgard Varèse (biography), Seghers (Paris), 1966, translated by Derek Coltman, Orion Press, 1968, revised version edited by Christian Bourgois, Seghers, 1989.

Les Actes retrouvés: Essais (title means "Recovered acts"), HMH, 1970.

Depuis Novalis: errance et gloses (essays; title means "From Novalis"), HMH, 1973.

Journal dénoué (autobiography; title means "Unbound diary"), Presses de l'Université de Montréal, 1974, l'Hexagone, 1988.

Écrire en notre temps (essays; title means "To write in our time"), HMH, 1979.

Ouvertures, l'Hexagone/La Librairie Bleue, 1988.

(With the Centre Francophone Canadien, PEN Club International) *L'Écrivain, Liberté et Pouvoir*, Les Éditions du Pélican/Septentrion, 1989.

Commencements: dans l'art et la peinture, à paraître, forthcoming.

Also author of film commentaries for the l'Office National du Film, 1955–59. Author of text for cantata by Pierre Mercure, "Psaume pour abri" (title means "Psalm for a shelter"), produced by Radio-Canada, 1963. Work is represented in more than a dozen anthologies, including *Twelve Modern French-Canadian Poets,* edited by G. R. Roy, Ryerson, 1958, *How Do I Love Thee: Sixty Poets of Canada (and Quebec) Select and Introduce Their Favourite Poems from Their Own Work,* edited by John Robert Colombo, Hurtig, 1970, *The Poetry of French Canada in Translation*, edited by John Glassco, Oxford University Press, 1970, and *Anthology of Contemporary French Poetry*, edited and translated by Graham Dunstan Martin, Edinburgh University Press, 1972. Contributor to numerous periodicals. Cofounder and editor of *Liberté,* 1958, member of editorial board, 1958—. Producer of Radio-Canada, 1960—.

Robert Phillips

1938-

Robert Phillips, 1990

There's an old vaudeville routine that begins, "I was born in the hospital because I wanted to be near my mother." (What's vaudeville? I hear younger readers asking.) I was born in Milford Memorial Hospital, Milford, Delaware, because that's where the family physician practiced. But home was Laurel, Delaware—a town further down Sussex County on the Delmarva Peninsula. I was a premature baby, weighing only three pounds, four ounces at birth (a fact many would find difficult to accept today; for the past several decades I have apparently been compensating for my early lack of weight). I spent my first months in an incubator with a growth light bulb, like a baby chicken. I was so little, my father said I would fit in a shoe box. My mother was not well, and after I was born the doctor lanced one of her breasts and drained "a cup of pus." Literature is made of particulars. I've always been fascinated by the fact that it was precisely "a cup." I didn't picture a measuring cup. I saw a tea cup.

Life on the Delmarva Peninsula in the thirties and forties and the early fifties was extremely parochial. This was before the Bay Bridge connected the western shore of Maryland with the eastern; before the Delaware Memorial Bridge connected Delaware with New Jersey; and long before the tunnel bridge connected the eastern shore of Maryland with Virginia. Consequently, the peninsula was pretty isolated from interstate traffic, commerce, and what passes today for "progress." In my hometown there were still some streets paved with oyster shells. Every spring a scissors grinder went door to door, sharpening scissors and knives. There were separate schools for "colored" and whites.

While I was growing up, the state of Delaware built one major highway, Route 13, popularly called "The Dual" because it consisted of two parallel lanes, separated by grass, running from Wilmington in the north to Delmar in the south. In Sussex County there were no trees or plantings to beautify the roadway, just two slabs of cement running down the flat state. I used to call it "Dual in the Sun," after the lurid Gregory Peck–Jennifer Jones Western film. But few picked up on my little joke. I wrote about that highway in the prologue to my first book of short stories, *The Land of Lost Content* (1970):

> Once you have crossed the canal up north, there is little of interest on Route 13, except perhaps for the state's one private college, a

junior college long on Jesus and short on funds . . . Poverty and wealth sit side by side in ironic juxtaposition: the house trailer that pulled off the road in the middle of the night seems to have camped for years on the plantation's perimeter; the jerry-built shack disgraces the drive where Cadillacs roar and raise dust in finny disdain. Zoning is unheard of here. It is as if the good Lord took a mixture of the very wealthy and the very poor, shook them up, and hurled them down upon this sandy, flat, gray, barren landscape.

The Eastern Shore was at once a fine place to grow up and (for me) a miserable place. What was fine were the splendid Atlantic Ocean beaches just thirty miles from my home, particularly Rehoboth Beach and Bethany Beach. Ocean City, Maryland, in those days was wonderful too—miles of unspoiled sand dunes and white pines. During the Lyndon Johnson administration, Bobby Baker built his infamous Carousel Motel north of Ocean City—and it signaled the beginning of the end for the Ocean City I loved. Today it is mile after mile of condos, co-ops, hotels, motels, gambling casinos, what have you. The Washington crowd finds it a diversion. For one who grew up there loving the uncluttered beaches, it is a disaster. I wonder if boys still go crabbing at Indian River Inlet the way I did, casting nothing but a string

Young Bob in front of the family home, Laurel, Delaware

with a chicken wing tied to the end, and pulling it in laden with blue crabs, shaking them into a bushel basket, and casting again? One could get a basketful within a half hour. Then I'd lug the basket back, and mother would boil the crabs in beer. They never tasted quite the same if you didn't eat them off newspapers spread on the table.

Another good thing about the Shore which has not changed is the abundance of good produce. Local sweet corn, strawberries, tomatoes, cantaloupe, watermelons—all were available at roadside stands as well as in the markets. Chicken farms were on every horizon, and long before Frank Perdue became a television personality selling his name-brand chickens, we were buying his oven-stuffers locally. One problem with raising chickens on the Eastern Shore was the summer heat and humidity. With temperatures over 100 degrees days in a row, it was not uncommon to read of thousands of chickens suffocating.

More suffocating than the henhouses, for me, was the cultural climate—or, more precisely, the lack of one. At the early age of five I wanted to take piano lessons. My parents didn't own a piano, but my paternal grandparents, who lived in the same town, did—a towering cherry-wood upright. It stood in their front parlor, a room closed off from the rest of the house by folding glass-paneled doors. In the winter it was freezing in that parlor. But I would practice for hours after elementary school, my fingers blue with cold. My parents, sufficiently impressed by my diligence and determination, eventually bought a secondhand upright for twenty-five dollars. It was installed in my parents' dining room. My mother felt its presence would disrupt the living-room decor.

She had very strong ideas about decoration and decorum. She was born in Roanoke, Virginia, in 1911, and had met my father when he left Laurel after high school to attend Virginia Polytechnic Institute in Blacksburg. He was taking a degree in metallurgical engineering while my mother was secretary to the dean of engineering. My father worked briefly as an engineer, but when the depression broke there were no such jobs. His father made inquiries at the local high school in Laurel, and as it happened, they needed someone to teach chemistry and physics. So my parents moved to Laurel, as a stopgap, my mother thought. My father ended up teaching in that school until he took early retirement decades later. My mother never adjusted to the town until the day she died in 1984, and never adjusted her expectations that my father should be doing something "better." My poem "Vertical and Horizontal" explores the relationship:

Mother grew up in the Blue Ridge,
thriving on the various landscape,
Southern sounds, the thin air.
He married her, brought her heirlooms,
antiques, pretensions back to Delaware,
back to the only town he ever knew
or felt comfortable in. Mother fell
in love with a uniform, not knowing
how uniform life could be.

Ensconced, immediately she felt oppressed
as teacher's wife, and by the heavy air.
(Could a soufflé ever rise in it?)
"It's not so much the heat," she remarked,
"it's the humility." The landscape?
Unrelentingly flat—not one hill
within ninety miles. The natives'
accent? Flat. The townspeople? Flat-
footed. Even the songbirds songed off-key.

Father never noticed—he,
whose favorite catch was flounder.
Every morning for decades she rose,
deflated, a vertical soul snared
within an horizontal landscape,
knowing a steamroller had run over her life.
And once a year Mother returned
to Virginia, head lifted high, and pretended
she never had come down in this world.

I grew up close to my paternal grandparents. Their home was only a few blocks from the public schools, and my grandmother would have me to lunch every weekday, a treat compared to the fare at the school cafeteria, especially since my grandparents had their main meal of the day at noon. There would be fried or stewed chicken or roast rabbit, and dessert was usually homemade pie—coconut cream, sweet potato, custard, or a fruit pie.

My grandfather Phillips was a self-made man. Born in 1886, he never went beyond sixth grade, because he had to drop out to work on his father's farm. But whatever he touched he made a success. After he tired of running the farm in Bethel, he got a tenant farmer to run it for him and moved to Laurel, where he started a confectionery store. It soon became the local adult hangout, with a soda fountain in the front room and tables with checkerboards in the back. And when Grandfather tired of *that,* he went into the timber business. He owned tracks of timber all over Sussex County, as well as real estate holdings. He became president of the Town Council. He was a much-respected man, as well as a generous one. Often there would be a knock on the back door, and it would be one of his employees, looking for an advance or a handout. He never refused them, even when my grandmother insisted they would "drink it up" immediately. He was also generous to our family. Knowing the limitations of a schoolteacher's salary, Grandfather would always provide us with a new appliance, even a new car when needed.

Which did not cut much ice with my mother, particularly on Sundays when my grandparents' big green Buick would pull into our drive. Every Sunday for decades they would arrive just after church— around noon—and stay until the end of the Ed Sullivan Show on TV—at 9 P.M. My mother always said she felt "just like a prisoner in my own house!" Every Sunday we had them for supper, except for holidays, when they would entertain us. We would then be joined by Great-grandfather Phillips, who lived on the Bethel farm with the tenant couple. He perpetually wore a Band-Aid across his left temple, covering a sore which would never heal. When I was a youngster, his nickname for me was "Old White-head," because my hair was platinum blond. Whenever I visited the farm to ride the horses or help pick beans, he'd yell out, "Old Whitehead will get there! Old Whitehead will do it!" Great-grandfather died in 1956, the year I was graduated from high school. He was eighty-nine.

In addition to music, I also developed a strong interest in art. But Laurel offered nothing in either field, there was no concert hall, no art museum, no performing theatre. There were bowling alleys and skating rinks and baseball diamonds and pool parlors. But for culture one had to drive ninety miles north to Wilmington, and certainly my father was unwilling to contemplate a 180-mile round-trip just to look at some pictures or hear someone play the piano. So I'd save my allowance and buy classical records—usually heavy RCA Red Seal 78 RPM records that broke if you dropped them. You couldn't buy them in Laurel. There were no record shops, no bookshops. You had to drive to Salisbury, Maryland, to find them. But my father liked jazz. He'd played trombone in the VPI band, and played a bass fiddle in a local dance band on weekends. So once in a while together we'd visit Watson's Smoke Shop in Salisbury, which had a back room devoted to records. I bought Liszt's "Second Hungarian Rhapsody" and Tchaikovsky's symphonies and "Scheherazade"—all the entry-level classics a junior-high-school kid would admire.

In my quest for the arts, I would scan the entertainment pages of the *Philadelphia Inquirer*, the Sunday paper we took. Sometimes I'd see a concert I had to attend—Eugene Ormandy directing the Philadelphia Orchestra, playing Bartok and Sibelius, for example. My parents actually let me take the bus to Philadelphia alone, find the concert hall, sit rapt for hours, only to run for the last bus back to the Eastern Shore. The trip was three hours each way. I wouldn't get home until three or four in the morning.

I kept up my piano playing, and following my father's example, I too joined a dance band, the Herbie Dayton Quartet. We were piano, drums, trumpet, and tenor sax. Occasionally we were joined by a bass-fiddle player when we could find one. We played for dances in American Legion homes, Elk homes, Moose lodges, firehouses, high-school gyms, wherever. Usually we played from nine until one, but sometimes it was ten until two, and occasionally—if the crowd really liked us—they would pass the hat around and we'd play an extra hour until three. It was late driving back to Laurel from Easton or Cambridge, but it never occurred to me this was an unusual life for a junior-high student. I was happy to be playing the piano, happy to earn the money. Sometimes I earned as much as thirty dollars an evening. That seemed good money then. Later I formed my own group and had a one-hour live program every Saturday morning over WSUX, the local radio station. The call letters were an abbreviation of Sussex County; it was only later I came to think of that station as WSUCKS. The format for my program was for listeners to call in requests, which we would improvise on the spot. All went well until someone requested "Hindustan," which none of us had heard of. But usually we were able to play what the audience wanted to hear. The program had sponsors, and we got paid every week. I could use the money. There were four children in our family, and my father earned around five thousand dollars a year teaching school. Mother wrote the weekly "Society Column" for the town paper, the *State Register*. She spent a lot of time on the telephone, finding out who was visiting whom and who had entertained at bridge. Some regularly called her with their "news," but mostly she had to ferret it out through endless phone calls. When I first saw Tennessee Williams's *The Glass Menagerie*, and witnessed the character Amanda Wingfield attempting to sell magazine subscriptions by phone, I was reminded of my mother's journalistic efforts.

When I wasn't taking the bus to Wilmington or Philadelphia, I often would drive our family car to no particular destination. I just had to drive, to get somewhere, to ward off my boredom. These drives

*"My mother and father, Katheryn S.
and T. Allen Phillips"*

are recounted in what has become my most antholo-
gized poem, "Running on Empty":

As a teenager I would drive Father's
Chevrolet cross-county, given me

reluctantly: "Always keep the tank
half full, Boy, half full, ya hear?"—

the fuel gauge dipping, dipping
toward Empty, hitting Empty, then

—thrillingly!—way below Empty,
myself driving cross-county

mile after mile, faster and faster,
all night long, this crazy kid driving

the earth's rolling surface
against all laws, defying physics,

rules and time, riding on nothing
but fumes, pushing luck harder

than anyone pushed before, the wind
screaming past like the Furies . . .

I stranded myself only once, a snowy
night with no gas station open, ninety miles

from nowhere. Panicked for a while,
at standstill, myself stalled.

At dawn the car and I both refilled.
But Father, I am running on Empty still.

One reason I was so determined to succeed in
the arts was that I knew I couldn't compete with my
older brother, Thomas Allen Phillips, Jr., who was a
star athlete, particularly in basketball. He was six feet,
four-and-a-half inches tall, tall for a high-school
basketball player then. He went on to play varsity
basketball at the University of Maryland. My younger
brother, Burns Elwood Phillips, played a mean trumpet and went to the University of Delaware. And the
baby of the family—a girl at last, Mary Elinor
Phillips—perhaps shared the most interests with me,
particularly literature. Today she teaches college
English.

I was an omnivorous reader. We had some
poetry volumes in the house, inherited from my
mother's side of the family—leather-bound, with
marbleized endpapers and black-and-white etchings
of the poets. It was from this home library that I first
encountered Wordsworth, Longfellow, Tennyson,
and—oddly enough—Jean Ingelow. Despite the fact
the town was a cultural desert, there was a fine public
library. The president of Du Pont in Wilmington, Mr.
Walter S. Carpenter, Jr., had married a lady from
Laurel. When she died, he wished to establish a
memorial in the town. It was agreed that a library
should be built, and Mr. Carpenter contributed one
hundred thousand dollars toward its building and
collections. I visited that library every Saturday. The
librarian, Mary C. Thomas, had her own ideas about
which books were "suitable" for circulation. I recall
requesting *The Catcher in the Rye*. She gave me a
baleful look, walked back to her office, and removed
the book from the bottom drawer of her desk, where
it was kept under lock and key. Mailer's *The Naked
and the Dead* occupied the same drawer. I read them
both.

The luckiest break I had during my high-school
years came when a local businessman, William J.
Hopkins, met and married a Boston Brahmin and
brought her to Laurel to live. She was attractive,
plump, and blue-eyed, and obviously came from
wealth. Her clothes, jewelry, and accent were impeccable. More so than even my mother, Lilian Beaulieu
Hopkins felt estranged in that town. She had been a
concert pianist and had taken part in Boston's rich

cultural life. I think to keep from going mad, she announced she would take "a few select pupils." She interviewed and auditioned a number over a period of weeks. Happily I made the cut. Mrs. Hopkins made a big difference in my life. I couldn't wait for Monday afternoon at four—our appointed hour—to sit before her big, black Baldwin grand, lid raised, and play. She was strict about tempi and fingering, and she frowned at my penchant for using too much pedal. But she could be lavish with her praise when she felt it was earned. Together we romped through the entire first volume of *Beethoven Sonatas.* Sometimes at the end of a lesson she would play for me:

Piano Lessons

The best times came when we exchanged places
	and she sat before the keyboard, hands
		poised,
then tore into "Soaring," "Carnival," or
	"The Waldstein." Former pupil of
		Gebhardt,
fellow pupil with Bernstein, she mumbled
	apologies if she fumbled a trill,

an arpeggio. No apologies
	needed—she filled that long rectangular
room with the first live classical music
	I'd heard. Rubenstein could not have
		thrilled me
more. As her fingers flew across the grand,
	she was transported to Back Bay Boston
of her girlhood, I was transported to
	any place but where I had to grow up.

For all my enthrallment with piano, it was art that occupied most of my time when I wasn't doing homework. My high-school yearbook states I was going to attend Pratt Institute and study painting after graduation. But late in my senior year I reread the Pratt catalogue and realized that, with the exception of Freshman English and History of Art, all my courses would be studio courses. I felt much too ignorant to begin to specialize so early. In May of my senior year I began to make applications to liberal-arts colleges—Swarthmore, Haverford, Syracuse among them. There was no guidance counselor, and luckily I was ignorant of the odds against any good

"Mother, Mary Elinor, Burns, me, and T. Allen, Jr."

school admitting me for September matriculation at that late date.

At commencement exercises I won more than my share of awards, including the English key for the highest average in English for four years (which I deserved), the Music key (which I also deserved), and something called Best All-Around Senior Boy Award (which I decidedly did not deserve. If anything, I was much too one-sided with my passion for the arts. I never played a single varsity sport). But receiving that award proved the faculty had admired my work over four years. Shortly afterward I got a letter of acceptance from Syracuse University. Their financial aid had all been dispersed by then. But they would give me a place in the freshman class and a job in the dining hall. I was ecstatic. Syracuse was the northern-most school to which I'd applied, and I wanted to put a great deal of distance between me and the Eastern Shore.

Syracuse University, it turned out, was a good place for me. Ernst Bacon and Louis Krasner were on the faculty of the School of Music, Ainslee Burke and Robert Marx taught in the School of Art, Jerome Reidenbaugh directed a dynamic School of Drama, and the English department was filled with professors whose courses were an inspiration. These included Mary H. Marshall on Shakespeare, Sanford B. Meech on Chaucer, Arthur W. Hoffman on the eighteenth century, Cecil B. Lang and Edwin Harrison Cady on the nineteenth, and Donald A. Dike, Walter Sutton, and David Owen on the twentieth. George P. Elliott, the fiction writer, and Philip Booth, the poet, were among the first faculty of the newly formed Creative Writing Program. Later they were joined by Delmore Schwartz (who in turn was succeeded by Donald Justice, W. D. Snodgrass, and Hayden Carruth). Saturday afternoons Jimmy Brown and Ernie Davis scored touchdowns for the Orangemen in Archbold Stadium. The football team went to the Cotton Bowl in 1959.

Tuition, room, and board at Syracuse totalled over two thousand dollars, a hefty fee for a school-teacher to pay. I washed dishes in Sims Dining Hall for free board. I hated working in that kitchen, but never told my parents. And one day before work I sat down at the piano in Sims and started to play. Mrs. Theresa DeNio, the dining-hall head, heard me. She came over and said, "How would you like to play for your supper?" "What?" I replied. "How would you like to supply dinner music instead of washing dishes?" I jumped at the chance, of course. Every evening for four years I put on tie and jacket and

played piano in Sims. And in my sophomore year I was declared the Western Electric Scholar, a scholarship I held for the next three years. That took care of tuition. I only had room and books and spending money to contend with. My father sent me as much as he could, usually twenty-five dollars. The rest I earned in summers—by being a busboy in the dining hall and piano player in the cocktail lounge of the George Washington Hotel in Ocean City. I lived in a free basement room in the hotel and took free meals in the kitchen. I bussed breakfast and dinner, and played piano until 2 A.M. Afternoons I sacked out on the beach, where my fair skin invariably got burned. I never really tanned, but when I returned to campus each fall I knew I looked healthy. This was in the years before skin cancer scares. Today I am more cautious.

Looking back on my undergraduate years, I see that I overcompensated for the paucity of activity in Laurel. I enrolled in a dual program and earned undergraduate degrees in both English and journalism. This entailed taking as many as twenty-one credit hours each semester. I was editor of the undergraduate literary magazine, a senator in student government, vice president of my class, member of a social fraternity, member of the marching band, and member of ROTC. I wonder now where I found time to study, but study I did. It was while an undergraduate that I began writing seriously, and took writing workshops from Donald A. Dike. Dike was short and wiry, red-faced and grey-haired, a boozer and a horseman. On more than one occasion he had to leave class because he'd received a call from the farm that his horses had broken out of the corral. Once he was kicked in the face by his horse Major de Spain (named after a Faulkner character, naturally). For months, Dike's broken jaw was intricately wired. He claimed when he talked he sounded like an aeolian harp. I was terrified of Dike, but waited for his praise. A major influence on my work at the time was the poetry of the Imagists. I kept producing tight little imagistic verses. In exasperation Dike wrote across one poem, "It is now time for you to attempt a poetry of *statement!*"

Two of my classmates in writing workshop were Joyce Carol Oates, who was to become a lifelong friend, and Judith Bloomingdale, who was to become my wife. By the time she was a junior, Oates already was a legend on campus. She produced novel-length manuscripts while we piddled with brief stories and poems. It was rumored that when she completed one novel, she would turn the stack of paper over and write another on the back. Once done, she'd discard

At the piano in Sims Hall, Syracuse University, 1957

both. She was very shy, and refused to read her works in class. Rather, she sat looking distressed while Dike gleefully read them aloud in his raspy voice. He was the first to recognize her genius.

Bloomingdale was a beauty and a gifted poet. It was she and Oates who won most of the annual literary awards at Syracuse, not me. She and I dated from our sophomore year through graduate school. Later she published poems in *Prairie Schooner, Modern Poetry Studies, Ontario Review,* and other quarterlies, and had a poetry collection accepted by Vanderbilt University Press, until a stroke stopped her writing in 1972. She has not written since. The poetry collection was never published. Other classmates included Ted Koppel, the news commentator; Suzanne Pleshette, the actress; Dick Allen, the poet; Barry N. Malzberg, the science-fiction writer; and Michael Herr, author of *Dispatches,* the best book to come out of the Vietnam war.

One influence on my life at this time was neither classmate nor professor. He was Lester G. Wells, the curator of rare books at the Arents Research Library on campus, and coeditor of Stephen Crane's *Love*

Letters to Nellie Crouse. I originally met "Deke" Wells at a function at our fraternity house, Delta Upsilon. (His nickname was Deke because originally he had pledged the Deke house, Delta Kappa Epsilon. Then he saw his mistake and pledged DU.) During Stephen Crane's brief tenure at Syracuse he also had been a member of DU, and I lived in the same room Crane supposedly had inhabited. I always hoped some of his genius would rub off onto me, by a process of osmosis from the walls. It never did.

Wells offered to show me the library's holdings of Crane manuscripts, letters, photographs, and first editions. I made an appointment and showed up the next day at the Arents Room. It was the first of many visits and the beginning of a strong friendship. I loved our long chats surrounded by first editions, oil portraits, silver bowls. It was he who introduced me to Saint Paul's Episcopal Church in Syracuse. When Wells died in 1971, he named Judith and me his heirs. We took possession of his personal library, furniture, and oriental carpets. My strong ties with the Syracuse University Library date to my meeting Wells. It was a proud moment, in the spring of 1990, when I was presented the same Post Standard Award for service to the Syracuse libraries that had been presented to Wells in 1966.

In the 1950s, poetry readings were relatively rare. They had become part of the literary scene as recently as January 1950, when Dylan Thomas made his first reading tours of America. But during my years at Syracuse, I attended readings by Robert Frost, E. E. Cummings, Robert Lowell, Richard Wilbur, Richard Eberhart, William Meredith, Robert Francis, and—of all people—Ayn Rand. Frost made the greatest impression. By then he had become the Grand Old Man of American Poetry. His "reading" largely was him saying his poems aloud by heart, head thrown back, eyes closed. It was quite an act. For his appearance Hendricks Chapel was filled to capacity.

My graduation from Syracuse in June 1960 was a big event in my family's life. My mother, father, and grandfather Phillips drove up from Delaware in Grandfather's Buick. Grandmother Phillips was not well enough to travel; she would live only four more years, whereas my grandfather survived until 1972. The family stayed at the then-grand Hotel Syracuse. My mother's big dilemma was deciding between two hats she had bought for the occasion. She settled upon a big, straw picture hat with artificial flowers. Commencement speakers were Adlai Stevenson and Sir Charles P. Snow. The valedictorian was Joyce Carol Oates, whose perfect *A* average was best of a class of two thousand. But she never got to deliver her valedictory address. The ceremony was held in Archbold Stadium, and halfway through the proceedings it began to rain furiously. There was no indoor facility large enough to accommodate the crowd, so everyone disbanded. My mother's new straw hat was seemingly ruined. Our diplomas arrived weeks later by mail.

During my senior year at Syracuse, I had made an unexpected decision. I felt I had to continue my education on the graduate level. I applied to numerous English departments—Cornell, University of Pennsylvania, University of Massachusetts, and Minnesota among them. I received an offer of financial aid from each. But Syracuse came up with the best package: a teaching assistantship for free tuition plus a salary, and a resident advisorship in one of the undergraduate dormitories for free room and board. My master's degree not only wouldn't cost anything, but I would be making money. I don't think I've ever felt so rich before or since! I actually had money in my pocket most days. (The teaching assistantship paid eighteen hundred dollars over nine months.) Judith, who graduated in the same 1960

class as I, left the university for a time and became an editor at General Electric in Syracuse. But after six months of editing technical data about the Atlas missile, she fled GE and returned to campus, taking a pleasant apartment on Euclid Avenue with a screened-in porch on the second story overlooking the women's playing fields. (At Syracuse everything from gymnasiums to dormitories was segregated in those days.) Judith applied for and received a teaching assistantship while she took her master's.

To escape the noise of the freshman dormitory where I was proctor, I'd take my work to Judith's apartment. There was a breeze on the porch, a stereo in the living room, and a well-stocked refrigerator in the kitchen. I had three sections of Freshman Composition to teach. Each class had thirty students. That meant ninety compositions to read and correct every week. If I gave a test, that meant an additional ninety papers. And of course I had to prepare three lectures a week—lectures on "structural linguistics," a subject about which I knew little. Further, I was supposed to have six conferences with each student each semester. Could that be 540 conferences? I remember vividly sitting on Judith's porch, correcting mountains of papers on autumn afternoons, while below my students drifted toward the stadium to watch a home football game. It seemed unfair I couldn't join them. My decision not to pursue an academic career dates from those days.

But I thoroughly enjoyed graduate school and my fellow graduate students, most of whom came to Syracuse from other schools. I spent most time with Willy Henry from Yale, Robert Alan Hastings from Harvard, Robert Emmet Long from Columbia, and Don Sturtevant from University of Vermont. I also made a lasting friendship with David H. Zucker, who later coedited with Dike the *Selected Essays of Delmore Schwartz.*

Delmore, as everyone called him, came to Syracuse in August of 1962. We had of course read his famous poems such as "The Heavy Bear" and "In the Naked Bed in Plato's Cave" in many anthologies. Judith was working in the periodical room of the Carnegie Library on campus that summer, and Delmore would drift in often to tease her—he had an eye for pretty women—and to "check out what his enemies were saying about him" in the quarterlies. He'd especially thumb *Partisan Review* and the *New Republic,* two of his power bases from which he was now estranged.

When Delmore first arrived on campus he was charming and a continuous source of fascinating

"My wife, Judith," 1970

conversation. He always wore shirt and tie, the city boy uncomfortably transplanted upstate. Physically he no longer was the handsome prince of the early photographs. But he also was not the haggard, haunted-eyed poet displayed on the back jacket of his 1959 selected poems, *Summer Knowledge,* which had won the Bollingen Prize. (About that jacket photo W. H. Auden had said, "Nobody should look that unhappy.") With his large, noble head—a little too large for his body?—and his peculiar complexion—it sometimes seemed gold, other times green—he was an unmistakable figure striding across the quadrangle, his tongue sometimes working outside his mouth. His body seemed bloated, as if from drink. Evenings he would hold court in the Orange, an off-campus bar where students would jockey for position in his booth. Among the students he befriended was Lou Reed, who later formed the Velvet Underground rock group. Long into the night at the Orange, Delmore would tell stories of "Cal" Lowell and "Lizzie" Hardwick and the like. He had a special store of spurious stories about T. S. Eliot's sex life. He called

me "the other Phillips," since he had worked with William Phillips on *Partisan Review.* He claimed to be working on a cycle of related short stories, called *A Child's Universal History,* which has never surfaced.

Every fall semester Delmore was a brilliant teacher. As the year ground on toward Christmas, he began to disintegrate. His classes, when he met them, were chaotic. He would often sleep in his office or on the sofa in the graduate-student lounge in the basement of Hall of Languages, rather than returning across the city to his flat in the chic Skyline Apartments. But Delmore would become less than chic. His clothes became wrinkled and messy, his speech a slur. This is from my first book of poems:

Writer in Residence

Schizoid poet, lumber up College Hill
Breathing like a dolphin, looking sad—
Too many bottles, too many pills,
Too little writing, too little, too bad.

The school you teach for, back-water,
The pupils you preach at, dull.
Genius-in-residence, desolate,
Try to hold conference with fools.

Fawning Circes (wanting to be
Writers, not wanting to write)
Encircle you at smoky teas;
Bitches in heat, about to bite.

Your last book, last testament, ten years ago
Cool critics picked and sheared to shreds.
So smile for students, placate Ego and Head,
Then homeward drag, to bottle, to bed.

In alcohol books get written,
In slumber fey critics swoon.
Bankrupt poet—gray, balding, stricken—
You wake haggard at dawn in some rented
     room.

The university recognized the problem, and had Delmore placed in a private mental hospital. The chairman or Dike would assume his classes. By springtime, Delmore was back on campus, much his old self. Then in the fall, the cycle would begin again. This pattern repeated itself until January of 1966, when Delmore left campus for the last time. Instead of entering a hospital, however, he fled to New York City and took residence in a series of seedy hotels. He died, alone, of a heart attack on July 11, 1966, after taking out his garbage in the Columbia Hotel.

Another faculty poet I greatly admired was Philip Booth. Physically and literarily he was the opposite of Schwartz. He had been a varsity skier at Dartmouth and looked the part. His poems were lean and trim as his frame, whereas Schwartz's late effusions were Whitmanesque catalogues. Booth's poems were filled with images of sailing and the soil, while Schwartz was a poet of the city. Booth was Judith's thesis advisor (she wrote on Eliot's *Four Quartets*) and he befriended us both. It was he who, after reading a group of my poems, suggested I send them to Harold Vinal for his magazine, *Voices*. I did, and Vinal accepted four, which appeared in the September-December 1962 issue (number 179). My self-perception as a poet dates from that time. I was grateful to Booth, whom I'd always regarded as an admirable figure—totally independent of "po-biz" and literary politics, never cutting the figure of his poems to fit current fashions.

Because Judith had begun graduate studies a year after me, I took my degree sooner. We had become engaged, and to bridge the time when her studies were complete, I took a job within the university as assistant director of admissions. This entailed interviewing prospective students on campus and visiting various high schools and prep schools. I also had to pass on thousands of applications for places in the freshman class. The work was pleasant enough. It was while driving to New Jersey to attend a Friday college night that I heard, over the car radio of my rented car, that President Kennedy had been shot. Everyone, I suppose, remembers where he or she was and what he was doing when news came that the president had died. I was on the New Jersey Turnpike in a rented Oldsmobile. The college night was cancelled and I drove back alone to Syracuse.

In the spring of 1963 Judith's degree was completed. We were married on June 16. It was a big wedding in Hendricks Chapel, where we'd heard Frost. Arthur Poister, professor of organ, played Widor's thunderous Tocatta and Fugue. We honeymooned on Nantucket, where neither of us had been. We stayed at the old, shingled Sea Cliff Inn, with its winding staircase and stained-glass windows. The inn has since been demolished, as has the White Elephant, another Nantucket landmark of the time.

One autumn day we took a bus from Syracuse to Manhattan. We began to apartment-hunt. We both felt, with our master's degrees in English, we'd have no trouble finding jobs in Manhattan, but we couldn't do it from upstate. We got off the bus, bought a *New York Times*, and began to circle apartment listings within our price range. Or rather, within what we assumed our price range would be, once employed. The first apartment we looked at was at 111 East Thirty-sixth Street, between Park Avenue and Lexington. It was a third-floor rear apartment overlooking a garden. There was a large ailanthus tree outside the bedroom window. The apartment had fourteen-foot ceilings, parquet floors, a marble fireplace and crystal chandelier in the living room, and a workable kitchen. The only drawback was lack of closet space. But we felt the charm and spaciousness more than offset that. The block was lined with trees, and the brownstone itself was well maintained. Later we found out it had been either Commodore Perry's or Admiral Dewey's—we've both forgotten which. Down the block was the house Franklin and Eleanor Roosevelt first occupied after their marriage, and on the far corner was the Morgan Museum. We took the apartment—perhaps the only couple to come to Manhattan and engage the first apartment they saw!

The rent was two hundred dollars a month, which sounded very high to us. (Judith had paid ninety a month for her large apartment in Syracuse, and that included a garage.) When relatives asked how much rent we were paying, we always lied and said, "A hundred dollars a month," which they still felt was exorbitant.

After paying several months' rent in advance, the moving van, phone and utility deposits, our resources were precariously low. We had to find jobs soon. As luck would have it, within a week Judith had a job as an editor on the Literary Heritage series of textbooks with the Macmillan Company. She started work in the handsome old Macmillan building on the corner of Fifth Avenue and Twelfth Street. Her office overlooked a churchyard. Today the building is the Forbes Building; Macmillan moved uptown to occupy a glass box on Third Avenue. For all of a week I went into a blue funk—Judith was working and I was not. Then the next week I had a job as a copywriter with Benton and Bowles advertising agency at 666 Fifth Avenue. When I contemplate how long it takes individuals to find an apartment and a job in New York today, I realize how markedly times have changed. I also realize we were incredibly lucky and naive.

We were very happy in Manhattan. I walked to work, Judith took the bus. Friday nights we dined out at Brews, one of the neighborhood restaurants on Thirty-fourth Street. We saw a lot of theatre and films. Some days I walked home for lunch, read the mail, did a little writing, then returned to the office. Years later that apartment figured as one of the residences in my "Tree Sequence":

. . . In New York the ailanthus
in the private courtyard
tapped upon our glass.
Favorite food of silkworms,
tree of the gods, good omen,
companion, reality, it bore
great shade and mythology.
We set our newly married roots
into city cement. Manhattan
was the center of the universe.
There was nothing we would not try.

It was in that apartment I put together the manuscript of my first book of poems, *Inner Weather,* which was accepted by a small New England press. That should have made me happy, but I've always felt its publication was premature. I hadn't yet found my own voice. There are echoes of Hardy, Robinson, and Ransom. Someday I'd like to take a tour of America's libraries, and wherever I find a copy of *Inner Weather,* smuggle it out and destroy it.

It was also in that apartment that our son, Graham Van Buren Phillips, was conceived. Graham was my mother's mother's surname. Van Buren had been Judith's family name until they changed it in the nineteenth century to conform to the name of their upstate New York farm, "Bloomingdale." (The Van Burens had come to America on the *New Amsterdam*

in 1633, and Judith wished to restore the name to the family tree.) Graham was born on January 27, 1967, in Doctors' Hospital in Manhattan. He was a big buster of a baby, weighing eight pounds, four ounces. Later that year, with crib, playpen, bassinet, bathinet, and toys occupying every corner of our one-bedroom apartment, we realized we should either look for a bigger place in the city, or move to a house in the suburbs. We decided the logistics of raising a child in the city were pretty formidable as well as expensive. We looked northward to Westchester County. We would, of course, miss aspects of our apartment on Murray Hill. (Twenty years later, in conversation with the photographer Star Black, I realized she had bought our very apartment. She loved it too—but complained about the lack of closet space.)

I knew Westchester County fairly well. My mother's mother, Mary J. Schaeffer, the composer (her most famous songs are "Do You Hear What I Hear?" and "Start the Day with a Smile," which Liberace used as a theme song), had remarried a steel tycoon named Mark Kenneth Frank and taken residence in Rye. As a youngster I used to visit Rye in the summers. We'd be driven around in Mr. Frank's Stutz Bearcat or his Lincoln, and go swimming at the Westchester Country Club. But by the time Judith and I were looking, Rye seemed too built-up and suburban for our tastes. We looked in Northern Westchester, fifty miles out of the city, and bought two wooded acres with a stream, waterfall, and lake rights. My salary was only eight thousand dollars at the time, but somehow we built a new four-bedroom house, at 16 Nash Road in North Salem. The house had a deck overlooking the waterfall, and during good weather, Judith and Graham would go down to the lake. We made a great mistake, however, in building on the north side of the hill. It seemed the driveway was covered with ice from Thanksgiving to Easter. Often I had to park at the bottom of the hill and walk up with bags of groceries. In the spring melting snow and rains would make the stream swell, bringing branches that blocked the drain under our driveway, flooding it. Three times I had to replace the bridge. Being on the north side, the house was also dark inside. You could have grown mushrooms in some of the rooms.

Every weekday I would drive to the Goldens Bridge or Katonah train station and commute to the city. This established a rhythm which has been interrupted for only two years during the last twenty-four years (when we lived in Europe, 1971–72). I got in the habit of doing most of my reading and some of

With son, Graham, Falmouth, Massachusetts, 1969

my writing on the train. This may account for the prevalence of poetry over prose in my oeuvre; it was easier to write a short poem on the train than to juggle the manuscript of a novel.

The house on Nash Road was a contractor's house, but Judith and I customized it in many ways. One change was to have what was to be a large "family room" downstairs divided to form a guest room and a den. It was in that den that I wrote most of the stories in *The Land of Lost Content,* the book of fifteen short stories published in 1970. The stories were all set in a town I called "Public Landing." The characters, for the most part, were totally imagined. A few were partially based upon people I'd known in my hometown. Reaction to the book on the Eastern Shore was heated. At one time my parents wrote me there was a waiting list of 350 people at the Laurel Public Library. I wrote back, "Can't they afford to buy a second copy?" The peculiar thing was, the characters I'd based on real people largely went unnoticed. It was the purely fictitious characters at which people took umbrage. One lady swore I'd libelled her, and that I'd better not set foot in Laurel again. But of her private life I knew nothing at all. Perhaps I was highly intuitive.

The book was published by Vanguard Press, an old New York firm (sometimes mistaken for Vantage Press, a vanity publisher. But Vanguard was far from that. They'd discovered and published James T. Farrell, Saul Bellow, Nelson Algren, Calder Willingham, Dr. Seuss, and my friend Joyce Carol Oates, whose first book of fiction Vanguard accepted while she was still a student). I was proud of the association, and went on to publish with Vanguard a critical anthology, *Aspects of Alice* (1971), and a poetry anthology, *Moonstruck* (1973). *Aspects of Alice* was and is an international success, published not only in the United States in hardcover by Vanguard and softcover by Vintage, but also by Gollancz in the United Kingdom and by Penguin in forty-four countries. It's still in print. When Graham did a college paper on Lewis Carroll, his professor assigned *Aspects of Alice.*

It was only after Evelyn Shrifte at Vanguard rejected the manuscript of my first mature poetry collection, *The Pregnant Man,* that I parted ways with the firm. That book wasn't taken by a publisher until 1978, when Stewart Richardson at Doubleday accepted it. I went from 1966 until 1978 without a poetry collection—twelve years of intense poetry writing and intense self-doubt. I was placing poems in all the best magazines, but somehow couldn't place a book. When *The Pregnant Man* finally was published, I sent Evelyn Shrifte a note quoting Psalm 118, verse 22:

"The stone which the builders refused is become the headstone of the corner." (She later told me she'd made a mistake in not publishing the book, which was good of her.) And in a way, *The Pregnant Man* is the cornerstone of my poetic career. The book established the style and voice and many of the subjects of all that was to follow. The first section, of a dozen poems, was based on the notion that all human emotions can be prefigured in the parts of the body. The poems on the head, the heart, and the hand remain some of my most characteristic work.

I'd written so many poems since *Inner Weather,* I had nearly a complete third manuscript, which is how *Running on Empty* (1981) could follow *The Pregnant Man* with such rapidity. Doubleday was happy to publish it. They'd sold three thousand copies of *The Pregnant Man,* which I'm told is like *Gone with the Wind* for a poetry book.

All these books were written while I held full-time jobs in advertising. I had served my apprenticeship at Benton and Bowles, then after three years moved on to become a creative supervisor at McCann-Erickson—a firm I did not much like. After two years there I went to Grey Advertising, a highly competitive environment in which I seemed to thrive. After six years at Grey I was asked by management if I'd consider a two-year assignment in Grey's new Düsseldorf, West Germany, office. Grey had purchased a successful German domestic agency, Gramm, and wanted a professional from New York to help organize the creative department. In essence, I was sent to hire and fire and to raise the creative product to New York standards. Prior to leaving the States I was sent to a total-immersion program in German at the Berlitz School, and would continue my language studies once abroad. Judith had taken both high-school and college German and was fluent.

The job turned out to be a thankless assignment. The Gramm agency had been very successful, or else Grey would not have bought it. Then they find this "ugly American" in their midst, criticizing in his broken German their product and operation. It is no wonder I found cooperation lacking. I was also expected to write advertising for some of the agency's international clients: Procter and Gamble, British American Tobacco, BMW automobiles among them. This was the best part of the job. I would write in English, and work with a translator to ensure it could be turned into good, idiomatic German. During my entire stay I wasn't called upon to use much of my own German; most of the staff wanted to practice their English on me. And their worst English was far better than my best German.

Judith, Graham, and I flew from New York to Scotland, then reboarded and flew direct to Düsseldorf. We were met by two agency staff members, Winfried Kilp and Nigel Jones. (Kilp was nicknamed "The Sweater Boy," because he wore wool sweaters all year around; Jones was a transplanted Britisher.) They presented Judith with flowers and Graham with chocolates. They also helped us whisk our orange tabby cat, Pekoe, through Customs. No one had told us pets were not allowed into the country except after extensive quarantine. Somehow Kilp managed to charm the officials, and the cat carrier emerged from the airport with us and all our luggage.

I'll always remember the first morning we awoke in Düsseldorf. It was July 4, 1971. The fact that we were on foreign soil on the Fourth of July was not lost on us. The first sounds we heard in our hotel room were the cries of several roosters. Someone was raising chickens in the middle of the city! We rose, took a typical German breakfast in the dining room— fruit juice, cold cuts, cheese, bread, real butter, milk, fruit—then strolled about the city. Roosters and chickens aside, it seemed an elegant and sophisticated place. The main shopping boulevard had a canal from end to end. There were outdoor cafes on each side. About eighty percent of the city was new, having been rebuilt since the war. But there was a charming Old Town still standing near the waterfront, including an ancient cathedral, Saint Lambertus, with a curiously twisted spire.

We would live in the hotel as guests of the agency until we found suitable accommodations. By "suitable," it was deemed we would want to spend a rental equivalent to our monthly mortgage payments on the house in North Salem. This meant we would live quite handsomely, because the exchange rate at the time was four Deutsche Marks to a dollar. (By contrast, today there are only 1.5 Marks per dollar.) A realtor with the amusing name of Mr. Nussbaum (Mr. Nut Tree—we were guilty of making literal translations of all names) drove us to the charming village of Benrath, located between Düsseldorf and Cologne. There we were shown a three-story stucco home with a red tile roof, hanging geraniums in the window boxes, an extensive rose garden, and a pool in the rear. The house was directly across from a park, on the exclusive Melies Allee—a boulevard lined with large homes. When we asked how much it would cost, we discovered it was easily within our means. We were delighted.

Mr. Nussbaum showed us the immediate neighborhood. Two blocks away in one direction was the Rhine, with its fascinating boat traffic. Two blocks in the other direction was Schloss Benrath, former hunting lodge of Empress Josephine's brother, Joachim Murat, Grand Duke of Berg, now a state treasure. The grounds were landscaped with topiary and mirror pools in the French fashion. There were black and white swans and all manner of duck. The *schloss* was open for tours. It was a wonderful neighborhood for our son to explore. I wrote several poems about its enchanted nature:

> In Düsseldorf the linden,
> German lime-tree, lifted limbs
> to cathedral the park paths.
> The heart-shaped leaves
> and flowers of cream and gold
> clusters, fairytaled us away.
> What deep shadows, what mystery!
> Angels and birds in its foliage,
> lions, stags, unicorns under its shelter.
> A pink palace beckoned beyond.
> We would live forever . . .
>
> (from "Tree Sequence")

And this:

> In Europe they lived like princess and prince,
> not in a palace, though one graced the block,
> and on Sundays they strolled in its gardens.
> They gazed Narcissus-like into the pools,
> their daughters chased mallards and rare black
>   swans.
>
> Their own house was a redone half-mansion
> they couldn't hope to occupy in the States;
> a winding staircase spun three stories high,
> the windowpanes told bright, stained-glass
>   fables,
> the latticed gazebo in the back yard
>
> bore roses which she watered every day
> *"Jeden tag!"* their avuncular landlord
> ordered, and she groaned but watered daily.)
> Participants in some vague fairy tale,
> they walked the Rhine with the dressed-up
>   Germans . . .
>
> (from "Once Upon a Time")

The best part of my German assignment was the travel. There were no facilities for filming commercials in Düsseldorf, so every time the agency sold a TV spot to a client, I was sent to London, Paris, Munich, Rome—wherever the commercial could be shot—all expenses paid. In Milan I stayed directly opposite La Scala, and attended opera. When I wasn't travelling for the agency, my small family and I would pack up our Peugeot 504 and drive to New Amsterdam, Brussels, Bohn, some destination never terribly far away. Every place seemed a short distance from Düsseldorf. Judith was an excellent driver, and had no fear of the speeders on the Autobahn. Given that, plus her superior reading knowledge of signs in German, I gladly let her do most of the chauffeuring. One day on the Autobahn she made the witty quip, "In Germany, all roads lead to Ausfahrt!" ("Ausfahrt" is German for "Exit").

Our good American friends the William Heyens were in Hannover during the same years. Bill was a visiting professor of American literature at the university. We visited and Bill and Hannelore showed us the extraordinary Herrenhausen gardens, formal and French on one side, informal and English on the other. We spent our first Christmas abroad in Paris, staying at a friend's apartment on the Rue de la Pompe near the Arc de Triomphe. Daniel Stern, the American novelist, and his wife Gloria were living in Paris and we visited them. On New Year's Eve Graham watched me set off firecrackers on the quay, adding our own light to the City of Light.

It was in Paris that Graham, only five, asserted his feelings about museums. "I hate museums!" he cried. "I get hungry. I get thirsty. My feet get tired." Unfortunately the morning he took this stand was the morning we were scheduled to visit the Louvre. Finally I lied, saying, "Today we're going to a gallery." "Galleries are okay," he said.

So we took a cab to the Louvre. After we climbed the steps and entered the massive building, Graham's head swiveled and his face assumed an expression of abject betrayal. "This is a *museum!*" he screamed, and flung himself to the stone floor in tears. The three of us did the world's fastest tour of the Louvre—rushing past the Mona Lisa, whizzing by the Madonna of the Rocks. It should be in *The Guinness Book of World Records*. But Graham was correct. We were expecting too much of him at his age.

Yet another holiday was spent in London, at my cousins' apartment overlooking Hyde Park. He was managing director of Du Pont in the United Kingdom. They had gone to Switzerland for their vacation and turned the large flat over to us for two weeks. I felt enormously at home in London. No doubt this was due to a lack of any language barrier. But I also had a number of friends there, including the poet and critic John Lehmann, with whom I had corresponded for years, and Joyce Carol Oates and her husband

Raymond J. Smith, who were in London during the same period.

When not travelling, I stuck to a strict schedule. Every morning in Benrath I rose, took a bath in an enormous claw-and-ball-footed tub—there was no shower, the one amenity I missed—and waited for the mailman, a blond youth who arrived on a yellow Deutsche Bundespost bicycle between eight-thirty and quarter of nine. Having put the most interesting mail from the States into my briefcase, I boarded the streetcar which paralleled the Rhine. It was a picturesque ride from Benrath into Düsseldorf, and the streetcar stopped directly in front of my office. At noon I would take lunch in one of the many small restaurants near my office. Even on a holiday, such as Saint Martin's Day, when I would order the traditional fare of roast goose, red cabbage, potato pancakes, and beer or white wine, it was difficult to spend more than five dollars. If I'd had a quick lunch, I'd then haunt one of several bookshops that carried English-language publications. Most of the books I bought were Penguin paperbacks. At one point, my living-room shelves were lined with identical orange spines. In the evening I took the streetcar back to the suburbs. Graham would have spent a half day at the American International School and by now was riding his bike, waiting for Daddy. He wore a black-and-white German police officer's cap, and the moment he saw me would break into a smart salute. At age six he was mad about hats. I brought him a large Italian policeman's hat from Milan, and he wore it despite the fact he could barely see above the brim, which kept sliding to his nose.

Each day while I was at the office, Judith would drive Graham across the city to the school. Since it was a long trip each way, usually she remained in the school's vicinity. She discovered a hospitable cafe where she could sit next to the radiator and drink coffee or chocolate and work on poems. Hours later she'd transport the boy home. I think we both were influenced by tales of expatriates—the Scott Fitzgeralds, Hemingway, the Gerald Murphys—scribbling away in cafes. I too wrote a lot during these European days, largely prose. I completed both *The Confessional Poets* (1973) and *Denton Welch* (1974) while in Germany. Pekoe also had her own schedule. Every morning she would carefully check the traffic on both sides of the Melies Allee, and make her way to the ducks and swans in the park across the way. At mealtime she'd cross the boulevard and return. Pekoe was one shrewd cat. She travelled all over Europe with us, and lived to be fourteen. Of the dozens of cats we've had, she is the only one I was moved to write a poem about. "Poem for Pekoe" can be found in *Running on Empty*.

After a difficult entry, I soon found myself accepted by most of the German staff at the office. By the time my designated term was to end, the director asked me to remain indefinitely. He showed me a large company apartment which could be mine rent-free. It was extremely luxurious. He mentioned a large BMW company car. He spoke of a financial raise and bonuses. I felt briefly like Jesus being tempted by the Devil. Judith and I decided against it. It was time for Graham to enter first grade in the States. He was speaking more German than English. He'd forgotten both sets of grandparents. We felt it was time to return and "Americanize" him. Besides, unless I was totally committed to the European advertising scene (and I wasn't), I felt I should continue my career in New York.

I'd saved most of my vacation time for the end of the second year. In early November we sent most of our belongings, including the Peugeot, back to the States by boat, and we left Düsseldorf by train for our grand tour. Judith, Graham, Pekoe, and I travelled from Düsseldorf to Munich, where we stayed some days; then Munich to Vienna, stopping again; Vienna to Venice, where I got ill and never saw the Doge's Palace; Venice to Florence; and Florence to Rome. We especially loved Florence. It seemed much more contained and manageable than sprawling Rome. We had to get acclimated to the late supper hours in Italy. Often we'd feed Graham in our hotel room at five or six, take naps, then the three of us would visit a restaurant when it opened at nine. Graham would crawl beneath our table and fall asleep. Hours later I'd arouse him, and carry him out thrown over my shoulder, much to the amusement of the other diners, who had been unaware of his presence. The previous year in London, Graham had seen Queen Elizabeth and Emperor Hirohito. (He was disappointed the queen was not wearing her crown.) This year in Rome he saw the Pope. Unfortunately, today he doesn't remember any of these travels. One day just before our return to New York, a chambermaid in Rome left our hotel-room door propped open for airing. When we returned, Pekoe was nowhere to be found. I frantically searched the hotel. Both Judith and Graham were hysterical at the cat's disappearance. Finally a young Italian elevator boy said to me, "If I were a cat, I would go up to the roof." I took the elevator to the roof garden and found Pekoe stalking pigeons. *Famiglia* Phillips had a tearful reunion with Pekoe. I never knew if the elevator boy was intuitive,

With Graham, Katonah, New York, about 1980

or if earlier he'd given the cat a lift to the roof. The next day we flew to New York.

Christmas week 1972 was spent in the Summit Hotel in Manhattan because we'd rented out the North Salem house through the end of the year. Christmas Day we were guests of William Goyen, the writer, his actress wife, Doris Roberts, their son, Michael, and Doris's mother, Ann. They gave Graham a big, shiny red fireman's hat with a badge. He could not have been happier. In January, I returned to work at Grey, at 777 Third Avenue. And in February, disaster descended. We'd been back in the North Salem house less than two months when, one wintry day, Judith suffered her stroke.

I had left for the commuter train. She had just put Graham on the school bus and turned to walk up our driveway. Suddenly she experienced an unbelievable headache. Once inside the house she looked for aspirin, but couldn't find any. She called the neighbor across the road and asked if she had any. The neighbor said she'd bring two over shortly. The next thing Judith knew, she was losing her vision. She went to the telephone to dial our family doctor, but couldn't see the numbers. She was standing there trying to get help when I did something I've rarely done before or since—I called home as soon as I reached my office. The moment Judith began talking I realized something very serious was wrong. She was slurring her words to the point they were indecipherable. I told her to stay put and I'd call the doctor.

When I reached him, the doctor stated it sounded as if Judith had a migraine headache, and she should take two aspirin, lie down, and he'd visit her after his office hours were concluded. I asked when that would be, and he said four in the afternoon. I screamed at him. "There's something seriously wrong with her! Get an ambulance out there right away. If I'm wrong, I'll pay for it. Just get her to the hospital." I called Judith back and said an ambulance was on the way. Then I took the next train home.

When I got to the house, there was no sign of Judith, just two aspirin atop the milk box on the front step. I learned later our neighbor had left them there. Then I called the hospital. After some delay they said a Judith Phillips had been admitted.

At the hospital I learned she had been admitted first as a regular patient. It was only after some time she was diagnosed as having had a stroke and placed in Intensive Care. It wasn't until noon she was given anticoagulants. That meant she had been hemorrhaging massively in the brain for four hours.

The weeks that followed were a nightmare. She was misdiagnosed as having a brain tumor. I began to live with the "knowledge" she would soon die. Then the diagnosis was changed. What they had read on the X ray as a tumor was, in fact, the mass of blood that had accumulated in her cranium. Now they said she had had an aneurysm. A blood vessel, probably congenitally weak, had burst. No one seemed to know the prognosis for her recovery. There was, they said, always the possibility of a reoccurrence. Patricia Neal, the actress, was also an aneurysm victim. She had had a total of three strokes.

Eventually Judith began to regain her speech. It was slurred, but it was speech. There were, however, long lapses when either the words would not come, or the thoughts behind the words. After some weeks she was able to take steps around her room. Her right side had been considerably weakened. She lost all peripheral vision in her right eye. Her doctor thought that might return. It never did.

From that day in 1973 forward, our lives were never the same. Judith's personality changed. Once a poet, editor, and voracious reader, Judith no longer functioned in the literary world. Even on a practical level our lives changed. While other suburban mothers were carting their kids about to ball practice, band

practice, and the like, Judith no longer could drive. And since I was at my job five days a week, some very elaborate planning had to be made in order to get our son where he had to go. Consequently, Graham has grown up to be very strong and independent. From the time he was six, he had to do certain things on his own. In high school he was in the band, played two varsity sports, had his own rock band, and wrote and distributed a rock newsletter. He graduated cum laude from Boston University, and today is in law school at Syracuse. He's my best friend.

We had planned to sell the North Salem house on our return from Europe. Our dear friends Charles and Nancy Willard were moving to Connecticut, where Charlie was to teach in the law college at Yale. We'd always admired their blue French farmhouse situated directly on the Cross River Reservoir. It had a southern exposure and was full of sun—the opposite of our North Salem home. Originally the house had been built in 1919 as the summer home of the Fulton family, owners of the Fulton Fish Market in Manhattan. In addition to its charm and location, the house was in the town of Katonah, which had a school system superior to North Salem's. We were negotiating for the house at the time of Judith's stroke.

The Willards handsomely came forward and said that, under the circumstances, they would understand if we withdrew our offer. That was one of the most difficult decisions I've had to make. On the one hand, Judith loved the blue house; it was where she wanted us to be. On the other hand, she would be surrounded by friends in our old North Salem neighborhood; we knew no one on the Reservoir. Another consideration was the expense of buying and closing and moving to a new house on top of our hospital and medical bills. I found out my medical insurance didn't cover practical nurses, and I was paying for a practical nurse at the rate of one thousand dollars a week. Ultimately, I think, it was logistical matters that pushed me to continue with the purchase. Except for a bedroom overhead in the remodeled attic, the house was all on one floor—whereas the North Salem house was a split level with two flights of stairs. The doctors weren't at all certain Judith would be able to walk properly again. Further, the house had a "maid's room" just off the kitchen, where a nurse could live without disturbing our lives at the other end of the house.

That was eighteen years ago, but it seems much longer. Physically Judith made a remarkable recovery. She had youth on her side, being only thirty-two at the time. Psychologically she is still recovering. I have never written a poem or story about her illness.

It is the one topic I have not been able to address. Also, sometime during the years following, I stopped playing piano. I can't say exactly when that happened, it just happened. I went from playing every day to not playing at all. This may have been the result of my schedule—leading, as it were, a double life: commuting to the city to a full-time job by day, commuting to the country to run the house and do my writing by night. But I have another theory. I think I stopped playing piano when Judith became ill. A certain joy had left my life.

Once I almost resumed practicing piano. The telephone rang one evening, and it was Lilian Hopkins, my former piano teacher. She was now a widow, not in good health, and planned to enter a Methodist nursing home. There was no room for the ebony Baldwin grand. She spent a lot of time thinking about who she wanted to have it. She was determined not to let her stepdaughter have it. (The stepdaughter apparently had not fully accepted her when the father remarried.) Finally Mrs. Hopkins decided to pass it along to me. Her memories of our lessons together were as fond as mine. As soon as her home was sold, she would call me to send a moving van for the grand.

I was touched by her offer, and excited by the prospect of having my own Baldwin grand. Judith and I discussed where the piano would be placed. I would always keep a vase of fresh flowers on it, as Mrs. Hopkins did. I would slowly regain my repertoire—Chopin, Debussy, Bach, and especially Beethoven.

Then one night Mrs. Hopkins called again. Was she ready for me to fetch the piano? No, there was no piano to fetch. One afternoon she was having luncheon at the country club. Outside, an electrical storm was in progress. When she arrived home, she found fire trucks parked in her driveway. Lightning had struck her house. It quickly burnt to the ground, destroying everything—all her furniture, clothes, photo albums, record albums, music, and "my" grand piano. "Well," she said philosophically, "it certainly will make moving to the nursing home a lot easier."

I never resumed playing. But I always seemed to be writing poems. By 1985 it was time to bring out another collection. But Doubleday, who had published my last two, suddenly declared that they were "out of the poetry business." They weren't even going to continue publishing James Dickey, who went

Cross River Road, Katonah, New York

back to his earlier publisher, Wesleyan University Press. Again I needed a publisher.

It was my friends the Raymond J. Smiths who came up with the idea of my not just publishing a collection of new poems, but putting back into print those I wanted to preserve from my earlier books. (Both *The Pregnant Man* and *Running on Empty* were out of print; perversely, *Inner Weather* remained available for years.) Ray and Joyce offered to bring out an edition of my new and selected poems in both hardcover and paperback from their Ontario Review Press, which was thriving in Princeton. They already had published poetry collections by Albert Goldbarth, Richard Moore, Eavan Boland, Tom Wayman, John Ditsky, and Oates herself. I was happy to join their list.

My original title for the book was *Personal Effects,* but a sensational novel came out with that very title. So I had to change it. (I'd already run into problems with the title *Running on Empty;* some people ordered it, only to receive a nonfiction study of our dwindling petroleum resources!) It was Ray Smith who came up with *Personal Accounts,* and I've liked the title ever since. He's an excellent editor.

The poems were arranged not chronologically but by topic. In putting it together I saw I'd continued to explore certain concerns—preoccupations—from book to book. So the book's progress was not from poem to poem, but chapter to chapter. These "chapters" included poems on childhood in Delaware, middle age, lives of great artists, our travels in Europe, works of art, the parts of the body, and, above all, survival. A good embodiment of this theme is found in "The Stone Crab," a poem admired by Howard Moss, John Logan, Horace Gregory, and others:

Delicacy of warm Florida waters,
his body is undesirable. One giant claw
is his claim to fame, and we claim it,

more than once. Meat sweeter than lobster,
less dear than his life, when grown that claw
is lifted, broken off at the joint.

Mutilated, the crustacean is thrown back
into the water, back upon his own resources.
One of nature's rarities, he replaces

an entire appendage as you or I
grow a nail. (No one asks how he survives
that crabby sea with just one claw;

two-fisted menaces real as nightmares, ten-tentacled nights cold
as fright.) In time he grows another—

large, meaty, magnificent as the first.
And one astonished day, *Snap!* it too
is twigged off, the cripple dropped

back into treachery. Unlike a twig,
it sprouts again. How many losses
can he endure? Well,

his shell is hard, the sea is wide.
Something vital broken off, he doesn't
nurse the wound. Develops something new.

Through the years I continued to write short stories as well as poems. But I'd come to consider my stories my poor little orphans. For one thing, I could always publish my poems, and in good magazines—the *New Yorker, New Republic, Nation, Hudson Review, Paris Review, Poetry,* and so on. But my stories were more difficult to place. This may be because I had no reputation as a story writer, whereas I was becoming known as a poet. It also may be because the stories were inferior to the poems—but I refused to think so. After all, reviews of *The Land of Lost Content* were unanimously favorable.

So I kept accumulating my stories, about half of which were rural tales set in "Public Landing," the other half urban and suburban stories about a character named Fallick. In the summer of 1989 I was on the staff of the Wesleyan Writers' Conference, and the poet Robert McDowell was also teaching there. Recently he had established his Story Line Press, and he asked if I had a manuscript to submit. It was only then I realized nineteen years had gone by since I'd published a story collection. No one could accuse me of rushing my fiction into print! I collected all the new Public Landing stories, and it will be published by Story Line in 1991 as *Public Landing Revisited.*

The Fallick stories, on the other hand, continue to get written. I don't want to rush that book, either. Someday it will all fall into place as an episodic novel. I once had a contract for it, with Vanguard Press. There was even a dust jacket designed, with the title *Fallick: A Fiction.* I liked that title. It dances around the issue of whether or not the book is a novel or a collection of stories. It also reminds me of Updike's *Bech: A Book,* another episodic "novel" I greatly admire. But my editor at Vanguard, Bernice Woll, took issue with the ending I'd given the book. I took issue that she took issue. Eventually I asked my agent, George Wieser, to withdraw the book. That was several years ago, and I'm still working on it—the book and the ending. Woll may have been right after all. Vanguard has since been bought by Random House for their backlist and is no longer a

Receiving the Arents Pioneer Medal from Chancellor Melvin Eggers, Syracuse University, 1988

functioning publisher. Wherever Fallick lands, it will be with a different house. Some readers of the manuscript have told me the book is profoundly sad. I think it's the funniest thing I ever read. Whichever, it is meant to depict the alienation of man in his modern universe. Toward the conclusion, Fallick is riding a subway late at night. He drunkenly oversleeps his stop at Grand Central Terminal:

> Fallick awakes because he is so cold. Opening his eyes suddenly, he looks down and is startled at what he sees. As the subway races through the upper Bronx, as the snow falls heavily from the sky, Fallick is wearing only his undershorts. His topcoat is gone, his suit is gone, his shirt and tie are gone, even his undershirt is gone. It goes without saying that his wristwatch, ring, and wallet are gone. Fallick panics and wonders, What will he do now?

In addition to my own books, I've edited a number of works by others. Sometimes this occurred because a writer-friend seemed stymied and I offered to make a book where he or she didn't see one. This was the case with at least three books of which I am the unacknowledged editor: William Goyen's *Collected Stories,* Isabella Gardner's *That Was Then: New and Selected Poems,* and Marya Zaturenska's *The Hidden Waterfall.* I also silently edited *Collected Stories of Noël Coward.* Sir Noël was not a friend; we never met. I

simply wanted to have all his stories together in one volume, so I did the job myself. Other books were requested by publishers, as when E. P. Dutton engaged me to collect and introduce the stories of Denton Welch, and when University of Texas Press requested an edition of the letters of William Goyen.

The most ambitious of these projects came as a consequence of my accepting the literary executorship of the Estate of Delmore Schwartz. After Delmore died in 1966, I kept waiting for someone to bring out his last book of poems. He'd published many in quarterlies and newspapers that were uncollected. No such book appeared. I learned that Dwight Macdonald was the self-appointed executor. I approached him at a party, asked if he were editing a posthumous volume. He claimed he was far too busy with his own projects. (Macdonald was attempting to write his literary and political memoirs, but had a terrible block. He never got very far.) I asked if he'd give me permission to edit such a volume, and he enthusiastically agreed.

Last and Lost Poems of Delmore Schwartz appeared as a Vanguard hardcover in 1979, and as a New Directions paperback in 1989. Since then there have been French, Italian, and Japanese translations. After Macdonald's death, Schwartz's heir, his brother Kenneth Schwartz, asked if I'd assume the executorship. At the time I didn't know what a literary executor did—but I found out fast.

Since then I've done my best to see that Delmore receives his share of attention. So much of a poet's reputation depends upon whether or not his work is available. Robert Lowell and John Berryman, for instance, were still being read and reviewed because Farrar, Straus and Giroux was keeping all their work in print. Since the *Last and Lost Poems,* I've edited and had published Delmore's *Letters* (1984) and *The Ego Is Always at the Wheel: Bagatelles* (1986). In preparation are Schwartz's critical book on T. S. Eliot (to be published by Illinois University Press), his five verse plays (to be published by BOA Editions), and selected correspondence between Delmore and his New Directions editor, James Laughlin (to be published by W. W. Norton). A writer in *Partisan Review* accused me of making "a cottage industry" of Delmore Schwartz. In a way this is true. One does not do all this work for money, however. There is little to be gained. But I admit to considerable pride when the volume of *Letters* was favorably reviewed on page one of the *New York Times Book Review* by Elizabeth Hardwick and called "an excellent edition."

Much has been made of my literary friendships, by Robert McPhillips in his essay on my life and work in *Dictionary of Literary Biography* and others. I have been fortunate to know many of our preeminent writers. As a young man I was introduced to James T. Farrell. He lived in the same Manhattan apartment house as my maternal aunt. I was excited to meet Farrell. I had first read *Studs Lonigan* one summer on the beach at Ocean City. I thought it one of the best American novels I'd read. I reread it for pleasure a number of times, and at Syracuse it was required reading for David Owen's course on the twentieth-century American novel. Farrell was very supportive of my fiction, and once gave Evelyn Shrifte a blurb for my book of stories—a blurb which, to my knowledge, was never used. It's possible she thought Farrell's name would "date" the book. It was through Jim Farrell I met Horace Gregory and his wife, Marya Zaturenska. Our friendship with this couple is recorded in my memoir "Visiting the Gregorys" (*New Criterion*, September 1990). I met Isabella Gardner through the poet Barbara Harr, who was an editor at Macmillan with Judith in the 1960s. Belle and I became fast friends, and we were good critics of one another's work. Her sudden death in 1981 occasioned one of my best poems, "Queen Anne's Lace," a poem I thought I would never stop writing. Its revisions became an obsession, as if no version would be good enough to serve her memory. I later wrote a prose memoir of her life and critique of her work, titled "The Democracy of a Universal Vulnerability" (*Chelsea*, 48, 1989).

I never met Philip Larkin, but our correspondence and his cantankerousness are recorded in my piece "'Interviewing' Mr. Larkin" (*Syracuse University Library Associates Courier*, XXIV, 1, Spring 1989). William Goyen was one of my closest friends. I like to think I helped get him writing again. We met when he was senior trade editor at McGraw-Hill Publishers, a post he held for seven years. During that time he didn't write one word of fiction. He owed Doubleday a book by contractual agreement. One April, I photocopied all his short stories—those collected in books, those uncollected in magazines and manuscript—put them in a box with a title page on top, COLLECTED STORIES OF WILLIAM GOYEN, and gave it to him on his birthday. He cried. Then he gave it to Doubleday, who readily accepted it. Its publication put Bill back on the literary horizon after a long absence. He quit McGraw-Hill and began writing again. My edition of his letters, when it appears, will surprise many with its impassioned eloquence about the nature and role of the artist in twentieth-century America. They are more than letters, they are arias. And laments.

Karl Shapiro and his brilliant wife Sophie Wilkins have been generous and are always fun to be with. It was Karl who was responsible for my invitation to read at the Library of Congress in 1987. They spend half the year in California, and I eagerly await their letters. Imagine receiving a new Karl Shapiro poem in the mail as soon as it is finished! My interview with Karl appears in *Paris Review* (Spring 1986).

Elizabeth Spencer is a special supporter—loving, sympathetic—everything a friend should be. My selected poems is codedicated to her, as it should be. I'm proud to say her collected stories was dedicated to me. That's how it is with us, back and forth. I goaded Elizabeth into putting that collected stories together at a time when she was convinced her next book had to be a novel. It too was reviewed on page one of the *New York Times Book Review,* and it won for Elizabeth the Gold Medal for the Short Story from the American Academy and Institute of Arts and Letters. She was elected to the Institute shortly after.

Other literary friendships should be recorded here—Stanley Burnshaw, Robert Francis, Dana Gioia, William Heyen, John Logan, Jerome Mazzaro, Howard Moss, A. Poulin, Jr., Raymond J. Smith, Thomas Victor, Richard Howard, William Jay Smith and his wife Sonja. But I'll mention in detail just one more: Joyce Carol Oates. From our days as undergraduates at Syracuse to the present, she has been a loyal friend and a soul mate. As I had with Delmore Schwartz, I've always regarded Oates as a true genius. The range and variety of her literary output is truly astonishing. Rather than being put off by this, I've always found it invigorating. There is something new in her conversation every time we talk. However, since we've never lived in the same town since 1960, we more often write than talk. Recently I presented Syracuse University Library with over three hundred of her letters. I suspect there is an equal number from myself to her. In 1990 Oates established the Joyce Carol Oates Papers at the Syracuse University Library. I think of both sides of our correspondence, dating back to 1957, sitting there cheek by jowl.

One nonliterary friend who has been important to my life and work is the painter DeLoss McGraw. By "nonliterary" I simply mean he is not a writer. But actually he and his work are highly literary. McGraw has painted entire series of works around poems by Dante, Emily Dickinson, Lewis Carroll, W. D. Snodgrass—and myself. It came about this way:

One night a few years ago my telephone rang. "Mr. Phillips, you don't know me, but I'm DeLoss McGraw, and I'm a painter. I was on vacation in Arizona recently, and I got hold of your *Personal*

Accounts in a bookstore. I was much taken with your poems, particularly the one called "The Wounded Angel." Would you mind if I painted a few pictures based on it?"

"No, why would I mind?" I replied.

"Thank God," he said, clearly relieved. "I've already finished two dozen!"

Those twenty-four paintings went to dealers in London and Munich, and every piece sold. And McGraw wasn't through. The next year in Los Angeles he had another big show, again based on "The Wounded Angel." I was invited to the opening to read that and other poems. It was a singular experience to stand in those big rooms surrounded by bright images and painted words taken from my poetry. One of the largest paintings—a triptych—was bought by the actor Gregory Peck. It's in his living room in Beverly Hills.

My friendship with McGraw continues. But our work relationship has changed. It began with him doing paintings from my poems. Now he sends me work and I do poems from his paintings. One example is the following. McGraw presented me with a large painting of "Robert the Poet" trying on

masks. It has the place of honor at home over our mantel.

Robert, the Poet: Wearing Tools of the Trade
(After the painting by DeLoss McGraw)

Observe the vividness of his hues.
Has faint pastel too long been my muse?

Now consider the wealth of choices—
Ten different masks, ten different voices.

That red one resembles Mickey Mouse.
The yellow one drives bargains like Faust.

Or assume the elephantine face
with the wisdom of an ancient race.

Or the maw of the man-eating shark,
elan of a green dog with no bark.

Some have shell-like ears like a girl,
some grimaces that make blood curdle.

Some, round glittering eyes that glare,
some, sly slitty eyes barely there.

There's a wolf to wear over sheep's clothes,
a creature with Pinocchio's nose.

"With the artist DeLoss McGraw in front of his paintings from my poems," Los Angeles, 1987

And just behind all this new headgear,
the palimpsest of an Old Master,

gold madonna and infant boy-child,
from an age when art was never wild.

I ask, What is the function of art?
Not to mask, deceive or counterpart.

So all I do is strap one in place?
Doesn't fit the mood, another face?

With so many various guises,
my poems should be full of surprises.

I have not said much about my day-to-day work in the business of advertising. It has been, for the most part, fun. The advantage has been that it pays better than teaching. The disadvantage is the total lack of job security. An account leaves an agency, or two agencies merge creating an account conflict, and people are immediately fired with total disregard for their longevity, ability or loyalty. It has happened to me more than once, and I'm one of the best writers in the advertising business, apparently, because I've received three Clios, the industry's equivalent of an Oscar. Moreover, the Monday through Friday, nine to six or later, routine clearly does not leave as much time and energy for writing as an academic schedule. I sometimes envied my teaching friends their long summer vacations and sabbaticals. I've never had more than two weeks' vacation in nearly thirty years. Perhaps once our son is out of law school, I can reduce my working hours in the city and spend more time at home writing. I'd also like to travel more. Travel always occasions new writing. I hope to produce more poetry, finish my novel about Fallick, and live long enough to see my grandchildren. Maybe even my great-grandchildren. Chances are one will be a towhead, and—for old time's sake—I'll call him "Old Whitehead."

BIBLIOGRAPHY

Poetry:

Inner Weather, Golden Quill, 1966.

The Pregnant Man, Doubleday, 1978.

Running on Empty, Doubleday, 1981.

Personal Accounts: New and Selected Poems, 1966–86, Ontario Review, 1986.

The Wounded Angel (etchings by DeLoss McGraw), Brighton Press, 1988.

Fiction:

The Land of Lost Content, Vanguard Press, 1970.

Public Landing Revisited, Story Line Press, 1991.

Criticism:

Aspects of Alice: Lewis Carroll's Dreamchild (anthology), Vanguard Press, 1971; Gollancz, 1972.

The Confessional Poets, Southern Illinois University Press, 1973.

Denton Welch, Twayne, 1974.

William Goyen, Twayne, 1979.

Editor:

Moonstruck: An Anthology of Lunar Poetry, Vanguard Press, 1974.

Last and Lost Poems of Delmore Schwartz, Vanguard Press, 1979, revised, New Directions, 1989.

Collected Stories of Noël Coward, Dutton, 1983.

Letters of Delmore Schwartz, Ontario Review, 1984.

The Stories of Denton Welch, Dutton, 1985.

Delmore Schwartz, *The Ego Is Always at the Wheel: Bagatelles*, New Directions, 1986.

Triumph of the Night: Tales of Terror and the Supernatural, Carroll & Graf, 1989.

Delmore Schwartz and James Laughlin: *Selected Correspondence*, Norton, 1991.

Delmore Schwartz, *Shenandoah and Other Verse Plays*, BOA Editions, 1991.

Other:

The Achievement of William Van O'Connor (bibliography), Syracuse University Library, 1969.

Contributor to *Isak Dinesen: Storyteller*, edited by Aage Jorgensen, Akademish Boghandel, 1972; *Natives: An Anthology of Contemporary American Poetry*, edited by Ed Ochester, Quixote Press, 1973; *The Achievement of William Styron*, edited by Robert K. Morris and Irving Malin, University of Georgia Press, 1975; *Old Lines: New Forces*, edited by Morris, Fairleigh Dickinson University Press, 1975; *Sylvia Plath: The Woman and Her Work*, edited by Edward Butscher, Dodd, 1978; *New York: Poems*, edited by Howard Moss, Avon, 1980; *The Pushcart Prize IV: Best of the Small Presses*, edited by Robert Henderson, Pushcart Press, 1979; *Anthology of Magazine Verse and Yearbook of American Poetry*, edited by Alan F. Pater, Monitor Book Co., 1981; *A Green Place*, edited by William Jay Smith, Delacorte, 1981; *The Generation of 2000*, edited by William Heyen, Ontario Review Press, 1984.

Also regular reviewer for *North American Review*, 1965–69; contributor of poetry, fiction, and essays to the *Boulevard, New Yorker, Hudson Review, Partisan Review, Paris Review, Poetry, New American Review,*

American Poetry Review, New York Quarterly, Commonweal, Southwest Review, New York Times Book Review, Los Angeles Times Book Review, Saturday Review, Studies in Short Fiction, Encounter, Nation, New Republic, America, and *New Criterion.* Book review editor, *Modern Poetry Studies,* 1971–78; associate editor, *New Letters* and *Ontario Review;* contributing editor, *Paris Review.*

Felice Picano

1944-

My mother used to tell us stories. Growing up in eastern Queens during the fifties in the midst of a middle-class, television-age, melting-pot neighborhood, my mother used to tell us stories of growing up a generation before in New England.

Her storytelling was immediate and fully recalled—"That reminds me of the time I was working on Westminster Street when the hurricane hit," she'd begin, just like that. It was limpidly related, unbound by extraneous facts or irrelevant information, rising to a climax—"We had to stay in the building all night, without electricity, watching the Providence River rise above the tops of cars. We laughed and lit candles and sang. But were we scared!" Sometimes she ended with a moral, not always, but you always knew the end—"You can still see the high-water mark from the '38 hurricane on some downtown buildings!"

I knew some characters in her stories: my mother's mother was alive until 1955 and Grandpa outlived her by twenty years. My uncles Billy and George and Rudy visited with their wives and children, as did my mother's nephew Henry, oddly enough her age, who'd been her escort in adolescence. But they had minor roles: my mother's stories were about her boyfriend Bill, whom she always called "Sourpuss," and Clemmy, short from Clementine. My mother had a nickname too—"Anna Banana"—because of the long, drooping curls she'd worn as a girl. And since her stories ranged willynilly, day to day, from her earliest years to just before she and my father married, we were sometimes confronted by confusions, mysteries.

How did our parents know each other? Visiting our grandparents in Thornton, Rhode Island, we could see from the second-floor bedrooms our other grandma—Soscia's—chicken coops, vegetable garden, and, hidden in peach trees, her house. My mother sent us to our grandma Soscia's house, though she never went herself. We'd walk down State Street to Fletcher Avenue around the hill. Coming back we'd cut through the connecting gardens and climb the tall, grassy hill, under which lay an old

Felice Picano, "the author as Angel,"
seven years old

Indian graveyard, where we'd hunt shards and shreds of anything in the least bit old.

We knew our grandparents—adjoining neighbors—weren't friendly. Knew that our parents' marriage was one (but not the only or the earliest) reason why not. That was one mystery.

We knew why Grandma's name was Soscia and not Picano: she'd remarried after her husband died of the Spanish flu in 1918, remarried and had three more children, Betty, Mike, and Little Tony—to distinguish him from Anthony Picano, known as Big Tony. But there was more mystery. My father's stories weren't about growing up in Rhode Island, but in New York: Ozone Park, though his siblings had grown up in Thornton and he'd once been my mother's classmate in an early grade. Why? My father's face would darken when he spoke of his stepfather, a man he hated with an intensity undiminished to this day. So my father's evil stepfather became another character in my mother's stories, with clever, gloomy, fortunate Sourpuss, and humorous, daring, social Clemmy.

When the Second World War was over and gasoline no longer rationed, we'd drive up to Thornton in a new, wooden-backed station wagon, along new highways spun like black ribbons through Connecticut's green hills, and we'd see and confirm places from my mother's stories—the trolley along Plainfield Street to funny-sounding Onleyville, Farmer Smith's fields stretching for miles, the orchards on the cliff above Atwood Avenue; in Providence itself, we'd play in Roger Williams Park, walk along Broadway, where a great-aunt lived in a huge Victorian house, or ascend Benefit Street on College Hill, where another aunt lived near Brown University, not far from where Poe and H. P. Lovecraft had resided. We'd drive to Barrington, where cousins lived on the waterside, or down to Bristol and Newport, or directly south to Rocky Point Amusement Park and Scarborough Beach, or further to Point Judith and Galilee. We'd even spend a July in a cottage in Petasquammscut, until it seemed we'd reclaimed all our mother's past and then some.

The more we reclaimed, the more the mysteries grew. Who was the boy in that old photo and why would no one speak of him? Who was that Air Force captain in that other photo? Why had we never heard of him? How come, if our mother was engaged to Sourpuss for so many years, she'd ended up marrying our father? Why was it some relatives hadn't spoken to each other in decades? Why was it our father had as a boy gone to live with Aunt Carrie and Uncle Recco? Why did we live not in Rhode Island, but in Queens? Not near my father's uncles and cousins, but an hour away, away from all relatives, at the city line?

I and my older brother and sister and cousins would pool rumors and data and try to figure it out, pushing into that treacherous, ultimately unknowable area of "what grown-ups do"—and why. We seldom came up with the answers.

Now, decades later, I've realized how those daily examples of my mother's storytelling and her sense of the importance of those stories have influenced me, perhaps decided me, to become a writer. Equally, unconsciously, influential for me in terms of *what* I'd write were my attempts to solve those mysteries in

"My mother, Anne Picano," 1939

and between our parents' families—and our physical distance, even exile, from the rest of them.

I was born in New York City at midnight between the 22d and 23d of February in 1944, the third child of Phillip and Anne Picano. I have three birth certificates for two days giving three times. My mother was awake at my birth and said it was just before midnight, and I was the easiest birth of her children despite my size—ten-and-a-half pounds. With my father home asleep, she named me—after my paternal grandfather.

My father had also been Felice, son of Felice, son of Felice, etc., all the way back to mid-nineteenth-century Itria, a mountain town known for olive oil in the province of Roma. In Italy, Felice is a common male name, as I discovered when I lived there; one with literary connotations: poet Felice Romani wrote libretti to operas by Verdi, Bellini, and Donizetti that every Italian knows. My father didn't grow up in Italy, but here, and he'd often fought over his name—in effect over being Italian. He'd legally changed his name. He didn't want any child of his to suffer from the same prejudice.

For my mother, with her New England sense of tradition, a family name, no matter how odd or difficult to bear, must be passed to the next generation. She had a point: after my books were published in England, Argentina, and France, I received letters from Picanos there tracing their lines back to one or another Felice Picano from Itria. And an archeologist placed my family name with geographical exactitude. She'd come across it in a story in an Italian grade-school reader. More recently, in *Smithsonian Magazine,* I found a forebear—Giuseppe Picano. In an essay on Neapolitan wood sculpture in the eighteenth century, art critic Hilton Kramer wrote that Giuseppe had moved from Itria to Naples and for several decades dominated his field with crucifixions, *pietàs* and carved *baldachins,* some still extant in local churches.

I've never fought over my name: people have been befuddled by it, misspelled and mispronounced it (Fuh-leese is right); people have asked if I'm Spanish or Greek or if it's a *nom de plume.* Due to my name, I've been instantly unique from early on in life. Later I realized being special for a name wasn't enough: spoiled by the attention, I sought a way to solidly earn it.

For my generation, being Italian was limited to a name and a few guarded family recipes my grandma Soscia gave my mother, herself a fine cook with an international cuisine. Being Italian was reduced to biannual visits to my father's relatives in Ozone Park, where Italian was spoken by adults when they didn't want us to know something, and where Uncle Recco read Italian-language newspapers while the tantalizing odors of lemon and anise and hazelnut arose in the kitchen, preceding delicious confections served with tiny cups of *espresso,* candy-covered almonds, and doll-sized glasses of sherry. Catholic icons, calendars, and a cousin who became a nun completed the exoticism of these visits, and we never tired of correcting adults who referred to someone nonItalian as "American," saying, "We're American too. All of us!"

Until I was three years old, we lived in Richmond Hill, Queens, in an apartment above a supermarket my father and my uncle Tony owned and which flourished during the war, even when Tony went off to become a much-decorated hero in the Pacific theater, and despite the fact that (as my parents insisted) they thought black-market sales unpatriotic. When the city took over the block to build the Van Wyck Expressway, my father bought land for a store off one new service road, and a house further away, in eastern Queens.

My brother Bob and sister, Carol, two and three years older than me, recall the apartment and store and our neighbors on Liberty Avenue. They recall trolley cars on the street and weekly serial shows on the radio. I don't. My awareness begins later, on long blocks of single and attached houses with front and backyards, grass, bushes, trees, a neighborhood rife with kids on skates and bikes, playing in the street at all seasons of the year, or in furnished basements watching TV. This defines me as Post War, in the van of the largest baby boom in history that would change our country, and eventually the world.

I led a cushioned life until the fourth grade. There, one day, quite by accident, I had my first encounter with unreasoning prejudice, and met my first life enemy.

In the book titled *Ambidextrous: The Secret Lives of Children,* published in 1985, I wrote of this encounter in detail. It centered on my ambidexterity. I'd learned to read and write on my own, using my older siblings' schoolbooks and notebooks. I watched them

"My father, Phillip Picano," 1939

write and taught myself that too. My mother—pregnant with my younger brother, Jerry—would correct me. By the age of four I read at first-grade level; when I entered kindergarten, I was reading third-grade books. One reason for my early success in any subject I was interested in was that I'd learned alone, forging my own methods. I used both hands to write and was very fluid in printing and script. I'd begin a sentence with my left hand and continue it with my right hand. In drawing, I'd shade and color-in using two crayons simultaneously.

My fourth-grade teacher, a middle-aged man, opposed my ambidexterity, my creativity, anything in fact but using my right hand. He went further, he used me as an example of everything wrong with a child. The more intolerant he became, the more I resisted. My parents didn't believe me when I told them of his irrational behavior. His persecution worsened. I was appalled by the injustice of my situation, trapped, on my own for the first time in my life. No one, not even my God, seemed able to help me. I began to rebel, in school and out. An explosion

*"Carol, Bob, Jerry (in front), and me,"
about 1950*

between my teacher and I was inevitable and it occurred. I was ten years old. I'd been a perfectly behaved child at home and at school—but when our little war was over, I'd become a monster of egotism and suspicion, filled with hatred.

And I was forever left-handed.

I settled more warily into a new class with a new teacher and got through the next two years easily. Following some quite high IQ tests, I was offered a chance to enter a special program in junior-high school: doubled science, music, art, social studies, two foreign languages, and tons of extracurricular activities. In recompense, we'd be socially and intellectually at the top of the school—and we'd skip the eighth grade!

I found I could learn at this advanced, subject-crammed, condensed level with only a bit more effort, since it depended so much upon autodidacticism, at which I was already a past master.

In *Ambidextrous,* I also wrote about my coming to sexuality, which happened between the ages of ten and thirteen, and involved several neighborhood girls and one boy. My third affair at the age of thirteen, recounted in the book, had more importance in that it led to my first piece of recognized writing, and my first artistic crisis.

The situation, briefly put, was that I realized one day that the surprising sexual relationship I'd been having with our ninth-grade class's "Ice Princess" had been completely set up and was being directed and watched by her father, an optics expert confined at home to a wheelchair by wounds suffered in the war. I ended the relationship.

Shortly later, when our English teacher had us write stories for a city-wide fiction contest, I wrote up what had happened with the girl and her father, greatly toning down the content, but not the situation nor its denouement. My story was much admired and picked to represent our grade in the contest. To my amazement, the story was sent back. The contest committee deemed it disrespectful of adults, in bad taste, overly mature, and even thought it was plagiarized. My teachers and even our dean weren't able to help me.

As a result, I became cynical and hard. It would be another decade and a half before I wrote fiction or showed it to anyone.

I had no special teacher in high school or college who intuited I had what it took to be a good writer and encouraged me.

Dr. Beringause conveyed his love for poetry: his clear, vivid analyses opened up the inner workings of poetry. Dr. Day's course in eighteenth-century British literature was sheer delight due to his legerdemain in making long-dead authors and their writings live again. James Wilhelm's seminar on Dante's work, life, and times was memorably comprehensive.

Though I was an art major—painting, sculpting, making collage—by my junior year I began to minor in cross-departmental literature using my alleged command of foreign tongues. I read six books a week, trying to keep plots and characters of Leskov and Genet apart from those in Henry James, William Faulkner, and Tolstoy.

Three students in most of my lit. courses were Steve, Barry, and Alan, who I joined during breaks between classes talking—arguing—in the "Little Caf," a small, older dining area favored by the bohemian elements on campus at Queens College, among which I suddenly found myself. But no matter how much Pinter or Proust that Alan or Barry or Steven read, they lived for, all but breathed, film. Not "movies," but film—experimental American film and any foreign-language one they could find. For them the novel was dead; literature completely moribund: film was the art form of the future. A few years younger and more restrained, I was less sure.

I had loved movies since I was two years old and awakened in a movie theater, stood on my mother's seat, being bottle-fed and watching Marlene Dietrich as a gypsy wrestle another actress for Gary Cooper in *Golden Earrings*. Now, living in lower Manhattan, I was closest to the cinemas that showed Resnais, Bergman, Fellini, and Mizoguchi: my apartment became a meeting place for the group—one teacher called us the "Hell Fire Club"—and my roommate Michael was also swept up in our cinema-madness.

Graduation neared and I still had no idea what I wanted to do with my life. I'd passed tests for the Peace Corps, but I wavered. The dean of the English department recommended me for a Woodrow Wilson Fellowship. That would mean more school: a masters and Ph.D. degree, then becoming a professor. I didn't think I wanted that. I'd written amusing and original term papers, so I'd been recommended for the Writing Workshop at the University of Iowa, and had been accepted. But Iowa looked so flat, so treeless, and I was so tired of going to school!

That spring, 1964, I'd accompanied my friend Ruth Reisiger when she'd applied for a job with the New York City Department of Social Services. I'd taken the tests and interviews too. Ruth had trained to be a social worker but I was less altruistic. Even so, when I discovered I'd be able to fulfill my military duty working for the Vista program—an American inner-cities version of the Peace Corps—I took the job.

At twenty, I was by no means a saint, but I'd been touched by several incidents bringing home our nation's social injustice. In 1962, the Black Muslim leader Malcolm X was to speak at Queens College. I knew he'd been a pimp and thief who'd become an eloquent speaker for Negro Rights (as it was called). One day before his appearance, the college administration cancelled it, calling Malcolm X "detrimental."

The uproar among students was immediate. The school had barred us from our First Amendment rights, although it insisted it was acting "in loco parentis"—in the place of a parent—protecting us.

In the sixties, Queens had as intellectual and liberal a faculty as any college in the country. They agreed it was a free-speech issue and joined our protest. When the administration failed to restore Malcolm X's speaking date, we organized a boycott of classes, marching around the campus's main quad with signs, chanting slogans, filling up the dean's office. The boycott spread to the rest of the City University system. We were assailed on all sides—our education was paid for by city taxes!—but we held firm, and the administration was embarrassed into letting Malcolm X speak. To my knowledge this was the first such student action in the country.

One result was that the implicit racism of the school, the city government, much of the public and the press was made explicit. The college's Student National Coordinating Committee chapter grew in size and activism. We organized sit-ins at lunch counters in the tri-state area where we heard of *de facto* segregation. I joined, was arrested, and experienced firsthand the oiled heat of bigotry. That summer and the next, SNCC sent students down South to enrol Black voters. I had to earn my living and didn't go. One pal and classmate, Andrew Goodman, did go—and paid with his life.

Despite this background, by the time my two year "hitch" as social worker was over, I'd become disillusioned: I could only see the program's lacks and failures. Oddly, others thought I did a great job: they wanted to promote me, to pay my tuition to get a graduate degree in social work.

This was also a time of personal crises—among them my need to investigate my sexuality more fully, which I knew would be difficult to do in the sexually repressive U.S. I quit work and went to Europe.

In the second volume of my memoirs, I've written in detail about this period and of my return. I merely note here that I returned to a new apartment in Greenwich Village, a new group of friends, mostly involved in the arts, and mostly homosexual. Nineteen sixty-six to 1971 were to be my years of experimentation: with different groups of people, life-styles, sexual and other relationships—and with psychedelic drugs.

Several people I met in this time influenced me greatly: among them the painter Jay Weiss, the writer Joseph Mathewson, the actor George Sampson, and Arnie Deerson. We—and others—were drawn by the charisma and generosity of Jan Rosenberry and formed a sort of group in 1968 and 1969. Jan was an advertising executive who tried to close the gap between the corporate world and rock music by befriending musicians and inviting them into TV commercials. Jan also opened his Manhattan flat to many people. It became a second home for some, an urban commune. His generosity toward me lay in his encouragement and his intelligent enthusiasm over any piece of writing—no matter how small or shallow—I showed him.

I'd written one story since the ill-fated one in junior high. In the "catalogue of my works," begun in 1974, it's listed as "Untitled: approx. 2,000 words, set in Cape Cod," with "artist from New York, and pre-teen local child" as characters. The subject is "betrayal." The entry reads: "August, 1966—MS missing. No typed copy." I.e. lost. I haven't a clue what it could be about.

As a social worker I'd written case histories, one of them complex enough to end up in the teaching manual. My next job was as a junior editor at a graphic-arts magazine. But there my writing was ephemeral, even the feature articles: not worth saving. My next job was at a bookstore. As was the next. At the latter store I wrote an introduction to an exhibit of Jiri Mucha's works—and an interview with the Czech artist's son translated from the French, the only language we more or less shared.

My little catalog shows other works I'd deemed important: one-act comedies written in the summer of 1968, with titles like "The Persistence of Mal-Entendu," and that fall, an unfinished novella that would become the seed upon which I built a career.

I was overqualified and overcompetent for any job I might land. It never failed—within months I'd be told I was the best employee, pushed into promotion, into pension plans and stock-sharing, my future in the company all laid out.

No way! I saw this period differently: as a time of testing and tasting and trying out. I would work as long as needed to save enough money to cover six to nine months of bills. Then I'd quit, giving as much advance warning as possible.

If asked, I'd say I was becoming a writer and needed time. And it's true that during these hiatuses from employment I taught myself the rudiments of poetry. I'd analyze, say, metaphor, then write a poem stressing metaphor—any topic would do—metaphor was what counted. Or I'd study form, say Spenserian Rhyme Royal, and use it to write a poem about my coffee cup or the first telephone call of the day—anything! Ditto with drama or comedy: I'd take any situation and turn it into a fifteen-page play. I'd even use authors I was reading, turn them into characters—with appalling results!

What I mostly did between stints of work was read, listen to music, go to movies and concerts, hang around with friends—anything but write. When a friend said it was an excuse for not working, for not tying myself to the "establishment," I couldn't deny it.

In the late winter of 1971, I was twenty-seven years old. I'd travelled, I'd had adventures, I'd lived in a variety of places among an assortment of people. A few months earlier I'd left the first bookstore I'd worked at, not only earlier than intended, but somewhat under a cloud, and with less savings than I would have liked. At the same time, a complicated and emotionally wrought romance with the late painter Ed Armour had begun to distort into something even more incomprehensible and unsatisfactory: I saw no way out but to end the relationship.

It was in this state of virtually total life crisis that I decided to become a writer. I dared myself: I staked everything on it.

I looked through notebooks and diaries, read scraps of plays and stories and finally lit on the 1968 novel fragment. After some scrutiny it seemed to hold up. A bit of thought and I began to outline it more fully. Amazement! I found I had characters, a plot, scenes, everything! As pieces of the novel began to fall into place in my outline I became excited. Certain scenes played themselves out in my mind—I could hear what my characters were saying to each other, could feel as they did, could see, smell, taste, know what it was like to *be* them.

Halfway through the outline, I threw it away and bought a hardcover notebook. I recopied the opening pages of the fragment from years before, crossed it out and began again. It took ten tries but I finally found the first line I wanted, then the first paragraph, the first page, the first chapter.

I wrote continuously after that, daily, whenever I could, whenever I wanted to. Late into the night sometimes, playing Bach's *Well-Tempered Clavier* on the stereo, letting his sense of structure and rhythm and Wanda Landowska's style subconsciously influence my own. When Bach became too rigid or monochrome, I'd switch to Solomon playing Beethoven's piano sonatas, or to Cortot's Chopin mazurkas.

Keyboard music—because the protagonist of my novel was a pianist. He'd been a child prodigy before the turn of the century, the toast of Europe in short pants, playing for Paderewski, Brahms, Sauer, Liszt. Now, in his midtwenties, living in New York, he'd returned to playing. A college acquaintance came to a recital and asked him to record for his new cylinder company. At the same time my protagonist had met a young European couple: a beautiful, charming, brilliant duo filled with extraordinary ideas, capable of anything!

My novel was unusual in other ways. It was set in New York of 1913, on the eve of the First World War. All that I'd read of that period's avant-garde convinced me that it was not too different than the late sixties I'd just gone through: bohemian life-styles, controversial art movements, experimentation with life-styles, sex, drugs. The young Hesse, Gide, and Ezra Pound seemed more my contemporaries than my grandparents—the half-century between their blossoming and my life a stupid waste filled with world wars.

It's not difficult to recall what writing that first novel was like for me: the same excitement, the same depth of concentration, the same trancelike, out-of-time sense that I'm on another plane of existence happens whenever I'm truly involved in writing. In an interview I once said that writing was one of the three physical/mental/emotional highs of my life—along with sexual climax and using LSD-25—and the only sustainable one.

One thrill in writing this first book was being in such full command of a fictional world that when I needed a minor character, one simply appeared at the tip of my pen, with her own personal quirks and demeanor, dress and history. I wondered how long this unexpectedly Olympian power could last.

Working at top speed to avoid its collapse, I completed a first draft in two months: a record I would never surpass, especially given that the ms. was 150,000 words long. I read it over, made notes for emendations, then typed a second draft over the next six weeks. On May 20 of 1971, I had two copies of a readable ms. in hand. I'd titled it *Narrative and Curse,* after the scene in Wagner's opera *Tristan and Isolde,* performed during the novel's climax.

I'd not told anyone what I was doing. Jan, Arnie, most of my friends from the Twelfth Street commune, had moved to California. I knew only one

"Grandma Soscia holding Cousin Nicky, and Uncle Tony—the World War II hero," 1949

person with enough experience, savvy, and connections to help me if what I'd written was at all good. I'd met Jon Peterson a few years before through Jay Weiss. He was intelligent, clever, and sophisticated: he'd produced plays off-Broadway, and introduced the actor Al Pacino. I phoned Jon and said I'd written a novel and needed an agent.

Jon was cautious. He would read the ms. first. He warned me not to be surprised if the agent turned it down. He was right in trying to calm me. But Jon read the novel quickly—and he loved it! He immediately got it to an agent friend, along with all of his enthusiasm. The agent read it and decided to represent my work.

In four months, I'd changed my life. Or so I thought.

By the time my savings ran out, my book still hadn't sold. I took part-time work and tightened my belt. As editor after editor turned it down, I saw I'd have to find a job. Through Dennis Sanders's recommendation I began work that fall at Rizzoli Bookstore.

Unlike the other bookstore I'd worked at, Rizzoli was unique. Truly international, its employees had to speak one or more foreign languages fluently. As a result our staff was unusual, many foreign-born, or Americans brought up abroad: many younger ones were biding their time while awaiting a break in their true careers as writers, painters, musicians—our manager had trained as a concert pianist. After I'd been there some months they seemed like a family— caring and close, but also emotional and irrational. Working at Rizzoli could be like a party where business also happened; at other times it was like being caught in the final act of some demented nineteenth-century opera.

After a year, my agent returned my ms. to me, unable to sell it. I was disappointed, but continued to work at the bookstore, and write.

Writing this novel had been creatively explosive: as though I'd been chock-filled with poems, stories, essays, plays, films, entire novels trying to get out. Among them would be my first published story, poem, and novel. But I'm getting ahead of myself.

For the next two-and-a-half years I continued at Rizzoli, moving steadily upward in its hierarchy—my usual course—and becoming steadily discouraged about finding a new agent or selling my novel. One poem I wrote in this time is titled "The Waiting Room," which pretty much sums up how I felt—on the brink of, but held back.

Our children's book manager, Alex Mehdevi, had written and published *Tales from Majorca*, folk stories from his homeland. When I told Alex of my frustration at being unpublished he was kind enough to have his own literary agent read my novel.

Jane Rotrosen phoned me before she'd even finished reading my ms. The title should be changed, she said, and she had other minor suggestions but she agreed to represent the book—even with its previous history! She spoke fast and made an appointment for us to meet.

The Kurt Hellmer Literary Agency office on Vanderbilt Avenue was a warren of small, dark rooms filled with manuscripts and shelvesful of books. Jane and I went to the Pan Am Building, where we sat thirty floors above Park Avenue and she talked about my novel with all the detail, expertise, immediacy, and enthusiasm I could hope for. As soon as I made those minor changes, she would send out the book. We sealed the deal with a handshake—and Jane has been my literary agent ever since.

Months went by, yet no editors seemed willing to take the ms. Jane couldn't get a fix on why not. Was it too new? Its combination of fictional world, characters, and style *too* different?

In February of 1974, Jane took me to dinner for my thirtieth birthday. My novel remained unsold. Meanwhile at Rizzoli, I'd been promoted to store manager and my boss had just explained the company's expansion plans, and my role in them. I'd said what I'd told each employer—I was a writer: the first book contract I got, I would leave. He and I knew the chances of this happening diminished daily. His offer included salaries and positions beyond my expectations. I told Jane this and of the decision I faced: I wanted to be a professional writer!

We returned to my apartment and Jane asked what was in the notebooks atop my nonworking fireplace. Unfinished works. She went through them, and stopped at the outline and opening chapters of a novel I'd titled *Who Is Christopher Darling?*

I'd begun it in the summer of 1972, basing it on the Greek myth of Phaeton—son of Apollo who'd driven his father's chariot across the heavens far too close to the sun, and who had to be destroyed. My updating retained the allegory with a sharp twist, and it was told as a psychological thriller. Its ideas reflected my interest in child prodigies and savants, and in the language and mores of Elizabethan and Jacobean England.

Jane thought it publishable. If I wrote up a fuller outline detailing characters and scenes, she'd get it to editors already intrigued with my work.

In a few weeks Don Fine, publisher of Arbor House, signed me to finish the novel. It was to be retitled *Smart as the Devil*, a more commercial title, he and Jane thought (I didn't). I'd receive an advance against royalties large enough to pay my bills while I left my job and wrote the book. My boss was surprised when I told him all this but the money involved was so small he gave me leave and agreed to keep all our future plans open.

From March through early October of 1974, I worked on the novel, moving out to Fire Island Pines that summer into a cottage I shared with Jon Peterson and two new friends, lovers named Nick Rock and Enno Poersch. As they all worked part- or full-time, I had the place to myself and was able to make real progress. I wrote two drafts, revised a bit after Jane had read it, and again after Don Fine read it.

Smart as the Devil was published by Arbor House on February 28, 1975, my mother's birthday. It wasn't given a large printing, and was not well advertised or promoted. It was excellently if not

"At the studio apartment watched by woman voyeur!"
age twenty-two

extensively reviewed, picked by the Mystery Guild book club, and paperback rights were sold to Dell, giving me somewhat more income. The book became one of five finalists for the Ernest Hemingway Award—for the best first novel of the year—partly due to the uniqueness of entire sections having been written in seventeenth-century English. It didn't get the award, but the nomination gave my reputation a boost.

I returned to Rizzoli after finishing the novel, but I had a new book I was eager to write, based on a personal experience. When I'd returned from Europe I'd moved into a studio apartment in the "Village," its two windows facing the street. One night, I got a phone call from a young woman. After a variety of questions and answers, it turned out I didn't know her.

She knew me, plenty about me, virtually everything about me! It took a while to figure it out; then I realized, she had binoculars—I was being watched! Whenever she phoned after that, I tried to elicit information from her—I'd lived in London too! I

found out little. One night a young woman slept over with me. The next day my voyeur phoned: her words and tone of voice angry and bitter. I found that odd, given how flip she'd been about the many more young men who'd slept over. When I pointed this out, she said it was because she didn't take the men seriously as rivals.

Clearly this went beyond sport: she'd developed a fantasy life about me. I was flattered—and freaked! As a social worker I sought help for her. She refused and threatened blackmail. I said I didn't care who knew what I did in my own home. I warned her not to call anymore—it was harassment, a Federal offense. From then until I moved, I would flinch every time my phone rang—was it her?—even though I'd changed my phone number and it wasn't listed. I kept my window shades down, but I felt aware at all times that I was being watched—that I might be in danger.

But I wondered what would have happened if I'd been different: if I'd been a young man as needy of a relationship as she seemed to be. What if the relationship had bloomed, become complicated by hidden neuroses, even psychoses in her and by his growing determination to know who she was and to find her?

That was the basis of *Eyes,* which Jane, Don Fine, and Linda Grey, the editor at Dell who'd bought *Smart as the Devil,* all liked. I sold it on several chapters and an outline and wrote it during the summer and fall of 1975.

Eyes was published in 1976, following a falling out with my publisher. Editing my ms., he'd excised a short chapter describing a crucial secondary character. I deemed it necessary to give weight and color to this character, whose role was almost that of a fairy-tale witch in what was an otherwise minutely realistic narrative. When the book was published, I found out he'd not put back the chapter and I broke off relations. My editor at Dell agreed to replace the chapter and it first appeared in the paperback edition.

This second published novel was well received, sold better than my first, got more attention—reviews from several women's magazines—and earned higher book club, paperback, and foreign advances. As the book became read by more people, I realized that in attempting to investigate an incident in my own past, I'd come to symbolize in my female voyeur the questions so many young women were facing themselves—how they could be equal to men yet still feminine; how be sexual and emotional yet intelligent; how be themselves yet appropriate companions.

When the paperback was published in 1977, Peter Caras's artwork—a woman's hands in close-up, holding binoculars through which a half-naked man can be seen looking back—was stunning and appropriate. It helped the book become a best-seller, though word-of-mouth played an even larger role.

Eyes sold well here and in England until quite recently. It was translated into French, German, Spanish, Portuguese, and Japanese. Several television and filmmakers were interested in it, and it was under option for over a decade. Even so, the "unhappy" ending—the only realistic one for the story—kept it from being produced. That and the fact that a woman's p.o.v. is required to make it work. I'd suffered over that while writing the book: had to, in effect, become a mentally disturbed woman to have it come out without compromise or faked emotion.

Even before *Eyes* was published I'd begun another novel. Some years before, a friend, Nunzio D'Anarumo, avid collector of Cupids and haunter of antique stores, sent me a copy of a New York *Telegraph* from St. Patrick's Day, 1900. The paper was yellowing and cracked but one front page article couldn't fail to catch my attention, accompanied as it was by a dramatic drawing of a man shooting a pistol in a crowded court building.

"Prosecutor Shoots Defendant!" The headline was datelined the previous day from a large city in Nebraska. I read it with interest and found it strange yet very much of its time and place. I put the aged newspaper away and thought I'd forget it.

The story continued to haunt me. Partly because it was bizarre and sensational: it wasn't every day a noted lawyer attacked the man he was prosecuting for conspiracy and murder. Partly because of the characters: the defendant was shady. He'd once used hypnotism for "painless dentistry" in the poorer section of town but had become influential through his connection with a woman—beautiful, wealthy, and recently widowed under odd circumstances. As intriguing were minor characters: the dead husband; his housekeeper; the handsome con man's old assistant. I found it easy to assess the social and business classes of a Midwest boomtown; its mores and its amusements.

I mentioned it to my agent, who thought it had possibilities. I began to research the story and discovered it had been written up in many national papers of its day and in even greater detail in Midwestern ones. The more I read, the more bizarre the story, its major and minor characters and their relationships became. I was certain I had a classic American tale: one never told before. My plan was to go to Nebraska and research the book where it happened then write it up as a nonfiction novel, the form popularized by Truman Capote.

Almost immediately, I hit snags. The town hall with the trial records had burned down in 1910. No local and no state library had existed to keep copies. Only one newspaper of the time was still in business and its archives didn't go back that far. The state's Historical Society forwarded data to me—it was jejune: I wanted those aspects of character and motive I thought essential for a book. I tried contacting survivors of the families involved but they wrote back saying either they wouldn't help or knew nothing.

After a time, I was able to put together my own idea of what had happened in that Nebraska town three quarters of a century before; not only during the course of the trial, but in the years before—and after.

I knew it contained mystery and color and humanity—enough for a good novel! That's what I'd write. I pored over letters and diaries of the year for the spoken tongue, then medical journals for what was known about psychology and how it was discussed by those who practiced it—*crucial* to my story. I even consulted a specialist in Territorial and Early State Law at the A.L.A. to get the correct trial law.

I wrote the novel throughout 1976. *The Mesmerist* was published by Delacorte in September of 1977, with excellent cover art—again by Peter Caras—which also appeared on the paperback. My original title was "The Mesmerist and Mrs. Lane," which I still think superior. *The Mesmerist* was chosen as an Alternate Selection by the Literary Guild. It was better promoted and advertised than my previous books, more widely and better reviewed. It sold triple the earlier books in hardback but eventually less in paperback—*Eyes* was such a runaway seller. *The Mesmerist* was translated into six languages and published widely abroad. The biggest immediate change for me was that I'd sold hardcover and paperback rights to Delacorte/Dell and in England and come up with a big enough sum for me to quit work at Rizzoli, move into a larger flat, keep a summer place myself, travel, even invest.

By mid-1978, I was launched as a writer. Bookstores held fifty-unit displays of my recent books. Even so, my first novel languished in a drawer, unpublished, unread, and I couldn't understand why.

I was leading a double life—at least in publication. Since my return from Europe in the late sixties I'd been living in Greenwich Village: my associations predominantly gay men. After the Stonewall Riot of 1969, the Village became a mecca for lesbians and gays. Stonewall had begun as another police raid

"At a publicity tour in downtown L.A.," 1979

upon another Village gay bar. For many gays, fed up with outmoded laws and constant harassment, it was the last straw. Once word spread, the raid became a pitched battle on the streets in which police were outnumbered, overwhelmed, and humiliated. Riot squads were required to keep the peace in the area the entire following week. The true importance of the event became clear the day after the raid when a thousand gays—myself and my friends among them—gathered at Sheridan Square to protest the harassment. Protests continued, a political-action group formed—the Gay Liberation Front—and eventually splintered to include the more radical Gay Activists Alliance. Within weeks, a political agenda was devised. The GAA began to meet, ironically, in a former firehouse on Greene Street: a minority had begun to empower itself.

And to celebrate itself. If Black was Beautiful! as the slogan had it, then Gay was Proud! Weekly meetings at the Firehouse were attended by larger groups and ended in a dance, helping to attract, centralize, and allow people to celebrate themselves. Out of the Firehouse rose other, less political gay and lesbian clubs. The first totally gay dance club was the

Tenth Floor, a "private party" stressing Black and Latin Rock and Soul music in Manhattan's West Twenties, which attracted a crowd involved in music, design, and fashion. This same group had begun to transform Fire Island Pines into a stylish, unambiguously gay resort.

By 1975, a new gay social set had emerged, quite different from "Activists" with their academic and political background. Defined by membership in the arts, the media, recording and design professions, it was known as the "Pines-Flamingo Nexus," after the resort and the new discotheque with its five hundred members that had become its Manhattan center. This small, homogenous, sophisticated, self-conscious group began many trends in the next decade in fashion, music, and social behavior. Their imprint on gay life was instant, long-lasting, and ultimately international.

Some feared such "ghetto-ization," ergo the proliferation of more heterogenous clubs—among them Le Jardin, Twelve West, the Paradise Garage, Les Mouches, and Studio 54. The latter, Steve Rubell and Ian Schrager's glitzy club, caught the public's imagination, and soon designers, movie stars, and

Social Register hopefuls were joining gays on its dance floor and in its lounges—and in summer, crowding the Botel and Sandpiper at Fire Island Pines. This same mixture of gays, jet setters, entertainers, personalities, and talent formed a highly creative social and artistic community that gave the seventies a distinctive high-gloss style, culminating in the "Beach" party of 1979, a charity drive at the Pines that commanded a full page of the "Society" section of the *New York Times* the following day.

I'd become a part of this group almost from its inception: in Manhattan as a member of the dance clubs, in the Pines as a full-time summer resident from 1975 on. Since others were offering their photography, music, sculpture, illustration, and design, I decided to offer my poetry and fiction.

Magazines of gay writing had begun: Andrew Bifrost's *Mouth of the Dragon* in New York, and Winston Leyland's *Gay Sunshine Press* in San Francisco. Even Manhattan's *Gaysweek* began a bi-monthly "Arts and Letters" section. Most of my earliest published poems and short stories appeared in these journals. Other gay magazines were *Fag Rag* and *Gay Community News* in Boston, *Body Politic* in Toronto, *New York City News, Christopher Street,* the *Native, Mandate, Stallion, Blueboy,* et al. in New York, the *Advocate* and *Drummer* in California. I wrote for them all—reviews, poems, stories, essays.

I—and other writers—began to give readings of poetry and fiction at the newly started lesbian/gay groups mushrooming on campuses at Hunter College, Columbia, Princeton, and Stanford universities.

A question now arose: I had a book of poetry, another volume of short stories, all written out of and addressing my experiences as a gay man: how could I get these books out where they could be read?

The answer, according to my agent Jane, my editor Linda, and my friend Susan Moldow, who also worked in book publishing, was that I couldn't! Few gay-themed books were published—and they had always been special: Vidal's novel, Rechy's *City of Night,* Isherwood's *Single Man,* Baldwin's *Giovanni's Room.* No one could live off writing them, and no publisher would put out books by unknown gay writers, dramatists, or—heaven forbid!—poets. I was told to forget it, told to do what gay writers had done for years: keep them to myself, and continue writing nongay novels.

That struck me as unfair; worse, as usufructage; even a species of slavery. I'd begin my *own* publishing house and publish *nothing* but the work of gays. I'd hire, utilize, and work only with gays—artists, typesetters, printers, binders, distributors. I'd stock my books in lesbian/gay-owned bookstores. The company would be called the SeaHorse Press—named after the marine species in which the male bears and gives birth—and I felt it would work.

SeaHorse Press's first title was my *Deformity Lover and Other Poems*—chosen because the author didn't have to be paid. George Stavrinos's cover illustration and the high quality of all aspects of the book got it noticed. In the gay media, reviews were lengthy and laudatory—from its first line, the book *assumed* the reader and writer shared the gay experience and went on from there to detail and particularize that world. Critics also appreciated the book's range of styles and forms: lyric, epistle, ode, sonnet, dramatic monologue were all represented.

When the book was reviewed by nongay media, the reaction was far more mixed—some tried to but were unable to hide their prejudice. For others it was simply too different, too alien. One bright woman poet couldn't grasp why I would opt for rhythms that sounded to her like "popular music: phonograph songs!"—which was *exactly* what I wanted. The poet/translator Richard Howard encouraged me, and the late Howard Moss, poetry editor of the *New Yorker,* thought the work strong and asked to see new poems; but he could never bring himself to publish any of my gay work. Others invited me to send work to those many small poetry quarterlies that seem to define American verse today.

I continued to write poetry and many newer poems were published in magazines and anthologies—a high-school textbook published one I thought fairly gay, "Gym Shorts," to illustrate "image."

Gym Shorts

You really look good in those gym shorts
now that they're worn
and you're filled out to fit them
so manly.
You used to look good way back then, too.
Was it ten years ago?
That long?

Yes. I saw the games. I was watching.
Watching those gym shorts
grip muscled sides
as you dribbled and sped
playing king of the court.
Watched how the gold stripe you alone wore
marked you apart from the bodies rising
when you netted the ball
as if picking a rose.
How your shorts sort of fluttered

against trembling thighs
when you sprang to the floor
and ceiling spotlights stroked you.

You were sweat and smiles and modest lies
leaning on the railing
at halftime.
You shivered. So I loaned you my coat.
You thanked me.
Those gym shorts were new then,
shining blue
like childrens' Christmas wishes.

Three poems appeared in *The Oxford Book of Homosexual Verse.* I've only had one more book of poems published, a chapbook, *Window Elegies,* by the Close Grip Press at the University of Alabama in 1986, but I was pleased and honored to read it at the Poetry Society of America, a usually less adventuresome organization.

SeaHorse Press, however, was launched. Especially as my book went through four printings. The second title was *Two Plays by Doric Wilson,* the third, *Idols,* poems by the talented Dennis Cooper, then Kevin Esser's man-boy love novel *Streetboy Dreams.* Clark Henely's hilarious *Butch Manual* became a best-seller, and in 1980 I edited an anthology of poetry, drama, and fiction by lesbians and gay men, *A True Likeness.*

As the press continued to grow, so did its list— Alan Bowne's play *Forty-Deuce,* a collection of stories by Brad Gooch, *Jailbait* (cover photo by Robert Mapplethorpe), poetry by Robert Peters, Rudy Kikel, Gavin Dillard, and Mark Ameen, George Stambolian's interviews, *Male Fantasies Gay Realities,* and a translation from the French of gay novelist Guy Hocquenghem's novel *Love in Relief.* Later on, I'd use the prestigious SeaHorse imprint on titles I would edit for Gay Presses of New York—our reprint of the 1933 Charles Henri Ford/Parker Tyler novel *The Young and Evil* and Martin Duberman's *About Time: Exploring the Gay Past.*

The SeaHorse Press turned out to be a great deal of work, fun, and a way to meet lesbian and gay authors all over. But it didn't solve the problem of writing gay material and getting it to a wide readership.

While writing *The Mesmerist,* I was approached by a film producer at Universal Studios who wanted me to write a gay-themed movie. His idea was for me to explore the darker side of gay life in Manhattan. He offered a single image which, while striking, ended up remaining unused. There was a basis to his idea. Arthur Bell, openly gay columnist for the *Village*

Voice, had been writing a series on several bizarre and grisly murders of gay entrepreneurs. Bell was chasing leads and tying together clues when his life was threatened; he stopped the series.

Through my own contacts, I could go further: sex partners, acquaintances, and a close friend worked in the hierarchy of discos, bars, bathhouses, and private sex clubs which had sprung up in Chelsea. I began to ask questions and what I discovered began to intrigue me.

A former lover, the playwright Bob Herron, was a community leader in the Village through the Jane Street Block Association. He told me of an undercover unit of the New York City Police Department formed to investigate the seemingly related murders Bell had reported. I met a member of this unit who answered some of my questions. Shortly after, the unit was disbanded. It was supposed to be investigated itself, but that never happened.

I had more than enough material and some of it was very hot. But I knew that presenting as factual what I'd found out would lead to death threats or worse: I'd fictionalize it. I put together an outline and got it to the film producer.

He was horrified. It was so gay, so raw, so disturbing and violent he could barely read my outline. No doubt, he was being realistic about its chances of being filmed in a homophobic industry. Upon my return from California I mentioned the outline to my editor, Linda Grey, who read it and, bless her, said, "It'll be a terrific book!" I wrote a single, gripping, opening chapter and Delacorte bought it.

The Lure was my fourth published novel, my most controversial, and until recently the best known. Someone recently called it "pulp." Someone else "a cult classic," which seems pretentious yet in terms of sales and influence isn't inaccurate. The hardcover was well packaged, promoted, and advertised and it was the first gay-themed book sold by the Literary Guild: an Alternate Selection. It sold very well in hardcover and paperback and was translated into many languages. Its greatest foreign success was in Germany, where it sold steadily for a decade under the title *Gefangen in Babel.* "Warning: Explicit Sex and Violence," the ad read for the book club advertising *The Lure:* and it's true, I've never written anything quite like it again and have resisted all requests and demands for a sequel or to have it made into a film.

I wrote it in Manhattan and at Fire Island Pines throughout 1978. A long time, given how tightly plotted the book is and how fast it reads: many people

With Andrew Holleran at "Gaywyck," New Jersey, 1980

told me they were up all night reading it. Author Edmund White called it "hallucinatory—as though one were drugged."

Some gays hated *The Lure*—and me—for its uncompromising portrait of the sleazier scenes that had arisen out of Gay Liberation, of which few political activists were proud. To them, I was washing dirty laundry in public. Worse, I was providing damaging confirmation to those opposing gay rights. At the least I was betraying the movement.

My intentions were different: I'd wanted the reader—gay or not, male or female, young or old—to share what it was like being gay in Manhattan: experiencing fear, doubt, the constant questioning of one's own and everyone else's motives, yet joy and camaraderie and love too; and always, motiveless bigotry and hatred.

Most nongay reviews (*The Lure* was reviewed widely) and the mail I received confirmed that I'd succeeded in that task. No matter how badly I portrayed some gays or some aspects of gay life in the novel, no matter how thin a slice of gay life I'd concentrated on, I'd drawn it richly, in the round,

sympathetically, and without the usual knee-jerk judgementalism. And I'd portrayed those arrayed against gays worse: irrational, ruthless, often deadly. Years later when *The Lure* was being used in college courses about minorities or about psychology or even about urban life, I knew my critics had been wrong: I felt justified.

I'd also achieved something else. With *The Lure's* success I'd tied together that work I'd been publishing—classed as "commercial fiction" despite that Hemingway Award nomination—with my own private life and interests. It was the first time these two disparate, even opposing, forces would come together for me—and to date, the last!

I'd met Edmund White socially in 1976. He'd just published *The Joy of Gay Sex* with Charles Silverstein, but I admired more White's stories and his earlier novel, *Forgetting Elena.* I'd also met George Whitmore around this time, and we became friends. George told me of a remarkable novel he'd read in galleys. Titled *Dancer from the Dance,* the new book was about the Pines-Flamingo crowd by an unknown author—Andrew Holleran. I read it and confirmed for myself his talent and the book's truth, humor, and brilliance. A few weeks later, at a party at the Pines, I was introduced to Holleran: we've been good friends ever since.

Dancer was published in the autumn of 1978. My *Deformity Lover* had come out earlier that year, as had a fascinating nonfiction book, *After Midnight,* by Michael Grumley, author of *Hard Corps,* a study of the S/M leather scene. Michael's lover, Robert Ferro, had published a short enigmatic novel, *The Others,* in 1977. George Whitmore was writing poetry and articles. Edmund's lover, Chris Cox, was compiling an oral history of Key West. In the spring of 1979, White's *Nocturnes for the King of Naples* was published; that autumn my novel *The Lure.*

In the following months, we seven were constantly thrown together within the gay cultural scene and found out we shared many interests. I don't recall who suggested we meet on a regular basis to read and discuss our work. I know the first meeting was held at George's apartment on Washington Square. Casually, later on, we came up with a name—the Violet Quill Club—sometimes called the Lavender Quill Club.

No matter how light-hearted we were in talking about it, once together we were in earnest. We'd seen what happened to gay writers before us who'd not been able to write about the gay experience, forced to tailor their talent to the heterosexual majority—William Inge, Thornton Wilder, Tennessee Williams, Truman Capote, Edward Albee. Few of those who had succeeded in what Roger Austen called "Playing the Game" for the sake of their careers had escaped personal damage: alcoholism, psychosis, self-destruction, suicide. We refused to take that route, even though (especially for Edmund White and myself) a public coming out might well mean the destruction of our careers.

We knew not to expect our work to be critiqued fairly, even competently. The literarily powerful *New York Times* was virulently homophobic and reviews of gay-themed books were openly hostile, often written by "closeted" gay writers. But our books were sympathetically reviewed elsewhere, and other writers worked quietly in our cause.

Yet with public criticism on such a simplistic level, we lacked that dialogue we needed to grow in our work. The Violet Quill Club would provide it, as well as occasional technical aid in the niceties of prose fiction. We discovered we were all writing some sort of autobiography, but besides individual tales of growing up and "coming out" we hoped our gay-themed work could be enlarged to treat the "big" themes that have always attracted writers—love, death, how to live one's life.

Through appearances in *Christopher Street* and the *New York Native*, we became known as a group to other gay writers. As a group, we strengthened each other individually and began to wield influence. Those who admired our writing or our uncompromising stance called us the New York School. Those who felt excluded or threatened called us the Gay Literary Mafia. Many younger writers have told me that our work and our publicity lessened their own fear of ostracism and helped them define themselves as gay writers.

Our meetings were neither regular nor often: in all, no more than eight times over a year and a half. Like all groups with strong egos, the VQ Club eventually ended. With one exception, we all remained friends. In some cases even closer friends. In the years since, we would often meet together for "tea" or spend weekends at the Ferro family summer place on the Jersey shore, which we jokingly renamed "Gaywyck."

"Friends and Violet Quill Club members: George Stambolian, Robert Ferro (deceased), Michael Grumley (deceased), and me in front," Fire Island Pines, 1985

Felice Picano: "pensive," Gaywyck, 1985

As of this writing—summer 1990—only three of us are still alive, and one of those three is infected: AIDS has taken and continues to take its toll. But the group's importance should continue to live on. The curators of the American Literature Collection at the Beinecke Library at Yale University believe the VQ Club to have been the key group in producing, popularizing, and legitimizing gay fiction in America: they are collecting our manuscripts and papers.

The VQ Club was responsible for an efflorescence of new books by its members, among them White's *Boy's Own Story* and *The Beautiful Room is Empty,* Ferro's *Family of Max Desir* and *The Blue Star,* Cox's *Key West,* Holleran's *Nights in Aruba,* Grumley's *Life-Drawing,* and Whitmore's *Confessions of Danny Slocum* and *Nebraska.* I'd completed my novel *Late in the Season* (1981) when we began to meet, but my novella *An Asian Minor: The True Story of Ganymede* (1981), and several short stories which I eventually collected, were written or rewritten for VQ Club meetings. Our discussions gave me enough confidence to later write more autobiographical works.

Late in the Season was published by Delacorte, although with a tenth of the attention given *The Lure*—because it was a "smaller" book. It was in fact something new: an "idyll," a love story about two attractive, successful middle-class gay men during one late summer month as their "marriage" is tested by, among other things, one of them having an affair with a young woman.

I'd written the book from a double p.o.v. as I had in *Eyes,* and in a way, it's a companion piece to that book. Except that it's a series of prose poems: aquarelles, even. It opens like this:

It was a perfect day for composing. The morning mist had finally burned off the ocean, unfurling the blue sky like a huge banner of victory. Kites were fluttering at various levels of the warm, balmy air. From down the beach came the sweet-voiced distortions of children's cries in play—the last children of the season—adding extra vibrancy to their sounds, piercing the scrim of post-Labor-Day-weekend silence that had softly dropped a week ago. Already the first dying leaves of an autumn that came early to the seashore and would blaze madly for a mere month of picture-book beauty had flung themselves at the glass doors this morning. They had saddened Jonathan then, perched over his large mug of coffee, feeling the hot sun on his closed eyelids. But now the morning felt so clear and sunny, so absolutely cloudless, he felt he might strike it with the little glass pestle in the dining room bowl, and the day would ring back, echoing crystal, like a gamelan orchestra.

The novel's poetry has made it a lasting favorite among my readers. While it was sold to British and German publishers, *Late in the Season* attained a smaller, if more discriminating, readership than my earlier novels. It fell out of print at Dell and was reprinted in a trade paper edition by Gay Presses of New York, where it's been a steady seller.

As has been my gay short-story collection, *Slashed to Ribbons in Defense of Love,* published by GPNY in 1983, now in its third printing. I'd gathered all my stories from gay magazines, added the novella "And Baby Makes Three," and a final, autobiographical tale, "A Stroke." The book was published at a time when the short story was making one of its periodic comebacks. Besides fine reviews in the gay media, it was well received in general. *Writer's Digest* listed it along with collections by Barthelme, Carver, and Beattie as the best of the year.

Gay Presses of New York was put together in 1980 by myself, Larry Mitchell, who'd begun Calamus Press, and Terry Helbing, who'd begun the JH Press. Our idea was to combine administrative and overhead costs and to publish one new title per year. Our first book was a play in three parts the author wanted printed as one and produced in a single evening. Harvey Fierstein's *Torch Song Trilogy* still hadn't been produced as a trilogy when GPNY bought publication rights. The book came out in 1981, the play opened off-Broadway in 1982, where its successful run led it to Broadway, and it received the Tony Award in 1983.

The great success of *Torch Song Trilogy* allowed GPNY to flourish. We spread our net wide, pulling in lesbian authors, gay dramatists, nonfiction writers, novelists, etc. The 1985 catalogue showed 75 titles in print. I knew GPNY was secure when my partners bid for *my* new works along with commercial publishers. We continued to encounter bigotry: book clubs wouldn't purchase rights directly from us, a large distributor wouldn't do business with us. Prejudice dies hard.

Throughout, GPNY has been hard work with little or no profit, done as a challenge and as a service to the readers and writers of the lesbian/gay community. When *Newsweek* ran a cover story on gay writing coming into the mainstream in 1989, it completely ignored GPNY and SeaHorse and Calamus, as well as other important lesbian/gay presses—Daughters Ink, Gay Sunshine Press—who were fully responsible for the inception and continued existence of a lesbian/gay literature.

I was happy enough for GPNY to publish my first book of memoirs. *Ambidextrous: The Secret Lives of Children* (1985) is a true story in the form of three novellas covering three years in my life, from the ages of eleven to thirteen. I began the first, "Basement Games," in the summer of 1983, driven by a need to deal with the most difficult problem I'd ever faced and the people involved. When I'd written it, I realized it was only one of three formative crises that had determined who I would become as a person and writer. I wrote "A Valentine" in the next few months, and spent the first third of 1984 writing the third and most complex section, "The Effect of 'Mirrors'."

The reception of *Ambidextrous* was strong enough for me to consider writing another volume. While I planned to be chronological, I didn't want a full sequential account. Like most lives, mine had gone through long fallow periods followed by sudden times of action: only those "highlights" would be my material.

I was impelled by more than memory and self-healing. I'd begun to feel increasingly limited and caged inside the novels I'd been writing. The tight, suspenseful plots and fully rendered p.o.v.s of characters required to drive my *House of Cards* (1984) and especially *To the Seventh Power* (1989) were making writing less "fun," more work. I tried other areas of writing: in 1985 and 1986 I worked on a screenplay of *Eyes* with director Frank Perry. I adapted my novella *An Asian Minor* at the request of director Jerry Campbell and it had a good off-Broadway run in 1986 as the play *Immortal!* That same summer my one-act play *One O'Clock Jump* was also produced off-Broadway.

Despite these distractions, I still wanted to use the individual "voice" I'd found in my poetry and short fiction and develop it into a more supple, varied, sophisticated prose. I was searching for new structures too, capable of the closest detail, yet open enough for sudden wide shifts in time, place, and character.

A short version of "The Most Golden Bulgari," the first part of the second book of my memoirs, appeared in George Stambolian's excellent anthology *Men on Men* in 1986. "A Most Imperfect Landing," the second part, was written in May 1987 and first published in a gay literary magazine, the *James White Review*, in 1989. I wrote the final part, "The Jane Street Girls," in the spring of 1988.

Gary Luke, editor of the Plume line at NAL, bought paper rights to *Ambidextrous* and hard/soft rights to *Men Who Loved Me*—as I'd cheekily titled the sequel. They were published together in the fall of 1989 and are the books I'm most proud of: they contain all I've learned so far of style, form, and technique in rendering the funny, tragic, sad, frustrating, incomprehensible, and ambiguous quotidian of our lives.

Not all reviewers grasped my purpose. While some found the books "distinguished" or "brilliant," others called them "bad jokes," "put on tell-alls." Unsurprisingly, complaints have been leveled at my prose for daring to mix "high" and "low" styles; also at the contents of the books for mixing the "popular" and "literary." Some British critics called the books flat-out lies, assuring their readers and me that children never have sex. But I'll continue to experiment with and develop this new style. At this time I'm utilizing it in a novel about the complex love-hate relationship of two gay friends over a busy, incident-filled, thirty-five-year period.

Looking over these pages, I see many deal not with myself, my life, my family, my friends, my work, but with larger issues: social and political forces—the Civil Rights and Student movements in the sixties, Gay Liberation and the world created by gays in the seventies. In a review of both memoirs in a Boston newspaper, Allan Smalling wrote: "Picano bids us to see his experiences as exemplary . . . Whether good or bad, his life experiences virtually define what it meant to come of age in America in the 'Fifties and 'Sixties."

The seventies and eighties too—once I feel I'm able to write about those decades—not an easy or happy task and not one I look forward to or think myself equal to. One example of the problem I face, think on this: two of my Fire Island Pines housemates and friends were among the first known American men to have been stricken with and died of AIDS. This past decade has been one in which I've watched my entire community, an era, an entire way of life—as rich and full as any I've known—swept away by disease as utterly as the Holocaust swept away European Jewry, and with about as little response from the rest of the world.

As those few friends left to me continue to sicken and suffer and die, I often wonder if that's the reason I lived through those times, knew those people, suffered those losses, became a writer, learned the value of storytelling from my mother—so that eventually I might bear witness to that era, those people, this great loss, and make it literature.

BIBLIOGRAPHY

Fiction:

Smart as the Devil, Arbor House, 1975.

Eyes, Arbor House, 1976.

The Mesmerist, Delacorte, 1977.

The Lure, Delacorte, 1979.

(Editor) *A True Likeness: An Anthology of Lesbian and Gay Writing Today*, SeaHorse Press, 1980.

An Asian Minor: The True Story of Ganymede, (novella), SeaHorse Press, 1981.

Late in the Season, Delacorte, 1981.

Slashed to Ribbons in Defense of Love and Other Stories, Gay Presses of New York, 1983.

House of Cards, Delacorte, 1984.

Ambidextrous: The Secret Lives of Children (memoir), Volume 1, Gay Presses of New York, 1985.

To the Seventh Power, Morrow, 1989.

Men Who Loved Me: A Memoir in the Form of a Novel, NAL, 1989.

Poetry:

The Deformity Lover and Other Poems, SeaHorse Press, 1978.

Window Elegies, Close Grip Press, 1986.

Contributor:

Winston Leland, editor, *Orgasms of Light*, Gay Sunshine, 1979.

Michael Denneny, editor, *Aphrodisiac: Fiction from Christopher Street*, Coward, 1980.

Ramsey Campbell, editor, *New Terrors Two*, Pan Books (England), 1980.

Frank Coffey, editor, *Modern Masters of Horror*, Coward, 1981.

Ian Young, editor, *On the Line*, Crossing Press, 1982.

Florence Grossman, editor, *Getting from Here to There: Writing and Reading Poetry*, Boynton/Cook, 1982.

Charles Ortleb and Denneny, editors, *The Christopher Street Reader,* Coward, 1983.

Stephen Coote, editor, *The Penguin Book of Homosexual Verse,* Penguin, 1983.

Young, editor, *The Male Muse, Number Two,* Crossing Press, 1983.

Martin Humphries, editor, *Not Love Alone,* Gay Mens Press (London), 1985.

George Stambolian, editor, *Men on Men,* New American Library, 1986.

Graham Masterton, editor, *Scare Care,* Tor Books, 1989.

Stambolian, editor, *Men on Men,* Volume 3, New American Library, 1990.

Other:

Immortal! (play with music; based on *An Asian Minor: The True Story of Ganymede*), produced Off-Off Broadway, 1986.

One O'Clock Jump (one-act play), produced Off-Off Broadway, 1986.

Author of the screenplay "Eyes," based on Picano's novel *Eyes,* 1986. Author of numerous short stories, including "One Way Out," "Absolute Ebony," "Spices of the World," and "Why I Do It." Author of many poems, including "Birthmarks," *"Nach Sommerwind,"* "Three Men Speak to Me," "In a Provincial Airport," "Swept to the Ground in Four Frames Flat," "An Artist to the Skin," and "After the Funerals."

Contributor of articles, poems, stories, and reviews to periodicals, including *OUT, Mouth of the Dragon, Islander, Cumberland Review, Connecticut Poetry Review, Cream City Review,* and *Soho Weekly News.* Book editor, *New York Native,* 1980–83. Founding editor of SeaHorse Press, 1978—.

Carolyn M. Rodgers

1942-

Carolyn M. Rodgers at work, 1982

Beginning

In 1972, I wrote a poem titled "For Our Fathers." I always liked that poem, even though it was written for *Ebony* magazine's special issue on black men that excluded my mother's role in the family's coming from Little Rock, Arkansas, to Chicago; it tells, in the best way I know how to this day, the history of my family's beginnings in Chicago. The poem read thus in part:

The wind blew my father from the south to the
    north.
He came with a heart as deep and as wide as a
    tunnel—

he came with a dream and a hope for a beautiful
    harmonious future.
He came. Daddy was a prayer, a jitterbug hymn
    and a collard/
cornbread sweet potato/green country
    psalm . . .

the city sifted him like wheat from chaff
like corn from husks, and the wind that blew
him here blew him down, blew him around,
    while
the flashing lights glazed his eyes and
    rechanneled
his heart in a new direction. He became a new
    dimension

He learned how to lock and close doors and bar
windows. He
bought dogs not to love, but for protection. He
learned to
carry guns not for harmless hunting but for
restraining men.
He learned how to be cool, not country, to be
stiff and serious and
silent. Laughter was reserved for home and
homebodies, homefolk.
He was a tree, with cautious and displaced
roots, walking the streets
with feet that hurt, with feet too big for
computerized shoes that
tapped the rhythm of concrete, and not the
loving crush of green grass.

So, for the first fifteen years of my life, I lived on
the south side of Chicago. I was baptized into the
African Methodist Episcopal Church (AME). What
that means is that the services were Methodist with an
African twist. Every Black that ever walked through
the AME church door was told the story about
Richard Allen, the free slave who started the church
in the eighteenth century, after being refused prayer
privileges at the altar of the White Methodist church
of which he was then a member.

When Allen protested such discrimination, he
left the church and took with him other men of color
who had suffered like or similar injustices. He then
started and became the first bishop of the African
Methodist Episcopal Church in America.

My mother was an avid churchgoer, so my early
years revolved around church activities. Three or
four times a week, my two sisters and brother and I
were there when the doors opened, and since we lived
only two houses away from the church, we often
opened the doors because we had been given the
keys. I was at one time a member of the Junior Choir,
the Junior Missionaries, and the Junior Usher Board.
I went to Sunday school every Sunday without fail.
No if's and but's were acceptable, unless death was
imminent or impending from a cold, a stomachache,
or the like. It wasn't difficult or unpleasant. It was
life—the way things were for us.

Part 2

We lived on Forty-sixth and Evans, closer to
Forty-sixth than the infamous flashing lights on
Forty-seventh Street; but not far enough to escape
the Forty-seventh Street influences, on the mind, the

soul, and the brain. I wrote this poem about Forty-
seventh Street children:

dark children
running in the streets
joyscreaming about a kite
dark children
clomping up and down on
half heels no heels half soled shoes
dodging chunks of glass
joyscreaming about a kite
a kite
that flies no higher than
the two story liquor store
they stream in front of.

don't these children know
that kites will fly
higher
much higher
than two story liquor stores?

*"One Sunday after church in a place where all
the kids went for milk shakes and music,"
about 1958*

There were nightclubs all along Forty-seventh Street for people to drink and laugh in. There were beauty shops, barbershops, flower shops, and privately owned drugstores; there were pawnshops, mortuaries, and little grocery stores stocked full of delicious candy and pickles for neighborhood children to buy. There was a whole world on Forty-seventh Street, and I had eyes for all of it.

At night, during the summers, the nightclub doors would stay open. Halfway down the block on Forty-sixth and Evans, you could hear Muddy Waters, Guitar Slim, Bobby "Blue" Bland, or Junior Wells singing in the 708 Club. I knew what the famous club looked like. It was as if magic was inside those doors. The rooms were red like blood, and the bottles and glasses sparkled and shone like expensive jewels. Music, laughter, and glamorous people were in there, living the good life, the easy life, or so it seemed to my child eyes.

But there was also a touch of fear about what lurked inside those rooms. Women and men who went inside were so often changed. They seemed to lose their lives to something in those rooms. They never came back the same way. Sometimes, red eyes and purple lips and an indescribable elusive sadness told the other side of the story; the sorry side that was often covered up by the glitter and the loud laughter. People who had lost themselves in the rooms of the clubs lived upstairs, next door, and around all the corners, and the entire community always seemed to be in some secret, private mourning for them; unless the lost ones had been designated by the gods, who bore their souls away to be the objects of everyone's ridicule and scorn. As a child, I would be awakened all year long, no matter the season, at 1 A.M. in the morning to hear them leave the clubs as they wandered through the streets, going someplace, perhaps home, laughing, talking, singing, or arguing.

So many people who grew up in the ghetto wrote about the misery, the poverty, and the deprivation there. It wasn't so bad for us, then. Maybe it was because I grew up in the forties in this country. Whatever it was, it was good. We laughed a lot. We tried to make ice cream out of snow in the winters. We had sleds and dogs. At nights in the summers when it was too hot to sleep, we all sat out on porches and the men and women talked while the children played. We had lightning bugs, grasshoppers, and caterpillar trees. We played hopscotch and we jumped rope. We played hide-and-seek and when we began to grow up, we played catch-a-girl, kiss-a-girl. True, we, all of us, ate plenty of cheap greens and fatback, the latter better known to me as salt pork.

True, we ate a lot of beans and corn bread to get full; and we had neck bones a-plenty, and chicken backs, necks, gizzards, and livers in soups. I thought everybody ate that way. Mostly, I loved the food that we ate. Except for the greens—all children hated greens, and all adults loved them. One way to tell whether or not a Black had arrived at adulthood was whether or not they liked greens yet. To children, greens were bitter. To adults, that bitter was sweet. It meant that you had survived.

Part 3

We lived in a stove-heated two-flat house. There was a kerosene one in the dining room, and there was a coal-and-wood-burning one in our kitchen. Those stoves were the sources of such fear. We children were warned about the dangers associated with the fire-burping beasts. One dripped kerosene all the time and woe to the soul that could light a match casually around it. The dining-room floor always smelled like kerosene and those droplets were always smearing up the linoleum floor. But you could warm your hands on this stove when you came in from the winter's cold. The stove never got very hot and gave off only a small amount of heat. The stove in the kitchen was the real death threat. The threat of kerosene wasn't real to me. You could never touch the stove in the kitchen unless absolutely nothing was burning in it. It would get red hot and there was always the possibility that some part of your body would accidentally touch it; or maybe a person would fall on it when it was lit. Any burn from that stove would have been serious. Miraculously, throughout the years, even though it almost happened, it never did.

*

I was the last of four children. The oldest was my now-deceased brother, Bobby. Next there was Nina and Gloria; and then I came along, after the family had moved from the South to the North. Being born in the North earned me the title of "city slicker" for years when I was growing up.

When my mother and father first migrated to Chicago from the back roads of Arkansas, I was in the womb. My father's sister had come up first and was occupying an apartment on Chicago's south side, where they would all live until after I was born. I think now about how spunky my mother must have been. She came north with three small children and one on the way, all by herself. My father had come

Mother, Bazella Cato Colding Rodgers, about 1946

earlier in the hopes of finding employment and was living with his sister.

Of course I don't remember anything about the first apartment, except my mother's stories about it having steam heat and how hot and wonderful that was. I'm sure it was my mother's first acquaintance with it. I actually grew up believing that steam heat was the closest thing a body had to heaven—in the winters of Chicago.

I was born December 14, 1942, at Provident Hospital, a small colored hospital on the south side of Chicago. Many people who had been born at Provident were ashamed of it. Some felt it was comparable to being born for free at the County Hospital where, of course, people went who did not have the money to pay. In elementary school, I remember the different children proudly and shamefacedly telling where they had been born.

It was my mother who told me to be proud of the little colored hospital. It was she who was proud and refused to give one inch to anyone who denigrated it, or belittled their nurses, the doctors, and the services given there. Throughout the years, she stood firm

against the insinuations, the insults outright, and the snickers. She stood firm and resolute. They had been good to her, she insisted happily, and they had been clean and caring.

*

I never knew how my father ticked, when I was growing up. His existence has always been a mystery to me. When I was young and he was young too, he was the tall, dark, and handsome man my mother had married; he was my father, but so often he was my mother's husband. I felt like I knew nothing yet everything about him. I knew that he had left school in the eighth grade, because unlike my mother, who had graduated from high school and attended some college, school had bored him. I knew that he loved to sing more than anything I could think of. I knew for a fact that he had desperately wanted the gospel quartet he sang with, the Eastbound Travelers they called themselves, to hit the big time like the Gospel Chimes and the Five Blind Boys had. They never did.

He had three girls and one boy, and so he had also wanted to be like Pop Staples, and he wanted all of us to be his Staple Singers. Throughout the years, he would coax us and chide us about our musical talent and how we could put it to some sensible use, if we just would. But it was all to no avail. I was the only one who had any desire like his to sing, and sing, and sing. Although all three of the girls played piano some and could sing a little, we didn't share his desire, ambition, or dream enough to put in the serious, long practice hours needed. As a matter of fact, I was the only one who even came close to professional singing.

During the sixties, when Joan Baez, Bob Dylan, and Odetta were popular, I made myself into a mini-Odetta and sang, and became quite well known in the coffeehouses of Chicago. That was a far cry, however, from what he had in mind, and he never cared much for what I was singing. He did eventually kick in and give up some laudations for the nylon-string guitar I learned how to play.

Several good things stand out in my mind as I think about my father and how he was when I was growing up. He was a hard worker. He started out as a cook when I was under the age of five. Meanwhile, he attended night school and learned welding. He then got a job at International Harvester. After he had been there for four or five years, he needed a second job to pay for a loan he had cosigned for. He found a dairy where he could work four hours a day. When the owner found out that my father had four children, he began to bombard us with milk, eggs, and butter. All of it, of course, went into happy, thankful mouths. My father worked those two jobs right up to his retirement at age sixty-five. He didn't change jobs the entire span of my life. It provided a wonderful example of stability for me. My father gave me the last check International Harvester gave him for a good-luck piece. I framed it in one of my half-dozen or so scrapbooks.

Because of my father's being such a hard worker, we always had more than enough to eat. We had so many dairy products, mother and daddy began to bake lots of pies, cakes, breads, biscuits, and rolls to use it up. My father could cook very well, having done it for a time for a living, and he and my mother used to have contests to see who could make the best pie or cake. They were always vying with each other and comparing recipes. I loved it. I learned an affection for cooking that is probably pretty hard to match—even to this day.

We were four children and two adults with only two bedrooms. Such was the house on Forty-sixth and Evans that my family moved to from the apartment of steam heat with my aunt on South Prairie Street. The big apartment building was big-city living where people were stacked on top of each other, or so my parents felt. But the house we moved to had a big backyard for all us children to play in, and vegetables could always be planted in certain parts of it. We children could run and play and shout and not worry about irate neighbors.

My oldest sister slept in one bedroom with whatever relative that happened to pass through, while my other sister and I slept on a Hide-a-Bed in the dining room. My brother slept on a fold-up cot in the living room. Then my grandmother on my mother's side came to live with us. I was ten years old. Grandmother, who had been living with my mother's older sister in Little Rock, had had a stroke. To this day, I don't know exactly why it was decided that she should come and stay with us for any reason other than that it was my mother's turn.

Once I met her, I was happy that my grandmother came to stay with us. Since both of my parents worked (my mother went to work as soon as I started school), frequently, only we children were in the house. Once my grandmother was there, someone was always in the house who was an adult. To me, this meant that the house would always be warm.

My grandmother was in her seventies, and because of the stroke, she was frail. But she was gentle and loving. She knew how to make patchwork quilts, and she gave hugs and dimes, and she hummed good old church hymns. She stayed with us for about a year

before she had a second stroke. I remember this part well because one time after the stroke she was trying to go to the bathroom. Her left side had been left partially paralyzed so she had some trouble with her bladder and bowels.

After the initial shock had set in, she insisted on doing some things for herself. This particular day, I had been standing close to her, watching her, waiting to help if necessary. She was doing okay, easing along the wall until she almost got to the bathroom, where she had to let go of the wall. Then, she almost fell on the hot pot-bellied stove. I leaped forth and caught her. For months, for years, every time I thought about it, I wanted to die, it had frightened me so. I kept thinking, suppose I hadn't been there to catch her. I had saved my grandmother from falling and surely burning herself. I shudder even today as I think back.

As soon as my mother came home from work, I related the entire incident to her. So, soon after that, it was decided that she should return to the South to again live with my mother's older sister, who by this time had had a rest from the tremendous and

Father, Clarence Rodgers

awesome responsibility. Less than a year later she died. I remember how my mother cried when they called her on the phone and told her.

Growing up, it always made me feel sad when I thought about her, and does so even now. She was old and kind of alone, living with my mother, her youngest child, one year, and then with her other children the others. Before she died, she had been rotated from sibling to sibling, and I knew that she hadn't liked it very much. Still, she had known how to love and laugh and smile, and sew and piece her quilts. I carry those gifts with me today, even the knowledge of how to piece a quilt. By the time she passed on, I was twelve years old. She had taught me many valuable lessons during the brief period she was in my life. I never mastered, though, how to use a thimble, even though I tried and tried, as she patiently strove to teach me. So, Bessie Cato Colding, widow of Abraham Colding, mother of eight plus one, my mother, Bazella Cato Colding Rodgers, passed on to hopefully happier, I believed most definitely higher ground, as I entered into my teens.

"Our first house in Chicago on Forty-sixth and Evans"

Part 4

As a grammar-school student, I was an avid reader of books, books, books, and even more books. I used to bring them home from the local library in shopping bags. I either disliked math because I wasn't good at it, or I wasn't good at it because I disliked it. I've never been sure. The years were uneventful, and I did the things most young Black children growing up do, except, perhaps, for one important and major exception.

By this time, the aunt on my father's side who had come to Chicago first decided to move to a town in Michigan. She purchased a farm and began to raise turkeys, chickens, ducks, and goats and there were wild pheasants on her land. Every summer, or almost every summer, my parents would pile the four of us children into a car and drop us off. During those summers, I drank goat milk, learned how but couldn't wring a chicken's neck. Ran barefoot and wild. Picked berries for money. Found out that I was deathly afraid of moths, and that at night, there are trillions of stars in the sky if you live in the country. Septembers would find me happy and fatter, although I have never been anything but thin.

One of my sisters and I were given dramatic-arts lessons. This too was definitely a highlight of my growing up. At the Lucas School of Dramatic Arts, we studied Boleslavsky and Paul Lawrence Dunbar. I became an elocutionist. I dramatized poems at many

church functions and became a paid performer. During my pre-adolescent years, different church groups were always asking me to read on their programs and it was not long before they began to give me small honorariums to encourage me. Boy, did it. Money for reading poetry. That's how early I began. I was in the fifth, sixth, seventh, and eighth grades. Still, I never dreamed of being a writer.

I never became serious about "elocutions," better known as acting. Even though I joined the high-school drama club and got major parts, for some reason, I never took any of it seriously, until years and years later.

*

Only one other thing stands out in my mind as I think about those years I spent in the old neighborhood. I remember it because it became the inspiration for my first attempts at writing fiction.

I used to walk a blind man home. He would come by my house and ring a tin cup that had a pebble in it. I was twelve or thirteen years old. In my first short story, "Blackbird in a Cage," I wrote about those days. I used to walk the old man past all the taverns, beauty shops, greasy-spoon restaurants, store-front churches, and barbershops to his home in a basement apartment right off an alley. He would come by my house at five or six o'clock every evening. He would have been working all day long, shaking his cup for money on the various corners along Forty-seventh Street. One day I was returning home from the grocery store on Forty-seventh Street and I saw him struggling to cross the street all by himself. I could not bear not helping him. After that, I became his guide. Years passed and I forgot how it all ended. Maybe it was when I was fifteen and we moved. I don't know.

Then one day in 1968, I saw a blind man with a cane and he was old and his clothes were tattered and soiled, like my childhood friend Simon's used to be. And the memory of Simon and myself flooded me. At first I tried to write a poem about it because that was the only genre I was accustomed to working in. But I couldn't fit all the details in without them appearing awkward, and on the advice of a friend, I decided to try my hand at a short story. It was published in *Negro Digest* in 1968. It was my second professional publication. A poem was my first.

When I was fifteen years old, two important events occurred. My parents bought a home in a racially changing neighborhood, and I had to have my appendix taken out. The former was the more important occurrence of the two. In the new neighborhood, many things were different. The house was small but spotlessly clean, with honey hardwood floors and woodwork. For the first time, I lived in a house where the kitchen and bathroom were white-tiled. Again there was a backyard, but this backyard was filled with rosebushes and trees. It was neatly sculptured and there was a garage. The entire scene looked like something out of Dick-and-Jane books.

By this time I was in high school, and for years my mother had been struggling to get up the courage to change her job. The factory where she had worked since I was in kindergarten was a literal hell to her. She told us how, in the winters, many days there was little or no heat. Sometimes there was standing water on the factory floors and her feet would be damp or outright wet, all day long. She would keep a cold. Some days, the workers would have to take turns and sit and guard an unsafe furnace in lieu of actually working. My heart stayed tight with fear for her throughout the years as she faithfully went to work and saved pennies for us, to have and to do the things she thought would better our lives.

In the new neighborhood there were more Black people who were trying to move up in life, so my mother got lots of encouragement from her new neighbors and friends to change her job and her life. My mother had wanted to become a teacher when she was a young woman in Arkansas. However, as the years passed and my two older sisters willingly moved into those positions, due to her leading and her help, she fastened her dreams on becoming a school-crossing guard. Eventually she altered her desire and decided to be a teacher's aide for handicapped children. She studied, took the state exam, passed it, and just like that my mother changed her life. No more was she a factory worker. No longer did she have to come home and cry about her many chipped fingernails, rough and chapped hands, and a less-than-minimum-wage paycheck. The little girl from Little Rock who had not had enough money to complete college beyond the first semester had achieved an aspect of her life's goal. She was a teacher of sorts. Our entire family celebrated and rejoiced with her.

The new neighborhood introduced me to the Catholic church which was just around the corner from our new house. We were miles and miles away from the church I had grown up in. I was maturing and I was beginning to be curious about different kinds of religious experiences. Not that I no longer loved the African Methodist Episcopals; I just wondered about something different. The Catholic church was there, ready and willing to interest me. The church actively recruited the new Blacks in the neighborhood, and even though they did not get anyone else in my family, they did get me.

I used to see the nuns pacing in the church courtyard, their rosaries dangling from their fingers, their lips moving as their long black habits billowed in the soft breezes. They paced and prayed, summer, spring, and fall, and only in the cold Chicago winters did they completely disappear from sight. The church was called Saint Raphael and it had a beautiful grotto. I had never seen one before and I had never seen statues of Mary and other saints that Catholics give homage to.

When other churches were closed, this church's doors always seemed to be open. I used to long to see the sanctuary inside, and one day the door was just open, and, like a thief, I crept in. It was empty inside, except for the cantor, who was in the choir loft, singing in a high, sweet tenor voice. He was practicing Georgian Latin chants for what was then called high mass. There was the sweet, heavy smell of incense in the air, and over the altar, the red candle that is still always lit glowed.

Something in me liked it all. It was so peaceful and different from the church I knew. On many other occasions after the first time, I would slip into the church and sit and listen to the cantor sing. One day I met a priest there and he talked me into taking instruction. Then I was baptized and later confirmed Carolina Maria. As I look back over the years now, I marvel that my mother let it happen. I was still a sixteen-year-old child and I suppose she could have stopped me; but even though she objected strongly and was almost heartbroken by my conversion, she let it be. She probably thought better that than nothing.

I was in my second year at Hyde Park High School when I converted. I was just average in my studies, which were all college preparatory. For extracurricular activities, I took orchestra, where I played the violin and I sang with great gusto in the Senior Acappella Choir. These were the ultimate joys in my high-school life, especially the choir. We learned Latin songs, spirituals, carols, and anthems. We studied Bach, Beethoven, and Mozart, and we listened to different operas while we studied the composers. My little world broadened. In this artistic milieu, I began to write poems and I also started keeping a diary. I hid them and would probably have tried to die if I thought anyone had read them. I never thought of myself as a writer. I was just a high-school student spewing guts.

I graduated from Hyde Park High School in 1959 and I promptly enrolled in the prelaw program at the University of Illinois Chicago campus. I lasted there exactly one year. My grades were so poor I had to transfer to a city junior college. What a relief that was. At the University of Illinois, there had been a lot of pressure to succeed or excel. There was always talk among students about someone who had flipped out because of the competitiveness and the awful pressure.

City College was a breeze. It was flunked-out heaven for scores of students and I began to relax there and enjoy the college life. I joined the Rimer's Club. We were the school's fledgling poets. We wrote and read to each other. We laughed, cried with, and encouraged one another. I was published for the very first time in the Rimer's poetry quarterly magazine. I participated in the club's poetry presentations to the school populace. I'll never forget the last reading program I read in. One of the drama instructors sent a message to me through the Rimer's Club academic advisor. He said that out of the eight or nine poets reading from the club, he felt only two of them expressed real talent. I was one of the two. I was very happy about that, but I still didn't understand the handwriting on the wall. I had no thoughts or dreams even of being "a writer." I just wrote stuff I liked and I wanted other people to like it too. That's how I viewed what I did. When I read the "stuff" I was

writing then, I marvel that any of my instructors were able to recognize my budding talent. I still like the work, and I think that it is good, but I never expected anyone else to. I earned my first *A* in college there at City Junior, and it was from a creative writing class. I must have been catharting right.

From City College, I went to a four-year institution in downtown Chicago. My stint at Roosevelt University was mostly miserable. Again, I lost myself. I didn't really know who I was there, and I sure didn't know what I wanted to be in life. Not much happened while I was at Roosevelt, but this one event is noteworthy.

The English department held a reception for Gwendolyn Brooks, the first Black author to ever win a Pulitzer Prize; an author I had heard nothing about. Since I was the founder and coordinator of the Poetry Club at the school and a few select people in the English department knew that I wrote poetry, they thought that I should attend the reception.

It was given in the school's beautiful Sullivan Room, a place with blue satin curtains and French Provincial furniture. I was afraid of "the room." As a student, I would occasionally pass by the open doors when affairs were in progress, and I would see all the expensive-looking White people, laughing, drinking, and chatting with each other. I was terrified about going into "the room." But I went because they said that she was Black.

What a warm, wonderful surprise she was! She read many of her most famous poems and I found that she was earth I could touch. I could look at her and know something of myself. I was an English major and I had read Whitman, Millay, Sandburg, Frost, Eliot, Dickinson, and Cummings, to name only a few. *These* were my favorite poets. I had heard of Paul Lawrence Dunbar and Langston Hughes, only because in my youth my dramatic-arts teacher had taught them to us. By then on my own I had read Paul Lawrence Dunbar and Langston Hughes, and a wee bit of James Baldwin. That was all. My head was full of the White writers that I was studying in school, and a person could see their influences in all my works. But here was a real live Black author. A woman—who radiated a "Negro Awareness" in and about her works.

So, when the poetry reading was over and she was standing off to the side, alone for a second, I inched up to her and timidly asked if I could send her some of my poems to look at and pass comment on. She said I could and she gave me her home address. I don't remember much else about the reception. After I told her how much I liked her work and asked her

*Gwendolyn Brooks in profile, inscribed
"With best wishes to an exciting writer,"
July 21, 1967*

about looking at mine, everything sort of blurred into an ecstatic haze.

When I left the reception, I thought I would dash right home and prepare some poems to send Ms. Brooks. I do not know how or even exactly when fear and doubt set in, somewhere along the way . . . It was actually a full two years after that day before I sent her anything. By then, I had read all of her works and as many other Black authors as I could find. I was a totally different individual, changed by my entrance into a world I had never dreamed existed.

The balance of my time at Roosevelt University was spent with me on an emotional roller coaster. I wanted to meet the man of my dreams and marry him. It was supposed to happen in college, wasn't it? All the right people and books said that. But even though I dated plenty of nice guys who would

probably have made decent husbands, when the stardust settled, I always seemed to end up going my own way. I was very unhappy, to say the least. Relatives and friends were always hinting and questioning me about my plans for the future. Eventually, I was labeled as too hard to please. I sadly agreed.

Then I left college and found out I was still young and could enjoy a single life. I had lots of company too; young Black men and women who couldn't marry easily. We formed a group and I learned to love my life, without a husband, babies, or the black picket fence. I couldn't meet a dream man for my family and friends and I slowly, painfully, learned how to live with that knowledge.

I left college in my last semester when, right before graduation, they discovered that I needed one more course to fulfill the academic requirements. I cried and begged and petitioned, but all to no avail. I walked out then on the entire college scene. I found a job working with high-school dropouts, since I figured I knew what made dropping out happen.

I wasn't wrong, either. It was a good job for me. The students were aged sixteen to twenty-one and I was still in my early twenties. I knew about some of the students' problems with school protocol and bureaucracy. I started out as a group leader, but after a few months, they promoted me and I became a language arts instructor. I began to use the works of James Baldwin, Langston Hughes, Richard Wright, and, of course, Gwendolyn Brooks in my classroom. I had unwed mothers and fathers; kids who were desperately trying to grab ahold of the lifeline the YMCA had thrown them by creating the program.

Not too long ago I wrote a poem where I called myself "A Bleeding Heart." That's what I was back then. I met students who came from the housing projects. Some of them had never known a father or mother's love. Some had been neglected and abused, while others had run afoul of the law because of drug or alcohol problems. Kids were there who were mentally retarded; there were those who had mental problems, discipline problems, adjustment and coping problems. Any and all of it; we dealt with it.

I saw it. I wrote about it and I bled about them until I learned that they were tough and had good survival instincts if they had found their way into our program. I had grown up in a two-parent home. I had been nurtured by a positive and supportive church environment. I had been inundated with books, concerts, museums, tutors, elocution lessons, piano lessons, and good schools. I was, even so, everything that they were, while I was everything that they were not. I read poetry to them. I took them to Canada to the Shakespearean festivals. I got some of them back in school by talking to counselors and principals and other school officials. Many went into training programs.

I began to write about them. They would come to me and tell me their sad stories. The more I wrote, the less I wanted to punch a time clock to work. Perhaps destiny was calling me? Whatever. One day I just stopped going. I called them and told them I was quitting. I declared myself a full-time writer. It was the most frightening thing I had ever done. I did not know how I was going to clothe or feed myself, let alone pay my rent, since by that time, I had my own apartment and roommate. Then I hooked up with Gwendolyn Brooks and told her what I had done. She said I was very brave, and she began to help me where I was hurting the most. In my pocketbook. I can never be grateful enough to her for having done that for me. It gave me the confidence in myself that I needed. She believed in me and my talent; I believed in myself.

Part 5

Before I left the high-school dropout program, I used Ms. Brook's poetry with my students. They loved her, and during the course of time, I remembered my meeting with her at Roosevelt University. I wrote her a letter telling her about my students and my new vocation and I sent her seven or eight poems. She wrote back a letter which told me that even though I sounded like all the White writers I had ever read, I had a poem or two that sounded like me and only me. She advised me to get the *Writer* magazine and find someone looking for poetry. Then she told me to submit work until "somebody took something."

Not long after I received her letter, I met Hoyt Fuller. I had never dreamed that I would meet a famous author/editor. While I was working for the YMCA School-Dropout Program, they would have fund-raising events. One such affair was a cabaret party held at the once-famous home of upcoming Chicago Black jazz musicians such as Ramsey Lewis: the Sutherland Hotel.

Some of my friends knew that I wrote poetry, and after we all had a few drinks, they told me that an editor from Johnson Publications was there. They told me to talk to him and see if he would agree to look over some of my work. I had no nerve for it, but with them egging me on, I did it. He said he'd be glad to see my work. Happily, I related this to my friends. I found I was very nervous about what he might say. I spent the next two working days at home, typing, revising, fussing with my work and recreating. I finally sent him three pieces: my first short story about the blind man, "Blackbird in a Cage," a poem, "Song To U. of C. Midway Blues," and "The Headscarf," my first attempt at writing a play.

He responded in record time, I think, now that I know how long editor's replies can take. About four weeks later, my entire life was changed. I'll never forget the first words of the long letter he sent me.

He began the acceptance letter with these words, "Well Carolyn, you can write." I died over those words a million times in the days, the months, even the years that followed. He took the poem and the short story. He declined the play, but I didn't really care. He told me how much money he would pay for each piece that he accepted. I couldn't believe it. Money for my writing. He informed me about what months each piece would appear in *Negro Digest,* the popular little literary magazine of John H. Johnson that had published all the Black literary giants. I was still in my twenties, and I was on my way.

From that day on, I began to take my writing seriously. I never really had before. It had just been something that I did and hid in a closet of my room or my soul. Inspiration began to pour through me as I wrote through all the hurting things that had ever existed in my Black life. Eventually, under the leadership of Mr. Fuller and Ms. Brooks, I learned to extend my hurts and concerns to the Black world around me. For the first time in my life, Black people's needs, desires, fears, and concerns dominated my works. I felt connected to something larger and more important than myself. To me, it was an awesome way to begin.

Not too long after I met Hoyt Fuller, he began a workshop for beginning Black writers. The workshop was called OBAC (Oh-Bah-See), which meant the Organization of Black American Culture. I was a founding member, as were Jewel Latimore (later renamed Johari Amini), Don L. Lee (Haki Madhubuti), Walter Bradford, Mike Cook, Peggy Susberry, Alicia Johnson, Jim Cunningham, Cecil Brown, and Ronda Davis. We met with many other local writers, but we were the core group, the officers, and the ones who planned readings and fund-raising events. One night a week we came together to read our work to each other, to criticize and support each other, and to learn from our wonderful mentor, the late Hoyt W. Fuller.

Shortly after OBAC was started, Gwendolyn Brooks began a workshop also, for beginning young Black writers, and all of us, the above, ended up in her living room, at least one night each month, officially, and many other wonderful days and nights throughout the following years, reading to each other, laughing, crying, and talking about anything and everything.

*

I used to go to Margery Peters's Writing Workshop in Hyde Park on the south side of Chicago, also. Mrs. Peters must have been in her seventies, at least. Yet without fail, every Tuesday night around eight o'clock, she would call us into the living room of the old mansion where she lived. She would call us, future writers of America, in from the dining room or the parlor, where we would be chatting while eating cake or cookies and drinking tea or coffee.

She would always wear a green velvet floor-length gown with long sleeves, tapered at the wrists. The high neck of the gown was saucer-round with a white lace collar, and there was white lace, pinafore style, down the front of the gown. Her thin, once-blond white hair would be piled high on her head,

and she had small, very blue eyes. She was a tiny woman, weighing less than 120 pounds and barely standing five-foot-three-inches tall. She was regal, even so. She looked as if she had stepped into the living room from another era, perhaps the Victorian one.

In the winters, the fireplace in the living room would be lit, and we would sit, as dry logs crackled and popped, in a haphazard circle or semicircle. Sometimes she would read our works, if we were too fragile or dogmatic about their intent. Other times, we would read. There weren't many Blacks who attended. I was often the only one.

With the three workshops, I learned how to skillfully critique a literary work so that I was able to write book reviews first for *Negro Digest,* and later on for the *Chicago Daily News* and *Sun-Times.*

At that time, Harry Mark Petrakis was her star pupil and he was already published for his Greek novels. Ofttimes, we would sit spellbound as he read. They always rolled out their red carpet for him and it was exciting just to be there. When I would become impatient with her comments about my work, she

Receiving the first Conrad Kent Rivers Writing Award from Hoyt W. Fuller,
at Johnson Publications office, 1969

would always remind me that Gwendolyn Brooks had once been a student of hers. Ms. Brooks told me that this was true.

Even so, when I began to get published on a regular basis in mostly Black periodicals, I stopped attending her workshops and concentrated on the other two. They were so much more exciting to me. People my own color and age were there, and some famous Black author or artist was always stopping by to visit and share with us.

*

Instead of mailing poetry to publishers around the country, I and the others in the workshops were exhorted "to do our own thing." So in 1968, I gathered up about fifteen poems and fashioned them into a little book, tentatively called *Paper Soul*. I sent them to Gwendolyn Brooks with a couple of other titles to choose from. She said I had twelve poems which were worth publishing, and agreed with me on my favorite title, *Paper Soul*.

I asked Hoyt Fuller to write an introduction for me and he did. Then I took the poems to a printer, after I found an artist to do a jacket cover. Approximately five hundred copies were printed. The response to the little book was more than I had hoped for. It surprised me to find that people accepted my work as having been published, even though I did it myself. Soon after I had the finished copies in my hands, I was distributing copies in Black and White bookstores around the country. I began to get invitations to read at different colleges. Reviews popped up in Black and White periodicals. It was, of course, reviewed in *Negro Digest*, but *Publishers Weekly* also gave it some space. The libraries agreed to stock copies of it. I began to get requests for certain poems to be included in the anthologies which were coming out, heralding the new Black poets of the 1960s and their poetry.

In 1970, I did a second book of poetry, called *Songs of a Blackbird*. People began to use the poems in dramatic programs. Once again a book of mine was well received. For this volume, I won the Poet Laureate Award of the Society of Midland Authors and I received a National Endowment for the Arts Award for many of the poems in the two combined volumes.

In 1971, I went to Albany State College as a resident poet for one month. It was a first for me. I had to write and to present myself as a living, writing,

published young Black author. I had no classes to teach and my only other commitments were to give occasional readings in English classes or in the school auditorium. I grew a bit bored, so that when I returned home and was offered the teaching position as the first writer-in-residence at Chicago's Malcolm X City College, I eagerly took it. It was my second teaching job at the college level. My first had been at Columbia College in 1969. At that time, Don L. Lee (Haki Madhubuti) and I had been asked by Gwendolyn Brooks to take over her classes at the college in Afro-American literature. She was then besieged with requests to lecture and read her poetry in all kinds of places throughout the country and the world. I had felt very privileged to be one of the people asked to fill in for her.

At Columbia, I had had few Blacks in my classes since the school was predominately White. Teaching Afro-American literature had been a real challenge to me. Malcolm X College, as evidenced by its name, was a product of the Black revolution, and full of young, eager, vociferous Blacks from the gutbucket of the Black community. Few Whites dared or cared to matriculate there. What Malcolm X students wanted, I was oddly enough able to give because of my teaching experiences at Columbia. They wanted to know who they were and how to get along in the White world. They wanted to know who Shakespeare was and how he fit into their lives, as well as the James Baldwins and the Langston Hughes. I resided at that school for a little over a year. I left in 1973, once again on my own, after the untimely, unexpected murder/death of my only brother.

Losing him made me feel lost and afraid in the world. I had not married. I had no children and I was thirty. I felt I needed to reevaluate my life and my goals. I was still so oriented as to believe that a woman's most noble goal in life was to marry and have children. I struggled with awful feelings of inadequacy. A friend that I had met at the high-school dropout program suggested that I try the church for the resolution of some of my painful feelings. Instead of going into the folds of the Catholic church, however, I opted to return to the church of my youth, the AME church.

The church helped me a lot. They had scores of single women who had been "in the world" and were "saved" or, as many call it, "born again." At first, I went skeptically, but ultimately I found some peace, acceptance, and fellowship as I continued to wait, hope, and search for my life and its meaning,

I learned there to love other people's children, and came to realize that I was, at least, half-blessed

Carolyn (left) and Maya Angelou at Maya's house, Oakland, California, 1980

not to have to endure the agonies of having had any, even if I was missing the ecstasies.

Part 6

It wasn't until 1976 that I met someone I cared about enough to marry. At the last minute, I backed out because he had serious social problems, and I had been told again and again by various church members that with the specific problem my intended had, it was highly unlikely that I could maintain a relationship with any church. That pronouncement didn't frighten me; it traumatized me. I was torn, emotionally, but in the end, I severed the serious side of our relationship and settled for friendship, after about six months of anger from his end.

I could not bear to lose the approval of the church. I had experienced such understanding from them. I had found peace in the walls, the pews, the hymns, the rituals. One important thing I came away with from the relationship with my boyfriend was that I knew the who in the world I could love, and I found out how it was that I myself loved.

*

I was living simply as a writer on the college lecture circuit. Not ever believing that I could fix my beloved beans and corn bread so many different ways. In short, I was always in the pawnshops, hocking this piece of jewelry or another. Some people never knew how hard it was for me financially. They thought I was hiding a private stash or acting out eccentric roles. But the poverty was real.

Then in 1974, I was invited to a conference in Mississippi. The Phillis Wheatley Conference was held at Jackson State University and was host to a myriad Black women writers of the previous decade. I was terrified of flying and rarely flew anywhere. Everyone knew that but still flight tickets came in the mail for me to read poetry or give a lecture on Afro-American literature or criticism. I rationalized. I was going to be in good company. All the Chicago poetesses were booked on the same flight. I decided I would fly to Mississippi. It was a monumental decision. For weeks preceding the conference, I boosted myself with anecdotes about people who had licked the flying phobia. Alas! It was all to no avail, even though I flew Bible in lap, tranquilizers in stomach, and drink in hand; I was as nervous as it was possible to be. My eyes were pried wide, my mouth was dry in between sips, my heart pounded at an ungodly rate. My hands were fists one minute, and clutching anything available the next. To make matters worse, it started to rain really hard, and the little DC-7 bounced up and down like a ball on a tennis court. I was catatonic, which is to say, hysterical with fear. I did not fly back, but insisted that the conference convert my flight ticket to a train ticket for the trip home.

The conference was wonderful though. Writers like Toni Cade Bambara, Sonia Sanchez, Alice Walker, Mari Evans, Audre Lorde, June Jordan, and of course the organizer of it all, Margaret Walker, were there. All of us read and the entire event was something like a dream, or a page out of a history book. I met so many new people there, I lost track of names and faces. Therefore, it came as a surprise to me when I got a call from a Doubleday editor after my arrival home. She reminded me that we had talked and I had promised to consider doing a book with them.

I was overjoyed. I quickly sent them some prerequisite poems, and was rewarded with a contract and a modest advance for what turned out to be *How I Got Ovah: New and Selected Poems.* The title of the volume came from the wonderful Negro spiritual Mahalia Jackson made famous:

> How, I got ovah, how I got ovah,
> Lawd, my soul looks back and wonders
> how I got ovah . . .

The title, the words, seemed right for me.

Putting together this book was my biggest single literary effort up to that time. I was a little scared. I was told that I needed at least forty poems. Well, I certainly had that many written, but I was sure Doubleday would not have received many of them well, since quite a few had been written during the turbulence and fire of the militant sixties. The poems were hostile and frequently inappropriate.

During the sixties, I had accustomed myself to writing a large number of position poems as well as the traditional protest poems. These poems addressed specific local or national Black problems and concerns and were often viewed by White critics as more propaganda than art. I had been taught to subjugate the art-for-art's-sake poems to an inferior or even nonexistent status in my repertoire. I had been schooled and indoctrinated by older Black critics and authors to write art for a Black revolution's sake, for Black people's sakes. But I had never wanted anyone to believe that that was all there was to me as an author, even a Black author.

I got busy and I started writing new works, while collecting various others which had been shuttled into hidden corners because they were too tame for anyone's taste other than my own. I did include in the compilation poems from my self-printed volumes, which by that time were some people's favorites and had become so well known they were almost synonymous with my name. I wanted to show the world who I was in a total sense. I was not just a Black militant woman whose main quest in life was social change and revolution. I was not that altruistic, and I didn't want people to think that I was. I was a person, aside from all the social rabble and babble; like Zora Neale Hurston, like Gwendolyn Brooks and Margaret Walker or Maya Angelou were. I felt an extra pressure to show the world what my otherness was like since I had no husband or children to obliquely reflect me.

The book was published in 1975 in hardback and in soft cover in 1976. I never got a lot of money from it like I thought I would. Or from much else in the literary field for that matter. When I heard what other people's advances and royalties were, I was always more than a little envious. But there was the joy of having the book published by such a large, prestigious house, of having it reviewed in places where my small press would never have been received, and, finally, of having it receive a nomination for the National Book Award in poetry for the year 1976.

When I got the nomination, Doubleday took out a huge ad space with a copy of the book-jacket cover and my picture in the *New York Times.* They advertised that I was their only author that year to receive such a distinction. So even when I didn't win the award, I was not greatly let down. It had been altogether a tremendously rewarding experience. I figured I was a newcomer. The prize went to John Ashbury, a poet who had worthily earned so much respect in the poetic field, his name alone was virtually venerable.

*

By the time the paperback edition of *How I Got Ovah* came out in 1976, I was writing new poems for my next volume. That book, *The Heart as Ever Green,* was not published until 1978, and it ended my publishing existence with Doubleday, even though the book got very good reviews. They never brought it out in paperback because they said that hardcover sales were too low. My original editor left and I never hit it off with her replacement.

During this period of time I was again at loose ends. I traveled every now and then, but my pocketbook was either filled with enough money for only beans or, diametrically, caviar. I was up one month and way down the next. I could never balance and I was beginning to realize that I was not going to be the poet who was lucky enough to live off royalties, permission fees, and even appearance honorariums. Right before my first editor left Doubleday, the planning committee for the Thirty Year Salute to Israel asked if Cicely Tyson could read one of my poems on the Satellite TV broadcast. I, of course, agreed. That was in 1978. I thought that the publicity from that would surely earn me a permanent spot in the hearts of the moneychangers. But even though the accolades fell on my ears in enchanting torrents, no real money or change in status came with it.

The college circuit wasn't a bad way to make a living. I was still scared of flying, but periodically, I would accept a flight ticket and actually use it. I flew to Amherst to a feminist poetry festival, and I can never forget that on 7-7-77 I flew to Emory University and back in one day. A first for me. I usually needed time between flights, but the date was too meaningful to pass by. I think now I should have been scared to death on such a date, but flying makes me completely crazy or completely sane. Somewhere in between those two extremes, I emerge as holy. I always fly with a Bible in my lap.

I began to want that bachelor's degree that I had never earned. When I found out that after all those years, I still only needed one course to obtain it, I enrolled in the English department at Chicago State University in the fall of 1980 to pick up the credits. I finally got my degree in English in January of 1981. That same year, I got a tiny grant from the Illinois Arts Council to publish a little book of poetry called *Translation*.

Then in 1982, Ruby Dee and Ossie Davis put together a gospel tribute to me with Billy Preston. They used all my religious poetry in a hand-clapping, foot-stomping presentation with a Dallas, Texas, gospel choir. Billy Preston sang, and Ruby and Ossie gave dramatic renditions of my works.

The show ran on educational television stations from coast to coast, and again I was hailed in the *New York Times*. Yet no real change occurred in my purse strings, though my popularity zoomed way up.

Also in 1982, Woodie King, a New York producer/director, contacted me. He told me that a friend of his, Shauneille Perry, had collected some forty poems of mine and choreographed them into an off-Broadway production. So, in 1982, I alone went off to New York City to see a great little troupe of dancers, singers, and dramatists whip through some of my best poetic works. The show ran for three weeks and ended with excellent reviews. My hopes that it would be picked up for Broadway never wavered, until that last production night.

Part 7

After my show closed, I did some serious thinking again. I knew that there was no silver-lined route out of poverty for me, and I had always been too sickly to work forty hours a week. Though I have not mentioned it before now, after my appendix was removed when I was fifteen, various problems plagued me throughout the following years. I had to have an operation for adhesions caused by the appendicitis surgery. Then I developed fibroid tumors and those had to be removed. The three surgeries left my body in a weakened condition, and I knew that I needed at least one more college degree if I was going to acquire a job of any permanence, in a capacity I could physically withstand. I decided to go for a master's degree.

"With my mother," 1983

I made that decision specifically and emphatically after I was invited to teach a class in Afro-American literature as a writer-in-residence for the summer of 1983 at my dear old alma mater, Roosevelt University. For eight weeks, for three hours, five days a week, I stood before a small, select group of students and taught them what I knew about the literature and ideology of the 1960s, in this country and in the African diaspora.

To top it all off, the English department arranged a parting reception for me in the still-beautiful Sullivan Room, the same room where some twenty-odd years before I had met Gwendolyn Brooks when I inched up to her to timidly inquire if she would preview some of my poems. The reception for me was a moving, momentous occasion. Newsmen and photographers were there from local newspapers to cover the event. That September, I started attending the University of Chicago graduate school of English on scholarship.

In June of 1984, I was graduated. I returned to Chicago State University, diploma in hand, and was hired as a part-time instructor with a salary lower than the non-degreed clerk typist working in the English department office. I walked, after a few months of misery due both to illness and poverty. Straight back to the University of Chicago I went, and enrolled in a second master's program, which promised big bucks for me if I could get through it. Alas! The department was small and tightly knit, and I could not break through the social or ethnic barriers. I left before finishing, and it was at that time I decided that I had had enough of Chicago. I decided I would follow in the footsteps of an old school friend who had moved to the Bay Area of California.

It was a major decision for me to make. I felt like I was planning to move to the other side of the world. I had never planned to live so far away from family, yet and still, in August of 1986, I left Chicago for what I thought would be forever. My plans were to occasionally visit family and friends, but to keep a safe distance away, otherwise.

I lived in Oakland exactly thirty-three months before I returned to Chicago. Happy, free, very productive, illuminating months. I learned a lot about myself, away from the people and places I had known all my life. I had *never* known how independent I could be, even though people had always told me that I was. I learned that it was true what some people had told me; that independence was indeed my bane and my blessing.

I was incredibly homesick when I returned, and I was elated to see the changes that that short span of

The author today

time had wrought in the city, family and friends, and not the very least, myself in relationship to it all.

The entire time I was in California, I worked on a novel, wrote several short stories, kept a journal, and wrote scads of poetry about the West Coast scene.

Part 8

When I left Chicago for California, I left three rooms of furniture in storage. Once settled, I thought I would simply send for it. I had all kinds of visions of family and friends visiting me and complimenting me on how well I had done, living away from the nest. California, however, though a wonderful, wonderful place to live for awhile, was not the place I finally wanted to be for the rest of my life. I was too far away from my aging parents and the rest of my family ever to be comfortable. Then too, I began to miss home places and faces, and when I finally returned, I had experienced a homesickness I had not even known was possible.

About three months after my return, I started working at Columbia College again, the first college I taught at in 1969 when I had filled in for Gwendolyn Brooks. I am presently there. So to end.

Eight months after I came home, a funny thing happened to me on the way to the rest of my life. On a perfectly gorgeous, sunny, blue-skied day in October, I returned from visiting my parents (who live in the suburbs) to my sister's house, where I was temporarily staying. The fall air had turned lusciously cool, and we thought we would just turn the furnace on for awhile to ease a slight chill from the rooms.

That evening we almost died, because the chimney was clogged, and deadly carbon monoxide fumes seeped into the house. That night, I wound up having desperately fought, hooked up to an oxygen mask, a cardiac monitor, and intravenous feeding apparatus, with my blood being drawn every few hours to determine the carbon monoxide level. What a way to end a day which I had thought was the most beautiful and productive that I had had since returning home from East Bay. How ironic it turned out to be.

Before I had passed into a state of semi-consciousness, I had managed to call my parents, who then called 911. The fire department rescued us. While in the ambulance, coming somewhat to, I had fought death so hard, I was exhausted, when I saw something like a vision. I saw only my head and neck with two sheaths of color circling them. First, there was an ethereal-like yellow-white light nearest to me; and surrounding it was the most beautiful blue I have ever seen. I felt completely safe and peaceful and warm. It lasted about two seconds, and then it was gone, but I see it again and again in my mind's eye. Oh, how I cherish life now, not that I had not before.

I write a lot now and at least half of it is religiously oriented and motivated. I was born into the Christian faith and I remain Christian still, for love, for nothing less than that or better. But I have studied religions like Buddhism and Islam, and I have for years wondered about karma, nirvana, and heaven. I have had cerebral love affairs with Krishnamurti Hesse, Camus, Kierkegaard, Sartre, Hegel, and many of the other existentialists. I have believed in life after death, and I have strongly suspected that there are many heavens and hells on this our earth.

I have tried to grow in the various levels of light I have been given. Finally, there is more, so much more I go on trying to say. I hope I have time to say it all.

April 28, 1990

how i got ovah

i can tell you
about them
i have shaken rivers
out of my eyes
i have waded eyelash deep
have crossed rivers
have shaken the water weed out
of my lungs
have swam for strength
pulled by strength
through waterfalls with electric beats
i have bore the shocks
of water deep deep
waterlogs are my bones
i have shaken the water free of my hair
have kneeled on the banks
and kissed my ancestors of the dirt
whose rich dark root fingers rose up reached
  out
grabbed and pulled me rocked me cupped me
gentle strong and firm
carried me
made me swim for strength
cross rivers
though i shivered
was wet was cold
and wanted to sink down
and float as water, yea—
i can tell you.
i have shaken rivers
out of my eyes.

Portrait

mama spent pennies
in uh gallon milk jug
saved pennies
fuh four babies
college educashuns

and when the babies
got bigger they would
secretly "borrow" mama's
pennies to buy candy

and pop cause mama
saved extras
fuh college educashuns
and pop and candy

was uh non-credit in bad teeth
mama pooled pennies
in uh gallon milk jug
Borden's by the way

and the babies went
to school cause mama saved
and spent and paid
fuh four babies
college educashuns
mama spent pennies

and nickels
and quarters
and dollars

I Have Been Hungry

1

and you white girl
shall i call you sister now?
can we share any secrets of sameness,
any singularity of goals. . . .
you, white girl with the head that
perpetually tosses over-rated curls
while i religiously toss my over-rated behind
you white girl
i am yet suspicious of/
for deep inside of me
there is the still belief that
i am
a road
you would travel
to my man. :120

2

and how could you, any of you
think that a few loud words and years
could erase the tears
blot out the nightmares and knowledge,
smother the breeded mistrust
and how could any of you think that i
after being empty for so long
could fill up on fancy fierce platitudes. . . .

some new/old knowledge has risen in me
like yeast
but still old doubts deflate

am i—really—so beautiful
as i sweat and am black and oh so
greasy in the noonday sun

the most beauty that i am i am inside
and so few deign to touch
i am a forest of expectation.
the beauty that i will be is yet
to be defined

what i can be even i can not know.

3

and what does a woman want?
what does any woman want
but a soft man to hold her hard
a sensitive man to help her fight off
the insensitive pangs of living.
and what is living to a woman
without the weight of some man
pulling her down/puffing her out

do not tell me
liberated tales of woman/woeman
who seek only to satisfy them selves
with them selves, all, by them selves
i will not believe you
i will call you a dry canyon
them, a wilderness
of wearying and failures
a fearing of hungerings from
and deep into
the wonderment of loneliness
and what makes any woman so.

4

as for me—
i am simple
a simple foolish woman.
all that i have ever wanted
i have not had
and much of what i have had
i have not wanted

my father never wanted three girls
and only one son, one sun. . . .
God, how he wished his seeds
had transformed themselves into
three boys and only one girl—
for heaven's sake, only one good for nothing
wanting needing love and approval seeking
bleeding
girl.
and so, i have spent my days
so many of my days seeking the approval
which was never there
craving the love
i never got

and what am i now,
no longer a simple girl
bringing lemonade and cookies
begging favor
    and what am i now
no longer a world-torn woman
showering my "luck" in a
cold bottle of cold duck

and—who—am i now
but a
saved
sighing
singular thing. a woman. . . .
ah, here i am
and
here have i been
i say,
i
have been hungry,
ravenously hungry,
all
my
years

Some Me of Beauty

    the fact is
that i don't hate any body any more
    i went through my mean period
    if you remember i spit out nails
        chewed tobacco on the paper
and dipped some bad snuff.
        but in one year
just like i woke up one morning and
        saw my mother's head gray
and i asked myself/could it have turned
        overnight?
knowing full well the grayness had been
        coming and had even been there
        awhile
just like that i woke up one morning
    and looked at my self
        and what i saw was
                        carolyn
        not imani ma jua or soul sister poetess of
                the moment
        i saw more than a "sister" . . .
            i saw a Woman. human.
                            and black.
        i felt a spiritual transformation
            a root revival of love

and I knew that many things
        were over
and some me of—beauty—
            was about to begin. . . .

A Brief Synopsis

at fifteen
pain
called me.
i went to one of the
accounting departments,
the hospital
tallied up
came home
with an appendix in a jar
all swollen, pickled and pinkened

each year after that
i reported in
for some kind of
duty.

by 18,
i had grown something else
with a lot of adjectives
like a notebook,
i was a running account
of cuts and bruises
a writer
you might say . . .

every three years
after 21
i helped somebody
doctors, lawyers and various other kinds of
    chiefs . . .
the last hospital
sent me home
in a cab
well pilled and still
very much preserved.

i can list so many
scars and abrasions
they make a fine cross
word puzzle
in my consciousness
i tell all my admirers
i'm a different kind of
poet.

i
told Jesus
be allright

if he
changed
my
name.

Recollections, Towards a Stream

and when i first
went back to church
i was not there. only a thin
wisp-o-will
stood softly in the corridors
swayed in the pews and clapped
hands and patted feet to the
rhythm of salvation. and everywhere
i went i saw the light leading me,
guiding me home towards some unknown hill
or stream of rest.
now i am quieted.
there is a stillness in me
working its way out towards life.
live, it whispers incessantly to me.

it is the only way to die.

With Malice Toward None

when divers sorts of people
want to know about me,
for obvious reasons that is
not love or liking
asking in a manner that is not kind,
    or sincere
i dream of telling each person something
    different
and arranging for them all to meet
        and letting them be ashamed
by what when they speak of me
they know about themselves.

Feminism

our mothers,
when asked
may speak of us
in terms of our accomplishments.
my daughter is a flower
shedding buds of brown babies.
she holds two diplomas in
her fists as she shows her
obliqueness to a world that

only cares for credentials.
what is your claim to fame?
what is your claim to life—
when there are no diplomas
to be lauded,
no husband to be pillared upon,
no buds to be babied.
when does the wind blow on your face
and in what direction do you turn
when it rains?

Contemporary/ Psalm

tenacity was my youth
with a certain hull
on the heel of my happiness.
hollow came later
and i yet bloomed like some sunflower in
the open spree of life.
i gathered storms in my fists
and threw them at the sky.
they rained back on me as fruit
which became my dreams
and now, who
not i can speak of dreams anymore
without speaking of wooing.
i woo the dreams that will not
ripen easily, i woo the dreams,
and eyes—yes
i woo the eyes of storms
and people,
with the flute of tears
when there is no laughter
as i wish me some someplace distinctly different
still i bloom right here right here as i am
like some perennial sunflower
the reap of many toils and seasons. and

yesterday
i saw my own becoming—
a diverse disunity/a leavened grace/a silken
    thirst
a Dahomey thread of
what i have always been.
and i knelt at the foot of
mercy/the well and i cried out to
God.

(Poems from *How I Got Ovah*
and *The Heart as Ever Green*)

BIBLIOGRAPHY

Poetry:

Paper Soul, Third World Press, 1968.

Songs of a Blackbird, Third World Press, 1969.

Two Love Raps, Third World Press, 1969.

Now Ain't That Love, Broadside Press, 1969.

For H. W. Fuller, Broadside Press, 1970.

For Flip Wilson, Broadside Press, 1971.

Long Rap/Commonly Known as a Poetic Essay, Broadside Press, 1971.

How I Got Ovah: New and Selected Poems, Doubleday/Anchor, 1975.

The Heart as Ever Green: Poems, Doubleday/Anchor, 1978.

Translation: Poems, Eden Press, 1980.

Eden and Other Poems, Eden Press, 1983.

Finite Forms: Poems, Eden Press, 1985.

Morning Glory: Poems, Eden Press, 1989.

Fiction:

A Little Lower Than the Angels, Eden Press, 1984.

Other:

Love (play), first produced by Woodie King, Jr., at Louis Abrons Theatre, New York, June 3, 1982.

Contributor to numerous anthologies, including *We Speak as Liberators, Brothers and Sisters, Spectrum in Black, No More Masks, Black Spirits,* and *Sturdy Black Bridges.* Contributor of poems to numerous magazines, including *Journal of Black Poetry, Ebony,* and *The Black Scholar.* Also contributed essays and short stories to such periodicals as *Essence, Negro Digest,* and *Black World.* Former reviewer for *Chicago Daily News* and *Chicago Sun-Times,* and columnist for *Milwaukee Courier.*

W. A. Swanberg

1907-

SOME THINGS THAT HAPPENED

The joke was on me one day in 1960 when I was researching a biography of William Randolph Hearst. His son, William Randolph Jr., then running the vast empire left by his father, gave me warm cooperation though cautious about the pater's private life. Once he took me to lunch at the snooty 21 Club on Manhattan's West Fifty-second Street—a place where a hamburger dinner cost twenty-one dollars and I couldn't afford on my own. I had my notebook with me, intending to continue my questioning as we ate.

As we sat down, a youngish and glamorous lady came by, said hello to Bill, and he invited her to join us. He introduced us but my hearing aid failed me and I didn't catch the name. She looked quite familiar. Where had I seen her? Anyway, she made such chatter with Hearst that my note-taking was nil. As he drove me back to his office, I asked him who she was. He stared at me and burst out laughing. "Didn't you know her? That was Zsa Zsa Gabor."

Thereafter I was celebrated in the Hearst office as the man who had lunch with Zsa Zsa and didn't know it.

I was also given an interview with Mrs. William Randolph Hearst, aged widow of the late titan, in her sumptuous apartment overlooking Central Park. This took diplomacy, since years earlier she had been replaced in Hearst's affections by Marion Davies and had refused him a divorce. Yet she was left millions by her errant husband, which she spent in worthy charities.

I knew better than to utter the name of Miss Davies. I hoped she would. Mrs. Hearst, kindliness personified, served tea as she spoke of the husband who, as the whole world knew, had abandoned this mother of his five sons in favor of the screen beauty. Did she give the old boy the business? Not at all. Never mentioning Miss Davies, she praised her late husband's skill as a newspaperman, his politics and his patriotism, and gave me eight interesting letters he had written her at the time of the Spanish-American War.

W. A. Swanberg, 1971: "This harassed expression perhaps arose from long work on a very difficult subject, Henry Robinson Luce."

Again, when I worked on a biography of Theodore Dreiser, who easily outdid Hearst in philandering, I interviewed six of the many women who had been his mistress at one time or another—some simultaneously. All but one spoke candidly of her affair with him, told of his eccentricities and his kindnesses, one explaining much in a single sentence: "He was a great lover."

This though he had no spark of handsomeness, was paunchy, clumsy, sometimes surly. His good friend and sometime admirer Carl Vechten told me,

"Dreiser was devoid of taste of any kind—in clothing, manner, speech, romance, and often in his writing."

His second wife, Helen, inured to his side affairs, decided that he was unable to write without them— that it was these intrigues that released his genius. Several times, when they lived in Hollywood, she got late-night calls from the madam of a brothel on Western Avenue saying Dreiser was there, drunk and troublesome, and would someone please come and get him? His next-door neighbor, the actress Jane Wyatt, told me she was occasionally aroused in the small hours by boisterous Dreiser parties, and one night he was seen in pajamas chasing an unknown woman around the yard.

Yet the old rake could be charming when at his best. And had he not written the incomparable *Sister Carrie* and the towering *American Tragedy,* among other works? What biographer could fail to be fascinated by such a character? Or could do more than show the powerful inner conflicts, the great gifts and great faults which made his writing range from close to crude to the most moving poetry? How to "explain" the genius who could be selfish and cruel, yet who expressed such sympathy for the downtrodden in his writings?

I did my best—and was as astonished as I was pleased when the book had four Scribner printings, another for the Readers Subscription, and a Bantam paperback issue.

When our two children were grown my wife, Dorothy, joined me in cross-country research tours— time-consuming and expensive, what with airline fares, hotels, and meals—but as engrossing as they were essential. Dorothy, a short-hand whiz, recorded important letters by day and transcribed them at night in our hotel. I interviewed witnesses by tape recorder by day and likewise transcribed them by typewriter at night. This often meant a twelve- or fourteen-hour day, but what fascination! Handwritten letters were often close to indecipherable. The missives of such Dreiser friends as James Farrell and Llewelyn Powys seemed scrawled in some other language—usually too much for me—but Dot had a gift for hentracks and could translate them.

M‌y place of birth, involuntary as with everybody, was St. Paul, Minnesota, in 1907. That's a long time ago. Teddy Roosevelt was president, Rudyard Kipling won the Nobel Prize, Oklahoma became our forty-sixth state, and Henry Ford had almost perfected the Model T, which he would bring out the next year and of which he would ultimately sell fifteen million.

"Father, Charles Henning Swanberg, and Mother (née Valborg Larsen) at their marriage," St. Paul, 1892

Father had emigrated from Sweden at nineteen and become a skilled cabinetmaker, designing and building beautiful furniture of rare woods. Mother had emigrated from Norway at eighteen to become a fancy seamstress in St. Paul, where the two were married. Norwegian and Swedish are similar but not identical. As I grew up with my two brothers and two sisters (all older), our parents' language became a Norwegian-Swedish blend, finally becoming English, with an accent.

Father, a Socialist, read the *Literary Digest,* the *St. Paul Daily News,* the Socialist *Appeal to Reason,* and the Little Leather Library. He wanted me to become a cabinetmaker. I aimed to be a newspaperman, but he thought it a foolish waste of time for me to go to the University of Minnesota. Mother, on the other hand, had an innocent faith in education, and my sister Helen was on my side, but he held the purse strings. Much argument. At last he agreed to furnish board and room, but other expenses were mine.

College for me was a wild race between classes and part-time jobs. I made twenty-five dollars a month as janitor at the Midway Club in St. Paul, mopping floors and tidying up. I clerked for the YMCA, painted houses, and in summers handled freight for the Great Northern Railroad at a glorious $3.84 a day six days a week. More important, I dated Dorothy Green, two years behind me at the university but ahead of me otherwise, always taking her to football games to watch mighty Bronko Nagurski, greatest footballer of the era.

Alas, I graduated in 1930 after the market crash had sunk the nation in depression, and the Twin Cities newspapers where I had hoped to land said Sorry, bub, we're laying off old hands. The *St. Paul Daily News* and *Minneapolis Star* did permit me to review books for them, sole payment being a byline and the books reviewed. Well, didn't I have my foot in the door for a reporting job? No. Not a chance in that desolate time of mass unemployment. Back I went to the Great Northern and $3.84 a day, certainly being the only book reviewer also loading sacks of sugar and boxes of canned goods. But there

was satisfaction even in this work, the commonest of labor. It was outdoors, muscular and healthful, making one feel good and eat like a horse. And it required homely skills. Pulling a two-wheel truck loaded with hundreds of pounds of freight would throw you and the truck unless you balanced it as you rolled along. By now I was expert at it. I knew what common labor meant. And I became friendly with dozens of laborers—Poles, Russians, Germans, Hungarians, and others, including a kindly Lithuanian stevedore whose English was precarious but whom I still remember fondly.

Alas, people weren't buying. The volume of freight dwindled so that finally I was needed only a day or two a week, then not at all.

Unemployed again except for unpaid book reviews. Father said, "See? What good is that B.A.?"

In those parlous days one pulled every string to get work, with not a particle of shame. A college friend of mine now with a construction company hired me as laborer on a small building going up in St. Paul. Three dollars a day—not bad. It was pick-and-

"Little Willie Swanberg, age three (top right), with brother Henning (top left), sisters Helen and Almeda, and brother Carl," 1910

"As Bachelor of Arts, 1930, hoping vainly for newspaper work in that grim Depression year"

shovel work requiring no finesse, until we began pouring concrete.

This involved wheeling a concrete buggy, a creation of the devil consisting of a huge two-wheeled bucket containing six hundred pounds of wet concrete. Let me tell you, that buggy had to be balanced exquisitely or the whole cargo would be dumped and wasted. For all my skill with a freight truck, this was a new challenge. I was working with seasoned men who made it look easy. I dumped one buggy and got sharp profanity from the foreman. By the time I mastered it the job was finished and I was out of work again.

Dorothy had graduated with honors in 1932 and was a private secretary in the attorney general's office in the state capitol in St. Paul. Twenty dollars a week every week—terrific. But her betrothed, aged twenty-four, was now down to house painting, lawn mowing, window washing, and whatnot. How long would she put up with this? So far she had parried other beaux, including one scoundrel who not only had a steady job but a snappy Pontiac convertible.

Well, her father, a civil-engineer executive with the state highway department, sympathized and landed me as a chainman on a highway survey party. I started with a party working in International Falls, on the Canadian border 296 miles north of St. Paul. I even entertained the ignoble suspicion that he had arranged this to get me away and let some more qualified suitor replace me.

Our party consisted of the engineer in charge, an instrument man skilled at the transit, a rodman, and two lowly chainmen. There were things to learn. The chain, for example, was actually a one-hundred-foot steel tape which had to be handled with care and could be wound into a compact thick circle for easy transportation. Sounds easy, but winding the tape was a cute maneuver that had to be learned.

The pay was sixty dollars a month plus thirty dollars for subsistence. I found I could live for forty dollars a month, renting a room for five dollars a month and eating good twenty-five-cent restaurant dinners—meat, potatoes, salad, pie, and coffee. Yes—so it was in the Depression. As I wrote Dot (who saved all my letters over the decades), "The washlady here washed & ironed 3 shirts, one pair of pants, 6 underwears, 6 pairs of sox & 2 pajamas. That was 45¢, she said—imagine! I made her reluctantly accept 6 bits. She needs the money."

Running a line for a projected road was simple, though when it ran through woods we cleared brush and chopped down trees so the instrument man could see the rodman. But surveying for a new highway in actual construction was more complicated. There we operated ahead of the road builders and there'd be hell to pay if we held them up. We set stakes for grade not only at centerline and both edges of the finished road, but also stakes at the extreme edge of the fill. Figuring a two-to-one slope of gravel from the road edge to the constantly changing level of land on either side required quick basic mental math.

Our crew developed a warm camaraderie, working and eating together and—let's be honest—occasionally drinking together on Saturday nights. This was during Prohibition, but liquor of course was available. On one occasion our instrument man, who had a taste for alcohol, could barely stagger into the truck when we picked him up in the morning. Luckily, the engineer in charge was elsewhere. Our rodman took over the transit while the culprit snoozed in the truck until he was functional.

Five months of this, during which I saw Dot only in dreams and cherished her letters. Then—hallelujah!—we moved to a new project in Glenwood, only 135 miles from St. Paul. *And* my salary was raised $10 a month! Recklessly, I bought for $210 a usable 1929 Chevrolet. Life became glorious. I saw Dot every other weekend and otherwise traveled in search of a news job. The *St. Paul Daily News* still sent me books to review, but my foot in that door got no farther. I tried country weeklies in the Glenwood area—at Long Prairie, Sauk Centre (Sinclair Lewis's hometown), Alexandria, Wadena, and elsewhere, to no avail. Ditto at the other Twin City dailies and advertising firms. I consulted University of Minnesota journalism professors, but they admitted things were bleak all over.

At Glenwood, Roosevelt's National Recovery Administration was at work. Our survey party supervised nearby farmers—all once prosperous, now in straits—in gravelling and improving smaller side roads. The columnist Mark Sullivan thought better times might come in two or three years—discouraging indeed.

In September 1935 my blessed college friend George Scullin—working for Fawcett Publications in Minneapolis, the lucky fellow—opened a door. He was driving east to work in Fawcett's New York office. "Bill," he said, "come along with me. You might even land with Fawcett's there."

Father protested, "In times like this you're foolish to leave a steady paycheck for a dream." "Dad," I said, "I've had it. I'm going to be foolish."

With $185 in my pocket I said good-bye to Dot and was off on a long, long chance. In New York I took an eight-by-ten cell at the Sloane House YMCA—$5 a week. No room for me at Fawcett's, worse luck, but through George's good offices I got occasional freelance assignments for their *Modern Mechanics* magazine. On the side I tried cowboy stuff—actually sold one to *Popular Western* for $65. Job-hunting, I pounded pavements that were lined with the destitute, selling apples, toys, or pornography, shining shoes, playing an accordion in hopes for a nickel, or merely begging. On the subway one ragged beggar walked along with a tin cup, muttering a prayer as he stuck it in one's face. Another sang Irish ballads infamously and gathered a few pennies. Such open, widespread poverty I had never seen and hope never to see again.

I tried the tony slicks—even the *New Yorker*, imagine!—the *New York Times* and the rest of the papers, the book publishers too. Some were kindly, some impatient, but all said No. Maybe Father was right. I lowered my sights, tried less prestigious magazines, *Redbook, Collier's, American, Liberty* among them. No dice. Then the ripsnorting pulps such as

Argosy, Amazing Stories, Weird Tales, and the whole string of thrillers published by Street & Smith.

My freelance trickle saved me. I was down to forty-seven dollars in December when I walked into the Dell Publishing Company at 149 Madison Avenue.

There George T. Delacorte himself talked with me for a half hour in his luxurious office. I've never had such a lucky day. It happened that one of his assistant editors had left. It happened that he had worked on three magazines, two of them Westerns. How fortunate that I had studied Western pulps, had that one published Western to show him, and could talk knowledgeably about that field. The third was known in the trade as a "dick mag," *Inside Detective,* about which I knew less but discussed confidently.

I had a job, salary twenty-five dollars a week, as assistant editor of *Western Romances, All Western,* and *Inside Detective.* The editor under whom I worked, genial though I had much to learn, was often absent because of angina attacks. I worked for three months,

"Dorothy Upham Green was my fiancée, but marriage was painfully postponed by my lack of husbandly employment."

Swanberg on road survey crew near International Falls, Minnesota, "almost three hundred miles from Dorothy, in St. Paul"

still selling occasionally on the side, built a nest egg, then married Dorothy at long last and brought her to New York. Three cheers and a tiger!

"Delacorte is the most charming of men," I noted in my diary, "handsome, intelligent, brisk but kindly." Though already very wealthy, he had not yet reached the opulence and fame of later years as enormously successful book publisher who gave millions to his Columbia University alma mater and the city of New York.

In 1937 my editor left for health reasons and I was boss at forty dollars a week. Delacorte kept raising my pay so that I felt treasonous to be looking vainly for work at magazines of some literary pretensions. In 1939 he also put me in charge of *Foto,* a schlock imitation of the enormously successful *Life* magazine. I now had a private office, a secretary, and two assistants.

By then I was making fifty-five hundred dollars a year—very comfortable in those still depressed times—plus added revenue from occasional outside

writing. We bought a house (with mortgage) in Connecticut, a brand-new Chevrolet, and were living well when the Hitler war in Europe began to look menacing. The Depression, which had blighted the nation for ten dreary years, suddenly ended at last as a preparatory Uncle Sam built planes, tanks, jeeps, and guns at such a rate as to recruit millions of women at welding and other roughneck jobs formerly the exclusive property of men.

When we entered the war in 1941 the Dell personnel changed visibly as the younger men enlisted or were drafted. Soon my best assistant was gone to Fort Bragg and I had trouble replacing him with one who could spell—who was in fact a capable, thirtyish woman.

I was thirty-four, father of two, had impaired hearing, and was rejected by the army. In 1943, however, I enlisted in the Office of War Information and after a course of training was sent to England as an "information specialist," i.e., propagandist. The flight to Shannon on a huge four-prop China Clipper hydroplane took twenty-three-and-a-half hours, with a long stop in Newfoundland. I reached London on June 16, 1944, shortly after the Eisenhower landings in France and one day after the first Nazi buzzbombs hit the city.

Soon I was working in OWI publications in Grosvenor Square, across from the U.S. embassy, a unit headed by Harold Guinzburg, owner of Viking Press and the most benign of men. Visible from our office were blitz-ruined mansions of this loveliest of Mayfair squares. The top two stories of one four-story building were totally gone, and the only evidence of its original height was a fourth-story porcelain water closet supported only by its vertical piping. The hard-pressed Britons had had manpower only for meager emergency repairs. The WC, swaying slightly, was proof of this and of the excellence of British plumbing. The Toilet, as our group of editor-writers capitalized it, was a rousing symbol of durability and courage etched against the sky, heedless of danger and giving promise of victory. Yet rusting pipes would inevitably topple it. Imagine the ignominy of the unlucky passerby flattened by the falling Toilet instead of being gallantly erased by a buzzbomb.

Well, the bombs were numerous and dangerous, we were busy ten hours a day sending air-dropped publications to Nazi-occupied France and elsewhere, and a bit of levity was essential. With a colleague, Bill Bennett, I had an apartment at 2 Whitehall Court with a valet named Kendal. This luxury was shameful in grim wartime, but he came with the building and

"Pounding out copy for a Delacorte Western"

we could not have the apartment without him. My hurried diary for July 2 reads:

> The 3 most striking aspects of life here are the Toilet, our valet & the bombs. Kendal is a gem, wounded & decorated in WW1, grateful to us Americans for our help in this war, insistent on drawing our baths, polishing shoes, mending, despite our protests that we can do this ourselves. The buzz-bombs (also called V-1's, pilotless planes, flybombs, doodlebugs & less genteel names) are historic—world's first bombardment by self-propelled missiles. Are launched from Nazi-held Pas-de-Calais 90 miles away. Some shot down by coastal guns but hundreds get through at 400 mph, only about 4000-foot altitude, easily visible by day & by night by flaming exhaust. They roar in until timing device stops engine over London. They drop & explode high-blast warhead. Sirens alert us 10–20 times daily. Wild rumors say London more dangerous than frontlines. One concerns injured English-

woman pulled from wreckage and asked where husband was. "He's at the front, the bloody coward," she purportedly replied. Necessary fish story: I write nervous Dorothy at home doodlebugs are insignificant.

It was of course a civilian terror weapon. Years later, Winston Churchill wrote: "This new form of attack imposed upon the people of London a burden perhaps heavier than [the earlier blitz]. Suspense and strain were more prolonged. Dawn brought no relief, and cloud no comfort. . . . The blind impersonal nature of the missile made the individual on the ground feel helpless. There was little that he could do, no human enemy that he could see shot down."

We were sending persuasive material to Frenchmen behind the German lines about Eisenhower's steady advance, though there was the hitch that some of Ike's shells and bombs were wrecking French towns and killing Frenchmen. London was catching it worse, giving the Nazis their own propaganda weapon, as my July 9 entry shows:

Hitler aim is to cause such devastation & fright as to collapse the Londoners & the Brit govt. itself. Destruction is such that a million women & children are evacuated beyond the city—enormous project that can't be hidden. The Nazis' Joe Goebbels exults by press & radio that London is "an inferno," its people fleeing, & England will soon have to capitulate. Indeed, total evacuation of London was considered for a time. "What a brainwash scoop this is for Goebbels," Bennett says rightly.

Our own propaganda concentrated on the Allied advance and the certainty of victory. A buzzbomb fell in Conduit Street, four blocks from our office, leveling many buildings and crashing our east windows. Our crew invented wry parodies of popular songs: "Nothing could be fina / Than to be in Carolina / Far from bombing"; and, "In a little English town 'twas on a night like this; / Bombs were ricocheting down 'twas on a night like this." English newspapers were permitted only to declare each day that bombs fell on the "south of England," though all but a few misfires hit London. Nothing was printed until after the war about the bomb that fell June 20 on the Guards' Chapel in Westminster, killing 119 Sunday worshipers, many of them ranking officers, and injuring many more, though everybody heard about it via the grapevine.

Kendal treated Bennett and me almost with reverence as emissaries of Roosevelt and Eisenhower who were "saving Britain." He addressed us as Sirs, though we threatened to call him Lord Mayor Kendal or Sir Knight of the Garter Kendal. He woke us gently in mornings, raised the blackout curtains, and gave us a summary of late news he heard on BBC. A widower who had lost his only son in this war, alone in the world, he was kind father to us. He wore his World War I medal only on days of celebration. My August 26 entry:

Kendal woke me, wearing medal, aglow with news of Allied liberation of Paris after 4 Nazi years. "Isn't it wonderful, sir! Your Gen. Eisenhower is simply splendid!" The OWI Directive on policy, usually so cautious, breaks into song: "The end of the war is in sight. . . . The Allies are on the road to Berlin."

Entry for August 29, three days later:

"As writer-editor for Office of War Information during World War II, visiting U.S. Air Force bomber base near Ipswich, England," 1944

Hallelujah!—Allies took Pas-de-Calais from which doodlebugs are fired—now beyond range of London. No more bombs. Repeat: NO MORE BOMBS. City radiates relief. Min. of Works Duncan Sandys proclaims "battle of London is won." Newspapers glow with ecstatic headlines. Sleepers quit bomb shelters & deep Underground stations. Bennett pointed across Gro. Sq.— indomitable Toilet still proudly aloft despite some close doodlebugs. We gave her a cheer. Someone invented new parody: "Joyful all ye scribblers rise, / No more buzz-bombs in the skies. . . ." Got fine letter from Delacorte—wants me back.

Short-lived relief, as my September 8 entry noted: "Heard several bomb explosions today. How come????"

These were soon identified as the new Nazi terror weapon, the first of many V-2's. A monster 12-

ton rocket, 47 feet long and 5 feet in diameter, it carried 2,200 pounds of explosives, more than double V-l's. Momentously, V-2 inaugurated the present rocket-missile age, soaring 50 miles high at 4,000 miles per hour. With its 200-mile range, it was now being launched from Holland, still in Nazi hands. September 21 diary entry:

> Eerie V-2 begets new psychology of terror making noisy & visible V-l's genial by comparison. Can't be seen or heard—no warning possible. Can strike anywhere any time. London fearful again, yet still sparks of humor. Berkeley Sq. chemist shop has sign: "BISMUTH AS USUAL DURING ALTERCATIONS." Kendal says "We must concede, sir, that the Nazis are expert at machines of terror."

One of them wrecked Selfridge's big department store, killing many—no word of it in the press. The invincible Toilet, only two blocks away, stood fast. My November 23 entry:

> My 37th birthday, freezing. Coal shortage keeps office & apt. around 50°. We see our breaths, wear long Johns, 2 wool sweaters. Today stayed in bed, fierce cold. Kendal treats me with vile remedy of his own, fixed me hot soup. Am now in charge of publication for Nazi-occupied Norway, must get back to work tomorrow. Feel sorry for myself—Dorothy & kids 3,000 miles away on my birthday, dammitall. All right—think of GI's in France, poor bastards, getting shot at, no Kendal to nurse 'em.

At Christmas, darkened terribly by the smashing Nazi counterattack in the Ardennes, Bennett and I gave Kendal goodies from our U.S. Post Exchange: cigarettes, costing Britons the equivalent of eighty cents a pack but seventeen cents a pack in our PX; and chocolate bars, chocolate being virtually unobtainable in England. To this we added a five-pound note, equaling about twenty dollars then. Such gratitude! But later he left the money on my dresser, this overreaching his firm British code. We worked all Christmas Day, Bennett inventing a new parody: "Holy Night, Silent Night, / All is ruin, all is blight."

At last the Nazis were hurled back, the Rhine was bridged, and by February Patton's force began its race into Germany and the great Russian army was in Prussia. I noted March 18, 1945:

Germans still fight on—pure fanaticism. V-2's still fall in England's 289th week of war. That's 5½ years. Some comment about huge Regent's Park zoo—what if bomb should liberate tigers & bears? BBC Symphony still plays at Albert Hall. Only remote mention of bombs in the press, but they plug great national event, the hearing of the first spring cuckoo in Sussex. So far only 4 OWI people bomb-injured, mostly by flying glass.

Then the discovery of the reeking Nazi slave camps—a true symbol of Hitler's world order. On April 13 Kendal woke me sorrowfully. "I have sad news, sir. President Roosevelt is dead. What a pity that great man missed seeing victory." All England went into mourning, with memorial services at every church in the land. Better news April 30—Mussolini was shot with his mistress, then both hanged in Milan as a public spectacle.

Best of all news May 8, when Kendal woke me at 6:30, his face blithesome, his medal shining: "It's all over, sir! All over! Peace at last!" V-E Day saw half-ruined London's greatest celebration, with bands, parades, bells, foghorns, fireworks, dancing in the streets, and such a raid on the pubs that we OWI men, working until two, found not a drop, all pubs closed.

That blessed Toilet, our lucky talisman, had come through it all, and now towered grandly over cheering crowds in the square.

There was of course still a matter of beating the Japanese. OWI was finished in Europe, but I was now a member of the U.S. Information Service and sent to Copenhagen, Oslo, and Stockholm to publicize the bitter remainder of the war to the Scandinavians. I was in Oslo when the papers headlined "ATOMBOMBEN ER EN FAKTUM," which could be loosely translated "The Atom Bomb Is for Real." Japan quit August 14, but not until late October 1945 did I sail on the GI-packed *Aquitania*, tingle at the sight of the Statue of Liberty in New York Harbor, and rejoin my precious Dorothy, daughter, Sara, and son, Jack. How the kids had grown in a year and a half!

I had had enough of editing pulps, but the everkindly Delacorte gave me freelance work and I spread to other magazines—*True, Modern Mechanics, This Week, Redbook*, yes, even the *Woman's Home Companion*. Not until 1953—I was a balding forty-six—was I financially able to subtract time from articles and work on my first book, *Sickles the Incredible,* about an astonishing Civil War general, killer of his wife's lover and famous wheeler-dealer. Scribner's bought it, and here I first met their top editor, Burroughs Mitchell, successor to the legendary Maxwell Perkins and my warm friend for a quarter century. Anthony West gave *Sickles* an enthusiastic review in the *New Yorker* and I was off and running, or at least loping.

So I was happily associated with a proud house founded in 1846 which had published work by such as Mark Twain, Kipling, Edith Wharton, Stephen Crane, and William Dean Howells. Later, under the miraculous Maxwell Perkins, had come that unimaginably rich and profitable stream of books by authors including Hemingway, Fitzgerald, Ring Lardner, Thomas Wolfe, and Max Eastman. At Scribner's I was walking on hallowed ground, including the spot where Hemingway and Eastman, meeting there by chance and in sharp literary disagreement, fought and rolled on the floor before being separated. Now, despite an occasional best-seller and the great sale of James Jones's *From Here to Eternity,* profits had leveled.

I got a literary agent, the nonpareil McIntosh & Otis, permitting me to say I had the same agent as such an eminent writer as John Steinbeck. From then on I was always working on a book. Each took from two to four years, so I sandwiched in magazine articles for ready cash. My second effort, *First Blood,* was a Book-of-the Month selection, reviewed enthusiastically by John P. Marquand, and did well indeed. Then came *Jim Fisk,* about the most colorful of rascals, which was featured on the cover of the *Saturday Review* but for all that made only a modest profit.

Next, *Citizen Hearst,* a job taking me almost four years but worth it. It made the *New York Times* bestseller list for twenty-six weeks, was a Book-of-the-Month selection, won the Frank Luther Mott award for research, then went through three successive paperback issues and was also published in England and France.

Surprise: the book was nominated by the advisory board for the Pulitzer Prize, normally making the prize automatic. Not so this time. The Columbia University fathers, jury of last resort, rejected it on the ground that Hearst lacked the qualities of principled patriotism decreed by the donor, Joseph Pulitzer. Never having happened before, this made quite a newspaper stir. My daughter, Sara, said truly, "Congratulations, Dad, sort of." Scribner's foxily advertised it as "Unanimously recommended for the Pulitzer Prize."

Then, after the Dreiser tome already mentioned, I worked on that same Joseph Pulitzer, Hearst's bitterest rival—a book that was a Literary Guild selection, winner of the Van Wyck Brooks Award, and with a paperback issue was nicely profitable.

On research travels one meets informants and librarians who become lifelong friends. At home I made steady use of the great New York Public Library and the Yale Library. Newspapers dating back decades were vital in the research, and mind you, this was before they were microfilmed. Libraries kept them in bundles of their original sheets, yellowed, dusty, and sometimes tattered. Occasionally I found a valuable news story whose ending, confound it, was torn away and lost. One needed an immediate shower after fighting those grimy bundles.

Advertisement in New York Times *for* Citizen Hearst, *best-selling of author's ten Scribner books, 1961*

One peril in writing biographies is the humiliating realization of one's own humdrum life compared with those of his electrifying subjects. One must be content with the secondhand excitement of research. And research requires the fastidious organization of literally thousands of notes, short and long, differing in time and context.

At home came the job of transferring the finished notes to hundreds of eight-by-five file cards in chronological order of the subject's life. Then the question—how to organize into a smooth story this immense goulash of notes ranging from a sentence or two to scores of paragraphs. And to evaluate each source, a close friend of the subject being more credible than a mere acquaintance, the *New York Times* being more reliable than some others. And to reconcile conflicting evidence—*that* could make you tear your hair.

Then the challenge—combing that formidable bushel of cards and beginning the script. The protagonist as infant could be quite dull. It is usually better to start with him involved in a climactic event of his later career. This gives the reader an immediate picture of the adult subject and (one hopes) seizes his interest. A universal law of narrative, from pulp fiction to serious writing, is that to bore the reader at the start is fatal.

My first draft was a mess, useful in organization and in solving interpretive problems along the way. The second was improved but still crying for repair. The third was the best I could do—for the Hearst book almost six hundred pages long—to be handed to Burroughs Mitchell with the hope that he would say "Good."

On a biography of the late Henry R. Luce I was caught in dilemmas. Born in China of Presbyterian missionaries, Luce had won fame and millions with his powerful *Time-Life-Fortune* trio. I knew of course that they slanted the news, but didn't know the half of it until I had studied their treatment of world affairs going back almost a half century. Early on Luce had cheered Mussolini and seen fascism as a brilliant new idea in effective government. His Calvinist terror of godless communism would rule him lifelong so that his magazines became foxy organs of cold-war, far-right propaganda.

While I was as anti-Red as anyone, fascism was as frightening. I had seen personally how it worked. Truth in news is obviously the first essential in a democracy. We wanted no *Pravda* or *Völkischer Beobachter* here. *Time's* liking for Mussolini soon spread to Hitler as a promising force in Germany, soft-pedaling the blood purges.

I was in a pretty pass. I received kindness and cooperation at Time Inc.'s skyscraper. *Life* had published a feature on my Hearst book and paid me handsomely. I was given my own desk in the archives room, jammed with letters and records open to me. The top people there, along with veteran staff men and women who had worked under Luce for years, gave me helpful interviews, as did his relatives, his first wife, and his widow, Clare Boothe Luce.

So? What else to do but tell the truth as I found it, let the chips fall. I had wanted to be a newspaperman, never made it, but had strong feelings about truth in news.

Not all of Luce's staff assented to this newsdoctoring, known as the meat-grinder. Archibald MacLeish, a dear Luce friend and top writer, told me of his disgust at this partiality for dictators as foes of communism. This principled man—later to win three Pulitzer prizes and hold high government office—complained uselessly to Luce and quit. The former *Time*man John Barkham related how dispatches from foreign correspondents were often thrown away in New York while the meat-grinder recast them in the Luceline. Theodore White told me of seeing his cables from China redone in New York to laud the corrupt—but Christian—Chiang Kai-Shek, who appeared on *Time's* cover six times. He quit, as did Walter Graebner in London. Dwight Macdonald quit over this propaganda called news. So did Merle Miller, so fed up that he attacked it in public lectures. Luce's mighty general manager, Ralph Ingersoll, quit to found a liberal newspaper opposing the *Time*slant.

John Hersey, long *Time's* Moscow man, delivered the supreme crusher. He told Luce that *Time* contained about the same amount of truth as *Pravda*, and left for more honest work.

Yet Time Inc. won Luce millions and great political power. To appear on *Time's* cover was the ultimate mark of greatness, inspiring gratitude among those so honored. In 1952 Luce sailed to England with his friend and highly paid contributor to *Life* Winston Churchill (thrice on *Time's* cover), discussed world problems with him, and informed the home office that England was too amiable toward the Soviets. He then crossed to Paris to confer with General Eisenhower, busy there in the formation of NATO and the likely Republican candidate for president. Ike had been six times on the cover, once as Man of the Year, and was nothing if not cordial. Luce's aim was partly to find if Mamie Eisenhower's drinking might be an intolerable embarrassment.

Perhaps more important was his wish to ingratiate himself with the man he knew he could help elect president.

He had a wistful desire to be a frequent White House caller, a presidential crony (as he certainly had never been under Roosevelt and Truman). He also wanted high public office. He got along grandly with Ike, and also felt that Mamie's rumored weakness was not a hazard. The later Lucepress championing of Ike was so vividly biased (as was its contempt for the Democrat Adlai Stevenson) as to outrage one of Luce's top editors, Thomas Griffith, already straining over meat-grinder journalism.

After Ike's landslide election, he chatted with Luce in the White House and asked what job he would like. Luce said the only post he really wanted was Secretary of State, though he modestly admitted he was not sure he was sufficiently qualified. No argument about that, and Luce's good friend John Foster Dulles, with highest anti-Communist credentials, got the job. But Luce's wife Clare wanted to be ambassador to Italy, and was so named.

Luce's perpetual propagandizing of his primary political-moral passion—fear and hatred of communism—so troubled a group of liberal staff men that he received their unsigned protest at *Time*'s "descent to the Communist propaganda level by using semantics, unproved rumors, and hate and fear appeals." They disliked seeing "*Time* condone (as it has) objectionable foreign parties and governments just because they are anti-Communist." Yet many staff people, some agreeing with Luce or not politically concerned, enjoyed Luce's kindliness, generous salaries, and the prestige widely associated with working for him. There was often bitter feeling between these two camps.

"I am for God, big business, and the Republican party," Luce said frankly. Though he disliked Senator McCarthy's methods, "If you find one Red under your bed, or in the State Department, you disqualify the term 'witch-hunt.'"

He was incensed by the report of a sage investigative body, the Committee on the Freedom of the Press, which castigated the Lucepress without naming it. It said in small part that the press "should assume the duty of publishing significant ideas contrary to their own." It "should identify the sources of its facts, opinions, and arguments so that the reader can judge them. . . . Identification of source is necessary in a free society." (*Time* was so notorious for quoting unidentified "observers" giving Luce opinions that competing newsmen called them "Delphic Oracles.") More, "The plugging of special color and 'hate' words . . . performs inevitably the same image-

making function." And "Of equal importance . . . are the identification of fact as fact and opinion as opinion . . ."

In a bristling speech to the *Time* staff after the Eisenhower election, Luce said, "I am literally your boss," adding that "moral truth" was essential and the idea that correct objectivity meant that "a writer presents facts without applying any value judgment to them" was "strictly a phony." The vital thing in newswriting was "having a correct value judgment."

"Moral truth" and "value judgment" were of course his names for his opinion-propaganda, not so identified. *Time* editor Thomas Griffith noted the boss's ability to "disconnect his conscience momentarily, as one might a hearing aid." Griffith agreed with Democratic charges that *Time* was "the 'house organ' of the Eisenhower regime." He dared to write Luce an angry memo about its national news:

> It is dishonest, and its dishonesty is spreading a cynicism through the rest of the magazine. . . . *Time* used to 'cheat' a little in the campaign's final month . . . now it's a four-year proposition. [It amounted, he added, to saying] the Republican Party interest is the National interest. . . . We are getting into worse and worse habits; and like dope users, increasing the dosage.

No use. The dosage was increased further in the endless, tragic Vietnam War, fought of course against Communists. Luce put our General Westmoreland on *Time*'s cover and lauded his brilliant command, though it seemed to get nowhere despite heavy losses. As A. J. Liebling observed, Luce had some good correspondents "but he has never been able to believe them unless they tell him what he already thinks."

The cabled dispatches of *Time*'s Vietnam correspondents Charles Mohr and Merton Perry telling of American setbacks were recast in the New York meat-grinder with enthusiasm for U.S. progress. They complained uselessly, then finally resigned to take jobs with other journals that would believe them. So too with Robert Anson, a *Time* youngling in Vietnam who wrote so vividly of the American bombings and the My Lai Massacre that *Time*—Hedley Donovan was Luce's heir as top boss—had his dispatches purified. A cable to Anson said, "the reader has a right not to be confused as to where *Time* stands." The word "stands" is emblematic of the value judgment. Anson quit to become a freelancer.

"The two Swanberg collaborators, at home in Newtown, Connecticut, approaching end of a long, long book script for Scribner's"

Years later, in retirement, Donovan made interesting admissions in his 1989 autobiography. In a private talk with Luce he had broached the touchy subject of the meat-grinder. He reports saying that many academics and intellectuals "loathed" *Time*—felt it should be honestly called "a journal of opinion." Further, he told the boss that "it is possible to be too opinionated," that *Time* "could be shallow and was often unfair," that it "did not always let the 'other side' make its case."

True indeed, but asking Luce to renounce the "value judgment" was as to ask the Pope to disown Christ, and Donovan got nowhere. In fact he himself strongly supported the Vietnam bloodbath, in which *Time* invariably followed administration taradiddle about victorious progress, rewrote its own Vietnam correspondents' unhappy cables to fit the victory line, and assailed doubters.

Donovan's support for the war continued after Luce's death and he had become top man. He made several trips to Vietnam, bringing back rosy reports. At long last, with terrible casualties and mass public protest growing thunderous across the land (and perhaps threatening *Time*'s circulation), Donovan finally saw it as ruinous, writing, "I wish I had been wiser sooner."

That was something, as the cliché goes, that he could say again. No telling how much *Time*'s influential cheerleading extended a senseless war that (aside from countless Vietnamese) cost us some 56,000 Americans dead, 304,000 wounded, and $111 billion in mere money. All for naught despite those engraved stones in Washington. My own son, Jack, served four years in Vietnam as an air officer and, thank God, came home alive. Earlier I was offered an honorary degree by Northwestern University—a salute I would have prized—but rejected it because of the then widespread university acquiescence to the war.

Donovan writes, "W. A. Swanberg put a prodigious amount of research into *Luce and His Empire*. The result is disappointing. Swanberg has claimed that he set out to write an 'objective' biography, but says he abandoned that idea . . . because he became persuaded that Luce had been a thoroughly sinister force in American opinion and policy. That . . . is the thesis of his book, which includes lurid exaggerations of the influence of Luce and Time Inc., considerable though they were."

Considerable indeed. On Luce's death, Donovan himself wrote that "he came to be called the most influential private citizen in the country." Is that a lurid exaggeration?

I'm delighted at *his* book, *Right Places, Right Times: Forty Years in Journalism Not Counting My Paper Route,* which gives a lovely though involuntary example of how years of Lucework makes it hard for a Luceman to throw off the meat-grinder. Does he mention the departure of Archibald MacLeish and Ralph Ingersoll out of disgust at it? Or the similar exit of Merle Miller, Dwight Macdonald, Merton Perry, and others? No. Or Thomas Griffith's squawk to Luce about *Time*'s "dishonesty" and its "increasing the dosage like drug users"? Or the Free Press Committee's emphasis on the duty to report opposing opinion? Or the *Time* staff protest against "descent to the Communist propaganda level"? Or Hersey's remark that *Pravda* and *Time* were about equally truthful?

He skips such embarrassments. And is Donovan, paid handsomely by Luce for many years despite his own nagging scruples about *Time*'s "unfairness," qualified to complain about "objectivity" or "exaggeration"?

What do you think?

I'm happy to get into that, for my Luce book was examined by a Pulitzer advisory board composed of distinguished journalists. Does Donovan mention this? No. And that the advisory board did not find the book "disappointing" or filled with "lurid exaggeration"? In fact that they actually *liked* it and disagreed with him and agreed with me so categorically that they awarded *Luce and His Empire* the Pulitzer Prize for 1973—this time approved by Columbia University?

No. That's another "opposing opinion" he overlooks.

Do you suppose that his failure to mention this award might have been caused by the intuition that it would tend to, shall we say, invalidate his opinion? And was not the failure to publish opposing opinion—in fact to attack and smear it—the abiding bane of the Lucepress?

Dear reader, I leave it to you.

I dwell on this at shocking length because the three years I spent on Luce were among the hardest of my life. It is not easy for a puny inkslinger to challenge a colossus of such wealth and prestige. I checked and rechecked records and interviews until I was blue in the face to make sure I was right. It was worth it.

Yet Donovan must at least be credited with having qualms about the news-doctoring, however much he had felt forced to comply with it. After Luce's death *Time* began to soften the meat-grinder and the dosage—very gradually, no doubt to avoid bewildering readers—and the "newsmagazine" became a relatively honest woman. I like to think that the shock of my "lurid" book, with the salute given it, its wide sale, and the comment it caused, had just a teeny bit of influence in that direction. I think *Time* now a reasonably dependable publication, not inclined to manipulate news, damn all opposition, or push us into war.

The 720-page Luce script I finally handed in to Burroughs Mitchell was the eighth book I had done for him in eighteen years. We were warmest friends, seeing eye to eye. The book was printed exactly as written and he took me to a celebratory dinner at Côte Basque, with wine, when it won the prize.

Mitchell, out of Bowdoin College, had worked under Maxwell Perkins's wing only a year and a half before the great editor died, but had absorbed much of his finesse. He had discriminating judgment, a fine sense of narrative, and could instantly pick out a clumsy passage or a single inappropriate word. He worked on books by many others, including P. D. James, Morton Thompson, C. P. Snow, and the brilliant but unpredictable James Jones. After Jones's tremendous, best-selling army story *From Here to Eternity*—which became an equally smashing motion picture—he worked on his *Some Came Running,* a long complexity rampant with obscenities not then accepted as they are now. Mitchell visited him at his Illinois home in an effort to improve the story, becoming involved in typical Jones carouses, during which Jones invariably fell on his face. *Some Came Running* was a loser for all that, though Jones would recover later and turn out fine fiction, but for another publisher.

Charles Scribner Jr., was the third—or was it the fourth?—Scribner to run this fine house. A St. Paul's and Princeton man, he was handsome, cordial though reticent, but there were times when I thought he looked worried. The firm had prospered during the fabulous Hemingway-Fitzgerald era decades earlier, but neither Scribner's nor anyone else had such a glorious stable of writers now. The famous Scribner bookstore right downstairs in the 597 Fifth Avenue building had growing competition.

Unknown to me then, later evidence indicated that profits were declining. They needed new Hemingways and Fitzgeralds and did not have them. The Jones book, after such high hopes, was a great disappointment and financial loss, and evidently there were others. The fast rise of television stole reading time from the public, reduced book sales, and distressed all publishers. Though there was no open bewailing at Scribner's, and Burroughs Mitchell seemed his old cheerful self, trouble was brewing.

Meanwhile Dorothy and I and the children made annual auto trips to Minnesota, the homeland. There were warm reunions with our families and old friends. And how wonderfully self-satisfying to be interviewed by the Twin Cities newspapers where I had once been unable to buy a job, including the *St. Paul Daily News* and *Minneapolis Star,* for which I had once reviewed books gratis. And to receive the Minnesota North Star Award for my writings at a grand dinner at the St. Paul Hotel, with the governor and other eminent people present. And to see that Father no longer thought me foolish for not becoming a cabinetmaker; vindication at last.

But he was bewildered by the singularities in publishing and advertising. He had read in his St. Paul paper an article I had written for *This Week,* the Sunday supplement appearing in many newspapers. *This Week* had paid me four hundred dollars for it.

"But they give us *This Week* free with the paper," he exclaimed. "How can they possibly pay you for it?"

I visited the University of Minnesota, chatted with a few of my old professors, and was interviewed on the university radio. This was years ago, and there was still a provincial feeling that one who had gone to glittering Gotham and published books must be rich and famous. Several of my old college friends had done far better financially than I—one as a prosperous physician, others in business.

Every man to his own. Each book involved problems quite apart from research and writing. How many pages would the subject require? How many pictures were available, and should they be bunched in a group or scattered to coincide with events in the story (the latter more expensive)? And how about title?—very important. A dull title could kill. I thought *Citizen Hearst* excellent, *Luce and His Empire* only passable, and the single-word title *Dreiser* dreadful—yet we could think of nothing better.

And clerical work: one must get written permission to quote from private letters and earlier books or risk getting sued. One also needed a basic sense of libel on books involving people still living. For safety's

sake the finished script was given to Scribner's lawyer, who went over it line by line to find comment which might cause lawsuits—especially in the Luce book, critical of a whole large organization and people in it. I recall only a few cautious changes, and there was never a lawsuit.

The documentation, with hundreds of footnotes, was itself a tricky job. And the Author's Note, in which he gave some idea of his aims and also acknowledged the help of many scores of witnesses and librarians whom he must not forget. And the Index, which could be done for a fee by a professional but which Dorothy and I compiled ourselves and actually enjoyed. And the promotion, requiring powwows with the firm's publicity director and a special script or two.

Then the jacket, the jacket! It had to be both attractive and meaningful. On these I had many parleys with Scribner's splendid art director, Greta Franzen.

After Luce, I worked on a biography of the late Norman Thomas, a genial giant whom I had once heard speak superbly at a Minnesota convocation. Six times Socialist candidate for president, he had been snowed under each time. Though I felt socialism utopian, Thomas was so fearless in tactics that he managed to make honesty and principle exciting. He was steadily attacked, hounded, defamed by conservatives who—yes—falsely linked him with communism. He was turned on by old friends, disowned by his dear alma mater, Princeton, suffered physical blows, and was even jailed briefly. If mistaken, he was nevertheless a paragon and hero, a model of intelligence and decency in politics.

Now, deciding on a print order for a book is anything but a scientific matter. If one only knew how many readers would buy a book, what waste would be avoided, how much simpler publishing would be. The Thomas print order was entirely for Charlie Scribner and Burroughs Mitchell to decide. Doubtless influenced by the Luce success and prize, they ordered far too many thousands.

Alas, poor Norman Thomas lost this election too. The book, though widely praised and with a sparkling review in the *New York Times,* mildewed on the bookstands and lost money. Ironically, it later won the coveted National Book Award—recognition that seemed at any rate to absolve me of doing a poor job.

That big print order was not my fault, but Charlie Scribner seemed less affable thereafter. I had been warmly loyal, having declined attractive offers from McGraw-Hill, Atheneum, and Harcourt Brace

Jovanovich. My old friend Burroughs Mitchell was retired for reasons unknown to me. In some perplexity I worked three years on my last book, about the astonishing Whitney family of New York. My new editor, luckily, was the charming and thoroughly capable Laurie Graham. The book got fine reviews in the *New Yorker* and *Wall Street Journal,* which Charlie used in advertising. It did very well and was a Book-of-the-Month selection. End of story, almost.

At seventy-three I settled comfortably with my family in Newtown, Connecticut, fifty-five miles from New York. I gardened enthusiastically, reviewed books for the *New York Times, Washington Post, Chicago Sun-Times,* and others, selling articles now and then to magazines, including *American Heritage* and *Yankee.* It was nice not to be pressed.

Then it happened. In 1984 Scribner's, along with two others, was sold to big Macmillan, though keeping its own famous imprint. A few years later the whole Macmillan agglomeration was bought by the huge, English Robert Maxwell firm. One had to say

that the Scribner imprint had lost much of its 140-year independent identity.

It has happened to almost all of them. Simon & Schuster became part of Gulf & Western, as did Prentice-Hall, Summit, Fireside, Pocket Books, and others. The revered Alfred A. Knopf, along with Pantheon, was taken over by Random House (of which more later). Harper's, of long prestige, took over Crowell and Lippincott, then was ingested by the Rupert Murdoch empire—the man who owns publications and television stations in several countries and has a sharp eye on profit.

More: Holt, Rinehart & Winston—itself a merger of three independent publishers—became the property of CBS. The international Penguin book colossus now owns Viking, Dutton, Signet, New American Library, and others. The Hearst Corporation bought Morrow, Arbor House, Avon, and nine other imprints. World Publishers became a subsidiary of the big Times Mirror complex. Time Inc. (itself a huge book publisher) purchased Little, Brown and the Book-of-the-Month Club, and Time then merged with Warner Communications.

"Swanberg parents with son, Jack, now a naval reserve captain, and daughter, Sara, now living in Oregon with her own family," 1981

And my old benefactor George T. Delacorte, Jr., whose Dell Publishing Company had long since become a thriving book publisher and had bought out Dial Press and others, sold out to big Doubleday, owner also of Bantam. Now hear this: Doubleday also owned the New York Mets baseball club—an odd literary linkage but perhaps giving them books about Met stars. And later Doubleday (but not the ball club) was sold to the huge German publisher Bertelsmann, which fired several hundred Doubleday people and is now owner of thirty-six imprints.

There have been many other buy-outs, but these will do. Let's get back to important Random House, which was bought by the vast $10 billion Newhouse multicompany, owner of forty American newspapers, seven TV stations, and prestigious magazines—the *New Yorker, Vogue,* others.

If you're still with me, through Random House, Newhouse accumulated a raft of once independent publishers, including Times Books, Vintage, Schocken, Crown, Fawcett, Ballantine, Villard, Clarkson Potter, and a few more.

Came the explosion of 1990, when one of the herd of Newhouse-Random House imprints, the respected Pantheon Books, was in the red. Its boss was fired, there were other layoffs, and a Newhouse deputy arrived to restore profits. Four senior editors resigned in protest at being "Newhoused." Forty editors and managers issued a statement attacking the "Newhousing." The head of the Authors' Guild lamented the "increasing pile-up of publishing power into the hands of fewer people." An unprecedented publishing storm arose, causing headlines.

In the highbrow *New York Review of Books* appeared a full-page denunciation of Newhouse's "assault on editorial independence and cultural freedom," which "chills the intellectual environment." It was signed by 288 writers, including such stars as Nadine Gordimer, John Hersey, Arthur Miller, William Styron, and Kurt Vonnegut. They did not say that Newhouse would rather publish best-selling junk than risky quality. But the *New York Times* noted that authors, including E. L. Doctorow, feared that because of conglomerate publishing "the commercial may be trampling on the creative in a drive to make publishing just another industry," a similar thought.

The best-selling Studs Terkel was among Random House writers who threatened to find another publisher. And James Michener—that eighty-three-year-old author of smash hits by the dozen—said he was "devastated" by the Random House uproar and talked of leaving it for "some small house obedient to the old traditions." But the old traditions have pretty

well faded, as have the small houses. An angry Newhouse partisan described complaining writers as "charity seekers" wanting a "free ride on Newhouse money."

Sure, books were always sold for a profit, but let us not confuse the great old publishers with their conglomerate preemptors. Such editors as Max Perkins and Burroughs Mitchell would be jobless now. They sought a good sale, to be sure, but demanded high quality. Many present editors yearn for quality but understand that they are first and foremost salesmen.

Hats off, say I, to the late great Archibald MacLeish, who rebelled when his longtime publisher considered an offer of purchase from a conglomerate also selling farm machinery. "I want to be published by a *publisher,*" he snapped, "not by a maker of farm machinery." And as Gerald Howard, an editor with the eminent and still independent W. W. Norton publishing house, wrote in the *American Scholar:*

> . . . today almost all the houses bearing the great names of American publishers are either huge corporations themselves or smoothly integrated into vast corporative combines. They now dance to the tune of big-time finance, and it's not a fox-trot; it's a bruising slam dance.

And now the other end of publishing—the selling of books—has also been invaded by corporate biggies. Dwindling is the dear old bookstore where the book-loving owner read his stock and told customers all about it. Now we have such huge chains as Waldenbooks, owning twelve hundred bookstores, seeking blockbusters that can be read in an hour or two, uninterested in important works that might sell less than thirty thousand copies—once considered a rousing sale. The chains now sell about half of all books sold and hence have great impact on publishers, who naturally reject some fine books not likely to be best-sellers in favor of quickies. Thus we are flooded with unbuttoned shockers replete with scandal, and ghosted "autobiographies" of football linebackers, rock singers, and raunchy film folk.

No wonder the respected *Publishers Weekly* called the eighties the "roller-coaster decade" of "sometimes reckless growth," and 1989 a year that "often seemed to be more about money than books." As did Arthur Lumsden, head of Dodd, Mead, who said, "It's time to throw the money changers out of the temple."

"Three grandchildren—Jessica, Caleb, and Zachary Spiegel, Sara's children—cluster around Grandmother Dorothy at a celebration of her seventy-fifth birthday," 1985

The hard-sell unloading of books has an ideal accomplice in radio and TV hype. A prime example was Jacqueline Susann's *Valley of the Dolls,* described by one critic as "literary trash." But Ms. Susann was so active on the air that it was said that "the only thing you could turn on without getting her was the water faucet." She sold 350,000 hardcovers and 22 million paperbacks. For years Merv Griffin, Johnny Carson, Mike Douglas, and others puffed books—many of them regarded as junk—and sold them fast. Now books and authors are whooped-up on hundreds of nationwide and local programs. The emcees range in great numbers from Larry King to Dick Cavett, who promote books and authors almost every night in the week.

Publishers now depend heavily on this. Authors are expected to appear on many programs, are coached on how to charm the public and warned to have a copy of the book to show the cameras, since the emcee has often never seen it, much less read it. And again, publishers—like the chain bookstores—favor sensational scripts intriguing to mass audiences and often reject superior scripts lacking in cheap thrills. As the veteran bookman Oscar Dystel said, "The penalty is that books of quality are being shoved off the stands."

Hence the visible cheapening of book publishing, so long our lamp of enlightenment, reason, and civilization. But am I a pot calling the kettle black, having spent some years editing cowboy and detective stories not notably intellectual? At any rate they were clean if not brainy, and I try to excuse myself on the ground that the Depression gave one little choice and I did aim higher when the opportunity rose.

Well, how lucky can you get? I retired just before the publishing slam dance. I never had to write for a machinery manufacturer or a conglomerate. I now recall with affection my years with Scribner—a bookworld almost gone. I've given appreciative attention to membership in the Authors' Guild, PEN, and the Society of American Historians. A heavy majority of the members are unhappy about the publishing decline, but no one has a remedy.

How to cope with old age, often libeled as "life's parody," "mere oblivion," and nastier pleasantries?

More affirmative are Solon's "I grow old learning something new every day," Seneca's "The evils of idleness can be shaken off by interesting work," and Walter Scott's advice, "Too much rest is rust."

And Boswell's chastening remark, "That dearest of all subjects, myself." Myself hitting eighty was a landmark enjoyed with my fifty-four-year collaborator, Dorothy, our children, and congratulatory friends, spiced by this octogenarian's agreeable surprise to be still breathing, still active, shall we say, in an easygoing way.

I never expected to live to such antiquity, but I find coping with age not bad at all. For one thing, I correspond joyfully with writers I've known for decades, topped by my oldest friend, George Scullin, who gave me my start and began his own distinguished New York magazine career when he drove me east fifty-five years ago.

In fact, writing is habit-forming. It's hard to stay away from the typewriter. Mine is an ancient electric that still seems new to me after pounding for years on those famous old muscle machines—Remingtons, Underwoods, Royals—but is old hat in this day of word processors. I avoid the "rest that brings rust" and hammer away without deadline tension, selling occasional articles and reviewing books. That's an exciting craft requiring judgment in analysis and giving one an agreeable sense that someone regards him as an oracle.

Not much loafing, but I had resolved never to get caught again in the intensive research-and-writing complexities of a full-length biography. That's too much. It tends to commandeer one's life, interrupt his meals, disturb his sleep, make him freaky and inattentive, and remove him from the normal niceties of social communion.

So what happened? Old man habit grabbed me again. At eighty-three I'm far along on a biography of William Eugene "Pussyfoot" Johnson (1862–1945), a character so overflowing with adventure and humor as to keep me fascinated.

But will he fascinate some corporate manufacturer-publisher in these glitzy latter days? I wonder. For all his uproarious exploits and his frequent terms in jail, he never played football, sang rock, or had extramarital affairs.

Nevertheless, Pussyfoot has commandeered me and I have great fun with him. I'll try to get him between covers as he deserves. If that fails, his astonishing career will suffer the ignominy of being hidden among my papers at Columbia University.

BIBLIOGRAPHY

Nonfiction, published by Scribner's:

Sickles the Incredible, 1956.

First Blood: The Story of Fort Sumter, 1957.

Jim Fisk: The Career of an Improbable Rascal, 1959.

Citizen Hearst, 1961.

Dreiser, 1965.

Pulitzer, 1967.

The Rector and the Rogue, 1968.

Luce and His Empire, 1972.

Norman Thomas: The Last Idealist, 1976.

Whitney Father, Whitney Heiress, 1980.

Contributor of narratives to the "Image of War: 1861–1865" series, Doubleday, 1981. Contributor of articles to periodicals, including *American Heritage, Life, New Yorker, Omnibook, Redbook, True, Woman's Home Companion, Yankee,* and others.

Robert Sward

1933-

Robert Sward, 1990

Part I
Four Incarnations—An Overview

Born on the Jewish North Side of Chicago, bar mitzvahed, sailor, amnesiac, university professor (Cornell, Iowa, Connecticut College), newspaper editor, food reviewer, father of five children, husband to four wives, my writing career has been described by critic Virginia Lee as a "long and winding road."

1. Switchblade Poetry: Chicago Style

I began writing poetry in Chicago at age fifteen, when I was named corresponding secretary for a gang of young punks and hoodlums called the Semcoes. A social athletic club, we met at various locations two Thursdays a month. My job was to write postcards to inform my brother thugs—who carried switchblade knives and stole cars for fun and profit—as to when, where, and why we were meeting.

Rhyming couplets seemed the appropriate form to notify characters like light-fingered Foxman, cross-eyed Harris, and Irving "Koko" of upcoming meetings. An example of my switchblade juvenilia:

The Semcoes meet next Thursday night
at Speedway Koko's. Five bucks dues, Foxman,
   or fight.

Koko was a young boxer whose father owned

Chicago's Speedway Wrecking Company and whose basement was filled with punching bags and pinball machines. Koko and the others joked about my affliction—the writing of poetry—but were so astonished that they criticized me mainly for my inability to spell.

2. Sailor Librarian: San Diego

At seventeen, I graduated from high school, gave up my job as soda jerk, and joined the navy. The Korean War was underway; my mother had died, and Chicago seemed an oppressive place to be.

My thanks to the U.S. Navy. They taught me how to type (sixty words a minute), organize an office, and serve as a librarian. In 1952, I served in Korea aboard a three-hundred-foot-long, flat-bottomed Landing Ship Tank (LST). A yeoman third class, I became overseer of twelve hundred paperback books, a sturdy upright typewriter, and a couple of filing cabinets.

The best thing about duty on an LST is the ship's speed: eight to ten knots. It takes approximately one month for an LST to sail from Pusan, Korea, to San Diego. In that month I read Melville's *Moby Dick,* Whitman's *Leaves of Grass,* Thoreau's *Walden,* Isak Dinesen's *Winter's Tales,* the King James Version of the Bible, Shakespeare's *Hamlet* and *King Lear,* and a biography of Abraham Lincoln.

While at sea, I began writing poetry as if poems, to paraphrase Thoreau, were secret letters from some distant land.

I sent one poem to a girl named Lorelei, with whom I was in love. Lorelei had a job at the Dairy Queen. Shortly before enlisting in the navy, I spent fifteen dollars of my soda-jerk money taking her up in a single-engine, sight-seeing airplane so we could kiss and—at the same time—get a good look at Chicago from the air. Beautiful Lorelei never responded to my poem. Years later, at the University of Iowa Writers' Workshop, I learned that much of what I had been writing (love poems inspired by a combination of lust and loneliness) belonged, loosely speaking, to a tradition—the venerable tradition of unrequited love.

3. Mr. Amnesia: Cambridge

In 1962, after ten years of writing poetry, my book *Uncle Dog and Other Poems* was published by Putnam in England. That was followed by two books from Cornell University Press, *Kissing the Dancer* and

Thousand-Year-Old Fiancee. Then in 1966, I was invited to do fourteen poetry readings in a two-week stretch at places like Dartmouth, Amherst, and the University of Connecticut.

The day before I was scheduled to embark on the reading series, I was hit by a speeding MG in Cambridge, Massachusetts.

I lost my memory for a period of about twenty-four hours. Just as I saw the world fresh while cruising to a war zone, so I now caught a glimpse of what a city like Cambridge can look like when one's inner slate, so to speak, is wiped clean.

4. Santa Claus: Santa Cruz

In December 1985, recently returned to the U.S. after some years in Canada, a free-lance writer in search of a story, I sought and found employment as a Rent-A-Santa Claus. Imagine walking into the local community center and suddenly, at the sight of four hundred children, feeling transformed from a skinny, sad-eyed self into an elf—having to chant the prescribed syllables, Ho, Ho, Ho.

What is poetry? For me, it's the restrained music of a switchblade knife. It's an amphibious warship magically transformed into a basketball court, and then transformed again into a movie theater showing a film about the life of Joan of Arc. It is the vision of an amnesiac, bleeding from a head injury, witnessing the play of sunlight on a redbrick wall. Poetry comes to a bearded Jewish wanderer, pulling on a pair of high rubber boots with white fur, and a set of musical sleigh bells, over blue, fleece-lined sweatpants. It comes to the father of five children, bearing gifts for four hundred and, choked up, unable to speak, alternately laughing and sobbing the three traditional syllables—Ho, Ho, Ho—hearing at the same time, in his heart, the more plaintive, tragic, Oi vay, Oi vay, Oi vay.

Part II
From the Kitchen Floor to the Kitchen Table

At age three, before I knew the alphabet, I would kneel or lie on the kitchen floor and draw pictures on large sheets of colored craft paper. One night, as she was preparing dinner, my mother turned and pointed to some of my scribblings.

"Those look like letters of the alphabet."

"What's 'alpha-bet'?"

"A, B, C . . . it's like what you're drawing right now. One day you'll write words and make up stories on paper."

What my mother was suggesting seemed to me beyond magic, beyond anything . . . I'll wait and see if she's right, I thought. She could just be making it up.

That was my earliest memory.

My interest in literature began with the linoleum on the floor of my bedroom. Imprinted on this linoleum and, as a consequence, on my mind, were a half-dozen Mother Goose rhymes with illustrations of Jack and Jill, Old King Cole, Little Jack Horner, the Old Woman Who Lived in a Shoe, Little Bo Peep, and Humpty Dumpty. One reason I mention the linoleum is that in the 1960s, I used Humpty Dumpty as a persona, a stand-in for Uncle Sam and America itself as I saw the country during the Vietnam War. Humpty Dumpty became Horgbortom Stringbottom, the title character in a book-length poem, *Horgbortom Stringbottom, I Am Yours, You Are History* (Swallow Press, 1970).

But I'm getting ahead of myself. At age five or six, going to bed at night, and waking up in the morning, I'd lean over the side of my bed and dreamily reflect on the linoleum as, years later, I would contemplate Hindu and Buddhist mandalas. In any case, I began reading linoleum Mother Goose rhymes before I began reading books. Indeed, I began reading books in order to escape the linoleum, which had begun to embarrass me.

My mother supplemented the linoleum with real books. I remember her reading aloud from *Gulliver's Travels, Thousand and One Nights, Alice in Wonderland, Pinocchio,* and *The Jungle Book.* After being run over by the MG in 1966 and my subsequent memory loss, some of this literature stayed with me. For example, a year after the accident, I began thinking of myself as something of an amnesiac Gulliver, an ingenuous new arrival in a strange land, when I worked on my novel *The Jurassic Shales.* In fact, there are elements of all five "children's" books in the novel.

*

At birth I weighed twelve pounds and, right from the beginning, my father complained I was more than my poor mother could handle. Fifty years later, my sister, Betty, and Aunt Leah recall stories of a drunken obstetrician, unsterilized forceps, an infected ear, and a generally mangled-at-birth Bobby Sward. At eight, I was healthy, though a pain in the neck. I was moody, shy, and yet prone to "talk back."

In addition, while my blonde, blue-eyed, five-year-old sister, Betty, earned money modeling tricycles and clothes for Montgomery Ward catalogs, I developed eczema on my hands, face, and legs. The condition grew so bad, I sometimes wore cotton gloves to school so I'd remember not to scratch myself. I had inherited my mother's large, hazel-brown eyes and so was nicknamed "Banjo Eyes," after the singer Eddie Cantor. Friends joked about my name: "The Sward is mightier than the Sword." And because I had a zany imagination, I had only to say, "Hey, I have an idea," and other eight-year-olds would collapse laughing. I was regarded as an oddball, an outsider. I had few friends. To this day I can remember the names of my grade three buddies: Junior Pucklewartz, Alan Stencil, and Eddie Greenberg.

Twelve years later, in 1952, home on leave from the Korean War, I sat down at the kitchen table and wrote a poem called "Pozzolana" about volcanoes in Italy and strong, slow-hardening cement. That was my first published poem. On the table or on the floor, kitchens are still my favorite place to write.

Family portrait: (clockwise, from bottom right) the author's father, Irving Michael Sward, age eight, Grandmother Bessie, Aunt Leah, age six, Grandfather Hyman David Swerdloff, and Uncle Morris, Goshen, Indiana, about 1912

Part III
A Long and Winding Road

My mother, Gertrude (née Huebsch), was born into a wealthy Chicago family and grew up on the South Side, pampered and protected. She had three brothers, Richard, the unlucky-in-love, tormented violinist; Harry, the finagling liquor salesman who always lived in hotels; and Irwin, an embittered, wounded-in-action, World War I veteran.

A tall, striking brunette with enormous, hazel-brown eyes, champion swimmer and diver, my mother was runner-up for Miss Chicago in the 1920s. Her father, Max Huebsch, grew up in Vienna, Austria, was an inventor, a speculator in the Chicago real estate market, and, for a time, a millionaire.

Like H. L. Mencken, the so-called Sage of Baltimore, Max Huebsch complained his way through the 1930s and '40s. He was narrow-minded, cantankerous, and looked down on any person who happened to be less fortunate than himself. Again, like Mencken, whom he resembled physically, Grandpa had a go-it-alone approach to living. His impassive, dry, bourbon-colored face would become purple-red, hot, and sticky at the mention of any social welfare program. Grandpa would foam at the mouth and sputter in English, with lapses into German, as he heaped invective on Franklin Roosevelt and the New Deal. He blamed Roosevelt for all that was wrong with the world.

In 1953, before my discharge from the navy, I visited Grandpa Huebsch. Neatly groomed in a well-ironed uniform, I told stories of my experiences in the Korean War and managed to pass the old man's inspection. He had known me as a dreamy, moody, "difficult child," and had urged my mother to send me to a military academy so I could learn discipline. She resisted. Max Huebsch was Teutonic, implacable, anti-youth, anti-life, anti-poetry.

I must have redeemed myself in his eyes by joining the navy and going to war. When Max Huebsch died in 1957—at age ninety-nine, after chain-smoking Camels and drinking straight shots of bourbon for over twenty years—he remembered me in his will. I inherited enough money to buy a used 1954 Plymouth, to attend the Bread Loaf School of English in Middlebury, Vermont, and to buy time to complete some of the poems included in *Advertisements* (Odyssey Chapbook Publications, 1958), *Uncle Dog and Other Poems* (Putnam and Company, London, 1962), and *Kissing the Dancer* (Cornell University Press, Ithaca, New York, 1964).

What's in a Name?
Poltava, Russia—New York City

My grandfather, Hyman David Swerdloff (1880–1929), was an orthodox Jew, father of my father, and the first Sward. In 1905, in the company of other survivors of government-sponsored pogroms, Hyman and his family journeyed from Poltava, Russia, to New York City. There the Russian "Swerdloff" became the more American "Sward," a word meaning "greensward, turf green with grass." In Sir Walter Scott's *Ivanhoe*, for example, the poet speaks of "A thick carpet of most delicious greensward." So it was that a twenty-five-year-old Russian-Jewish tailor immigrated to America to have thrust upon him a poetic name with Old English roots dating back to A.D. 900.

Leah Gold, my aunt, describes her father as a humorous, generous, but cautious man. "He loved making us laugh, never let us leave the house without asking if we had money in our pockets, and, if he noticed something too near the edge of a table, he'd pick it up and place it in the middle."

An entrepreneur with limited resources, Hyman Swerdloff employed several apprentices. He used to joke about having people work for him, "You've got to hire someone to take the blame."

In 1903, Hyman was conscripted and forced to serve in the Russian army as a quartermaster. His humor stood him in good stead with his fellow soldiers. Hyman, however, kept silent about his sympathies for the anti-czarist revolutionary movement. For decades, Jews in Poltava had been terrorized—many were killed—by czarist troops. On one occasion, Hyman's wife Bessie narrowly escaped death while waiting outside a prison for her brother, a revolutionary, to be released. In 1905, fearing they would become victims of the Russo-Japanese War, the Swerdloffs joined the stream of emigrants to the United States.

The Immigrant and the Beauty Queen

My parents met in 1927 and married in 1929, just in time for the Depression. My sister, Betty, jokes they simply fell in love with one another's good looks. In photographs from the 1920s, my father looks like a cross between Charlie Chaplin and Errol Flynn. Ambitious and hardworking, he longed to become a physician, but because of the Depression and family responsibilities, he cut short his studies and became a podiatrist. Dad was a poor businessman

*"Bobby Sward out in the cold,"
age nine months, Chicago, 1934*

and, though he loved his work, he had to struggle to make a living in Chicago. Late in life, he moved to Palm Springs, California. At age seventy-six, still a workaholic, he passed the state board exam to practice in California. Even in his eighties, after open-heart surgery, he continued to work.

Part IV
Uncle Dog: The Poet at 9

There was never a time, growing up in Chicago, when I didn't own a dog. There was Fluffy the golden cocker spaniel, Spot the wirehaired terrier with eczema worse than mine, gentle, unassuming crossbreeds and curs, dogs and dog-dogs, some of whom I found on the streets of Chicago without collars or identification and introduced to my parents saying, "He followed me home and we're going to keep him." I even fantasized about dogs, dogs like the garbageman's sharp-looking, fox-eared cur who I nicknamed "Uncle Dog." Cocky, aristocratic in manner, Uncle Dog appeared to laugh on occasion.

Certainly he carried himself with dignity and wore an ever-alert, amused expression on his face. In 1957, I wrote a thirty-nine-line poem for him titled "Uncle Dog: The Poet at 9." An excerpt follows:

> Uncle Dog had always looked
> to me to be truck-strong
> wise-eyed, a cur-like Ford
>
> Of a dog. I did not want
> to be Mr. Garbage man because
> all he had was cans to do.
>
> Uncle Dog sat there me-beside-him
> emptying nothing. Barely even
> looking from garbage side to side:
>
> Like rich people in the backseats
> of chauffeur-driven cars, only shaggy
> in an unwagging, tall-scrawny way . . .

First published in the *Chicago Review,* "Uncle Dog: The Poet at 9" served as title poem for a collection of my work brought out by Putnam in England in 1962. "Uncle Dog" was reprinted in Robert Kelly's *A Controversy of Poets,* Mark Strand's *The Contemporary American Poets,* George MacBeth's *The Penguin Book of Animal Poetry,* and a dozen other anthologies and textbooks.

At nine, I read books on the care and feeding of dogs and once, out of curiosity, fed Fluffy a can of Campbell's vegetable beef soup while I sampled Fluffy's horsemeat Rival dog food. Indeed, my interest in health foods began in the 1940s when, shopping for dog food, I began reading labels. Who would have guessed that this early interest in dogs, dog food, and soup would lead me, years later, to become not only a vegetarian, but a professional food-reviewer?

There's a photo of me at age nine with thirty-nine other Peterson Elementary fourth-graders. All the kids in the photograph are smiling at the camera over their left shoulder. I'm the only one in the photograph facing in the wrong direction. And, instead of a cheerful, cheesy smile, I have a dreamy, abstracted look on my face. I was nearsighted, had a bad overbite, and, when crimes or misdemeanors were committed around the school, was the kid most likely to be punished. Guilty of some offenses, not guilty of others, I spent more than one period outside the classroom sitting in my locker.

One thing I liked about Peterson Elementary School was the library. What a relief to escape harassed teachers and Depression-era classrooms crowded with forty or more students. The library is where I discovered Albert Terhune's *Lad: A Dog* and

Jack London's *Call of the Wild.* As author of "Uncle Dog," "Alpha the Dog," "Clancy the Dog," "Letter to His First Dog," "Classified—Pets," "Pet Shop," "I Have Just Bought a House," and other poems in which dogs play a central role, I have to acknowledge Terhune and London as two of my early mentors. London's ability to get inside the mind of Buck the dog, and to write convincingly from an animal's point of view, struck me as uncanny. I found I cared more for Buck the dog than I did for Lou Gehrig and the sports heroes my friends read about. However, I didn't want to be laughed at and so kept quiet about my affection for Jack London and his ability to turn dogs into true heroes of fiction.

Bells, Bells, Bells . . .

In grade five, our teacher asked us to memorize two poems, "The Raven" and "The Bells," by Edgar Allan Poe. At age ten, standing up in class and reciting lines like "Tintinabulations of the bells bells bells" was enough to make us enemies of poetry forever. Further, to hear a teacher with no feeling for poetry announce that "Edgar Allan Poe is a great, great poet" aroused in us a feeling of contempt for the melancholy, tubercular versifier. Without a word to anyone, full of confidence, I decided to rewrite "The Raven" and "The Bells" and improve them. After going through those two poems line by line, word by word, I had to admit that even the verses that most embarrassed me could not be improved upon. I came away from the experience with a grudging respect for my adversary, the no-longer-boring Edgar Allan Poe. After that, I surrendered to the task at hand and memorized the two poems. Next, I began reading more of Poe and making up verses of my own. If you can't beat 'em, join 'em.

Part V
Switchblade Truman Cold War
Rhapsody in Blue

In 1947, I began attending Chicago's Von Steuben High School on the city's North Side. Von Steuben? Right. Our largely Jewish high school was named after a German general, Baron Friedrich Wilhelm Von Steuben, Washington's military advisor during the Revolutionary War. Germany had been our enemy since the rise of Hitler in the early 1930s. Two years after the war, many of my classmates continued to have nightmares about Nazi death

camps. Little surprise that the name *General Friedrich Wilhelm Von Steuben* made us vaguely uncomfortable.

Von Steuben was then an academically lax, "country club" high school with a student body of first- and second-generation Americans. Many of my classmates had moved up to conservative, middle-class Albany Park from Chicago's West Side. In the late 1950s and '60s, as these people prospered, they bought homes in suburbs like Skokie and Highland Park. In 1947, my mother said, "Bobby, you'd better start studying and come home with good grades. Don't you want to become a doctor or lawyer so you can live in Highland Park?" Ambitious for me, she wanted me to take music lessons. A fan of Gene Krupa, I asked for a set of drums. She suggested I try an accordion. Eventually we settled on a piano.

In upwardly striving, postwar Albany Park, we experienced the Truman years as no less hypocritical, conservative, and stifling than the grin-and-wave Eisenhower era that followed. At fourteen, I wanted no part of Skokie or Highland Park. Like my buddies,

Mother, Gertrude Huebsch, and father, Dr. Irving M. Sward, before their marriage, Elkhart Lake, Wisconsin, about 1928

I got myself a ducktail haircut, wore Levi's, blue suede shoes, and navy blue "hoodlum" shirts purchased at Smokey Joe's on the South Side. I listened to singers like Chicago-born Frankie Laine ("Mule Train") and Vaughn Monroe ("Racing with the Moon") and, when no one else was around, I'd play classical music, including recordings of George Gershwin's *Rhapsody in Blue* and *An American in Paris.* I also read Irving Shulman's *The Amboy Dukes* and carried a switchblade knife. Anti-Semites started fights after Von Steuben basketball games and, sometimes, at Sonny Berkowitz's Lawrence Avenue poolhall. At fourteen, I was already 6'1" and weighed 160 pounds. Because of my size, I was obliged to fight several times on my friends' behalf with my fists—I never used a knife. Invited to join a club called The Regular Fellas, I made a fateful decision. I chose, instead, to become a member of a gang called the Semcoes.

One rainy evening, after a seven-day initiation ritual, ten teenagers—I among them—raced on hands and knees across a muddy football field. As we raced, we were pelted with hell-night, week-old fruit and vegetables. Covered with tomatoes and mud, but winner of the race, I was told to flag down the Chicago Transit Authority's Foster Avenue bus. Ah, the rewards of winning! As the bus pulled to a stop, I leapt aboard and, pretending to carry a gun, shouted, "This is a holdup. Stick 'em up!" I believed myself to be well-disguised. The driver and bug-eyed passengers put their hands in the air. Some older, more experienced riders, used to being robbed, began removing their wristwatches and rings. As they held out their wallets and valuables, I made a quick career decision. I wanted to be in the Semcoes, but understood I was no Billy the Kid. I jumped off the bus as the driver sped into the night. My friends were suitably impressed and I became a gang member in good standing.

The mud, tomatoes and filthy clothes proved to be an inadequate disguise. At school the next day, a girl asked me, "Robert, wasn't that you last night on the Foster Avenue bus?"

As a gang member, I spent hours hanging out with my friends, eating Twinkies, drinking soda pop, and playing billiards at the poolhall. One night we drove to Gary, Indiana, to a brothel. I was impressed both by the sex I enjoyed that night, an unexpectedly tender initiation, and the near-visionary experience of seeing fire erupting from the local steel mills. Excited by my first sexual escapade and the sight of the Indiana sky exploding with hellfire and brimstone, I tried to explain to my friends that seven-eighths of everything is invisible. I argued that there is a difference between appearance and reality, and that we Semcoes were just punks who didn't know anything about anything. A messenger bringing unwelcome news, my days as a gang member were numbered.

*

In early 1948, my athletic, vivacious, forty-two-year-old mother began taking medication for a goiter condition. As months passed, she became morose and irritable. Then she told me she had to undergo some "routine" surgery. On July 3, 1948, my mother died while being operated on for an enlarged thyroid gland. I know she was concerned about having a dreamy, abstracted son. Hence her last words to my father: "Keep his [Robert's] feet on the ground." Gertrude Sward died ten days after my fifteenth birthday and, for what it's worth, my height (6'1") and weight (160 pounds) have remained constant from that day to the present.

Addressing my father at the funeral service, the rabbi said, "Now, Irving, you're going to have to be both a father and a mother to your children." Seeing my father wince with confusion, I understood that my sister and I were, in fact, going to have to raise ourselves. I asked myself, Were my mother and father ever who I thought they were? Who were my parents, really? I knew for certain that my mother had been an agnostic. Following her death, I felt anger with God, with my mother, with my father, and myself.

My mother's death turned me into a scholar. From 1948 to 1951, I devoted myself to my studies and began earning straight *A*'s. At sixteen, I decided I really did want to go to college. I wrote to Harvard to find out what I had to do to get into law school. Their reply: Be first in your class and come with lots and lots of money. My father, meanwhile, had begun drinking and his practice had fallen off. I realized I would have to work my way through college. At the same time, I was trying to make whatever sense I could of my life. I found myself making up song lyrics and poems. However, I was too embarrassed to write them down. I took on the position of corresponding secretary for a gang of hoodlums because it offered me what seemed a legitimate opportunity to write. I became the gang's resident mad poet. And, the truth is, no member of the Semcoes objected to receiving rhyming reminders of meetings.

I wrote an original rhyming message to each Semcoe—no two alike! I didn't care that I was assured of only one reader for any given poem. Better an audience of one than none, I thought.

After my mother's death, I began taking long walks along the lakefront near Navy Pier. I felt drawn to Michigan Boulevard and often visited Chicago's Art Institute. Sometimes I'd go read and warm myself in the Chicago Public Library. Entering the library one winter afternoon, I passed through the Art Room on the main floor. There I saw a number of men browsing in the works of the great masters. They resembled figures out of the opera *La Bohème*. I fantasized that they were Bohemians, brooding geniuses, the neglected artists of America. Most likely they were homeless men from West Madison Street. However, I saw them as artist-monks who had risked everything, who had taken vows of poverty on behalf of their calling. Could I do that? I wondered. Could I take a vow of poverty and dedicate myself to writing or painting? And live in a garret as these people did, to be discovered only in the last years of my life? I wasn't so sure.

Part VI
The Korean War (1950–1954)

Growing up in Chicago during World War II, I felt elated but also oddly disappointed when the war ended. I was a patriotic twelve-year-old in 1945, and had expected to go overseas as a sailor or marine. In 1941, the Japanese had caught us unawares and bombed Pearl Harbor. The murderous Nazis had plans to conquer the world. There was a captured German U-boat tied up at the dock by Navy Pier that caught my imagination. I once toured that submarine and a U.S. Destroyer Escort tied up nearby. Each evening our family listened to the radio for news of the war. I had grown up with visions of German troops marching into Chicago. If that happened, I planned to work with some resistance group and perform acts of sabotage against the enemy.

In 1949, ten months after my mother died, my father remarried. My stepmother immediately began telling my father, my sister, and me how to live our lives. It was as if, with the death of my mother, I had lost my father too. To make matters worse, I had two stepbrothers and their dog Satin, a dog I disliked, sharing my bedroom. It was time to think about leaving home. At seventeen, I enlisted in the naval reserve and began attending weekly meetings at Navy Pier. In 1950, the Korean War started, and in 1951, I graduated from Von Steuben. Fearing I would be drafted, I visited a navy recruiter who promised if I volunteered I'd get the G.I. Bill to pay my way through college. I signed up.

In 1952, stationed on Coronado Island, working at the headquarters of the commander of the Amphibious Fleet, I was feeling safe and secure. I mulled over stories I'd heard of servicemen in World War II who had done "easy duty" for four years and grown fat and lazy.

A few months later, bored with filing and sorting mail for the admiral, restless to see the world, I volunteered to go to Korea to serve in the combat zone. I expected weeks to pass before my application was approved. Surprise! Twenty-four hours after I filed my request, I was on the USS *Menard,* an Attack Transport, heading for Korea. In addition to the regular crew, we were carrying two thousand combat-ready marines.

Two weeks later, I was designated editor of the ship's newspaper. My job was to select and edit from a mass of incoming news dispatches those likely to be of interest to sailors and marines. Once I included a story about the launching of a nuclear-powered submarine. President Dwight D. Eisenhower had termed the submarine "a weapon for peace." I felt obliged to editorialize on the cold war. I wrote that there was something contradictory in the president's phrase "weapon for peace." Having uncovered that contradiction, I busied myself rewriting all news reports that contained evidence of "newspeak." There was much to do. Unfortunately, this was also the time of Senator Joseph McCarthy's crusade against communism. One evening, when the executive officer found me writing poetry on the ship's typewriter, he coolly asked if I was a Communist.

A few weeks later, on maneuvers off the coast of Red China, the ship's radar operator noted an unidentified aircraft. I happened to be out on deck reading a World War II Armed Forces Edition of the poetry of Edgar Allan Poe. When the battle alarm sounded, everyone seemed to disappear at once. All the ship's hatches clanged shut and the *Menard* began steaming into some combat formation. Alone on deck, unable to reach my position in the radio tower, I began pounding on the watertight hatches yelling to be let in. No one heard me. Seeing the *Menard* was in no immediate danger, I curled up outside the ship's radio tower and continued reading poetry.

The day after we arrived in Japan, I was transferred to Landing Ship Tank (LST) 914, an ugly, three-hundred-foot-long, flat-bottomed relic from World War II. Crew members joked that the price of a modern missile was greater than the price of a recommissioned LST. We drew reassurance from the fact it would be uneconomical for an enemy submarine to sink us.

*"Seaman Sward," age eighteen, Great Lakes
Naval Training Center, 1951*

Again I was made editor of the ship's newspaper (readership: 110). And, as yeoman third class, I found myself typing up "clean" copies of the ship's deck log with notations on weather conditions and cloud formations. I became the vessel's chronicler, a nineteen-year-old diary-keeper for an amphibious warship. But best of all, I became overseer of twelve hundred World War II surplus books—stashed in one of the holds. One incredible day the commanding officer told me to haul out the books and create a library of the ship's Armed Forces Editions.

U.S. servicemen and women in World War II were among the first readers of quality paperback books. Realizing many military people *(a)* have a certain amount of spare time, and *(b)* enjoy reading books, the government began providing "little paper books to fit in a soldier's pocket," as Isak Dinesen put it. In 1956, in her interview with the *Paris Review,* she remarks, "The book [*Winter's Tales*] had been put into Armed Forces Editions . . . suddenly I received dozens of charming letters from American

soldiers and sailors all over the world." I am proud to say I was one of those sailors.

In 1958, at the Bread Loaf Writers Conference, I heard publishers crediting the Armed Forces Editions with preparing the way for what has become known as the paperback revolution. In 1952, before I even heard of Lawrence Ferlinghetti and his City Lights Paperback Bookstore (founded in 1953), I was one of many librarians managing a City Lights at sea, a City Lights Quality Library in a War Zone—and I was my own best customer.

I had a few friends, access to a desk, a typewriter, paper, and all the books I could read. On the other side of the bulkhead was the ship's kitchen. Each day I enjoyed the fragrance of coffee, fresh-baked bread, down-and-dirty (but generally edible) meat and potatoes. Evenings, restless and lonely, oddly stirred, I'd write letters or wander about on deck, looking at the stars. New to poetry, a raw recruit to literature, I scribbled away my months at sea, happy and madly productive, as I'd be years later at the MacDowell Colony, at Yaddo, and the Djerassi Foundation. In 1958, William Meredith, my colleague at Connecticut College, suggested a poet could do worse than spend twenty years sailing around the world with all expenses paid by the U.S. government. Meredith himself had served as a navy pilot during World War II.

It took thirty years for me to begin writing about my experiences in the Korean War. In 1986, I sent the poem "On My Way to the Korean War" to Dr. Martin Bax in London, England. Martin, a physician and magazine editor, ran the poem in *Ambit* 106.

> On my way to the Korean War,
> I never got there.
>
> One summer afternoon in 1952,
> I stood instead in the bow
> of the Attack Transport *Menard,*
> with an invading force
> of 2,000 battle-ready Marines,
> watching the sun go down.
> Whales and porpoises,
> flying fish and things jumping
> out of the water.
> Phosphorescence—
> Honolulu behind us,
> Inchon, Korea, and the war ahead . . .

The poem goes on to tell how a half-dozen sailors, I among them, converged on the bow of the ship, where, each evening, composed and silent, we'd maintain our vigil until sunset. One evening, suddenly, unaccountably, I felt extraordinarily joyful, peaceful, secure in a way I had never felt before. At the same time I seemed to lose all sense of personal history. I felt myself merging with every atom, every visible and invisible thing. I felt if I chose, I could simply step out into space and, sink into the ocean or soar into the sky, all would be well. I'd joined the navy to see the world. One thing I hadn't counted on was achieving union with the world I'd gone to see. I came out of the experience believing I had been initiated in some way, that I was beginning to wake up.

> In-breathe, out-breathe, and leave,
> in-breathe, out-breathe, and leave.
> Leave your body, leave your body,
> leave your body, leave your body,
>
> We sang as we went out
> to where the light went,
> and whatever held us to that ship
> and its 2,000 battle-ready troops, let go.
> So it was, dear friends, I learned to fly.
>
> And so in time must you
> and so will the warships,
> and the earth itself,
> and the sky,
> for as the prophet says, the day cometh
> when there will be no earth left to leave.
>
> Oh me, O my
> O me, O my
>
> goodbye earth, goodbye sky.
> Goodbye, goodbye.

My association with Dr. Martin Bax goes back to 1961. As editor of *Ambit* and a fan of "Uncle Dog: The Poet at 9," Martin arranged several poetry readings for me in London pubs and coffeehouses. Thirty years later, Martin says he still uses "Letter to his First Dog" and other poems of mine "when we do Jazz Recital." It was Martin who, in 1961, suggested I contact John Pudney, then senior editor at Putnam in London. I had been unable to find a publisher in the States. As William Meredith wrote in his introduction to *Kissing the Dancer* (1964), "These poems are unusual . . . in a number of ways, but what strikes me first about them is that they are the only book of poems I know about . . . that has been turned down by a lot of publishers over a good many years because they are so original as to be unrecognizable as poetry by a conventional eye. They have gone off to respectable publishers with praise from Stanley Kunitz, Louise Bogan, even Robert Lowell, and come

back with the embarrassed confession that they simply escaped the respectable editors."

I was fortunate. Putnam published *Uncle Dog and Other Poems* in 1962, about the same time John Pudney took on the writer Jeff Nuttall, another indication of his open-minded approach to poetry.

But I'm getting ahead of myself.

Part VII
Iowa Writers' Workshop (1956–1967)

In 1956, the year I graduated from the University of Illinois, Paul Engle offered me a fellowship to attend the Iowa Writers' Workshop. A year later, at the University of Iowa, I was writing up to ten poems a day and assaulting *Poetry Northwest*, the *Chicago Review*, and the *New Yorker* with an almost constant barrage. In 1957, Carolyn Kizer published three of my poems in *Poetry Northwest* and George Starbuck accepted "Uncle Dog: The Poet at 9" for the *Chicago Review*. I became a regular contributor to the *Antioch Review*, the *Beloit Poetry Journal*, *Best Articles & Stories*, *Carleton Miscellany*, *Chelsea Review*, *Epoch*, the *Nation*, *New Orleans Poetry Journal*, and *Poetry Chicago*. I persevered, and eventually even the *New Yorker*, and the *Paris Review* printed my poems.

For a period of about ten years, from 1957 to 1967, I typically had twenty "packets" of poems (five or more poems per packet) circulating at any one time. Only rarely did I send the same poems out to two magazines at the same time.

In 1957, I submitted satires on *New Yorker* advertisements to two Chicago-based magazines, Rob Cuscaden's *Mainstream* and Ron Offen's *Odyssey*. Rob had begun his mimeographed effort in 1955, and Offen later joined him as coeditor.

Originally, as Ron tells it, the outlook of *Mainstream* was to "present poetry that was in the 'mainstream,' poetry that was being written by 'real' poets rather than academics. Later, when we became *Odyssey*, this changed somewhat. Then our inclination was to feature poets that were neither 'neat' nor 'beat.' So we published people who didn't seem to be part of either school, like Charles Bukowski, Imamu Amiri Baraka (then LeRoi Jones), Michael Benedict, Judson Crews, Fred Eckman, Curtis Zahn, and Robert Sward."

When I began work on this autobiography, I contacted Ron Offen, who, after all, published *Advertisements* (Odyssey Chapbook Publications) in 1958. I asked Ron how it was that he and Cuscaden chose to invest money and energy in producing a collection of my satires at a time when I was "odd man out" in

Iowa City and little known outside the Midwest. I also wanted to know how they, as magazine editors, viewed the literary climate at that time.

Ron Offen replied:

> Both of us had a profound distrust of poems about poems, poems about myths, and poems with cryptic Greek epigraphs. On the other hand we had a certain respect for form—we were close to the Angry Young Men of England in that respect—and were suspicious of the Beats' insistence on spontaneity, a freedom from artistic control that seemed too often "typewriting" rather than "writing," to paraphrase Capote's criticism of Kerouac's work.

> Robert Sward, like most of the poets we published, seemed to fit somewhere between the two influences. As a quasi-academic, he was studying at Iowa . . . he was very conscious of craftsmanship (although he rarely used conventional forms), and his stance was ironic rather than engagé. But like the Beats he wrote about his own experiences as a kid in Chicago or aimed satiric barbs at the last phase of the Eisenhower beehive-hairdo-and-airhead culture.

> In addition, we were enthralled with Sward's wacky and marvelous sense of humor (something most of the arid academics and earnestly spiritual Beats lacked). And the spirit of humor carried beyond his work into his life. For example, he once wrote us that the reason we couldn't reach him by phone was that Ma Bell had yanked out his phone when he offered to pay his bill with a sonnet sequence (syllabic sonnets, mind you!).

Because Cuscaden and Offen had already published some of my poems on *New Yorker* magazine advertisements, and knew I had others, in 1958 they offered to publish a chapbook titled *Advertisements.* Poet Fred Eckman wrote an introduction, Ron Offen designed the cover, and, availing themselves of a 1250 Multilith press, Odyssey Chapbook Publications printed 368 copies of the book. "My guess is we sold about 25 at a buck a pop," says Offen, who now runs a California-based magazine called *Free Lunch: A Poetry Journal.* Offen hasn't given up on me yet. After thirty years, he still publishes my quirky poems.

A jazz aficionado, I drew on funky blues, gospel music, and Middle America speech rhythms. I wrote in a variety of forms—including sonnets—but most of my work was in unrhymed syllabics and free verse. I loved poets as diverse as e. e. cummings, Marianne Moore, Wallace Stevens, and W. H. Auden, writers who found it in their souls to integrate "seriousness" with playfulness and humor. But the Iowa cornbelt metaphysicals took themselves very seriously. In those years, 1956–58, all the Iowa poets seemed to be jabbering about Franz Schubert, German art songs of the nineteenth century, Baudelaire, the Flowers of Evil, the fountains of Rome, and the well-wrought urn. I was reading Whitman's *Leaves of Grass,* Mark Twain's *Life on the Mississippi,* and the *Des Moines Register.*

*

In 1967, George Starbuck invited me to teach at the Iowa Writers' Workshop. I was privileged to have students like James Tate, Alan Soldofsky, Michael Dennis Browne, Jon Anderson, and Michael Culross in my classes. In 1989, Michael Culross let me see a copy of his book, *The Lost Heroes.* There, on page twelve, I read a poem titled "Robert Sward":

With sister, Betty, Chicago, about 1967: "The house in the background was 'home' when I attended Von Steuben High School and belonged to the Semcoes"

how unlike your poems
you are. You should
live as they do

in exotic lands
and major cities, but you
hide behind a beard

in some forgotten farmhouse.
All the fiery lines
you've ever written

are wasted
when you make
apologies for them.

Return to your poems.
Take them seriously.
Emulate

your characters:
fly around a room
or out to sea;

take two or more wives
at once, and several
lovers; fling yourself

across life-size pages
in uneven lines;
become endless, unlikely,

remarkable verses
even Robert Sward
would never dream of.

I no longer have a beard, but I do live now in a
beautiful, exotic land—dangerous, mad Santa Cruz,
after a 7.1 earthquake. And, as my second, third, and
fourth wives will testify, I've overstepped the boundaries and, yes, have flung myself "across life-size
pages / in uneven lines."

Have I become "endless, unlikely, remarkable"?
Perhaps it's time, dear Michael, for us to become
better acquainted.

Part VIII
Recollections of an Amnesiac:
The New England Poetry Circuit

The best thing that ever happened to me
    besides everything else
        was briefly having amnesia and enjoying it
            at least briefly.
How instructive are our illnesses. How
    instructive is madness and

losing one's mind precisely the moment one
        had begun
    overvaluing that mind . . .

(from "Scarf Gobble Wallow Inventory")

Cornell published *Thousand-Year-Old Fiancee and Other Poems* in 1965. In the winter of 1966, I was at the MacDowell Colony writing poems and preparing to embark on the New England Poetry Circuit. Holly Stevens, coordinator of the series, had made arrangements for me to visit fourteen colleges and universities in Connecticut, Massachusetts, Maine, and New Hampshire. The day before I was scheduled to give my first reading, I trekked around Cambridge seeing friends and visiting bookstores. Early in the afternoon, I stepped out from between two snowbanks to cross a street and was run over by a student driving an MG. I regained consciousness in the backseat of the car as we drove to Massachusetts General Hospital. Looking at the young man and woman in the front seat, I wondered, Who are these people? Seeing blood on my jacket, I touched my head and realized my ear had come loose. I didn't know my name or the names of the driver and his beautiful female companion. But look at that blue sky and the sunlight on that redbrick wall, I remember thinking. Amazing. Unfortunately, I didn't know what city I was in. I didn't know the day, year, or anything to do with my personal history. Was I married or single? Were there children to be noti-fied? How had I become a bloodied passenger in the cramped backseat of a classy green sports car?

At the hospital, a doctor sewed my ear back onto my head. I was conscious the entire time. Next, I was transferred to a ward filled with heart-attack and gunshot victims, a three-hundred-pound man with a bleeding ulcer, and others, like myself, with less dramatic ailments. Once I settled in, I rang for a nurse. "I've been run over by a car and I've lost my memory," I said. "I'd like someone to talk to." She looked into my eyes, glanced at the bandage holding my ear in place, turned and walked away without a word. Moments later she returned with a giant television set mounted on an enormous tripod. The television set was wheeled to the front of the ward so all the patients could watch. The program she select-ed was a movie, *The Three Faces of Eve*. She cranked up the volume. Again, I rang for a nurse and explained I wanted someone to talk to. Looking frightened, the second nurse also disappeared. Then my survival instinct must have kicked in. Slowly I began to remember things.

Early the next morning, I convinced the doctors I was ready to leave. Released from the hospital, my head wrapped in bandages, I went to see a lawyer. "Don't do the poetry readings," he advised me. "Cancel the poetry tour. Go home and have yourself a rest. Claim you were too badly injured to perform. That way you can sue for lots and lots of money. If you don't take my advice, there's not much I can do for you."

"I've committed myself to all those colleges," I said, blinking as my memory continued to return. "I'm primed to do the readings. So I'm going to go ahead and give them."

The lawyer shrugged and turned away. But I was thinking of Holly—Wallace Stevens's daughter—and the work she did to make the series possible. Memory or no memory, stitches in the head or no stitches in the head, I made up my mind to give those readings.

You may ask, How can you remember back to a precise time in 1966 and recall so many details, particularly if you had been run over by a car and lost your memory?

Good question. One of the first things I wanted to do after recovering my memory was to write about the experience. For whatever reason, I'm happy to say, I can recall more details about that particular day than any other day in my life—with the possible exception of October 17, 1989, when Santa Cruz experienced a 7.1 earthquake. Nothing like a near-death experience to wake one up, to shake loose all those mental cobwebs. Where was I? Oh, yes, I did all fourteen readings. The New England Poetry Circuit proved to be an intense and, certainly, a memorable experience.

In 1989, I did a reading at the Berkeley YMCA. Ruth and Artie Daigon, editors of *Poets On,* came to the reading and laughed as they recalled my visit to the University of Connecticut in 1966. "You had an audience of 225 people waiting for you. You arrived late. You trotted into the hall smiling and wearing a big white bandage on your head. You had a beard and you were waving your arms. You were very physically active in your reading."

Following the New England Poetry Circuit, I returned to the MacDowell Colony, where I worked on my journals. "I find myself perplexed at my sexual response at a time when I was physically injured," I wrote. "What is the connection between sex and violence? There I was, unconscious in the backseat of the MG that had nearly killed me. Then, as I regained consciousness, I found myself physically attracted to the young woman seated in front of me. I didn't know then that it had been she who had run me over. After

a brief fantasy in which she was my partner, I realized I was bleeding. Even as an amnesiac I couldn't go five minutes without a sex thought. Only after that fantasy did it occur to me that I didn't know my own name. Otherwise, if I had been able to remember my name, I might have introduced myself."

What does it say about me that in this instance, as in many other instances in my life, the sexual impulse overrode everything else?

Once is enough, of course, but I have never regretted being an amnesiac. I know I'm lucky to be alive. I know too I was fortunate to be at the MacDowell Colony to recover. There I sought answers to the question: Who am I?

I spent hours walking in the woods, reading Dag Hammarskjold's *Markings,* and listening to Bob Dylan, the Beatles, and the Mamas and the Papas. A year or two later, I began work on the novel *The Jurassic Shales* and the longish "Scarf Gobble Wallow Inventory." The latter is a poem of personal stock-taking, a way of dealing with amnesia, loss, marriage and the family, space exploration, and the afterlife.

> How hungry and for WHAT are the people this
>   season
>   predicting the end of the end of the end of
> I've only just come home after having been
>   away
> The world sends its greetings and the greetings
>   send
>   greetings
> Hello goodbye, hello goodbye . . .

The experience of being run over by a car still haunts me. In the early 1980s, living in Toronto, I wrote another poem about losing my memory. It's called "Mr. Amnesia," and it starts:

> Even an amnesiac remembers some things
>   better than others.
> In one past life I was a subway conductor
> for the Chicago subway system.
>
> In another I was . . . Gosh, I forgot!
>
> . . . I don't know about you, but I hardly
>   unpack
> and get ready for this life and it's time
>
> To move on to the next . . .

Part IX
Welcome to Victoria, B.C. (1969–1979)

During the late 1960s and early '70s, American men arriving in Canada were automatically assumed to be Vietnam War protestors, draft dodgers, or deserters. American veterans of World War II, Korean War veterans, even bona fide academics and unsuspecting tourists were regarded with disapproval.

In 1969, I was a married, thirty-six-year-old, honorably discharged and decorated Korean War veteran. I was also the father of four children. I was not subject to the draft and had been specifically invited to the University of Victoria to teach. However, the circumstances of my arrival meant nothing to anti-American nationalists.

Canada is a beautiful, wonderfully raw, exciting country, an inspiringly sane, peaceable kingdom compared to America. There are many valid reasons for citizens of the country to be nationalistic. But why the prejudice against foreigners? Why the fear? Why so little generosity of spirit? Why believe that invited guests, for example, come for dishonorable rather than honorable reasons?

At a faculty party in September 1969, I found myself in conversation with a portly, red-faced, rather jowly steak-and-kidney-pie academic, the head of the university's freshman English program. "Well, what do you think of Victoria?" he asked, pouring me a drink. "It's dull, provincial, quiet, friendly, and clean," I replied. "I'm amazed that every house I've seen so far has a flower garden."

Then I told him how English poet Michael Dennis Browne laughed when he saw Victoria. "England hasn't looked like this for over twenty years," he said. "Victoria is a facsimile of an England that exists now only in peoples' imaginations."

I felt angry with Michael for saying this. Who wants to live in an imitation of someone else's homeland, garden city of Canada or not? But maybe Michael was right. I wanted to hear what the steak-and-kidney-pie Canadian had to say. The Professor harrumphed with annoyance. He ignored my question. Instead he asked me, "What brought you to British Columbia? Are you a Vietnam War draft dodger?"

"I was invited to read my poetry here in February. This was the last stop for me on the Northwest Poetry Circuit. Your colleagues said Victoria was narrow and self-centered. They said they wanted an 'intense American-type, someone whose adrenalin is moving,' to replace Robin Skelton. They even paid my moving expenses. What brought *you* here?" I

asked. "My family moved here from New England. We left because of the Revolution."

At first I thought the Professor was saying he too was a new arrival. Maybe an older, more established person fed up with Lyndon Johnson and the Vietnam War. Maybe someone who decided America was a violent country on the brink of revolution? Or was he perhaps an individual so outraged at the 1968 police riot in Chicago that he had left the country? Science-fiction writer Judith Merril, and others, had left America for that reason.

"What do you mean, Revolution?" I asked.

"The American Revolution. My ancestors left America after the Boston Tea Party. We're United Empire Loyalists," he said proudly. He was very impressed with himself.

"Professor, you mean you've been here for over two hundred years? That's incredible. By the way, how long does it take to get tenure at UVic?"

It never occurred to me there existed in this world an outpost of people who, more than two hundred years after the event, still regarded the dumping of tea into Boston Harbor as a criminal act, who believed Paul Revere to be "the enemy," and who, though they lived twenty minutes from Seattle, felt an emotional bond with King George III (the crazy one) and Queen Elizabeth II.

And here I was, a Chicago-born, bearded, academic hippie drinking Bristol cream sherry with United Empire Loyalists in a city named after dowager Queen Victoria. A couple years earlier, I had written, "Iowa, what am I doing in Iowa?" Now the question was, "Canada, what am I doing in Canada?"

Suddenly America seemed very far away.

"Is anything wrong?" asked the chairman. "All the color's left your face."

Oh, my God, I thought. ·

*

I came to Victoria to give a fifty-minute poetry reading. I accepted a teaching position that was supposed to keep me in British Columbia for nine months. I wrote poems about Canadian alligator matrons, prehistoric English crocodiles, tea-drinking Royalists, Tories in their glory. To my surprise, I was rehired to teach a second year. My daughter Hannah was born in 1970, and I purchased a three-story, tudor-style home in quiet, stodgy Oak Bay for $18,500. In 1971, I was promoted to assistant professor, given a bonus, a new two-year contract and other inducements, and so stayed on two more years. In 1973 I met, and in 1975, married, a French-Canadian artist (see "Barbara Walters Interviews a

Much-Married Man"). What started out as a fifty-minute, Northwest Poetry Circuit appearance led to my living in Canada for fifteen years.

Part X
Soft Press, Canada (1970–1979)

"The spirit in man is soft.
It can go anywhere."

I am in debt to William Stafford for the name Soft Press. It was Stafford who said, "The spirit in man is soft. It can go anywhere." I am also indebted to Ram Dass (Dr. Richard Alpert), who, in 1968, was living an hour or two from Peterborough, New Hampshire. I was in residence at the MacDowell Colony when I learned that Ram Dass, recently returned from India, was now a "neighbor." I immediately phoned asking if I could visit.

Ram Dass reportedly lost his job at Harvard for experimenting with LSD. In one of his experiments, he included the sons of a Harvard dean. The afternoon of my visit, Ram Dass spoke of how he had gone back to Harvard and, by chance, encountered the two young men.

"What was it like running into them?" I asked.

"They were soft," he said, meaning gentle, at peace with themselves.

For some reason I was struck by the positive emphasis he placed on the word "soft." Up until then I tended to think of "soft" in a negative way.

Months later, when I arrived in Victoria, B.C., to begin teaching, there was a letter waiting for me.

"I have consecrated Vancouver Island in advance of your arrival. Many beautiful people with much light," it read. And was signed, "Ram Dass."

Soon after Ram Dass's letter arrived, poet and publisher Larry Raferty asked if he could store a one-hundred-year-old treadle-operated Cropper platen letterpress in the basement of our Oak Bay home. I said yes and, a few weeks later, purchased two thousand pounds of lead printing type. A novice, it took me up to eight hours to prepare the press, set the type, and print one page of poetry. Nonetheless, for about seven years that press was the heart of our 1050 Saint David Street house.

I reflected on the meanings of the word "soft." Could I accept the challenge of using the word when I named a publishing company? That, briefly, is how Soft Press came into existence.

In 1973, we produced a hand-set, signed limited edition of William Stafford's *In the Clock of Reason.* Stafford's poems were followed by our most ambi-

tious project, an anthology titled *Vancouver Island Poems.* Canadian artist Pat Martin Bates contributed cover artwork and our poets included Dorothy Livesay, Earle Birney, P. K. Page, Susan Musgrave, Victor Coleman, and Gary Geddes.

Soft Press published twenty-one books of poetry, most of which were well-received, and won some small grants from Canada Council. From 1970 to 1979, I supported the Press with my salary as a university professor and, later, as an editor for a commercial publishing house.

I was publishing widely in the early 1970s, was popular with my students, but some of my colleagues complained: "Isn't four years long enough for a Visiting [American] Poet, particularly one who has been much-married, whose poetry is incomprehensible, and who employs controversial teaching methods?" In truth, my colleagues had a point. One day the chairman of the English department visited my classes. I describe the experience in "Mr. Amnesia":

An instructor in Modern Poetry, I once
lectured

For four weeks as if each class was the first class
of a new year. When the genial Chairman,
manifesting polite alarm,

Visited my classes the occasion of his being
there
gave me the opportunity to teach
as if those classes, too, were new classes.

Promoted, given a raise, a bonus and a new two-
year contract,
even I was confused. Each class I taught became
one
in an infinite series of semesters, each semester

Lasting no more than fifty minutes.
I don't know about you, but I hardly unpack
and get ready for this life and it's time

To move on to the next . . .

"Mr. Amnesia" stretches the truth. In 1973, my appointment ran out and I decided to devote myself to writing poetry, managing Soft Press, and working for a commercial publishing house.

*

Why is it that hard-nosed businesspeople are regarded as the embodiment of sanity? Because they dedicate their lives to a quest for money

With daughter Cheryl Cox, Vancouver Island, Canada, 1978

and power? Because in our society we believe rational behavior and the possession of money and power go hand in hand? The question intrigues me because, in my experience, businesspeople—publishers, for example—are often more idiosyncratic, if not notably irrational, than the people they publish.

In 1976, I became senior editor for a commercial book publisher. I accepted the position because I was going broke publishing poetry with Soft Press. I had another reason for taking the job: I wanted to learn all I could about the day-to-day operation of a nitty-gritty, seemingly successful publishing house. I had, and still have, dreams of starting a new publishing firm.

I was a loyal, hardworking employee. On one occasion, I learned that the company owed money to a printer. Therefore, I introduced my employer to a literary agent. The agent was ready to negotiate a fifteen-thousand-dollar purchase of some old letters and manuscripts the publisher regarded as "worthless, space-consuming garbage." A certain university library was prepared to buy this material.

"What's the agent like?" the publisher asked.

"He's honest and reputable, but he can be rude," I replied.

"Rude," bellowed the book publisher. "I'm rude. I'm the rudest man in Canada. There's no one ruder than I am."

I wasn't prepared for this response.

It's true I knew he was rude. It's true that once we'd argued over a manuscript I didn't want to publish. It's true he insulted me. It's true I lost my temper and hit him over the head with the three-hundred-page manuscript. But after two years of working in the industry, I assumed such unpleasantness was normal. He never protested being hit. I kept my job as editor and, some months later, asked for and received a raise.

So I'd forgotten how much he prided himself on being uncivilized. A self-proclaimed wild-and-wooly, businessman bully, bush airplane pilot, and "outback" filmmaker, he had a reputation to uphold. For some reason he needed to believe he was the rudest man in Canada. For me to suggest that there might be a rival, an individual more uncouth, more uncivilized, more barbarous than himself, was unacceptable. The publisher felt threatened.

I knew what was coming and made a point of being present when the two businessmen met. The publisher immediately accused the agent of being a swindler. The agent responded that the publisher was a noted boor with a reputation for publishing crap. The publisher counterattacked by ridiculing the agent for overvaluing the manuscripts he himself wanted to sell. Though the two were meeting for the first time, they were attacking one another's reputations with glee. If the stakes had been higher, would more insults and profanities have been exchanged? Who won? The publisher. He was more aggressive, threw out more damaging remarks, and, in the end, still managed to collect his fifteen thousand dollars.

What did I get out of it? A day off.

Part XI
Survivor of Four Marriages, Father of Five Children

I practised the Lamaze method and assisted at the birth of two of my children, Hannah and Nicholas. People speak of the "bonding" that occurs when one is present at the birth of a child. I know I felt it. It's somewhat ironic, in fact, that two years after her birth, I became both a father and a mother to Hannah. In 1972, Hannah's mother underwent a fit of wanderlust. "Robert, you can have legal custody," she said. "I think you'll be a better parent to Hannah than I can be."

So it happened that in my last full year of teaching at the University of Victoria, I became a single parent. I remember the first day that two-year-old, blonde, blue-eyed Hannah and I were alone together. We sat on the floor of a kitchen from which all the furniture had been removed. I had nothing original to say. "It's just you and me, kid," I joked.

From the time of her birth in Victoria, B.C., to her graduation from Santa Cruz High in 1988, Hannah lived and travelled with me continuously.

It's difficult to concentrate four or five hours at a time on poetry when there are children around. As father of five, I had to come up with a solution. One day in Peterborough, New Hampshire, my son Michael—then four years old—was playing in the attic with my six-year-old stepdaughter. Concerned for their safety, I didn't want to leave them alone. So instead of turning on the TV or yelling for them to shut up, I listened and took notes on what they were saying. That's how I began writing poetry with children.

"Monster Poem—Lagoon Goon"; "For Michael"; "Doctor in the Horse, House, Mouse"; "Elementary Fire Alarm"; and others were written for, and in some cases, with, my children. "Bebop a Rock"; "Blind Poet;" and "Lakes Can Die, Too" were inspired by teaching in elementary and high schools for the Ontario Arts Council in Canada, and the Cultural Council of Santa Cruz County in California. In 1979, when I first began participating in a Poet-in-the-Schools program, schoolchildren responded to my free verse poems by saying, "Poetry rhymes. If it doesn't rhyme, it's not poetry." For these students, my credibility as a poet and teacher depended on my ability to write poetry that rhymed. Assonance and consonance left them cold. *Scream-dream* was a rhyme. *Leaves-lives* was not. Alliteration was acceptable. Say *Ding-dong*, and you had their attention. Try to establish a musical connection between *steel* and *chill*, and you lost it. I could read a poem like "Honey Bear,"

> A pale blue light
> surrounds her toes as she waltzes
>
> By the clover and the mint.
> Lighter than air, heavier
> than a bear. Clear-skinned lady
> O fairest of the fair
>
> I bow to my honey bear.

and they were ready to write poems of their own.

In 1984, I learned how to operate a computer and began to do some desktop publishing. Since that time, I have worked with elementary, junior-high, and college students to produce inexpensive anthologies of the best of their prose and poetry.

How I Learned to Stand on My Head and Marry My Third and Fourth Wives

In December 1968, shortly before my third marriage, I began to find it difficult to breathe and went to see a physician. After an examination he said, "You have asthma. You need to reduce the stress in your life."

At that time I was in my fifth or sixth residence at the MacDowell Colony. I was working on my novel *The Jurassic Shales*. I didn't know it in 1968, but it was the fear of an impending marriage that was making it difficult for me to breathe.

Wayne Boohors, a New York painter—and a

fellow Colonist—introduced me to some basic yoga postures.

When it comes to breathing, I'm a pragmatist. I did the assigned bends and stretches and soon I was breathing normally. Okay, so yoga works, I decided. If yoga can help me breathe, what else can it do for me?

In 1969, I began taking yoga classes with a former British army officer who had spent twenty years in India studying meditation. I went to yoga retreats with Indra Devi, Swami Radha, Muktananda, and others. I studied Sanskrit. I read and reread Paramahansa Yogananda's *Autobiography of a Yogi,* the *Bhagavad Gita, The Upanishads,* W. Y. Evans-Wentz's *The Tibetan Book of the Dead,* Robert Payne's *The White Pony,* John Blofeld's *The Zen Teaching of Zen Huang Po,* Lao Tzu's *Tao Te Ching,* and everything else I could find on Eastern literature and religion.

When the British army officer retired from teaching, he asked me to take over his classes. So I began working as a book editor at the Authors and Eagles publishing house by day, and teaching hatha-yoga to British Columbia Civil Service employees at night. From 1976 to 1979, I also led a Siddha Yoga meditation center.

When the pressure became too much, I'd go off to a weekend yoga retreat. When that didn't work, I'd go off to a seven-day yoga retreat. After that I began attending month-long yoga retreats. Eventually—in my fourth marriage—I went to live in an ashram in Ganeshpuri, India.

My third wife disliked my involvement in yoga. She wasn't too keen on my writing poetry either. Each morning I'd get up at dawn, stroll outside, and stand on my head. Then I'd write in my journal. An hour or two later, I'd come into the house hungry for breakfast. She'd be waiting for me. "Have you taken out the garbage yet? How much money do we have in the bank? What kind of a husband are you?"

Once my third wife picked up a copy of Richard Wilhelm's translation of the *I Ching: Book of Changes,* the one with an introduction by Carl Jung, and threw it at me.

Well, imagine sharing your life with someone who scribble scribble scribbles every chance he gets. Imagine living with a partner who, when he isn't scribbling, is standing on his head. From her point of view, I was insufferable.

Ars longa, vita brevis. Art is long. Marriage is short.

Part XII
The Much-Married Man Moves to Toronto

In 1975, Toronto's Coach House Press sponsored a two-week workshop for small-press publishers. As publisher of Soft Press, and as organizer of a poetry-reading series at Open Space, Victoria, B.C., and at the University of Victoria, I had already met a dozen or more Coach House authors: Margaret Atwood, Douglas Barbour, George Bowering, Victor Coleman, Gerry Gilbert, Roy Kiyooka, Robert Kroetsch, Dorothy Livesay, David McFadden, Fred Wah, Phyllis Webb, David Young, and others. I had hopes of getting a book of my own published, a novel called *The Jurassic Shales.* In addition, I dreamed of moving to Toronto—Canada's answer to New York City—and the Coach House workshop was an opportunity to check it out.

One day, Coach House Press editor Victor Coleman invited me to a party. Victor lived in a

With daughter Hannah, age nine, and son Nicholas, age two, Toronto Island, Canada, 1979

community of about seven hundred people on the Toronto Islands, a mile-and-a-half ferry ride from downtown Toronto. Cars are not allowed on the Islands, and the main mode of transportation is the bicycle. The residents, a unique mix of writers, painters, musicians, workers in Canada's business and entertainment industry, all commuted to the city together on a ferry boat. A number of American expatriates live on the Islands, along with people from England, France, Germany, and Switzerland.

The Coach House Press party went on late into the night. It was two days before I got back to Toronto and, by that time, I had made up my mind to move to the Big City, and to live in the Island community.

Canadian poet Penny Kemp invited me to rent her house while she wintered in South America. Penny's house featured a staircase made out of tree branches and a full-size, indoor swing suspended from a swaybacked thirty-foot ceiling. Overly energetic swingers tended to crash into walls or against a stove, which sometimes set the house on fire.

I was living in Penny's house in 1980 when Swiss photographer Ursula Heller arrived on assignment for *Neue Zurcher Zeitung,* a German-language newspaper published in Zurich. Ursula invited me to interview twenty longtime residents of the community for a five-page feature story. My interviews were translated into German and published—with Ursula's photographs—on Valentine's Day, 1981. Meanwhile, *The Islanders,* a traveling exhibition of my poems and Toronto Island interviews, accompanied by Ursula's photographs, opened in Toronto City Hall. Specially typeset, enlarged, mounted on large, transportable panels, *The Islanders* exhibit was subsequently seen by more than sixty thousand people.

A year later, I received a Canada Council Explorations Grant to develop the interviews and to produce a book, *The Toronto Islands: An Illustrated History.* I spent weeks in the Toronto City Archives reading diaries from the eighteenth and nineteenth centuries, including accounts of the invasion of the Toronto Islands, and the burning of Toronto, by American troops in the War of 1812. The *Toronto Star* published numerous sections of *The Toronto Islands.* David Crombie, former mayor of Toronto and a member of Parliament, contributed an introduction and, in 1983, Dreadnaught Press published the book.

Torontonians generally support the community. But Metro Council and suburban politicians were mounting their forces at that time, as they had off and on for thirty years, to tear down the Islanders' homes and destroy the "Bohemian" enclave. In Canada, the Islanders have established a reputation for themselves as people who enjoy life. In cold climates, particularly, the enjoyment of life is sometimes subject to persecution.

When the book appeared, I was invited to appear on numerous radio and TV shows. I shared what I learned about the history of the Islands and talked about the controversy. Dreadnaught Press seized the opportunity to sponsor a publication party which was attended by several hundred people—and a TV crew. I became, by Canadian standards, a best-selling author.

The Three Roberts

Robert Priest, Canadian poet, rock musician, and singer-songwriter, was also a Dreadnaught author. Robert and I were both active in the Ontario Arts Council's Poet-in-the-Schools program. Both of us were involved in writing a series of children's poems. Robert Priest, with Bongo Herbert and the illustrator Rudi McToots, had even formed a performance group for children, the Boinks.

Robert and I met for lunch one afternoon at a Bloor Street falafel restaurant. I joked, "Let's do a stand-up comic poetry reading and call ourselves The Two Roberts." "No, no, that doesn't sound right," said Priest. "How about The Three Roberts?" "Good idea, but who's going to be the third Robert?" I asked. "There's this mad poet I heard the other night who writes in Hungarian and in English. He's also a radio broadcaster and film editor. We could combine poetry, music, and visuals."

According to Glenn Gould, Robert Zend [was] "unquestionably Canada's most musical poet." Immanuel Velikovsky said of him, "Robert Zend's feet are planted on the ground, his heart is forgiving, his head is in the clouds." William Ronald said of him, "Zend is a split personality, and I love him both."

I too came to love Robert Zend. Because I lived on the Islands, we talked often on the phone. One day Robert called me. I described the experience in a poem called, appropriately enough, "The Three Roberts":

> Ring, ring.
> "Robert, this is Robert."
>
> "Is this Robert?" "This
> is Robert, Robert." "Yes,
> Robert?" I say, "This

The Three Roberts: Robert Sward, Robert Zend, and Robert Priest, 1984

Is Robert, too." "Ah,
excuse me, I need
to find a match,"

says Robert Zend putting
down the telephone
and rummaging for matches,

granting me, a non-smoker,
the status of accessory
to his addiction.

All this occurring a few
seconds into an otherwise
scintillating conversation . . .

The three of us began to meet and rehearse. We spent hours playing together, establishing themes, introducing and juxtaposing poems. "This is the way musicians rehearse," said Priest. And that was the way we rehearsed for each of our readings.

On January 29, 1984, we read together at Grossman's Tavern, a few blocks from the University of Toronto. This reading, our first as a group, was arranged by Elliot Lefko, "founder of poetry concerts in Toronto, 'the mastermind of poetry cabaret,'"

according to the *Globe and Mail.* Elliot, one of Canada's literary entrepreneurs, did well by us. It was a cold, gray, miserable Sunday afternoon, but over three hundred people turned out. Priest led off with a musical set. We read individually, then as a group, alternating poems, playing out a series of variations.

In response to the demand for the poems we read, Robert Zend designed an edition titled *The Three Roberts, Premiere Performance.* HMS Press published and distributed the book in conjunction with a Toronto music magazine called *Shades.* Writers Judith Merril, Elizabeth Smart, and Sheila Wawanash praised the little publication and it sold well.

Next we did a reading at Major Robert's Restaurant near the intersection of Major and Robert Streets in Toronto. Our theme was Love and, in response to the demand for the poems we read, Dreadnaught Press published an edition titled *The Three Roberts on Love.*

Our third reading was on the theme of Childhood. We read at a small church a few steps from the Eaton Center in Toronto. Again, there was demand for our work. In 1985, Peter Baltensperger and Brenda Krewen issued *The Three Roberts on Childhood* with Moonstone Press (St. Catharines, Ontario). We did a fourth reading on the theme of War, but that "book" is as yet unpublished.

The group dissolved in 1985 about the time we were scheduled to appear on a Canadian Broadcasting Corporation radio show. Robert Zend, a one-man literary renaissance, underwent heart surgery and died a few months later. That same year I returned to the U.S.

Part XIII
How Whitman, Thoreau, and John Robert Colombo Sent Me Back to America

I met John Robert Colombo, Canadian poet and editor of *Colombo's Canadian Quotations,* in 1971. Friends for nearly twenty years, we sometimes browsed together in Queen Street, Toronto, bookstores. On one occasion, Colombo introduced me to a volume titled *Walt Whitman's Diary in Canada, with Extracts from Other of His Diaries and Literary Notebooks.* There's a certain irony in the fact Colombo, the "Master Gatherer of Canadiana," helped set me on a course which led me back to my American roots.

In any case, I learned that Whitman visited Toronto in 1880, and was favorably impressed. "The city made the impression on me of a lively dashing place," he wrote in a thick pocket journal he carried with him. Whitman went sightseeing on an omnibus and (as one might expect) rode on top with the driver. He wrote of "blue Ontario's waters, sunlit, yet with a slight haze, through which [I saw] occasionally a distant sail."

When I learned of Thoreau's visit to Canada ("What I got by going to Canada was a cold," wrote Thoreau), I began imagining what it might be like to live abroad for many years and then, homesick for one's native land, to be visited by two dear friends—albeit from the nineteenth century. How could one resist packing one's bags and returning with them? I wanna go home, I wanna go home. That was my underlying thought as I wrote a feature for the *Toronto Star* titled "Whitman Loved (But Thoreau Hated) Toronto."

Since 1969 I had lived exclusively on islands—Vancouver Island for ten years and Toronto Island for five. Reading Whitman's journals, rereading *Leaves of Grass,* I felt I was waking up after a long sleep. I was an expatriate Rip Van Winkle. "It's time to go home," I said. But my French-speaking Canadian wife and two children, Hannah and Nicholas,

didn't want to leave the safe and secure Toronto Islands and the "no automobiles allowed" community of seven hundred people. "Why leave?" they protested. "We own a home in an idyllic park with a view of Lake Ontario. Downtown Toronto is ten minutes away by ferry. We have everything we need right here."

But I was fifty years old and pining away for my American friends and children who still lived in the States. In addition, I missed the language. I missed the humor. Canadian speech is subtly different from American speech. As a writer, I craved the language I had grown up with. My French-speaking Canadian wife told me I resembled some extraterrestrial being, a Chicago-born E.T. destined to return to his home. I knew it was put up or shut up. Now or never. I began making plans to return to America and to bring my family. It was a less-than-democratic decision, and I paid a price.

"Where are we going to live? What about school? All our friends are here. America's a violent country. People shoot one another in the street for no reason. And what about money? Where are you going to get a job?"

"I'll meditate on it," I said.

In 1984, in the Hart House Debates Room at the University of Toronto, I went to see a white-clad yogi with an untrimmed beard who hadn't spoken a single word in more than thirty years. He understood English, but used a young "interpreter" to field questions and read aloud from a chalkboard on which he, the yogi, wrote the answers.

"What is the function of a master?" I asked.

As befits a man who has kept his mouth shut for three decades, the yogi had developed a skill for saying a great deal in the fewest possible words. "The function of a master is to show the path and leave," he wrote on his chalkboard.

"This is like having a conversation with a Chinese fortune cookie," I whispered to my wife.

The next day, I confronted my editor at the *Toronto Star* with former Harvard University professor Richard Alpert's description of the yogi in his book *Be Here Now:*

His arms are . . . tiny. But this little ninety-pound fellow . . . architecturally designed . . . temples and schools, supervised . . . the buildings and grounds . . . He slept two hours a night. His food intake for the last fifteen years had been two glasses of milk a day . . . yet when the workmen can't lift a particularly heavy rock, they call for "the little great king." As in a comic strip, he goes over and lifts the rock, just with one-pointedness of mind.

That did the trick. The editor came up with $300.00 so I could attend, and write about, a week-long yoga retreat at Sparrow Lake, about one hundred miles north of Toronto. My wife and children came with me. A week later, the *Star* ran an illustrated two-page feature under the heading, "He hasn't spoken for thirty years, but the wise words of Baba Hari Dass and five peaceful days at his yoga camp helped relieve a frazzled Toronto family's daily stresses."

Baba Hari Dass did more than relieve us of our stresses. As things turned out, he also proved to be my ticket back to America. Soon after the piece was published, I received a letter from the Mount Madonna Center inviting me to teach a couple of writing courses at Mount Madonna School in the Santa Cruz Mountains. The author of the letter neglected to mention that the school is located on the San Andreas Fault. In any case, my family and I were provided with a house, meals, a decent school for the children, and an opportunity to get reoriented to life in the U.S.A.

As my friend Mort Marcus wrote in his introduction to *Poet Santa Cruz,*

Now he has moved from Canada to California, taken up residence at Santa Cruz County's Mount Madonna . . . and the physical and psychical environment has taken him by the tongue to new spiritual heights, which have slowed his responses to a meditative stillness and (surprisingly) eased him back into such closed forms as sonnets and villanelles . . . This change shows in his new poems, "A Monk on the Santa Cruz Mountains"; "Castroville—California"; "A Coffee Shop . . ."; "Li Po"; and "The Emperor . . ."

*

In Part II of this autobiography, I write of my progress in moving from the kitchen floor to the kitchen table—a milestone. In January 1986, I moved from the mountains overlooking Monterey Bay to Santa Cruz, a seismically active community of forty-five thousand people located seventy-five miles south of San Francisco. Another milestone. Right, I was a wifeless, risk-taking man in his early fifties with little money in the bank. Back in the real world

working as a free-lance writer and teacher, it was time to do some stocktaking, time for another inventory.

Sometimes I imagine myself being interviewed by Barbara Walters.

Part XIV
Barbara Walters Interviews a Much-Married Man

INT: Robert, why four marriages?

RS: You mean, why four successful marriages? I know I may sound defensive, but I regard all my marriages as successful. They may have dried up in the end, but they weren't miserable marriages. I learned from each one. And they've produced five beautiful children.

INT: I stand corrected. Would you tell us what you were looking for in each of your marriages? Then, would you tell us what they were like and what went wrong?

RS: I wanted a devoted wife and muse, a nurturer and a general factotum all in one person. I was looking for the perfect partner—sexually, emotionally, intellectually. Because I came into my first two marriages with the traditional male script, I caused pain for the women, for my children, and for myself. It's sad, but true.

My first, an Iowa Writers' Workshop marriage, ended because of my immaturity. At some level, I didn't know what I wanted. My first wife and I had both grown up in the 1940s on the North Side of Chicago. There was something wonderfully warm and familiar about her. I remember how, on Saturday afternoons, we'd open all the windows in our two-room, Iowa City apartment, turn up the volume on the phonograph, and clean house while playing schmaltzy recordings of *La Bohème* and *Madame Butterfly.*

Then we'd invite friends over and make a big spaghetti dinner. I was happy but, at the same time, I feared I had lost my freedom. I was afraid I was being pressured into getting a regular job. In those days men who married instantly gained twenty or thirty pounds. I was afraid I was going to develop a potbelly and stop writing poetry. So I began willfully scribbling poetry all the time. I was a jerk.

INT: The late 1950s and early '60s were a productive time for you.

RS: I wrote "Uncle Dog: The Poet at 9" and many of the poems included in the Odyssey Chapbook *Advertisements*, the Putnam, England, edition of *Uncle Dog and Other Poems*, and *Kissing the Dancer*. I associate one, a zany poem titled ". . . I Have Just Bought a House," with my first marriage. That poem is in the form of a letter:

Dear George—George, I have just bought a
    house,
an eighty-seven room house. Also,
a twenty-one room house. And many
little houses. And eighteen trailers,
and nineteen cars (six with beds in them);
and wives for all the rooms, the trailers
the little houses, and the six cars
with beds in them,
        . . . and they all love me,
all my wives love me. They do, George . . .

INT: You must know that line from Emily Dickinson: "Is there not a sweet wolf in us that wants what it wants?"

RS: Yes, and there's a connection between that hot, aggressive, sweet wolf in me and the patriarchal role.

INT: And then, Robert, you married a second time.

RS: In an age when there weren't other alternatives, at a time when it was the right thing to do, my second wife and I were propelled into marriage by an unexpected pregnancy. She came from a well-to-do Washington, D.C., Greek Orthodox family. She was a fine mother, a fantastic cook. She loved to entertain. She created a terrific home. In fact, I didn't realize how important home was until the marriage ended. That was one thing I learned from the marriage: that I sincerely wanted a home, family, and children. I learned too that I tended to impose a script on women and limited their growth.

As much as I loved these women, I was callow, shallow, and disloyal, not ready for marriage. All the time I was going scribble scribble scribble. That wasn't so bad. But I was also pant pant panting around. I'd ask myself, What else is out there? What am I missing? I was like a heat-seeking cocky mocky poetry missile. I was a low-down, self-involved dirty dog. Woof, woof. I want. I want. That part of me that needed stability to write was at war with the part that needed to have adventure. And I thought the adventure would help my writing.

INT: In 1967, you left your second wife and ran off to London, England, to live with the British novelist Ann Quin, author of *Berg* and *Three*. By all accounts, you were very much in love with Ann. But then you decided to return to the States to be with your children. After all that, what possessed you to marry a third time?

Daughter Hannah and son Michael, 1988

Daughter Barbara Austin and granddaughter Robin, 1990

RS: After being run over by an MG, my reason was swept away by a gorgeous peaches-and-cream New York German-Jewish American stoned sardonic architect princess with a lovely sense of humor and the features of a playboy bunny. I was goo goo, ga ga, a love-hungry yummy dummy. And what a price I paid for that one! At once entertaining and informative, it was like being married for four years to a living technicolor Kama Sutra psychedelic fleshtone get-it-while-it's-hot chapter of American history, all the best and worst aspects of the sexual revolution.

A friend describes the marriage as a combination of thunder, lightning, and intercity rivalry: her New York The Big Apple First City Master Race Center of the Universe versus my pip squeak bourgeois Chicago Second City midwestern Eastern European origins. In her view, people who grew up in Manhattan and attended Music and Art High School are privileged humans, wiser, tougher, and more deserving than anyone else in America. So right from the beginning there was some tension.

In addition, I was formed by the 1940s and cautious '50s. She was formed by the zipless encounters of the 1960s. "I want an open marriage," she said. Wowwy powwy. "I want a sub-

scription to the *Saturday Evening Post,*" I replied. You know, Barbara, I'm more conventional than my resume might lead you to think. And after four marriages, I find each divorce hurts hurts hurts just as much, maybe more, than the one before.

INT: Hmm. You're referring of course to your marital resume. What goes around, comes around. It sounds to me as if you got what you deserved. But tell us, Robert, after all these years, are you for monogamy?

RS: Yes, I am. I have come to agree with Robert Graves, who says,

> the act of love is a metaphor of spiritual togetherness, and if you perform the act of love with someone who means little to you, you're giving away something that belongs to the person you do love or might love. The act of love belongs to two people in the way that secrets are shared . . . promiscuity seems forbidden to poets, though I do not grudge it to any nonpoet.

I feel I've done some of my best writing when I've been faithful, solid, and secure in a relationship. I need conventional, nitty gritty practicality in my life in order to write zany surreal crazy goofy musical moving tuneful poems and stories . . . and to have a place, a faithful goddess, a base to come back to. All that mindless careless joysticking didn't lead to much readable, let alone memorable, poetry.

INT: What poem of yours do you associate with your third marriage?

RS: There's one called "Scarf Gobble Wallow Inventory," which George Hitchcock published in *Kayak* 21. Robert Vas Dias reprinted "Scarf Gobble . . ." in *Inside Outer Space: New Poems of the Space Age* (Doubleday-Anchor). I mention the anthology because the poem is now out of print.

INT: How about a sample?

RS: All I am really hungry for is everything
The ability to hibernate and a red suitcase going
    off
        everywhere
Every cell in your body and every cell in my body
    is
        hungry and each has its own stomach . . .

Is the universe a womb or a mouth?
And what *is* hunger, really?
And is the end of the world to be understood in
    terms of
        hunger or gifts, or the tops of peoples'
            heads coming off?

The most complex dream I've ever dreamed I
   dreamed in
     London.
It involved in its entirety taking one bite of an
   orange . . .

Even now we are all saying, over and over,
I've never been so hungry in my life.
I want one more bacon-lettuce-and-tomato
   sandwich,
to make love and kiss everyone I know
   goodbye . . .

INT: *Inside Outer Space* . . . There's a science-fiction
aspect to that poetry anthology, isn't there?

RS: Yes, and there was a science-fiction, War-of-the-
Worlds aspect to my third marriage.

INT: Which leads us to your fourth marriage. You
were heavily into yoga in 1975, weren't you?

RS: Yes, and Wife Number Four was raised in the
Russian Orthodox tradition. She agreed to be
married by a yogi. I thought maybe that would
help. Mantras, incense, and a California marriage
license. Who knows, all that chanting and meditation may have done some good. That marriage
lasted what was, for me, a record-setting twelve
years.

When we married, I was forty-two and she was
thirty, an artist and a feminist. This time I became
the devoted spouse, muse, nurturer, and general
factotum. This time, while she complained of being
shackled and unfree, I did all I could to make the
marriage work. As much as I loved poetry, for
example, I began writing articles and features to
make money so we could survive and so she could
devote herself to her art.

INT: Then what happened?

RS: How does one support a family of four as a free-
lance writer? As much as I loved her, I was
frustrated: I had less and less time to write poetry.
And she was fed up living off my marginal income.
She was also bored and restless. Fortunately, when
the marriage ended, we were living in a spiritual
community in the Santa Cruz Mountains. I
thought, What good is a spiritual community if it
can't help you through a busted marriage? I began
by seeking advice from a yogi.

"How come she left?" I asked the yogi.
"She found you boring. She wants fun," he
wrote on a small chalkboard.
"Am I boring?"
"No. You have different natures. Women
leave you because they want excitement.

You are a writer. You live in an abstract
world which doesn't excite them."

Then he told me to get a job and make money.
He also told me that she had moved in with another
man and asked if I could accept that the marriage
was over. Well, it turned out he was right on all
counts. That happened in August 1985.

INT: After tying and untying the knot four times what
did you feel?

RS: I felt ready to jump out of my skin. I was burning
up and, at the same time, I felt I had just stepped
out of a freezer. When the yogi told me my fourth
wife found me boring, I thought, Here's a man
who's never been married. Would I trade places
with him? I thought, If I had to choose between
never marrying and paying the price one pays for
breaking up, no, no, better celibacy, better the life
of a monk than a much-married man singing the
blues.

INT: Fair enough. And how long did that resolution
last?

RS: It wasn't exactly a resolution. I lived in a cabin in
the Santa Cruz Mountains for six months looking
after a seventy-nine-year-old blind woman, a hat-
maker known as Mountain Mama. And I worked
on my *Collected Poems* and a novel, *How to Cure a
Broken Heart.* In 1986, I was ready to move back to
civilization.

INT: Santa Cruz is civilization?

RS: Santa Cruz is an exciting place to live. There's lots
going on. And, if nothing else, one can count on a
little geologic activity. In any case, I needed a job. I
found work as a newspaper editor and food reviewer. I taught some poetry courses and continued
working on the *Collected Poems.*

INT: And what about your children? How have they
turned out?

RS: My oldest daughter, Cheryl, is now a scientist. She
does research in limb regeneration and teaches at
University College in London, England.

Barbara is a graduate of Berkeley, where she
finished first in her class. Barbara lives near San
Francisco and works full-time as an environmental
scientist. She writes about air pollution and acid
rain issues. She's also married and has two children.

Barbara and my oldest son, Michael, are children
from my second marriage. Michael is a student at
Arizona University in Flagstaff.

Hannah's a dancer and actress. She's working for
a degree at Florida International University.

Nicholas, my youngest, is a junior-high student
living on Toronto Island. Nicholas's dream is to
play professional hockey.

Expensive as it is to travel, we do manage to see one another—though not as often as the old man would like. Nicholas, of course, is with me every summer.

INT: What were the worst and best times in your life?

RS: Before going to India, working for the Authors and Eagles publishing house, I used to jog every day on the beach. One day I found myself jogging and sobbing at the same time. I'd been in Canada since 1969. I was sobbing out of homesickness, out of love for America and my family and friends in the U.S.A. I was sobbing because I felt trapped and didn't know how to get back. I was sobbing because I was grieving for a marriage that had turned sour. I was sobbing because I was working at a stupid, ill-paying job to support a wife and two children and my writing career had gone off the track.

INT: And the best of times?

RS: Now. Being with Gloria. Finding time to write. Because writing is my passion. And teaching, because I love teaching and feel I'm giving more to it now than I ever did in the past.

Erica Jong writes, "At forty-five, you either perish or recreate yourself like a phoenix. I was chosen for the latter course." Barbara, I'm fifty-six years old, but I believe I too was chosen for the latter course. And this is the best of times, no doubt about it.

INT: Coffee House Press plans to publish your *Collected Poems* in 1991. We'll have to have you back when the book is in the stores.

End of fantasy.

Part XV
Compatibility Plus (1987—)

In October 1986, I was named editor of a weekly Santa Cruz County newspaper. As editor, I wrote a regular column, the lead news story, back-up stories, features, and profiles. In addition, I took photographs, wrote captions, and worked with the art department to lay out and produce the paper.

In February 1987, the publisher asked me to do a feature on "The Business of Love" for a special Valentine's Day edition. I began my story by phoning Allan Gleicher, a former Westinghouse engineer, and now director of services for Compatibility Plus, an introduction service for "selective single people."

Allan agreed to meet me at a coffee bar in the Capitola Book Cafe, "good neutral ground for a first date." Busy, successful people don't have time to date

around, he said. Where are they going to meet other successful people on their own level?

For $495, the matchmaker said he would personally screen a client, and their prospective mates, in order to save everyone time.

Going the Extra Mile for Love

Later, doing more research on love, I learned that the secret of the marriage-broker business (according to Genkichi Ishizaka, the most successful matchmaker in Japan) is "to get the right boy for the right girl so that their sexual energies will go bang and keep on going bang." To achieve this end, Genkichi Ishizaka says he seeks a combination of the opposites in temperament together with similarity in backgrounds.

To make a long story short, my Valentine feature was published. In March, now an honorary member of Compatibility Plus, I received a complimentary computerized printout with the phone numbers of three well-to-do, upwardly mobile clients. I called one of the three, but my heart wasn't in it.

In June 1987, Allan Gleicher phoned to say he had someone new, someone special he wanted me to meet, a beautiful, warmhearted, emotionally stable, talented woman, recently separated from her spouse. She too was from Chicago. Opposites in temperament, similarities in background, I thought.

"If she's been separated from him for less than a year, I don't want to meet her," I said.

"They've been separated over a year," Allan assured me. "Her name is Gloria Alford. She's an artist, and you were the very first person I thought of."

I decided I wanted to meet this woman.

According to Gloria, I appeared at her door looking like a *Saturday Evening Post* cover. "You were carrying a bouquet of flowers and a poetry book. You had a big innocent smile, and you were all dressed up . . . you had rosy cheeks and a bald spot surrounded with dark, curly hair like a monk . . . and that very first night you told me you had been married four times."

I handed Gloria one of my poetry books—*Half a Life's History*—and she handed me a copy of *Monterey Life* magazine with a profile of her and her artwork. So there we sat in her living room reading about one another. I liked what I read: "If an accepted belief doesn't make sense to her, Gloria will ignore it." Gloria was quoted as saying, "Why not take up new challenges in mid-life, or even in old age? Who

Artist Gloria Alford and Robert Sward, Santa Cruz, 1990

determines that youth is the only worthwhile life stage?"

"Gloria majored in social sciences at Berkeley . . . taking a few art classes . . . [and, later] decided to cut her own path [as a sculptor] and make use of new techniques and materials—vacuum-formed plastic, screen printing, computer graphics, and printed circuit boards . . . she's now in demand by museums and galleries across the country."

"I knew that night, I had no doubt at all that something very special had happened," Gloria says.

"Why would you be interested in a man who's been married four times?" I asked.

"You make a convincing case you've learned something from your marriages. You know what mistakes you made . . . and you made them all. You're a man who's had some of his rough edges smoothed out. Yet you seem not so much worn down with your four marriages as shined up. So to my eyes, you're more valuable . . . you know, the way certain antiques have a patina on them?"

In *Golden Oldies and New Releases*, there's a sequence written for Gloria. One of the poems is titled "For Gloria on Her 60th Birthday, or Looking

for Gloria in Merriam-Webster." The last two stanzas read:

> She has chestnut-colored hair,
> old fashioned Clara Bow lips,
> moist brown eyes . . .
>   Arms outstretched, head thrown back
> she glides toward me and into her seventh
>   decade.
>
> Her name means "to adore,"
> "to rejoice, to be jubilant,
> to magnify and honor as in worship, to give or
>   ascribe glory—"
>   my love, O Gloria, I do, I do.

BIBLIOGRAPHY

Poetry:

Advertisements (introduction by Frederick Eckman), Odyssey Chapbook Publications, 1958.

Uncle Dog and Other Poems, Putnam (London), 1962.

Kissing the Dancer and Other Poems (introduction by William Meredith), Cornell University Press, 1964.

Thousand-Year-Old Fiancee and Other Poems, Cornell University Press, 1965.

Horgbortom Stringbottom, I Am Yours, You Are History, Swallow Press, 1970.

Hannah's Cartoon, Soft Press (Victoria, British Columbia), 1970.

(With Mike Doyle) *Quorum/Noah*, Soft Press, 1970.

Gift, Soft Press, 1972.

Songs from the Jurassic Shales, Soft Press, 1972.

Five Iowa Poems and One Iowa Print, Stone Wall Press, 1975.

Honey Bear on Lasqueti Island, B.C., Soft Press, 1978.

Six Poems, League of Canadian Poets, 1980.

Twelve Poems, Island House Books, 1982.

Movies: Left to Right, South Western Ontario Poetry, 1983.

Half a Life's History, Poems: New and Selected, 1957–1983 (introduction by Earle Birney), Aya Press (Toronto), 1983.

(With Robert Priest and Robert Zend) *The Three Roberts: Premiere Performance*, HMS Press (Scarborough, Ontario) 1984.

(With Priest and Zend) *The Three Roberts on Love*, Dreadnaught Press (Toronto), 1984.

(With Priest and Zend) *The Three Roberts on Childhood*, Moonstone Press (St. Catharines, Ontario), 1985.

Poet Santa Cruz (introduction by Morton Marcus), Jazz Press, 1985.

Four Incarnations: New and Selected Poems, 1957–1991, Coffee House Press, 1991.

Fiction:

The Jurassic Shales (novel), Coach House Press (Toronto), 1975.

Nonfiction:

The Toronto Islands: An Illustrated History, Dreadnaught Press, 1983.

Audiotapes:

The Thousand-Year-Old Fiancee and Other Poems, Western Michigan University Aural Press, 1965.

"New Letters on the Air" (broadcast on National Public Radio; interview/reading), University of Missouri, 1985.

"Poem: For William Carlos Williams" (with music by Daria Semegen), Electronic Music Center of Columbia and Princeton Universities, 1965.

Other:

The Islanders (with photographs by Ursula Heller; traveling exhibition of poems on the Toronto Island community), opened in Toronto, 1980.

"Alpha The Dog," "Lagoon Goon," and "Toronto Island Suite" (with music by Davis Passmore; performed by the Tapestry Singers, Adelaide Court Theater, Toronto), on tour in Canada, May 1984.

Producer of three fifty-minute features for the radio show "Anthology," including "Spiritual Poetry in Canada: Interviews with Margaret Atwood, Earle Birney, Gwendolyn MacEwen, John Robert Colombo, David McFadden, and Joy Kogawa," 1984; "Poetry as Performance: Featuring the Dub Poets; Earle Birney Reading and Singing With Nexus; the Four Horseman; the Three Roberts; and Sean O'Huigin," 1984; and "Canada's Wandering Saintly Minstrel: An Evening with Leonard Cohen," 1985; all broadcast by the Canadian Broadcasting Corporation (CBC).

Contributor of stories, poems, and articles to many periodicals, including *Canadian Forum, Chicago Review, Globe and Mail, Hudson Review, Nation, New Yorker, New York Times, Paris Review, Quarterly Review of Literature*, and others.

Contributor to numerous anthologies, textbooks, and references, including *Controversy of Poets: The Anchor Book of Contemporary American Poetry*, Doubleday Anchor; *Contemporary American Poets: American Poetry since 1940*, World Publishing; *Inside Outer Space*, Doubleday; *Penguin Book of Animal Poetry*, Penguin; *New Yorker Book of Poems*, Viking; *The Now Voices*, Scribners; *Poets of Canada*, Hurtig; *Oxford Book of American Light Verse*, Oxford University Press; *To Say the Least: Canadian Poets from A to Z*, Press Porcepic; and others.

Karen Swenson

1936-

My mother pulled from the old black-and-brass trunk bundles and bundles of letters in tattered envelopes adorned with stamps from all the countries of Europe and North Africa. They were addressed in tendrils of copperplate handwriting, the black ink brown with age. "What's the point of keeping them? Throw them all out." Most foolishly I acquiesced, but that day in the attic I did save from her reordering hand her own travelogues. They consisted of fat bundles of postcards, each numbered and on its back a narrative of a part of her trip as well as pictures of the various men who had courted her enroute—Henri in Algiers who had been too possessive, Enrico in Florence whose mother had thought her too American, too liberated. Writing and traveling were the two obsessions of the women in my family, but in my life writing came first.

Writing meant the writing of letters and I started with thank-you notes after Christmas and my birthday to my gaggle of great-aunts in Fargo, North Dakota. The day after Christmas my mother would enforce the writing of these notes and I am convinced that it was from this exercise that my commitment to writing came. At first I was expected only to say thank you for each present and append a flattering comment on its size, color, or use. This I found a sufficiently ponderous exercise at the age of six, but, when I was eight, she upped the ante and urged me to write "something interesting. . . . Some news, Dear."

I was appalled at the potential size of the project and objected that I didn't know any interesting news. "Well, then, look out the window and describe what you see," she said, and left me to the terrifying solitude of the blank page that is refuge and dungeon to all writers.

I looked out the window and started to describe the bare-branched winter scene, the oak rattling its tatters of leaves, the snow crusting the hollows of the lawn. To my amazement I found I was enjoying myself. What was more amazing was that, when my mother came back to see how I was getting on, she actually praised what I'd written. My mother came from the school of maternity that believed expressions of praise and love were detrimental to the

Karen Swenson, 1982

characters of children, would make them arrogant, egotistical, and lazy.

The idea that I might wring praise from the lips of my mother, whom I adored and hated and have written about extensively in *A Sense of Direction*, published by The Smith, may have set my feet on the path to poetry.

Ironically, she gave me the tool that helped to heal me from the anguish of our difficult relationship. When she died in 1976, I was able to go back to the core incident that occurred between us and make it into the poem "The White Rabbit." Our tragedy was neither that she beat me nor that I killed the white rabbit, but that neither of us could admit to what we had done and on the basis of our mutual admissions

Karen, age four

create a basis for a relationship. The real corpse was not that of the rabbit but of the relationship we never allowed ourselves to have.

My father, whom I adored, was an architect, an alcoholic, and a lonely, frightened man. He also figures in a number of poems in both *An Attic of Ideals,* my first book, and *A Sense of Direction.* Over a period of fifty years he worked for the most famous architectural firms in New York, including Harrison and Abramovitz and I. M. Pei. My parents' marriage was often stormy. Every morning of my childhood I was awakened by the sound of my mother crashing the pots and pans around in the stove drawer while she argued with my father about money. Every year she would drive out to Fargo to see her relatives, and, as I learned later, to escape from the claustrophobic relationship she had with her husband.

I always pled to go because, though I did not like writing to my great-aunts, I loved being with them in the old house with its gables shaded by the arms of the elm. I loved the trip out there through the New York farmland, a smidgen of Canada (so I could say I'd been out of the country), and up and over the

Michigan peninsula with its beautiful countryside. These trips were the beginnings of my travels.

Sometimes we went by train, the Twentieth Century Limited with its elegant dining car decked out in white linen and flowers on each table. The compartments were wonderful private worlds, full of interesting gadgets, cozy places to curl up in and alternately read a book and watch the country flow by. There was a suspension of being on a train that I found delightful. I suspect that was another reason my mother traveled. She had very little rebel in her soul, but I don't think she was comfortable in her societally assigned roles, or her perceptions of them, which were very narrow. Traveling temporarily broke her out of those rigid confines.

The summer I turned eleven I was in Fargo with my great-aunts when I received a letter that subtly changed my life. I had only one close friend in school, a boy named Billy Bliss. We did everything together: walked to school, came home from school, adventured in the woods during the summer.

Billy would get cross if I became too bossy and ordered him around when we rearranged the boulders in the creek bed. I wouldn't talk to him for a couple of days after he washed my face in snow. But we always came back to each other. It was the one relationship in my childhood in which I had complete trust. His mother wrote to tell me that Billy had died after an appendix operation. I found the news incomprehensible and decided to wait until the fall when I would be back in my hometown of Chappaqua to understand what it meant.

That September I stood at the end of my drive waiting for Billy to join me for our walk through the woods to school. His brother Eddy showed up but, of course, Billy didn't and I began to understand. That day I decided Billy had been cheated out of his life and that, therefore, I had to lead my life for the two of us. I would have to have a girl-boy life to make up for what Billy had missed. I think, looking back in middle age, that is what I've had.

The summer that Billy died I read every book on pirates that they had in the Fargo library. The frustration of my young life was at that point twofold: *a)* there were no more pirates; *b)* there were no women pirates. I was beginning to become aware that in all the fields I was interested in, there were no women. The women in my family, and in my suburban community, Chappaqua, outside of New York, offered few role models for any profession other than ladyhood. Worse than that, they were critical to sneering of women who worked. A woman in town who was a lawyer had a retarded child, and was spoken of as though her child's retardation was directly traceable to her profession. My mother spoke disparagingly of both her older sister's career teaching in private schools and her previous career as a dancer on Broadway with Al Jolson and in Ziegfield productions. Indeed, my mother had had a successful career as a buyer at Macy's before she married. My great-aunts lived very social lives going to rounds of club meetings, luncheons, and teas, although they had, in their youth, all worked in the family furniture store in various capacities.

But now, when they were not involved in the Fargo social round, they were happy to tell me stories of their childhood. My great-aunt Olivia had been on a train immobilized by swarms of locusts which were ground up by the wheels, making the tracks so slippery that the train couldn't move, while inside the cars, even with the windows shut, the locusts flew about eating people's clothes and hair. Great-aunt Claire had stories about Indians coming around to sell strawberries and wild rice. Great-aunt Ann played

"My mother, Dorothy Trautman Swenson, at age eighteen"

"My father, Howard Swenson, in Grandfather August Martin Swenson's arms, and my uncle Lorenzo Swenson"

elephant with me, a game in which I leapt out of the dark curve of the kitchen stairs yelling "I am an elephant" and scared her. Most of them had been to Europe and written those letters in the attic that we threw out.

My great-aunt Claire had wanted to take her little Irish harp and travel around Ireland playing in small towns, but a woman, her parents told her, could not travel alone. My great-aunt Ann had wanted to go to Paris to study painting, but her father and mother had quashed that idea. Instead, she had married a man who, when she needed new shoes, taunted her, telling her to go ask her rich family for shoes. Ashamed, and having no money of her own, she returned milk bottles and saved until she could buy a cheap pair.

In their seventies my great-aunts traveled to San Francisco to see their one surviving brother, to Mexico, to New York. They came, after all, from traveling stock. Their parents had come here first by boat from Hamburg, then across the plains to North Dakota when it was still the Northwest Territory. On the other side of the family there were stories that the ship on which my Danish grandmother had come to America alone had been attacked by pirates. Perhaps that was linked with my desire to be a pirate. The gift these women gave me, particularly my great-aunts, was a firm belief that the last of life was the best. My mother, so it seemed to me, was always kowtowing to the requisites of society. My great-aunts bowed to no one, not even New York City taxi drivers. Great-aunt Claire in the late 1940s once tipped a taxi driver a nickel. He held it in his palm and asked in mock bewilderment, "Hey, lady, what's this?" She whipped it off his palm stating crisply, "If you don't want it, I do."

My mother and her sister, my aunt Liz, were more daring. My mother traveled to North Africa to Tunisia and Algeria and was even alone for a few days in Tunis while she waited for her uncle, who was buying rugs for the store, to join her. My aunt went to Central America and ended up teaching at the American School of Monterrey in Mexico when I was fifteen and took me with her the first year she was there. Everything was wonderful—I loved the food; Liz let me read at the dining-room table; she even understood when I went groggy for two days because of my nonstop reading of *Gone with the Wind;* there was sunshine every day and flowers everywhere— except that I was the only genuine, pale-skinned,

green-eyed redhead for about five hundred square miles in a Spanish culture.

I lost my anonymity the moment I stepped out the door every morning. When I walked down the street I was followed by a continuous stream of male comment. I learned to curse them out under my breath. They would follow in cars behind my bus when I came home and then park outside the apartment while, terrified, I locked all the windows and doors. For years I had traveled alone into New York City, the only child my age in Chappaqua who was allowed to do so. I had always felt perfectly safe there. But in Monterrey, I was not anonymous as I was in New York, and the raw sexuality of the attention I received was frightening to me. It was largely because of the attention from men and because I was homesick for New York City that I returned home the next year. But the year in Mexico created a bond between my aunt Liz and me that lasted until she died at ninety-nine.

When I returned to Chappaqua I had a teacher, Miss Curzon, whom I adored. She made the world of literature a vast treasure hoard of authors all of whom I wanted to read at once. I also wanted desperately to impress her. I did book reports on Dante's *Inferno.* She tried to pry me off the top of the intellectual ladder and even urged children's books on me, which I dutifully, if disdainfully, read and reported on for extra credit.

The Lugar "Girls": (from left) Great-aunts Olivia, Julia, Amelia, Grandmother Elizabeth Trautman, Great-aunts Claire and Ann

She also had us write small creative pieces. If she liked your piece, she would read it aloud in class and comment on it. I burned to have her read one of my pieces. I was sure there was some trick involved. By the age of ten I had decided that all adults talked in code and that you could not believe anything they said. Once in a while, not often, I would run into an adult who said what he or she meant and I would be totally astounded. Therefore, when Miss Curzon said we were to write about anything we wanted, that we should write about what was important to us, I was sure she didn't mean it. I listened carefully to those pieces she read, but that didn't help much. The only one I can remember at this distance in time was by a girl named Janet about how she loved her family's tractor. I thought it was weird.

Still every Thursday I would try. I wrote about pathetically dying dogs, about fires aboard capsizing ships. I was very dramatic and, I thought, interesting. She never read any of them in class. One afternoon when the creative assignment was due the next day, I gave up. I couldn't think of anything interesting. So I did what my mother had taught me so many years before. I looked out the window and began describing what I saw. The first snow of the year was falling and I incorporated into my description memories of the excitement the first snow had brought to me when I was younger. I recalled its promise of Christmas and sledding and skating, and concluded by saying that, while the first snow was still exhilarating, it had lost its magic. Miss Curzon read it in class, praised my descriptions and the tone of the piece. She said it was one anyone could identify with. I became, of course, her slave for life, and joined her after-school Creative Writing Club, but I was totally mystified. I knew that piece truly was full of my feelings and my voice.

My experience had taught me that no adult wanted to hear a child's real voice. Miss Curzon had said what she meant, and I was totally confused. I had a wonderful time in her club, however, and even won a national *Scholastic* magazine award for one of my stories.

By the time I got to college I had run out of plots and, therefore, turned to poetry, which I felt didn't need a plot, just a surplus of emotion. I have since found in teaching creative writing many young people with the same misunderstanding of the craft.

I was admitted to Barnard, which I was sure was a mistake. In my first few weeks on campus I kept expecting the dean to call me in to say that they had made an error in judgement. But she didn't. I was too

Elizabeth West (a stage name), the author's aunt

frightened to take a course in writing poetry, although Bob Pack was teaching there then. But I did manage to get enough courage to take a creative-writing course in prose. I'm not sure what I was afraid of, perhaps that the professor would tell me I was no good, and then what would I do? Professor Kauenhaven taught the course I did take, and he did me an enormous service by having us write five hundred to a thousand words five days a week in a journal. The sheer quantity meant that I lost my self-consciousness about writing. After a while I found I wasn't sitting about gnawing on pencils but instead writing fairly fluently. The only people I told about my writing ambitions were my roommates and my boyfriends.

My roommates had no particular reaction and my boyfriends were unanimously discouraging. Why in the face of this I continued to write, I can't imagine, but I did. What I did not do, and it has taken many years and some psychiatry for me to understand why I did not, was to seek out other people who wrote and make friends with them. My father, who was an architect, had always spoken of artists as people who were utterly alone in the world, and he acted as though that were true. He had no architect friends. I followed suit.

By my junior year I was terrified of what would happen when I graduated. I had no belief in myself and thought that I would graduate, never be able to find a job, and die of starvation. Logically, I dropped out of school. After all, if you are going to starve to death, why not do it now? In that year, 1957, I worked at the Hayden Planetarium bookstore. I was there the night the Russians put up *Sputnik,* which was enormously exciting.

The other thing I did was to get married to a very handsome man with whom I had nothing in common. He liked motorcycles. I liked books. He also had an alcoholic parent. We were both very frightened people. The trouble with a marriage based on each person looking for a raft to float them through life is that no one has the raft. In the first years of our marriage we lived in a series of fascinating places.

The first was an unheated, sixth-floor walk-up loft on Center Street in lower Manhattan, in the used machinery district a block away from police headquarters. Our landlord gave us a huge pot-bellied stove and my husband lugged fifty-pound sacks of coal up the stairs. I spent winter Sundays under a quilt doing the crossword puzzle in gloves. In those days lofts were not legal residences; therefore, taking your garbage out was always an adventure. You looked around carefully for a policeman before dumping it into a public trash can.

Our next residence was on Broome Street in a tenement in Little Italy. My neighbors taught me how to cook Italian dishes, and we had wonderful times together talking, usually about sex, children, and the Mafia. We again lived on the sixth floor, but we never locked our door because the fourth landing was patrolled by an insomniac grandmother who inspected everyone who went by and told our panting guests, in Italian, that they had two more flights to go.

Our third habitation was diagonally across the street from number two, over the bakery of a cafe owned by a Mafioso who was discovered, some years later, in a New Jersey swamp in two pieces. It was an old brownstone-type building with marble fireplaces coated with layers of enamel paint. Though there was no furnace, there was a space heater and the warmth did come up from the bakery below. While we were there, our marriage began to crumble seriously. We did what we felt was the logical thing. We decided to have a baby. I, more or less unilaterally, decided that we were going to spend the pregnancy in Europe. I started saving money—I was working for the Doubleday bookstore in Penn Station—and when we had

enough I got pregnant. In none of these fascinating locations did I do any writing.

The eight months we spent in Europe were sheer heaven for me, but, I suspect, sheer hell for my husband. We took a freighter over from Baltimore to Newcastle upon Tyne, and then a train down to where he had relatives outside of London.

They kindly put us up while we waited for our car, a Morris-Mini Minor. When that appeared we were off, first all over England, then on to France and Spain. In Morocco we visited an old friend of mine, today a famous chef, Paula Wolfert. We recrossed the Straits of Gibraltar and headed over to Italy, where we spent a month in Florence. I put on weight happily through the months, but my husband, who must have been worried sick about what we were going to do when we returned to New York, got thinner and thinner. Finally we came home, just in time for John F. Kennedy's inauguration and our son's birth in February 1961.

That was the end of my traveling for almost ten years, but I had been enthralled by the experience. We settled into an apartment in Brooklyn which had an elevator, radiators, and tile in the bathroom. The marriage got worse and worse. We were two people who should never have been married in the first place. The reason we stuck it out was, on my side, a Catholic upbringing that abhorred divorce. On his side, I suspect that as a child of a divorce he felt guilty about repeating the pattern. All together we hung on for thirteen years. The two greatest favors my husband did for me were supporting me until I was grown up enough to support myself and, in a rage one night, saying to me, "You'll never write. You talk about it, but you never do it."

The next day, after delivering my son to nursery school at the local temple, I started to write. But I had no one to share my work with. A friend told me about a group of people on Canal Street who met in a loft to read their work to each other. I did that for a while, and then, when that disintegrated, I moved on to Saint Marks on the Bowery, where I met Judy Sherwin and some of the New York poets—Paul Blackburn and Diane Wakowski.

I was very lucky and quickly was accepted by the *New York Times,* my first acceptance anywhere. That was in the days, much mourned, when there were poems on the *Times* editorial page. Then I began to appear in literary magazines—the *Beloit Poetry Journal, Texas Quarterly, Denver Quarterly,* and *Prairie Schooner.* What I longed for, however, what probably every poet in the United States longs for, was to be accepted by the *New Yorker.* One day in 1968, with my arms full of groceries, I found an envelope with the *New Yorker* letterhead in my mailbox. Doing a dance of joy, I dropped a quart of Coke in a grand smash all over the foyer of the apartment house. I didn't even mind cleaning it up. I opened it to find a letter from Howard Moss tentatively accepting a poem of mine and suggesting some changes. About 50 percent of them looked good to me. I made them, and the poem was accepted.

Not long after that, in 1974, my first book, *An Attic of Ideals,* was accepted by Doubleday. It sold exceptionally well, twenty-five hundred copies in two years, but at that point a new law prohibiting publishers from deducting warehoused books from their taxes was passed. As a result, I was shredded with the best, including Carolyn Kizer and Hugh Seidman. The book received good critical notices, of which my favorite was one in *Commonweal* which said, "Swenson's uncannily powerful imagery causes us to sit in her skin."

By then my marriage had come to a close. To celebrate the beginning of a new personal era I took a

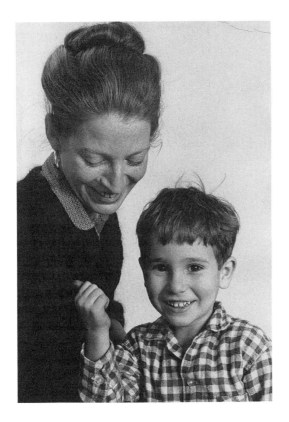

Karen Swenson with her son, Michael Shuter, Jr.

trip to Denmark, the country of my grandmother who had been pursued by pirates. I had a wonderful time touring Viking sights, out of which came "The Viking Grave at Ladby" in *Attic.* I also made the important discovery that I could manage without much difficulty traveling alone even when I did not speak the language of the country.

I was teaching at the City College of New York up in Harlem. It was enormously exciting work in the late sixties and early seventies. I had students who had never hoped to get to college, who were trying to be the first in their family not only to have a college education, but to get off welfare after a generation. I had students from every country in the world. There was an openness and a hopefulness in those years that made it easy to teach, because students wanted to learn since there seemed to be no boundaries on their future. The other joy of teaching there was my colleagues, who were warm, argumentative, and supportive. I am still close to many of them. Money was tight in those years, but I had a sudden bonanza when I sold a piece of furniture at Sotheby's which I had acquired for nothing years before. I brooded over my little pile trying to decide whether to save it, since the storm clouds of bad times were gathering on the horizon, or blow it on a trip to Iran.

Luckily I decided to blow it and took my son and myself to Iran, where we visited a colleague, Leo Hamalian, teaching in Teheran. From there we traveled by bus around Iran seeing Isfahan, Persepolis, and the far eastern ruin of Bam. I have never regretted that trip.

However, in 1976 the storm hit and New York City had severe financial trouble. There were cutbacks occurring everywhere. I joined the ranks of the cut. I had finished my M.A. and was beginning to write the thesis of my Ph.D. on *Beowulf* when the ax fell. I decided not to pursue the Ph.D. but, instead, to try to find jobs as Poet-in-Residence. My son was fifteen and, I thought, capable of looking after himself most of the time. My first job was at Clark University through the kind recommendation of Maxine Kumin, whom I had met at Bread Loaf. That carried me through Christmas, but, after that, not only was I unemployed, but my mother died in January, blowing the lid off my Pandora's box full of resentment and guilt toward her. My father was lost without her and reached out to me, hoping I would fill her place. All that year and part of the next, while sending out a thousand resumes all over the country, I spent every other weekend with my father going through my mother's belongings and trying to make him comfortable. He had always been dependent on her ability to make friends and now, without her, he led an isolated, desperately lonely life with only his bottle as his friend.

The next September I taught at Skidmore College in Saratoga Springs. The English department was small and companionable. Bob and Peg Boyers, who between teaching, writing, and *Salmagundi* work harder than galley slaves, became my treasured friends and still are. During this time of my own personal diaspora I always felt desperate and terrified as I looked for the next job and feared I wouldn't find it. I had been raised, after all, to wear white gloves and pass the hors d'oeuvres, not to engage in the hurly-burly of the real world. But those years brought to me many good, kind friends who helped to see me through.

I decided that when the year ended at Skidmore, since they could not afford to retain me, I would drive across the country stopping at universities and talking to people in hopes that something would turn up, since I had no job for the fall. I was teaching at a number of summer writers' conferences and I had a few readings scheduled as well. I read in Saint Cloud,

Swenson in 1972

Minnesota, and then went on to see Aunt Liz in Fargo, now at quite an advanced age. She encouraged me but also worried about me continually. All the years I was on the road, wherever I was, her letters, full of love and advice, followed me.

In Idaho I visited a wonderful woman, Bitsy Bidwell of Boise, who was in charge of the Artists-in-the-Schools Program for the state. Bitsy crammed herself into my little Honda Civic with her legs doubled up on top of a carton of books and hung onto the cat, who was trying to commit suicide by leaping out the window. She kindly did not comment on the odor in the car from the cat's pan. We went off to have lunch and mull over the possibility of my teaching in Idaho.

From there I went to Aspen to teach at the writers' conference. One of my colleagues was William Matthews, who endeared himself to me forever by arranging a meeting between me and Barbara Neal, who was then in charge of Artists-in-the-Schools in Colorado. The result of all this was that at the end of the summer I had Poets-in-the-Schools work in Colorado, Montana, and Idaho. It was an incredible year.

The bad part was driving through the passes in the Rockies in all kinds of winter weather. Surely, I had some sunny days on those passes, but in retrospect it seems I always drove in a snowstorm or thick fog. I set the driving, the loneliness, and the radio voices down in "The Itinerant Poet's Road Song" in *A Sense of Direction.*

It was an adventure in which I got to see parts of the country I would never have otherwise seen and meet people I would never have otherwise known. I taught in a three-room schoolhouse outside of Glacier National. The children came to class bursting with excitement at the birth of animals on their farms. People put me up in their homes and handed me from family to family in this landscape of dark firs and glittering snow. In Idaho, I spent fourteen weeks in a papermill town rancid with the odor from the plant. Again and again as I taught in the town's schools and made friends among the students at the local college, I ran into cases of abused children and battered wives. In Colorado, I taught in a town in the south near the Sangre de Cristo Mountains, where the people were descendants of those who had come over with Spanish land grants. I lived in a frigid, abandoned nunnery with three young women who were working for Catholic Charities. My first night they asked me to help them change a lightbulb. I thought it was some variation on a Polish joke. But it turned out the ladder they had had only three legs.

Howard Swenson, age forty-two, 1955

Three of us held the ladder up while the fourth changed the bulb. There were a number of other things wrong in the barn of a house and I suggested to my housemates that they ask the local priest over for dinner and I would urge him to do some repairs. He came to dinner and I made my suggestions, which were accepted grudgingly. At the end of dinner one young woman said, "Father, we have a wonderful dessert for you."

"I couldn't," he groaned. "I've eaten far too much already."

"Well, just look at it, Father," she urged. Going out to the kitchen, she returned with an enormous head of lettuce which rolled about on the plate like a gargantuan green marble, frozen solid by the malfunctioning refrigerator.

The refrigerator was repaired the next day.

In this town I had the most talented student I have ever had at the high school level. He was a senior and able to write poetry in either Spanish or English and sometimes he wrote half in one and half in the other. A handsome young man, he had three deep slashes on his cheek. Puzzled, I asked his teacher

how he had acquired them. She told me, as she might have explained the installation of a new kitchen in her house, that in seventh grade he had decided he was an atheist and, therefore, had to be marked. He had then taken his razor and made the three slashes in his cheek, which he opened up periodically so that they would form a scar. It was then that I realized that I was in the territory of the Penitentes of the Southwest.

The people I met during these years of traveling enriched me with their friendship. We continue to correspond and when I can get out to see them or they pass through New York we have a reunion. A chapbook came out of this period, *East-West,* published by Confluence Press, which was then headed by the inimitable and hilarious M. K. Browning. But many more poems came out of that time and are included in *A Sense of Direction.*

At the end of my diaspora, after teaching at the University of Idaho and Denver University, I taught for two years in California at Scripps College. By that time my father had moved in with me in New York and occupied the downstairs apartment in the building he had bought for me. Ours was not a smooth relationship but I could not have refused to live with him. My son was now in college. At the end of my first year at Scripps I drove back across the country stopping off, as I always did, to relieve the loneliness with Barbara Neal in Denver and Hilda Raz of *Prairie Schooner* in Lincoln, Nebraska. Arriving in Brooklyn, I had just turned off the engine of my car when a neighbor stuck her head in my window and announced that my father had died of a heart attack in the street the day before.

I spent the summer with his death, figuring out what I should do next. I decided to return to Scripps, finish my contract there, then come back to New York to teach again at City College. Reluctantly I said good-bye to the friends I had made out there, particularly Jean Burden, the poetry editor of *Yankee,* a fine poet herself, and Ann Stanford, who died shortly after. I also decided that as my time driving across the United States was coming to an end, I should start traveling outside the country again.

My mother, in 1961, had traveled around the world. When she returned I asked her which country she had liked best. She endorsed Thailand as the most exotic place on earth. Her approbation made me interested in traveling in the East. The semester I had taught at the University of Idaho I had learned about an anthropologist from the University of Washington who was taking a group to Nepal. I went with them that summer, had a wonderful time, and found myself

"With a couple of my Thai girlfriends," Bangkok

falling for the East. Next to my experience in Nepal, Europe looked like a reproduction of the United States with a few eccentricities. I found I liked the excitement of being alien, of not comprehending the culture in which I found myself.

After my father's death my first trip was a tour of Russia. The best parts were in southern Russia, Uzbekistan, and Outer Mongolia, which has a magnificent rolling landscape of open pastureland flecked with flocks and horsemen and yurts. But I didn't like being constrained by a tour.

The next year, simply terrified, I set out alone for Thailand. It was part of my agreement with myself that I made no hotel reservations. I picked out a section of town near the Temple of the Emerald Buddha, found a hotel there, and took a taxi from the airport. That trip was three quarters over before I had overcome my fears and was able to travel the way I wanted to, that is, by staying in very cheap hotels and eating at food stalls. But I did it and went home with a sense of exhilaration.

Ever since then I have gone over for approximately two months every year. I have traveled in

Burma, Thailand, Malaysia, and Indonesia. When I started traveling in Indonesia, I asked PEN if I could do any work for them. They said that they were missing an author, the premier novelist of Indonesia, Pramoedya Ananta Toer. I didn't find him that year but the following year I did, and have since worked with PEN attempting to get him more freedom as well as the right to publish his work in his own country. My first time to Indonesia I traveled with a friend to Sumatra and Nias. The *New York Times* took an article on Nias for their travel section and I was launched as a travel writer. On another trip I went to the island of Sulawesi, formerly the Celebes, saw the Toraja area where people make effigies of their dead and set them up on balconies in cliffs overlooking their rice fields. It is a sort of living theater with the dead as audience. The *Times* also ran my article on this area. But beyond the Toraja I traveled alone by public bus and then in a jeep with seven men over rain-forest mud tracks cut from the jungle by Indonesian slave labor during the Second World War. Overcoming my fear had paid off. I crossed a lake surrounded by jungle and then flew into the Bada Valley by missionary plane to see the monoliths that dot the valley and for which no one has any explanation. The following year I went to Irian Jaya, the western half of New Guinea, and more recently to Laos, Vietnam, and Cambodia. The result of all this traveling has been my deepened involvement with human rights both with PEN and Asia Watch. I have given up teaching at City College so as to spend more time writing articles about my travels, human rights, as well as poetry.

In 1989, The Smith brought out my second full book of poems, *A Sense of Direction*. It covers the years between my mother's death and my father's death, when I was traveling around the country. With its publication I spent six months traveling to ten states to do twenty-eight readings. After such a long time without a book, it was gratifying to see many people around the country had been waiting for another book.

For the last few years I have been working on a new book, as yet untitled, about the people, places, and adventures I've had in Southeast Asia. Yaddo, the Albee Foundation, and the Millay Colony have all given me time and space in which to work, for which I am very grateful. Travel and poetry have, indeed, become entwined in my life.

BIBLIOGRAPHY

Poetry:

An Attic of Ideals, Doubleday, 1974.

East-West (chapbook), Confluence, 1980.

A Sense of Direction, The Smith, 1989.

Contributor to the *New Yorker, Nation, New York Quarterly, Texas Quarterly, New York Times, Prairie Schooner, Denver Quarterly,* and the *Beloit Poetry Journal.*

Frank Waters
1902-

THE CHANGING AND UNCHANGEABLE WEST

Frank Waters at his home in Tucson, Arizona, 1988

Mountain-bred, I was born at the foot of Pike's Peak in Colorado Springs, Colorado, in 1902. The small, sedate town of thirty thousand residents, popularly called Little London, was a noted scenic resort and health spa that drew visitors from all over the country. No liquor was sold within the city limits, and the Sunday newspaper refrained from including a comic section because it might keep children from attending Sunday school.

Our neighborhood didn't lie in the rich and fashionable North End but along Bijou Street and Shook's Run, where we gathered watercress. Life was never dull. The Pan Dandy bread wagon stopped at our house early every morning. It was drawn by a fast pair of sorrel mares, and in the winter my younger sister and I hitched our sled behind it for an exciting ride to Columbia School. In the summer we waited for the arrival of the ice wagon—its driver would chip off pieces of ice for us to suck through our handkerchiefs—and the knife-and-scissors sharpener, who set up his portable grinding stone on the curb.

These visitors didn't deter us from shopping at the corner grocery store, where we always were given a dill pickle from the barrel and often sent home with a free slab of "easy meat," or liver. An ice-cream cone cost a buffalo nickel, a licorice stick an Indian penny.

The standard coin of the realm was a silver dollar minted in Denver from Colorado-mined silver. No greenbacks, please.

High, snowy Pike's Peak dominated our earliest years. We learned early to foretell the weather from it. The usual Sunday outing for my sister and me was a streetcar ride with Father and Mother to Manitou Springs, six miles west. Here, at the base of the peak, we filled our bottles with iron-and-soda water gushing from the many springs. Often we rented a burro, or "Pike's Peak canary," from one of the crowded corrals to carry us children and our picnic basket up a mountain canyon threaded by a turbulent white-water stream.

My first ride on a train ended in a disaster. My father was taking us to Denver on the Denver & Rio Grande line. I was sitting in the coach, nose flattened against the window. Near Husted, a few miles north of our boarding point, I watched another train coming toward us around a curve. Then suddenly I was on the floor amid a jumble of baggage and overturned seats and a bedlam of shrieks and groans. The two trains had collided headlong.

Father got us out of the wreck to sit on the prairie under Mother's umbrella. Around us all afternoon lay other passengers, injured and dying. Doctors and nurses came driving out from Colorado Springs. Their help was generally refused upon the advice of railroad officials, because no medical fees or insurance would be paid to those who didn't wait for the railroad's own doctors. They finally came.

My left arm evidently had been injured. Throughout the winter Mother dutifully took me to the railroad doctor, who was unable to help me. To ease the constant pain I kept rubbing my forearm until it developed a growth. That spring, when I was in seventh grade, I broke the arm while playing baseball. That healed it as medical treatment couldn't.

An exciting event during those years was the lightweight championship fight between Freddie Welsh and Charlie White held in Colorado Springs one afternoon in 1914. I didn't watch it. I was the Fred Harvey newsboy at the new Santa Fe railroad station. But late that afternoon, while special trains were filling with the returning crowd of fight spectators, a truckload of newspaper extras arrived headlining double news. Freddie Welsh had won the championship, and during the bout the flimsy wooden stands had collapsed, injuring dozens of fans. Everybody screamed for a paper, thrusting quarters and dollars into my hand until my pockets bulged. It was my most profitable day.

Jack Dempsey, born in Colorado, was of course our boyhood idol. On the memorable Fourth of July, 1919, when he KO'd Jess Willard to gain the world's heavyweight championship, I stood in the immense crowd on Pike's Peak Avenue in front of the Gazette building. From a second-story window an announcer with a megaphone, reading the telegraphic dispatches handed him, called out every blow.

Beautiful and sedate as it usually was, Little London owed its imposing mansions in the North End not to the English money and taste that had laid out the town but to Cripple Creek, on the eleven-thousand-foot-high south slope of Pike's Peak. Gold had been discovered there as late as 1891; the "Cripple Creek Cow Pasture" quickly became the world's greatest gold camp, eventually producing some $450 million in gold at the then current rate of twenty-one dollars an ounce.

The pharmacist at our corner drugstore rushed up there on a Sunday morning, threw his hat in a gulch and dug where it fell. Thus was discovered the rich Pharmacist Mine. Jimmie Burns, a plumber, found an even richer vein, from which he extracted enough gold to build the new Burns Theater. Everybody was getting rich.

My grandfather Joseph Dozier, a prosperous pioneer building contractor, also succumbed to gold fever. He persuaded my father to help him open a series of exploratory tunnels. I often rode up there with them—a mile straight up and eighteen miles west—on the spectacular Cripple Creek Short Line Railroad.

Cripple Creek was everything conservative Little London wasn't. It was a madhouse of activity and extravagant hopes. The muddy roads between its major towns, Cripple Creek and Victor, were crowded with mule-drawn freight and ore wagons; muckers and drillers elbowed promoters and stockbrokers on every corner; ladies in long skirts and high-button shoes were jostled off board sidewalks by the prostitutes from Myer's Avenue. How exciting it was!

Grandfather and Grandmother often talked about Winfield Scott Stratton, whose discovery of the famous Independence Mine had opened the district. For seventeen winters he had worked for Grandfather as a journeyman carpenter, saving his wages to grubstake his prospecting through the summers. Destiny finally rewarded his persistence with the Independence, which he sold for ten million dollars before he died.

The "Midas of the Rockies" didn't forget his lean years. He devoted his great wealth to town improvements and to establish the Myron Stratton

Home for old, impoverished prospectors who had never struck it rich.

That Stratton had become a hopeless alcoholic and recluse didn't diminish Grandfather's hopes. None of his own workings ever struck pay dirt. He eventually lost all he owned except his house, whose title was in Grandmother's name. But still he borrowed money to open another unproductive mine, our Family Folly, the Sylvanite.

My father, Jonathan, was a man of space, not height, of open plains, not mountains. He was part Indian, Cheyenne. One of his best friends was an Indian vegetable huckster named Joe. Father often rode around with him on his rounds. The sight of Father, neatly dressed in a suit and polished boots, sitting on the plank seat of a rickety wagon beside an Indian huddled in a tattered blanket always infuriated Mother. She was even more disconcerted by Father's visits to the Ute encampment.

The Utes had been moved to a reservation farther west, but a band of them was permitted to return every summer to their former homeland nearby. Their encampment of smoke-gray lodges lay on a mesa just west of town. Respectable Little London avoided it, but Father frequently took me there of an evening. He would squat down cross-legged in the circle of men around the cooking fire. With the long-bladed knife he always carried, even to church, he would cut off a pink slice of steaming meat from the fire and eat it, as did they, in his fingers. I waited patiently with the women and children outside the circle for my turn at table.

The high peak rising above us was the Utes' sacred mountain, looming prominently in their creation myth. It had power. As they talked about it their dark, wrinkled faces in the flame light seemed to possess an inner glow. It darkened as they haltingly voiced their fears of how the mountain was being violated by the open trenches, glory holes, and abandoned tunnels and shafts. "This mountain sick," one of the elders ventured. "Pretty soon it lose all its power."

One summer Father took me with him to New Mexico to live for a time in the remote trading post of Hon-Not-Klee, "Shallow Water," in the immense Navajo reservation. My first impression of the trading post was of an island in a vast pelagic plain, a fortress in an empty wilderness.

The building was a thick-walled adobe with iron-barred windows. Its huge trading room was full of goods: salt and sugar and coffee, canned goods, bridles and ropes, bolts of flowered gingham and brilliant velveteen. In back were our living quarters, a storeroom for sheep pelts and huge sacks of Navajo wool, and a double-locked rug room piled with gorgeous Navajo blankets and exquisite Navajo silver-and-turquoise jewelry, which had been brought in for pawn or trade.

The master of this outpost, supplying the needs of perhaps a thousand square miles, was a man named Bruce. He was ill, and Father had come to help him manage the post, the Navajos' only contact with an alien, encroaching people.

All day they rode in—slim, arrogant men on horseback, women and children huddled in springless wagons. They impressed me with their independence, their air of barbarity, their love of color, and their reverence for the earth, their mother.

This was a natural life for my father. Bruce wanted him to stay, but he was recalled home to work with Grandfather in Cripple Creek and died shortly thereafter.

Times and customs by then were changing. Men's high stiff collars went out of fashion, and their Paris garters gave way to stretch socks. Uniformity decreed that I part my hair in the middle and plaster it down with Vaseline. I bought my first safety razor and waited impatiently for the time to use it.

My first fledgling flight from home carried me to Wyoming. I had worked my way through high school and three years in Colorado College as an engineering major before I realized I wasn't cut out to be an engineer. Leaving school, I rode the train to Casper, then hitchhiked a ride with a truck driver to the booming Salt Creek oil fields. There I got a job as a roustabout with a gang laying ten-inch iron pipe. For hitting the hooks all day we were paid fifty cents an hour. In turn we paid fifty cents each for breakfast and supper, and another fifty cents for the use of a cot in the bunkhouse. Lunch out on the prairie was simple and free, sandwiches and apples.

On Saturday nights we trudged five miles into the squatter town of Lavoye to spend our remaining wages for bootleg beer. With their two-story fronts of unpainted wood, Lavoye's ramshackle buildings looked like a movie set. Swarming with men, trucks, and machinery, all Salt Creek reminded me of Cripple Creek. The jackpot of one was gold, the other oil.

That fall of 1924 I met an old-time Westerner who had been a trapper, horse wrangler, and cowpuncher, and had worked as a guide for one of Theodore Roosevelt's Western jaunts. He had been offered a home with his daughter in California. With his savings he had bought a little Star roadster to drive there but had difficulty driving it. He persuaded me to drive him. "You won't have to buy an overcoat to wear in sunny California," he assured me. "And whenever you get hungry, all you'll have to do is pick oranges off the trees along every street."

We drove south through Wyoming and Colorado, then west through New Mexico and Arizona on U.S. Route 66, with frequent stops to change tires and cool the radiator. Many stretches of dirt road were unmarked and unfenced. Every evening we turned off to camp in the sage. What a wide, empty land! There were no large cities. Santa Fe was a little town of eleven thousand people and narrow cobblestone streets. Albuquerque's population was thirty-five thousand. The largest city in the Southwest was Phoenix, housing barely fifty thousand residents.

Along the way we passed through many Indian pueblos. The people in each were differently dressed, spoke their own tongue, and observed their own customs. Far to the north stretched the vast Navajo country I'd seen with my father. All this heartland of America's Indian country would become intimately familiar to me later.

Puttering along at thirty miles an hour, we finally topped the desert mountains above the old Arizona mining town of Oatman. Below us lay the muddy Colorado River. Beyond it and the Mojave Desert was the Promised Land.

The City of the Angels was a shocking disappointment. We drove into what the old cowboy remembered as the center of the city—the historic Mexican plaza at the north end of Main Street. In this shabby neighborhood of adobe buildings there were no orange trees. We divided our last few dollars, and he drove on to his daughter's house near San Diego, while I rented for four dollars a week a room in a squalid hotel on the plaza.

From its grimy window there was no sign of the blue Pacific. I had yet to discover uptown a newer, more modern Los Angeles, or to find a job. But none of this belittled my great accomplishment. I had crossed the entire breadth of the American West and reached the last frontier city on the ocean's shore, the ultimate goal of that Manifest Destiny that had impelled America's westward expansion.

Imperial Valley, on the California–Baja California border, where I was sent some time later to work as a junior engineer by the telephone company, lay 235 feet below sea level in the heart of the Colorado Desert. Mountain-bred, I was fascinated by the desert's tawny, treeless expanse under the pitiless sun. Yuma, Arizona, lay on the bank of the Colorado River to the east; water from there was channeled to the sea-level fields on the boundary of Mexico, whence it drained down into Imperial Valley.

Under irrigation, the valley's desert floor had become "America's Winter Garden," producing that year fourteen thousand train carloads of cantaloupes. Already by May 1 the first melons to reach the East's breakfast tables had been shipped. The little towns with their large packing sheds bustled with activity in desert heat of 106 degrees. All the valley seemed to be a boom camp resembling Cripple Creek and Salt Creek, its own symbol a round, ripe cantaloupe.

In El Centro, the largest town, the lobby of the Barbara Worth Hotel—named for Harold Bell Wright's popular, sentimental novel *The Winning of Barbara Worth*—was the focus of activity. Murals on the walls pictured scenes from the novel, and the hotel stationery and dining room silver carried portraits of the young lady herself under a fetching sombrero. Here thronged fruit brokers telephoning Kansas City, Chicago, and New York to order diversions of refrigerator boxcars as the market rose and fell with the thermometer. Ranchers in heavy boots stomped in, demanding trucks, railroad cars, more workmen. As a young engineer I was kept busy following all this activity, meeting the demand for efficient telephone service from overworked switchboards.

Yet in all the valley the place that intrigued me most was Mexicali, the Mexican border town adjoining the American town of Calexico—perhaps because it seemed so blatantly to manifest the dark, repressed domain in our Puritan-Anglo soul.

Mexicali was the bottom of the human barrel. Its portals were the Owl and the Southern Club, two great casinos offering bars, dining and gaming rooms, music and entertainment. To them every evening came the melon growers, brokers, well-heeled ranchers, and businessmen looking for a bit of fun. At nine o'clock the whistle blew for their exodus back across the international line. The gates clanged shut then. The lights went out.

Down the back streets beyond the two casinos lay ill-lit cantinas with names such as El Gato Negro, Tivoli, and Casa Blanca, and nameless dirt-floor drinking dens selling mescal and green tequila. And behind them were their cribs—open courtyards holding twenty or more shapeless women apiece in sweaty shifts. The alcoholic stench and acrid odor of urine filled the desert night.

Now was their hour. As if from deep underground emerged the petty criminals and refugees of both countries: pimps and prostitutes; all the mixtures of Indian, Mexican, and Anglo breeds—mestizos, coyotes, criollos, *cholos;* crawling beggars; Negro cotton pickers; giant Hindus with heads swathed in black turbans; Chinese hopheads. The barrio wasn't a safe place for the unwary. The women in any crib could strip you of your clothes in an instant, and a knife might be stuck in your back when you turned a dark corner.

Despite the savage brutality and perversions, I began to feel that all this teeming life, not yet informed with the qualities that mark more evolved human forms, does indeed gush up from a mysterious wellspring of all life, ever replenishing humankind with its brute strength and fresh vitality. This feeling, I must admit, may have been nourished by Tai Ling, the yogi of Cockroach Court.

He had been among the first of the Chinese who had been imported by shiploads to work in the great cotton fields south of the border, congregating here in a Chinese quarter that equaled in fact the storied Barbary Coast. It was known as La Plaza de las Cucarachas, "Cockroach Court," named for its swarming prostitutes called cucarachas.

Here stood Tai Ling's shop. He sat behind his abacus at the front window, a small man wearing a black sateen jacket and ragged trousers. I struck up a friendship with him and visited him often.

His shop was cluttered with barrels of rice, pinto beans and garbanzos, strips of dried meat, rolls of matting, packets and jars of lily roots, lichee nuts, herbs, silk panties, and American blue-denim trousers. Twice a week he distributed fresh fish brought up from the gulf. He marked and sold Chinese lottery tickets, and peddled cans of Rooster and Elephant-brand opium. His dark cellar, I found out, served as a station on the underground line that smuggled Chinese workers across the international border to Los Angeles's Chinatown and thence to San Francisco.

Tai Ling also traveled another, more difficult road. As a struggling yogi, he followed the path to spiritual illumination by meditating on the divine and undefinable, unbounded and indivisible Ultimate Reality, the Tao. He saw no conflict between his two paths, for as a yogi he accepted good and evil as equal parts of the universal whole and was partial to neither. He was an incomprehensible character whose magnetism kept drawing me back to him, but I could

Waters, with the 1966 Ford Galaxy he considers an extension of himself, Tucson, 1988

never quite make him out. Perhaps this is why, of all the important people I met in the Imperial Valley, to this day it is he I remember most vividly.

How different was the beautiful blue valley of Mora as I knew it several years later. I was no longer working at a salaried job and had come to write my first long novel in the valley's peace and seclusion. It was a world apart, tucked in the high Sangre de Cristo mountains of northern New Mexico. To drive to the nearest large town—Las Vegas, New Mexico, scarcely thirty miles south—took two hours, and the road over the pass to Taos was impassable a good part of the year.

The valley had first been occupied in 1835 by seventy-six Spanish colonial settlers from Mexico. Their descendants still spoke their mother tongue, adhered to their Spanish traditions, and worked their small family fields for a meager living.

Mora was the central village, surrounded by tiny settlements of a dozen or so houses in the enclosing mountains. During my two years there I lived in a rambling, eighteen-room adobe hacienda known as the Butler Hotel. It was without plumbing, furnished with walnut-spool feather beds and wardrobes brought from the officers' quarters of abandoned Fort Union.

The hotel was owned by a middle-aged woman, Sybil Butler. Her husband, Monte, had been a professional gambler who had fled there from Indian territory with a price on his head. Going blind, he had taken in a half-Cherokee named Ralph, also a refugee from the law. Monte patiently taught Ralph how to deal cards and all the other tricks of the gambler's trade. Now, after old blind Monte had died, Ralph stayed on, running the hotel for Mrs. Butler. His only earnings were his winnings from the poker games he conducted every night for passing cattle buyers, surveyors, and occasional state officials.

The only other permanent guests beside myself were a couple, Fran and Ed Tinker. One of their two rooms was a kitchen. I took supper with them there, because Mrs. Butler only cooked breakfast before retiring to her own room for the rest of the day.

Ed was a black sheep, part Osage Indian, whose brother was the famous major general shot down at Midway (Tinker Airfield in Oklahoma City is named after him). A handsome six-footer, Ed dabbled in local politics, occasionally rebuilt a washed-out bridge, and generally relied on his wife's wages.

Fran, a woman whose small stature and unassuming manner gave no evidence of her resoluteness and capability, was one of the most remarkable people I've ever known. Her father had been a judge in Santa Fe, and she spoke colloquial Spanish as fluently as English. Her job—part of the federal Work Projects Administration program—was to teach families in these remote canyons to use pressure cookers to preserve meat, vegetables, and fruit for winter instead of drying them in the sun, but other problems always confronted her. I often accompanied her on her rounds, impressed by her abilities and her compassion as she delivered babies, broke fevers, and taught the medicinal uses of native herbs and plants.

I loved them both.

My only other friend of non-Hispanic stock, who readily joked with me in English, was Peter Balland. A one-legged Frenchman, he and his family ran the general-merchandise store opposite the hotel. He was a shrewd trader. When an impoverished family had run up a bill it couldn't pay, he would stomp on his wooden leg to their dirt-floored adobe and take down from their wall the painted image *(santo)* or carved wooden figure *(bulto)* of a Christian saint. "I will just take this in payment for your debt," he would say. "Now you will have no more worry about it, no?"

These old, primitive, and rare santos and bultos covered the walls of his rear butcher shop. He kept offering them for sale to the museum and university in Santa Fe, with no success. Eventually his collection was taken to the Fine Arts Center in Colorado Springs, which showed it in traveling exhibitions throughout the country.

These were my fellow passengers on what, during winter especially, seemed like a ship becalmed in a protected harbor, undisturbed by the waves of outer change. Past my window ebbed the earthy people of the valley, going to mass or market. Theirs was still the life that had given the Southwest its distinctive Spanish culture, projected from the past into the present.

But already a storm was gathering outside.

The development of the first atom bomb on Los Alamos mesa northwest of Santa Fe, and its detonation in the desert of southern New Mexico, changed all our lives, the entire world. It ushered in the Atomic Age.

I had served a short stint in the army at the beginning of World War II before being released to write analyses of events in Latin America for the Office of Inter-American Affairs. Soon after the war ended, Russia unexpectedly exploded its own first atom bomb, then another war began in Korea. Under the threat of these events the Los Alamos Scientific Laboratory began developing a series of new fission bombs, which increased the explosive power of its first A-bomb tenfold. These new nuclear weapons were tested in the desert sixty miles north of Las Vegas, Nevada.

I accepted the offer of a job as information consultant at the laboratory. I worked at Los Alamos during the winter, and each spring accompanied the scientists to Nevada for the test series. From their control point, a huge blockhouse, I witnessed the awesome detonation of almost a hundred bombs in the "Valley Where the Giant Mushrooms Grow"—a searing experience I can neither forget nor describe.

When I finally resigned to return home and resume my life at the typewriter, I became aware of what had been happening elsewhere. The entire West was undergoing developments that would change its face forever.

Precious uranium, the life force of the Atomic Age, had been discovered in New Mexico. It opened the entire West to the greatest prospecting rush since the scramble for gold of the century before. Men carrying Geiger counters were penetrating deep mountain canyons, plodding through empty deserts, and across the immense Colorado Plateau. The last undeveloped area in the nation held the greatest uranium deposits in the world. Six hundred mines were producing ore; mills were going up. Little villages I had once known were suddenly thriving towns; cities were expanding miles outward and bursting with prosperity.

In my own middle life I went to the dead center of this maelstrom of activity, to live for almost three years among the Hopi Indians in northern Arizona. It was the perfect counterpoint to the events swirling about me, a period of personal introspection as rewarding as the perspective on the outer world I had gained.

I had written in 1942 a novel of pueblo life, *The Man Who Killed the Deer,* and in 1951 a nonfiction study of Navajo and Pueblo Indian ceremonialism, *Masked Gods.* Both had reflected my empathy with Indians and my study of their lives, but neither had broken through the traditional secrecy that veiled the Indians' innermost religious beliefs from outside observers. Now, another decade later, I began writing a third book, *Book of the Hopi,* which would give the Hopis' own account of their creation myth and continental migrations and explain the esoteric meanings of their annual nine great ceremonies—the only true indigenous mystery plays in America.

Such a book would break new ground. The Hopis always had been considered the most secretive of all tribes and a puzzle to a generation of rational white anthropologists and ethnologists, who couldn't fathom the aura of myth and mysticism enshrouding them.

While gathering information for the book I lived at Pumpkin Seed Point, overlooking New Oraibi on Third Mesa, in a little house without plumbing, heated by a butane gas stove and lit by a kerosene lamp. I took my meals at the nearby house of my Hopi research assistant and interpreter, Oswald White Bear Fredericks, and his white wife.

The Hopis claimed to be the first inhabitants of this New World, the fourth successive world they had occupied. Disputed as this claim was by anthropologists, their pueblo of Oraibi, dating from A.D. 1100 or earlier, was admittedly the oldest continuously occupied settlement in the United States. Unlike the nomadic Navajos, they were a sedentary people who occupied, in all, just nine villages or pueblos on top of three rocky mesas a hundred miles north of the small white towns along U.S. Route 66. Their patches of corn, beans, and squash lay in the sandy desert below. Without irrigation, they depended upon their prayerful ceremonials to bring infrequent rain.

I was fortunate in gaining the confidence of thirty of them, who related to me their world view and the esoteric meanings of their rituals. They spoke willingly, wanting to leave for their children and grandchildren a record of their people's beliefs. Most of them were older men and women. I still in sleepless hours of the night see their dark, wrinkled faces and gnarled hands, hear their low measured voices that seemed to rise out of the depths of an archaic America we have never known, out of a fathomless racial unconscious.

One of the first I met was an aging man in a ragged red sweater and baggy pants, whose straggly gray hair fell to his shoulders. He was Dan Qochhongva, religious leader of Hotevilla Pueblo. His father, Chief Yukioma, had once been dubbed the American Dalai Lama and jailed for seventeen years by the government Indian agent for inciting the Hopi Traditionalists, or "Hostiles," against the Progressives, or "Friendlies," who had welcomed the incoming white people.

Old Dan first viewed me with suspicion. "If your heart is right and you are sincere, you will have four dreams," he concluded. One by one they came to me, as I have related elsewhere, resulting in his sponsoring my research. I hadn't yet witnessed the Hopi ceremonials, nor did I know their meanings. But each successive dream symbolically, as it were, initiated me into them before they took place.

The author, with the Sacred Mountain of Taos Pueblo as seen from his front yard in Taos, New Mexico: "Next time, by hook or crook, make sure you're born with a mountain in the front yard."

Old Dan I saw frequently. Although I couldn't understand Hopi any better than he could understand English, our curious relationship continued until I left.

My closest Hopi companion was John Lansa of Oraibi. Seventy years old, alert and tireless, he tended a flock of sheep that provided his livelihood. He was head of the Badger clan, which controlled the important Niman kachina ceremony. He took me with him on one of his arduous pilgrimages to gather spruce for the rituals, and accompanied White Bear and me to Mesa Verde and Chaco Canyon, homes of the long-ago Indian cliff dwellers. Not only could he speak good English, he was also able to read the ancient petroglyphs on the cliff walls.

Mina Lansa, his small, frail wife, was the adopted daughter of Chief Tewaquaptewa of Oraibi and custodian of the Bear clan sacred tablets, the ancient Hopi titles to their land. The old chief died while I was there, leaving no Bear-clan successor. His position of *kikmongwi* reverted by right of clan succession to Mina's Parrot clan. She thus became the symbolic

mother of the Hopis, as Tewaquaptewa had been their father.

She also became the leader of the Traditionalists, the former "Hostiles," who were opposed to the modern "Friendlies," now dominated by the federal government's Bureau of Indian Affairs. With failing strength she fought the bureau's ever-growing control of tribal matters until she died. John remained my close friend, visiting me in Taos and Tucson until he, too, died years later.

The intimacy I shared with White Bear and his wife helped to carry our project to a successful end. But it was the thirty elderly Hopis who finally opened to me the door to all Indian America, a world that once extended unbroken from Central America up through Mexico and the American Southwest, and which still endured here on the Hopi mesas.

What separated Hopi life from our own Anglo culture wasn't ethnic differences, but modes of thinking. Accepting Robert Ornstein's current explanation, we Anglos, being predominantly concerned with the material aspects of the world, rely almost wholly upon the rational, intellectual function of the human brain's left cerebral hemisphere. From our first arrival on this continent we have viewed the land as a vast treasure house of inanimate nature to be plundered at will. The Indians, on the other hand, from pre-Columbian times, were geared to the brain's right hemisphere, which controls intuitional and spiritual perceptions, reflecting their holistic orientation in space and time.

Whatever the reason, the Hopis were the last island of Indian America not yet submerged in the ocean of Anglo materialism. They still existed in a realm whose elements were dream, myth, and mysticism. To them the earth was their living mother. Stones, stars, the corn plant and the spruce, all birds and animals, the locust and the ant, were likewise imbued with a universal inner spirit as well as a physical form. One did not kill a deer or fell a lofty pine without first ritually asking its consent to its sacrifice for the good of all. The spiritual components of these things remained alive as sources of psychical energy, manifesting themselves during ceremonials as masked kachinas.

The nine great annual ceremonials with their symbolism, rituals, dances, songs, and prayers unfolded like stages of consciousness expanding to a vision of universal unity. They seemed to me to be as soundly conceived and executed as the scientific processes developed at Los Alamos, meant not to test a hypothesis of releasable physical energy from divisible matter but to assert a thousand-year-old belief in the indestructibility of the spiritual energy that informs all inert matter and breathing forms. Here on the Hopi mesas I found the indigenous culture of America, still preserving those transcendent values of universal wholeness and unity so desperately needed by our fragmented world today.

Now my heart's home base, as it has been for almost forty years, is my adobe house and back pastures in the Sangre de Cristo mountains of northern New Mexico. It repeats features important to me in my past: Pike's Peak has been replaced by the Sacred Mountain of Taos Pueblo, a horseback ride through the pueblo reservation. The ceremonial dances here are among the best in the Rio Grande pueblos, and the religious leaders have been my close friends for many years.

The little village of Arroyo Seco, a mile down the dirt road, is as wholly Spanish as is Mora, and a century older. It once had the reputation of harboring *brujas*, or witches, as well as horse thieves and other offenders escaping the clutches of the sheriff. When I first settled here, despite the extravagant

tales of witchcraft and wickedness matching the actual evils once found in Mexicali, I was the only Anglo in the vicinity. I found it conservatively peaceful, and my neighbors have always looked after me.

My wife Barbara and I, taking our evening walk up the mountain slope, can see the twinkling lights of Los Alamos. I think of the friendly, peace-loving scientists I worked with there and in Nevada, the men who achieved the release of atomic energy, only to have it used today as an agent that threatens the obliteration of all mankind. The sky is darkening with pollutants and particulates drifting here from the Four Corners area to the west. There huge power plants and the strip-mining monsters of powerful energy corporations are exploiting the land as ruthlessly as did the men at Cripple Creek, Salt Creek, and the Imperial Valley.

Change. Constant change is the law of life. Everything is different, yet everything is the same. The American West reflects this paradox. It shows the ever-changing present, and somehow embodies an eternal existence at the same time. We can hope that, as the Hopis say, the spirit that imbues the land will outlast the change.

This essay is reprinted in entirety from *Growing Up Western*, edited by Clarus Backes.

BIBLIOGRAPHY

Fiction:

The Wild Earth's Nobility: A Novel of the Old West (also see below), Liveright, 1935.

Below Grass Roots (also see below), Liveright, 1937.

Dust within the Rock (also see below), Liveright, 1940.

People of the Valley, Swallow Press, 1941.

The Man Who Killed the Deer, Swallow Press, 1942.

(With Houston Branch) *River Lady*, Swallow Press, 1942.

The Yogi of Cockroach Court, Swallow Press, 1947.

(With Branch) *Diamond Head*, Farrar, Straus, 1948.

The Woman at Otowi Crossing, Swallow Press, 1966.

Pike's Peak: A Family Saga (contains *The Wild Earth's Nobility: A Novel of the Old West, Below Grass Roots,* and *Dust within the Rock*), Swallow Press, 1971.

Flight from Fiesta, Rydal, 1986.

Nonfiction:

Midas of the Rockies: The Story of Winfield Scott Stratton and Cripple Creek, Covici-Friede, 1937, reprinted, Swallow Press, 1971.

The Colorado, Farrar & Rinehart, 1946.

Masked Gods: Navajo and Pueblo Ceremonialism, University of New Mexico Press, 1950, reprinted, Ballantine, 1975.

The Earp Brothers of Tombstone: The Story of Mrs. Virgil Earp, C. N. Potter, 1960, reprinted, University of Nebraska Press, 1976.

Book of the Hopi, Viking, 1963.

Leon Gaspard (monograph), Northland Press, 1964.

Pumpkin Seed Point, Swallow Press, 1969.

To Possess the Land: A Biography of Arthur Rochford Manby, Swallow Press, 1974.

Mexico Mystique: The Coming Sixth World of Consciousness, Swallow Press, 1975.

(Editor with Charles L. Adams) W. Y. Evans-Wentz, *Cuchama and Sacred Mountains,* Swallow Press, 1981.

Mountain Dialogues, Swallow Press, 1981.

Frank Waters: A Retrospective Anthology, edited by C. L. Adams, Ohio University Press, 1985.

(Contributor) *Growing Up Western,* edited by Clarus Backes, Knopf, 1989.

Also author of *Fever Pitch.* Contributor of book reviews to *Saturday Review,* 1950–56; contributor of articles to *Yale Review, Holiday,* and other periodicals. *River Lady* was made into a motion picture by Universal-International, 1949.

Donald E. Westlake

1933-

ME

Around the turn of the century, a favorite sunny Sunday pastime in Albany, New York, and in its sister town of Rensselaer, across the Hudson River, was to promenade between the two towns on the DeWitt Clinton Bridge. One Sunday, one of these promenaders was a young man named Edwin Bounds, born in County Cork, Ireland, emigrated to America in his teens, then a factory worker in Albany. Seeing a lovely young thing promenading toward him, he murmured as they passed one another, "What a pretty girl." But being shy he said it in Gaelic, not to risk offense.

"Thank you very much," she replied, in Gaelic.

Her name was Josephine Fitzgerald. She too had been born in County Cork, had emigrated as a teenager, and was then a housemaid in Rensselaer. They of course soon married, and among their one son and three daughters was my mother, Lillian Bounds.

By the time I came along, in 1933, the glow from that first romantic meeting was long gone. My maternal grandparents had not lived together for many years, though, being cowed Catholics, divorce was out of the question. My grandmother shared an apartment with my unmarried aunt Peg, the youngest child, while my grandfather lived some sort of raffish, unacceptable life downtown. So far as I know, I never met the man, though I did see him once.

This would be around 1943; he would probably have been in his sixties. My sister Virginia and I were eight or ten years of age—something like that— riding in the backseat of the family car, my parents in the front, my father driving. (My mother didn't learn to drive till after his death; then I taught her, a horrible experience.) We were driving along South Pearl Street, then a very louche part of downtown indeed; so disreputable in fact that it was the part of the city specifically earmarked for destruction by Nelson Rockefeller when, as governor of New York State and therefore willy-nilly resident of the capital, Albany, his Ozymandias side took over and he built all those gray-horror public buildings.

Donald E. Westlake

"There's your father," my father said conversationally to my mother, though I think I knew at the time that he was being sardonic, even nasty, in that innocent remark.

"Bert!" my mother said. "Not in front of the children."

I looked out the side window, then out the back. Across the street, in bright sunlight, was a used-clothing store with a line of weary garments hung from the front edge of the long awning and crammed dark windows beneath. At the left side of the wide storefront was the entrance. Seated beside the entrance, taking the sun in a chair tilted back against the brick wall, was a stout old man wearing a black suit, the coat draped wide open and a white shirt open at the collar. I had a glimpse of a round, puffy, unfriendly face.

My mother would never talk about him, and I never saw him again.

A few years later, at the movies, I first saw W. C. Fields; it was the same man.

My paternal grandmother's maiden name was one of the most beautiful I've ever heard: Annie Tyrrell. There's a lilt to it, like a quick little mountain stream; you can't say it aloud without a ripple.

Annie Tyrrell came from Dublin, and when I knew her she was tiny and wise and humorous; a fairy-tale grandmother. She fumbled about for a number of years without making any fuss about the fumbling, and then one day, out walking, she spied a pair of eyeglasses discarded in somebody's trash, tried them on, and was delighted. She could see! The glasses were lopsided, and one wing was repaired with tape, but she could see so much better with them on that she wore them ever after.

When my father, long a grown-up with kids of his own, found out about this and tried to get Grandma to have her eyes tested so the *right* glasses could be made, at his expense, she refused. She was so happy with the new clarity these secondhand specs gave her, why should she want any more?

I decided after a while, when I'd grown used to my grandmother's smiling, wrinkled face behind the lopsided glasses, that a leprechaun had left them for her; professional courtesy. I still believe it.

Annie Tyrrell moved to America at some point in her young life and married an American named Joseph Westlake, of English heritage. (My father once told me that one of my female forebears, married to a Westlake a few generations back, was a Mohawk Indian, a knowledge—or belief—that played a great part in getting me through my childhood, but I have no proof or verification of this. The Mohawk Indians are famed in New York City for their fearlessness about heights, which led to their being the preeminent construction workers on skyscrapers, and on that basis my Mohawk blood must be either extremely thin or actually nonexistent. I have a perfectly rational fear of heights. It's not like a fear of balloons, or the dark, or going outdoors. If you fall, you get hurt.)

Joseph Westlake was a carpenter, as tall as Annie was short, equally thin, a narrow, silent, unhumorous man who was very good with his hands and, from a pesky child's point of view, very quick with his hands,

Mother, Lillian Bounds Westlake, 1930:
"Before me"

too. He never showed warmth directly, but he had one indirect way, which I insufficiently understood at the time. For each of his grandchildren, of whom he had fifteen, he constructed a small child-size rocking chair, very solid, very well-built, and very comfortable. The particular child's name formed the chair back. I don't mean he etched or carved the name into a piece of wood, I mean he shaped and glued pieces of wood to spell out the name—usually twice, horizontally and vertically, crossing in the middle letter—so that the back of my chair looked like this:

The meaning of those chairs is much clearer to me now, of course. An inarticulate man who was manually talented, this was his only way to express his love for his grandchildren. Giving them *chairs* ex-

Father, Albert Joseph Westlake, about 1930

pressed his equally inarticulate desire that they should all shut up and sit down for a while.

When our family disintegrated some years later, our chairs—Virginia's said GINIA on the back—were among the things we lost track of. Much of life, I believe, is spent remembering the things we used to have.

W hat I know of my family is mostly little and late. There is mystery, for instance, concerning the meeting between my mother and father. When Virginia and I were growing up, the general impression we were given was that our parents had both been living and working in New York City, had met there, and had been part of a large, party-loving group which frequently made the rounds of the speakeasies. (This was Prohibition, apparently a pretty bad time to have been in America but a pretty good time to be in New York, a not-infrequent situation.) Then, according to this version, they fell in love, married, and continued to have a fine time until they started having children (i.e., me). Then the marriage

turned bad, for which my mother never forgave us (i.e., me).

It was after my mother's death that this story broke down. Virginia and I were clearing out my mother's apartment—this was 1956, three years after my father's death, and a part of the disintegration and vaguing of youthful tangibles—when we found a missal with the name "Lillian Steuber" written in it, in what was without question my mother's handwriting. (I knew my mother's handwriting, having forged it on any number of report cards.) She had been born Lillian Bounds and had married Albert Westlake. Who was this Steuber?

None of the relatives on my mother's side would talk about it. If I asked anything at all, my aunt Peg would say only, "I'm sorry you ever saw that," and clench her jaw.

Finally, a relative on my father's side told me what little she knew, which was all hearsay. As she understood it, by the time my mother had reached the age of twenty or twenty-one—something like that—her father had already abandoned his family, which was supported exclusively by the work of my mother's mother, a lady who would naturally have somewhat negative views about both men and security. A considerably older man, a landlord named Steuber, wanted to marry my mother, who resisted but was at length persuaded by her mother to accept the match. There would be financial security with Steuber. And as for waiting for romantic love, in my grandmother Bounds's view, the road from the DeWitt Clinton Bridge led all downhill.

My mother, then, was apparently a more-or-less contented hausfrau in Albany, was Mrs. Steuber, for several years. She had no children; at least none that I know of. Then, one day, a door-to-door salesman came to call. He was handsome, he was ebullient, he was cocky and cheerful, and he had the gift of gab.

My father was always a good salesman.

There was an affair. There was a leaving of Mr. Steuber and a departure—perhaps flight—to New York. The time frame for all of this I know nothing about, but the last act, apparently, was a pregnancy. A while after finding the missal, my sister and I found the divorce papers, which we foolishly showed my aunt Peg, who immediately destroyed them. But Steuber—I don't even know his first name—in March of 1933, divorced his wife, Lillian. Albert Westlake was named in the papers. Lillian and Albert married the instant the divorce was granted. And, on July 12, 1933, surrounded by ambiguity and mystery, arriving to a not-unmixed welcome, there came me.

There were other mysteries and ambiguities in the family. My father, like my mother, was one of four children; in his case, two boys and two girls. The youngest, considerably younger than my father, was Edwin, and in him hope was the most heavily invested. He was an excellent student, and for high school attended Christian Brothers Academy in Albany, a prestigious military school in which he became cadet colonel (the highest student rank) and valedictorian, and was voted Most Likely To Succeed.

That was the high-water mark of his life. By 1947, he was living a bit further upstate, in Amsterdam, New York, with a wife and four young children, had a history of incomplete achievements, and was employed as driver of a fish market's delivery truck. One night his wife awoke to find Edwin packing. "I have to get out of town tonight," he told her, looking and sounding scared. "I'll send you a card when I know where I am."

He was never heard from again.

Another mystery concerns my father. I learned it in two chapters, at two different times, and do not know the ending.

Some time after my father's death, my mother told me this story: It was around 1930. My father and mother and another couple were in a speakeasy in New York. Three men entered the joint, one tall and cadaverous and wearing a too-short black suit, the other two remaining behind him with their hats on their heads and their hands in their topcoat pockets. As the three started toward the rear of the place, the man in front saw my father and exclaimed in pleased surprise, "Al! How are you?"

"Fine, Bill. Good to see you."

Bill sat with them, called the waiter over, and ordered champagne "on my tab." The two men with him remained standing and did not take part in the conversation. While waiting for the champagne, Bill and my father talked about the Giants, my father being a mad baseball fan (and one-time semipro third baseman) and the Giants being his team.

The champagne arrived. Bill stayed long enough to toast the table and take a polite sip, and then he said, "See you, Al," patted my father on the shoulder, and left. He and his two friends went on to the rear and through the door to the back room.

My mother said, "Bert? Who was that?" (My father was feckless "Bert" at home, popular and able "Al" outside.)

"Bill Bailey," my father murmured. (Bill Bailey was a New Jersey bootlegger, an associate of Dutch Schultz.) "I'll tell you about it later." But he never did.

Chapter two came after my mother's death, when Virginia and I were trying to deal with the things they had left behind. In the cellar was my father's old trunk, into which he would put whatever he no longer needed but didn't want to throw away. It existed in archaeological levels, receding in time from top to bottom, with the lowest level containing his First World War uniform, neatly folded. And *below* that, the only item out of chronological order, was a cluster of clippings from New York City newspapers in 1931, describing the death of Bill Bailey. He'd walked into a northern Manhattan hospital at five in the afternoon, saying he didn't feel well, and was admitted. At two the next morning, he was pronounced dead of pneumonia. Not impossible; not likely.

Aside from a clipping about me winning an essay contest in grammar school, those are the only newspaper clippings I know of my father having saved. They're certainly the only ones he hid. How did he know Bill Bailey? Why was Bailey's death of such surreptitious interest to him? I'll never know, will I?

"My mother and father, with me"

The Depression treated our family about as badly as it treated everybody else. My father had various bookkeeping jobs, for less and less money, and eventually succumbed to the temptation to supplement his income using his access to the firm's books. He was found out, of course, but hadn't hit them for much, and was good old Al, and was not prosecuted. But he was let go.

When I was four, we moved from Manhattan to Yonkers, where I started school in more ways than one. The rear of our backyard abutted the side of a yard behind a house around the corner. A boy my age was back there, and through the fence he asked me if I could come around to his yard to play. I asked my mother. It involved no crossing of streets. I would be out of sight briefly while walking around the corner but would be in my mother's view again once I attained my friend's backyard. She said yes.

Thrilled, I started out on my first adventure, walking on a sidewalk all on my own. I made it around the corner and partway up the drive beside that other house—two strips of concrete, with gravelly weeds between—where my friend met me. "My name's Donald," I said.

"*My* name's Donald," he said, and hit me on the nose.

I sat down on the gravel. My nose started to bleed. He ran into his house crying. I ran around the corner and into my house, crying and bleeding.

We didn't make it up later.

When I was six, our financial situation became so dire that we moved back to Albany, where all our relatives lived and mutual assistance might be found. I don't think anyone involved wanted to make this move, but there wasn't much choice.

My parents lived in Albany the rest of their lives, constantly squabbling—my mother droned, my father maintained silence or, on rare occasions, became violent—occasionally separating (we'd be farmed out to relatives or, for six awful months one time, put in a Catholic orphanage over in Rensselaer), and never, I think, managing to find peace.

Not at home, anyway. My father was active in the Veterans of Foreign Wars, becoming post commander, then state commander, then regional commander, and healed himself with the esteem he earned out there. I don't know that my mother ever found a palliative at all. In any event, the drama was fought out in Albany, and that's where I grew up.

Albany is small, dark, dirty, corrupt, and tired, and William Kennedy found a hell of a lot more there than I ever did. When I entered high school, the joke going around was, "If they ever gave New York State an enema, they'd put the tube in Albany." We didn't have to have experience of anywhere else to know what we had.

Albany is like the kind of terminally ill patient who would die if somebody pulled the plug. In Albany's case, the plug is state government. Pull that, and it's all over. There hasn't been a reason for Albany to exist since the Erie Canal stopped being the principal route to the West.

Some years ago, I was asked to speak at the Albany Public Library—my first time back in that city for over twenty years—and with some free time I showed my wife some of where I grew up, ending in the bar where I'd misspent my later teens. "I haven't been in here in twenty-eight years," I told the bartender. "You haven't missed a thing," he said; *boom,* like that.

Later, in the car, my wife said, "Does that man have any idea what he just said about his own life?"

Maybe.

I knew I was a writer when I was eleven; it took the rest of the world about ten years to begin to agree. Up till then, my audience was mainly limited to my father, who was encouraging and helpful, and ultimately influential in a very important way.

Neophyte writers are always told, "Write what you know," but the fact is, kids don't *know anything*. A beginning writer doesn't write what he knows, he writes what he read in books or saw in the movies. And that's the way it was with me. I wrote gangster stories, I wrote stories about cowboys, I wrote poems about gold prospecting—in Alaska, so I could rhyme with "cold"—I wrote the first chapters of all kinds of novels. The short stories I mailed off to magazines, and they mailed them back in the self-addressed, stamped envelopes I had provided. And in the middle of it all, my father asked me a question which, probably more than any other single thing, decided what kind of writer I was going to be.

I was about fourteen. I'd written a science-fiction story about aliens from another planet who come to Earth and hire a husband-wife team of big-game hunters to help them collect examples of every animal on Earth for their zoo back on Alpha Centauri or wherever. At the end of the story, they kidnap the hero and heroine and take them away in the spaceship because they want examples of *every* animal on Earth.

Now, this was a perfectly usable story. It had been written and published dozens of times, frequently with Noah's Ark somewhere in the title, and my

*"My father, my sister, and me, around the
time I sighted my grandfather Bounds"*

version was simply that story again, done with my
sentences. I probably even thought I'd made it up.

So I showed it to my father. He read it and said
one or two nice things about the dialogue or whatever,
and then he said, "Why did you write *this*
story?"

I didn't know what he meant. The true answer
was that science-fiction magazines published that
story with gonglike regularity and I wanted a story
published somewhere. This truth was so implicit I
didn't even have words to describe it, and therefore
there was no way to understand the question.

So he asked it a different way: "What's the story
about?" Well, it's about these people that get taken
to be in a zoo on Alpha Centauri. "No, what's it *about*?"
he said. "The old fairy tales that you read when you
were a little boy, they all had a moral at the end. If
you put a moral at the end of this story, what would it
be?"

I didn't know. I didn't know what the moral was.
I didn't know what the story was *about*.

The truth was, of course, that the story wasn't
about anything. It was a very modest little trick, like a
connect-the-dots thing on a restaurant place mat.
There's nothing particularly wrong with connect-the-
dots things, and there's nothing particularly wrong
with this constructivist kind of writing, a little story or
a great big fat novel with nothing and nobody in it
except this machine that turns over and at the end
this jack-in-the-box pops out. There's nothing wrong
with that.

But it isn't what I thought I wanted to be. So that
question of my father's wriggled right down into my
brain like a worm, and for quite a long while it took
the fun out of things. I'd be sitting there writing a
story about mobsters having a shootout in a nightclub
office—straight out of some recent movie—and the
worm would whisper, Why are you writing *this* story?

Naturally, I didn't want to listen, but I had no
real choice in the matter. The question kept coming,
and I had to try to figure out some way to answer it,
and so, slowly and gradually, I began to find out what
I was doing. And ultimately I refined the question
itself down to this: What does this story mean to *me*
that I should spend my valuable time creating it?

And that's how I began to become a writer.

We were lace-curtain poor, which meant we
didn't surrender to our poverty but spent all
our time—at least my mother spent all *her* time—in
little strategies meant to hide the poverty from
outsiders. And no strategy was too little. My mother
smoked Pall Mall cigarettes at home because they
were longer for the same price, but Lucky Strike
outside so no one would think she was cheap. Life
under the constant surveillance of four billion hostile
eyes can get tense.

By the time she was a teenager, my sister
Virginia had pretty much fled this half-strangled
existence to hang out farther downtown with people
whose poverty was open and uninhibited; they even
had crude accents, the better to flaunt their "have-
notitis." But while Virginia was fleeing outward, I was
fleeing inward. If the world was intolerable, that's
okay. I had others.

In school, I was always very bright and also
always in a whole lot of trouble. If I was so smart, why
couldn't I do things *right* once in a while? I didn't
know, and it was a severe torment to be so able and
yet so unable at the same time.

Years later, I read a book that made the point
that what artists and criminals have in common is a

capability for strong concentration of brainpower on a short-term project—a landscape in oils, a bank robbery—combined with an almost ludicrous inability to do anything requiring long-term planning or follow-through. (Think of artists' marital histories, or all those escaped cons who never get farther than the nearest culvert.) Pity I hadn't had that book in grade school; I could have brought it to class in lieu of all those notes from my exasperated parents.

There were three Catholic high schools in Albany at that time. They all cost money. We didn't have any money, but I was to attend one of them. Cathedral had a merit scholarship that was rather easy to get; I got it. Vincentian had a scholarship that was relatively tough to get; I got it. That year, for the first time in its history, Christian Brothers Academy (where Uncle Edwin had so excelled) offered two scholarships, to be awarded following a quite rigorous exam. Short-term concentration: I was always a killer on tests. I won the first scholarship CBA ever gave out. Good for me; bad for them.

CBA was a religious school *and* a military school. That I was there at all merely demonstrates the depth of my lack of self-knowledge at that time. This was the only high school in America from which, until 1945, it had been possible to graduate as a second lieutenant in the United States Marine Corps. (A small contingent of marines were still there, in my time, as ROTC instructors.) Even then, I knew that the endless honor roll of the glorious defunct in the main hallway was a record of horror: foreshortened lives, snuffed promises, entire histories thrown away for the good of somebody else's short-term political advantage.

If you did something wrong at CBA, like forgetting to wear your collar stay (I always forgot to wear my collar stay), you got demerits, which you walked off after school, marching around the flagpole with a rifle on your shoulder (a World War I Enfield). I did not receive the most demerits of anybody in my school while I was there; I came in second. Tommy, who got the most, was my best friend. He was also hilarious, a jokester to his toenails. He earned his demerits the right way, by being the clown prince, the very spirit of anarchy, the irrepressible soul and essence of the individual in the face of two monoliths: the Church and the Marines. I got mine the wrong way, by being a goofball.

My friendship with Tommy was typical. All through school and beyond, I was never the funniest kid, but I was always the funniest kid's best friend. I was a great appreciator. And of whom does the

teacher take disapproving notice? Is it the trickster, or the laugher? Ah, trouble, trouble.

I lasted two-and-a-half years at CBA. Midway through the third year, the principal called me in to point out that I had averaged two days a week in school that year, that my alleged notes from home were an insult to any pedant's intelligence, and that the school's indulgence (I was their very first scholarship child, and how awful this must have been for them) was nearly at an end. Then he made a mistake. Like a Toon, I've never been able to resist a punch line. Heartfelt though the principal's message may have been, his delivery system was unalloyed cliché; everything principals say, he said. And so, when at last he said, "Don't you like it here?" what I said was, "No." I hadn't intended to, honest.

I finished my high school at Vincentian, a coeducational school, but with the sexes separated, the girls' classes taught by nuns on the top two floors, the boys' classes taught by brothers on the bottom two floors. (That's how much they knew.) There were three coeducational classes, journalism, art, and typing, and I took all three.

Sister Mary Carmel, the journalism teacher, accepted me on my own terms and let me get on with my writing. I will always be grateful to her. And I will always continue to bear in mind her injunction that the key to readable writing is to use active verbs. "He strode" is so much better than "He walked determinedly" as to not even be in the same league. The verb is the engine of the sentence; be sure it's powerful enough to push the whole sentence forward. Right.

After high school, given our family's finances, there were very few choices to be made. Of those few, there's one I still very much regret.

A Catholic university in St. Louis had begun a creative writing program and offered merit scholarships based on submitted written work. The trick was, the scholarships were for only one year at a time. They offered ten freshman scholarships; the entire freshman class could later compete for seven sophomore scholarships; the entire sophomore class could try for five junior scholarships; and the entire junior class had to claw one another to bits for three senior scholarships.

I submitted a semi-neat parcel of stories and poems and some time later received a letter from the school saying that I had come in eleventh and that, since students often applied to several colleges at once, there was every likelihood that one or more of the ten winners would not accept the scholarship. I was at the top of the list to replace any such person, but only if I sent the school a letter saying I was still interested. If I sent no letter, my name would be dropped from the list. And here is where my father gave me advice I still regret; regret his having given it, my having taken it.

A word about my father. He had been a smart, attractive, confident, outgoing guy. My grandmother showed me talented charcoal portraits he had done in his youth. With an incomplete high-school education, he had nevertheless completed the hotel-training school at Cornell. When I knew him, he did no drawing or painting; he had never worked in a hotel. Defeat had come to live in his breast at some point, for some reason, and he never found the strength to evict it. On the road in a selling job, or at the VFW post, he was still gregarious and intelligent—not a heavy drinker, oddly enough—but at home he could not hide from his assessment of himself as a failure. Only once did the timidity of his conviction of failure ever spill over into his dealings with me, and it was in this question of the scholarship to St. Louis.

If I went there, he pointed out, I would be over a thousand miles from home. We had no money. If I got sick, or if I was unhappy with the school, it would be hard for my family to be of help from so far away. And the scholarship was for only one year; wouldn't it be worse, if I *did* love the place, to have to leave after only one year? And after all, in the competition for the second year's seven scholarships, wouldn't I be struggling against eight or nine fellow students who'd already demonstrated their superiority to me? And even if I snakehipped my way into the second year, what about the even narrower third? We won't even mention the fourth.

When faced with an agonizing decision, it's always easiest to do nothing. I sent no letter to St. Louis.

This was 1951. At the end of World War II, a number of colleges had been created by New York State to deal with the sudden influx of veterans: I went to one of these, a liberal arts college in Plattsburg called Champlain, for two hundred dollars tuition a semester, plus I forget how much for food, plus the cost of books. The tuition included a shared (three-person) dormitory room.

The summer after high-school graduation, I worked for the New York Central railroad as a gandy dancer (track-repair crew) and with supplemental help from my parents raised enough money for my freshman year. They also sent me two dollars a week for expenses.

Plattsburg was then a very poor town in the poorest corner of New York State. In the year and a half I was there, I found only one job, as helper on a beer truck, and that was only for a month or two in the spring and fall. Christmas vacation, I did another two weeks on the railroad track gang, and spent the next summer there as well, but it wasn't enough.

A classmate of mine—not a roommate—was a fellow from New York City with the same last name as a well-known gangster. He at times claimed the gangster was his uncle, at other times denied it. He was a premed student and usually a bright and funny guy, but with one quirk: he always wanted somebody to come commit burglaries with him. He talked about these burglaries all the time but never did them, so far as I then knew. (It later turned out he *had* been doing them.) One day in December 1952, the week before Christmas vacation of my sophomore year, I was seated in my room counting up my money and realizing there was no way to put together next semester's cash—needed in early February—when Joe came in and said, "I got a great way to get into the chem lab. We can pick up a couple microscopes, pawn them when we get home."

"Done," I said.

He wasn't at all surprised at my agreement, and the job was as easy as he'd said it would be. In Albany, over Christmas vacation, I got forty dollars for the microscope from a pawnshop, much less than I'd hoped for. I also worked on the track gang again, and when I got back to school early in January, Joe and I were arrested for burglary.

Okay. I spent five days and four nights in the town jail. The low point of my life—still—was when my father came to visit me there. He wasn't mad; he was sad.

He was also practical. Somehow, though he could rarely do much for himself, he could always find solutions for other people's problems. He went on the assumption that the local state legislator would be a lawyer. He was, and my father hired him, borrowing money from anywhere he could to cover the fees. At the end of the day, the court produced a sealed indictment; in other words, if I remained law-abiding for a year—or however long the judge decided—the indictment would be quashed and the arrest would cease to exist in the records, but if I were arrested for any other crime in that period the indictment would be unsealed and I'd be in double trouble.

I managed to be totally law-abiding for a year and five months, and at last the indictment was quashed, and there now exists no record of the

In the Air Force

incident anywhere, except in this account. I could have forgotten the event, ignored it; but it's part of how I became the writer I am. And, regardless of any other consideration, I'm still pleased that I thought enough of myself to steal for me; I wasn't defeated. And I still believe you only play fair—as I am doing here—if you can afford to.

During the year and a half under indictment, I worked for New York State as a temporary clerk and went to night school at Russell Sage. I knew I'd be going into military service once the indictment was quashed (citizens under indictment cannot enlist or be drafted) so my life was on hold, and the time seemed endless. I finally found the right image for it—I felt like a boxcar on a siding, watching the trains go by, month after month after month—and as usual the right image, the right words, did help. But not enough.

I did a lot of writing in that time, short stories aimed at every known genre, and at last got one accepted. I was nineteen, but the story wasn't published till I was twenty, so I didn't make my goal of being a published writer in my teens. But it was okay anyway.

My breakthrough was a science-fiction story, or a fantasy, really, and a gimmick at that. The idea was, when Patrick Henry said, "Give me liberty or give me death," he meant the United States. Therefore, so long as America remained a free country, Patrick Henry wouldn't die. He would, however, develop ailments linked to losses of liberties in this country. He was blind during the Alien and Sedition Acts, for instance, and during Prohibition he had terrible bursitis and couldn't bend his elbow. The story was about the death of Patrick Henry.

Now, I happen to know why I wrote that story, and it was merely because it was a joke I got a kick out of. I wasn't using it as a vehicle for a political statement or anything like that. (My distrust of authority and of law was tucked away inside it, but was given no emphasis.) The story was merely a gag, and I'd told it well enough to get it published, and that was fine.

Over the years, with every rejection of a story, I had been given a rejection slip, sometimes with a word or two penned on it. I never knew what to do

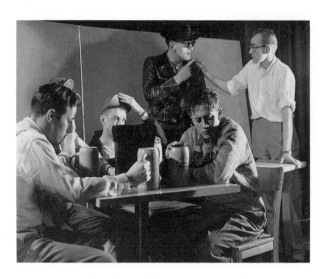

Westlake (far right), "performing in a short play I had written in the Air Force."

with the rejection slips but couldn't bring myself to throw them away, and eventually I tacked them to the wall over my desk, making patterns as their numbers grew and promising myself to throw them out when I finally got something accepted. I did just that when "Or Give Me Death" sold, counting them as I took them down—there were just over two hundred—and keeping one from the *New Yorker* to represent the lot. That last one is still over my desk.

During my time under indictment, my mother was a clerk for the local Army-Air Force recruiting office. The recruiting sergeants, knowing she had a fresh calf at home, kept wangling dinner invitations, and the Air Force sergeant must have been very good. He convinced me the Air Force was better than the Army; okay, why not? But he also convinced me, and this was genius, that a four-year enlistment in the Air Force—the only term possible—was better than two years in the Army; that four years in the military was better than two years in the military. Why, if that fellow had turned his talents to good, he could have brought about world peace by now.

The Air Force did nothing to challenge my belief that authority was not to be trusted. The euphemism there was "personality conflicts," and when enlisted men have personality conflicts with officers the result is rarely pretty. Trouble, trouble. I hung out, as usual, with the wits and the wise guys and merely tried not to get myself in enough trouble to earn Leavenworth. (The stockade, or jail, at my last

base of assignment, to which somehow I was never remanded, contained the notice over the entrance, "Obedience to the law is freedom." Just in case you were unsure what we're fighting for.)

My first military year was spent in training in upstate New York and Illinois, followed by assignment to a radar hub near Syracuse, New York; close enough to spend weekends at home. Then I was sent to Germany, where I spent the next year and a half, and would have spent three years if it were not for the American Congress.

Congress cut the Air Force appropriation that year, a shocking surprise to everybody. Having to cut back, for that fiscal year only, the Air Force invented a new one-time discharge to thin the ranks at their very lowest level. The discharge was only obtainable by enlisted men who were in the second half of their first enlistment, had completed at least half of their overseas assignment, had never risen above the rank of airman third class, would sign a declaration of their firm intent not to reenlist, would request the discharge, and who were "unadaptable to the military service." The form of severance was a General Discharge under Honorable Conditions, leaving the recipient eligible for all veterans' benefits.

This was no off-the-rack discharge; this thing was tailored precisely to my proportions. All I had to do was request it, be evaluated by a staff-level (that is, major or above) officer from outside my direct chain of command (the officers receding upward in a direct line from the clot of an adjutant to the president of the United States), and my life of personality conflict would be over.

As soon as I heard of this door through the clouds that had been created, I went to my immediate commander, a gentleman named Major Gilstrap, whom I'd always liked, and requested it. The major was a serious and an honest man; he was troubled that I could be so ambiguous about my duty. "Why don't you take twenty-four hours to think this over?" he asked me.

Well, there it is; I can't resist a straight line. "What time is it?" I said, and watched Major Gilstrap's face close against me, which it had never done before. I regretted the line, but not the result. Twenty-four hours later, he made no comment when I repeated my request, and the march of paperwork began.

The staff-level officer who came to evaluate me was another major. In my military experience, majors are the only even remotely sensible officers. They've made that incredible leap up out of junior-officer rank—a whole lot of also-rans repine as captains their entire careers—and are too far from generalship to have been driven mad by the possibility, as all colonels, without exception, are. (Generals, of course, are like movie producers, but with the power to kill.)

During my time in Germany, other military organizations had (with my connivance) requested I be transferred to them, but all transfers had been blocked by my personality-conflict friend, who wasn't finished with me. These included the Public Information Office for the Air Force at SHAEF Headquarters in Wiesbaden, the Eighty-sixth Fighter-Interceptor Wing magazine called *Raider* at Landsruhe Air Base across the road, and Armed Forces Network, which wanted me as a radio writer/announcer and would have housed me in their headquarters in a castle in Frankfurt.

The evaluating major offered me a guaranteed transfer to Armed Forces Network if I would withdraw my request for the discharge. I thought it over, having to make another difficult decision, and finally said, "I'm sorry, Major, even a month or two ago I would have jumped at it, but right now, all I want out of the Air Force is me."

My father had died of a heart attack at fifty-seven shortly before I went into the Air Force, and my mother's heart went at fifty-six while I was in. I took my discharge at Manhattan Beach Air Force Station in Brooklyn, found an apartment near Prospect Park, and wrote a novel about the Air Force. It

"With my firstborn, Sean," about 1960

wasn't published, but a few short stories were, and a few months later I went back to college, this time upstate in Binghamton, at a place then called Harpur College (a sister institution to my first school, Champlain College, and the last survivor of those postwar educational Levittowns) and now called State University of New York at Binghamton.

A classmate, learning I was a writer, inveigled me into doing a three-act musical comedy for the Spring Revue; book and lyrics by me, music by another guy. In the course of that production I met my first wife, who aspired to be an actress. It was, in fact, to further her career and not mine that we soon moved to New York City. (I had by then four years of college at three schools and had finally made junior; thus ending my formal education.)

For a theatrical career, Nedra had to be in New York City, available for auditions and classes and showcases and agents and all of that. I used to say, "I can write anywhere on earth there's a post office," and I suppose that's true. Nevertheless, New York loosened some muscles inside me, invigorated me in some way, made a true difference in the already-accepted fact that I was a writer.

My wife's New York experiences, on the other hand, were not happy. It was from watching her, and a few other people, that I've developed my basic criteria for success in either the creative or interpretive arts. I believe there are three things you absolutely have to have for long-term success: talent, ambition, and luck. There are people who've gone partway with only two—in particular, ambition and luck without talent have made some people quite plausible ninety-day wonders—but to turn aspirations into career, I think, you need all three.

My first wife had talent to spare; I've seen her on stage, and I've seen what she could do to an audience. We'll never know if she had luck, because her ambition just wasn't strong enough to carry her forward.

Ninety-eight percent of an actor's experience is of rejection. If you are going to spend your entire life being too short, too dark, too old, too thin, too intense, too nasal, too young, too pale, with wrong-colored eyes and wrong-shaped hands and the wrong walk and the "Oh, I don't know, there's just something not quite *right* but we do thank you for coming in"—you'd better have a strong ego.

For about three months, my wife cried herself to sleep every night. Every night. When she found she was pregnant, she abandoned hope with oceanic relief.

In October of 1958 I answered a blind ad in the *Times* for an "associate editor at a literary agency." The agency turned out to be Scott Meredith Incorporated, a part of whose business has always been as reader, for a fee, of amateurs' stories. (I'd sent them one story and five dollars myself, at around the age of fourteen.) I became a fee reader, and for the next six months read approximately sixty short stories or eight novels or some mix thereof every week, writing letters for Scott's signature about how *this* story doesn't quite make it but shows really amazing talent and do try us again with another story and another check.

The other fee reader at that time was a guy named Hal, who has subsequently made a good career as screenwriter and television writer. Back then, he was the funniest guy around and inevitably became my best friend. On my first or second day on the job, Hal said, "See that guy over there? That's Henry. If he ever asks you, 'Do you know anything about . . . ?' and mentions horror stories or westerns or war stories, say yes and you'll get an assignment."

(Henry turned out to be Henry Morrison. For many years he was my agent, and is still my friend.)

A couple of weeks later, Henry came over and said, "Do you know anything about confession stories?" and I said, "Oddly enough, yes. My roommate and I in college did a content analysis on confession magazines for a sociology course."

Yes was all the answer Henry had needed. He told me to type three one-paragraph story ideas on a sheet of paper, which he would send to the publisher, who would checkmark the one he wanted, which I would then write at three thousand words for fifty dollars. So I went home, dragged out the content analysis, typed out one-paragraph versions of the three most frequent stories in the fifty magazines Bill Coons and I had read and analyzed, and turned it in. That was the only time the publisher ever checkmarked all three stories. I wrote them the next weekend and collected my hundred and fifty dollars.

A while later, Henry came over and said, "Do you know anything about sex novels?" and I said, "Yes," although the true answer was, "No." Henry said, "Bring in ten thousand words and an outline. If they okay it, you write a fifty-thousand-word book and they'll pay six hundred dollars."

That was in the morning. I waited till afternoon before going to Henry and saying, "Henry, in my childhood there were staplebound paperbacks with titles like *Impatient Virgin,* and the girl almost does it

all the way through the book, and finally does do it at the end. Is that what you mean?"

Utter disgust. "No," he said, and took three paperbacks from a shelf and gave them to me. "This," he said.

In 1959 these were called sex novels. I don't know *what* they'd be called today; euphemism novels, maybe. They didn't contain any of the taboo words, and their sex scenes were nowhere near as graphic as, say, your automobile owner's manual. They weren't part of any other genre, not westerns or mysteries or anything like that, but were sort of subnormal novel-novels. Characters had affairs; marriages broke up; people betrayed each other and sought vengeance. They were soap opera in their outlook, except that they came to an end. And the nice thing about them was, it's easy to get to fifty thousand words when you can't call anything by its rightful name.

I still at that time didn't know what particular kind of writer I was. I'd written all kinds of stories that had not been published. I'd published mystery stories and science-fiction stories and humorous stories and magazine nonfiction, and now these bottom-of-the-barrel things for Henry. I still submitted stories to the *Atlantic* and *Sewanee Review* and hither and yon, and they still came back. But the stories that were getting published were more and more frequently mystery stories, and I think it's a natural tendency to go where you're liked, so the next time I tried to write a novel it was a mystery novel. (That's when I began to describe myself as a writer disguised as a mystery writer, a remark I continued for ten or fifteen years, until the face grew to match the mask.)

There were two serious major hardcover publishers of mystery novels then, Simon and Schuster and Random House. Simon and Schuster rejected the book, and so did Random House, except that the Random House editor, Lee Wright, phoned the Scott Meredith office—Scott had transmogrified from my employer to my agent—to say to Henry, "I wish the author lived in New York. I'd like to talk with him about the book."

"He lives in New York, he lives in New York," Henry said, and called me to say, "You're going there to pick up the manuscript and bring it back. *Listen* to the woman."

Lee Wright was at that time the cream of the mystery editors and had been for years. She's the best editor I've ever had—though I've had a couple of other very good ones—and I was extremely lucky to have reached her on my very first try. (Now all we need is talent and ambition.) We talked for an hour

"Inside a beard," about 1970

and a half, and at the end of it she'd agreed to look at a revised version of the book. She bought the revision, after further revisions, and became my editor for the next ten years.

The problem was, at that time the mystery novel was viewed with contempt by the publishing industry. Just one mark of that contempt was that, at almost every hardcover publishing house, the mystery editor and cookbook editor were the same person. (The idea of Lee Wright as cookbook editor was comedy at its blackest. As she once said, "If I ever walk into a kitchen, my thumb immediately starts to bleed, and I haven't even touched the can opener yet.") Writers in the mystery ghetto were not to be taken seriously.

Ah, well. I wrote what I thought was a serious novel. It was called *Memory*, and that's what it was about. At the beginning of the novel, an actor on tour is hit on the head and hospitalized. His brain is damaged, so that his long-term memory goes; his memory loss is accelerated; last month is lost to him. By the time he comes out of the hospital, the touring company is long gone and so is his past, though he has enough memory to function in normal ways, and has fitful glimpses of a brighter and more interesting yesteryear. The book is about the functions and uses and glories of memory, and about the slow despair of the hero. (When he finally makes it back to New York and the awful public humiliation of an audition, we

learn just how much of himself he has lost. Memory is the actor's primary tool, not only for remembering lines in a play but for the ability to note and replicate people's movements and emotions.)

Lee Wright tried to get Random House to take *Memory* seriously, even though I was a cook and she the cookbook editor. Donald Klopfer, an owner of the place—Bennett Cerf's more mature partner—read it and wrote, "It's the only American novel I've ever read with the inevitability of the Russians." He also said he couldn't see any way to sell it.

Memory was submitted to Helen and Kurt Wolff, who said they loved it but had had such a heart-wrenching experience with the commercial failure of Günter Grass's *The Tin Drum* that they didn't want to risk their emotions on another such experience. (Hard to think of *The Tin Drum* as a commercial failure.) Bob Gotlieb, now at the *New Yorker*, then I forget where, praised it for a couple of paragraphs, said he couldn't sell it, and described it as the best novel he wouldn't publish that year and much better than many he would.

All in all, eight to ten of the most respected hardcover book editors in New York said how much they loved it and how little they could sell it, and compared it to everybody from Dostoevsky and Kafka to Twain and Thomas Wolfe (the previous one). All expressed their self-serving conviction that someone else would surely solve the commercial aspects.

For those who can dine on praise, this was a feast. The book was never published.

I was extremely prolific in those early years, and began to use pen names to take the overflow. One of those names was for a while more successful than I. The name was Richard Stark—"Richard" from Richard Widmark, whose Tommy Udo in *Kiss of Death* defined a generation of villains, and "Stark" because that's what I wanted the writing to be—and the first book Richard Stark wrote, in 1960, was about a professional crook named Parker who avenges a betrayal and is then caught by the police.

I had been aiming for Gold Medal, then the premiere publisher of original paperback genre novels, but Gold Medal rejected the book. Then an editor at Pocket Books named Bucklyn Moon phoned and said, "Is there any way you could let Parker escape at the end of the story and then give me three books a year about him?"

It had been very hard to get Parker caught in the first place. I'd practically had to stick an authorial foot into the manuscript and trip him. (I'd thought villains *had* to get caught.) So it was easy to let him escape, and it later turned out to be easy to write further about him. In the next fourteen years, Richard Stark wrote sixteen novels about Parker, eight for Pocket Books and then four for Gold Medal and then four (in hardcover!) for Random House, plus an additional four books about a compatriot of Parker's named Grofield.

Richard Stark's success was and is an astonishment to me. The last Richard Stark novel was published in 1974, and now in 1990 I still cannot enter a bookstore for an autographing session without three or four people asking me when Parker will reappear. Six of the sixteen books have been made into movies, including one seminal major film *(Point Blank,* 1967, John Boorman directing, with Lee Marvin) and one very good minor film *(The Outfit,* 1973, John Flynn directing, with Robert Duvall).

I don't know why Richard Stark retired. In 1974, and subsequently, I tried several times to put him back to work, but he was tired and leaden. His imagination was gone, the simplicity of his prose was gone, the coldness of his view was gone. It never worked. (On the other hand, I've learned from embarrassing experience never to make absolute statements about the future.)

It can't be that time left the character behind— Parker, so very Dillingeresque, was twenty-five years obsolete when I started him—so it must be something in myself. Maybe by 1974 I no longer felt so much the need to brace myself and prepare for the worst. By then I'd been through my two flawed marriages and had found the person who would help make the third one last, I had fathered my children, had become fairly successful and maybe even somewhat known as a novelist, had written screenplays and seen one turned into a movie *(Cops and Robbers,* 1973, directed by Aram Avakian), and had become the homeowner-breadwinner-settler against which Parker had been the rebuttal.

Or maybe it was merely that *nobody* could take Parker at face value any more. The most recent film adaptation *(Slayground,* 1984, Terry Bedford directing, with Peter Coyote) was a pretentious mess, reeking of art. One thing you could say for my Parker: he was never self-conscious.

My first five books for Random House were variations on traditional genre tunes: private eye, innocent unjustly accused, psychological suspense. The sixth was supposed to be the same, one more innocent-on-the-run story, but it started coming out funny. There were no funny mystery novels,

hadn't been since the death of Craig Rice some years before, so I was naturally worried, and phoned my agent.

Henry and I had both left Scott Meredith by then; Henry had started his own agency, and I was his first client. (The basic problem with Scott Meredith was that he thought of himself as a dairy farmer and the writers as his cows. For instance, he sold the French rights to one of my early books to a smaller company for less money, because it might improve the *agency's* relationship with that publisher, whereas all it could do for me was make me less money and offer me narrower exposure.)

Henry urged me not to give in to this manic muse, and all his arguments were commercially sound. But it was happening anyway, despite the two of us, this jaundiced view of the conventions of the genre bubbling out of me. "It isn't taking long, Henry," I said, "and I'll just do this one, and then go back to doing it right."

The fact is, despite a couple of humorous short stories, it had never occurred to me that *I* could write funny. I wasn't the funniest kid around, I was the funniest kid's best friend. So what this book was trying to do I had no idea, but I followed it, and it kept on being funny. I called it *The Dead Nephew,* which Lee didn't like (one of her few errors), so Random House published it as *The Fugitive Pigeon* and it doubled the sale of preceding books and did very well in foreign and ancillary markets. And I never looked back. Well, occasionally I've looked back.

In 1970, trying to think of another story for Richard Stark to tell about Parker, I came up with a situation in which he would have to keep stealing the same thing over and over. There was something lunatic about the idea, though, and I soon realized that for Parker it would never do. The worst thing that can happen to a tough guy is to be laughed at; his credibility immediately disappears.

So Parker couldn't be the character, and Stark couldn't be the storyteller, but the story was still appealing. I put together another group, less dangerous, led by a woeful fellow called John Dortmunder, named after a German beer *(Dortmunder Actien Beer,* with that word which is almost "action" but isn't, and a kind of long-nosed mournfulness in "Dortmunder" which seemed apt, somehow), and with a partner called Andy Kelp, named for a seaweed. (When William Goldman was writing the screenplay based on the book resulting from all this, called *The Hot Rock,* he told me I had a very unfortunate knack in naming my characters. *His* were called Butch Cassidy and the

"At the New York Public Library, gesturing hypnotically at Robert B. Parker (left), William F. Buckley, Robin Winks, and Stanley Ellin," 1987

Sundance Kid; mine were called Dortmunder and Kelp. There was something in what he said.)

I never had any intention of making Dortmunder and Kelp series characters, or I might have named them differently: Butch Dortmunder and the Algae Kid, maybe. *The Hot Rock* was, after all, the thirteenth novel under the Westlake name, and none of the previous twelve had contained characters who felt they had more to say and do once their original tales were told. But in 1972, I saw a bank on Route 23 in New Jersey which was being temporarily housed in a mobile home while its original building was torn down and replaced, and it occurred to me that an enterprising fellow could back up a truck to that bank and *drive it away.* Dortmunder and Kelp were obviously the only people for the job.

Over the last twenty years, while writing other books and stories and screenplays and whatnot, I've done seven novels and three short stories about Dortmunder and Kelp, and now they have taken Richard Stark's place as the corner of my empire which outshines the rest. Plaintively I point out that my other novels contain complete sentences, too, that

some of them—like *Kahawa,* a 1982 novel set in Idi Amin's Uganda—are closer to my heart and more full and novelistic, but there are people who simply won't read anything I write unless Dortmunder and Kelp are in it. I begin to understand why Conan Doyle eventually snuck up behind Sherlock Holmes at the Reichenbach Falls. Except that I, too, like Dortmunder and always enjoy our outings together.

Twenty years ago, a movie producer said these two sentences to me in a row: "I made sixteen movies the past six years. I never made a film I didn't care deeply about." I've mocked the man behind his back for that, but don't I feel the same way about my novels? There've been more than seventy of them in thirty years, and I never wrote a book I didn't care deeply about. *While writing it.*

Over the years, my talent has been whatever it is, my ambition has been to never do anything but write, and my luck has been fitful. Should I agonize for years because *Memory* never found an editor capable of doing his or her job and with the support of his or her employer? Or should I care deeply about the book I'm writing *now?*

That's my job. Once the book is done, it is up to agents and publishers and editors and booksellers and readers. I'll do my job the best I can. They'll do their jobs as they see fit.

In the meantime, from unlikely and iffy beginnings, without an uncle in the business and with no conviction that my message to the world was of overriding importance (nor eagerly awaited), I've managed to stay at this typewriter, more or less undisturbed, for more than thirty years. It's what I wanted. It's what I got. The only thing that keeps this from being a happy ending is that it isn't the end.

BIBLIOGRAPHY

Fiction:

The Mercenaries, Random House, 1960.

Killing Time, Random House, 1961.

361, Random House, 1962.

Killy, Random House, 1963.

Pity Him Afterwards, Random House, 1964.

The Fugitive Pigeon, Random House, 1965.

The Busy Body, Random House, 1966.

The Spy in the Ointment, Random House, 1966.

God Save the Mark, Random House, 1967.

Philip, Crowell, 1967.

(Compiler with Philip Klass) *Once against the Law,* Macmillan, 1968.

The Curious Facts Preceding My Execution, and Other Fictions, Random House, 1968.

Who Stole Sassi Manoon?, Random House, 1968.

Somebody Owes Me Money, Random House, 1969.

Up Your Banners, Macmillan, 1969.

Adios, Scheherezade, Simon & Schuster, 1970.

The Hot Rock, Simon & Schuster, 1970.

I Gave at the Office, Simon & Schuster, 1971.

Under an English Heaven, Simon & Schuster, 1971.

Bank Shot, Simon & Schuster, 1972.

Cops and Robbers (also see below), M. Evans, 1972.

(With Brian Garfield) *Gangway,* M. Evans, 1972.

Help! I Am Being Held Prisoner, M. Evans, 1974.

Jimmy the Kid, M. Evans, 1974.

Brothers Keepers, M. Evans, 1975.

Two Much, M. Evans, 1975.

Dancing Aztecs, M. Evans, 1976, published in England as *A New York Dance,* Hodder & Stoughton, 1979.

Enough, M. Evans, 1977.

Nobody's Perfect, M. Evans, 1977.

Castle in the Air, M. Evans, 1980.

Kahawa, Viking, 1982.

Why Me (also see below), Viking, 1983.

Levine, Mysterious Press, 1984.

A Likely Story, Penzler Books, 1984.

High Adventure, Mysterious Press, 1985.

Good Behavior, Mysterious Press, 1986.

(With Abby Westlake) *High Jinx,* McMillan, 1987.

(With A. Westlake) *Transylvania Station,* McMillan, 1987.

Trust Me on This, Mysterious Press, 1988.

Sacred Monster, Mysterious Press, 1989.

Drowned Hopes, Mysterious Press, 1990.

Under pseudonym John B. Allan:

Elizabeth Taylor: A Fascinating Story of America's Most Talented Actress and the World's Most Beautiful Woman, Monarch, 1961.

Under pseudonym Tucker Coe:

Kinds of Love, Kinds of Death, Random House, 1966.

Murder among Children, Random House, 1968.

Wax Apple, Random House, 1970.

A Jade in Aries, Random House, 1971.

Don't Lie to Me, Random House, 1972.

Under pseudonym Richard Stark:

The Hunter (also see below), Pocket Books, 1963, published as *Point Blank,* Berkley, 1973, reprinted under original title with a new introduction by the author, Gregg Press, 1981.

The Man with the Getaway Face (also see below), Pocket Books, 1963, published as *The Steel Hit,* Coronet (London), 1971, Berkley, 1975, published under original title, Allison & Busby, 1985.

The Outfit (also see below), Pocket Books, 1963.

The Mourner (also see below), Pocket Books, 1963.

The Score (also see below), Pocket Books, 1964.

The Jugger, Pocket Books, 1965.

The Handle, Pocket Books, 1966, published as *Run Lethal,* Berkley, 1966.

The Seventh (also see below), Pocket Books, 1966, published in England as *The Split,* Allison & Busby, 1984.

The Dame, Macmillan, 1967.

The Damsel, Macmillan, 1967.

The Green Eagle Score, Fawcett, 1967.

The Rare Coin Score, Fawcett, 1967, reprinted, Schocken, 1984.

The Black Ice Score, Fawcett, 1968.

The Blackbird, Macmillan, 1969.

The Sour Lemon Score, Fawcett, 1969.

Deadly Edge, Random House, 1971.

Lemons Never Lie, World Publishing, 1971.

Slayground, Random House, 1971.

Plunder Squad, Random House, 1972.

Butcher's Moon, Random House, 1974.

Stark Mysteries (contains *The Hunter, The Man with the Getaway Face, The Mourner, The Outfit, The Score,* and *The Seventh*), G. K. Hall, 1981.

Screenplays:

(With Michael Kane) *Hot Stuff,* Columbia, 1979.

The Stepfather, New Century/Vista, 1986.

The Grifters, Miramax, 1990.

Also author of screenplays *Cops and Robbers,* upon which Westlake based the novel, and *Why Me,* based on the novel.

Cumulative Index

CUMULATIVE INDEX

For every reference that appears *in more than one essay*,
the name of the essayist is given before the volume and page number(s).

INDEX

INDEX

INDEX

INDEX